Contents

Bibliography

ECO Volume B (2nd and 3rd Editions)
Chess Informant 1-71
NIC Yearbook 1-45
Correspondence Chess Yearbook 1-14
Accelerated Dragons, J.Donaldson and J.Silman (Cadogan Chess 1993 and 1998)
Sicilian Accelerated Dragon, D.Levy (Batsford 1975)
Beating The Sicilian 3, J.Nunn and J.Gallagher (Batsford 1995)
ICON: Sicilian Accelerated Dragon, J.Donaldson (ICE 1995)
Sizilianische Verteidigung: Drachen-System, E.Gufeld (Rudi Schmaus 1985)
52 – 54 – STOP – Fernschach, F.Baumbach (Sportverlag 1990)
New In Chess Magazine – 1982 through 1998

Abbreviations

ch	Championship
ct	Candidates tournament
izt	Interzonal tournament
zt	Zonal tournament
ol	Olympiad
corr	Correspondence game

The Sicilian Accelerated Dragon

Peter Heine Nielsen and Carsten Hansen

B. T. Batsford Ltd, *London*

First published 1998
© Peter Heine Nielsen and Carsten Hansen 1998

ISBN 0 7134 7986 8

British Library Cataloguing-in-Publication Data.
A catalogue record for this book is
available from the British Library.

Typeset and edited by First Rank Publishing, Brighton
and printed in Great Britain by
Creative Print & Design (Wales), Ebbw Vale
for the publishers,
B. T. Batsford Ltd,
583 Fulham Road,
London SW6 5BY

A BATSFORD CHESS BOOK
General Manager: David Cummings
Advisors: Mark Dvoretsky, Raymond Keene OBE,
Daniel King, Jon Speelman, Chris Ward

Preface

The Accelerated Dragon had lived a life of semi-obscurity for many years, when Bent Larsen revitalised the black side of the Maroczy Bind with his impressive performances against Karpov and Short in the 1987 SWIFT tournament in Brussels. For a while this boosted the popularity of the entire system before new ways were found for White, and slowly the system faded away once again.

But in recent years, continued use by players such as Tiviakov, Anand, Alterman, Petursson, Andersson and Larsen has once again brought attention to Black's chances.

In this book we have tried to cover every variation thoroughly with plenty of examples, new ideas and explanations to give you, the reader, a close feel for the typical plans, tactics and strategies in each line. In some chapters we have particularly emphasised the explanation of typical ideas and plans, as these should help you if you meet an unfamiliar move or move order and guide you to a safe position.

The history of the Accelerated Dragon is long – you will find examples by Lasker dating back to the last century – but nowadays the theory is developing so fast that it can be difficult to keep track of the newest moves in each line. However, we still feel that this book should be a helpful companion for several years to come and will hopefully bring you many points whether you play the white or black side.

Although both of us have a deep attachment to the black side of this system, we have tried to be as objective as possible. Sometimes it may still shine through that we prefer Black, but this probably comes from having a solid belief in Black's chances. However, this should not keep White players from trying out our suggestions and recommendations.

Several people have helped us throughout this project. Allan Holst, Jacob Aagaard, Ove Ekebjerg, Stephanie Alexander, Bent Hansen and Uffe V. Nielsen all deserve to be thanked for their contribution; without them this project would have taken even longer to finish. Last, but not least, we would like to thank our publishers, Batsford, for their patience and belief in the book.

This book is the first either of us have written. It has been a lot of hard work, involving countless hours at the chessboard and on the computer.

We hope that you, the reader, will find our work useful whether you are interested in only one chapter or decide to work your way through the whole book. Should you have any questions, new ideas or criticisms, please address these to Batsford Chess, so that they can be forwarded to us.
Good luck!

Peter Heine Nielsen and Carsten Hansen
May 1998

Introduction

The starting position for the Sicilian Accelerated Dragon occurs after **1 e4 c5 2 ♘f3 ♘c6 3 d4 cxd4 4 ♘xd4 g6**

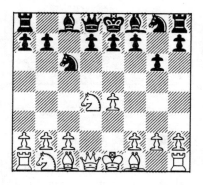

For years, White's most feared weapon was the Maroczy Bind, initiated by 5 c4, and many people seemed to believe this set-up was just 'good for White'. As already highlighted in the Preface, however, Black has many resources at his disposal nowadays, and can look forward to a dynamic yet solid position. Nevertheless, the Maroczy is still White's most popular choice, and is covered in the first eight chapters of the book.

Black can choose a range of set-ups against the Maroczy, each of which has its own unique flavour.

The three mainstream options are:

a) The 7...♘g4 system (Chapter 1), entered via the move-order 5...♗g7 6 ♗e3 ♘f6 7 ♘c3 ♘g4.

b) The Classical Maroczy, 5...♗g7 6 ♗e3 ♘f6 7 ♘c3, which is given extensive coverage in Chapters 3-5.

c) The Gurgenidze Variation 5...♘f6 6 ♘c3 d6 followed by ...♘xd4, analysed in Chapter 8.

In addition, two slightly more offbeat configurations for Black are the double fianchetto system (Chapter 2) and the lines with an early ...♘h6 (Chapter 6). Meanwhile, White's attempts to avoid the bulk of Maroczy theory by an early ♘b3 or ♘c2 are covered in Chapter 7.

Chapters 9-13 give full coverage of the lines where White plays 5 ♘c3, avoiding the Maroczy. These variations have an affinity with the Dragon Sicilian, with the key difference that Black has delayed moving his d-pawn, so can often play ...d7-d5 in one go.

Early deviations by Black such as the Semi-Accelerated Dragon and the Hyper-Accelerated Dragon are covered in Chapters 13 and 14, while Chapter 15 is a guide to the transpositions from queen's pawn or flank openings.

Key Ideas in the Accelerated Dragon

In the Maroczy Bind in particular, there are several common themes, of which players of either side should be aware. By studying these plans and strategies carefully, you will gain a better understanding of the opening, and you will then know what to strive for and what to strive to avoid.

If you have never played the Accelerated Dragon before, or if you want some help to find which games are particular useful, here is a brief summary of the key themes and the games which best illustrate them.

Black's Dark-Squared Strategy

This is a common idea throughout the entire opening complex, but it is most evident in the Classical Maroczy and the Gurgenidze variation. It also frequently occurs in 7...♘g4 system and in the main lines with 7 ♗c4 ♕a5.

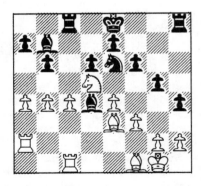

Important games for the understanding of this theme are Games 6, 7, 23 and 43.

Good Knight vs. Bad Bishop

This is one of Black's strategic goals, and occurs when the dark-squared bishops are exchanged and Black succeeds in swapping his light-squared bishop for one of the white knights. It happens very frequently in the Classical Maroczy, the Gurgenidze variation and the main lines with 7 ♗c4 ♕a5.

See Games 22, 36, 38 and 53.

White's Space Advantage

The nightmare scenario for Black is where he is simply crushed by White's oncoming pieces and pawns. This is a potential feature in many lines of the Maroczy Bind.

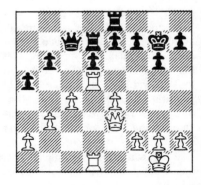

Games 12, 16, 19, 21, 25, 28 and 77 illustrate how White can best make use of his space advantage.

Black's Backward e-pawn

With Black eager to reach a middlegame or endgame with good knight vs. bad bishop, he often has to exchange his light-squared bishop for a white knight on d5. After White recaptures with e4xd5, the backward black e-pawn is slightly vulnerable. On the positive side, however, this pawn may also be used to break the center open.

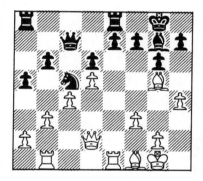

Please see Games 39, 77 and 81 for illustrations of this scenario.

The ...b7-b5 Break

With White controlling more space in the Maroczy Bind, Black often has to use this break to open up the queenside and gain counterplay. In the Gurgenidze variation, this is often Black's only way of releasing himself from White's pressure. From time to time, Black even sacrifices a pawn in the process, hoping to prove sufficient compensation in the form of open files on the queenside. However, when breaking with ...b7-b5, Black can also weaken his queenside, something White may be able to exploit.

Please study Games 3, 41, 50 and 66 for a deeper understanding on this common theme.

The ...f7-f5 Break

When Black has chosen a more modest set-up on the queenside and therefore does not have the ...b7-b5 break at hand, he can choose to break with ...f7-f5. Black, however, must bear in mind that in doing so, he drastically weakens his kingside and vital squares in the centre.

Games 11, 37, 44, 51, 57, 62 show some of the pros and cons of this break.

1 Maroczy Bind: 7...♘g4 System

Chapter Guide

1 e4 c5 2 ♘f3 ♘c6 3 d4 cxd4 4 ♘xd4 g6 5 c4 ♗g7 6 ♗e3 ♘f6 7 ♘c3 ♘g4 8 ♕xg4 ♘xd4 9 ♕d1

9...e5
  10 ♘b5! 0-0 11 ♕d2
        11...♕h4 – *Game 1*
        11...♕e7 – *Game 2*
  10 ♗d3 0-0 11 0-0 d6
       12 ♕d2 – *Game 3*
       12 a4 – *Game 4*

9...♘e6 10 ♖c1
   10...♕a5 11 ♗e2 b6
       12 ♕d5 – *Game 5*
       12 ♕d2 – *Game 6*
      12 0-0 ♗b7 13 f3 g5
          14 a3 – *Game 7*
          14 ♖f2 – *Game 8*
    11 ♗d3 b6
        12 0-0 – *Game 9*
        12 ♕d2 – *Game 10*

   10...b6 – *Game 11*
   10...d6 – *Game 12*
  10 ♕d2   – *Game 13*

This system is often known as the Exchange variation or the Simagin variation, after the Soviet GM Vladimir Simagin who popularised it in the early fifties. From the mid-sixties until 1987 the entire system was regarded with a certain degree of suspicion, but the games Karpov-Larsen and Short-Larsen from the SWIFT tournament in Brussels 1987 (both of which can be found in this chapter) changed the general opinion and made the variation fashionable again.

The system is still often played, but once again most people tend to prefer White's chances, although theoretically Black is certainly doing fine.

It is almost impossible to generalise about the entire 7...♘g4 system, as the sub-variations are so different: some are extremely complicated, while others are based on sound positional understanding. We therefore recommend that the reader study the different games to get a better understanding of the specifics of each variation.

We start with a classic encounter from the early 1970s.

Game 1
Gufeld-Espig
Sukhumi 1972

(1 e4 c5 2 ♘f3 ♘c6 3 d4 cxd4 4 ♘xd4 g6 5 c4)

5	...	♗g7
6	♗e3	♘f6
7	♘c3	♘g4!?

For a long time this was considered dubious, but when Larsen used it to obtain an advantage against Karpov in Brussels 1987, it became popular again.

8 ♕xg4

Occasionally 8 ♘xc6 ♘xe3 9 ♘xd8 ♘xd1 10 ♘xd1 (to avoid ...♗xc3+) 10...♔xd8 is played, but with the pair of bishops and no counterpart to the dark-squared bishop, Black is much better, as in for example Villegas-Réti, Buenos Aires 1924.

8 ... ♘xd4

8...♗xd4 has been tried and is in fact very logical, since it is a very common theme in the Maroczy Bind for Black to exchange dark-squared bishops. The idea is to post a knight on d4, protected by a pawn on e5. Normally this gives Black good play, but here White is ready for a direct assault, and unless a major improvement can be found for Black, then 8...♗xd4 must be considered unplayable.

After 9 ♗xd4 ♘xd4, 10 0-0-0! is now possible (if 10 ♕d1 then 10...e5 is fine for Black), since once the bishop on g7 has gone, the queenside is a safe haven for the white king. After 10...e5, 11 ♕g3 d6 12 f4 f6 White has tried 13 h4, but the more convincing 13 f5! was introduced in the game Mestel-Karlsson, Las Palmas izt 1982. On that occasion Black played 13...♔f7, but he did not have much to smile about after 14 ♘b5!, which gets rid of Black's only good piece. After 14...♘xb5 15 cxb5 ♕c7+ 16 ♔b1 ♗d7, instead of 17 b3?!, Mestel gives 17 ♖c1 followed by ♗c4+ and ♕d3 as stronger, and this does indeed look awful for Black. However, Mestel still won after the game continuation. In a subsequent game, Black later tried 13...gxf5 (instead of 13...♔f7) and survived after 14 ♕g7 ♖f8 15 ♘d5 ♖f7 16 ♕g8+ ♖f8 17 ♕xh7 ♕d7

(17...♗d7 lost immediately to 18 ♖xd4! ♖f7? 19 ♕h8+ ♖f8 20 ♕h5+ 1-0 in Z.Almasi-Marosi, Hungary 1992) 18 ♕g6+ ♔d8 19 ♕h6 ♕f7 20 ♗d3, when White offered a draw in Samarin-Lysenko, Briansk 1984. But 18 ♕h6!, as given by Silman and Donaldson, wins after 18...♕f7 19 ♖xd4 exd4 20 ♗e2 ♔d8 21 ♗h5 ♕g8 22 ♘f6, as neither 22...♕h8 23 ♘h7! nor 22...♕xc4+ 23 ♔b1 offers Black any chance of survival. Black's last hope may be Mestel's recommendation 13...0-0, but after 14 fxg6 it is difficult to believe that Black's attack, involving the moves 14...♗e6 followed by ...♖c8 etc., should be as dangerous as White's attack on the kingside.

9 ♕d1

9 0-0-0 has been played on a few occasions, but it looks very risky. In Cherepkov-Gufeld, USSR 1961, Black played 9...e5 and stood better after 10 h4?! d5 11 ♕g3 dxe4 12 h5 ♗f5. Much stronger is 10 ♕g3, intending 10...0-0 11 ♘b5, which is much better for White.

It is much more logical to play 9...♘c6, opening the diagonal for bishop on g7 and threatening both ...d7-d5 and ...♗xc3 followed by ...♕a5, ...d7-d6, ...♗e6 and ...♘e5. 10 ♘d5 is the only way to counter both of these ideas, when after 10...e6 White can return with 11 ♘c3 since after 11...♗xc3 12 bxc3 ♕a5 13 ♔b2 White has ideas like ♕f4-f6, and Black does not have the standard attack with the pawn already on e6. Therefore Black should meet 11 ♘c3 by 11...♕a5 12 ♗d2 0-0 13 ♔b1 d5 with attacking chances. Note also that 13

♕h4 can be answered with 13...d5!?, as after 14 exd5 exd5 neither 15 ♘xd5 ♕xa2 nor 15 exd5 ♘d4 is scary for Black. In summary, the seemingly aggressive 9 0-0-0 actually offers more attacking chances for Black than White.

After 9 ♕d1 Black has to choose between positional play with 9...♘e6 or 9...♘c6 or the more tactical positions after 9...e5.

9 ... e5

At one time this move was very popular, but since the main line seems to give White a clearly better game, interest has faded. Now and then Black comes up with a new idea, but so far none of these have stood the test of time.

Apart from the standard 9...♘e6 (see Games 5-13) Black has also tried 9...♘c6 a few times. However, the knight is misplaced here, and Black can do little to counter White's quiet development with ♕d2, ♖c1, ♗e2, 0-0 and ♖fd1, after which White will have strong pressure. Black is as solid as always, but compared to the main system, not only is the knight less active on c6 than on c5 (after ...♘e6-c5) but it also takes away the c6-square from the light-squared bishop. Furthermore, Black cannot prevent his opponent from playing b2-b4 with ...a7-a5, since ♘d5 will exploit the weakening of the b6-square. A good example is Gavrikov-Pribyl, German Bundesliga 1993/94: 10 ♕d2 d6 11 ♗e2 ♗e6 12 b3 0-0 13 ♖c1 ♕a5 14 0-0 ♖fc8 15 ♖fd1 ♘e5 16 h3 ♔f8 17 f4 ♘c6 18 ♗f3, when White had a large space advantage and Black no counterplay. White expanded with f2-f4, which is normally impossible due to Black's pressure against the e4-pawn from a knight on c5 and/or a bishop bearing down on the long light-squared diagonal.

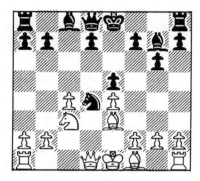

10   ♘b5!

The most ambitious attempt to refute the 9...e5 line. Larsen once claimed that the only reason why 10 ♗d3 is played so frequently is that White players are afraid of the complications after 10 ♘b5!, but only because they are complicated, not for any intrinsic reason. With 10 ♗d3 (Games 3 and 4) White goes for a small but safe advantage, whereas if he dares enter the complications of 10 ♘b5! he should be rewarded with a clear edge.

10   ...   0-0
11   ♕d2!

Two other moves have often been seen here:

a) The greedy 11 ♘xd4? is refuted tactically by 11...exd4 12 ♗xd4 ♕a5+ 13 ♔e2 ♖e8 14 f3 d5 15 ♗xg7 ♖xe4+ 16 ♔f2 (16 fxe4 ♗g4+) 16...♕c5+ 17 ♔g3 ♕e3! (threatening ...♖g4+) 18 h3 ♕f4+! 19 ♔f2 ♔xg7 20 ♕c1, and here for some reason Aizenhstadt-Aronin, USSR 1961, was agreed drawn, but if Black plays 20...♕f6 he keeps

the queens on and obtains a fantastic attack after 21 cxd5 ♗d7 followed by ...♖c8.

Instead of 16 ♔f2, 16 ♔d3 was played in Brunner-Ekström, Switzerland 1990. After 16...♖xc4 White found 17 ♔e3!? which wins an exchange, but after 17...♕c5+ 18 ♔d2 ♔xg7 19 ♗xc4 dxc4 Black had more than sufficient compensation. The white king cannot escape and Black won in 28 moves.

b) 11 ♗e2 seems to be sufficient to gain a slight pull, as for example in Ivanchuk-Korchnoi, Monaco (rapid) 1994: 11...♘xb5 12 cxb5 d6 13 0-0 ♗e6 14 ♕a4 ♕d7 15 ♖fd1 ♖fc8 16 ♖d2. It is not a lot for White, but the d6-pawn is weak and Ivanchuk managed to win this particular game. 14...♕h4 instead of 14...♕d7 is possibly an improvement, since then ...d6-d5 is a threat and if 15 g3 ♕e7, and Black is then ready to play 16...f5 with counterplay.

Instead of 11...♘xb5, 11...♕h4?! seems logical, but this is exactly what White is hoping for. In Gaprindashvili-Servaty, Dortmund 1974, play continued 12 ♘xd4 exd4 13 ♗xd4 ♕xe4 14 ♗xg7 ♕xg2? 15 ♕d4! ♕xh1 16 ♔d2 ♕xa1 17 ♕f6! 1-0. 14...♕xg2? was clearly bad, but 14...♔xg7 15 0-0 is also depressing.

To summarise, 11 ♗e2 is solid and contains a nice little trap, but it should not bother Black too much.

11   ...   ♕h4

11...♕e7 is seen in the next game. Kuzmin has suggested 11...d6 12 ♗d3 (12 ♘xd4 exd4 13 ♗xd4 ♕h4 14 ♕e3 ♗h6 15 ♕f3 ♖e8 16 ♗d3 f5 wins for Black) 12...♗e6 with equality. However, after 12 ♘xd4 exd4 13 ♗xd4 ♕h4 White simply plays 14 0-0-0 ♕xe4 15 ♗xg5 ♔xg7 16 f3 with a safe extra pawn.

12   ♗d3

Vaganian must have feared an improvement in the main line, since he chose to diverge here with 12 ♘d6 against Espig, German Bundesliga 1990/91. After 12...♕e7 13 ♘xc8 ♖fxc8 14 ♗d3 a5?! 15 0-0 ♕b4 it seems as if Black will reach an equal ending, but after the surprising yet instructive 16 ♕c3! Black had to go back to d6, since an exchange of queens would have simply dropped the b7-pawn. Still, White did not have a lot here, although he later managed to play f2-f4 under favourable circumstances and went on to win. Instead of 14...a5?!, we recommend 14...♘e6 with the idea of ...♗f6-g5 to play for the dark squares, when Black is doing fine.

12   ...   d5

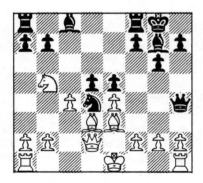

Black has to rely on tactics, otherwise he will just be positionally worse.

13   cxd5!

The only try for an advantage. In reply to 13 exd5, Black has the fantastic 13...♗h3! which guarantees a draw. After 14 ♗xd4 (14 0-0 ♗xg2) 14...exd4 15 gxh3 a6 16 ♘a3, Espig played 16...♖fe8+ against Luther, German Bundesliga 1994/95, and won a spectacular game: 17 ♔d1 ♗h6 18 f4?! ♗xf4 19 ♕g2 ♖e3 20 ♔c2 ♗d6 21 ♘b1?! ♖ae8 22 ♘d2 ♖xd3 23 ♔xd3 ♖e3+ 24 ♔c2 d3 25 ♔b3 ♖e2 26 ♕f3 ♖xd2 27 ♖hf1 f5 28 ♕e3 b5 29 ♖ac1 ♖e2 30 ♕xd3 ♕e7 31 ♖f3 bxc4+ 32 ♕xc4 ♕b7+ 33 ♔a4 ♖e4 0-1. However, it is better to play 18 ♕c2, when we do not see a convincing continuation of the attack. Neishtadt recommends 18...♖e5 'with compensation', but White can defend with 19 f4!, as after 19...♕xf4 20 ♕g2 followed by ♔c2 or 19...♖e3 20 ♕d2 followed by ♔c2, we have not found anything for Black, although intuitively you feel that there must be something. Also if 21 ♘b1?! is replaced by 21 ♖ad1, it is difficult to believe that Black has sufficient compensation.

So perhaps Black should go for the forced draw given by Boleslavsky: 16...♗h6 17 ♕c2 ♖ae8+ 18 ♔d1! (18 ♗e2 d3! 19 ♕xd3 ♖e3 followed by ...♖fe8 wins for Black) 18...♕xh3 19 ♗e2! (19 ♖f1 ♖e5 20 f4 ♖e3 and 19 ♗e4 ♕h5 20 f3 f5 both win for Black) 19...♖xe2 (else ♕d3 will follow) 20 ♕xe2 d3 21 ♕e4 f5 22 ♕e6+ ♖f7 and White has to settle for the perpetual.

It is worse to play 13 ♘xd4 dxe4 and Black is already better, or 13 ♗g5 ♕g4 again with fine prospects for Black.

13   ...   ♘xb5

Here 13...♗h3 unfortunately loses to 14 ♗xd4, so Black has to

14   ♗xb5   ♕xe4
15   0-0

After 15 f3 ♕h4+ 16 ♗f2 ♕f6 17 0-0 ♖d8 18 ♖fd1 ♗f5, Black easily held the draw in Schmidt-Espig, German Bundesliga 1992/93

15   ...   ♖d8
16   ♖fd1

Black has got his pawn back and the d-pawn looks weak, unfortunately he is not able to make use of it tactically. Instead it turns out that the d-pawn, in fact, is a strong passed pawn and White is better. White has also tried the direct 16 d6 with some success. After 16...♗e6 17 ♖ad1 ♗f8 18 f3 ♕h4 19 ♗g5 he won the exchange in Corral-Jimenez, 1967. Stronger is 16...♗d7 17 f3 ♕f5, when Black seems to be okay, since the d6-pawn is solidly blockaded and may even be a weakness.

16   ...   ♕f5

Unfortunately 16...♗e6 runs into 17 f3!, since 17...♕xd5? 18 ♕e2 traps the queen in the middle of the board. Also 17...♕h4? 18 ♗g5 ♕h5 19 ♗xd8 ♖xd8 20 ♕a5 1-0 Joksic-Werner, Biel 1975, was not much fun for Black either. Relatively best is 17...♕f5 18 ♗d3, which 'only' wins an exchange, as in Penrose-Lees, British ch 1965.

17   ♖ac1   ♗d7
18   ♗e2   e4

White's threat was 19 g4, after which the black queen would be in trouble. 18...♗c6 again runs into 19 ♗d3, when the endgame that arises after 19...e4 20 dxc6 bxc6 21 ♗xe4 ♖xd2 22 ♗xf5 ♖xd1+ 23 ♖xd1 gxf5 24 b3 is very bad for Black.

19   ♖c7   ♗c6

Necessary, since both 19...♗e6

20 ♗c4 and 19...b6 20 ♗g5 ♗f6 21 ♗xf6 ♕xf6 22 d6 are really bad for Black. The d-pawn is too strong.

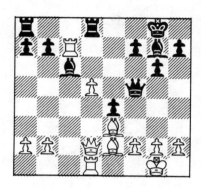

20 · dxc6!

Forced, because 20 ♗c4 and 20 d6 are both answered by 20...♗e5 with good play.

20   ...   ♖xd2
21   ♖xd2   bxc6
22   ♗c4

This position has been considered clearly better for White ever since this game, but Espig must believe that it is possible to make a draw, as he has repeated the line recently.

22   ...   ♗e5!

After 22...♖f8 23 ♖xa7 White keeps his dark-squared bishop, and Black is lost.

23   ♖xf7

In Quist-Espig, Berlin 1993, White did not believe the endgame advantage was sufficient to win and tried 23 ♖b7 instead, but after 23...♖f8 24 ♖xa7 ♗f4! 25 ♖a3 ♗xe3 26 ♖xa3 ♔g7 27 ♖de2 ♖d8 28 ♗b3 ♖d4 29 ♗c2 ♕c5 30 ♗xe4?? (Black would of course have played ...f7-f5 next, after which he would be fine) 30...♖d1+ 31 ♖e1 ♕xe3! 32 fxe3 ♖xe1 33

♔f2 ♖a1 34 a3 c5 35 ♗d5 ♖d1 36
e4 ♖d2+ 0-1. It seems that after
24...♗f4! Black has solved most of
his problems, and the game should
be drawn with normal play.

| 23 | ... | ♛xf7 |
| 24 | ♗xf7+ | ♔xf7 |

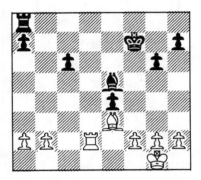

This ending is critical for the assessment of 11...♛h4. It certainly
looks bad for Black, with so many
weak pawns. But Espig believes
Black is holding on, and so far nobody has proved him wrong in
practice.

25   ♖d7+

After this Black seems to be
holding his own, so perhaps 25
♖c2!? is more critical. Black must
play 25...a5 26 b3 a4! (passive defence is very dangerous, since if
White can consolidate then the
black pawns will become easy targets) 27 ♖xc6 axb3 28 axb3 ♖a3
29 b4 ♗c3 30 g4 ♗xb4 31 ♖c4
♗e7 32 ♖xe4. Black is a pawn
down, but should be able to draw
with careful play. 26 ♗c1!? may be
stronger, since Black will find it
problematic to find targets for his
counterplay and White simply
threatens to centralise with ♔f1-e2
etc. Certainly Black is under a lot

of pressure, but whether White's
chances to win are superior to
Black's drawing chances is difficult
to say.

| 25 | ... | ♔e6 |
| 26 | ♖xh7 | |

If 26 ♖xa7 ♖xa7 27 ♗xa7 ♗xb2
Black's centralised king guarantees
him the draw, e.g. 28 ♔f1 ♔d5 29
♔e2 c5 followed by ...♗d4.

26   ...   a5!

Not 26...♗xb2 27 ♖xa7.

27 b3 a4 28 bxa4

28 b4 ♖d8 followed by ...♖d1-a1
is too dangerous for White, and
both 28 g4 axb3 29 axb3 ♖b8 and
28 ♖a7 axb3! 29 axb3 ♖b8 are
nothing to worry about for Black.

28...♖xa4 29 ♖a7 ♖b4 30 ♔f1?

30 g3 keeps the extra pawn, although Black still might save the
rook ending after 30...♗d4.

30...♖b1+ 31 ♔e2 ♗c3!

This must be what White missed
when he played 30 ♔f1? The threat
is ...♖e1 mate!

32 f3

32 f4 ♔d5 is too risky.

**32...♖b2 33 ♔f1 exf3 34 gxf3
♖xh2 35 a4 ♖a2 ½-½**

It seems to us that after 11...♛h4
Black has to defend some really
unpleasant endings, and although
he may succeed in making a draw,
it is certainly not much fun for him.

Game 2
Serper-Sermek
Tilburg 1994

(1 e4 c5 2 ♞f3 ♞c6 3 d4 cxd4 4
♞xd4 g6 5 c4 ♗g7 6 ♗e3 ♞f6 7
♞c3 ♞g4 8 ♛xg4 ♞xd4 9 ♛d1 e5
10 ♞b5 0-0 11 ♛d2)

| 11 | ... | ♛e7 |

A move which has enjoyed something of a renaissance lately.

12   0-0-0

White has two main alternatives:

a) 12 f3 was played in Yemelin-Silman, Budapest 1994. Black responded sharply with 12...f5, but after 13 ♗d3 d6 14 ♗g5 ♗f6 15 ♗xf6 ♕xf6 16 ♘xd4 exd4 17 0-0 all he had to show was weak pawns. As usual 12...♘xb5 13 cxb5 d6 14 ♗c4 is positionally suspect for Black, so maybe 12...♖d8!? should be given a try. The tactical point is 13 ♘xd4 exd4 14 ♗xd4 d5! 15 ♗xg7 dxe4! 16 ♕c3 exf3+ 17 ♔f2 ♕c5+!, when Black gets a perpetual check. Also 17 ♕e5 ♕xe5+ 18 ♗xe5 ♖e8 19 0-0-0 ♖xe5 20 ♖d8 ♔g7 21 exf3 b6 22 f4? ♖e1+ 23 ♔d2 ♖b1! is fine for Black. Probably White should go for 13 ♘c7, trying to prove that the rook on d8 is misplaced, but since Black retains the knight on d4 he has a playable position.

b) 12 ♗e2 was played in Tal-Pähtz, Halle 1974, when Black reacted badly with 12...b6? 13 ♘xd4 exd4 14 ♗xd4 ♕xe4 15 ♗xg7 ♕xg2? 16 ♕d4! ♕xh1 17 ♔d2 ♕xh2 18 ♗xf8 ♔xf8 19 ♗f3

d5 20 ♗xd5 ♖b8 21 ♖e1 ♗e6 22 ♖xe6 1-0.

12   ...   ♘xb5
13   cxb5   d5
14   exd5   ♖d8!

The new move which has revitalised the 11...♕e7 variation. 14...♗f5 was played in Smyslov-Jimenez, Havana 1963, but Black had nothing to show for the pawn after 15 ♗d3 ♖c8+ 16 ♔b1 ♕d7 17 ♗xf5 ♕xf5+ 18 ♕d3 e4 19 ♕b3, and White won easily.

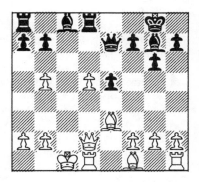

15   d6

Forced, as 15...♗f5 followed by ...♖ac8 was a big threat. The point behind 14...♖d8! is that Smyslov's plan of defence (♗d3) is no longer possible, since the d-pawn can then simply be taken.

15   ...   ♕e6
16   ♔b1

Also possible is 16 ♕b4, since 16...♕xa2? loses to 17 ♗c4 ♕a1+ 18 ♔c2 ♗f5+ 19 ♔b3, and if Black parries White's threat of ♗c4 with 16...♗d7, then White will play 17 ♔b1, when Black will never get rid of the d6-pawn. Still, the simple 16...♗f8! 17 ♗c4 ♕f6 gives Black equality.

16   ...   ♗f8

17 ♕c3

The critical test of Black's play. White returns the pawn and hopes that his better development will decide the game.

17 ♗c5 is less good. After 17...b6 18 ♗b4 ♗b7 19 h4, as in B.Lalic-Heim, Slough 1997, Black played the strong 19...♗xd6! 20 ♗xd6 ♖d7!, when White has no way of keeping his extra piece. 19 f3 has also been played, but again Black has 19...♗xd6 with at least equality.

17 ... ♖xd6

Probably taken by surprise, Sermek tries to defend an inferior position, instead of playing the more complex 17...♗xd6. He later won a nice game with this move against Dizdarevic: 18 ♗c4 ♕f5+ 19 ♗d3 e4 20 g4?! ♕xg4 21 ♕f6 ♗e6 22 ♗d4 ♔f8 23 ♗c2 (it looks like Black is in big trouble, but in fact everything is under control) 23...♕f5 24 ♕g7+ ♔e7 25 ♕xh7 ♖ac8 26 ♕h4+ g5 27 ♕xe4 ♖xc2! 28 ♕xc2 ♗xa2+ 29 ♔c1 ♗f4+ 0-1. Very impressive. Unfortunately, Serper points out the much stronger 20 ♗c4, when Black must settle for a bad ending after 20...♗e6 21 g4!, and now either 21...♕e5 22 ♕xe5 ♗xe5 23 ♗xe6 fxe6 or 21...♕f3 22 ♗xe6 fxe6 23 ♗g5! The point is that 21...♕xg4? loses immediately to 22 ♖xd6 ♖xd6 23 ♗h6. This is all very convincing and difficult for Black to improve upon. 19...♗b4?! is tricky, but simply 20 ♗xf5 ♗xf5+ 21 ♕c2! ♗xc2 22 ♔xc2 gives White a pleasant ending, since his b5-pawn combined with pressure against b7 guarantees him a huge edge.

Maybe Black's best chance is

18...♕g4!? instead of 18...♕f5+, when Serper regards 19 ♗d5 ♗f5+ 20 ♔a1 ♖ac8 21 ♕a5 as clearly better for White, although the position after 21...♗c2 seems unclear and playable for Black, since both 22 ♗xb7 ♗xd1 23 ♗xc8 ♖xc8 24 ♕d2 ♗b4 25 ♕xd1 ♕xg2 26 ♗xa7 ♕b7 27 b6 ♗a5 and 22 ♗f3 ♕d7 23 ♖d5 b6 24 ♖d2 ♕e7 25 ♖c1 ♗f5 are not better for White. Maybe 19 ♕b3 is better, keeping the pressure up. If this does not scare you, then 11...♕e7 is an interesting way of fighting for the initiative.

18 ♗c4 ♖xd1+
19 ♖xd1 ♕g4
20 ♕b3 ♗f5+

Sacrificing the f7-pawn, but if Black had tried to defend it he would have been left in a very passive position.

21 ♔a1 ♖c8 22 ♗xf7+ ♔g7 23 f3 ♕xg2 24 ♗e6!

With the idea of 24...♗c2? 25 ♕d5 ♗xd1 26 ♕xe5 mate!

24...♖d8 25 ♖xd8 ♗c2 26 ♗h6+!

Not 26 ♖d7 ♔h8 27 ♕xc2 ♕xc2 28 ♗g5 ♗e7!

26...♔xh6 27 ♕e3+ g5 28 ♕c1 ♗b4 29 h4 ♗g6 30 ♗g4 ♗e7 31 ♖d7 ♗f6 32 ♖d6 ♔g7 33 ♖d7 ♔h6 34 ♖d6 ♔g7 35 h5 ♕c2 36 h6 ♔f7 37 ♖d7 ♔e8 38 ♕c2 ♗e2 39 ♖b7 ♗d1 40 ♖a7 e4 41 ♗d7 1-0

Game 3
Polugayevsky-Piket
Aruba match 1994

(1 ♘f3 c5 2 c4 ♘c6 3 d4 cxd4 4 ♘xd4 g6 5 e4 ♗g7 6 ♗e3 ♘f6 7 ♘c3 ♘g4 8 ♕xg4 ♘xd4 9 ♕d1 e5)

10   ♗d3

10 ♗d3 is seen almost as frequently as 10 ♘b5, probably because many White players prefer a quiet game to entering complications familiar to their opponents. White tries for a small positional edge instead of attempting to refute Black's set-up outright.

10   ...   0-0
11   0-0   d6

11...b6 has been played with some success and is a viable alternative to the game move:

a) 12 ♕d2 ♗b7 and now:

a1) 13 ♖ad1 ♘e6 14 ♗b1 ♗c6 15 b4 ♖c8 16 a3 ♖c7 and Black has a solid position, Smyslov-Bagirov, Leningrad 1960.

a2) White tried 13 ♗h6 in Britton-Wells, Oviedo 1993; after 13...d6 14 ♗xg7 ♔xg7 15 f4 exf4 15 ♖xf4 ♘e6 16 ♖f2 ♕g5 17 ♗c2 ♕e5 Black had good play on the dark squares.

b) Another example of this theme is Bivshev-Simagin, Moscow 1952, which continued with 12 ♘d5 ♗b7 13 f4 exf4 14 ♗xf4 d6 15 ♕d2 ♘e6 16 ♗h6 ♗xh6 17 ♕xh6 ♗xd5! 18 exd5 ♘c5 19 ♖f3 f5 20 ♖e1 ♕f6 21 ♖h3 ♖f7, when

Black parried the attack and later won. His knight is clearly superior to the white bishop.

12   ♕d2

12 a4 is seen in the next game, while 12 ♖c1 was played in Smyslov-Botvinnik, Moscow 1956. After 12...♗e6 13 b3 a6 14 ♗b1 ♖b8 (14...b5 15 cxb5 ♘xb5! 16 ♖c6 d5 17 exd5 ½-½, Gulko-Seirawan, Key West 1994) 15 ♔h1 b5 16 cxb5 axb5 17 ♕d3 b4 18 ♘d5 ♗xd5 19 exd5 ♕a5 20 ♕c4 ♖b5 21 ♗d2 ♖fb8 22 ♕c8+ ♗f8 23 ♕d7 ♖5b7 24 ♕g4 f5 25 ♕h3 ♕xd5 Black was a pawn up, but only managed to draw.

12   ...   ♗e6
13   ♖ad1

In an earlier game of Polugayevsky's, against Bagirov, Leningrad 1963, 13 ♖ac1 was tried, which looks more logical since the other rook can then go to d1. Still, White had to concede an early draw after 13...a6 14 ♖fd1 ♕a5 15 ♗f1?! b5 16 cxb5 axb5 17 ♘xb5 ♘xb5 18 ♕xa5 ♖xa5 19 b4 ♖xa2 20 ♗xb5 ♖b8 ½-½. Later 15 b3 was suggested as an improvement, the idea being to answer 15...b5 with 16 ♘e2. But first of all, White has not got a whole lot after 16...♕xd2 17 ♖xd2 ♖fc8, and if this does not suit Black, then 15...♖fc8 preparing ...b7-b5 seems fine too.

13   ...   a6
14   b3

A necessary prophylactic move, defending a2. If 14 ♘e2?! then 14...b5!

14   ...   ♖c8
15   ♘e2   ♘c6!?

It is now difficult for White to find a reasonable plan, since 16 f4 will ruin his position, as Black gets all the dark squares, and an eventual b3-b4 will weaken c4 too much. White instead tries to attack the weakness on d6, but it turns out to be immune.

16	♗b1	b5
17	cxb5	axb5
18	♘c3	

Realising that the pawn cannot be taken (18 ♕xd6?? ♘d4! 19 ♕xd8 ♘xe2+ wins a piece), White tries to re-route the knight to d5 instead. However, 18 ♔h1, making the threat on d6 real, seems like a better idea.

18	...	♕a5
19	♘d5	b4
20	♗g5	f6
21	♗e3	f5
22	exf5	gxf5
23	♘e7+??	

An incredible blunder, losing a piece. With 23 f3 or f4, White would still have been okay.

| 23 | ... | ♘xe7 |
| 24 | ♕xd6 | ♔f7! |

Defending both e7 and e6 and thereby winning easily.

25 ♗g5 ♘g6 26 g4 e4 27 h4 ♗e5 28 ♕d2 h6 29 gxf5 ♗xf5 30 h5 hxg5 31 hxg6+ ♔xg6 0-1

Game 4
Smyslov-Fabriano
Rome 1990

(1 ♘f3 c5 2 c4 ♘c6 3 d4 cxd4 4 ♘xd4 g6 5 e4 ♗g7 6 ♗e3 ♘f6 7 ♘c3 ♘g4 8 ♕xg4 ♘xd4 9 ♕d1 e5 10 ♗d3 0-0 11 0-0 d6)

12	a4!?

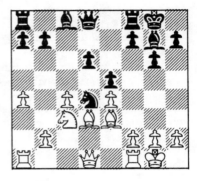

Played with the idea of seizing more space with a4-a5 and preparing 13 ♘b5, when White can take back on b5 with the a-pawn.

| 12 | ... | ♗e6 |

We believe that 12...a5!? is the right answer, and if 13 ♘b5 ♗d7! 14 ♘xd4 (14 ♘xd6 ♗xa4) 14...exd4 15 ♗d2 ♕b6 16 b3 ♗c6 followed by doubling rooks on the e-file, when Black is fine. White can do little, since he needs to keep the e4-pawn protected and must watch out for the f5-break. Instead, 12...a6 was played in Herbert-Sermek, Cannes 1995, but after 13 a5 ♗e6 14 ♘d5 ♖c8 15 ♘b6 White was much better.

13	♘b5	a6
14	♘xd4	exd4
15	♗d2	♖c8
16	b3	f5

Necessary at this point. If Black chooses to play quietly, he will not manage to attack the e4-pawn in time, and White will get in f4-f5 with an attack.

17	exf5	♗xf5
18	♕f3	d5

In Spraggett-Garcia, Candas 1992, Black played 18...♕d7, but after 19 ♖fe1 ♖f7 20 ♗xf5 ♖xf5 21 ♕d3 White was positionally much better and Black's kingside attack came to nothing.

19	♖c1	♕d7
20	cxd5	♗xd3
21	♕xd3	♕xd5
22	♖xc8	♖xc8
23	♖e1	

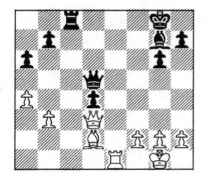

Since Black cannot use the c-file for anything constructive, and his d-pawn is blockaded, White stands better. All endgames will be a win for White, since the d4-pawn will become very fragile when the king comes to d3.

23	...	♕f5!?
24	♖e4	

It is too dangerous to immediately enter the endgame with 24 ♕xf5 gxf5 25 ♖c1 ♖xc1 26 ♗xc1 because of 26...d3.

24	...	♖f8

25	f3	♕c5
26	♖e1	♖c8
27	♖c1	♕f5
28	♖xc8+!?	

28 ♕xf5 ♖xc1+ 29 ♗xc1 gxf5 30 ♔f2 ♔f7 31 ♔e2 ♔e6 32 ♔d3 ♔d5 33 g4 is also much better for White, but is perhaps defensible for Black. So Smyslov keeps the queens on and centralises his king instead.

28...♕xc8 29 ♔f2 ♕d7 30 ♕c4+ ♔h8 31 ♔e2 ♗f6?

Now White suddenly gets a mating attack. But things were not easy for Black in any case. White was planning g2-g4 and ♔d3 followed by an attempt to exchange the queens, since now the black king will never reach d5.

32 ♗h6! g5 33 ♕c5 d3+ 34 ♔d1

Not 34 ♔d3?? ♕g6+.

34...d3 35 ♕f8+! ♕xf8 36 ♗xf8 ♗e5 37 g3 ♗c3 38 ♗h6 b5 39 axb5 axb5 40 ♗xg5 ♔g7 41 g4 ♔f7 42 h4 ♔e6 43 h5 ♔d5 44 ♗h6 ♔c5 45 ♗f8+ ♔d5 1-0

White will play h5-h6 and ♗g7 and then push the other pawns.

Game 5
Ribli-Rogers
Germany 1995

(1 ♘f3 c5 2 c4 ♘c6 3 d4 cxd4 4 ♘xd4 g6 5 e4 ♗g7 6 ♗e3 ♘f6 7 ♘c3 ♘g4 8 ♕xg4 ♘xd4 9 ♕d1)

9	...	♘e6

(see following diagram)

A safe alternative to 9...e5.

10	♖c1	

10 ♕d2 is the subject of Game 13, while Vaganian tried 10 ♗e2?! against Frias in St John 1988 and obtained excellent compensation

for the pawn after 10...♗xc3+ 11 bxc3 ♕a5 12 0-0 ♕xc3 13 c5! ♕e5 14 ♕a4! 0-0 15 ♖ac1 ♘f4 16 ♗f3 d6 17 ♖fd1, although he later lost. What Vaganian had in mind on the simple 10...♕a5 11 0-0 b6 is hard to say. The logical 12 ♖c1 just transposes to the main line, and although 12 ♘d5 has been recommended, 12...♗xb2 is good. It is very difficult for White to justify this pawn sacrifice. Finally, 12 ♕d5 is possible, though after 12...♕xd5 13 cxd5 ♘c5 White does not have much.

Still, perhaps even stronger, after 10 ♗e2?!, is 10...♗xc3+ 11 bxc3 ♕c7 followed by ...b7-b6 and ...♗b7. In Imanaliev-Lanka, Moscow 1979, Black was better after 12 0-0 b6 13 ♗d4 f6 14 ♖e1 ♗b7 15 ♗f1 d6 16 ♕g4 ♘c5 17 ♖ad1 ♕d7 18 ♕h4 ♕c6 19 f4 0-0, when White had too many weak pawns and no real attack. 13 ♗d4 looks wrong and direct action with 13 f4 was probably called for, though after 13...♗b7 we prefer Black, although it is a matter of taste.

In brief, 10 ♗e2?! should not worry Black at all. The only problem is how to choose between sev-

eral promising options.

10   ...   ♕a5

The usual move. 10...b6 is the subject of Game 11 while for 10...d6 see Game 12.

11   ♗e2

11 ♗d3 is seen in Games 9 and 10, while the immediate 11 ♕d5!? was played in M.M.Ivanov-P.H.Nielsen, Aars 1995. Here Black should not go for the endgame, since 11...♕xd5 12 cxd5 ♘d4 does not threaten to take on e2, and the knight is in danger. Black instead played the brave 11...♗xc3+ 12 ♖xc3 ♕xa2.

The game ended in a draw after 13 ♗c1! (necessary, because of 13 ♕d2 ♕b1+, when Black picks up the e4-pawn) 13...♕a4 14 ♗e2 d6 15 0-0 ♕c6 16 b4 a5 ½-½. Not very informative perhaps, but I remember we concluded in our post-mortem that Black is okay in the final position. Later I analysed the game with Miron Sher and we decided that 14 h4! would have given White the better prospects.

Instead of 13...♕a4, 13...d6, planning a quick ...♘c5 and ...♗e6, is possible. During the game I was afraid of 14 ♖a3?, but 14...♕b1 15 ♔d2 ♘c5 16 f3 ♗e6 17 ♕d4 f6 is a lot better for Black who will free himself with ...b7-b5 and ...♖c8. 14 ♕b5+ ♗d7 15 ♕xb7 ♖c8 is also fine for Black, as ... ♘c5 will come next, threatening both to take the e4-pawn and to play ♘b3. Finally, 14 h4!? is possible, when Black may try 14...♘c5 15 h5 ♗e6 16 ♕d4 ♖g8 with counterplay. It is clear that White has some compensation in the form of the pair of bishops and play on the dark squares. Still, by leaving the queen on a2 and developing quickly, Black seems to be doing fine.

| 11 | ... | b6 |
| 12 | ♕d5 | |

Now White forces his opponent to enter an endgame, since he is hitting the rook on a8. 12 ♕d2 is seen in the next game and 12 0-0 in Games 7 and 8.

| 12 | ... | ♕xd5 |

Since this does not equalise, attention should be paid to 12...♖b8, when:

a) 13 ♕xa5 bxa5 is fine for Black. The a-pawn is useful, preventing White from expanding on the queenside and Black can also play along the b-file. After 14 b3 Black should play 14...♗d4 with a fine position.

b) On 13 0-0, 13...♘d4?! unfortunately does not work. White plays 14 ♗xd4 ♕xd5 15 ♗xg7! ♕g5 16 ♗xh8, when it is more likely that White will open the position for his pieces, than that Black will consolidate and win the bishop. However, 13...g5, threatening 14...♘f4, seems to be okay for Black.

c) Finally, if 13 f3 then 13...♘d4 *is* possible, as 14 ♗xd4 ♕xd5 15 ♗xg7?? ♕g5 wins for Black.

In conclusion, 12...♖b8 probably

allows Black to execute his usual dark-squared strategy with a fairly even game and should be preferred to 12...♕xd5 which gives a somewhat inferior endgame.

| 13 | cxd5 | ♘d4 |

13...♘c5 was played in Dur-Plachetka, Austria 1991. Now after 14 f3 a5 15 d6 White was clearly better, since Black now had to play 15...e6 to keep a reasonable pawn structure, and then 16 b3!, which threatens 17 ♘b5, would have been tough to meet.

| 14 | ♗c4 | |

14 ♗xd4? ♗xd4 15 ♘b5 ♗xb2 16 ♘c7+ ♔d8 17 ♖c2 ♖b8 leads nowhere for White.

| 14 | ... | ♗b7 |
| 15 | ♔d2?! | |

Here White should play the simple 15 0-0 ♖c8 16 b3, which is slightly better for White according to Rogers. This is clearly a critical line for Black. If 16...e6, then simply 17 dxe6 is good, e.g. 17...dxe6 18 ♖fd1 ♘c6 19 ♘b5 is almost losing for Black. We have not found any way of making the black position playable, so we suggest Black tries 12...♖b8!?

15	...	e6
16	♖hd1	♖c8
17	b3	0-0
18	♔d3	exd5
19	♘xd5	♘c6
20	f4	♖fe8
21	♗d2	♘d4
22	♗e3	

(see following diagram)

Now instead of going for the draw with 22...♘c6, Rogers played

| 22 | ... | ♘e6 |

and won on time on move 40, after Ribli had misplayed a better position.

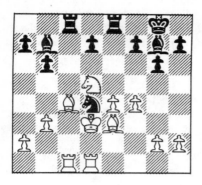

Game 6
Karpov-Larsen
Brussels 1987

(1 e4 c5 2 ♘f3 ♘c6 3 d4 cxd4 4 ♘xd4 g6 5 c4 ♗g7 6 ♗e3 ♘f6 7 ♘c3 ♘g4 8 ♕xg4 ♘xd4 9 ♕d1 ♘e6 10 ♖c1 ♕a5)

11   ♗e2

In actual fact Karpov played 11 ♕d2 b6 12 ♗e2. Perhaps he was afraid that (after 11 ♗e2) Larsen might grab the pawn with 11...♗xc3+ 12 ♖xc3 ♕xa2. Although Larsen has said that someday he will take this bait, we believe that it is much too dangerous for Black.

11	...	b6
12	♕d2	♗b7
13	f3	h5!

This was the new plan introduced by Larsen in this game. By playing ...h7-h5 and ...g7-g5, Black prevents his opponent from playing f3-f4. The e5-square then becomes an excellent outpost for the black queen; from there it combines with the knight on e6 and bishop on g7 to control the dark squares. Given the chance, Black will also advance his kingside pawns even further to attack the white king. Normally Black plays ...g7-g5 before ...h7-h5, but here White has not yet castled, and could then have replied 14 h4!?

14	0-0	g5
15	♖fd1	d6
16	♘d5	

Karpov goes for a typical endgame, which he has won so often, but as we shall see, Black is excellently prepared to counter his opponent's plans here. 16 a3, postponing the endgame for a while, was played in Kosten-Cebalo, Paris 1988. However, after 16...♔f8 17 ♕c2 ♕e5 18 b4 ♗c6 19 ♘d5 ♕b2, Black achieved his beloved ending anyhow and later won.

16	...	♕xd2
17	♖xd2	♗e5
18	b4	

Playing for f3-f4 with g2-g3 would merely weaken the e4-pawn, while the opening of the g-file may bother the white king.

18	...	♖c8
19	a4	h4
20	♗f1	

A necessary prophylactic move, since 20 ♖a2 ♗d4 21 ♔f2 ♗xd5!

22 exd5 ♗xe3+ 23 ♔xe3 ♘f4 would leave both the g2- and d5-pawns under attack.

20	...	f6
21	♖a2	

The only way to try to break through the black position, but since Black ends up with slightly the better position, White probably should have declined to play actively.

21	...	♗d4
22	♔f2	

22 ♗xd4 was played in Wolff-Miles, Philadelphia 1987, when after 22...♘xd4 23 ♖d1 ♘c6 24 a5 ♘e5 25 ♘e3 h3!

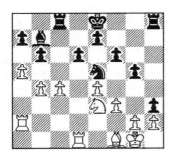

26 axb6 axb6 27 ♖a7 ♗c6 28 b5 hxg2 29 ♗xg2 ♗d7 30 ♘d5 ♖b8 31 ♘xb6 ♗e6 32 ♖d4 ♖h4 White was a pawn up, but his position was a tragedy. All his pieces are misplaced, doing nothing but defending some weak pawns. The game concluded 33 ♘a8 ♗xc4 34 b6 ♔f7 35 ♖a4 ♗b5 36 ♖a3 ♗c6 37 ♘c7 ♖xb6 38 ♖d1 ♖b7 39 ♘a6 ♖f4 40 ♖d4 ♖a7 0-1. This is a good example of Black's potential chances in these endgames. The idea of advancing the pawn to h3 is very difficult to prevent, since for White to play h2-h3 himself would amount to capitulation on the dark squares.

22	...	♔f7
23	a5	♗xd5
24	exd5	♗xe3+
25	♔xe3	♘f4
26	♔d2	

White had to watch out for ...♘xd5. The 'active' 26 ♖ca1 would have been bad after 26...♘g6 27 axb6 axb6 28 ♖a6 ♘e5 29 ♔d4? h3.

26...♖c7 27 axb6 axb6 28 ♖a6 ♖hc8 29 ♖xb6

Again 'active play' with 29 ♖c1 would be punished; this time with 29...b5.

29...♘xd5 30 ♖b5 ♘f4 31 ♖a5 ♘g6 32 c5!

White is worse. His c-pawn is weak, but Karpov manages to reduce the material and make a draw.

32...♘e5 33 ♖c3 dxc5 34 bxc5 ♖b8

34...♘d7 does not win a pawn, since White has 35 ♗a6 ♖xc5?? 36 ♗xc8 ♖xa5 37 ♗xd7.

35 ♗b5 ♖d8+ 36 ♔e2 ♘c6

Now it is a draw for sure, but White has had to defend well to hold everything together.

37 ♗xc6 ♖xc6 38 g3 ♖d4 39 ♖b5 hxg3 40 hxg3 ♖d5 41 g4 ♖c7 42 ♔e3 e6 43 ♖c2 ♔e7 44 ♖c3 ♔f7 45 ♖c2 f5 46 gxf5 exf5 47 ♔f2 ♔g7 ½-½

Naturally this game attracted a lot of attention. It is not often that someone gets a safe ending, with some chances to play for win, as Black against Karpov. Later in the same tournament, Larsen faced Short as Black. Since Short is not a player who backs away from a critical discussion, the line was duly repeated.

Game 7
Short-Larsen
Brussels 1987

(1 e4 c5 2 ♘f3 ♘c6 3 d4 cxd4 4 ♘xd4 g6 5 c4 ♗g7 6 ♗e3 ♘f6 7 ♘c3 ♘g4 8 ♕xg4 ♘xd4 9 ♕d1 ♘e6 10 ♖c1 ♕a5)

11	♗e2	b6
12	0-0	♗b7
13	f3	g5

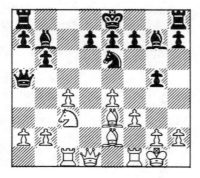

14 a3

This was Short's idea. By threatening 15 ♘b5 followed by ♗d2 he forces Larsen to put his queen on e5. Then Short can continue with ♕d2, b2-b4, ♘d5 etc., without exchanging queens. In a later encounter between the same two players, Short switched to 14 ♖f2!? (see the next game).

14	...	♕e5
15	♕d2	h5
16	♖fd1	d6
17	b4	h4
18	♘d5	♔f8
19	♗f1	♗c6

Here both players had probably achieved what they wanted. But now Short realised that things were not as rosy as he had expected.

Larsen intends to play 20...♗a4, after which White will have to misplace his rook.

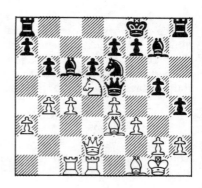

20 ♕d3 ♘f4

Now 20...♗a4 would be pointless after 21 ♖d2.

21 ♘xf4?!

Short should have admitted that he had nothing and settled for a draw with 21 ♕d2 ♘e6 22 ♕d3.

21...gxf4 22 ♗d4 ♕xd4 23 ♗xd4 ♗xd4+ 24 ♖xd4 ♖h5

White is still about equal, but his next move is over-ambitious.

25 c5? dxc5 26 bxc5 b5 27 e5 h3!

The usual undermining move.

28 ♖e1 hxg2 29 ♗xg2 ♖c8 30 ♖xf4 ♗d5 31 e6 f6 32 h4 ♖xc5

Larsen had again managed to achieve an edge against a world-class player. This time he won in 74 moves. Later the same year Short had his chance for revenge as White against Larsen in Hastings. This time Short came up with something more venomous.

Game 8
Short-Larsen
Hastings 1987/88

(1 e4 c5 2 ♘f3 ♘c6 3 d4 cxd4 4

♘xd4 g6 5 c4 ♗g7 6 ♗e3 ♘g4 7
♘c3 ♘g4 8 ♕xg4 ♘xd4 9 ♕d1
♘e6 10 ♖c1 ♕a5 11 ♗e2 b6 12
0-0 ♗b7 13 f3 g5)

14   ♖f2!?

With the idea of transferring the
rook to d2, where it will be excellently placed. White will then be
able to play a2-a3, b2-b4 and ♘d5
etc., without risking an exchange of
queens.

14   ...   h5

In this game, Larsen plays the
same plan as before, but he ends up
clearly worse. Subsequently, some
other ideas have been devised:

a) 14...♗e5 with the idea of exchanging bishops with ...♗f4 and
then following up with ...♕e5, is
positionally well justified. Yet in
Ikonnikov-Vokarev, Perm 1993,
White acted quickly: 15 g3 h5 16
♘d5 ♗xb2 17 ♖b1 and since
17...♗g7 18 c5 is terrible, Black
had to play 17...♕a3, after which
he never managed to co-ordinate
his pieces: 18 ♗f1 ♗xd5 19 ♕xd5
♘c7 20 ♕d2 ♗c3 21 ♕d3 ♗b4 22
♖b3 ♕a5 23 ♗h3 0-0-0 24 c5! and
Black was blown apart.

b) 14...♖d8!? is untried and deserves serious attention. We believe
that the position after 15 ♗f1 ♕e5
16 ♖d2 ♕b8 17 ♘d5 (otherwise
Black will play ...♗e5-f4, exchange
the bishops and then return to e5
with the queen) 17...♗e5 18 h3
(necessary, since 18 g3 h5 gives
Black too much play) is critical for
the whole assessment of Larsen's
plan. Black has a great deal of
dark-squared control on the kingside. Still, to make the attack real,
he needs to get in ...g5-g4, which
must be prepared by ...f7-f6, ...♔f7
and ...h7-h5. White's chances are
on the queenside, where he is in
control. As usual the standard plan
is to play for a4-a5. Another idea is
to open the b-file with first b2-b4
and then c4-c5, to answer ...b6xc5
with b4xc5, but since Black's king
is already on f7, he can simply play
...♗c6, ...♕a8 and ...♖b8 and play
on the b-file himself. In general, we
believe that Black has enough resources to hold the balance, and
that 14...♖d8!? promises an interesting game with difficult strategic
play for both sides.

15   ♗f1   ♕e5

In Hastings 1990, Larsen tried
15...♗xc3? against Chandler. In his
preparation for the game he must
have missed that after 16 ♖xc3 g4,
17 f4! ♗xe4 18 f5! is very strong
(if now 18...♗xf5 19 ♗d4! followed by ♖a3 wins a piece). Larsen
played 18...g3 19 hxg3 ♘c5 20
♖a3 ♕b4 21 ♕d4 ♖g8, but after 22
♗d2 his queen was lost and he resigned a few moves later.

16   ♖d2   d6

Another idea is 16...♗c6 17 b4
♖d8 18 ♘d5 ♕b8 19 c5 bxc5 20
bxc5 ♗e5 21 h3 ♖g8?! (more solid
is 21...f6 and ...♔f7) 22 ♕b3 g4 23

♕xb8 ♗xb8 24 hxg4 hxg4 25 f4!
♗xd5 26 exd5 ♗xf4 27 ♗xf4
♘xf4 28 ♖d4 ♘h5 29 ♖a4 ♘f6 30
c6, Stangl-Becker, German Bundesliga 1991/92. This approach is
quite similar to 14...♖d8 above and
also warrants consideration. As
already mentioned, we do not think
the plan with c4-c5 should be a
problem for Black.

17	♘d5	♔f8
18	b4	

We now see why it is more effective for White to place the rook
on d2 instead of the queen. First of
all, it is not possible for Black to
exchange queens, while on d1 the
queen defends the a4-square, which
means that a2-a4-a5 cannot be
stopped by ...♗c6.

18 ... ♗h6

Larsen tries to exchange the
dark-squared bishops. Although
this is normally a good plan in the
Maroczy, here it is ineffective.
White has too much space and the
standard plan of ...e7-e5 and ...♘d4
is impossible, because Black is so
poorly co-ordinated.

19	♕b3	g4
20	♗xh6+	♖xh6
21	♕e3	♕g7

22	**f4**	**h4?**

A bad move according to Larsen: It just weakens the g4-square.
However, in the end it is these advanced flank pawns that save
Black. From a practical point of
view it is understandable that Larsen did not want to defend passively.

**23 ♗e2 ♖c8 24 ♖f1 ♗xd5 25
♖xd5 g3 26 h3 b5?!**

Again Larsen prefers to go for
active, yet dubious, counterplay,
instead of sitting and waiting. The
neat point is 27 ♖xb5?? ♕d4! and
Black is nearly winning.

**27 cxb5 ♕c3 28 ♕xa7 ♕xb4 29
b6 ♘c5 30 e5 dxe5 31 ♖xe5 ♖e6
32 ♖xe6 fxe6 33 ♔h1 ♖d8 34 ♕c7
♖d6 35 ♕c8+??**

Larsen claims that 35 f5 would
have won for White. Now he manages to effect an escape.

**35...♔g7 36 ♕e8 ♘e4 37 ♕xe7+
♔g8 38 ♕h4 ♕xb6 39 ♕g4+ ♔f8
40 ♕g6 ♕d4 41 f5 ♘f2+ 42 ♖xf2
♕xf2 ½-½**

White has a perpetual.

Ever since this game, 14 ♖f2!?
has always been regarded as the
correct way to meet Larsen's plan
of ...g7-g5 and ...h7-h5. Still, we
suggest that after 14...♖d8!? Black
has no more to fear than in any
other line.

Game 9
Ljubojevic-Korchnoi
Tilburg 1987

(1 e4 c5 2 ♘f3 ♘c6 3 d4 cxd4 4
♘xd4 g6 5 c4 ♗g7 6 ♗e3 ♘f6 7
♘c3 ♘g4 8 ♕xg4 ♘xd4 9 ♕d1
♘e6 10 ♖c1 ♕a5)

11	♗d3

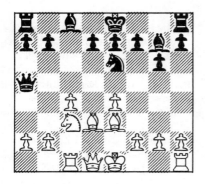

Actually Ljubojevic played 11 ♕d2, but we have taken the liberty of changing the move order in order to cover some of White's additional opportunities. As it turns out, the white plan connected with f2-f4 is very strong. Yet the immediate 11 f4 seems too direct. After 11...d6 12 ♗d3 ♘c5 White cannot play 13 ♗b1 because of 13...♗e6.

11   ...   b6

There seems nothing wrong with playing 11...g5 first, preventing plans based on f2-f4. Eric Prie has faced this idea twice. First he tried 12 h4 against Berend in Val Thorens 1989, but achieved nothing after 12...h6 13 hxg5 hxg5 14 ♖xh8 ♗xh8 15 ♕h5 ♕e5 16 g3 b6 17 ♕h7 ♕g7. Later in Moscow ol 1994, he played 12 ♕h5 against Vorontsov, when after 12...♕e5 13 g3 b6 14 0-0 ♗b7 15 ♖fd1 h6 16 b4 0-0? 17 ♘d5 White was better and went on to win. However, 16...0-0 is a mistake, and Black should be fine after both 16...♖c8 and 16...♗c6.

12   0-0

Here White might try 12 f4, when 12...♘c5 is now dangerous for Black, since after 13 0-0 ♘xd3

14 ♕xd3 his queen is in trouble. 12 ♕d2 is considered in the next game.

12   ...   ♗b7

Again we recommend 12...g5. An interesting attempt at a refutation is 13 ♘d5!?, which was played in Razuvaev-Ermenkov, Polonica Zdroj 1972. Ermenkov played 13...♗b7, but after 14 a4! ♗c6 15 b3 h5? 16 ♗d2 ♕a6 17 ♗xg5 White won easily. The critical continuation is 13...♗xb2, when 14 ♖b1 ♗g7! 15 ♗xg5 ♘xg5 16 ♘c7+ ♔d8 17 ♘xa8 ♘e6 is okay for Black.

13   ♕d2

Here White should play 13 f4!, after which it is difficult to see how Black can obtain any counterplay. In Horvath-Conquest, Budapest 1987, Black tried 13...♗d4, but after 14 ♗xd4 ♘xd4 15 ♘d5 ♗xd5 16 cxd5 b5 17 ♗b1 ♕b6 18 ♔h1 Black's knight on d4 only looks good; in fact it is very difficult to protect and Black soon lost.

Just as depressing for Black was Rodriguez-Hernandez, Camaguey 1988, when after 13...0-0 14 ♗b1 d6 15 ♖f2 ♖ac8 16 ♘d5 ♗xd5 17 cxd5 ♘c5 18 a3 ♘a4 19 b4 ♕a6 20 ♕b3 b5 21 ♗d3 ♕b7 22 c5 Black was lost. To make matters even worse for Black, Tukmakov played 14 a3 against I.Ivanov, Nuremberg 1994, and after 14...♗d4 15 ♗xd4 ♘xd4 16 ♘b5! ♘xb5 17 cxb5 a6 18 ♖c7 Black again found himself in a lost position. Since this plan seems very simple and effective, we recommend that Black prevents it quickly with ...g7-g5 as mentioned above.

13   ...   g5
14   ♖fd1   d6

| 15 | a3 | h5 |
| 16 | ♖c2 | |

Preparing b2-b4, which here would been met by 16...♕xa3 17 ♘d5 ♕b2, and the queen escapes via e5 with a pawn in the bag.

| 16 | ... | ♗d4!? |

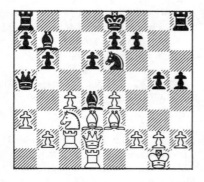

It was of course possible to play normally with 16...♕e5 etc. Generally, however, Black should exchange dark-squared bishops in the Maroczy, when given the chance. He must only be careful not to concede too much space.

| 17 | b4 | ♕e5 |

17...♕xa3 18 ♘d5 would leave the queen in big trouble.

| 18 | ♘d5 | ♗xe3 |

It was safer to play 18...♔f8, but probably Korchnoi did not foresee White's next move.

| 19 | fxe3!? | |

The 'normal' move was 19 ♕xe3, but with his excellent dark-squared control Black would have been fine. Now White tries to use the semi-open f-file for an attack.

19...♖c8 20 ♖f1 ♘g7!

Covering f5, which means the queen cannot be forced away from e5.

21 ♕f2 f6

If 21... 0-0, then 22 ♕g3! would be annoying.

22 ♕e1 0-0 23 a4 h4 24 ♕a1!

Realising that the black queen cannot be removed with violence, White exchanges it instead and tries to generate some initiative in the endgame with a4-a5.

24...♕xa1 25 ♖xa1 ♗xd5 26 exd5 f5?!

Here Black should have secured the draw with 26...a5, when 27 ♖b2 ♖c7 28 bxa5 bxa5 29 ♖b5 ♖a8 is fine for Black, since White cannot break through. Unfortunately it is not possible to activate the g7-knight, so Black cannot win either.

27 ♖f2 ♖c7 28 a5 ♔h7 29 g4 hxg3 30 hxg3 ♔g8 31 ♔g2 ♖f6 32 axb6 axb6 33 ♖a8+ ♖f8 34 ♖a6 ♖b8 35 b5 ♔f7 36 e4 ♔f6 37 exf5 ♔e5 38 ♖a4 ♘e8 39 f6!

If Black had had time for ...♘f6 he might even have been better.

39...♘xf6 40 ♖f5+ ♔d4 41 c5+ ♔xd3 42 ♖f3+ ♔c2 43 c6

Not 43 ♖a2+ ♔b1 44 ♖e2 ♖xc5!

43...♔b2 44 ♖aa3 g4 45 ♖fb3+ ♔c2 46 ♖e3 ♔b2 47 ♖ad3 ♔c2 48 ♖a3 ½-½

Game 10
Leko-P.H.Nielsen
Copenhagen 1995

(1 e4 c5 2 ♘f3 ♘c6 3 d4 cxd4 4 ♘xd4 g6 5 c4 ♗g7 6 ♗e3 ♘f6 7 ♘c3 ♘g4 8 ♕xg4 ♘xd4 9 ♕d1 ♘e6 10 ♖c1 ♕a5 11 ♗d3 b6)

| 12 | ♕d2 | ♗b7 |
| 13 | ♗b1 | g5 |

In the past Black has invariably responded with 13...♖c8 14 b3 f5, which was first seen in Tal-Rashkovsky, Moscow 1973, where

Black drew the endgame after 15 ♘d5 ♕xd2+ 16 ♔xd2. However, I saw no reason not to play the usual dark-squared strategy.

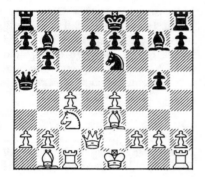

	14	b3	d6
	15	f3	h5?!

This gives White the chance to play 16 h4!, when 16...g4 17 f4 looks good for White. Leko feared 16...gxh4, but after 17 ♖xh4 all that Black has is a weak h-pawn. Probably I should have preferred 15...♕e5 or 15...♗e5.

16   ♘d5?!

Leko goes for an endgame, where White traditionally has good chances. Here, however, Black can easily generate counterplay because of his dark-squared control. In general, it is not the endgame that one should fear when playing Black in the 9...♘e6 variation.

	16	...	♕xd2+
	17	♔xd2	h4
	18	g3	hxg3
	19	hxg3	♔d7

Simply connecting the rooks and preparing to swap them on the h-file.

20 ♗d3 ♘d4 21 f4 gxf4 22 gxf4 ♘f3+ 23 ♔e2 ♘d4+ 24 ♔d2 ½-½

24 ♔f2 would have failed to

24...♖xh1 25 ♖xh1 ♘f5, so Leko had to give me an easy draw. This game shows how simple Black's game is, when White goes for the ending too quickly. Even a top player such as Leko did not manage to put the black position under any pressure.

Game 11
B.Lalic-Conquest
Hastings 1995/96

(1 e4 c5 2 ♘f3 ♘c6 3 d4 cxd4 4 ♘xd4 g6 5 c4 ♗g7 6 ♗e3 ♘f6 7 ♘c3 ♘g4 8 ♕xg4 ♘xd4 9 ♕d1 ♘e6 10 ♖c1)

| | 10 | ... | b6 |

| | 11 | ♕d2 |

The game Chandler-Larsen, Hastings 1987/88, was played in a later round of the same tournament in which Short introduced his 14 ♖f2!? (see Game 8). Since Larsen got a bad position in that game, he switched to the more conservative 10...b6 against Chandler, and after 11 ♗d3 ♘c5 12 ♗b1 d6 13 b4 ♘d7 14 ♗d4 ♗xd4 15 ♕xd4 0-0 16 0-0 ♗a6 17 ♘d5 ♖c8 18 ♖fd1 ♗b7 19 h3 ♖e8 20 ♕b2 ♗c6 a fairly standard position was reached, White being slightly better. Here something very instructive occurred. Instead of slowly trying to build on his small advantage, Chandler played 21 f4?? to grab more space. But when Black answered 21...e5!

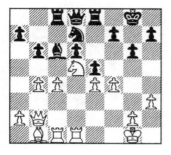

Chandler realised that he had irreparably damaged his position. White cannot prevent e5xf4, when Black will seize the e5-square for the knight. Then the c4-pawn is weak and the bishop on b1 simply misplaced. Since 22 f5 would leave Black with a classic good knight versus a bad bishop scenario after 22...♗xd5 23 cxd5 ♕g5, Chandler played the desperate 22 c5!?, but was soon a pawn down after 22...dxc5 23 ♘e3 ♕e7 24 b5 ♗a8 25 ♘g5 ♔g7, and Black later won.

11 b4!? may be the best answer to 10...b6, in order to keep the knight away from c5 and to gain space on the queenside. Black will never be able to open the queenside with ...a7-a5, since this will leave the b6-pawn very weak, and he will risk getting a very passive position. Suba-Taimanov, Bucharest 1979, continued 11...♗b7 12 ♗d3 0-0 13 0-0 ♘d4 14 ♗b1 ♘c6 15 a3 d6 16 ♕d3 ♖c8 17 f4, after which White

had all the play.

11	...	♗b7
12	♗e2	0-0
13	f3	f5!?

Very often the ...f7-f5 thrust only serves to weaken Black's position. Here, however, it is the only active plan, aiming for a combined attack on g2 with the bishop and rook. Still, White is very solid, and it is difficult to realise the attack.

14	exf5	gxf5
15	♘d5	♕e8
16	0-0	♕f7
17	b4	

In order to play 18 f4, since 17 f4 is met by 17...♘c5, when the knight heads for e4.

| 17 | ... | f4 |
| 18 | ♗f2 | ♘g5?! |

With the idea of ...e7-e5 followed by ...♘e6-d4, which Lalic easily prevents. According to Lalic, 18...♔h8 was better, in order to play down the g-file.

19	h4!	♘e6
20	♖fe1	♔h8
21	♗d3	♖ae8
22	♗c2	♖g8
23	♔f1?	

Here White could have entered a won ending with 23 ♕d3, when

Black's only chance would be 23...♗b2, since both 23...♗h6 24 ♖xe6 and 23...♘f8 24 ♕f5! win for White. After 24 ♖b1 ♕g7 25 ♕xh7+ ♕xh7 26 ♗xh7 ♔xh7 27 ♖xb2 b5 28 ♖d2 bxc4 all Black's pawns are weak and White should pick some of them up.

23...d6 24 ♕d3 ♗e5 25 ♖xe5 dxe5 26 ♖e1 ♘d4 27 ♖xe5 ♘xc2 28 ♕xc2 ♗xd5 29 cxd5 ♖c8 30 ♕d2 ♖g7 31 ♗d4 ♔g8 32 ♗b2 ♕g6?

The losing mistake according to Lalic; Black may have been able to survive with 32...♖c4!

33 ♖e4 ♖f7 34 ♗e5 ♕h5 35 ♗xf4 ♕xh4 36 ♔g1 ♖g7? 37 ♗h6 ♕f6 38 ♗xg7 ♔xg7 39 ♖e6 ♕h4 40 ♕e3 ♔f7 41 ♖e4 1-0

Game 12
Kasparov-Malshikov
USSR 1977

(1 e4 c5 2 ♘f3 ♘c6 3 d4 cxd4 4 ♘xd4 g6 5 c4 ♗g7 6 ♗e3 ♘f6 7 ♘c3 ♘g4 8 ♕xg4 ♘xd4 9 ♕d1 ♘e6 10 ♖c1)

| 10 | ... | d6 |

Another playable, yet passive, alternative to 10...♕a5.

11 b4!?

11 ♗d3 has also been played on many occasions. After 11...0-0 12 0-0 ♗d7 13 ♗b1 (best, since 13 ♕d2 is met with 13...♕a5, as in Kudrin-Larsen Hastings 1986, when after 14 b3 ♖fc8 15 f4 ♘c5 16 ♗b1 ♗c6 17 f5 ♘d7 Black parried the attack and won due to his positional trumps) 13...a5 both 14 ♕e2 ♗c6 15 ♖fd1 b6 16 ♘d5 ♘c5 17 ♗g5, as in Beliavsky-Velimirovic, Reggio Emilia 1986, and 14 f4 ♗c6 15 ♕d2 a4 16 ♘d5 ♘c5 17 e5, as in Kosten-Larsen, Esbjerg 1988, seem to give White a slightly better game although it should not bother Black unduly.

Instead of 12...♗d7, 12...♘c5 was played in Portisch-Petrosian, Palma de Mallorca 1974, when after 13 ♗b1 a5 14 ♕d2 ♗d7 15 ♗d4?! ♗xd4 16 ♕xd4 ♗c6 17 ♕d2 f6 18 ♖fd1 ♖f7 19 ♗c2 ♕b6 20 ♖b1 ♖d8 21 ♘d5 ♕a7 22 b3 Black was ready for the thematic 22...e5!, with slightly better prospects, since his knight is on its way to d4.

| 11 | ... | 0-0 |
| 12 | ♗e2 | b6 |

The most common. Although Velimirovic has had some success with 12...a5, it looks suspect, since the b6-square is left terribly weak. Yet, so far no one has managed to exploit that. After 13 a3 axb4 14 axb4 ♗d7 15 0-0 ♗c6, White normally plays 16 ♕d2 (16 ♘d5 was once tried in Kobas-Velimirovic, Zenica 1987, but Black won tactically with 16...♖a2 17 ♖e1 ♖e8 18 ♗g4 ♕b8 19 b5 ♗xd5 20 cxd5 ♘c5 21 ♗xc5 dxc5 22 ♖xc5 ♕f4 23 ♗f3 ♖d2 24 ♕c1 ♗d4 25 ♖c8 ♖xc8 26 ♕xc8+ ♔g7 27 ♔h1 e6

0-1, since ...♗e5 cannot be prevented), and after 16...♖a3 17 ♘d5, Velimirovic improved upon Portisch-Pfleger, Manila 1974, (where Black lost after 17...♔h8?!), with 17...♖e8 and had a fine position after 18 ♖fd1 ♘f8! 19 h3 ♘d7, since the active rook on a3 is annoying for White. Instead, 18 ♗b6 was tried in the 1985 correspondence game Rosanen-Rau, but after 18...♕a8 19 f4 ♖a2 20 ♖c2 ♖xc2 21 ♕xc2 ♗xd5 22 exd5 ♘d4 Black had absolutely no problems. It is worth noting that here the opening of the a-file was a big plus for Black. Normally it is White who tries to open it by playing b2-b3, a2-a3 and b2-b4, but here we saw just how much counterplay this can allow.

| | 13 | 0-0 | ♗b7 |
| | 14 | ♘d5 | ♘c7 |

Larsen tried 14...♕d7 against Adorjan, Hastings 1986/87, but faced a difficult position after 15 ♗g4 f5 16 exf5 gxf5 17 ♗h3 ♘c7 18 ♘xc7 ♕xc7 19 c5!

| | 15 | ♕a4!? |

In Cu.Hansen-Larsen, Esbjerg 1988, White played 15 ♗g5 and stood better after 15...f6 16 ♗e3 ♔h8 17 ♕b3 ♕d7 18 ♖fd1, although this clash between the two great Danes ended in a draw.

| | 15 | ... | b5? |

Not a good decision. 15...e6 was more solid, when Black should be okay.

	16	♕a5!	♘xd5
	17	cxd5	♕xa5
	18	bxa5	

Suddenly Black has a cheerless ending with no counterplay. He would be fine if he could play ...a7-a6 and ...♖fc8 in one move, but

since this is not legal White gets the c-file with a winning initiative.

18...♖fb8 19 ♖c7 f5 20 f3 ♗f6 21 ♖fc1 a6 22 ♖d7

Black's fortress looks impregnable, but the young Kasparov manages to organise a breakthrough.

22...♔f7 23 ♖cc7 ♗c8 24 ♖d8 ♗b7 25 ♖xb8 ♖xb8 26 ♗a7 ♖a8 27 ♗e3 ♗c8 28 g4 fxg4 29 fxg4 ♔e8 30 g5 ♗e5 31 ♔g2 ♗d7 32 ♗b6 ♗g7 33 h4 ♗e5 34 ♔f3 ♗c8 35 ♔e3 ♗d7 36 h5 ♗g1 37 ♗d4 ♗g1+ 38 ♔d3 ♗xd4 39 ♔xd4 ♔d8 40 ♖c1

It seems as if Black has escaped somehow, but White just breaks through on the kingside.

40...e5+ 41 dxe6 ♗xe6 42 hxg6 hxg6 43 ♖c6! ♔e7

43...♔d7 44 ♖xa6! ♖xa6 45 ♗xb5+ ♖c6 46 a6 ♔c7 47 a7 wins easily.

44 ♖c7+ ♔e8 45 a3 ♖b8 46 ♖c6 b4 47 ♖b6! ♖xb6 48 axb6 ♗c8 49 axb4 ♔d7 50 ♗g4+ ♔d8 51 ♗xc8 1-0

Despite White's strategic success in this game, the line with 10...d6 is a solid alternative to 10...♕a5. In particular, Velimirovic's plan with 12...a5!? deserves close study.

Game 13
Larsen-Petrosian
Santa Monica 1966

(1 e4 c5 2 ♘f3 ♘c6 3 d4 cxd4 4
♘xd4 g6 5 c4 ♗g7 6 ♗e3 ♘f6 7
♘c3 ♘g4 8 ♕xg4 ♘xd4 9 ♕d1
♘e6)

10   ♕d2

As we now know, this is not the
most exact move order, since in the
10...♕a5 systems, the queen does
not belong on d2. At the time of the
game, however, this had not been
recognised, and on 10...d6 Larsen
considered it more aggressive to
have the rooks on d1 and e1.

10   ...   d6
11   ♗e2   ♗d7
12   0-0   0-0
13   ♖ad1!?

13 ♖ac1 was played in Keres-
Petrosian, Zagreb ct 1959, when
after 13...♗c6 14 ♖fd1 ♘c5 15 f3
a5 16 b3 ♕b6 a well-known position from the Classical system had
arisen, but a tempo up for White.
Still, since the rooks are on c1 and
d1, instead of b1 and c1, one might

even argue that Black is in fact a
tempo up! Since that structure is
more relevant to the Classical system, we shall cover it in the relevant chapter (see Game 34).

13   ...   ♗c6
14   ♘d5   ♖e8?!

Too passive. It was better to play
14...♘c5, which was actually Larsen's own choice in Porath-Larsen,
Amsterdam 1964, when after 15 f3
a5 16 ♗d4? ♗xd4 17 ♕xd4 e5! 18
♕d2 ♘e6 Black had the usual ad-
vantageous structure and later won.
Petrosian feared 15 ♕c2, yet
15...a5! is strong, since 16 ♗xc5
dxc5 17 ♘f6+ ♗xf6 18 ♖xd8
♖fxd8 is okay for Black.

15   f4!?

A logical reaction to the rook
move. Now the f7-square becomes
a target.

15   ...   ♘c7

After the usual 15...♘c5, Petrosian feared 16 e5 ♘d7 17 ♘b4!
which looks strong. Yet, Larsen
suggests that after 17...♕c7 it is not
clear whether Black is worse than
in the game.

16   f5   ♘a6

Black tries to get the knight to
e5. Although it takes a lot of time
to get there, this is necessary since
the knight is badly needed in the
defence.

17   ♗g4?!

Larsen goes for the direct attack,
which is quite logical, since Black
is using a lot of time to manoeuvre
his knight. However, 17 b4! was
simpler, after which Black cannot
regroup, since 17...♘b8 18 b5!
♗xd5 19 ♕xd5 hits both f7 and b7.

17   ...   ♘c5
18   fxg6   hxg6
19   ♕f2   ♖f8

20   e5!

Very strong, but also absolutely necessary. 20 ♕h4 ♝xd5 21 ♖xd5 e6 or 21 exd5 e5 is not better for White. It is striking to see that although Black has lost a lot of time with his knight, his position is still very close to being tenable, and that only active tactical play breaks through.

20	**...**	**♝xe5**
21	**♕h4**	**♝xd5**
22	**♖xd5**	**♞e6?!**

The point behind 20 e5! is that 22...e6 would be answered with 23 ♕xd8 ♖fxd8 24 ♖xe5 dxe5 25 ♝xc5. Still, since Black has reasonable drawing chances in that case, he should have played it anyway. Also 22...♞e4 23 ♝f3 ♞f6 24 ♖b5 is positionally much better for White.

23   ♖f3   ♝f6?

The decisive mistake. Black could still have hung on with 23...f5 24 ♖h3 ♔f7!, after 25 ♝xf5 gxf5 26 ♕h5+ ♔f6 27 g4 ♞g7! After 28 ♝g5+ ♔e6 29 ♕g6+ ♝f6 30 gxf5 ♔d7 31 ♝xf6 ♖xf6 32 ♕xg7 ♕g8, when Black has real drawing chances. It seems incredible that White does not have anything decisive, but Larsen has not found anything and neither have we. Now, however, we have arrived at one of the proudest moments in Danish chess history, since it is not often that a reigning world champion is defeated like this.

24   ♕h6   ♝g7

25   ♕xg6!   ♞f4

Nothing works: 25...♞c7 26 ♕xg7+ mates and 25...fxg6 is very similar to the game.

| **26** | **♖xf4** | **fxg6** |
| **27** | **♝e6+** | **♖f7** |

27...♔h7 28 ♖h4+ ♝h6 29 ♝xh6 ♖f5 30 ♖xf5 gxf5 31 ♝f7! e5 32 ♖h3 mates.

28	**♖xf7**	**♔h8**
29	**♖g5**	**b5**
30	**♖g3**	**1-0**

Strong attacking chess, and a nice way to round off the 7...♞g4 chapter.

2 Maroczy Bind: Double Fianchetto System

Chapter Guide

1 e4 c5 2 ♘f3 ♘c6 3 d4 cxd4 4 ♘xd4 g6 5 c4 ♗g7 6 ♗e3 ♘f6 7 ♘c3 0-0
8 ♗e2 b6 9 0-0 ♗b7

10 ♘xc6!?	– *Game 14*
10 f3	

The double fianchetto system against the Maroczy Bind does not have the greatest of reputations, but nevertheless it is still played with Black by several grandmasters, e.g. Bellon, Rogers and Pigusov to mention but a few.

White must be aware that his opponent has several tricks up his sleeve, but if he avoids these, Black often ends up in an unpleasant, passive position with few prospects of being able to obtain active counterplay.

Game 14
Schlosser-Pigusov
Sochi 1989

(1 e4 c5 2 ♘f3 ♘c6 3 d4 cxd4 4 ♘xd4 g6 5 c4 ♗g7 6 ♗e3 ♘f6 7 ♘c3)

7   ...   0-0

8   ♗e2

This quiet development of the bishop is the logical way for White to continue. However, a couple of other approaches have also been tried, with the following practical results:

a) 8 h3 d6 9 ♗e2 ♗d7 (9...♘xd4 10 ♗xd4 ♗d7 11 0-0 ♗c6 12 ♕d3 a5 13 ♖ad1 was slightly better for White in F.Olafsson-Bouaziz, Nice ol 1974) 10 0-0 a6 11 ♕d2 b5 (Black has to play actively) 12 cxb5 ♘xd4 13 ♗xd4 axb5 14 ♖fd1 (Larsen gives 14 ♗xf6 ♗xf6 15 ♘b5 ♕a5 16 ♘c3 ♖fc8 17 ♖fc1 ♗xc3 18 ♖xc3 ♖xc3 19 ♕xc3 ♕xc3 20 bxc3 ♖a3 21 c4 ♗a4 with a level ending) 14...♗c6 15 ♗b5 ♘e4 16 ♘xe4 ♗xb5 17 ♗xg7 ♔xg7 with roughly equal chances in the game Larsen-Kavalek, Solingen 1970.

b) 8 ♘b3 d6 9 f3 ♗e6 10 ♘d5 (Black does not have any problems after 10 ♖c1 either: 10...♖c8 11 ♘d2 a6 12 ♗e2?! [12 ♘d5] 12...♘e5 13 b3 ♕a5, Murey-Afek, Montpellier 1985) 10...♘d7 11 ♕d2 a5 12 ♖c1 a4 13 ♘d4 ♗xd5 14 exd5 ♘xd4 15 ♗xd4 ♗xd4 with equality in Korchnoi-Van der Sterren, Netherlands 1977.

8 ... b6

This is the double fianchetto line, which has been laid to rest and then revived a couple of times. Its current status depends very much upon whether or not Black can find a way to meet 10 ♘xc6, which has been causing problems for the last couple of years. Aside from 8...b6, Black has 8...d6, which will be discussed in Chapter 3.

9 0-0

At this point White has tried a number of other ideas. Some of these are quite interesting but the first is completely useless:

a) 9 g4? (Where does White intend to put his king after this move?) 9...♗b7 10 ♘xc6 ♗xc6 11 ♕d3 d6 12 ♖g1 ♘d7 13 f3, Lus-

sault-Donaldson, Monaco 1977, and now 13...a6! intending ...b6-b5 would have been best, when Black would have had clearly the better chances.

b) 9 ♕c2 ♗b7 10 ♖d1 ♘xd4 11 ♗xd4 d6 12 h4 ♕d7 13 ♘d5 ♖ac8 14 ♖h3 ♖fe8 15 h5 b5 16 hxg6 hxg6 17 b3 bxc4 18 bxc4 ♗xd5 19 exd5 e5 20 dxe6 ♖xe6 21 ♔f1 ½-½ Speelman-Cebalo, Taxco izt 1985.

c) 9 f3 ♗b7 10 ♕d2 e6? (this move is not a good idea after 10 0-0 either – see Game 15; it is better to play 10...♖c8!? or 10...♘h5!? with a likely transposition to the main lines) 11 ♖d1 ♘e5 12 ♘db5 d5 13 exd5 cxd5 14 ♘xd5 ♘xd5 15 exd5 a6 16 ♘c3 ♘c4 17 ♗xc4 ♕h4+ 18 g3 ♕xc4 19 ♗d4 with a clear edge for White in the encounter Muco-Rantanen, Lucerne ol 1982.

d) 9 ♘xc6 dxc6 10 ♕c2 ♘g4 11 ♗g5 ♕d4?! (this is a bad idea that only brings problems; better is 11...♗e6) 12 ♗h4 ♕c5 13 h3 ♘e5 14 0-0 g5 (this seems to be a rather odd move, but better moves are hard to come by; White was threatening 15 ♘a4 ♕d6 16 ♖ad1 ♕c7 17 f4) 15 ♗xg5 ♘f3 16 ♗xf3 ♕xg5 17 ♕c1 ♕g6 18 ♔h1 ♔h8 19 ♕c3 when Black had some, but not quite sufficient, compensation in the game Zso.Polgar-Edelman, Münster 1993.

e) 9 f4!? and now:

(see following diagram)

e1) 9...♗b7 10 ♗f3 ♖c8?! (now Black ends up in a passive position; far better is 10...♘xd4 11 ♗xd4 ♖c8, e.g. 12 e5 ♗xf3 13 ♕xf3 ♘e8 followed by ...d7-d6 or ...f7-f6) 11 e5 ♘e8 12 0-0 ♘a5 13 ♗xb7

♘xb7 14 ♕e2 d6 15 e6 f5 16 b4! ♘f6 17 ♘d5 ♘g4 18 ♖ac1 ♕e8 19 ♘b5 and Black's position was downright awful in Mortensen-Kristensen, Denmark 1983.

e2) 9...e5!? 10 ♘db5 exf4 11 ♗xf4 ♘e8 12 0-0 ♗b7 (this position can also arise from 9 0-0 ♗b7 10 f4 e5 11 ♘db5 exf4 12 ♗xf4 ♘e8) 13 ♕d2 a6! 14 ♘d6 ♘xd6 15 ♗xd6 ♖e8 16 c5?! (better seems 16 ♕f4!?, putting pressure on the f7-pawn, which Black probably will have to sacrifice if he wishes to remain active) 16...♗d4+ 17 ♔h1 bxc5 18 ♗c4 ♖e6 19 ♗xe6 dxe6 20 ♕f4 f5 and Black's powerful pair of bishops provided him with more than enough compensation for the exchange in Rodin-Kron, Moscow 1991.

e3) 9...♘xd4 10 ♗xd4 ♗b7 11 e5 (or 11 0-0 d6 12 ♕d3 ♘d7 13 ♗xg7 ♔xg7 14 ♖ad1 f6 15 ♗g4 ♘c5 16 ♕d4 a5 with a passive but solid position for Black) 11...♘e8 12 ♗f3 ♗xf3 13 ♕xf3 ♘d6 (here both 13...♖c8 and 13...d6 were worth considering; Olafsson's approach is more direct and frees his position immediately) 14 exd6 ♗xd4 15 0-0-0 ♗xc3 16 ♕xc3 ♖c8 17 ♔b1 exd6 18 h4 b5 19 ♖xd6 ♖xc4 20 ♕d3 ♖e8 and Black had

solved his opening problems in Zso.Polgar-F.Olafsson, Vienna 1993.

9 ... ♗b7

10 ♘xc6!?

This move has gained in popularity in recent years and no wonder – White's results have been very impressive. However, as on move nine, White has tried an amazing variety of moves. For 10 f3, see the next game, while the other alternatives are:

a) 10 f4!? (this thrust is more difficult for Black to handle when played on the previous move, as Black can now stop e4-e5 with ...d7-d6) 10...d6 (10...e5!? 11 ♘db5 exf4 12 ♗xf4 ♘e8 transposes to Rodin-Kron above, but 10...♖c8 is too passive: after 11 e5 ♘e8 12 ♘cb5 [for 12 ♗f3, see Mortensen-Kristensen under 9 f4 above] 12...♘xd4 13 ♗xd4 ♖a8 14 ♕d3 ♘c7 15 f5 ♘xb5 16 cxb5 ♖c8 17 f6 ♗h8 18 ♗g4 ♖c7 19 ♖ae1, White was much better in Murray-Barbeau, Montreal 1981) 11 ♖c1 (also interesting is 11 ♘xc6 ♗xc6 12 ♗f3 ♖c8 13 ♖c1 e6 14 ♕d3 ♕e7 15 ♖fd1 ♖fd8 16 ♘b5 ♗xb5 17 cxb5 ♖xc1 18 ♖xc1 e5 19 ♖c6 d5 with equal chances in Hunt-Crouch, London 1994) 11...♖c8 12 b3 ♘d7 13 ♗f3 ♘c5 14 ♕d2?! (14 ♘de2 with equal chances deserves preference) 14...♘xd4 15 ♗xd4 ♗xd4+ 16 ♕xd4 e5 17 ♕d2 exf4 18 ♖cd1 ♕g5 and Black was a safe pawn up in Wallace-Silman, Phoenix 1990.

b) 10 ♘c2 ♖c8 11 f3 ♘e8 12 ♕d2 (or 12 ♘a3 f5 13 c5 ♘a5 14 exf5 ♖xf5 15 ♗d3 ♖e5 16 ♗d4 ♖h5 17 ♗xg7 ♔xg7 18 b4 ♘c6 with an initiative for Black in Scarella-Panno, Argentina 1995) 12...f5! 13 ♗h6 ♗xh6 14 ♕xh6 ♘e5 15 exf5 gxf5 16 ♖fe1 ♖c6 17 ♕e3 ♖e6 18 ♘d5 f4 19 ♕b3 ♖h6 20 ♗d3 d6 21 ♗e4, Wegner-Raaste, Berlin 1990, and now Black should have proceeded with 21...e6 22 ♘xf4 ♖xf4 23 ♗xb7 ♕h4 24 h3 ♕a3 (Wegner).

c) 10 ♘db5?! d6 11 f3 ♘d7 12 ♕d2 ♘c5 13 ♘d5 ♖b8 14 ♖ad1 a6 15 ♘a3 e6 16 ♘c3 e5!? 17 ♘d5 ♘d4 18 ♗xd4 exd4 19 ♘c2 ♗xd5 20 cxd5 d3 21 ♗xd3 ♗xb2 with a good game for Black in Ragozin-Mezentsev, Orel 1992.

d) 10 ♘b3?! d6 11 ♖c1 (or 11 f4 ♖c8 12 ♗f3 e5!? 13 ♘b5 exf4 14 ♗xf4 ♘e8 15 ♘xd6 ♘xd6 16 ♗xd6 ♗xb2 with fine chances for Black in Renet-Rantanen, Palma de Mallorca 1989) 11...♖c8 12 f3 ♘e5 13 ♘d5 e6 14 ♘xf6+ ♗xf6 15 ♖c2 ♗a6 16 ♕c1 d5 17 ♗h6 ♖e8 18 f4 ♘xc4 and Black had the luxury of an extra pawn in Hertneck-Hickl, Munich 1988.

e) 10 ♖c1? (a well-known mistake that, surprisingly, even strong grandmasters have been guilty of from time to time) 10...♘xd4 11 ♗xd4 ♗h6!

The point! (11...♘xe4?? loses a piece after 12 ♗xg7 ♔xg7 13 ♘xe4 ♗xe4 14 ♕d4+). White now loses material after either:

e1) 12 ♖c2 ♘xe4 13 ♗f3 ♘xc3 14 ♖xc3 ♗xf3 15 ♕xf3 ♖c8, Tseshkovsky-Bellon, Las Palmas 1976.

e2) 12 f4 ♘xe4 13 ♘xe4 ♗xe4 14 ♗c3 (or 14 ♗f3 ♗xf3 15 ♕xf3 ♕c7 16 b3 ♕c6, as in Yakovich-Antunes, Bayamo 1990) 14...♕c7 15 ♕c2 e5 16 ♖cd1 ♗xf4 17 ♕xd7 ♕xd7 18 ♖xd7 ♖fd8 19 ♖fd1 ♗e3, as in Kruszynski-Hernandez, Polanica Zdroj 1983.

e3) 12 ♗d3 ♗xc1 13 ♕xc1 d6 14 f3 ♘d7 15 ♕h6 f6 16 h4 ♘e5 17 ♗c2 ♖c8 18 ♗xe5 dxe5 and White had insufficient compensation for the exchange in Lichtenstein-Petursson, Stockholm 1981.

e4) 12 ♗f3 ♗xc1 13 ♕xc1 d6 14 ♖d1 ♘e8 15 ♕h6 e6 16 ♖d3 ♕e7 17 ♗g4 e5 18 ♗e3 ♖d8 19 ♘d5 ♗xd5 20 cxd5 ♘f6 21 ♗f3 ♘d7 and once again White did not have enough for the exchange in Tosic-Karlsson, Nis 1981.

e5) 12 e5!? ♗xc1 13 exf6 ♗g5 14 fxe7 ♗xe7 15 ♗f3 ♗c6 16 ♘d5 ♖c8 17 ♕d2 ♗xd5 18 ♗xd5 ♗f6 with a clear edge for Black in the encounter Hauchard-Bernard, Val

Thorens 1988.

f) 10 ♕d2? is the most common mistake by White in the 9...b6 system. White does not lose material, but Black obtains the pair of bishops, and the dark-squared bishop in particular helps him to secure a safe edge. Practice has shown that White does indeed face a difficult defensive task; the score is heavily in Black's favour after 10...♘xd4 11 ♗xd4 e5! (the trick)

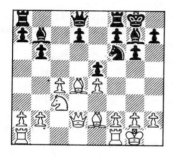

12 ♗xe5 ♘xe4 13 ♘xe4 (13 ♕d4? and 13 ♕f4? both lose to 13...♗xe5 14 ♕xe5 ♖e8) 13...♗xe5 and now White has tried:

f1) 14 f4 ♗xb2 15 ♕xb2 ♗xe4 16 ♗xf3 ♗xf3 17 ♖xf3 ♕c7 18 f5 ♕c5+ 19 ♔h1 ♕xc4 20 ♕d2 f6 21 fxg6 hxg6 22 ♕h6 ♕f7 23 ♖g3 g5 24 h4 ♕h7 25 hxg5 ♕xh6+ 26 gxh6+ ♔h7 27 ♖g7+ ♔xh6 28 ♖xd7 ♔g6 and Black went on to win the endgame in Parameswaran-Crouch, Calcutta 1994.

f2) 14 ♘d6 ♗c6 15 ♖ad1 (White seems to be able to equalise with 15 f4!?, e.g. 15...♗g7 16 ♖ad1 f5 17 ♗f3 ♕f6 18 b3 ♖ab8 19 ♘b5 ♗xb5 20 cxb5 ♖fd8 Hakki-Asmat, Novi Sad ol 1990) 15...♕e7 16 ♗g4 ♗xd6 17 ♕xd6 ♕e4 18 ♗h3 ♕xc4 19 b3 ♕c2 20 ♖d2 ♕c3 21 ♖d3 ♕a5 22 a4 ♖ad8

and Black went on to win in Eriksson-Rogers, Malmö 1993.

f3) 14 ♘g3 ♗c6?! (possibly better is 14...♕f6 15 ♖ab1 ♗c6, 15...h5!? or 15...a5!?, intending 16 ♕xd7 ♗c6 17 ♕d2 h5 with a powerful initiative) 15 f4 ♗g7 16 ♖ad1 a5 17 ♗f3 ♕f6 18 b3 ♖fe8 19 ♗d5 ♗h6 20 a4 ♖e7 21 ♕f2 ♗xd5 22 ♖xd5 ♖ae8, when despite his weak b- and d- pawns Black had the better chances due to his strong dark-squared bishop in Robovic-Rogers, Biel 1992.

f4) 14 ♘c3! ♖e8 15 ♖ae1?! (best was 15 ♖ac1) 15...♖c8 16 ♘d5 (not 16 f4 ♗xc3 17 ♕xc3 b5) 16...♗xd5 17 cxd5 ♕c7 18 ♗a6! ♖b8! 19 f4 ♗f6 20 a4 ♕c5+ 21 ♔h1 h5 22 ♗b5 ♕d6 23 ♖e2 ♖bc8 24 g3?! (preferable was 24 ♖fe1) ♔g7 25 ♖fe1 ♖xe2 26 ♖xe2? ♖c5 27 ♖e3 ♖xd5 and Black went on to win in Sion-Zsu.Polgar, Salamanca 1989.

10 ... ♗xc6

After 10...bxc6 theory gives White a preference, but in practice it has been a slaughter. For example, 11 e5 ♘d7 (11...♘e8? is even worse: 12 f4 ♕c7 13 c5 b5 14 a4 b4 15 ♘e4 a5 16 ♗c4 ♗a6 17 ♗xa6 ♖xa6 18 ♕g4 ♖a8 19 ♖ad1 ♖a8 20 ♕d7! and Black was torn apart in Kaidanov-Kristensen, Hastings 1990) 12 f4 (also of interest is 12 e6 fxe6 13 ♗g4, when Silman gives 13...♖f5 14 ♗xf5 exf5 with some compensation, but we prefer 13...♘c5, e.g. 14 ♗xc5 bxc5 15 ♗xe6+ ♔h8 when Black's dark-squared bishop compensates for the disrupted pawn structure; based on the obvious merits of 12 f4, White should not spend too much time on 12 e6) 12...♕c7 13 ♕c2 ♖fe8

(Black wants to activate his pieces with ...♘f8, ...♖ad8, ...♘e6 and ...c6-c5, but he never gets that far) 14 h4! ♘f8 15 h5 f6? (more sensible is 15...♖ad8) 16 hxg6 hxg6 17 c5! b5 18 ♕b3+ and White soon won, Wahls-Pigusov, Biel 1989.

11 f3 d6

Black has a few options to choose from, but this is the most solid. The alternatives are:

a) 11...e6 12 ♕c2 (with 12 ♕d2 d5 we would transpose to 10 f3 e6 11 ♕d2 d5 12 ♘xc6 ♗xc6 which, as we shall see in the next game, is better for White) 12...♕e7 13 ♖ad1 ♖ac8 14 f4 d6 15 ♗f2 with a small plus for White, Fedorowicz-Donaldson, Gausdal 1979.

b) 11...♘h5 12 ♕d2 (also possible is 12 ♖c1, as in Nunn-Ristoja, Malta ol 1980) 12...f5 13 exf5 gxf5 14 f4 ♘f6 15 ♗d4 ♖c8 16 ♗f3 e6 17 b3 ♖f7 18 ♖ad1 and White was very much in control, Smejkal-Rantanen, Novi Sad ol 1990.

c) 11...♕b8!? 12 ♕d2 ♖e8 13 ♖ac1 d6 14 ♘d5 ♕b7 15 ♗g5 (White forces some structural weaknesses on his opponent, but with the limited material left on the board, he has problems taking ad-

vantage of this; it was therefore better to play 15 b4) 15...♖ad8 16 ♘xf6+ ♗xf6 17 ♗xf6 exf6 18 ♖fd1 ♕e7 19 ♗f1 ♕e5 20 ♖c3 f5 21 exf5 ♕xf5 22 ♖d3 ♕c5+ 23 ♔h1 ♖e6 24 b4 ♕e5 25 ♖d4 ♔g7 26 ♔g1 h5 27 ♕f4 ♖c8 28 ♕d2 ♖d8 29 ♕f4 ♖c8 ½-½ was the game Nemec-Znamenacek, Czechoslovakia 1992.

12 ♕d2 ♖c8

Although nothing much seems to be going on, Black has to handle matters with care. In the game Chekhov-Martin, Barcelona 1984, Black ended up in trouble: 12...♕d7?! 13 ♖fd1 ♖ad8 14 a4 e6 15 a5 ♕b7 16 axb6 axb6 17 b4 ♕b8 18 ♗d4 d5 19 cxd5 exd5 20 e5 ♘e8 21 ♕e3 ♘c7 22 b5 ♗a8 23 ♗xb6 and White was winning. Also 12...♘d7 has been tried, Isupov-Balogh, Budapest 1994, saw 13 ♖ac1 a5 14 b3 ♘c5 15 ♖fd1 ♖a7 16 ♗g5 ♘e6 17 ♗e3 f5? (it was much better to repeat the position with 17...♘c5, although White is probably slightly better) 18 exf5 gxf5 19 ♘d5 ♖b7 20 f4 with a clear plus for White.

13 ♖fd1 ♖e8

13...♕d7?! would have been met with 14 a4!, as in Chekhov-Martin above.

14 ♖ac1 ♕d7

With the rook gone from a1, White no longer has the option of a2-a4.

15	♗f1	♕b7
16	♗g5	♘d7
17	♘d5	♘c5
18	♖c2	a5
19	b3	♖cd8

Black has equalised and the game was agreed drawn after a few more moves:

20 ♕c1 ♖d7 21 ♗g5 ♘e6 22 ♗e3 ♘c5 23 ♗g5 ♘e6 24 ♗e3 ♘c5 ½-½

Game 15
Wojtkiewicz-Bellon
Iraklion 1993

(1 e4 c5 2 ♘f3 ♘c6 3 d4 cxd4 4 ♘xd4 g6 5 c4 ♗g7 6 ♗e3 ♘f6 7 ♘c3 0-0 8 ♗e2 b6 9 0-0 ♗b7)

10   f3

10   ...   e6?!
Black hopes to get in ...d7-d5, thereby solving his problems through multiple exchanges. However, it is not quite so easy as that.

Black has a number of other options here on the 10th move, and in this game we shall take a look at most of them: 10...♘xd4, 10...♘e8 and 10...d6. The next game will deal with 10...♖c8 and Game 17 with the two most popular choices 10...♘h5!? and 10...♕b8!? Although the latter two moves constitute the lines in which Black has the best chance of equalising, the others are often played and not without interest. However, with correct play White should obtain an advantage. Here are the lesser lines:

a) 10...♘xd4? (very passive) 11 ♗xd4 d6 12 ♕d2 ♘d7 13 ♗xg7 ♔xg7 14 f4 ♖c8?! (probably better is 14...a5, although White also has a clear edge after 15 ♖ac1 ♘c5 16 ♕e3 e5 17 ♖cd1 ♕e7 18 f5 f6 19 h4, Boleslavsky-Pirc, Belgrade 1956) 15 ♖ad1 ♘f6 16 e5 dxe5 17 fxe5 ♘g8 18 ♕e3! ♕c7 19 e6 fxe6 20 ♘b5! ♕c5 21 ♕xc5 ♖xc5 22 ♖xf8 ♔xf8 23 ♖d7 with a decisive advantage for White, Cvetkovic-Cebalo, Yugoslavia 1985.

b) 10...♘e8?! (originally this was devised as an attempt to play ...f7-f5, but this advance just creates weaknesses; Black players then came up with an alternate plan of sending the e8-knight via c7 to e6, but this idea is very slow and Black usually ends up in an inferior position without counterplay) 11 ♕d2 (11 ♖c1 also seems good) 11...♘c7 (as mentioned above, 11...f5?! does more to create weaknesses than generate counterplay; after 12 exf5 gxf5 13 ♖ad1 ♖c8 14 ♖fe1 e6 15 ♘b3 ♖f7 White was clearly better in Korelov-Bannik, USSR 1962) 12 ♖ad1 ♘e6 13 ♘c2 (also interesting is 13 ♘db5)

13...d6 14 b3 ♚h8 15 f4 f5 16 exf5 gxf5 17 ♗f3 ♕d7 18 ♖fe1 ♘cd8 19 ♗d5 and White was very much in control, Magem Badals-Tatai, Andorra 1987.

c) 10...d6?! (this move used to be the main line, but after the game Gheorghiu-Bellon, Las Palmas 1976, the entire line was discredited) 11 ♕d2 ♕d7 (the alternatives are 11...♘d7 12 ♚h1 ♘xd4 13 ♗xd4 ♗xd4 14 ♕xd4 a5 15 f4 ♘c5 16 ♕e3 e6 17 ♖ad1 ♕e7 18 ♗f3 ♖ad8 19 b3 with a small edge for White, Timoschenko-Apicella, Bucharest 1993, or 11...♘xd4 12 ♗xd4 ♘d7 13 ♗xg7 ♚xg7 14 f4 ♖c8 15 ♖ad1 ♘f6 16 e5 dxe5 17 fxe5 ♘g8 18 ♕e3 with a clearly better game for White, Cvetkovic-Cebalo, Yugoslavia 1985) and here White has tried several different ideas:

c1) 12 ♖fe1 ♖fd8 13 ♗f1 ♘e8 14 ♘xc6 ♗xc6 15 ♗g5 ♖ac8 16 ♖ac1 ♕b7 17 b4 f6 18 ♗e3 ♘f7 19 ♕f2 ♗e8 20 ♖ed1 ♘a6 21 a3 ♗f7 22 ♘d5 e6 23 ♘c3 ♘c7 24 ♖c2 ♗f8 with equal chances, Csom-Bellon, Indonesia 1982.

c2) 12 ♘db5 ♖fc8 13 ♖ac1 a6 14 ♘a3 ♕d8 15 ♖fd1 ♖ab8 16 f4 ♗a8 17 ♗f3 ♕e8 18 ♕e2 ♗f8 19 ♘d5 ♘d7 20 ♗f2 e6 21 ♘e3 ♕e7 is also equal, Portisch-Garcia Gonzalez, Lucerne ol 1982.

c3) 12 ♖ad1 ♖ad8 13 ♖fe1 ♘e8 14 ♗f1 ♕c8 15 ♘d5 ♖d7 16 ♘xc6 ♗xc6 17 ♗g5 ♕b7 18 b4 with a small edge for White, Tukmakov-Bellon, Madrid 1973.

c4) 12 ♖fd1 ♖fd8 13 ♗f1 ♘xd4 14 ♗xd4 e6 15 a4! (this is a standard plan in such positions; White puts pressure on the weak black queenside and sometimes even

sacrifices the a-pawn to weaken Black's pawn structure and loosen his control over the c5-square) 15...♕c7 16 a5 bxa5 17 ♘b5 ♕e7 18 ♕xa5 ♖d7 19 ♕a3 ♘e8 20 ♗xg7 ♚xg7 21 ♕e3 and Black was scrambling to defend, Ciocaltea-Forintos, Titograd 1982.

c5) 12 a4! e6 13 ♖fd1 ♖fd8 14 ♘xc6 ♕xc6 (Black would also have problems after the superior 14...♗xc6) 15 a5 bxa5 16 ♘b5 a6 17 ♘xd6 ♘e8 18 c5 ♖d7 19 ♕xa5 ♗xb2 20 ♖ab1 ♘xd6 21 ♖xd6 ♖xd6 22 exd6 ♗f6

23 ♕c7! 1-0 Gheorghiu-Bellon, Las Palmas 1976.

11 ♕d2!

This simple move is the best way for White to play for an advantage. However, there are some other moves of interest:

a) 11 ♘db5!? d5 (if 11...♘e8? then 12 ♕d2 a6 13 ♘a3 and Black has more weaknesses that he can cope with) 12 cxd5 exd5 13 exd5 ♘b4! 14 d6 ♘fd5 15 ♘xd5 (Black does not have any problems after 15 ♗f2 either: 15...♕g5!? 16 ♘xd5 ♘xd5 17 ♘c7 ♘e3 18 ♗xe3 ♕xe3+ 19 ♚h1 ♖ad8 20 ♖e1 ♕f4 21 ♕b3 ♖xd6 with a clear edge for Black, Bramkamp-Znamenacek, Dortmund 1990) 15...♘xd5 16

♗d4 ♗h6! 17 ♗c4 ♘e3 18 ♗xe3 ♗xe3+ 19 ♔h1 ♕h4 20 g4 ♗f4 21 ♕e2 a6 22 ♘c7 ♖ad8 23 ♖ad1 ♗xd6 and Black's strong bishops gave Black much the better chances in Kamyshov-Simagin, Moscow 1947.

b) 11 ♘xc6!? ♗xc6 12 ♕b3! (White obtained an advantage after 12 ♖c1 ♕e7 13 ♕b3 ♖ac8 14 ♖fd1 ♗a8 15 ♕a3!? ♕xa3 16 bxa3 ♗c6 17 c5 bxc5 18 ♗xc5 ♖fd8 19 ♗xa7 ♖fd8 20 ♗c5 ♖dc8 21 ♗e7 in Vitolins-Bielczyk, Riga 1981) 12...d5? (possible is 12...♖c8!? 13 ♖ad1 ♕c7 14 ♘b5 ♗xb5 15 ♕xb5 ♖fd8 16 ♖d2? d5 with an edge for Black, Mokry-Kristensen, Belgrade 1985) 13 ♖ad1 ♕e7 14 e5 ♘d7 15 cxd5 exd5 16 f4 ♘f6 17 ♗d4 with a clearly better game for White, Illescas-Bellon, Linares 1991.

c) 11 ♖c1!? ♘xd4 12 ♗xd4 ♗h6 13 ♖c2 ♘e8 14 ♖e1 d6 15 ♗f1 ♘c7 16 ♗xe3 ♗xe3 17 ♖xe3 ♕g5 18 ♖d3 with a slight advantage for White, Polugayevsky-Bellon, Logrono 1991.

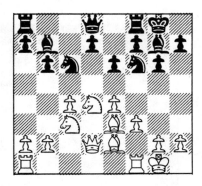

11 ... ♕e7!?
The old main line is 11...d5, but Black has been under a lot of fire in this variation and it seems that he

will have to give up that concept altogether. After 11...d5 the line continues with 12 ♘xc6 ♗xc6 13 cxd5 exd5 14 e5 ♘d7 15 f4, when Black's attempts so far have been in vain:

a) 15...f5? 16 ♗b5! ♗b7 17 e6 ♘c5 18 f5 a6 19 ♗xc5 bxc5 20 ♗d7 ♕a5 21 ♕d3 d4 22 ♘a4 ♖ad8 23 ♕c4 ♔h8 and Black resigned, Chiburdanidze-Pinal, Havana 1985.

b) 15...g5?! 16 ♘xd5 ♘xe5 17 ♖ad1 gxf4 18 ♗xf4 ♘g6 19 ♗c4 ♕h4 20 ♗b3 ♗xd5 21 ♗xd5 ♖ac8 22 ♗d6 ♖fd8 23 ♗g3 ♕e7 24 ♗xf7+ ♔h8 25 ♗d6 and Black was being crushed, Panchenko-Teilman, USSR 1988.

c) 15...♘c5 (Black's best chance but he is nowhere near equality) 16 ♖ad1! (White also has 16 ♖fd1!? and 16 ♗xc5) 16...f6 17 ♘xd5 fxe5 18 ♗c4 ♔h8 19 fxe5 ♖xf1+ 20 ♖xf1 ♕h4 21 ♖f4 ♕h5 22 ♘e7 ♗b7 23 b4 ♘e4 24 ♕d7 ♖b8 25 ♘c8! ♖xc8 26 ♕xb7 ♖d8 27 ♕xe4 ♗xe5 28 ♗e2 1-0 was the encounter Kuporosov-Malisauskas, USSR 1985.

12	♖fe1	♖fd8
13	♗f1	♘xd4
14	♗xd4	♘e8
15	♗xg7	

A better way for White to continue was shown in the subsequent game Panno-Bellon, Buenos Aires 1994: 15 ♗f2 ♘c7 16 ♖ad1 d6 17 a4 ♗e6 18 ♖a1 ♖ab8 19 a5!? bxa5 20 ♖xa5 a6 21 ♖ea1 ♖b3! 22 ♖1a2 ♖db8 23 ♘d1 ♗e5, when White was slightly better.

15 ... ♔xg7 16 ♔h1 d6 17 ♖ac1 ♘c7 18 ♕e3 e5
Black wants to play ...♘e6-d4.
19 ♘d5 ♘xd5 20 cxd5 ♖dc8 21 ♗b5 ♖c5 22 ♗a4 ½-½

Game 16
Nunn-Karlsson
Helsinki 1981

(1 e4 c5 2 ♘f3 ♘c6 3 d4 cxd4 4 ♘xd4 g6 5 c4 ♗g7 6 ♗e3 ♘f6 7 ♘c3 0-0 8 ♗e2 b6 9 0-0 ♗b7 10 f3)

10   ...   ♖c8

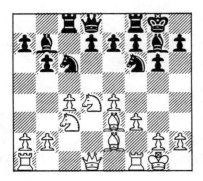

This move enjoys a quite large following, but with best play White should be able to develop an edge. White must not underestimate his opponent's resources, however, as the black position is both dynamic and solid. Unfortunately, it is close to impossible for Black to make any winning attempts if White does nothing.

11 ♕d2!

Natural and best. White takes charge of the c1-h6 diagonal and thereby stops any tricks involving ...♘xd4 followed by ...♗h6. The vast majority of games with 10...♖c8 feature 11 ♕d2, but White does have some alternatives:

a) 11 ♘xc6!? ♗xc6 12 ♕b3 e6 13 ♖ad1 ♕c7 is Mokry-Kristensen, which can be found under 10...e6 11 ♘xc6 in the notes to Game 15.

b) 11 ♖c1 ♘xd4! (Black takes control of the c1-h6 diagonal) 12 ♗xd4 ♗h6! 13 ♖c2 ♘h5 14 g3 ♘g7 15 f4 f5 16 ♖d2 ♗c6 17 e5 ♘e6 (at first glance White seems better, but in fact he is struggling to keep the position under control) 18 ♗e3 (18 h4 to avoid ...g6-g5 was tried in Sznapik-Pytel, Polanica Zdroj 1982: 18...♘xd4 19 ♖xd4 ♗g7 20 ♕b3 ♔h8 21 ♖d2 ♕c7 22 ♖d1 and now 22...d6 23 exd6 exd6 24 ♖xd6 ♖cd8! 25 ♖xd8 ♖xd8 26 ♖xd8+ ♕xd8 27 ♕d1 ♕e7 is difficult for White; Black's strong pair of bishops and the vulnerable white king give him more than enough compensation for the pawn) 18...g5! 19 ♗f3 ♕e8 20 ♗h5 ♕d8 21 ♗f3 ♕e8 22 ♗h5 ♕d8 (now 23 ♗f3 would have been a draw by repetition, but White tries for more and gets burned) 23 ♘b5 gxf4 24 gxf4 ♔h8 25 ♖ff2? ♖g8+ 26 ♔f1 ♖g7! 27 ♘xa7 ♕g8 28 ♔e2 ♘xf4+ 29 ♗xf4 ♕xc4+ 30 ♖d3 ♗xf4 31 ♘xc6 ♕e4+ 32 ♔f1 ♖cg8 and Black was winning, Browne-Benjamin, Lone Pine 1980.

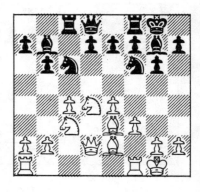

11   ...   ♖e8

Black, and in particular GM Lars Karlsson, has done well with this move, but it is still questionable whether it is Black's best. Alternatives are:

a) 11...♕c7 12 ♖ac1 ♕b8 13 ♖fd1 ♖fd8 14 ♗f1 ♘xd4 15 ♗xd4 ♘e8 16 ♘d5 ♗xd4+ 17 ♕xd4 ♗xd5 18 exd5 e5 19 dxe6 dxe6 20 ♕h4 a5 21 ♖d4 ♖xd4 22 ♕xd4 ♕d6 23 ♕xd6 ♘xd6 24 b3 ♔f8 ½-½ was Pieper Emden-Bischoff, Germany 1989.

b) 11...♘e8?! (this move should not be trusted; Black hopes to play ...f7-f5, but this just weakens his position) 12 ♖fd1 (12 ♖ad1 is also good) 12...♘d6 13 b3 f5 14 exf5 gxf5 15 ♘xc6 ♗xc6 16 ♖ac1 ♔h8 17 ♘d5 ♖g8 18 ♗g5 ♗xd5 19 ♕xd5 ♕f8 20 ♗f4 ♕c5 21 ♕d2 ♗e5 22 ♗xe5+ ♖xe5 23 f4 ♕a8 24 ♗f1 ♖e6 25 b4 with a clear edge for White, Liang-Qi, China 1981.

c) 11...♘h5!? is possibly Black's best chance. He intends to throw in ...f7-f5 at the right moment and also plans ...♘h5-f4 to take advantage of the e3-bishop's obligations to protect the d4-knight. White has now tried:

c1) In Zso.Polgar-Sosonko, Aruba 1991, White scored a quick victory with 12 ♘c2 d6 (Black's position after 12...f5 13 exf5 gxf5 14 ♖ad1 ♘f6 15 ♘d5 ♘e5 16 ♘xf6+ ♗xf6 17 b3 d6 18 ♘b4 ♘f7 19 ♘d5 was very unappealing, Hendriks-Van den Bosch, Enschede 1995) 13 ♖ab1 ♕d7 14 ♖fd1 f5 15 exf5 gxf5 16 ♗h6! (before playing f3-f4 to fix the black pawn structure, White exchanges the dark-squared bishops) 16...♘e5 17 b3 f4 18 ♗xg7 ♔xg7 19 ♕d4 ♔g8?? 20 ♕xe5 1-0.

c2) 12 ♘db5 should be harmless, but things got out of control in

the game Ghinda-Pavlov, Predeal 1988: 12...♘e5 13 c5!? a6 14 ♘a7 ♖xc5 15 ♗xc5 bxc5 16 f4 ♗h6 17 ♗xh5 gxh5 18 ♕f2 ♘g6 19 f5 ♘e5 20 f6 exf6 21 ♕xc5 with unclear complications.

c3) 12 ♖fd1 (the most common choice) and now:

c31) Black successfully took charge with 12...f5 in Boesken-Doncevic, Germany 1987: 13 exf5 gxf5 14 f4? (this drops a pawn without compensation; 14 ♘d5, 14 ♘c2 or 14 ♕c2 were worth considering) 14...♘xf4 15 ♗f3 ♘g6 16 ♘db5 ♘ge5 17 ♗d5+ ♔h8 18 ♗g5 ♕e8 19 ♘xa7 ♖a8 20 ♘ab5 ♕g6 with an initiative for Black.

c32) 12...♘e5 is quite popular, but against best play Black has big problems to face: 13 b3 f5 14 exf5 gxf5 15 ♘d5! ♗xd5 16 cxd5 f4 17 ♗f2 ♕e8 18 ♗d3?! (as Nunn and Gallagher point out, 18 d6 is better, e.g. 18...exd6 19 ♘b5 ♕g6 20 ♖ac1 or 18...e6 19 ♘b5 ♕g6 20 ♖ac1 in both cases with a clear edge for White) 18...♘xd3 19 ♕xd3 ♕g6 20 ♕xg6 hxg6 21 ♖ac1 ♖xc1 22 ♖xc1 ♗xd4! 23 ♗xd4 ♖f5 and White was struggling in Sherzer-Edelman, New York 1993.

c33) 12...♘f4! (the sane move) 13 ♗f1 ♘e6 14 ♘cb5?! (this just encourages Black to exchange everything; 14 ♘c2, preserving some tension, is probably better) 14...♘exd4 15 ♘xd4 ♘xd4 16 ♗xd4 ♗xd4+ 17 ♕xd4 d6 18 e5 dxe5 19 ♕xe5 ♕c7 20 ♕xc7 ♖xc7 21 ♖d2 ♗c8 22 ♖ad1 ♔g7 23 b3 ♗e6 24 ♔f2 g5 ½-½ Tatai-Makropoulos, Budva 1981.

d) 11...d6 (this is similar to, but perhaps somewhat more accurate than, 10...d6, but Black's winning prospects are about the same, close to none!) and now:

d1) 12 ♘xc6 ♗xc6 13 a4 a5 14 ♗d3 ♘d7 15 ♗c2 ♘c5 16 ♖ad1 ♗d7 17 ♗h6 ♗xh6 18 ♕xh6 f6 19 h3 ♖f7 20 b3 ♕f8 21 ♕h4 f5 22 exf5 gxf5 23 ♘d5 ♖b8 24 ♕g3 ½-½ De Firmian-Benjamin, USA ch 1985.

d2) 12 ♖fd1 ♘d7 13 ♘xc6 ♗xc6 14 ♖ac1 a5 15 ♘d5 ♘c5 16 ♖b1 a4 17 b4 axb3 18 axb3 ♖a8 19 ♗f1 ♖e8 20 b4 ♘d7 21 ♕f2 with a tiny edge for White, Taimanov-Cebalo, Titograd 1984.

d3) 12 ♖ac1 ♘d7 (Black equalised smoothly in Sammalvuo-U.Andersson, Sweden 1994, after 12...♘xd4 13 ♗xd4 ♘d7 14 ♗e3 ♖e8 15 ♖fd1 ♕c7 16 ♗f1 ♕b8 17 ♕f2 ♗e8 18 ♘d5 e6 19 ♘c3 a6 20 ♕d2 ♗f8, and was even more successful with 12...♖e8 in Bang-Callergaard, Copenhagen 1988: 13 ♘b3 ♘e5 14 ♘d5 e6 15 ♘xf6+ ♗xf6 16 ♖fd1 ♗a6 17 ♕b4 d5 18 exd5 exd5 19 ♖xd5 ♘c6 20 ♖xd8 ♘xb4 21 ♖xc8 ♗xc8 22 ♔f2 ♗xb2 with a clearly better game for Black) 13 ♘xc6 ♗xc6 14 ♖fd1 ♘c5 15 ♘d5 ♕d7 (15...a5!?) 16 b4 ♘e6 17 f4 f5 18 ♗f3 ♔h8 19 ♖e1 ♘c7 20 exf5 ♗xd5 21 cxd5 gxf5 with a clear advantage for White,

Am.Rodriguez-Pazos, Moscow ol 1994.

12 ♖ac1

Another excellent move is 12 ♖fd1, after Black risks ending up in a joyless position even if he is careful. His best chance is 12...♕c7 13 ♖ac1 ♕b8 and here White has tried the following:

a) 14 ♘db5 ♕b8 15 ♗f1 a6?! (15...♘e5 16 ♘d5 ♘ed7 seems better) 16 ♘a3 ♘d7 17 ♕f2 ♘b4 18 ♘ab1 ♗a8 19 a3 ♘c6 20 ♘d5 with the better chances for White, Mulivanela-Taborsky, Prague 1993.

b) 14 b3 ♘h5 15 ♗f1 ♗e5 16 g3 ♗g7 17 ♗g2 ♘f6 18 ♕f2 h5 19 ♘de2 ♘e5 20 h3 d6 21 ♘d4 ♘ed7 22 g4 a6 23 g5 ♘h7 24 h4 ♘hf8 25 ♗f1 e6 26 ♘de2 ♗a8 27 ♗d4 ♗xd4 28 ♖xd4 ♘e5 29 ♖cd1 ♖ed8 30 ♗h3 ♘c6 31 ♖4d2 b5 32 cxb5 axb5 with mutual chances, Borik-Karlsson, Randers zt 1982.

c) 14 ♗f1 ♘h5 15 ♘de2 ♘e5 16 ♘f4 ♘xf4 17 ♗xf4 d6 18 b3 ♗c6 19 ♘d5 ♖cd8 20 ♗g5 f6 21 ♗e3 e6 22 ♘c3, Sznapik-Ristoja, Helsinki 1981, and now instead of 22...f5? 23 ♕c2 fxe4 24 ♘xe4 d5 25 cxd5 exd5 26 ♘g5 with a big advantage for White, Black should have remained calm and continued 22...♖d7 with approximately even chances.

d) 14 ♘c2 d6 15 ♘d4 (although White was successful with this, it can hardly be called a refutation of Black's play) 15...♖cd8 16 ♘xc6 ♗xc6 17 b4 ♘d7?! (the start of a series of strange moves; simple and better was 17...♖d7, intending ...e7-e6 and ...♖ed8 to meet a wing attack with a counter-thrust in the centre) 18 a3 ♘f8?! 19 ♕a2 h6?! 20 ♗f1 ♘d7 21 ♘b5 ♖c8 22 a4 a6 23 ♘d4 ♗b7 24 ♘b3 ♗a8 25 a5 bxa5 26 ♕xa5 ♘e5 27 ♘d4 ♘c6 28 ♘xc6 ♖xc6 29 b5 axb5 30 cxb5 ♖xc1 31 ♖xc1 ♖c8 32 ♕a7 with a comfortable edge for White, A.Martin-Haik, Manchester 1981.

Finally, White can play 12 ♘db5, but after 12...a6!? 13 ♘a4!? axb5 14 cxb5 d5! unclear complications arise. Kudrin-Karlsson, Hastings 1983/84, continued: 15 bxc6 ♗xc6 16 ♘xb6 ♖b8 17 e5! ♘h5 18 ♕d4 f6! 19 ♕c5 ♗h6! 20 ♗xh6 ♕xb6 21 ♕xb6 ♖xb6 22 ♖fc1 ♖xb2 23 ♖xc6 ♖xe2 with a level game.

12	...	♕c7

13　　b4!

Black has no problems after 13 ♘d5 ♕b8 14 ♘b3 d6 15 ♖fd1 ♘d7, as in Jansa-Karlsson, Yugoslavia 1981, which finished 16 ♘d4 e6 17 ♘xc6 ♗xc6 18 ♘b4 ♗f8 19 ♘xc6 ♖xc6 20 b3 ½-½.

13	...	♘h5?!

This is a waste of time and just leads to a position where White has everything he wants. It was better to follow the standard plan of 13...♕b8, intending ...d7-d6, ...♖cd8, ...e7-e6 and ...♖d7 with a solid position.

14	♘xc6	♗xc6
15	♘d5	♕b8
16	f4	♘f6
17	♗f3	d6
18	♗d4!	b5
19	e5	♘xd5
20	cxd5	♗d7
21	♕e3	

White dominates the entire board, and makes no mistake whilst taking the last few steps to the full point:

21...a6 22 e6 ♗xd4 23 exf7+ ♔xf7 24 ♕xd4 ♖xc1 25 ♖xc1 ♖c8 26 ♖e1 ♖c4 27 ♕e3 ♕d8 28 a3 ♗c8 29 h3 ♗f5 30 g4 ♗c8 31 f5 gxf5 32 ♕h6 ♔e8 33 ♕h5+ ♔f8 34 ♕xh7 ♔e8 1-0

After 35 gxf5 followed by f5-f6 it is all over.

Game 17
Saltaev-Pigusov
Katerini 1993

(1 e4 c5 2 ♘f3 ♘c6 3 d4 cxd4 4 ♘xd4 g6 5 c4 ♗g7 6 ♗e3 ♘f6 7 ♘c3 0-0 8 ♗e2 b6 9 0-0 ♗b7 10 f3)

10	...	♘h5!?

After the relative demise of the old 10...e6 and 10...♖c8, this has now become the preferred move. With the knight out of the way, it is easier to play ...f7-f5, which stirs things up a little and avoids the passive positions that arise after virtually any other 10th move. We have already looked at a number of other ideas for Black here, all of which have been around for some time. However, in 1990, Morovic introduced a new idea in his game against Kir.Georgiev at the Novi Sad Olympiad. His new move was 10...♕b8,

which does not seem to make much sense at first glance. The deeper point is revealed when you see the next couple of moves, where Black usually continues with 11...♖d8, 12...d6, 13...♖d7, 14...♕f8 and 15...♖ad8. Black thus builds up a fortress which is not easy to break down, and given the opportunity he will open up the position with a timely ...d6-d5.

Let us take a look at the present status of this line: 11 ♕d2 (11 ♖c1 allows immediate equality with 11...♘xd4 12 ♗xd4 ♗h6! 13 ♖c2 ♗f4 14 g3 ♗xg3+ 15 hxg3 ♕xg3+ and ½-½ due to the perpetual, Milu-Moldovan, Bucharest 1994)

11...♖d8 and now:

a) 12 ♘c2 d6 13 ♔h1 ♖d7 14 ♖ac1 ♕f8 15 b3 ♖ad8 16 f4 e6 17 f5?! exf5 18 exf5 d5! 19 ♗g5 dxc4 20 ♕f4 cxb3 21 axb3 h6 22 ♗xf6 ♗xf6 23 ♘e4 ♗e5 24 ♕g4 ♕e7 25 f6 ♕f8 with an extra pawn for Black, as in the game Timoshenko-Moldovan, Calimanesti 1992.

b) 12 ♘db5 d6 13 ♖ad1 e6 (13...♖d7!?) 14 ♔h1 ♘e8 (14...♖d7) 15 f4 ♘e7 16 ♗f3 a6 17 ♘a3 ♗c6 18 ♘c2 with a good game for White, I.Gurevich-Rodriguez Andrez, Maringa 1991.

c) 12 ♖ad1 d6 13 ♕e1 ♖d7 14 ♕h4 ♕f8 15 ♔h1 ♖ad8 16 ♖d2 ♘xd4 17 ♗xd4 ♘e8 18 ♗xg7 ♘xg7 19 f4 f5 20 ♗e3 e5 21 ♖df2 ♖f7 with roughly equal chances, was Kramnik-Moldovan, Arnhem 1991.

d) 12 ♖fd1 (the most common move) 12...d6 and now White has tried a variety of moves:

d1) 13 ♘b3!? e6! 14 a4 ♘a5! 15 ♘xa5 bxa5 16 ♘b5 d5 17 cxd5 a6 18 ♘c3 exd5 19 ♗f4 ♕a7+ 20 ♗e3 ♕b8 21 ♗f4 ♕a7+ 22 ♗e3 ½-½ Moldovan-Milu, Bucharest 1991.

d2) 13 ♖ac1 ♖d7 14 ♘c2 ♕f8 15 b3 ♖ad8 16 f4 e6 17 ♗f3 ♕e7 18 ♕e1 ♘e8 with slightly better chances for White, Tundirar-Kahyai, Teheran 1991.

d3) 13 ♘db5 ♖d7 14 ♖ac1 ♕f8 15 ♗f1 ♖ad8 16 ♕f2 e6 17 ♘d4 ♘e5 18 h3 ♕e7 with equal chances was Kir.Georgiev-Morovic, Novi Sad ol 1990.

d4) 13 ♕e1 ♖d7 and now:

d41) 14 ♖ab1 ♕f8 15 ♔h1 ♖ad8 16 ♘cb5 ♘xd4 17 ♘xd4 ♘h5 18 ♗f1 e6 19 ♖d2 d5 with a promising game for Black, P.H.Nielsen-

Moldovan, Mamaia 1991.

d42) 14 ♕h4!? ♕f8 15 ♘db5 ♘e8 16 ♖ac1 ♗f6 17 ♗f2 e6 18 f4 ♖ad8 19 ♖d2 ♘c7 20 ♖cd1 ♘xb5 21 ♘xb5 ♕e7 22 ♗f3 ♗g7 with a passive but solid position for Black, where White is slightly better, Brodsky-Moldovan, Bucharest 1994.

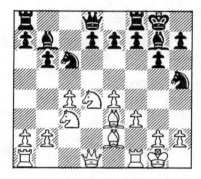

11   ♘xc6

This is probably White's best shot at an advantage; he eliminates all of Black's tricks involving ...♘f4, and since ...f7-f5 is rarely of any use, it leaves the black knight on h5 looking quite silly. Apart from the text move, White has a number of alternatives, however, not all of which are to be recommended:

a) 11 f4? (this loses a pawn) 11...♘xf4! 12 ♖xf4 (12 ♗g4 ♘e6 [12...♘xd4 is simpler; now White goes for an ill-fated attack] 13 ♘f5 gxf5 14 exf5 ♘c5 15 f6 ♗xf6 16 ♖f3 ♘e5 17 ♖h3 e6 18 ♗f5 exf5 19 ♕h5 ♖e8 20 ♕xh7+ ♔f8 21 ♗h6+ ♔e7 22 ♕xf5 ♖g8, when it was soon all over in Kosten-Pytel, England 1981) 12...♘xd4 13 ♗xd4 e5 14 ♖f3 exd4 15 ♘d5 ♗xd5 16 exd5 ♕g5 17 ♖g3 ♕e5 18 ♕d2

♖ae8, and Black is on top, Raaste-Rantanen, Jarvenpaa 1985.

b) 11 ♔h1 f5 12 exf5 gxf5 13 f4 ♘xd4 14 ♗xd4 ♘f6 15 ♗f3 ♗xf3 16 ♕xf3 ♖f7 17 ♖ad1 ♖c8 18 b3 ♖c6 19 ♗e5 ♕e8 20 ♘b5 ♘g4 with roughly equal chances, Agnos-Rogers, London 1991.

c) 11 ♘b3 f5 (11...♗xc3!?) 12 exf5 gxf5 13 c5 ♖b8 14 ♕d2 ♘f6 15 ♖fd1 ♔h8 16 ♔h1 ♗a8 17 cxb6 axb6 18 ♗d3 e6 19 ♘b5 d5 20 ♘3d4 ♖e8 21 ♖e1 ♕d7 22 ♖ac1 ♖bc8 23 ♗h6 ♘h5 with equal chances, Rotman-Garrido, Mamaia 1991.

d) 11 ♘db5 a6 (or 11...d6 12 ♕d2 ♕d7 13 ♖ad1 ♖ad8 14 ♗h6 ♖ac8 15 ♗xg7 ♘xg7 16 f4 a6 17 ♘a3 ♖b8 18 ♘d5 ♗a8 19 b4 a5 with good play for Black, Veres-Certek, Slovakia 1993) 12 ♘a3 e5 (in Timman-Yusupov, Linares 1992, Black ran into trouble after 12...♖b8 13 f4 ♗xc3 14 bxc3 ♘f6 15 e5 ♘e4 16 ♕e1 d6 [better was 16...f5, when White is only slightly better] 17 ♗f3 ♘a5 18 f5! with a clear edge for White) 13 g3 ♘d4 14 ♘c2 ♘xe2+? (Silman and Donaldson's suggestion of 14...♕c7 seems to be the correct way to continue, as 15 ♘xd4 exd4 16 ♗xd4 can be answered with 16...♘xg3 and 15 ♔g2 with 15...♘xc2 16 ♕xc2 f5 with unclear play) 15 ♕xe2 f5 16 ♗f2 ♕g5 17 ♔h1 b5 18 cxb5 ♘f6 19 ♘b4 fxe4 20 fxe4 axb5 21 ♕xb5 ♖ab8 22 ♕d3, when Black does not have enough for the sacrificed pawn, Wirthensohn-Hernandez, Lucerne ol 1982.

e) 11 ♕d2 ♘f4 (other moves lead to a comfortable edge for White: 11...f5 12 exf5 gxf5 13 ♖ad1 f5 14 ♗f2 ♘e5 15 ♖fe1 ♕e8

16 ♗d3 ♘xd3 17 ♕xd3 ♕f7 18 b3
♖ad8 19 ♘db5, Ilincic-Haik,
Vrnjacka Banja 1986, or 11...♘xd4
12 ♗xd4 ♗xd4+ 13 ♕xd4 ♘f4 14
♖fd1 d6 15 ♗f1 ♕c7 16 b4 ♖ac8
17 ♕e3 ♘h5 18 a4 ♘f6 19 ♘b5
♕b8 20 a5, Panno-Milos, Villa
Gesell 1985) and now White has
tried:

e1) 12 ♘xc6 ♘xe2+ 13 ♘xe2
dxc6 14 ♕c2 ♕c7 15 ♗f4 e5 16
♗g5 f6 17 ♗e3 f5 with some initiative for Black, Larrosa-A.Martin,
Alicante 1991.

e2) 12 ♗xf4 ♘xd4 13 ♗d3 ♖c8
14 ♗e3 d6 15 ♖ad1 ♕c7 16 b3
♖fd8 17 ♗b1 ♘e6 18 ♖c1 ♘c5 19
♔h1, Kudrin-Ramos, Seville 1990,
and now instead of 19...a5?! 20
♖fd1 with a clear advantage for
White, 19...♖d7 would have been
the right way to continue.

e3) 12 ♖ad1 ♘e6 (12...♘xe2+ is
better) 13 ♘c2 d6 14 ♗h6 ♖c8 15
♗xg7 ♔xg7 16 f4 f5 17 exf5 gxf5
18 ♗f3 ♘a5 19 b3 with a clear
edge for White, Meyers-Hergott,
Biel 1993.

f) 11 ♖e1 ♘f4 12 ♗f1 ♘e6 and
now:

f1) 13 ♘ce2 ♖c8 14 ♕d2 ♕c7
15 ♖ad1 (15 b3 is also equal)
15...♗e5 16 ♘xc6 dxc6 17 f4 ♖cd8
18 ♕c1 ♗g7 19 ♘c3 ♖xd1 20

♖xd1 ♖d8 21 e5 ♖xd1+ 22 ♕xd1
f6 23 exf6 exf6 24 ♘e4 f5 25 ♕d6
♗c8 with equal chances, Uhlmann-
Zsu.Polgar, Aruba 1992.

f2) 13 ♘de2 f5 (also adequate is
13...d6 14 ♕d2 ♖e8 15 ♖ab1 ♖b8
16 ♖ec1 ♗a8 17 ♘d5 ♖c8 18 b3
♘c5 19 ♖d1 ♘e6 20 ♖bc1 ♖b8 21
♕e1 ♕c8 with equality, Magyar-
Pigusov, Budapest 1989) 14 exf5
♖xf5 (14...gxf5 is a viable alternative) 15 ♕d2 ♘e5 16 ♘d4 ♘xd4
17 ♗xd4 ♕c7 18 ♘d5 ♗xd5 19
cxd5 ♖af8 with excellent chances
for Black, Ekabson-Terentiev,
USSR 1983.

g) 11 ♖c1 ♘f4 12 ♖f2?!
(alternatively, 12 ♕d2 ♘xd4?!
[both 12...♘e6 and 12...♘xe2+ are
superior] 13 ♗xd4 ♗xd4+ 14
♕xd4 ♕c7 15 ♔h1 e5? 16 ♕d2
♔g7 17 ♖fd1 ♖fd8 18 ♗f1 ♘e6 19
b4 ♗c6 20 ♘b5 ♕b8 21 ♘d6 with
a big edge for White, Smirin-
Grechinin, Smolensk 1992, or 12
♗xf4 ♘xd4 13 ♕d2 d6 14 ♗h6
♗xh6 15 ♕xh6 e5 16 ♗d3 ♘e6 17
♖fd1 a6 18 ♕e3 ♗c6 19 ♘e2 ♖b8
20 ♗b1 ♕e7 with equal chances, as
in Schinzel-Pytel, Poland 1980)
12...♘xd4 13 ♗xd4 ♗h6! 14 ♖c2
♘e6 15 ♗f1 ♖c8 16 ♘d5 ♘xd4 17
♕xd4 e5?! (17...d6! would have
given Black a slight pull) 18 ♕d3
♗xd5 19 cxd5 ♕g5 20 ♖fe2 ♖fd8
21 g3 ♗f8 22 ♗h3 ½-½ Gulko-
Yusupov, Groningen 1994.

11   ...   dxc6

This is the most natural recapture. Black returns the pawns to a
symmetrical configuration. However, in Khuzman-Hergott, Biel
1993, Black did not experience
many problems after 11...♗xc6
either: 12 c5 b5 13 g4 ♘f6 14 ♕c2
e5 15 a4 a6 16 ♖fd1 ♕e7 17 ♖d2

♖fd8 18 ♖xd8 ♖xd8 19 axb5 axb5 20 ♖a7 ♖d7 21 b4 ♘e8 22 ♔g2 ♗c8 23 ♖xd7 ½-½.

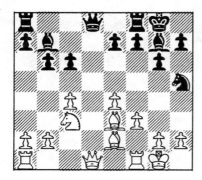

12 f4

Possibly better is 12 c5, when in Grunberg-Certek, Bratislava 1992, Black was crushed after 12...♕b8? 13 f4 ♗xc3 14 bxc3 ♘f6 15 ♕c2 b5 16 ♗d4 ♘d7 17 f5 ♘e5 18 f6 ♕c7 19 ♕d2 exf6 20 ♖xf6 ♕e7 21 ♖ae1 ♖ae8 22 ♕h6 ♗c8 23 ♖1f4 g5 24 ♕xg5+ ♘g6 25 ♖h4 ♗e6 26 ♖xh7 ♔xh7 27 ♕h5+ 1-0. In fact 12...♕b8? is not necessary; 12...b5 is much better, when Silman gives 13 f4 b4! 14 ♘a4 ♘f6 15 ♗f3 ♗a6 16 ♖f2 ♗b5 and 15 ♗d3 ♕a5 with good play for Black in both cases.

Nunn/Gallagher suggests that White is better after 15 ♕c2, but 15...♕a5 is still fully adequate for Black.

12 ♕b3?! has also been tried, but after 12...♗d4! 13 ♗xd4 ♕xd4+ 14 ♔h1 ♘f4 15 ♖fd1 ♕e5 16 ♗f1 ♖fd8 17 a4 ♘e6 18 ♘e2 ♘c5 19 ♕c2 a5, Black was better in Kuznetsov-Silman, USA 1986.

12	...	♗xc3
13	bxc3	♕xd1
14	♖fxd1	

14 ♖axd1 c5 15 ♗f3 ♘f6 16 e5 ♗xf3 17 gxf3 ♘h5 18 ♖d7 ♖fd8 is also fine for Black.

14	...	c5
15	e5	♖fd8
16	a4	♘g7

16...♔f8 is inaccurate. Magem Badals-Apicella, Moscow ol 1994, saw 17 ♖xd8+ ♖xd8 18 a5 ♗e4 19 ♔f2 ♘g7 20 g4 f5 21 exf6 gxf6 22 axb6 axb6 23 ♖a6 with a small advantage for White.

17	a5	♖xd1+
18	♖xd1	♘e6
19	♔f2	h5!
20	♖a1	♗e4
21	♗f3	♗xf3
22	♔xf3	♖b8

½-½

3 Classical Maroczy: Introduction and Early Deviations

Whilst other systems have had their ups and downs over the years, the Classical system has remained quite popular. Black first strives to exchange a set of knights and the dark-squared bishops on d4; then the plan is to transfer the f6-knight to c5, put the light-squared bishop on c6, play ...a7-a5 and the rest depends on the particular set-up chosen by White.

Like most other systems in the Maroczy, Black gets quite a solid position, but here Black also has chances to play for a win, which probably explains why the system has remained a popular choice. It has been a favourite of Larsen's for several years, while Anand and Petursson are also happy to take the black side. This chapter deals with early deviations from the main lines with 9...♗d7 10 ♕d2 or 10 ♖c1, which are dealt with in the following two chapters.

However, Black must be careful with his move order, as we will see.

Game 18
A.Sokolov-Nemet
Bern 1992

(1 e4 c5 2 ♘f3 ♘c6 3 d4 cxd4 4 ♘xd4 g6 5 c4 ♗g7 6 ♗e3 ♘f6 7 ♘c3 0-0 8 ♗e2)

8	...	d6

The immediate 8...a5 has been tried on a few occasions. The most direct attempt at refutation was 9 0-0 a4 10 c5!?, as played in Nunn-Haik, Paris 1983, when, after 10...d5 11 cxd6 ♕xd6 12 ♘db5 ♕b4 13 a3 ♕a5 14 f4 e5 15 fxe5 ♘xe5 16 ♖xf6 ♗xf6 17 ♘d5 ♗d8?, White won in great style. It was much better to play 17...♖a6, when it is not clear whether White can break through. If White plays a move other than 10 c5!?, then Black will play ...♕a5, defending the a4-pawn, and then simply develop normally. An interesting way to prevent this is 9 f3!?, defending the e4-pawn and planning to meet 9...a4? with 10 ♘xa4. The standard answer to f3, 9...♕b6, can be met by 10 ♘cb5, as Black cannot kick the knight with ...a7-a6! Black will probably have to play 9...d6 transposing to Andersson-Larsen in the notes to Game 30.

9	0-0	♘xd4

The plan with ...♘xd4, ...♗e6

and ...♕a5 is not very logical here, since White can take back on d4 with the bishop. Compared to the lines where White has to capture with the queen on d4, losing time since the queen cannot stay in the line of the bishop on g7 forever, he now has the chance to grab more space, which should give him an edge.

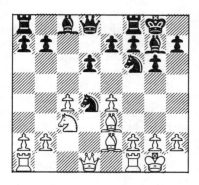

10	♗xd4	♗e6
11	f4!?	

The most direct approach, but White has other good moves, too. Smyslov played the prophylactic 11 ♔h1!? against Gheorghiu in Moscow 1967 and was successful after 11...♕a5 12 ♕d3 ♖fc8 13 b3 a6 14 f4 b5?! 15 cxb5 axb5 16 ♘xb5, since Black does not have enough compensation for the pawn. With 11 ♔h1!? White avoids the plan with ...♕c8 and ...♗g4 since he is not yet committed to f2-f4 and can simply reply f2-f3. Gheorghiu's play was in fact quite logical, trying to punish the 'slow' 11 ♔h1!?, but as it turned out to be insufficient, it seems that 11 ♔h1!? is an excellent move, forcing Black to show his cards.

11 ♕d2 is also possible, but after

11...a6 White should not play as in Larsen-Browne, Siegen ol 1970, where after 12 ♖ad1?! b5! 13 cxb5 axb5 14 b4 ♕b8 15 ♖fe1 ♖c8 White could not win the b5-pawn for tactical reasons. Realising that if he did nothing, Black would put something on c4 with the much better position, Larsen tried 16 ♗f3 ♘d7 17 ♗xg7 ♔xg7 18 e5 ♖a3 19 exd6 ♖axc3 but did not have enough for the piece, although he later managed to swindle his way to a draw. Maybe White should have played 12 a4 instead, to control the queenside, and try to exploit the weakening of the b6-square. In general, White stands better in this line since he is well prepared to meet any action on the queenside.

11   ...   ♖c8

More in the spirit of 10...♗e6 is 11...♕a5, but after 12 ♔h1 ♖ac8 13 b3 ♖fe8 14 ♕d3 the logical question is: What next, Mr Black? Ornstein's answer against Tukmakov in Yerevan 1976 was the 'positionally logical' 14...♘d7??, but unfortunately after 15 f5! ♘c5 16 ♗xc5! White won a piece, since 16...dxc5 17 fxe6 ♗xc3 18 exf7+ picks up a rook. But Black already has a bad position, e.g. 14...a6 is simply answered with 15 a4, and Black has no useful plan.

11...♕c8, with the idea of exchanging bishops with ...♗g4, has been tried a few times. After 12 b3 ♖d8 13 ♕d3 ♗g4 14 ♗xg4 ♕xg4 15 f5 ♕h4 16 h3 a6 Black was okay in Panno-Najdorf, Buenos Aires 1968. 14 ♖ad1 was later suggested as an improvement, keeping the pressure up and not activating the black queen. Yet Silman and Donaldson's 13 h3!?, preventing the bishop exchange and seriously questioning the value of ...♕c8 and ...♖d8, seems even better.

12   b3   ♗d7?!

Better is 12...♕a5, as in Korchnoi-Granda Zuniga, Buenos Aires 1993. After 13 f5 (13 ♔h1 transposes to Tukmakov-Ornstein above) 13...♗d7 14 a3 ♕d8 15 b4 b6, White has more space but after 16 ♕d3 ♗c6 17 ♖ad1 ♖c7 18 ♕e3 ♕a8 Korchnoi could find nothing better than 19 ♗xf6 ♗xf6 20 ♘d5 ♗xd5 21 ♖xd5 with an okay position for Black. 17 ♕e3!? is interesting, with the idea of replying to 17...♖c7 with 18 a4, since White still has his rook on a1. If 17...♘d7, then 18 ♗xg7 ♔xg7 19 ♖f3 with an attack on the kingside.

13   e5!

Black was trying to put his bishop on c6 with a normal position, but White wants more, well motivated by the fact that Black has lost too much time.

13   ...   dxe5
14   fxe5!

Now White gets an isolated pawn, but since it can be used aggressively, this is not a big problem.

14   ...   ♘e8
15   ♕d2   ♗c6
16   ♖ad1   ♕c7
17   ♕e3

Black is suffering; his pieces are not co-ordinated, and the knight on e8 gets in the way.

17   ...   ♖d8

Threatening 18...♖xd4, when Black will get the e5-pawn and a lot of play on the dark squares; then he might even be better.

18   e6!

Now Black has the chance to enter an endgame, but in return White gets rid of his weak e-pawn. Black, on the other hand, is still left with a big problem: how to control the white queenside majority.

18 ... 罝xd4

18...f5 is positionally well justified: Black will swap twice on d4 and put the knight on d6. But after 19 臭xg7 ⃞xg7 20 豐xa7 ⃞xe6 21 豐e3 ⃞g7 22 ⃞d5 White keeps the advantage.

19	罝xd4	臭xd4
20	exf7+	罝xf7
21	豐xd4	罝xf1+
22	臭xf1	⃞f6

Black hopes to become active after 23 豐xa7 豐e5 followed by ...⃞g4, but White is not so easily distracted.

23 c5!

Simple and effective. The c4-square is freed, and the pawns can start rolling.

23...e5 24 豐c4+ 零g7 25 b4 臭e8 26 a3 a6 27 臭e2 豐d8 28 豐d3!

Black needs his queen to create counterplay. Without the queens White will simply advance his pawns, which in combination with a centralised king, gives excellent winning chances.

28..豐e7 29 臭f3 a5 30 ⃞e4 axb4 31 axb4 臭c6 32 豐d6! 豐xd6 33 ⃞xd6 e4 34 臭e2 ⃞d7??

Losing a piece, but Black was probably lost anyway. The white king will attack via f2-e3-d4.

35 b5 臭xb5 36 臭xb5 ⃞xc5 37 零f2 零f6 38 零e3 零e6 39 ⃞xe4 1-0

It seems to us that if Black wants to play for ...臭e6, ...豐a5 and ...罝c8, he should rather prefer the line 1 e4 c5 2 ⃞f3 ⃞c6 3 d4 cxd4 4 ⃞xd4 g6 5 c4 ⃞f6 6 ⃞c3 d6 7 臭e2 ⃞xd4, since here White has too many promising ways of countering it.

Game 19
Lautier-Koch
Lyon zt 1990

(1 e4 c5 2 ⃞f3 ⃞c6 3 d4 cxd4 4 ⃞xd4 g6 5 c4 臭g7 6 臭e3 ⃞f6 7 ⃞c3 0-0 8 臭e2 d6 9 0-0)

9 ... ⃞xd4

The idea of this move order is to avoid the systems with 10 ⃞c2 or 10 ⃞b3, hoping simply to transpose to the main lines.

10 臭xd4 臭d7

11 ♕d3!?

This seems to be the only way to exploit Black's move order. White gets the same kind of position as in Game 28, without having wasted time on ♖b1.

11 ... a6?!

Since Black is unlikely to get ...b7-b5 in, this seems rather pointless. More logical was 11...♗c6, as in Smyslov-Pirc, USSR 1956, when after 12 ♖fe1 ♘d7 13 ♗xg7 ♔xg7 14 b4! White had a clear edge. 12...a5 would have been better, in order to gain space on the queenside. White probably should go for 12 b4!? and Black for 11...a5!, when he seems to be okay, as ...♘d7 will come next with a normal kind of position.

12 ♕e3 ♗c6
13 b4!

This move would have been pointless on move 11, Black would simply reply 11...♗e6 and start attacking the c4-pawn. However, now that the bishop is on c6, this idea is not possible anymore. Therefore, White seizes space on the queenside.

13 ... ♕b8
14 b5 axb5

15 cxb5 ♗d7
16 a4 ♗e6
17 a5 ♘d7
18 ♗xg7 ♔xg7
19 b6

White has made considerable progress on the queenside, and Black must prevent the white knight from getting to c7. Although he can manage that, as is often the case with passive defence, one can defend one flank but disaster often strikes on the other.

19...♘c5 20 ♘b5 ♘a6 21 f4 ♗d7 22 ♘c3

Lautier suggests that 22 ♘d4! was even stronger, but the text does not ruin anything.

22...♗c6 23 f5 ♘c5 24 ♗c4 ♕d8 25 e5 ♘d7 26 exd6 exd6 27 ♗d5 ♖c8 28 ♖ad1 ♗xd5 29 ♘xd5 ♖c5 30 ♖f3 ♖e8 13 ♕f4 ♘e5 32 ♖h3 h5 33 f6 ♔h7 34 ♕g5 ♖e6 35 ♖xh5 1-0

Again a clean sweep by White. In the last two games the White players were clearly more skilled than their opponents. Still, the games are important for the understanding of typical Maroczy positions, since one can see how things can go wrong for Black, if he does not manage to time his counterplay correctly.

Game 20
Short-Larsen
Naestved 1985

(1 e4 c5 2 ♘f3 ♘c6 3 d4 cxd4 4 ♘xd4 g6 5 c4 ♗g7 6 ♗e3 ♘f6 7 ♘c3 0-0 8 ♗e2 d6 9 0-0)

9 ... ♖e8!?

An idea that Larsen said he thought of over the board. The idea is, that while ...♖e8 will always come in handy, White will now have to show his intentions first, and Black can then react accordingly.

10   a3?!

Short decides to make a semi-waiting move as well, but in the game the pawn structure with a2-a3 and b2-b4 just seems to be weak. He should probably have gone for one of the options mentioned in the next game.

10	...	♗d7
11	f3	a6
12	b4	

This is very weakening, but having played a2-a3, White can hardly do without it, e.g. 12 ♖c1 ♖c8 13 ♕d2 ♘a5! wins for Black since ...e7-e5 follows.

12	...	♖c8
13	♖c1	♘xd4
14	♗xd4	♗h6!

(see following diagram)

A common theme in the 9...♖e8 system. With the rook on e8, f2-f4 can always be answered with ...e7-e5, after which Black will pick up the e4-pawn.

15	♖c2	♗e6

Black is already much better

since his pieces exert strong pressure on White's weaknesses. White has no choice but to play as in the game.

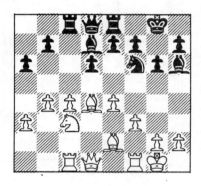

16	♘d5	♘xd5
17	exd5	

Playing for symmetry and a draw with 17 cxd5 will just give Black control of the c-file after 17...♗d7. The bishop on h6 controls c1.

17	...	♗d7
18	♖c3	e6
19	dxe6	♖xe6

Black is very active, but White is hardly lost yet. 20 f4 seems like a good idea, preparing ♗f3 as well as closing the c1-h6 diagonal. Instead, Short tries to liquidate to a draw, but is hit by some powerful tactics.
20 c5? ♗a4! 21 ♕xa4 dxc5! 22 bxc5 ♖xe2 23 ♕c4??

(see following diagram)

Dropping a piece, but the position was tragic anyway.
23...b5! 0-1

Since Black seldom wins such tactical miniatures in the Maroczy, this game attracted a great deal of attention, and 9...♖e8 became quite fashionable for a while.

Game 21
Cu.Hansen-P.H.Nielsen
Copenhagen 1995

(1 e4 c5 2 ♘f3 ♘c6 3 d4 cxd4 4 ♘xd4 g6 5 c4 ♗g7 6 ♗e3 ♘f6 7 ♘c3 0-0 8 ♗e2 d6 9 0-0 ♖e8)

10   ♕d2
Numerous other moves have been tried here:

a) In the tournament in which the previous game was played, Andersson played 10 f3 against Larsen. After 10...♘d7 11 ♕d2 ♘c5 12 ♖fd1 Larsen tried the provocative 12...♕a5 with the idea of 13 ♘b3!? ♗xc3 14 bxc3 ♕a3, which seems very dangerous to us. Of course, Andersson played his usual solid chess, trying to squeeze something out of the endgame with 13 ♖ab1 ♘xd4 14 ♗xd4 ♗xd4+ 15 ♕xd4 ♘e6 16 ♕f2 ♗d7 17 f4 ♕c5. He did not succeed, and in the end it was Larsen who had some winning chances, before the game finally ended peacefully after 55 moves. A simpler approach for Black would have been 11...♘xd4 12 ♗xd4 ♗xd4+ 13 ♕xd4 ♕b6. White has nothing after 14 ♕xb6 ♘xb6 15 ♖fd1 ♗e6. In Stohl-Ftacnik, Trencianske Teplice 1985, 11 ♖c1 was played instead of 11 ♕d2, although after 11...♘c5 12 ♕d2 ♕a5 13 ♖fd1 ♗d7 14 ♖b1 ♘xd4 15 ♗xd4 ♗xd4+ 16 ♕xd4 ♘e6 White did not believe in his position and agreed a draw.

b) Speelman tried 10 ♖b1 against Larsen in Hastings 1988, but after 10...♗d7 11 ♕d2 a6 12 ♖fd1 ♖c8 13 f3 ♘xd4 14 ♗xd4 ♗e6 15 ♘d5 ♘xd5 16 cxd5 ♗xd4+ 17 ♕xd4 ♗d7 18 ♖bc1 ♕a5 19 a3 ♗b5 Black had equalised.

c) 10 ♖c1 is possible, e.g. 10...♘xd4 11 ♗xd4 and now:

c1) 11...♗h6!? and:

c11) 12 ♖c2 e5 (12...b6!? is interesting, since White will find it difficult to co-ordinate his pieces and the 'misplaced' bishop on h6 is very disturbing for him; after 13 f3 ♗b7 14 ♕e1 ♘h5 15 g3 e5 16 ♗f2, as in Pyhala-Rantanen, Pori 1986, Black has an excellent position with a pleasant choice between the positional ...♘g7-e6 or the aggressive ...f7-f5) 13 ♗e3 ♗xe3 14 fxe3 is very good for White, since Black cannot consolidate. A good try was 14...♔g7 15 ♖d2 ♕a5 16 ♖xd6 ♗e6, as in Veingold-Hergott, Manila ol 1992. After 17 ♕d2 ♖ad8 Black was close to getting some counterplay, but Veingold responded aggressively, and after 18 b4 ♕b6 19 ♖d5! ♘xd5 20 ♘xd5 ♗xd5 21 exd5 Black could not stop the pawn-roller.

c12) 12 f4!? e5 13 ♗e3 is more testing, when 13...♗e6 seems unfortunate, since after 14 ♕d2 exf4 15 ♗xf4 ♗xf4 16 ♖xf4 Black has problems: ♘b5 is a threat as well as simply ♖d1 when the d6-pawn will be lost. Black played 16...♖c8? in Escalente-Williams, Dubai ol 1986, and lost a pawn after 17 e5! Better is 13...♗d7 when 14 ♕xd6 ♗c6 will regain the pawn.

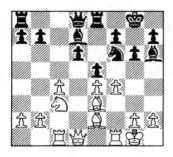

Here 14 ♕d3 was tried in Kolev-Cid, Tortosa 1992, and after 14...♗g4? 15 f5 White was much better. 14...exf4 15 ♗xf4 ♗xf4 16 ♖xf4 ♗c6, however, seems okay for Black. Although 17 ♖cf1 looks strong, after 17...♘d7 White cannot take on f7 because of ...♘e5, 18 ♕xd6 ♕b6+ followed by ...♕xb2 also seems fine, while after 18 ♕h3 ♘e5 19 ♖h4 ♗d7 Black also holds sufficient resources. 14 ♕d2 is another idea, intending 14...exf4 15 ♗xf4 ♗xf4? 16 ♕xf4 and wins, so Black should play 15...♗g7, since he now attacks the e4-pawn, and should therefore be fine.

c2) If this scares you, then follow Wolff-Larsen, London 1989, when after 11...♗d7 12 ♕d2 ♗c6 13 f3 a5 14 b3 ♘d7 15 ♗e3 ♘c5 16 ♖fd1 ♕b6 it seems like Black has lost time, since the rook on e8 will have to go to c8, but as we will see later, the white rooks are better placed on b1 and c1, so one might argue that Black has actually won a tempo and not the opposite!

d) 10 ♘c2 is logical, since ...♖e8 is hardly ever played in the ♘c2 systems. After 10...♘d7 11 ♕d2 White has played ♗e3 and ♕d2 directly, and not first ♗d2 as in the ♘c2 systems. The game Wolff-Cebalo, Croatia 1991, continued 11...♘c5 12 f3 and now Cebalo played 12...b6. However, this looks too passive, so we recommend 12...♕a5, intending to take on c3 and play ...♘a4. 13 b4 does not work since after the continuation 13...♘xb4 14 ♘d5 ♘c6 15 ♕xa5 ♘xa5 White will not win the exchange with ♘c7; he has to move the queen's rook first.

10   ...   ♘g4

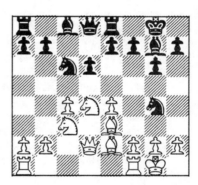

Demonstrating another point of the move 9...♖e8; the bishop now goes straight to g4.

11   ♗xg4   ♗xg4
12   h3

In the 9...♗d7 system the rook would have been on f8, when 12 f4! would be strong. However, this can now be met by 12...♘xd4 13 ♗xd4 e5! with excellent prospects for Black, as in Mohring-Topakian, Eger 1988, when after 14 fxe5 dxe5 15 ♗e3 ♕xd2 16 ♗xd2 ♗e6 17 ♘d5 ♖ac8 18 ♖ac1 f5 Black is fine. If White avoids this ending and goes for 14 ♗e3 instead, simply 14...exf4 15 ♗xf4 ♗e6 is okay for Black, since his bishops are strong. Finally, 12 f3 was played in Magem Badals-P.H.Nielsen, Moscow ol 1994, when after 12...♗d7 13 b3 ♕a5 14 ♔h1 ♖ac8 15 ♖ad1 a6 16 ♖fe1 ♘xd4 the game was agreed drawn.

12	...	♗d7
13	♖ad1	♖c8
14	♘xc6!?	

This forces Black to take with the rook, since 14...♗xc6 15 ♗xa7! is bad for Black. 14 b3 would meet with 14...a6 followed by ...b7-b5, which should equalise.

14	...	♖xc6
15	b3	♕a5
16	♗d4	♗e6?

This turns out badly. Better would have been 16...♗xd4 17 ♕xd4 a6, going for ...b7-b5 again.

17	♗xg7	♔xg7
18	f4!	f6?

The standard way of parrying the white kingside attack. Now 19 f5 ♗f7 keeps things under control. Unfortunately, Black had missed some other tactics.

19	♘b5!

Strong play! Black cannot exchange queens due to the attack on a7 as well as the threat of ♘d4, winning the exchange.

19...♕b6+ 20 ♔h1 ♗f7 21 e5! dxe5 22 dxe5 ♖e6

22...fxe6 23 ♕c3 was awful as well, so Black hopes to get some play along the e-file.

23 exf6+ exf6 24 ♘d6!

Stopping Black's dreams of activity in their tracks. 24...♖8e7 25 ♘c8 is embarrassing, but now it is clear that the difference between the knight on d6 and bishop on f7 will decide the game.

24...♖f8 25 b4 ♕c7 26 c5 b6 27 ♕f2 bxc5 28 bxc5 ♖b8?

The final mistake, but Black was lost anyway.

29 ♖ae1 ♕e7 30 ♕g3

30 ♘f5+ wins as well.

30...♖xe1 31 ♖xe1 1-0

Black's disaster in this game cannot be blamed on 9...♖e8, which does seems to be playable.

Game 22
Annakov-P.H.Nielsen
Buenos Aires 1992

(1 e4 c5 2 ♘f3 ♘c6 3 d4 cxd4 4 ♘xd4 g6 5 c4 ♗g7 6 ♗e3 ♘f6 7 ♘c3 0-0 8 ♗e2 d6 9 0-0)

9	...	♗d7

The immediate 9...a5 has also been tried here, but Andersson showed the right antidote against Larsen in Linares 1983. After 10 f3! ♘d7 11 ♘db5 ♘c5 12 ♕d2 a4 13 ♖fd1 ♕a5 14 ♖ac1 ♗e6 15 ♘d5 ♕xd2 16 ♖xd2 Black has very few active options. Still, the black position is very solid, and with careful play such as 16...♖fd8 and 17...♔f8 White is only slightly better. Larsen decided to be active with 16...♗xd5 17 cxd5 ♘b4, but the normally very careful Swede now aggressively gave up the exchange with 18 ♖xc5! and won after 18...dxc5 19 ♗xc5 ♘xa2 20 ♗xe7 ♖fc8 21 f4 ♗f8 22 d6 ♘b4 23 ♗h4 ♖c1+ 24 ♔f2 ♘c6 25 ♘c7 a3 26 bxa3 ♖xa3 27 e5 h6 28 ♗f6 ♗g7 29 ♗e7 ♗f8 30 ♘d5 ♖a8 31 h4 ♖c5?? (White was winning anyway) 32 ♘f6+ ♔g7 33 ♗xf8+ ♖xf8 34 ♘d7 1-0.

10 f3?!

A common mistake, White tries to be prophylactic and defends the e4-pawn. Yet Black has a trick!

10 ... ♕b6!

The standard move is 10...♘xd4, transposing to the main lines, but since White has played inaccurately, why not punish him?

11 ♘a4

Several other moves have also been tried:

a) Worse is 11 ♕d2? as played in Leko-P.H.Nielsen, Kecskemet 1991, when after 11...♘xd4! 12 ♕xd4 ♕xb2 Black was already nearly winning, and achieved an easy victory.

b) For some reason 10 f3?! seems to be popular among young prodigies. In Gistrup 1997, the Russian U-12 champion Vladimir Belov played 11 ♘cb5 against P.H.Nielsen, and was nearly winning after 11...a6 12 ♘c2 ♕a5 13 ♘c3 ♖ac8 14 f4 b5? 15 c5!, although Black later managed to swindle a draw. 14...♗e6 is much better, when Black is fine.

c) 11 ♕d3 was played in Cuijpers-Rausis, Nimes 1991, when after 11...♕xb2 12 ♖ab1 ♕a3 13 ♖xb7 ♘e5 14 ♕d2 ♖ac8 Black was better.

d) White's best is 11 ♔h1!, as in the game ·Rychagov-P.H.Nielsen, Norway 1997. The idea is that after 11...♕xb2 12 ♘a4 ♕a3 13 ♗c1 ♕b4 14 ♗d2 ♕a3 15 ♘b5 Black's queen is trapped. Since 12...♕xa1 13 ♕xa1 ♘xd4 14 ♗xd4 ♗xa4 15 f4 also looks good for White, I played 12...♕a3 13 ♗c1 ♕xa4 14 ♕xa4 ♘xd4 15 ♕d1 ♘xe2? 16 ♕xe2 ♘xe4, overlooking 17 ♗a3!, which gave White a winning position: he wins the e7-pawn. Still, this line is playable since Black has 15...♘xe4!

The point is 16 ♗b2 ♘xe2 17 ♗xg7 ♘4g3+ 18 hxg3 ♘xg3+ 19 ♔g1 ♔xg7, which is excellent for Black. 16 fxe4 ♘xe2 17 ♗g5 ♘c3 18 ♕d3 f6! also seems fine for Black, who has some pawns and two pieces which in this position is enough for the queen. White has no targets, and Black, if given time, simply attacks c4 and e4 and could easily be better.

11 ... ♕a5
12 ♘c3

This looks clumsy, but the white position is still very solid.

12	...	♘xd4
13	♗xd4	♖fc8
14	♕d2	♗e6
15	b3	b5!

Now White wins some time, but Black gets the c5-square for his knight!

| 16 | b4!? | |

16 cxb5 ♘xe4 gives Black a good game, since he gets the c-file.

16	...	♕xb4
17	♖ab1	♕a5
18	♖xb5	♕d8
19	♘d5	♘d7!

The usual strategy, but here even better than normal, since the knight will become a monster on c5.

| 20 | ♗e3 | ♘c5 |
| 21 | ♘d5 | ♗xd5 |

More ambitious was 21...f6 and then ...f6-f5 later.

| 22 | cxd5 | ♗f6! |

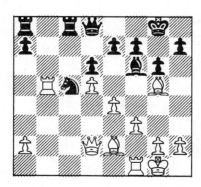

A typical trick, Black always wants to exchange bishops, which will magnify the imbalance between the knight on c5 and bishop on e2. The threat is 23...♗xg5 24 ♕xg5 e5!

| 23 | ♗xf6?? | |

A positional blunder but a very common one. White imagines that he is wrecking Black's pawn structure as well as getting the b-file. But as Larsen has once explained, Black gets rid of the weakness on e7 and has the e-file combined with the break ...f6-f5. As we will shall see, White's play on the b-file is an illusion: the knight on c5 will defend the b7-square forever. Much better would have been 23 ♗e3 when White is okay.

23...exf6 24 ♕d4 ♕e7 25 ♖b2 ♕e5 26 ♕xe5 fxe5 27 ♗b5 ♖ab8 28 ♖fb1 f5 29 exf5 gxf5 30 ♗c6 ♖xb2 31 ♖xb2 ♔g7

White might seem to be active, but neither the bishop nor the rook can do anything active, since this will give Black control over the b-file.

32 g3 ♔f6 33 ♔g2 ♖g8 34 ♖b4 e4 35 f4

Keeping the black king away from e5.

35...h5 36 ♖b1 h4 37 ♗b5? h3+!

The pawn cannot be taken, since ...♖b8 wins a piece, as in the game.

38 ♔f2? 0-1

This loses a piece. 38 ♔f1 was necessary, but of course Black wins the ending after 38...♖b8 39 ♗d3 ♖xb1. The knight is far superior to the bishop. After 38 ♔f2 ♖b8 39 ♔e3 ♖b7! and ...a7-a6 will pick up the bishop! It is worth noting that the knight on c5 never moved. It never had to, since White could not threaten it in any way. On c5 it simply controlled everything.

Game 23
Kapetanovic-Petursson
New York 1987

(1 e4 c5 2 ♘f3 ♘c6 3 d4 cxd4 4 ♘xd4 g6 5 c4 ♗g7 6 ♗e3 ♘f6 7

♘c3 0-0 8 ♗e2 d6 9 0-0 ♗d7)

10   f4!?

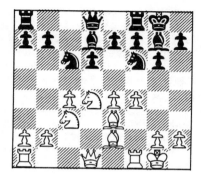

Ambitiously trying to seize space.

10   ...   ♘xd4

Here 10...♕b6 is pointless, as after 11 ♘c2! ♕xb2 12 ♘a4 White wins the queen. However, 10...a6 is possible, e.g. 11 ♖c1 ♖c8 12 ♕d2 ♖e8 13 ♖fe1 e5! with a good position for Black, as in Antoshin-Boleslavsky, Moscow 1957. Later the right plan was found for White: 11 ♔h1 ♖c8 12 ♖c1 ♖e8 13 ♘b3! ♘a5 14 e5! ♘xc4 15 ♗d4 ♘xb2 16 ♕d2 dxe5 17 fxe5 ♘c4 18 ♗xc4 ♖xc4 19 exf6 exf6 and Black's compensation is insufficient, Grooten-Vladimirov, Graz 1981. This probably means that 10...a6 is too ambitious. If White avoids exchanges, Black has problems with the co-ordination of his pieces.

11   ♗xd4   ♗c6
12   ♗f3   a5
13   ♖f2   a4!

White's 10 f4 showed that his intentions are on the kingside, so Black seizes as much space as possible on the queenside. This is

nearly always a good idea, unless White has prepared some quick action on the queenside, such as b2-b4, which is clearly not the case here.

14   ♕d2

A useful move which includes a small trap: 14...♕a5 15 ♘d5 is embarrassing.

14   ...   ♘d7

Black is running out of useful waiting moves, so he sticks to the standard plan.

15   ♗xg7   ♔xg7
16   ♖d1   f6!

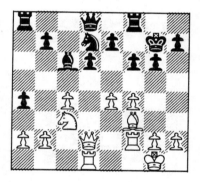

This looks like it weakens the light squares, but as we shall see Black's counterplay on the dark squares is more important.

17   ♗g4   ♘c5
18   ♕e3   ♕a5
19   ♖fd2   ♕a7!

Forcing an exchange of queens, which signals an end to White's dreams of an attack.

20 ♗f3 ♘e6 21 ♕xa7 ♖xa7 22 g3 ♖a5 23 ♘d5 ♗xd5 24 ♖xd5 ♖xd5 25 ♖xd5 ♘c5 26 ♗d1 a3!?

Brave. It would have been safer to activate the king and rook first.

27 b4 ♘xe4 28 ♖a5 ♖c8 29 ♗b3 ♘d2 30 ♖xa3 ♘xb3 31 axb3 b5!?

32 cxb5 &f7 33 &f2 &b8 34 &a5
&b7 35 &e3 e5 36 &d3 &e6 37
&c4 &e7 38 &d3 &b7 39 &c4
&c7+ 40 &d3 &d7 41 &a6 h5 42
b6 &c8 43 fxe5 fxe5 44 &e4 &c1
45 &a7+ &c8 46 &d5 &c2 47 &g7
&xh2 48 b7+ &b8 49 &c6 &a7 50
&c7 &c2+ ½-½

Although Black did not win this
game, we once more saw an example of his chances, including a con-
sistent dark-squared strategy.

Game 24
Korchnoi-Anand
Wijk aan Zee 1990

(1 e4 c5 2 &f3 &c6 3 d4 cxd4 4
&xd4 g6 5 c4 &g7 6 &e3 &f6 7
&c3 0-0 8 &e2 d6 9 0-0 &d7)

10   &b3!?

This looks clumsy, but since after 9...&d7 Black clearly intends to
trade knights and play ....&c6, there
is some point in preventing this.

10   ...   a5!?

Certainly the most direct way of
meeting 10 &b3, although other
moves have been tried:

a) 10...&a5 was a non-starter in
Short-Hamdouchi, Lucerne 1989,

after 11 &d2 a6 12 &c1 Black
found nothing better than 12...&c6
13 a3 e5?! 14 &b3, which Short
did not have any problems in converting into a full point.

b) 10...b6 has some points, be-
sides preventing the c4-c5 break. In
Polugayevsky-Ljubojevic, Roquebrune 1992, Black managed to
draw after 11 f3 &e8 12 &d2 &c8
13 &ac1 &e5 14 &d5 e6 15 &f4
&e7 16 &fd1 f5 17 exf5 &xf5 18
&d4 &f8, although his position
seemed suspicious. After 11 &c1
Black, obviously inspired by our
main game, managed to get the
usual knight versus bishop middlegame after 11...a5 12 &d2 &c8! 13
&b3?! &b7 14 f3 &d7 15 &d4
&xd4 16 &xd4 &c5 17 &xg7
&xg7 18 &d4+ f6 19 &d5? e5 20
&d2 &xd5 21 cxd5 &d7 22 b3 b5
and won easily in Vescovi-
P.H.Nielsen, Buenos Aires 1992.

11   &d2

11   ...   &c8!?

Very original play by Anand. He
believes that the knight is placed
less well on d2 than on d4 and now
transfers the knight to c5 with comfortable play.

12   &c1

12 c5!? was tried in Sion-Vilela, Cuba 1991, but this 'unbinds' the Maroczy and should not worry Black, who equalised with 12...dxc5 13 ♗xc5 ♗e6.

12	...	♘d7
13	♘b3	b6
14	♘d4	

Not very impressive, but the knight was indeed clumsy on d2.

14	...	♘xd4
15	♗xd4	♗h6!?
16	f4	

After 16 ♖c2, 16...e5!? 17 ♗e3 ♗xe3 will destroy the white pawn structure.

16...♗b7 17 ♗e3 ♘c5 18 b3

18 ♕c2 ♗g7 would leave the e4-pawn weak anyway.

18...♘xe4 19 ♘xe4 ♗xe4 20 ♕d4 ♗c6 21 f5!

A strong pawn sacrifice which Black wisely rejects. 21...♗xe3+ 22 ♕xe3 followed by ♕h6 is really dangerous.

21...♗g7 22 ♕xb6 ♕d7 23 fxg6 hxg6 24 ♗g5 a4 25 ♕e3 axb3 26 axb3 ♖a2 27 ♖f2 ♕e6 28 ♗f3 ½-½

10 ♘b3 seems to misplace the knight somewhat, so if you want to avoid 10...♘xd4, 10 ♘c2 is certainly our recommendation.

Game 25
Short-Andersson
Wijk aan Zee 1990

(1 e4 c5 2 ♘f3 ♘c6 3 d4 cxd4 4 ♘xd4 g6 5 c4 ♗g7 6 ♗e3 ♘f6 7 ♘c3 0-0 8 ♗e2 d6 9 0-0 ♗d7)

10 ♘c2!?

An interesting and quite logical way of side-stepping the main lines by not allowing 10...♘xd4. Compared to the normal ♘c2 systems, an additional plus is that plans with ...♗xc3 are dubious for Black, since the knight on c3 will be defended simply with ♕d2, given that the bishop is already on e3.

10 ... ♕a5?!

To us this just seems to provoke White to seize more space by hitting the queen. One might argue that White thereby weakens his position, but here this seems less important than the extra space. 10...a6 is seen in Games 26 and 27.

11 f4!?

Ambitious. More usual is the solid 11 f3, when after 11...♖fc8 12 ♕d2, Lutz-Vokac, Dortmund 1991, continued 12...♗e8?! 13 ♖ac1 a6 14 ♖fd1 ♖ab8 when Lutz simply played 15 ♘d4!?, claiming that the two tempi spent by ♘d4-c2-d4 had been used poorly by Black, since his queen and the bishop on e8 seem misplaced. Vokac played 15...♘d7 16 ♘b3 ♕d8, and although he lost the game, it seems to us that by playing ...a7-a5, ...b7-b6 and ...♘c5 here, Black would have been fine, since he reaches the normal solid structure.

Similar to our main game is the

encounter Ribli-Qi, Bled 1979, which might in fact have been the game that inspired Short: 11 a3 ♖fc8 12 f4!? ♗e6 13 ♔h1 ♕d8 14 ♖b1 ♕d7 15 ♕d2 b6 16 b3, when White controlled a lot of space, and if Black does nothing, he risks being suffocated. After 16...♖f8 17 ♗g1 ♘e8 18 ♗f3 ♖c8 19 ♘d5 f5 20 ♖be1 White won easily.

11	...	♖ac8
12	♖b1	a6
13	b4!?	

Again very committal. Now the c4-pawn will be very difficult to defend if it is attacked, but since both a5 and e5 are unavailable for the black knights, White can afford to play like this.

13	...	♕d8
14	♕d3	

Even more ambitious would have been 14 h3, not allowing Black to trade bishops.

14	...	♗g4
15	♔h1	♗xe2
16	♕xe2	e6?!

Why not 16...♘d7, when Black's position would still be reasonably healthy?

| 17 | c5! | |

Short offers to exchange the weak d6-pawn, but for example 17...dxc5 18 ♗xc5 ♖e8 19 ♖fd1 would mean serious problems for Black's queen.

17	...	d5
18	♖fd1	♖e8

Played to discourage e4xd5, since now this would give Black some activity along the e-file.

19	a4	♕e7
20	b5	axb5
21	e5	♘d7
22	♘xb5!	

Excellent play. After the standard 22 axb5, the white pawns might end up as weaknesses, but now ♘d6 is threatened.

22...♖b8 23 ♘d6 ♖f8 24 ♘d4 f6

The only chance. Black cannot sit around and watch his queenside collapse.

25 ♘xb7 ♘xd4 26 ♗xd4 fxe5 27 fxe5 ♖f4 28 c6 ♖xd4 29 ♖xd4 ♘xe5 30 ♖db4 ♘xc6 31 ♖b6 ♘d4 32 ♕g4

White has everything under control. The a-pawn is a winner.

32...♖f8 33 a5 ♗e5 34 a6 ♕f6 35 ♖g1

Not 35 a7?? ♕f1!

35...♗c7 36 ♖bb1 ♕e5 37 ♕h3 ♗b8 38 ♘c5 ♕d6 39 ♖b7 h5 40 ♘d7 1-0

This game, along with Ribli-Qi (see note to White's 11th above), indicates that 10...♕a5?! is rather dubious. By playing ambitiously, White can secure a large space advantage.

Game 26
Anand-Larsen
Roquebrune (rapid) 1992

Normally we would not consider using a rapid game as one of the main games, but with two real experts on the Maroczy playing each other, we hope you will forgive this exception.

(1 e4 c5 2 ♘f3 g6 3 d4 cxd4 4 ♘xd4 ♗g7 5 c4 ♘f6 6 ♘c3 d6 7 ♗e2 0-0 8 0-0 ♘c6 9 ♗e3 ♗d7 10 ♘c2)

10 ... a6!?

Black claims that with 10 ♘c2, White has weakened his control of b5. Now White will constantly have to worry about the ...b7-b5 break. It is not an immediate threat, but since White has no immediate plan either, Black has enough time to prepare it.

11 ♕d2

11 f3 is the subject of the next game.

11 ... ♖e8!?

Anyone else would have played 11...♖c8, preparing an attack on the c4-pawn. However, Larsen claims that the rook will be useful on e8. It defends e7 and if, at some point, a white knight is exchanged on d5, and White recaptures with a pawn, Black has the ...e7-e6 break, opening the e-file. As we saw in Game 20, this long-term plan can suddenly become a reality.

12 f3 ♖c8
13 ♖ac1 ♕a5!

Now this is an excellent square for the queen. White will not get in both f3-f4 and b2-b4, since Black will attack the c4-pawn in the meantime.

14 ♖fd1 ♘e5
15 ♘a3

15 b3 b5! was not an option for White.

15 ... h5!?

Again typical Larsen, who believes that this is nearly always useful. It gives the black king some air and controls the g4-square, while under favourable circumstances the h-pawn might march on and create weaknesses in the white camp. Other players have claimed that, at best, ...h7-h5 is just meaningless, losing a tempo and creating a potential weakness! In general, we agree with Larsen, and indeed here, since both sides are manoeuvring, Black can afford the luxury of a tempo. However, it is important to stress that ...h7-h5 is not essential for Black in the Maroczy, but only useful if Black's forces are already well placed.

16 ♔f1

A clear indication that White is experiencing difficulties in finding a useful plan.

16 ... ♗a4!?

(see following diagram)

Again a surprising decision. Black offers his opponent the bishop pair, since this would mean an exchange of the well-placed knight on c3, leaving White with only the ugly knight on a3.

17 ♖e1 ♗c6
18 ♘d5

White goes for the classical end-game edge, but Black is well armed for immediate counterplay.

18	...	**♕xd2**
19	**♗xd2**	**♘d7**
20	**b4?!**	

Too optimistic. This turns out just to weaken the white position; 20 b3 was more sensible.

20	...	**e6**
21	**♘e3**	**♘b6**
22	**h3**	**♗h6!**

Now it is getting unpleasant, as White's position is becoming rather loose. Black has no immediate threat, but given time he will double on the c-file and put pressure on c4.

23 c5 dxc5 24 ♖xc5 ♖cd8 25 ♗c1 ♘d3 26 ♗xd3 ♖xd3 27 ♘ec4 ♘xc4 28 ♘xc4 ♗f8 29 ♘e5 ♗xc5 30 ♘xd3 ♗f8

White has just about managed to avoid losing material, but this does not mean an end to his suffering. The black pair of bishops will win a queenside pawn, unless White plays as in the game, which on the other hand is also highly unpleasant!

31 a3 ♗b5 32 ♔e2 ♖c8 33 ♖d1

Losing material, but 33 ♔d2

♗h6+ is even worse.

33...♖c2+ 34 ♔e3 ♖xg2 35 ♘c5 f6 36 ♘d7? ♖e2+ 37 ♔f4 ♗xd7 0-1

Winning a piece. 38 ♖xd7 is met by the thematic 38...♗h6+.

Game 27
Short-Petursson
Tilburg 1992

(1 e4 c5 2 ♘f3 ♘c6 3 d4 cxd4 4 ♘xd4 g6 5 c4 ♘f6 6 ♘c3 d6 7 ♗e2 ♗g7 8 ♗e3 0-0 9 0-0 ♗d7 10 ♘c2)

| 10 | ... | **a6!?** |

Usually 10...♖c8 just transposes, but some games have taken an independent course. For example, after 11 f3:

a) 11...♘a5!? might be a strong option, when 12 ♘a3 is met by 12...♗e6!, as in Holmsgaard-Hoi, Aalborg 1992. The idea is 13 ♘d5 ♘xd5 14 cxd5 ♗xb2! Here Holmsgaard gave up the exchange with 15 ♘b5, but his position was bad anyway. 12 b3 seems more logical, but after 12...a6, ...b7-b5 is a threat and 13 ♕d2 b5 14 cxb5 ♕c7 15 ♗d4 axb5 16 ♘b4 ♕b7 seems fine for Black.

b) 11...♗e6, as in Miles-Piket, Groningen 1992, is inferior, when after 12 ♕d2 ♘d7 13 ♖ac1 ♕a5? (better is 13...a5, as in Serper-Hracek, Jakarta 1994) 14 b4! ♘xb4 15 ♘d5 ♗xd5 16 exd5 ♘xc2!? 17 ♕xa5 ♘xe3. Although Piket has two pieces and a pawn plus a lot of play on the dark squares, a queen is a queen, and Miles duly won the game. In order to avoid the 'Hoi' plan, 11 ♕d2 or 11 ♖c1 first and then a later f2-f3 should probably be preferred.

11 f3 ♖c8

11...♘e5 was tried in Petrosian-Rytov, Tallinn 1979. After 12 b3 ♖c8 13 a4 ♕a5 14 ♕e1 ♗c6 15 ♖d1 ♘ed7 16 ♔h1 ♕c7 17 ♘d4 b6 18 ♗d3! ♘c5 19 ♗c2 ♗b7 20 ♕h4 Petrosian had the queenside under control, and later broke through on the kingside.

12 a4

Like Petrosian, Short wants to keep the queenside under control, but here the knight is still on c6, from where it controls some dark squares. Petursson is able to make excellent use of that in the game. The less committal 12 ♘a3 was tried in Tempone-Spangenberg, Trewel 1995: 12...♘e5 (possible now, since with the knight on a3, White cannot get the pawn to a4 easily) 13 ♕d2 ♗c6 14 ♖ac1 ♖e8 15 b4 b6 16 ♖fd1 ♘ed7 17 ♗f1 ♕c7 18 ♕f2 ♕b8 led to a typical hedgehog structure, with reasonable chances for Black.

12 ... ♗e6
13 ♘d5 ♘d7
14 ♖b1 a5

For some reason, Petursson chose to vary from the game P.Cramling-Petursson, Reykjavik

1984, in which he was successful with 14...♘c5 15 b3 a5 16 ♘d4 ♗xd5 17 exd5 ♘xd4 18 ♗xd4 ♗xd4+ 19 ♕xd4 ♕b6 20 ♖fd1 ♘d7. Here Black has the classical, very favourable ending, with a strong knight versus a bad bishop, which he converted into a full point. Short would hardly have played 16 ♘d4, but we cannot see what else he had in mind.

15 b4

Not very frightening. Black is well placed to meet this direct attempt, but Short was probably already happy with simplifications and a draw.

15	...	axb4
16	♘cxb4	♘a5
17	♗d4	♗xd4+
18	♕xd4	♘c6
19	♕e3	♖a8
20	♘d3	♖xa4
21	♖xb7	♖a3
22	♕d2	♗xd5
23	cxd5	♘d4
24	♖fb1	½-½

Simple play by Black, but still enough to make a comfortable draw against a world championship finalist. 10 ♘c2 is certainly a reasonable weapon for White if he wants to avoid the main lines, but after careful study of the games of Larsen and Petursson, players of the black pieces should not be scared.

Game 28
Larsen-J.Sorensen
Aalborg 1989

(1 e4 c5 2 ♘f3 ♘c6 3 d4 cxd4 4 ♘xd4 g6 5 c4 ♗g7 6 ♗e3 ♘f6 7 ♘c3 0-0 8 ♗e2 d6 9 0-0 ♗d7)

10	♖b1!?

Typical Larsen. Most people play 10 ♖c1, so of course he has to play 10 ♖b1. It is hardly better but it is different!

10	...	♘xd4
11	♗xd4	♗c6
12	♕d3	a5
13	b3	♖e8
14	♖fd1!	

White wants to meet ...♘d7 with ♗xg7, so it is very important to keep pressure on the d6-pawn to prevent Black from playing the standard plan of putting his pawn on e5 and then directing the knight to d4 via c5-e6.

14	...	♘d7

15	♗xg7	♔xg7
16	♖d2	b6?!

Too passive. Black tries to play solidly, but this square belongs to the queen. After 16...♕b6 Black would have had more options than in the game.

17	♕e3	♕c7
18	♖bd1	♖ac8?

A very instructive mistake. The knight belongs on c5, and should go there immediately.

19	♗g4!

It is nearly always favourable for White to exchange his light-squared bishop in the Maroczy. He already has several pawns on the light squares.

19	...	♖cd8
20	♗xd7	♖xd7
21	♘d5	♗xd5
22	♖xd5!	

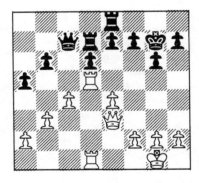

It was Mikhail Botvinnik who first pointed out that with only the heavy pieces left on the board, it is much easier to break through with e4-e5 after recapturing with the rook on d5, than to get any advantage from the pressure on the e-file after e4xd5. And so it is in this game, where Black is indeed in big trouble. White easily combines threats of a breakthrough, while Black can only sit and wait.

22...♖ed8 23 h4 f6 24 a4 e6 25 ♖b5 ♖b8 26 h5 ♖b7 27 ♕h3 ♖e7 28 ♕g3 ♖d7 29 ♕g4 ♖e7 30 ♖d3 ♕b8 31 hxg6 hxg6 32 ♖h5 ♕g8 33 ♖g3 ♔f7 34 ♖h6 ♔e8 35 ♖xg6 ♕f7 36 ♕f3 ♔d7 37 e5 1-0

It is important to note how bad Black's position was after 19 ♗g4! in order to avoid ending up like this. White simply won numerous tempi by attacking the weak spots in Black's position, and in the end smashed through efficiently on the kingside.

4 Classical Maroczy: White Exchanges the Dark-Squared Bishops

Chapter Guide

1 e4 c5 2 ♘f3 ♘c6 3 d4 cxd4 4 ♘xd4 g6 5 c4 ♗g7 6 ♗e3 ♘f6 7 ♘c3 0-0 8 ♗e2 d6 9 0-0 ♗d7

10 ♖c1 ♘xd4 11 ♗xd4 ♗c6 12 ♕d3 – *Game 29*
10 ♕d2
    10...a5   – *Game 30*
    10...♘xd4 11 ♗xd4 ♗c6
        12 ♗d3   – *Game 31*
        12 f3 a5 13 ♔h1 ♘d7 14 ♗xg7 ♔xg7 15 f4
                15...f6   – *Game 32*
                15...a4   – *Game 33*

This chapter and the next feature the main lines of the Maroczy Bind, Classical system. An important early decision that White has to face is whether or not to allow the exchange of the dark-squared bishops. This choice has a crucial effect on the future shape of the game. First of all, in this chapter, we deal with lines in which White allows the exchange, while Chapter 5 covers positions where he avoids the bishop-trade. If White intends to play a system with ♗xg7, we believe that 10 ♕d2 is more precise than 10 ♖c1, since having exchanged dark-squared bishops, White's only attractive plan is to attack the weakened dark squares around Black's king.

Game 29
P.Cramling-Petursson
Reykjavik 1984

(1 e4 c5 2 ♘f3 ♘c6 3 d4 cxd4 4 ♘xd4 g6 5 c4 ♗g7 6 ♗e3 ♘f6 7 ♘c3 0-0 8 ♗e2 d6 9 0-0 ♗d7)

10	♖c1	♘xd4
11	♗xd4	♗c6

(see following diagram)

    12   ♕d3!?

White tries to get the same kind of position as in Game 19, but here she has wasted time on 10 ♖c1. However, when Black plays the 9...♗d7 move order, there is nothing that White can do about this. Black is ready to play ...a7-a5 with the standard dark-square strategy.

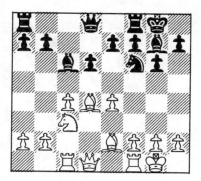

Instead, White can also play 12 f3, with the exchange of dark-squared bishops in mind. Here it is important for Black to respond with 12...a5, since 12...♘d7? was severely punished in Razuvaev-Honfi, Cienfuegos 1976. After the thematic 13 b4! ♗xd4+ 14 ♕xd4 ♕b6 15 ♕xb6! ♘xb6 16 e5! dxe5 17 b5 ♗e8 18 c5 ♘d7 19 ♘d5 e6 20 ♘e7+ ♔g7 21 c6 Black was unable to stop the c-pawn.

But if Black does play 12...a5 it seems that ♖c1 is not a particularly useful move. For example, 13 b3 ♘d7 14 ♗xg7 ♔xg7 15 ♕d4+ ♔g8 16 ♖fd1, as in Andersson-Christiansen, Hastings 1978, and now Black could have obtained an equal ending with 16...♕b6, but who wants to play an ending against Andersson? In Dokhoian-Glek, Bonn 1994, Black instead played 15...f6!? in order to control the dark squares. After 16 ♖fd1 ♘c5 17 ♖b1 ♕b8 18 ♗f1 ♖d8 19 ♕e3 e5! 20 ♖d2 ♘e6 21 ♖bd1 b6 22 g3 ♖a7 23 ♗h3 ♘g5 24 ♗g2 ♘e6 a draw was agreed. Black has equalised with the standard dark-squared strategy.

12   ...   a5!

The correct move order. 12...♘d7?! was punished by 13 ♗xg7 ♔xg7 14 b4! in Smyslov-Golz, Polonica Zdroj 1968, when White has achieved a typical advantage.

13   f4

The logical plan. It is now far more difficult for White to seize space on the queenside.

13   ...   a4!?

This is a very interesting idea. Normally, this move would be met by b2-b4, ...a4xb3, a2xb3, with an opening of the queenside favourable to White. But here the rook has left a1, which means that Black gets counterplay along the a-file. The 'standard' 13...♘d7 is also playable, which after 14 ♗xg7 ♔xg7 leads to structures very similar to the main lines where White takes on g7. Normally White must play his pawn to f4 in two moves, but here White has played ♕d3, where it is not well placed in this kind of structure. Timman-Wedberg, Amsterdam 1984, continued 15 ♔h1 f6 16 ♖cd1 ♕e8 17 ♕d4 ♕f7 with equality.

14   ♔h1   ♕a5

Black again delays ...♘d7,

keeping White guessing, while making useful moves.

15 ♕e3

15 ♘d5 might be a better idea, when Black has a choice of captures:

a) White was successful in Dolmatov-Petursson, Reykjavik 1988, when after 15...♘xd5 16 exd5 ♗xd4 Dolmatov played 17 dxc6!? ♗xb2 18 ♖c2 ♕b4 19 cxb7, and Black blundered with 19...♖a5?? 20 ♖xb2 ♕xb2 21 ♖b1 with a lost position. It was probably better to play 18...a3, which seems okay for Black. It is noteworthy that White did not like the attractive 18 ♕xd4 ♗d7 19 ♗d3 followed by f4-f5.

b) Black had more success with 15...♗xd5 16 exd5 ♘d7 in the game Petrakov-Mololkin, Moscow 1994, when after 17 ♗xg7 ♔xg7 18 ♖fe1 ♖fe8 19 ♗f1 ♘f6 20 ♕d4 b6 21 h3 ♕c5 22 ♕d2 ♖a7 Black had a solid position. White now mistakenly played the 'active' 23 b4 axb3 24 axb3, and Black took the a-file with 24...♖ea8 and later won the game.

15 ... ♘d7

Now, finally, Black plays the standard plan.

16 ♗xg7 ♔xg7
17 ♗g4 ♕c5

Since this kind of ending is at least equal for Black due to White's bad bishop, Black wins time by threatening the exchange of queens.

18 ♕e2 ♘f6
19 ♗h3 e5!

A very strong move which probably gives Black the advantage. He now threatens ...e5xf4 followed by ...♖ae8, attacking the e4-pawn, which will be difficult to protect

with the bishop offside on h3.

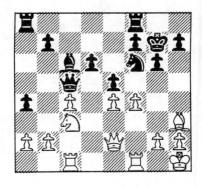

20 f5 g5!

Since the knight on f6 is a mighty defender, Black does not fear the possibility of a white king-side attack.

21 ♗g4 h6 22 h4 ♖h8 23 ♗h5 ♔f8 24 ♘d5 ♗xd5 25 cxd5 ♕a5 26 ♖c4 b5 27 ♖c3

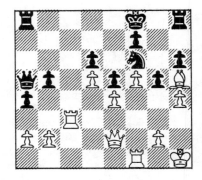

This is a very interesting position. Place the white h-pawn on h2 and the bishop on d3, and White would be winning. Yet here the pawn on h4 secures Black counterplay on the kingside, since White will never be able to close it comfortably. It is difficult to say who is better, but Black seems to have

more than sufficient counterplay.
27...♔e7 28 ♖fc1 ♖a7
Black defends c7, but White will break through eventually. The only question is: will Black be able to break through on the kingside?
29 ♗f3 ♖d7 30 a3 ♖b8 31 ♖c6 ♕d8 32 ♕e1 ♕g8
Black's last moves might seems passive, but now he is ready for 33...gxh4 and 34...♕g5. White cannot find a way to meet this.
33 ♕b4 ♖bd8!
Not 33...gxh4 34 ♖xd6!
34 ♗e2 gxh4 35 ♖6c3 ♕g5 36 ♗xb5 ♖g8
Finally it is Black who is making the threats.
37 ♗f1 ♕f4 38 ♖c7 ♖gd8!?
38...h3 was winning, but in time-trouble Black plays it safe. He will win in the end because his knight is so much stronger than the white bishop.
39 ♕e1 ♘xe4 40 ♖7c4 ♘g3+ 41 ♔g1 ♕xf5 42 ♖xa4 ♕g5 43 ♖c2 f5 44 ♗b5 ♖b7 45 ♗a6 ♖b3 46 ♕a5 ♖xb2 47 ♖c7+ ♔f8 48 ♖b4 ♖d2 49 ♖b1 h3 0-1
A hard-fought battle, where Black defended well. His knight on f6 kept things under control and then he went onto the offensive. White's ideas with ♕d3 are not particularly dangerous, but do lead to complicated struggles with mutual chances.

Game 30
Timman-Larsen
Las Palmas izt 1982

(1 e4 c5 2 ♘f3 ♘c6 3 d4 cxd4 4 ♘xd4 g6 5 c4 ♗g7 6 ♗e3 ♘f6 7 ♘c3 0-0 8 ♗e2 d6 9 0-0 ♗d7)

10   ♕d2

This is a more aggressive way of playing the dark-squared bishop exchange system than 10 ♖c1.
10   ...   a5
Now White will not be able to prevent Black from playing ...a5-a4 and ...♕a5, but on the other hand Black has lost time with 9...♗d7, since it is not clear whether this is the right square for the bishop in this line. With aggressive play White should be able to profit from this loss of time. The standard 10...♘xd4 11 ♗xd4 ♗c6 is considered in Games 31-49.
11   ♘db5!
Although 11 f3 is more common, it does not pose Black any serious problems. After 11...a4 12 ♖ab1 ♕a5 13 ♖fc1 ♖fc8 14 ♘db5 ♗e6 15 ♘d5 ♕xd2 16 ♗xd2 ♘xd5! 17 cxd5 ♘d4 18 ♗d3 ♗d7 Black was slightly better in two of Petursson's games. Not much better is 14 ♗f1 ♘xd4 15 ♗xd4 ♗e6 16 b3 axb3 17 axb3 ♕b4 with an easy game for Black in Smejkal-Larsen, Helsingor 1982. White did well in Cvetkovic-Mestel, Belgrade 1982, after 13 ♖fd1 ♖fc8 14 ♘db5, but only because Black got himself

into trouble with the passive 14...♗e8?! 15 ♗f1 ♘e5 16 b3 axb3 17 axb3 ♕b4 18 ♕f2. Probably better was 14...♘e5 15 b3 axb3 16 axb3 ♗xb5!? 17 ♘xb5 ♕xd2 18 ♖xd2 ♘c6 followed by ...♘d7 with a decent ending; Black controls the a-file, and the bishop on g7 is quite strong.

11	...	a4
12	f4	♕a5
13	c5!	

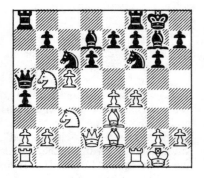

This is the move which has put the whole line under a dark cloud. White acts before his opponent can complete his development.

13	...	dxc5
14	♗xc5	

The more forcing 14 e5?! was played in the correspondence game Strand-Brezau, 1986, but Black survived the complications after 14...♘g4 15 ♗xc5 ♖fd8 16 ♗xg4 ♗xg4 17 ♕e3 ♖d7 18 h3 ♗e6 19 ♗b6 ♕b4 20 ♘c7 ♖d3! 21 ♕c5 ♕xb2 22 ♖fb1 ♕xc3 23 ♕xc3 ♖xc3 24 ♘xa8 g5 and later went on to win.

14	...	♗g4

This is necessary in order to get some room to breathe, and 14...♖fd8 15 ♕e3 would just make

things worse.

15	♗xg4	♘xg4
16	♕e2	♗xc3

On 16...b6 Timman suggests 17 ♗a3 ♘d4 18 ♘xd4 ♗xd4+ 19 ♔h1 ♗xc3 20 bxc3 ♕xc3 21 ♗xe7 ♖fe8 22 ♗h4 as clearly better for White, but after the obvious 22...♘e3 it seems to us that White is close to losing a pawn. A critical alternative is 21 ♗b2! ♕c8 22 ♖ac1 with compensation but probably not more. One strange line is 22...♕e6 23 f5 ♕xa2 24 ♖c2 ♘e3?! 25 ♕xe3 a3

26 ♗h8!! ♕xc2 27 ♕h6 ♔xh8 28 fxg6 mating. A beautiful variation, but 24...♖ac8 is better since 25 ♖xc8 ♖xc8 26 ♕xg4 ♕xb2 27 fxg6 ♖f8 28 gxf7+ ♔h8 29 ♕d7 ♕b4 is not clear. If you have the nerves for something like this, maybe you should give 10...a5 a shot, since most White players will probably play something safe and get nothing. And if they should dare to enter the complications, hopefully you will be the better prepared player.

It is interesting to note that the Maroczy expert Petursson has played 10...a5 several times since the Timman-Larsen game. Naturally he has an improvement ready, but since he has almost now completely left the chess world in favour of the world of law, we may never know what he had in mind.

17	bxc3	♘f6
18	♖ab1	♖fd8
19	♔h1	♖ac8
20	♗a3	♘e8
21	f5	

Black's problem is that, after the bishop on g7 has gone, his king feels exposed due to White's play on the dark squares.

21...♘c7 22 fxg6 hxg6 23 ♕f2 f6 24 ♕g3 ♔f7 25 c4 ♘xb5

This should have lost tactically. Better would have been 25...♘e6, helping with the defence of the king. White is still better, but if he does not break through, Black holds the positional trumps.

26 cxb5 ♘d4 27 ♗b4?

Timman must have been suffering from time pressure, otherwise he would not have missed 27 ♗xe7! ♔xe7 28 ♕xg6 ♖f8 29 e5 which wins immediately.

27...♕b6 28 e5 ♘f5 29 ♕f3 ♕e3

Since White cannot play 30 ♕xb7?? ♘g3 and ♖h8 mate, Larsen forces the exchange of queens, after which only Black can be better. Indeed, Larsen managed to get a close to winning position, but then it was his turn to blunder. The game ended in a draw after 63 moves.

Game 31
Beliavsky-Hjartarson
Reykjavik 1989

(1 e4 c5 2 ♘f3 ♘c6 3 d4 cxd4 4 ♘xd4 g6 5 c4 ♗g7 6 ♗e3 ♘f6 7 ♘c3 0-0 8 ♗e2 d6 9 0-0 ♗d7 10 ♕d2)

10	...	♘xd4
11	♗xd4	♗c6

12	♗d3!?	

A similar idea is 12 ♗f3!?, also intending to attack with the rook along the third rank. Geller-Abramovic, New York 1989, continued 12...a5 13 ♖fe1 ♘d7 14 ♗xg7 ♔xg7 15 ♖e3 ♘c5 16 ♖ae1 f6 17 ♗d1 e5, when Black slowly prepared ...f6-f5 and went on to win. In Luther-P.H.Nielsen, Bad Lauterberg 1991, Black played in even more solid fashion: 12...a5 13 ♖ae1 a4 14 ♘d5 ♘d7 15 ♗xg7 ♔xg7 16 ♖e3 ♘c5 17 ♗d1 e5, and again Black was fine. This indicates that if Black exercises some care, 12 ♗f3 is harmless.

The standard 12 f3 is seen in Games 32-49.

12	...	a5
13	♖fe1	♘d7

A interesting alternative is 13...♖e8, as in Mortensen-Larsen, Aalborg 1989, played shortly after our main game. The idea is that White cannot naturally continue his plan as long as the dark-squared bishops are still on the board. There followed 14 ♖ad1 a4, after which White got tired of waiting and played the positionally undesirable 15 ♘d5 (after the exchange of the dark-squared bishops Black threatens ...♗xd5 with the usual knight vs. bishop positions). The game continued 15...♘d7 16 ♗xg7 ♔xg7 17 b4 axb3 18 axb3 e5 19 ♗c2 (in order to take back on d5 with the queen) 19...♘c5 20 b4 ♘e6 21 ♘c3 ♘d4 22 ♘e2?? ♘xc2 23 ♕xc2 ♗a4 and Black was winning easily. Instead of 17 b4, 17 ♖e3, as in Sorokin-Nielsen, Cheliabinsk 1991, is more logical. White won after 17...♕a5 18 ♕c1 ♗xd5 (18...e5!?) 19 ♖h3 ♘f6 20 ♕h6+ ♔h8 21 exd5 ♕b6 (21...e5 seems to solve Black's problems) 22 g4 ♕d4 23 ♖h4 ♕xb2 24 g5 ♘d7 25 ♗xg6! Generally, when White wants to play ♗xg7 followed by a kingside attack, Black should not hurry with ...♘d7, but simply play useful waiting moves.

14	**♗xg7**	**♔xg7**
15	**♖e3**	

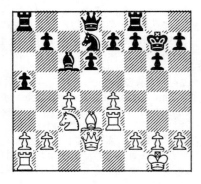

Interestingly, Beliavsky criticises this move in *Informator*, claiming that White should play on the queenside. We do not believe this. With the dark-squared bishops off the board, Black has too much

play on the dark squares, combined with the idea of manoeuvring the knight to d4.

15	**...**	**♘f6?!**

Probably not best. Black has two other options:

a) Larsen introduced 15...h6 against Milos, Mar del Plata 1993. The idea is to answer ♖h3 with ...♖h8, and then simply continue with the standard dark-squared strategy. After 16 ♖d1 ♕b6 17 ♘d5 ♗xd5 18 exd5 ♖fe8 19 ♖de1 ♕b4! 20 ♕e2 a4 (Black makes sure that he has targets on the queenside so that White never really threatens e7) 21 ♗b1 ♘f6 22 ♖d1 ♖ac8 23 b3 axb3 24 axb3 b5 25 ♗d3 ♖c7 26 ♖b1 bxc4 27 bxc4 ♕c5 28 ♕b2 ♖a7 Black had much the better position.

Sorokin-Spangenberg, Argentina 1994, saw 16 b3 instead of 16 ♖d1, but after 16...♕b6 17 ♘d5 ♕d4!? 18 ♖d1 e5 19 ♘c3 ♘f6 Black had solved his problems.

b) 15...f6 was tried in L.Hansen-U.Nielsen, Vejle 1994, and after 16 ♖d1 ♖f7 17 ♗e2 ♘c5 18 h4 ♕f8 19 h5 ♔h8 20 hxg6 hxg6 21 ♖h3+ ♖h7 22 ♖xh7+ ♔xh7 23 f3 ♕h6 Black was fine, although White later won.

16	**♖d1**	**♕b6**

In the simultaneous game Kasparov-Koch, Evry 1989, Black played 16...a4 and the world champion achieved nothing after 17 ♘d5 e6 18 ♘b4 ♕a5 19 ♗c2 ♖fd8 20 ♕c3 e5 21 h3 ♕c5 22 b3 axb3 23 axb3 ♖a3 24 ♕d2 ♕a4 25 ♘xc6 ½-½.

17	**♘d5**	**♗xd5**
18	**exd5**	**♖fe8**
19	**♗f1**	

Now the e3-rook might go to b3.

19	...	♕b4
20	♕d4	a4
21	b3	♔g8?!

This is dubious, Black should have gone in for 21...axb3 22 ♖xb3 ♕c5 23 ♕xc5 dxc5 24 ♖xb7 ♖xa2 25 ♖e1 ♔f8 26 ♖c7 ♖a5, when it is difficult to see how White can make progress.

22 ♖b1 ♘d7 23 a3! ♕xa3?

Another mistake, but the position was already bad, since 23...♕c5 24 ♕h4 axb3 25 ♖bxb3 ♘e5 26 ♖h3 h5 27 ♖bg3 is very dangerous for Black.

24 b4 ♕a2 25 ♕d1 a3 26 ♖c3 1-0

The queen will have to leave the board. An impressive performance by Beliavsky, but as we saw on moves 13, 15 and 16, Black has other options.

Game 32
Salov-Velimirovic
Szirak izt 1987

(1 e4 c5 2 ♘f3 ♘c6 3 d4 cxd4 4 ♘xd4 g6 5 c4 ♗g7 6 ♗e3 ♘f6 7 ♘c3 0-0 8 ♗e2 d6 9 0-0 ♗d7 10 ♕d2 ♘xd4 11 ♗xd4 ♗c6)

12	f3

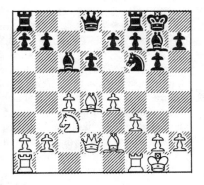

12	...	a5

In this position, 12...♘d7 has also been played, since 13 b4 is harmless. After 13...♗xd4+ 14 ♕xd4 ♕b6 15 ♕xb6 ♘xb6 16 e5 does not work, as the rook is not yet on c1 and 16 ♖fc1 ♖fc8 is just equal, Vaganian-Mariotti, Leningrad 1977.

Adorjan-Velimirovic, Budapest 1973, continued instead 13 ♗xg7 ♔xg7 14 f4 (perhaps White should try 14 ♔h1 which would transpose to the main game if Black answers 14...a5) ♕b6+ 15 ♔h1 ♕c5?! 16 ♘d5 ♗xd5 17 b4 ♕b6 18 cxd5 a5 19 ♖ab1 ♔g8 20 bxa5, when Black could have played the drawing 20...♕xa5 21 ♕xa5 ♖xa5 22 ♖xb7 ♖xa2. Anyway, safer was 15...♘f6, hitting the e4-pawn, as given by Silman and Donaldson, and if 16 ♗f3, then 16...♕c5 targeting the c4-pawn. We believe this is fine for Black, since White has to waste time protecting his pawns. An example is 17 b3 e5!? 18 f5 ♕d4 19 ♕c2 g5!? with a good game for Black.

If the lines after 12...a5 do not suit you, this may be the way to play. Here White's attack is not nearly as dangerous as it may become after 12...a5.

13	♔h1

Sensible, and clearly the best way to keep the tension, waiting for Black to play ...♘d7. 13 f4 e5! is embarrassing, and other moves hardly help the white attack. 13 ♖ac1 is seen in Game 38 and 13 b3 in Games 39-49.

13	...	♘d7

This is what everybody plays, but as it is not clear what White will do next, it is quite tempting for

Black to make a useful waiting move instead. Unfortunately, this is easier said than done. 13...a4?! is strongly met by 14 b4 axb3 15 axb3, when White achieves easy play on the queenside. But 13...♖e8!? seems playable, and may be a way to force White to think independently, instead of just following mainstream theory. Although Black has excluded himself from using the defensive plan with ...f7-f5, it is not easy to say how White should try to exploit it. 14 ♖ae1 will be met by 14...a4! since the rook has left a1. One might play 14 b3 ♘d7 15 ♗e3 claiming that ♔h1 is more useful than ...♖e8, but not everybody would agree. And by playing 13 ♔h1 White was emotionally prepared for an attack, but would then have to hold fire.

14 ♗xg7 ♔xg7
15 f4

Other moves have been played but are clearly unambitious, since Black achieves good play with the standard set-up: ...e7-e5 and ...♘c5 etc.

15 ... f6
Black follows the classical dark-squared strategy. However, this may not be best here. Apart from 15...a4!? (see the next game), two other alternatives are worth considering:

a) 15...♘c5 has been tested twice in high level games. In Chandler-Petursson, Chicago 1983, White played 16 ♗g4!? and held the initiative after 16...e5 17 f5 f6 18 ♕e2 ♕e7 19 ♖f3 b6 20 ♖g3 ♖h8 21 ♗h5 g5 22 h4 h6 23 ♖d1 ♖d8 24 ♗g6 ♕b7 25 ♖e3 ♔f8 26 b3 ♕c7 27 ♔h2 ♔e7. Here Chandler's assessment of White being clearly better is a little excessive, since neither in the game nor in his analysis in *Informator* does he offer a plan by which White is able to break through. It is interesting to note that the white f5-pawn radically changes the position. Now Black cannot manoeuvre his knight to d4, but has to keep White busy by exerting pressure on the e4-pawn, which now requires constant protection. Clearly, Black has no active plan, but still has reasonable chances for a successful defence. Epishin-Kamsky, Leningrad 1989, saw the more conventional 16 ♗f3 a4 17 ♖ad1 ♕a5 18 ♕e3! ♕b4 19 e5! ♗xf3 20 ♖xf3 ♕xc4 21 f5 dxe5 22 ♖h3 ♖ad8 23 ♕xe5+ ♔g8 24 ♘d5 f6 25 ♕xe7 ♖d7 26 fxg6! h6 27 ♖xh6 ♕xd5 28 ♖h8+! ♔xh8 29 g7+ 1-0. Impressive, and a warning for Black to remember how important it is to keep his dark squares under control. Probably Black should have gone for 16...e5, although he may then end up in a somewhat passive, but solid position, as in Chandler-Petursson.

b) 15...♕b6 was played in Dolmatov-Gufeld, USSR 1985, when

16 ♖ae1 ♕b4 17 ♖f3 ♖ad8 18 ♗f1 a4 19 ♖h3 ♘f6 20 a3 ♕c5 21 ♘d5 ♗xd5 22 exd5 ♖fe8 23 ♖e3 ♘g4 gave reasonable play for Black, although he eventually lost.

| 16 | ♖ad1 | ♘c5 |
| 17 | ♕d4 | |

Actually, White would prefer to have his queen on e3, but after 17...♕b6 Black would threaten 18...♘a4 with simplifications.

| 17 | ... | b6?! |

This was criticised by Salov, who believes that Black should play more actively with 17...♕b6, hitting the b2-pawn. If 18 b3?, then 18...a4 with counterplay. In fact, this seems to give Black a reasonable position, since White cannot both defend b2 and stop ...♘a4.

18	♗f3	♕b8
19	♖d2	♖a7
20	♗g4!	

Black was intending to play 20...♖d7 followed by ...e7-e5, but to accomplish this now, he has to weaken the kingside with ...h7-h5.

20	...	h5
21	♗f3	♖d7
22	♕e3	

White could have won a pawn with 22 f5 g5! 23 ♗xh5 ♖h8, but now 24 g4 is forced, since otherwise Black has 24...d5 with the threat of mate on h2. White might still be better, but the bishop on h5 looks quite ridiculous.

22...♕b7 23 h4!

Splendid play. Now White really does threaten 24 f5. One might call 23 h4! weakening, but Black is in no position to take advantage of it.

23...♖dd8 24 ♔g1 e5 25 f5 ♕f7 26 ♘d5 ♗xd5 27 ♖xd5 ♖d7 28 ♖fd1 ♖fd8 29 b3

Now White is ready for a2-a3, b2-b4 etc., which will be terrible for Black. So instead he comes up with a clever pawn sac, hoping that his knight will give him sufficient compensation.

29...♖c7!? 30 ♖xd6 ♖cd7 31 ♖6d5 ♖xd5 32 ♖xd5 ♖xd5 33 cxd5 gxf5 34 exf5 ♕d7 35 ♗xh5 ♕xf5?

A better chance was 35...♕xd5, hoping for 36 ♕g3+ ♔f8 37 ♕g6? ♕d4+ with a perpetual. However, 36 ♗e2 secures White excellent winning chances.

36 ♕g3+ ♔h6 37 ♗g4 ♕e4 38 d6! ♕d4+ 39 ♔h2 ♘e4

39...♕xd6 40 ♗f5 is mate.

40 ♕f3 ♔g7 41 d7 ♘c5 42 ♕f5 e4 43 h5 ♕d6 44 ♔h1 ♔h8 45 h6 ♕e7 46 ♕d5 1-0

This game shows how important it is for Black to keep open some active options, otherwise he runs the risk of being suffocated.

Game 33
A.Sokolov-Haik
Lucerne 1985

(1 e4 c5 2 ♘f3 ♘c6 3 d4 cxd4 4 ♘xd4 g6 5 c4 ♗g7 6 ♗e3 ♘f6 7 ♘c3 0-0 8 ♗e2 d6 9 0-0 ♗d7 10 ♕d2 ♘xd4 11 ♗xd4 ♗c6 12 f3 a5

13 ♔h1 ♞d7 14 ♗xg7 ♔xg7 15 f4)

15 ... a4!?

This is more active than 15...f6, which we looked at in the previous game. Black wants to put his queen on a5, when he always has ...♕e5-g7 to cover the kingside after a white f4-f5. Also, White must defend the c3-knight; otherwise Black plays ...a4-a3 to undermine it.

16 ♖f3!?

White goes for a direct attack, which seems to be the only way to trouble Black, whose only worry is his somewhat naked king.

16 ... ♕a5
17 ♖h3 ♔g8
18 ♕e1?

A mistake that allows Black to use a clever defensive idea. 18 ♗f3 has been recommended by Hertneck, with the idea of meeting 18...f5? with 19 e5!, while 18...♕c5 19 e5! is also quite tricky, since 19...dxe5 20 ♗xc6 ♕xc6 21 fxe5 is critical for Black. It seems most sensible to switch to the dark-squared strategy with 18...f6, hoping to prove that the rook on h3 is offside. Of course, White hopes to

break through on the kingside, but ...♖f7 is a useful defensive resource. Meanwhile Black will attack on the opposite flank, and the c4-pawn should keep White busy. A complicated game thus lies ahead.

18 ... f5!

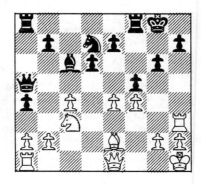

Ambitious and strong. Black claims that his opponent has been too direct, and counters efficiently.

19 ♗f3 ♖ae8
20 ♕h4 ♖f7
21 exf5

This helps Black to bring his queen to the main battleground, but since 21 ♞d5 e6 is nothing, and 21...a3 is a huge threat, there was no real choice.

21 ... ♕xf5

White must certainly have been depressed here, seeing his attack disappear so easily. Now he should worry about defending the f4-pawn, which was only possible with a passive strategy. White may have thought that he was still better, but a nasty surprise awaits.

22 ♞d5?! ♗xd5 23 ♗xd5 e6 24 ♖e3?

24 ♗xb7 was better, although 24...♖b8 followed by 25...♖xb2 is

unpleasant for White. Now he is just lost.

24...♘e5!

As this piece cannot be captured due to mate in two, White will lose material.

25 h3 ♕xf4 26 ♕xf4 ♖xf4 27 ♗xb7 ♘xc4 28 ♖e2 ♖b8 29 ♗a6 ♘e5

Black, of course, keeps his two passed pawns instead of going for the b2-pawn.

30 ♖c1 h5 31 ♖c7 ♖f7 32 ♖c8+ ♖xc8 33 ♗xc8 ♖f1+ 34 ♔h2 ♔f7 35 ♖e4 ♖c1 36 ♗a6 ♖c2 37 ♖b4 a3 38 bxa3 ♖xa2 39 a4 d5 40 ♔g1 d5 41 ♔f1 ♘c6 42 ♖b7+ ♔f6 43 ♗b5 ♘d4 44 g4 hxg4 45 hxg4 ♘xb5 46 axb5 ♖b2 47 ♔e1 ♔e5

48 ♔d1 ♖g2 49 ♖b8 ♖xg4 50 ♔c2 ♔d6 51 b6 ♔c6 52 b7 ♖e4 0-1

Black will exchange the g-pawn for the b-pawn, leaving him completely winning. The idea of defending actively with ...f7-f5 is certainly attractive, but 18 ♗f3 is critical. We think Black should be okay, but if this kind of position scares you, we recommend either 13...♖e8!?, or 12...♘d7!? which makes ♗xg7 less attractive. Black's counterplay then comes really quickly. However, this has had few tests at the very highest level. To us it seems to be reliable and offers Black good play, and hopefully it will be tested in practice soon.

5   Classical Maroczy: White Avoids the Exchange of Dark-Squared Bishops

Chapter Guide

1 e4 c5 2 ♘f3 ♘c6 3 d4 cxd4 4 ♘xd4 g6 5 c4 ♗g7 6 ♗e3 ♘f6 7 ♘c3 0-0 8 ♗e2 d6 9 0-0 ♗d7

10 ♖c1 ♘xd4 11 ♗xd4 ♗c6 12 f3 a5 13 b3 ♘d7 14 ♗e3 ♘c5
     15 a3 *– Game 35*
     15 ♕d2
          15...♕b6 *– Game 36*
          15...f5 *– Game 37*
10 ♕d2 ♘xd4 11 ♗xd4 ♗c6 12 f3 a5
     13 ♖ac1 *– Game 38*
     13 b3 ♘d7
          14 ♗e3 ♘c5 15 ♖ab1
               15...♕b6
                   16 ♘b5 *– Game 39*
                   16 ♖fc1
                       16...♕b4 *– Game 40*
                       16...♖fc8 17 ♖c2 ♕d8
                           18 ♗f1 ♗e5
                               19 ♘d1!? *– Game 41*
                               19 a3 *– Game 42*
                           18 a3
                               18...h5 *– Game 43*
                               18...♕f8 *– Game 44*
               15...e6!? *– Games 45, 46*
          14 ♗f2 ♘c5 15 ♖ab1
              15...e6 *– Game 47*
              15...♕c7 *– Game 48*
              15...♕b6 *– Game 49*

Here we examine in detail the lines where White avoids the trade of dark-squared bishops, a plan which can be adopted after either of the 10 ♖c1 or 10 ♕d2 move orders. White keeps as many pieces on the board as possible, since he has more space in which to manoeuvre. Compared to the lines with the exchange of bishops, Black's king is relatively safe, but White will use a different strategy now, intending slow manoeuvres and an eventual breakthrough on the queenside.

Game 34
Keres-Petrosian
Zagreb ct 1959

This game is not of current theoretical importance, since Black reaches the main line a tempo down. However, in this famous game Black introduced some strategic ideas which later became standard, so we feel it is relevant to include it.

(1 e4 c5 2 ♘f3 ♘c6 3 d4 cxd4 4 ♘xd4 g6 5 c4 ♗g7 6 ♗e3 ♘f6 7 ♘c3 ♘g4 8 ♕xg4 ♘xd4 9 ♕d1 ♘e6 10 ♕d2 d6 11 ♗e2 ♗d7 12 0-0 0-0 13 ♖ac1 ♗c6 14 ♖fd1 ♘c5 15 f3 a5 16 b3 ♕b6 17 ♘b5)

White is now simply a tempo up on the next game, as his rook is already on d1.

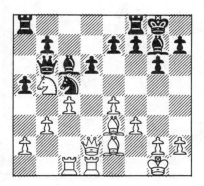

17...♖fc8 18 ♗f1 ♕d8 19 ♕f2

♕e8 20 ♘c3 b6 21 ♖c2 ♕f8

Hoping to exchange bishops with 22...♗h6.

22 ♕d2 ♗d7 23 ♘d5 ♖ab8 24 ♗g5 ♖e8

It may seem as if Black is playing very passively, but just wait and see. He is slowly preparing to expand.

25 ♖e1 ♖b7 26 ♕f2 ♗c6 27 ♕h4

White finds it difficult to form a plan, and tries to provoke some weaknesses. Having had no success so far, he finally tires of waiting and tries to attack.

27...f6!

This looks ugly, but the pawn will not stop here.

28 ♗e3 e6 29 ♘c3 ♖d7 30 ♗d4 f5!

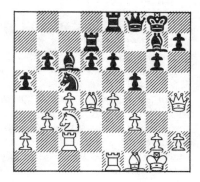

Black is on top now since the position is opening up, and he is better prepared for this. In particular the light-squared bishop on c6 is well placed for a coming kingside attack.

31 exf5 gxf5 32 ♖d2 ♗xd4+ 33 ♖xd4 ♖g7 34 ♔h1 ♖g6 35 ♖d2 ♖d8!

Not only defending d6, but simultaneously heading for the kingside.

36 Zed1 Zd7 37 Wf2 Wd8 38 We3 e5!?

Although this weakens the d5-square, since Black is threatening ...♘e6-d4, White has no time to exploit this.

39 f4 e4?

Very bad, blocking the bishop on c6. Much better was the dynamic 39...Wh4! which gives an ideal attacking game, with a huge edge for Black. Probably time trouble was a factor here.

40 ♘e2 Zdg7 41 ♘d4 ♗d7 42 a3

42 ♘b5 leads to an edge for White, as after 42...♗xb5 43 cxb5 White's bishop reaches c4 and the d6-pawn will also be under fire.

42... Wa8 43 ♔g1 h5 44 Zb1 h4 45 Zbb2 Zg4 46 Zf2 Wd8 47 b4 Zg3!

Just in time, otherwise Black's knight had to retreat.

48 hxg3 hxg3 49 Zfd2 Wh4 50 ♗e2 Zh7 51 ♔f1?

But even 51 ♗h5! Zxh5 52 ♔f1 ♘d3 wins for Black.

51...Wxf4+! 0-1

Not an error-free game, but a good illustration of how difficult it is for White to break through without the b3-b4 break, and of Black's attacking potential when he finally starts to expand.

Game 35
Ernst-Larsen
Sweden zt 1992

(1 e4 c5 2 ♘f3 ♘c6 3 d4 cxd4 4 ♘xd4 g6 5 c4 ♗g7 6 ♗e3 ♘f6 7 ♘c3 0-0 8 ♗e2 d6 9 0-0 ♗d7 10 Zc1 ♘xd4 11 ♗xd4 ♗c6 12 f3 a5)

13   b3

13 Wd2 transposes to Game 38, while at the 1990 Manila Interzonal

Shirov introduced a concept which had not been seen at the highest levels. He played 13 c5!?, a move which at first seems very illogical, since it reduces White's space advantage. Damljanovic responded well with 13...e5 14 ♗f2 ♗h6! 15 Zc2 d5 16 ♗h4!? d4 17 ♘b5 ♗e3+ 18 ♔h1 g5 and had a fine attacking game. Shirov would have done better to follow the stem game Filipenko-Rausis, Albena 1989, in which White picked up an exchange after 14 ♗e3! d5 15 ♗g5 dxe4? 16 Wxd8! Zfxd8 17 fxe4 ♘xe4 18 ♗xd8, which he easily converted into a full point. Much better was of course 15...d4, as in Todorovic-Abramovic, Cetinje 1992, but White was still somewhat better after 16 ♘b5 h6 17 ♗h4 Wd7 18 Wb3. Untried is 13...dxc5 14 ♗xc5 ♘d7 followed by ...a5-a4 and Wa5. This seems very reasonable for Black, and it would be interesting to see it tested in practice.

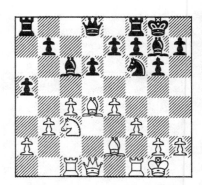

13   ...   ♘d7

At the time when 15 a3!? was considered critical for Black, Velimirovic came up with a very creative idea. Against Nunn in the

Szirak Interzonal 1987, he introduced 13...♗h6!?, when after 14 ♖c2 ♘d7 15 ♔h1 ♘c5 16 ♘d5?! ♗g7! Black had absolutely no problems. Nunn should have preferred 17 ♗g1 but instead he went for 17 ♗xg7?! ♔xg7 18 ♖d2 ♗xd5 19 ♖xd5 ♕b6, when Black was better. It might seem as if 13...♗h6!? just loses time, but it disrupted White's position and Black then got the typical knight versus bishop edge. Velimirovic tried out his idea again the following year: 14 ♖b1 ♘d7 15 a3 ♘c5 16 b4 axb4 17 axb4 ♘e6 18 ♗f2 ♖a3 with active play in Zelic-Velimirovic, Belgrade 1988. 13...♗h6 is certainly playable, but since 15 a3!? is not causing Black problems any more, it has remained a rarity.

14   ♗e3!?

Nowadays, this is generally accepted as the critical test.

14   ...   ♘c5
15   a3!?

A move which, for a while, was regarded as a clever way to prevent the rook from transferring to c8. 15 ♕d2 is covered in Game 36.

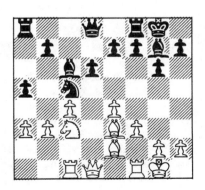

15   ...   h5!?

This is certainly the most fun. White might have thought his opponent had gone nuts! White is ready to break through on the queenside, and Black starts making strange moves on the other flank. The alternatives are:

a) 15...♕b6?! is met by 16 ♘b5, when 17 b4 is hard to meet.

b) 15...b6 is solid but passive. Van der Wiel-Petursson, Biel 1995 continued 16 ♕c2?! ♕b8 17 ♖cd1?! ♖c8 18 ♘d5 ♖a7 19 a4 ♗xd5 20 ♖xd5 e6 21 ♖d2 e5! and Black was fine. However, White's handling of the opening was hardly impressive.

16   ♔h1   ♔h7

Now White has no useful waiting moves left, so takes concrete action. Normally, White would play ♕d2, ♖d1 etc. first, but here this is not possible, since 15 a3!? has weakened the b3-square!

17   b4?!   axb4
18   axb4   ♖a3!

The key move. Since e3 would be hanging, White cannot move the knight from c3, but has to admit to the failure of his opening strategy. 17 b4?! is to blame for White's troubles, but as this is the logical follow-up, we have to conclude that 15 a3 is insufficient for an opening plus.

19   bxc5   ♗xc3
20   cxd6   exd6

20...♕xd6 was fully playable, leaving Black at least equal. But as always, Larsen is playing the Maroczy to win and prefers a middlegame to an endgame!

21   ♗d2   ♗g7
22   ♗b4   ♖a2

Black is not losing a pawn because of 23 ♗xd6? ♖xe2 24 ♗xf8

♕xd1!

23   c5

It is always a bad sign when your best move is to exchange your opponent's only weakness!

23...♖a4 24 ♕e1 dxc5 25 ♗xc5 ♖e8 26 ♗c4 f5

Opening lines for the rook on e8 and bishop on c6.

27 ♗f7 ♖e5 28 ♕g3 ♕f6 29 ♗b3 ♖xc5!

White is uncoordinated and, not surprisingly, Black can strike with a combination.

30 ♖xc5 ♖a1

Unbelievably, White must lose material. If 31 ♖c1 ♖xc1 32 ♖xc1 ♕b2 wins a piece, while 31 ♖e1 h4 32 ♕f2 ♕d4! also picks up material.

31 ♗d1

31...♕d4?

What a pity! Larsen was close to creating a classic, but here he slips up. 31...fxe4 was decisive, e.g. 32 ♕f2 ♕d6 33 ♖xc6 ♕xd1! Now White manages to escape.

32 ♖xc6 bxc6

If 32...♕xd1 then 33 ♕xg6+ is a perpetual.

33 exf5 gxf5 34 ♗e2

Now things are under control

again. Surely, it is a dead draw, but Larsen gets too ambitious.

34...♖xf1+ 35 ♗xf1 c5 36 ♕g5 h4?

Losing. 36...♕a1 seems like a better chance, hoping that Black's activity will compensate for the lost pawn.

37 ♕xf5+ ♔h6 38 ♗d3!

This was probably what Larsen had missed. Now 38...♕a1? 39 ♗b1! is nothing.

38...♕f6 39 ♕e4 ♗f8 40 f4 ♕f7 41 g4 fxg3 42 hxg3

Suddenly, White is completely winning. The rest is simple.

42...♗d6 43 ♔g2 ♔g7 44 ♔f3 ♕h5+ 45 ♔e3 ♔f8 46 ♗c4 ♕d1 47 ♕f5+ ♔e7 48 ♕f7+ ♔d8 49 ♔e4 ♕h1+ 50 ♔f5 ♕h3+ 51 g4 ♕e3 52 ♔g5 ♗e7 53 ♔g6 ♕e4+ 54 ♔h6 ♗d6 55 ♕g8+ ♔c7 56 f5 ♕f4+ 57 ♔h7 ♗e7 58 ♕f7 ♕h2+ 59 ♔g8 ♕h4 60 ♕g6 ♗g5 61 ♗e2 c4 62 ♕f7+ ♔b8 63 ♕xc4 ♕h6 64 ♕b4+ ♔c7 65 ♕c5+ 1-0

A tragic end for Larsen, who certainly deserved a better fate. Still, from an opening point of view, the game is very interesting, again stressing the fact that White should not expand too quickly, if Black is ready with immediate counterplay.

Game 36
Serper-J.Sorensen
Tunja 1989

(**1 e4 c5 2 ♘f3 ♘c6 3 d4 cxd4 4 ♘xd4 g6 5 c4 ♗g7 6 ♗e3 ♘f6 7 ♘c3 0-0 8 ♗e2 d6 9 0-0 ♗d7 10 ♖c1 ♘xd4 11 ♗xd4 ♗c6 12 f3 a5 13 b3 ♘d7 14 ♗e3 ♘c5**)

15   ♕d2   ♕b6

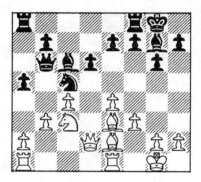

This is the most common plan in these positions, and it will be covered in detail. Black tries to restrain the potential b3-b4 break, and intends to put his king's rook on c8. In addition, he now threatens 16...a4 to break up White's pawn structure. 15...f5 is discussed in the next game.

16 ♘b5!?

Now 16...a4? 17 b4 wins a piece, but of course this is not the only idea behind 16 ♘b5!? White intends to stifle Black's active ideas on the queenside, and ...♗xb5 is hardly ever possible, since this kind of structure, as we shall see in Game 47, is quite depressing for Black. Therefore, Black must start manoeuvring, so that he will be able to counter b3-b4, when White is ready to play it.

| 16 | ... | ♖fc8 |
| 17 | ♖fd1 | ♕d8 |

As there is nothing left for the queen to do on the queenside, it returns to d8, hoping to re-emerge later on the a1-h8 diagonal.

18 ♘d4

18 ♗f1 has been tested twice against Petursson. First by Sax, Reykjavik 1988, when after

18...♕f8 19 ♘c3 b6 20 ♘d5 ♖ab8 21 ♖b1 ♗e5 22 ♗h6 ♗g7 23 ♗g5 ♖b7 24 ♖e1 ♘e6 25 ♗e3 ♘c5 26 ♖cd1 ♖cb8 27 ♖c1 e6!? 28 ♘c3 ♖d7 29 ♖ed1 ♕d8 30 ♕e1 ♗e5 31 ♘e2 ♗e5 32 ♘d4 ♗a8 33 ♕f2 a draw was agreed. White was not close to breaking through, since every time he created a threat, Black could easily meet it. Since White cannot make progress with piece play alone, he needs to use his pawns. De Firmian recognised this before his game against Petursson, Reggio Emilia 1989, and followed the game above until Black varied with 21...♖b7, preparing ...e7-e6 and ...♖d7 right away. Here De Firmian did not like 22 a3 a4! 23 b4 ♘b3 followed by 24...b5, when Black will be very active, so he played 22 b4 instead, but after 22...axb4 23 ♖xb4 ♗xd5! 24 cxd5 ♖a8 25 ♖db1 ♕d8 all Black's pieces were well placed, although the game ended in a draw. Again, we see that without an eventual b3-b4, White has no chance of breaking through. But we also saw that it is hard to accomplish! In conclusion, 18 ♗f1 should not scare Black.

18 ♖c2 was played in Karpov-Mariotti, Milan 1975. Normally, Karpov is very effective at using space advantages, but here he was less efficient: 18...b6 19 ♗f1 ♕d7 20 ♘c3 ♕b7 21 ♕f2 ♘a6! 22 ♖cc1 a4 23 ♘d5 ♗xd5 24 cxd5 axb3 25 axb3 b5 26 f4 b4 27 ♖c4 ♖xc4 28 ♗xc4 ♘c7 29 ♕e2 ♖a5 30 ♗f2 ♘b5 31 ♖c1 ♘c3 32 ♕d3 ♕a8 33 g3 ½-½. Karpov is usually a trend-setter but, not surprisingly, this approach has not found many followers!

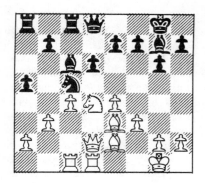

18	...	♛f8
19	♖b1	

This is probably White's only way to make progress, but then of course the rook should have gone to b1 in the first place, leaving White with an extra tempo. However, as we shall see in the notes to the next game, even this should not frighten Black.

19	...	♗d7

The game Nunn-Velimirovic, Dubai ol 1986 went 19...♗f6 20 a3 ♛g7 21 b4 axb4 22 axb4 ♘e6 23 ♘xe6 fxe6 24 b5 ♗e8 25 f4 ♗e8 26 e5! dxe5 27 fxe5 ♗xe5 28 c5 with a crushing position. Nunn recommends instead 18...♗d7 19 ♖b1 ♘e6 20 ♘xe6 ♗xe6 21 f4 with some edge for White. But Sorensen points out that there is no reason for the knight to leave the excellent c5-square, unless it is forced to do so! The big difference is that in the line given by Nunn, the queenside remains closed, and White starts to play in the centre. Here, however, he would have to play a2-a3 and b3-b4 first, when Black will exchange knights with ...♘e6, since the a-file, combined with the bishop on g7, secures him

sufficient counterplay. Compare with Jansa-Petursson in the note to White's 18th move in Game 39.

20	♖dc1	h5!?

An attractive idea. Instead of the typical ...♗f6 and ...♛g7, Black prepares 21...♔h7 either to exchange bishops with 22...♗h6, or simply to play ...♛h8 to play on the long diagonal.

21	♗d1	♔h7
22	♘e2	

On 22 ♗c2 with the idea of 22...♗h6 23 f4 e5 24 ♘f3, Sorensen had prepared 22...e5!? 23 ♘e2 ♗c6 followed by 24...♗h6 with excellent play for Black.

22	...	♗h6
23	♘f4	♗c6

Black is preparing ...e7-e5, which was not possible immediately due to 24 ♘d5.

24 ♘d5

White tries to avoid ...e7-e5, but it might have been the lesser evil.

24...♗xd5 25 exd5 ♗xe3+ 26 ♛xe3 ♖e8! 27 ♗c2 e6 28 dxe6 ♖xe6 29 ♛d2 b6 30 ♖e1 ♖ae8 31 a3 ♖xe1+ 32 ♖xe1 ♖xe1+ 33 ♛xe1

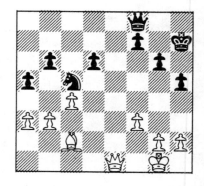

It may seem that White is on top due to his better pawn structure.

But since queen and knight work better together than queen and bishop, in fact Black has the advantage. He can also attack on the dark squares.

33...♕g7 34 h4 ♕b2 35 ♕d1 ♕xa3 36 f4?

White should have tried 36 ♕xd6, although 36...♕c1+ 37 ♕d1 ♕e3+ is clearly better for Black.

36...♘e6! 37 ♕xh5+ ♔g7 38 ♕d1 ♕c5+ 39 ♔f1 ♘xf4 40 ♕f3 ♕e5 41 g3 ♘e6 42 ♗d1 ♘d4 43 ♕d3 ♘f5 44 ♔f2 ♕c5 0-1

A pawn down with a bad position, White threw in the towel. Again White never accomplished b3-b4, since Black kept him busy with small positional threats.

Game 37
Vaganian-Yudasin
USSR 1988

(1 e4 c5 2 ♘f3 ♘c6 3 d4 cxd4 4 ♘xd4 g6 5 c4 ♗g7 6 ♗e3 ♘f6 7 ♘c3 0-0 8 ♗e2 d6 9 0-0 ♗d7 10 ♖c1 ♘xd4 11 ♗xd4 ♗c6 12 f3 a5 13 b3 ♘d7 14 ♗e3 ♘c5 15 ♕d2)

15   ...   f5!?

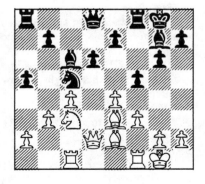

An interesting idea. Black is

aiming for similar attacking possibilities to Game 34, but he plays ...f7-f5 immediately, hoping that he can regroup later. It is thought of as a difficult line for Black, as while he regroups, White will be able to attack his weaknesses. But since no-one has actually proved this in practice yet, it is difficult to explain why 15...f5!? is not more popular.

16   exf5   gxf5!

A natural recapture – the g-file is potentially more dangerous than the f-file.

17   ♘d5

17 f4 prevents Black from pushing his own pawn to f4, but then the c6-bishop, combined with play on the g-file, would give Black attacking chances. After 17 ♖fd1, not 17...♖f7?? 18 ♗xc5 1-0 (Lerner-Urban, Berlin 1991), but 17...b6 with similar play to the main game.

17   ...   ♖f7
18   ♖fd1   b6

Since the queen is not heading for b6, and Black has already committed himself by playing ...f7-f5, it is sensible to fortify the strong knight. This move also opens up a different path for the other rook to the kingside.

19   ♗g5   ♖a7

Both defending the e7-pawn and preparing for a quick transfer to the kingside, which Black hopes will be the main battleground.

20   ♗h4?!

Yudasin was more afraid of 20 ♕e3!?, and rightly so. He was intending 20...♖b7, covering the b6-pawn, and after 21 f4 h6 22 ♗h4 ♗f8 23 ♗h5 ♖g7 he considers the position to be unclear, since Black plans 24...♕a8 and then 25...e5.

The position is indeed messy, but one cannot help thinking that White's centrally placed forces should offer him the better chances.

20 ... ♕b8!

This looks odd as the queen is moving away from the kingside, but Black needs to play ...e7-e6 to get rid of White's annoying knight. However, the b-pawn needs protection and that is why this must be the right square for the queen. In any case, the price is just one tempo, since the queen will later attack via f8.

21 ♗f1?!

This was criticised by Yudasin, who claims that 21 ♗g3 would hold the balance for White, the trick being 21...e6? 22 ♗xd6, but of course Black would play 21...♖d7 with excellent chances.

21 ... e6
22 ♘c3 ♖ad7

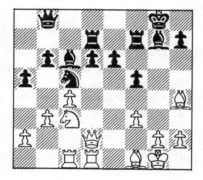

Black's position looks a little loose, but that is of no importance, as White has no quick way of attacking the weak spots. The only white plan is a2-a3 and b3-b4, but by the time White is ready for this, Black's dynamically placed pieces will already be tearing his kingside

apart.

23 ♖b1 ♗e5

Already threatening 24...d5. Should White play 24 f4, Black has the instructive 24...♗xc3! 25 ♕xc3 ♖g7 followed by doubling rooks on the g-file with a potentially winning attack.

24 ♔h1 ♕a8

Threatening 25...♗xf3.

25 ♘e2 f4!

This prevents 26 ♗g3, which would have eased the pressure a little.

26 ♘g1 ♖f5 27 ♕e1 ♖g7 28 a3 ♖h5 29 ♗d3!

Careful defensive play, not allowing 29 b4? ♘e4!!, when Black's last piece enters the attack with decisive effect.

29...♔f7!?

Black wants to break through with brute force and prepares some interesting sacrifices. Simple and good was 29...♘xd3 30 ♖xd3 ♕e8, bringing the queen to the kingside with decisive effect.

30 ♗c2 ♕g8 31 ♕f2 ♖g3!

'Trapping' the bishop on h4, and thereby forcing White to accept the offered material.

32 hxg3 fxg3 33 ♕e2 ♖xh4+ 34 ♘h3 ♕g7 35 b4

Since White cannot stop Black's attack anyway, he tries to create counterplay on the queenside. At least it forces Black to make some exact moves, as his knight is now threatened.

35...♕f6! 36 ♖f1

The only way to stop 36...♖xh3+ followed by 37...♗xf3.

36...♕h6!

It was important to lure White's rook to f1 first, as there it blocks the king's escape route.

37 ♖bd1 ♘a4??

Poor Yudasin. Having played such a great game, he messes it up in time trouble. 37...♗f4! won, as 38...♖xh3+ 39 gxh3 ♕xh3+ 40 ♔g1 ♗e3+ mating cannot be met.

38 ♗xa4 ♗xa4 39 f4! ♗xf4 40 ♖xd6 ♔e7 41 ♖xf4 ½-½

41...♖xf4 42 ♖xe6+ ♕xe6 43 ♘xf4 leads to a drawn ending. It is a pity that Black did not win after having generated such an attack, but still this game is a fine illustration of Black's potential chances, if he gets the attack rolling.

Game 38
Kristiansen-Larsen
Copenhagen 1985

(1 e4 c5 2 ♘f3 ♘c6 3 d4 cxd4 4 ♘xd4 g6 5 c4 ♗g7 6 ♗e3 ♘f6 7 ♘c3 0-0 8 ♗e2 d6 9 0-0 ♗d7 10 ♕d2 ♘xd4 11 ♗xd4 ♗c6 12 f3 a5)

13   ♖ac1?!

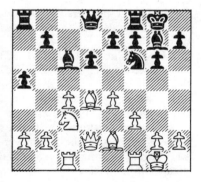

This is inaccurate. White should either play 13 ♔h1, exchanging on g7 and going for the attack (Games 33-34), or play slow positional chess with 13 b3 (Games 39-49). If

White insists on not playing b2-b3, he should not leave the a-file so that 13...a4 can be met by 14 b4!

13   ...   a4!

Now after 14 b4 axb3 15 axb3 ♘d7 Black has excellent play due to his control of the a-file, while the knight threatens to go to c5.

14   ♘d5?!

Perhaps we are too harsh in our criticism of White's play, but this was not one of his better days. On other occasions he has given the authors a lesson or two. This move is actually a quite common inaccuracy. White might have been hoping for 14...♘xd5, but Black was going to play 14...♘d7 anyway, so why force him to do it? Actually, White's knight does nothing on d5 and should have stayed on c3.

14   ...   ♘d7
15   ♗e3

15 ♗xg7 is a typical, but incorrect follow-up. Black recaptures, and tries to regroup with ...♘c5, ...e7-e5 and ...♘e6, when White will have to take his knight to e2 to keep the black knight away from the beautiful d4-square.

15   ...   ♖e8

Larsen loves this move, and for once it is immediately useful, releasing the queen from the defence of e7.

16   ♖c2   ♘c5
17   ♖d1   ♕a5

Since Black has gained some space on the queenside, he is not afraid of the endgame. It is difficult to see what White should play now.

18   ♗g5   ♕xd2
19   ♖dxd2   ♗xd5
20   cxd5   ♗f6

A typical trick, winning time.

21   ♗xf6?

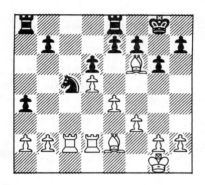

This is a positional blunder. First of all, Black gets rid of the weak e7-pawn, leaving him with an open e-file and a possible ...f6-f5 break. Second, the c5-knight cannot be challenged for a while, which means that the bishop on e2 is useless compared to the black knight. White should have played 21 ♗e3 with a perfectly normal position and retaining equal chances.

21	...	exf6
22	♖d4	♖e5
23	♖b4	f5
24	♖b6	

This square was probably what seduced White. It looks like he is exerting pressure, but Black can easily defend the pawn on d6.

24...♖d8 25 exf5 ♖xf5 26 ♗c4 ♖e5 27 ♔f2 ♖e7

Black is on the retreat, but his knight versus bishop advantage is permanent – no need to hurry.

28 b4 axb3 29 axb3 ♖c7!

Stopping White's plans of removing the knight with 29 b4, which would now lose due to the pin on the c-file after 29...♘d7.

30 ♖a2 ♔f8 31 ♔e3 ♘d7 32♖b4 ♖e8+ 33♔d4 ♖e1 34 ♖a8+ ♔e7 35 ♖a7 ♘c5 36 ♖b6 ♖c1 37 ♖a2

♖d1+ 38 ♔e3 ♘d7 39 ♖b4 ♖c1 40 ♔f2 h5 41 ♖e2+ ♔f8 42 ♖e1 ♖xe1 43 ♔xe1 ♔e7 44 ♔d2 ♔d8 45 ♖a4 ♘e5 46 f4?

Of course, White should have drawn this game, but he has been under constant pressure due to his bad bishop. This move only creates more weaknesses, which means more problems.

46...♘g4 47 h3 ♘f6 48 ♖a8+ ♔e7 49 ♖a7 h4!

Fixing the targets.

50 ♔e3 ♘h5 51 ♔f3 f5 52 ♔e3 ♔f7 53 ♔f3 ♔f6 54 ♔e3 ♔g7 55 ♗d3 ♖e7+ 56 ♔f3 ♘f6 57 ♗c4 ♘e4 58 ♔e3 ♔f7 59 ♔f3 ♘c3

Threatening 60...♘d1!

60 g3 hxg3 61 ♔xg3 ♔f6 62 ♔f3 ♖h7 63 ♔g2 ♖c7 64 ♔f3 ♘e4 65 ♔g2 g5!

Finally securing some asymmetry, which of course is good for the attacker.

66 fxg5+ ♔xg5 67 ♗d3 ♔f4 68 ♖a4 ♖g7+ 69 ♔f1 ♔e3 70 ♗xe4

In principle White would love to exchange his light-squared bishop for the knight, but here a new monster appears. However, there was no choice.

70...fxe4 71 h4 ♖h7 72 ♖b4 ♔f3 73 ♔g1 e3 74 ♔f1 b5 75 ♖d4 ♖c7 0-1

Not a great game perhaps, but it does contain some typical mistakes, as well as an illustration of Black's potential if he gets the knight versus bishop ending he so often dreams of in this line.

Game 39
Kudrin-Velimirovic
Thessaloniki ol 1988

(1 e4 c5 2 ♘f3 ♘c6 3 d4 cxd4 4

♘xd4 g6 5 c4 ♗g7 6 ♗e3 ♘f6 7
♘c3 0-0 8 ♗e2 d6 9 0-0 ♗d7 10
♕d2 ♘xd4 11 ♗xd4 ♗c6 12 f3 a5
13 b3 ♘d7 14 ♗e3 ♘c5)

15   ♖ab1!

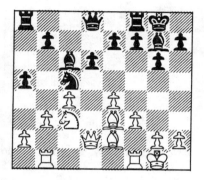

This certainly seems to be the
right square for the rook, since it
helps to prepare the b3-b4 advance.

15   ...   ♕b6
16   ♘b5

This used to be the main move,
but nowadays 16 ♖fc1! is more
common (Games 40-42). With the
text move, White puts an end to
Black's dreams of activity on the
queenside. But apart from that, the
knight is not well placed, and will
often simply retreat, having lost
some tempi.

16   ...   ♖fc8
17   ♖fd1

Other moves have been tried
here:

a) Adams-Larsen, London 1990,
saw 17 ♖fc1 ♕d8 18 ♘d4 ♗d7 19
♗d1?! ♕e8 20 ♗e2! (stopping
20...b5) 20...h5 and Black has a
good position. Instead of 18 ♘d4,
18 ♖c2 was tried in Kotronias-
Petursson, Komotini 1993. After
18...♕f8 19 ♗f1 ♗e5 20 ♘c3 b6

21 ♘d5 ♕d8 22 ♗g5 ♖a7 23 ♗h4
♖b8 24 ♖e1 ♗xd5 25 exd5 ♕d7 26
f4 ♗f6! 27 ♗xf6 exf6 28 ♖c3 ♖e8
29 ♖ce3 ♖aa8 a drawish position
had arisen. Again, White got nowhere by just manoeuvring around.

b) The direct 17 a3 was tried in
Cebalo-Petursson, San Bernardino
1989, but after 17...♕d8 18 ♘d4
♗d7 19 ♖fd1 ♕f8 20 b4 axb4 21
axb4 ♘e6 22 ♘b3 ♖a3 23 ♖b1
♗a4 24 ♗d1 ♖a8 White had to ask
himself whether opening the a-file
was such a great achievement.

17   ...   ♕d8
18   ♘c3

18 ♘d4 proved ineffective in
Jansa-Petursson, Naestved 1988.
After 18...♕f8 19 a3 ♗d7 20 b4
axb4 21 axb4 ♘e6 22 ♖a1 ♖xa1 23
♖xa1 ♖a8, White had absolutely
nothing, and went on to lose!

18   ...   ♕c7?!

Petursson would probably have
gone for 18...b6 19 ♗g5 ♖a7. Also
Sorensen's approach with 18...♕f8
and a later ...h7-h5 is worth a try,
although Black is a tempo down on
the previous game. 18...♗e5 was
played in Kudrin-Haik, Marseilles
1987, but after 19 ♗f1 e6?! 20
♘b5 ♗xb5 21 cxb5 ♕e7 22 ♗g5
♕c7 23 ♔h1 f6 24 ♗e3 f5 25 ♗c4
♕e7 26 ♗xc5 ♖xc5 27 f4 Black's
position was terrible and he soon
lost. 19...e6?! was premature, since
Black was not yet able to defend
the d6-pawn with a rook on d7.

19   ♗f1   b6
20   ♘d5   ♕b7
21   ♗g5   ♗xd5
22   exd5!

The only way to make progress.
22 cxd5 b5 would not get White
anywhere, and capturing with the
queen would ease the pressure.

22	...	♖e8
23	♖e1	

The structure is very similar to the previous game, but here White is ready to meet Black's counter-play, since he is several tempi up.

23	...	♕c7
24	h4!	

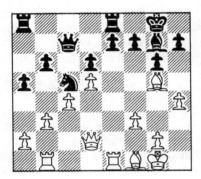

This is often a useful move to break through Black's defences. The pawn will march on, since 24...h5 would only weaken the black position. The difference between h2-h4 and ...h7-h5 is that here it is White who holds the initiative!

24...e5 25 dxe6 ♖xe6 26 ♖ad1 ♖ae8 27 ♖xe6 ♖xe6 28 ♕d5

This time it is White who is active. Black can only sit and wait, defending his weaknesses.

28...♕c8 29 g3 ♕e8 30 ♔f2! ♗c3 31 ♗d2 ♗g7 32 ♗f4 ♗e5 33 ♗xe5 dxe5 34 ♗h3 ♖e7 35 ♕d6

Black has got rid of his main weakness, the d6-pawn, but as often happens, some other problems have been revealed. White is about to break through via the d-file.

35...♖b7 36 ♕f6 ♖b8 37 ♔e3! ♕f8 38 ♖d5 ♕h6+ 39 ♕g5 ♕f8 40 ♕f6 ♕h6+ 41 ♔e2 e4 42 f4 ♕f8 43 ♔e3

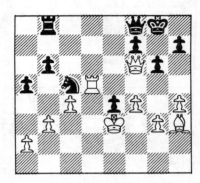

Complete domination. Black is hopelessly lost.

43...♘d3 44 ♕d6! ♕xd6 45 ♖xd6 f5 46 g4! fxg4 47 ♗xg4 ♘c5 48 f5 ♔f7 49 ♖c6 ♖b7 50 h5 g5 51 h6 1-0

The f-pawn will be a winner. Truly a model game for White, but Black went astray early in the middlegame, when correct play would have offered him reasonable chances.

Game 40
Gelfand-Anand
Manila izt 1990

(1 e4 c5 2 ♘f3 ♘c6 3 d4 cxd4 4 ♘xd4 g6 5 c4 ♗g7 6 ♗e3 ♘f6 7 ♘c3 0-0 8 ♗e2 d6 9 0-0 ♗d7 10 ♕d2 ♘xd4 11 ♗xd4 ♗c6 12 f3 a5 13 b3 ♘d7 14 ♗e3 ♘c5 15 ♖ab1 ♕b6)

16 ♖fc1!

Nowadays this is generally accepted as the right way to place the rooks against the ...♕b6 system. On b1 and c1 they will support a future b3-b4 break in the best possible way, while leaving the d1-

square free for manoeuvring the knight to the kingside.

21	♗f1	♗e5
22	b4	axb4
23	axb4	♘a4
24	♘e2	

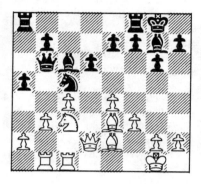

16	**...**	**♕b4**

This move is often criticised, but it is not so bad. At first sight, it seems as if Black is trying to prevent a2-a3 and b3-b4, but in fact the opposite is true. As we will see in the game, White has to play ♕c1 and a2-a3 to shift the annoying queen, after which she happily returns to b6, hoping to prove that White's a2-a3 has been played too quickly. For 16...♖fc8 see Games 41-44.

17	♖c2	♖fc8
18	♕c1	♕b6
19	a3	♕d8
20	♕d2	

As we now see, Black has not lost a tempo, but has in fact forced White to go for an immediate a2-a3. 20 ♕d2 was not absolutely necessary, but the queen is not very well placed on c1.

20	**...**	**e6**

An active choice. Black is planning to put the bishop on e5 to protect the weakened d6-pawn. Although this is a common idea, it is usually played without moving the king's rook to c8.

24	**...**	**♕h4?!**

This seems too ambitious. Black creates a long-term weakness, but it is unlikely ever to turn into anything concrete. The prophylactic 24...♗e8 seems to us to be a better move. Black intends to play 25...♘b6 next, hitting the c4-pawn and leaving the a-file open. This typical way of exploiting the open a-file secures plenty of counterplay. Such positions are normally given as slightly better for White, due to his space advantage, but practical play has not supported this.

25	g3	♕e7
26	♘d4	♗e8
27	♖bc1	♘b6?

Now Anand is going for the standard plan, but there is a tactical flaw. Gelfand recommends instead 27...♖c7 28 ♘b3 ♖ac8 29 c5!, when White is somewhat better, although it is not that scary.

28 ♘xe6 ♕xe6 29 ♗xb6 ♖a3?

Gelfand gives 29...d5 as a big improvement, hoping for compensation after 30 ♗f2 dxe4 31 fxe4

♖d8. It is true that Black is some-what active, but White will create a passed pawn on the queenside, which should bring him the win.

30 f4?!

Gelfand is not one to back off. Still, a pawn up, the more cautious 30 ♕f2 was wiser, leaving White a clear pawn up with no immediate targets.

30...♗g7 31 ♕d5 ♗c6 32 ♕xe6 fxe6 33 ♗g2 e5

Now Black is getting some counterplay together, since White's pawns are somewhat weak.

34 ♖d2 exf4 35 gxf4 ♗c3?!

After this move White takes control again by returning material. 35...♗h6 or 35...♖f8 was to be rec-ommended, going for the f-pawn. Although only White can win, Black could put up a tough fight for the half point.

36 ♖xd6 ♗xb4 37 c5 ♖f8 38 e5!

The key move. White is happy to return the extra pawn in order to regain the initiative.

38...♗xg2 39 ♔xg2 ♖xf4 40 e6

White now has a huge passed pawn, and since the b7-pawn is weak, the c-pawn could also turn into something.

40...♖e4 41 ♖d8 ♔g7 42 ♖d7 ♔h6

Forced. After 42...♔f6 43 ♗d8+!, Black could not take on e6 anyway, since 44 ♖e7+ picks up a rook.

43 e7 ♖e2+ 44 ♔f1 ♖aa2 45 ♗c7 ♗a3 46 ♖e1 ♖f2+ 47 ♔g1 ♗xc5 48 ♔h1 ♗xe7 49 ♖dxe7 ♖f5 50 ♗b6 ♖f6 51 ♗e3 g5 52 ♖g1 ♖f5 53 h4 1-0

Along with the previous game, this encounter really set the trend. Nowadays everybody puts their rooks on b1 and c1. Although this

is certainly sensible, Black has ways to kick back, and his defeat in this game was due to later mis-takes, not because of the opening.

Game 41
Vaganian-Ivkov
Moscow 1985

(1 e4 c5 2 ♘f3 ♘c6 3 d4 cxd4 4 ♘xd4 g6 6 c4 ♗g7 7 ♗e3 ♘f6 7 ♘c3 0-0 8 ♗e2 d6 9 0-0 ♗d7 10 ♕d2 ♘xd4 11 ♗xd4 ♗c6 12 f3 a5 13 b3 ♘d7 14 ♗e3 ♘c5 15 ♖ab1 ♕b6)

16   ♖fc1!

16   ...   ♖fc8
17   ♖c2

17 a3 does not work yet, as seen in Maksimenko-Marinkovic, Vrn-jacka Banja 1991, where Black was fine in the complications after 17...♘xb3 18 ♗xb6 ♘xd2 19 ♖b2 ♘c4! 20 ♗xc4 ♗d7! 21 ♗d5 ♗xc3 22 ♖bb1 ♗e5 23 ♗xb1 ♖xc1+ 24 ♖xc1 ♖b8 25 ♖c7 ♗e6 26 ♗a7 ♖e8, although White had enough compensation to draw.

17   ...   ♕d8

Since White is close to the a2-a3 and b3-b4 push, the queen has no further purpose on the queenside. It might seem strange to move back and forth, but in that way the black rooks can be placed on the a- and c-files, where they have useful pro-phylactic purposes, since White's standard plans will lead to the opening of one file or the other. Furthermore, the queen now goes to f8 or even h8, where it has a useful role.

18 ♗f1

The direct 18 a3 is the subject of Games 43 and 44. Vaganian plays more slowly, hoping his extra space will make it easier for him to manoeuvre.

18 ... ♗e5

Normally this is a useful move, simultaneously planning ...♕f8-g7 and ...e7-e6 and ...♕e7. The prob-lem is that the bishop is somewhat unstable on e5. Black would not mind if it were exchanged with ♗d4xe5, since after d6xe5 he will get a solid grip on the dark squares. However, if it is exchanged by the knight, White keeps his dark-squared bishop, which is unaccept-able for Black. This fact is skilfully exploited by Vaganian.

19 ♘d1!?

This weakens the grip on b5, but by the time Black gets ...b7-b5 in, White's attack is already at full speed. 19 a3 is seen in the next game.

19 ... ♕e8
20 ♘f2 b5?!

20...h5 would be the modern way of playing, and this would certainly have provided a much tougher test. In general, Black would be happy to push ...b7-b5, as it loosens White's queenside bind. Here, however, White shifts his attention to the kingside.

21 ♘g4 ♗g7
22 cxb5 ♗xb5
23 ♘h6+

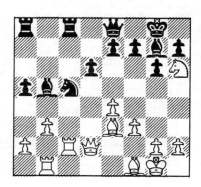

23...♔f8

Black is forced to this unpleasant square due to the weakness of f7.

24 ♗xb5 ♕xb5 25 ♕d5 ♕e8

Although it is bad, Black had to try 25...♗xh6, which would have left him with a small chance of a successful defence. Now White has a rarely possible, but in this case decisive break.

26 e5!

This move undermines the posi-tion of the strong c5-knight, which is Black's main defender, while opening up the black king.

26...♖d8 27 exd6 exd6 28 ♖e1!

The black queen now has no-where to hide.

28...♖c8 29 ♖xc5 ♖xc5 30 ♕xc5!
1-0

An attractive game, and it is no wonder that many players started copying Vaganian's approach.

Game 42
Khalifman-Hracek
Pardubice 1994

(1 e4 c5 2 ♘f3 ♘c6 3 d4 cxd4 4

♘xd4 g6 5 c4 ♗g7 6 ♗e3 ♘f6 7
♘c3 0-0 8 ♗e2 d6 9 0-0 ♗d7 10
♕d2 ♘xd4 11 ♗xd4 ♗c6 12 f3 a5
13 b3 ♘d7 14 ♗e3 ♘c5 15 ♖ab1
♕b6 16 ♖fc1 ♖fc8 17 ♖c2 ♕d8 18
♗f1 ♗e5)

19   a3!?

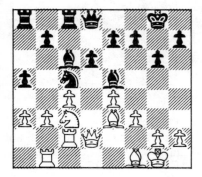

It is interesting to note that 19
♘d1!? neither attracts Khalifman
nor scares Hracek. The only possible reason for this must be that
20...h5, as mentioned in the previous game, is evaluated as okay for
Black by both players. If this is not
the case, then 18...♗e5 is indeed
dubious.

19   ...   ♕f8
19...♗e8 was played in
Wojtkiewicz-Bischoff, Altensteig
1995, but it seems dubious, since it
is difficult to see what Black can do
next if White keeps on manoeuvring – the bishop blocks Black's
traditional plans. In the game, however, it was fully justified, since
after 20 b4 axb4 21 axb4 ♘a4 22
♘e2 ♘b6 White agreed to a draw,
admitting that he had expanded too
quickly.

20   ♘d5
20 b4 axb4 21 axb4 ♘a4 22

♘d5 ♗xd5 23 exd5 ♕g7 simply
transposes.

20   ...   ♗xd5
21   exd5
21 cxd5? a4! 22 b4 ♘b3 gives
Black everything he could dream
of.

21   ...   ♕g7
This idea of putting the queen
behind the bishop on the long diagonal is a typical way of obtaining
counterplay. Black might already
be threatening 22...a4 23 b4 ♘b3
with counterplay.

22   b4   axb4
23   axb4   ♘a4!
Going for the dark squares at
any cost.

24   ♖b3   b6
25   ♖a3   ♕f8
White was threatening to double
rooks on the a-file, but now this is
met with 26...♕e8, when a later
...b6-b5 gives Black counterplay.

26   ♗d4
White tries to fight back on the
dark squares, hoping that after the
exchange of dark-squared bishops,
Black's ...b7-b5 sacrifice will not
be so effective, since he cannot use
the c3-square. The risk, of course,
is that he might end up with a terrible bishop versus knight endgame.

26   ...   ♗xd4+
27   ♕xd4   ♕g7!
White's threats along the a-file
were getting serious, but after the
queens disappear, Black is saved
by tactical means.

28   ♕xg7+
If the queen had gone anywhere
else, Black would have had counterplay with 28...b5.
28...♔xg7 29 ♖ca2 b5!
This is the trick that saves Black.
If White accepts the sacrifice with

30 cxb5, then Black responds 30...♘b6, and White will not find a way through Black's defences, since the knight offers a very effective blockade. White goes for more, which involves serious risks.

30 c5 ♖ab8

31 ♗xb5 was the threat, but now this would simply lead to a draw, which does not satisfy White.

31 c6 e6

White should now go for the draw with 32 ♗xb5, but he continues his ambitious approach.

32 ♖xa4 bxa4 33 ♖xa4 ♖c7

Black certainly will not allow b4-b5 and ♖a7.

34 b5 ♔f6 35 ♖a6 exd5 36 ♔f2

Sadly enough, there is no way for White to make progress, so he has to switch to defensive mode, hoping to make a draw.

36...♔e5 37 ♔e3 d4+ 38 ♔d2 ♔d5 39 ♖a1 ♔c5 40 ♖c1+ ♔b6

The time control has been made, and Black has achieved more than he could have hoped for. Before he seemed to have sufficient counterplay for a draw, but now he only need to solve technical problems to get the full point.

41 ♔d3 ♖a8 42 ♔xd4 ♖a2 43 ♖d1 ♖ca7 44 h3 f5 45 ♔d5 ♖a1 46 ♖xa1 ♖xa1 47 ♗c4 ♖d1+ 48 ♔e6 ♔c7 49 f4 ♖d4 50 ♗d5 ♖b4 51 g4 ♖xb5 52 gxf5 gxf5 53 h4 h6 54 ♗f3 ♖a5 55 ♗d5 ♖c5 56 ♗f3 ♖b5 57 ♗d5 ♖a5 58 ♗f3 ♖a3 59 ♗d5 ♖d3 60 ♗g2 ♖d2 61 ♗h1 ♖h2 62 ♗d5 ♖xh4 63 ♔xf5 h5 64 ♗e4 ♖h2 65 ♔g5 h4 66 f5 h3 67 f6 ♖f2 68 ♔g6 h2 69 f7 ♖f1 70 ♔g7 h1♕ 0-1

Again, this was absolutely not an error-free game, but Black kept finding clever resources, and in the end White was too ambitious.

Game 43
Ivanchuk-Larsen
Roquebrune (rapid) 1992

This was a rapidplay game, and it should be regarded as such. But even here, these players come up with moves that we mere mortals would be proud of producing in serious chess.

(1 e4 c5 2 ♘f3 ♘c6 3 d4 cxd4 4 ♘xd4 g6 5 c4 ♗g7 6 ♗e3 ♘f6 7 ♘c3 0-0 8 ♗e2 d6 9 0-0 ♗d7 10 ♕d2 ♘xd4 11 ♗xd4 ♗c6 12 f3 a5 13 ♖ab1 ♘d7 [With this particular move order, 13...a4 14 b4 axb3 15 axb3 ♘d7 16 ♗e3 ♘c5 17 b4 ♖a3 seems okay] **14 ♗e3 ♘c5 15 b3 ♕b6 16 ♖fc1 ♖fc8 17 ♖c2 ♕d8)**

18   a3

The model game for this move was Dimitrov-Abramovic, Prilep 1992, when White managed to expand on the queenside whilst keeping his opponent's activity to a minimum. The game continued 18...b6?! (this often turns out to be a weakness) 19 b4 axb4 20 axb4 ♘a4 21 ♘d5 e6 22 ♘f4 ♕e7 23 ♗f1 ♖d8 24 ♖b3! ♕b7 25 ♖d3 ♕b8 26 ♘e2! (preventing ...b6-b5) 26...♗e8 27 ♗g5 ♖c8 28 ♗e7 d5 29 exd5 exd5 30 ♖xd5 b5 31 c5 ♕b7 32 ♗g5 ♘b6 33 ♖d3 ♘c4 34 ♕f4 ♗d7 35 ♘g3 ♖e8 36 ♗f6 ♗c6 37 ♘h5! 1-0. An impressive performance. Black's problem was that he was unable to use the a-file for anything concrete, did not get any play on the a1-h8 diagonal, and had to keep the weak b6-pawn under control. It was better to play 22...♗e5 followed by 23...♕f6.

18   ...   h5!?

Typical Larsen: pawns on a5 and h5! The idea is, as mentioned before, ...♔h7, and then either ...♕h8 or ...♕f8 and ...♗h6. Furthermore, the h-pawn might be used to create counterplay, as we shall see later in the game. Again, the standard warning is that ...h7-h5 could be a weakness, but not many games have proven that it is. 18...♕f8 is seen in the next game.

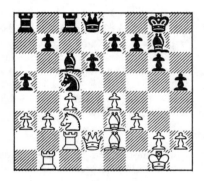

19   ♗f1

The direct 19 b4 was successful in Pytel-Sokolowski, Jadwisin 1985. After 19...axb4 20 axb4 ♘a4 21 ♘d5 e6 22 ♘f4 ♕e7 23 ♗f1 ♔h7 Black was almost okay but was then slowly outplayed. 22...♘b6 is a possible improvement, trying to make use of the a-file.

19   ...   ♗d7!?

This seems like a passive and rather odd move, but in fact it is very aggressive. Larsen is trying to show that White's early a2-a3 has its downside too. He intends to play 20...a4 21 b4 ♘b3 followed by ...e7-e5 and ....♗e6, or the immediate ....♗e6. Should White then put his knight on d5, it will be ex-

changed, and the b3-knight will promise Black good chances along the c-file.

20   ♘d5!?

Clever play. 20...a4 21 b4 ♘b3 22 ♕d3 would leave Black with a problem on b6.

20   ...   e6
21   ♘c3   ♕e7
22   ♗g5?!

White tries to provoke more weaknesses, but Black finds enough dynamic play to justify them. The natural continuation would have been 22 b4 axb4 23 axb4 ♘a4 24 ♘e2, hoping to control Black's active pieces, and then to cash in due to the space advantage. Still, there is nothing here that should scare Black – it is just an ordinary game.

22   ...   ♕f8
23   ♗f4   e5!
24   ♗e3   a4!
25   b4   ♘b3
26   ♕d1   ♗h6

Black wants to put his knight on d4, even at the cost of some material. 26...♘d4 27 ♗xd4 exd4 28 ♘e2 would have justified White's previous moves.

27   ♗xh6

Ivanchuk is not afraid to take up the challenge, but 27 ♗f2!? was certainly worth considering. Black would have then have problems with the d6-pawn, while the white knight is heading for d5. Black's only chance seems to be 27...♗e6!? 28 ♘xa4 ♖xa4 29 ♖xb3 ♖ca8 30 ♖a2 b5 with compensation, which should be enough for the draw.

27...♕xh6 28 ♕xd6 ♗e6 29 ♘b5

A tough choice. 29 ♘d5 ♗xd5 30 ♕xd5 allows ...♕e3+ and ...♖d8. My computer claims that White is winning here, but surely not many humans would like to play this position. White will be some pawns up, but, normally, when Black wins the a3-pawn, his own a-pawn will become a monster. Ivanchuk tries to keep things under control.

29...♘d4 30 ♘xd4 ♕e3+ 31 ♔h1 exd4

Black is very active and surely has enough compensation. But by some clever defensive moves White escapes.

32 b5 ♖d8 33 ♕b4 d3 34 ♖c3 h4!

It was not just for fun that the h-pawn was advanced...

35 ♖d1

35 h3 was risky, since after 35...♖ac8 36 ♖d1 ♕f2 37 ♖dxd3 ♖xd3 38 ♗xd3 ♕e1+ 39 ♔h2 ♖d8 Black has at least a draw, and maybe more.

35...h3 36 ♕b2 ♖ac8 37 ♖cxd3 ♖xd3 38 ♖xd3 ♕e1 39 ♕e2 ♕c1 40 ♕d1 hxg2+ 41 ♔xg2 ♕g5+ 42 ♔h1 ♔h7!?

Since 42...♗xc4 43 ♖d8+ was embarrassing, Black gets out of the way first, hoping that the white pawns are so weak that they will fall anyway.

43 ♖d4 ♕e3 44 ♖d3 ♕g5 45 ♖d4 ♕e3 ½-½

Black is very active, so White has to go for the repetition; 45 ♖c3 ♖d8 was too dangerous. A strange game, showing some active plans for Black. Although Black's play was on the edge of the unsound, he probably never crossed the line into a bad position.

Game 44
Filippov-P.H.Nielsen
Minsk 1996

(**1 e4 c5 2 ♘f3 ♘c6 3 d4 cxd4 4 ♘xd4 g6 5 c4 ♗g7 6 ♗e3 ♘f6 7 ♘c3 0-0 8 ♗e2 d6 9 0-0 ♗d7 10 ♕d2 ♘xd4 11 ♗xd4 ♗c6 12 f3 a5 13 b3 ♘d7 14 ♗e3 ♘c5 15 ♖ab1 ♕b6 16 ♖fc1 ♖fc8 17 ♖c2 ♕d8 18 a3**)

18   ...   ♕f8!?

| 19 | b4 | axb4 |
| 20 | axb4 | ♘e6!? |

The traditional path is 20...♘a4, but I wanted to use the a-file to generate counterplay.

| 21 | ♘d5 | ♖a3! |

Winning a tempo, as 22 ♘b6?? ♖xe3 picks up a piece.

22	♗f2	♖ca8
23	♘b6	♖a1!

Again Black defends actively. The trick is 24 ♖cc1 ♖8a2! White therefore has to allow his opponent to swap a pair of rooks, while leaving Black's other rook actively placed on the a-file.

24 ♖d1 ♖xd1+ 25 ♗xd1 ♖a1 26 ♗e3 ♖a3 27 ♗f2 f5!

A well-justified move. Black's position looks passive, as only the rook is active, but it is like a compressed spring and his pieces will soon be in command.

28 b5 ♗e8 29 exf5

This helps Black's queen to become active, but 29 ♕d5 ♗f7 30 ♕xb7 ♖a1 would have backfired.

29...♕xf5 30 ♘d5 ♔f8!

A last defensive move. Now Black is ready for ideas like 31...g5 and 32...♗g6 or 31...♘c5 and 32...♗f7.

31 ♖c1 ♕e5!

White was planning 32 ♗c2, which is now answered by 32...♖a2 with a nasty pin.

32 ♖b1

32 f4 ♕b2! would force a favourable ending for Black, as 33 ♖c2 ♕b1 24 ♖c1 ♖d3 is good for

him. White's pawns are weak and without the queens it will be impossible to defend them.

32...♖a1 33 f4 ♕e4 34 ♖xa1 ♗xa1 35 ♗f3?

A mistake under time pressure. Better was 35 ♕e3, hoping to make a draw in a worse ending.

35...♕xc4 36 f5 gxf5 37 h4

Admitting failure, but after 37 ♕h6+ ♘g7, White has to worry about a check on the first rank anyway.

37...♗xb5 38 ♕h6+ ♘g7 39 ♗g3 ♗c6 40 ♘xe7 ♗xf3 41 ♗xd6 ♔f7!

The key move. Black's attack now comes in first.

42 gxf3 ♗d4+ 43 ♔g2 ♕e2+ 44 ♔h1 ♕f1+ 45 ♔h2 ♗g1+ 0-1

White will soon be mated. It is difficult to say exactly what went wrong for White in this game. However, the knight manoeuvre clearly missed the target as Black's rooks managed to become active anyway. This game illustrates quite well that opening the a-file is risky for White, as Black gets plenty of play there.

In the last few games we have been focusing on the standard plan with ...♕b6, trying to slow down White's queenside actions. However, more direct plans have also been tried.

Game 45
Cu.Hansen-J.Sorensen
Denmark (rapid) 1996

(1 e4 c5 2 ♘f3 ♘c6 3 d4 cxd4 4 ♘xd4 g6 5 c4 ♗g7 6 ♗e3 ♘f6 7 ♘c3 0-0 8 ♗e2 d6 9 0-0 ♗d7 10 ♕d2 ♘xd4 11 ♗xd4 ♗c6 12 f3 a5 13 b3 ♘d7 14 ♗e3 ♘c5 15 ♖ab1)

15 ... e6!?

This is Sorensen's pet line. He aspires to the attacking chances associated with ...f7-f5, but prepares it with less committal moves such as ...e7-e6, ...♕e7 and ...♗e5 first, and only decides whether or not to go for ...f7-f5, depending on what White is doing.

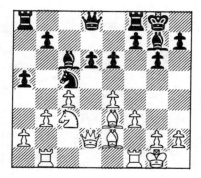

16 ♔h1

16 ♗d1!? has been regarded as the 'official' refutation of 15...e6 since Tringov-Haik, Vrnjacka Banja 1986, when White was much better after 16...f5 17 exf5 ♖xf5 18 ♘e2 b5 19 ♗c2 ♖f7 20 ♖fd1 ♖d7 21 cxb5 ♗xb5 22 ♘d4. But, of course, 17...gxf5! is the right move. Still, there was no reason to rush ...f7-f5, and 16...♕e7 looks sensible, when it is difficult to believe that 16 ♗d1 is such a great achievement.

16 ... ♗e5!

An excellent place for the bishop. It now defends the weak d6-pawn as well as having aggressive intentions on the kingside with 17...♕h4!? already in the offing.

17 ♗d4

Not very ambitious, but this seems to be the choice of many players when faced with ...e7-e6. Black could now simply have played 17...♗xd4 18 ♕xd4 e5! 19 ♕d2 ♘e6 with no problems at all.

17	...	♕e7
18	♖fd1	♖ad8
19	♗f1	♗xd4
20	♕xd4	f5!?

Again, 20...e5! is safe and solid with no risks.

21	exf5	gxf5
22	a3	e5!

This concedes White the d5-square for his knight, but gets d4 for Black's own knight. This is a good bargain for Black, as with the light-squared bishops on the board the d5-knight can be removed, whereas the one on d4 cannot.

23 ♕e3 ♘e6 24 axb4 axb4 25 axb4 ♕g7 26 b5 ♗e8 27 ♕b6 ♕d7 28 ♖a1 ♗h5

As always, it is difficult to evaluate the position when Black plays the ...f7-f5 break. The b7- and d6-pawns are not that easy to attack, and given a couple of free moves Black will have a rook on the g-file with a dangerous attack.

29 ♖d5 ♕e7 30 ♖ad1 ♘d4 31 ♘e2

31 c5! to simplify the position after 31...dxc5 32 ♕xc5! seems correct, with a probable draw.

31...♘xf3! 32 ♘g3

32 gxf3 ♗xf3+ 33 ♔g1 looks very dangerous for White, but as we cannot find a clear win, this was certainly preferable.

32...♕h4??

The simple 32...♘xh2! 33 ♘xh5 ♕h4! would have won immediately.

33 gxf3 ♗xf3+ 34 ♗g2 ♗xd1 35 ♖xd1 f4 36 ♗d5+ ♔h8 37 ♘e4 ♕h3? 38 ♘g5 1-0

39 ♘f7+ picks up material. A

tragic end for Black, but the middlegame was certainly fine for him. That 15...e6 holds direct threats, is well illustrated with the next game.

Game 46
P.H.Nielsen-Larsen
Danish ch 1997

(1 d4 ♘f6 2 c4 c5 3 ♘f3 cxd4 4 ♘xd4 ♘c6 5 ♘c3 d6 6 e4 g6 7 ♗e2 ♘xd4 8 ♕xd4 ♗g7 9 ♗e3 0-0 10 ♕d2 ♗d7 11 0-0 a5 12 b3 ♗c6 13 f3 ♘d7 14 ♖ab1 ♘c5 15 ♖fc1 e6!)

After a strange move order, we now have the main line with an extra tempo for White. 15...e6! is a strong idea here, as White's rook belongs on d1.

16 ♘b5 ♗e5 17 ♖d1??

Losing, and a very difficult mistake to explain. I had actually discussed this position with Sorensen, who told me about the combination that arises in the game. However, over the board I confused this line with another line I had analysed with ♗f2 and then ♘b5, which is quite strong (see the next main game).

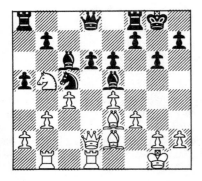

17...♕h4!

Winning immediately. In fact even 17...♘xe4 18 fxe4 ♕h4 should win.

18 g3

At least White gets an extra piece. 18 h3 ♘xe4 19 fxe4 ♕g3 with 20...♕h2+ and 21...f5 wins.

18...♗xg3 19 hxg3 ♕xg3+ 20 ♔h1

20 ♔f1 ♘xe4 21 fxe4 f5! wins, as 22 e5 ♗g2+ mates.

20...♘xe4 21 ♕d3

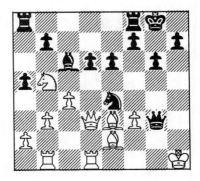

21...♕h3+?

21...♘f6 would have forced immediate resignation, as 22...♘g4 mating cannot be prevented without dropping too much material. 22 ♗g1 ♘g4 23 ♕xd6 ♕xf3+ 24 ♗xf3 ♗xf3+ would have finished the game in a proper way.

22 ♔g1 ♘g3 23 ♘d4?

23 ♔f2 would have offered some fighting chances, but this was really not my day.

23...♗e4!

A nice shot, winning material.

24 fxe4 ♕h1+ 25 ♔f2 ♘xe4 26 ♕xe4 ♕xe4

Normally, three pieces is enough for a queen, but here Black has too many extra pawns, and White will not be able to counterattack, as

Black's position holds no weak spots.

27 ♗f3 ♕h4+ 28 ♔g2 a4 29 b4 ♖ac8 30 ♖bc1 d5 31 cxd5 exd5 32 ♖c5 ♕e7 33 ♗f2 b6 34 ♖b5 ♖c4 35 ♔f1 ♕d6 36 ♖xd5 ♕xb4 37 ♖d7 ♕a3 38 ♗d5? ♕h3+ 0-1

Even without the last blunder, the game was lost. The Maroczy is known as a solid opening, but if White takes it too lightly, Black can still score dramatic wins.

Game 47
Hellers-Cebalo
Debrecen 1992

(1 e4 c5 2 ♘f3 ♘c6 3 d4 cxd4 4 ♘xd4 g6 5 c4 ♗g7 6 ♗e3 ♘f6 7 ♘c3 0-0 8 ♗e2 0-0 9 0-0 d6 10 ♕d2 ♘xd4 11 ♗xd4 ♗c6 12 f3 a5 13 b3 ♘d7)

14   ♗f2!?

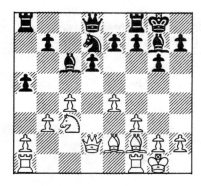

14   ...   ♘c5

The immediate 14...♕c7 has also been tried as well. It was not especially successful in I.Gurevich-Palatnik, New York 1992, after 15 ♖ab1 ♖fc8 16 ♖fc1 ♕d8 17 a3 ♘c5 18 b4 axb4 19 axb4 ♘a4 20 ♘e2, Black was outplayed, al-

though his position was probably okay. 17...b6 intending 18 b4 axb4 19 axb4 ♖a3! seems like a reliable alternative.

In Kengis-P.H.Nielsen, Gistrup 1997, White went for 15 ♖ac1 instead, but after 15...♖fc8 16 ♖fe1 ♘c5!?, Black switched back to the standard plan, as White was not ready to counter it with a2-a3 and b3-b4. The game continued 17 ♗f1 ♕b6 18 ♘b5 ♕d8 and now White played 19 e5!?, an unusual way of breaking through Black's fortress, using the fact that the knight on c5 seems insufficiently defended, and I have to admit that it was only through plain luck that I found the following resource: 19...a4!, the point being that 20 exd6 axb3 21 ♗xc5 ♗xb5 22 cxb5 bxa2 is good for Black. Kengis went for 20 b4 ♘e6 21 exd6, when a draw was agreed. The ending after 21...♗xb5 22 cxb5 ♕xd6 23 ♕xd6 exd6 is now okay for Black, as the a4-pawn, combined with an attack on a2, secures Black at least equality.

15   ♖ab1

Here we see the point of White's 14 ♗f2!?: if Black plays along the standard lines with 15...♕b6 16 a3, the trick from the 14 ♗e3 system, 16...♘xb3 does not work now because of 17 ♕d1, when White simply wins a piece as the bishop is now well protected on f2.

15   ...   e6

An aggressive move which seems slightly dubious. The solid 15...b6 was Serper's choice against Bischoff, Krumbach 1991, when White was a little better after 16 ♖fd1 ♖a7 17 ♗f1 ♗e5 18 ♘e2 ♕b8 19 ♘d4 ♗d7, but agreed to a draw after 22 moves. Indeed it is not easy for White to make progress, as Black is ready to exploit the open a-file which would arise if White should go for a2-a3 and b3-b4. Serper indicates that 20 g3!? followed by 21 ♗g2 and then 22 f4 is the right way to expand. This does indeed look like the way to play, but Black's position still looks solid enough. 15...♕c7!? is seen in the next game and 15...♕b6!? in Game 49.

16   ♘b5!

This looks like the right antidote to Black's plans, as the d6-pawn will come under immediate pressure. Less successful was 16 ♖fd1 ♗e5 17 ♗f1? (17 ♘b5!) 17...♕f6 18 ♖bc1 g5! 19 ♘e2 g4 20 ♕e3 gxf3 21 gxf3 ♕g6+ 22 ♗g3 f5, when Black had an attacking position in Ikonikkov-P.H.Nielsen, Cheliabinsk 1991, the game ending in a perpetual after 23 f4 ♘xe4 24 fxe5 dxe5 25 ♗g2 f4 26 ♗xf4 exf4 27 ♘xf4 ♖xf4 28 ♕xf4 ♖f8 29 ♕h4 ♖f2 30 ♖d8 ♔f7 31 ♖d7+! ½-½. In this game Black had the only chances, and White just managed to hold the balance.

17 ♖fd1!? seems more direct to us, as the threat to the d6-pawn forces 17...♗xb5 18 cxb5, which generally favours White. Actually, this was what I had intended in the previous game, but I was surprised by 17...♕h4, which is impossible here. Black was maybe intending 18...♕f6, planning 19...g5, with good control of the dark squares on the kingside, but then 19 ♗e3! is strong, as now 19...♕h4 20 g3 ♗xg3 21 hxg3 ♕xg3+ 22 ♔f1 seems to win for White. Maybe Black could try 18...g5, but 19 ♗e3 h6 20 h4! looks very good for White.

17	...	♕f6
18	♖bd1	♗f4
19	♕c2	♖fd8
20	g3	♗h6
21	♘b5!?	

This leads to the structure discussed earlier. Hellers indicates 21 ♘xc6 ♗xc6 22 f4 e5 23 f5 as somewhat better for White, but this does not seem all that clear to us, as suddenly Black's pieces are excellently placed, and he has the plan of preparing ...a5-a4.

| 21 | ... | ♗xb5 |
| 22 | cxb5 | |

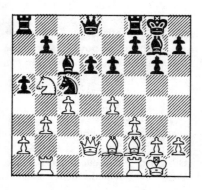

| 16 | ... | ♗e5 |
| 17 | ♘d4 | |

Now, however, it seems clear that White is much better. He has the simple plan of a2-a3 and b3-b4 which is very difficult to prevent, as without the bishop on c6, Black will find it very difficult to undertake any active play.

22...♖ac8 23 ♗c4!

Making sure that Black will never be able to push ...d6-d5.

23...♗g7 24 ♖d2 b6 25 ♕d1 ♕e7 26 ♕e2 ♗c3 27 ♖c2 ♕f6?!

An ambitious way of preventing White's plan of a2-a3 and b3-b4, but it seems to be insufficient. Better was 27...♗g7 28 f4?! ♕b7!, as indicated by Hellers, when Black gets in ...d6-d5 with counterplay.

28 ♖d1 ♗b4 29 ♔g2 ♕e7 30 ♗d4 e5 31 ♗b2 ♘e6 32 a3 ♗c5 33 ♗xe6!

It may seem illogical to exchange the strongly posted bishop, but Black was ready to occupy d4 with counterplay. Instead Black's bishop is about to be trapped, and he will lose a pawn.

33...♕xe6?

Better was 33...fxe6, when Black keeps control of d5. Rescuing the bishop will cost a pawn, but as White's extra pawn is the doubled b-pawn, Black retains some drawing chances.

34 ♖c4 h5 35 ♖d5 h4 36 g4 ♕f6 37 b4 axb4 38 axb4 ♗d4 39 ♖cxd4!?

Probably in time pressure, Hellers misses 39 ♗xd4 ♖xc4 40 ♕xc4 h3+ 41 ♔f2 ♕f4? 42 ♗xe5! However, he does not spoil anything.

39...exd4 40 ♗xd4 ♕f4 41 ♗xb6 ♖e8 42 ♗e3 ♖c2 43 ♗xf4 ♖xe2+ 44 ♔h3 ♖f2 45 ♖d3 ♖b8 46 ♗xd6 ♖xb5 47 ♔xh4 ♖g2 48 ♔h3 ♖c2 49 ♔g3 ♖b7 50 ♗c5 ♖b8 51 h4

♖a8 52 ♖d5 ♖b2 53 h5 ♔h7 54 hxg6 ♔xg6 55 ♖d6+ ♔h7 56 g5 ♖b3 57 ♖h6+ 1-0

There is no defence to 58 ♗d4. Although the 15...e6 plan is certainly interesting against 14 ♗e3, it seems less attractive against 14 ♗f2!?, as Black does not have the ...♕h4 trick as in the previous game, and therefore has to take on b5, which hardly ever is good.

Game 48
Leko-Spangenberg
Buenos Aires 1994

(1 e4 c5 2 ♘f3 ♘c6 3 d4 cxd4 4 ♘xd4 g6 5 c4 ♗g7 6 ♗e3 ♘f6 7 ♘c3 0-0 8 ♗e2 d6 9 0-0 ♗d7 10 ♕d2 ♘xd4 11 ♗xd4 ♗c6 12 f3 a5 13 b3 ♘d7 14 ♗f2!? ♘c5 15 ♖ab1)

15   ...   ♕c7!?

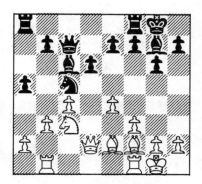

Black wants to play along standard patterns, putting his king's rook on c8, and then bringing the queen back to d8. However, here he uses c7 for the queen to sidestep a quick a2-a3 and b3-b4 by White.

16   ♖fc1   ♖fc8

White must now take care to avoid 17 a3? a4! 18 b4 ♘b3, winning an exchange.

17 ♖c2

The same tournament featured the game Renet-Spangenberg, in which White tried another way of preparing a2-a3 and b3-b4. After 17 ♗d1 ♕d8 18 a3 b6 19 b4 axb4 20 axb4 ♘d7 21 ♗b3 the bishop was well posted on b3, where it protects c4 and eyes f7. Although Black has a solid position, he went down surprisingly quickly after 21...♕f8 22 ♗e3 ♗f6 23 ♗h6 ♕d8 24 ♘d1 b5? 25 cxb5 ♕b6+ 26 ♘f2 ♗xb5 27 ♗e3 ♕a6 28 ♘g4 ♗g7 29 ♘h6+ ♗xh6 30 ♗xh6 ♘e5 31 ♕d4 txc1+ 32 ♖xc1 ♕a3 33 ♕c3 ♗d7 34 f4! 1-0. However 24...b5? was very bad and 24...♖a3 should be okay.

17	...	♕d8
18	a3	♕f8
19	♗e3	

Preventing 19...♗h6.

19	...	h5!?
20	b4	axb4
21	axb4	♘a4
22	♘d1	♗f6

A typical Maroczy position. White has managed to get in the classic b3-b4 break, but as we now know, this is absolutely no guarantee of success. Black's pieces are active, and he has reasonable control of the dark squares. A clear indication of White's difficulties is the fact that Leko now heads for a repetition, as he sees no way of making progress.

23 ♗h6 ♗g7 24 ♗e3 ♗f6 25 ♗h6 ♗g7 26 ♗e3 ♗f6 27 ♗h6 ♕d8!?

Black bravely decides to play on.

28 ♗e3 ♔h7 29 ♗f1 ♕h8

Now Black has excellent control of the dark squares, and White has to keep his knight on the clumsy d1-square, or else Black's knight will invade on c3.

30 ♔h1 ♖c7 31 ♖bc1 ♗d7 32 ♖a2 ♗e6 33 ♖ac2 ♖ac8 34 ♗e2 ♗d7 35 ♗f1 ♕e8 36 ♔g1 ♗g7 37 ♗e2 b5!?

Again Black chooses to keep the game alive instead of settling for a draw.

38 cxb5 ♖xc2 39 ♖xc2 ♖xc2 40 ♕xc2 ♗xb5 41 ♔f2 e6

Although the position is certainly drawn, Black keeps pressing his slight initiative by making pawn breaks in an attempt to unbalance the position.

42 ♕d2 ♗xe2 43 ♕xe2 d5 44 exd5 exd5 45 ♕d3 d4!? 46 ♗xd4 ♕d8 47 ♔e3 ♕g5+?

Better was 47...♕e7+!, getting the pawn back with a draw.

48 ♔e2 ♕xg2+ 49 ♘f2 ♘b2 50 ♕c3??

After 49 ♕e3! White would nearly be winning, as Black is close to losing his knight, e.g. 49...♘c4 50 ♕c3. Now, however, Black is rewarded for his willingness to take chances.

50...♕xf2+! 51 ♗xf2 ♗xc3 52 b5
♗e5 53 h3 ♔g8 54 b6 ♔f8 55 ♔e3
♔e7 56 ♔e4 ♔e6 57 b7 ♘c4 58
♗d4 ♘d6+ 59 ♔d3 ♘xb7 0-1

Not an error-free game, but one
that illustrates that b3-b4 is not that
great for White. 14...♕c7 and
15...♕c7 both seem reliable ways
to reach standard positions, reaching near equality.

Game 49
Hernandez-Petursson
Linares 1994

(1 e4 c5 2 ♘f3 ♘c6 3 d4 cxd4 4
♘xd4 g6 5 c4 ♘f6 6 ♘c3 d6 7
♗e2 ♗g7 8 ♗e3 0-0 9 0-0 ♗d7 10
♕d2 ♘xd4 11 ♗xd4 ♗c6 12 f3 a5
13 b3 ♘c5 14 ♗f2!? ♘c5 15
♖ab1)

15   ...   ♕b6!?

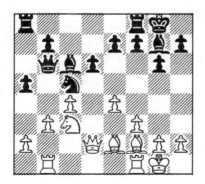

This was introduced by Larsen
in 1989 against Savon. When we
saw this move for the first time, we
were sure that Larsen had simply
played too quickly and was lucky
to escape. And when we saw him
play 15...♕b6 again three years
later we were rather concerned that
our national hero seemed to be un-

able to remember his own mis-
takes. Then, suddenly, Petursson
started copying it, and we began to
understand that they were actually
doing it on purpose!

16   a3   ♕d8!

Amazing! Two of the biggest
experts on the Maroczy consider
a2-a3 to be a weakness worth giving up two tempi for! The point is
that it is now very difficult for
White to regroup quietly before
undertaking anything active. The
main problem is that 17 ♖fc1 a4!
18 b4 ♘b3 loses an exchange. In
the two Larsen games, White tried
the critical 17 b4 axb4 18 axb4.
Against Savon, Palma de Mallorca
1989, he went for 18...♖a3 19 ♘b5
♗xb5 20 bxc5 ♗c6 21 cxd6 exd6
22 ♖fd1 ♗e5 23 c5 ♗a4 24 cxd6
♗xd1 25 ♖xd1 ♕f6, which looks
good for Black but ended in a
draw. Against Arnason in Oster-
sund 1992, he went for 18...♘a4
instead, reaching an equal position
after 19 ♘xa4 ♖xa4 20 ♖fc1 ♕a8
21 ♖c2 ♖c8. 17 b4 should not scare
Black at all.

17   ♗d1!?

Quite logical, as White wants to
keep b3 well under control, and
then start regrouping. In the game
I.Gurevich-Petursson, St Martin
1993, White tried 17 ♖fd1 instead,
which resulted in an fairly even
position after 17...♖e8 18 ♗f1 ♗e5
19 ♘e2 ♘e6 20 ♖bc1 ♕b8, as
Black is now ready for 21...b5.
White stopped this radically with
21 ♗b6, but after 21...♘c5 22 ♖b1
♖a6 23 ♗xc5 dxc5 Black's position was excellent due to his bishop
pair and control over the dark
squares, although active play by
White later secured him a draw.

| 17 | ... | **♛b8** |

Preparing ...b7-b5 and allowing the king's rook to go to c8.

| 18 | **♝c2** | **♜c8** |
| 19 | **a4!?** | |

An interesting decision. As 19 b4 axb4 20 axb4 ♜a3 certainly is okay for Black, White decides to stop a possible ...b7-b5 at the cost of closing the queenside. He now has hopes for an attack on the kingside, as with the queenside closed, he can now concentrate all his pieces over there.

| 19 | ... | **♜c7** |
| 20 | **♜be1** | **♛f8!** |

Black, of course, hurries to bring his major pieces to the kingside battleground.

| 21 | **f4** | **e6!** |

Securing e7 for the queen, which now seems an ideal square for it. Then the rook will go to f8 in preparation for a later ...f7-f5 break. Should White go for 22 f5, hoping for an attack, 22...♛e7 followed by 23...♝e5 gives sufficient counterplay on the dark squares.

| 22 | **♝xc5** |

Not a very ambitious decision, but it was not easy to see a convincing plan for White. 22 ♝h4!? looks like an idea, preparing 23 f5!, but 22...f5! seems like a convincing answer. Now the game enters a sharp tactical phase which peters out in a draw.

22...dxc5 23 e5 f6 24 ♛d6 ♛e7 25 ♘b5 ♝xb5 26 ♛xe7 ♜xe7 27 exf6 ♝xc4 28 fxe7 ♝xf1 29 ♜xe6 ♚f7 30 e8♛+ ♜xe8 31 ♜xe8 ♚xe8 32 ♚xf1 ½-½

15...♛b6 does indeed look suspicious at first sight, but it has some deep points, and so far White has not been able to come up with a convincing answer. It also has a psychological plus as White may believe that his opponent has just blundered, become over-optimistic, and overreact when trying to punish him.

6 Maroczy Bind:
Systems with an Early ...♘h6!?

Chapter Guide

1 e4 c5 2 ♘f3 ♘c6 3 d4 cxd4 4 ♘xd4 g6 5 c4 ♗g7 6 ♗e3

In this line Black strives for an early ...f7-f5, attempting to undermine the white centre. If Black manages to time his counterplay correctly, before his opponent can establish a strong hold on the centre, then he may be able to equalise. However, practice has shown that it is quite difficult for Black to handle these positions, and the line has therefore more or less disappeared from high level tournaments.

Game 50
Geller-Larsen
Monte Carlo 1967

(1 e4 c5 2 ♘f3 ♘c6 3 d4 cxd4 4 ♘xd4 g6 5 c4 ♗g7 6 ♗e3 d6)

The immediate 6...♘h6 has, of course, also been tried, but generally it just transposes. A few exceptions are mentioned in the next game.

7   ♗e2   ♘h6!?

First recommended by Simagin.

Of course, Tarrasch's maxims teach that it is bad to place the knight on the edge of the board, but here it does have some use. The only other square for the knight is f6, where it temporarily hinders Black by blocking the g7-bishop and the f-pawn.

8   0-0   0-0
9   ♕d2

At the time of the game, this move was considered good for White, but now it is not very highly regarded. The game transposes to the Classical system with 9...♖e8 without Black having played ....♖e8! In that variation Black plays 9...♖e8, waiting to counter 10 ♕d2 with 10...♘g4 but here Black gets a better version, since the rook is not urgently needed on e8 with this structure. The standard 9 ♘c3 is considered (by transposition) in the next game.

9	...	♘g4
10	♗xg4	♗xg4
11	♘c3	♕a5

Nowadays this is regarded as the main line. The alternatives are:

a) 11...♖c8 has been played on occasion. A horrible example is Bhend-Keres, Zurich 1959, when Black had a terrible position after 12 b3 a6 13 ♖ac1 ♕a5 14 h3 ♗d7 15 ♘xc6 bxc6? 16 c5! ♗e6 17 ♘d5!?, although Keres later managed to draw. Better was 15...♗xc6 16 ♘d5 ♕d8, followed by ...b7-b5 with reasonable play.

b) Langeweg-Velimirovic, Amsterdam 1974, saw 11...♗d7 12 f4 ♖c8 13 b3 ♕a5 14 ♖ac1 f5 15 exf5 gxf5 16 ♘de2 ♗e6 17 ♘g3 ♖fd8 18 ♖fd1 ♗f7 19 ♘b5! ♕xd2 20 ♖xd2 a6 21 ♘c3 e6 22 ♗b6 ♖d7 23 ♘a4 and Black has too many weaknesses. Normally Black is not afraid of endgames in the Maroczy, but if he has played ...f7-f5, they are in general dangerous for Black.

12 ♖ac1

Interestingly, Geller has no confidence in 12 f4!?, which had brought Petrosian a quick victory against Heinicke 12 years earlier. In that game Black had played 12...♘xd4 13 ♗xd4 e5 14 fxe5 dxe5 15 ♗e3 ♖ad8 16 ♕f2 f5? 17 ♗c5! ♖f7 18 h3 and White picked

up a piece. 12...♗d7 followed by ...♖c8 seems more logical, after which Black has reasonable play. A sign that 12 f4!? cannot be so bad for Black is the fact that Larsen was ready for it – and Geller did not dare play it!

12	...	♖fc8
13	b3	a6
14	♖c2?!	

Played to prevent ...b7-b5, but this move misses its objective. Better is 14 ♘xc6!, which was introduced by a young Kasparov against Ivanov, Daugavpils 1978, which continued 14...♖xc6 15 ♗h6! (trading Black's best piece, since 15...♗h8 16 ♘d5 ♕d8 17 ♕g5! is winning) 15...♖ac8 16 ♗xg7 ♔xg7 17 f4 f6 18 ♔h1 b5 19 f5 g5 with complex play. Kasparov writes that 17 ♕b2 is preferable, giving White an edge after 17...f6 18 ♘d5, though surely it is not a lot. This idea was tried out in Popovic-Abramovic, Novi Sad 1985, and after 15 ♗d4 ♗e6 16 ♗xg7 ♔xg7 17 ♕b2 f6 18 ♘d5 ♕d8 19 a4 ♖ac8 20 ♖cd1 ♖c5 Black's set-up was solid and he can try for ...b7-b5.

| 14 | ... | b5! |

Very strong. After 15 cxb5 Black has the pleasant choice between 15...axb5 16 ♘dxb5 ♘b4 17 ♖b2 ♗d7 with fine compensation, 15...♘xd4 16 ♗xd4 ♗xd4 17 ♕xd4 axb5 and the spectacular 15...♗xd4!? 16 ♗xd4 axb5, since 17 ♗e3 ♘b4 is annoying for White. It may seem odd to give up the dark-squared bishop, but White must defend his queenside and will not get a mating attack.

15	♘d5	♕xd2
16	♖xd2	♗xd4
17	♗xd4	♖ab8!

Black keeps things under control. If now 18 c5 ♗e6! 19 cxd6 ♗xd5 20 exd5 ♘xd4 21 ♖xd4 exd6, he gains a huge advantage due his control of the c-file.

18	♖c1	♔f8
19	♗b2	bxc4
20	♖xc4	♔e8
21	♖dc2	♔d7

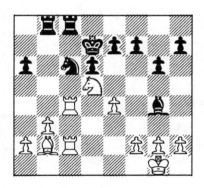

Black enjoys a slight edge. He has more central pawns and a centralised king, and can later play ...a5-a4. This may not be enough to win the game, but it is quite unpleasant for White.

| 22 | f3 | ♗e6 |
| 23 | ♖d2 | a5 |

| 24 | h4 | ♖b5 |
| 25 | ♖a4 | f6 |

Seemingly a very innocent move, but it contains a little trap which Geller walks right into.

26 ♔h2? ♗xd5! 27 ♖xd5 ♖xd5 28 exd5 ♘b4 29 ♖xa5 ♖c2

Now we see the idea behind 25...f6. Without it White would have had a perpetual with ♖a7+, but now the king hides on f7.

30 a3

Entering a difficult rook ending, but the alternatives were grim and in particular 30 ♗d4 ♖xa2 31 ♖b5? ♘xd5!! 32 ♖xd5 ♔c6 is beautiful.

30...♖xb2 31 axb4 ♖xb3 32 ♖a7+ ♔e8 33 ♖a8+ ♔f7 34 ♖b8 ♖d3 35 ♖b5 ♖d4 36 ♔g3 g5 37 hxg5 fxg5 38 ♔f2 ♖d2+ 39 ♔g3 h5 40 ♔h3 ♖d3 41 ♔g3 ♔f6 42 ♔f2 ♖d2+ 43 ♔g3 ♖d4 44 ♔h3 g4+ 45 fxg4 ♖xg4 46 ♖b8 ♖d4 47 ♖b5 ♖e4 48 ♖b8 ♖e5 49 ♖b5 e6 50 ♖b8 ♖xd5 51 b5 ♖d4 52 ♖h8 ♖b4 53 ♖h6+ ♔f7 54 ♖xh5 ♔g6 55 g4 d5 56 ♖e5 ♔f7 57 ♔h4 ♖xb5 58 ♖e1 d4 59 ♖a1 ♔f6 60 ♖a8 ♖d5 61 ♔g3 d3 62 ♖a1 ♔e5 63 ♔f2 ♔d4 64 ♖a7 e5 65 g5 e4 66 ♖a4+ ♔e5 0-1

Nice play by Black, who managed to carry out the Sicilian dream: proving that 3 d4 leaves Black a central pawn up!

Game 51
Wojtkiewicz-Hoffman
Valencia 1990

(1 ♘f3 g6 2 d4 ♗g7 3 c4 c5 4 e4 cxd4 5 ♘xd4 ♘c6 6 ♗e3 ♘h6!?)

| 7 | ♘c3 |

This gives Black an extra option. 7 ♗e2 is more exact, as then Black is more or less forced to play

7...d6, since the alternatives are dubious:

a) 7...0-0 8 ♕d2 ♘xd4 9 ♗xd4 is very troublesome for Black. The game Seirawan-Shirazi, Durango 1992, continued 9...f6?! 10 ♘c3 d6 11 0-0 ♘g4 12 ♘d5 ♗h6 13 f4 e5 14 ♗xg4! ♗xg4 15 ♗e3 ♗g7 16 f5! with a huge edge for White. Better is 9...d6, but it is still unpleasant for Black, since without the dark-squared bishops, plans involving ...f7-f5 are less attractive.

b) 7...f5? is too direct and can be refuted by 8 exf5 ♘xf5 9 ♘xf5 ♗xb2 (9...♕a5+ 10 ♘c3 ♕xf5 11 c5!) 10 ♘d2 gxf5 11 ♗h5+ ♔f8 12 ♕c2! and White was winning in Unzicker-Filip, Vienna 1957.

7 ... d6

An interesting alternative is 7...0-0 8 ♗e2 f5!? 9 exf5 ♗xd4 10 ♗xh6! ♖xf5 11 0-0 and now 11...d6 transposes to the next game, but Black also has the extra option of 11...♕b6!? This was condemned following Gurshevsky-Veresov, Moscow 1959, where White won brilliantly after 12 ♘d5 ♗xf2+ 13 ♔h1 ♕d4? 14 ♗g4! ♕xd1 15 ♖axd1 ♖f7 16 ♘xe7! ♘xe7 17 ♗e6!!, winning material. However,

in Marusenko-Turner, London 1994, Black was successful with 12...♕xb2. The game continued 13 ♖b1 ♕a3 14 ♗g4 ♖f7 15 ♘c7 ♖b8 16 ♘b5 ♕c5 17 ♘xd4 ♕xd4 18 ♗e3 ♕xd1 19 ♖fxd1 ♘e5 20 ♗e2 d6 and now White wrongly took on a7 and ended up worse after 21 ♗xa7 ♖a8 22 ♗d4 ♖xa2 23 ♗f1 ♘d7. Better was 21 c5 with sufficient compensation, but not more. Even 13...♗xf2+?! is not so easy to refute, although 14 ♔h1 ♕a3 15 ♗f3 looks dangerous. Still, White has to act quickly or he will be two pawns down for nothing. Although this is all very interesting, it is not so relevant if White plays 7 ♗e2.

8 ♗e2 0-0
9 0-0 f5
10 exf5 gxf5

This seems to be Black's best chance, as the alternatives are dubious:

a) 10...♘xd4 11 ♗xd4 ♗xd4 12 ♕xd4 ♘xf5 13 ♕d2 ♗d7 14 ♗f3 ♗c6 15 ♗d5+ ♔g7 16 ♖e1 e5 17 c5! gave White a huge edge in Tal-Kupreichik, Sochi 1970, which Tal easily converted into a win.

b) 10...♗xd4 11 ♗xh6 ♖xf5 and now:

b1) 12 ♗f3 is very good for White. In Kudrin-I.Ivanov, New York 1983, Black was outplayed after 12...♗g7 13 ♗e3 ♗d7 14 ♖e1 b6 15 ♗e4 ♖f7 16 ♗g5 ♗f6 17 ♗xf6 ♖xf6 18 ♕d2 ♕f8 19 ♖ad1 ♖d8 20 ♘d5 ♖f7 21 ♘c7. White rules on the light squares.

b2) 12 ♕d2 has also scored well in practice, but in that case 12...♕b6 seems reasonable. Black was better in Ilivitsky-Keres, Parnu 1955, after the weak 13 ♗e3? ♗xe3 14 fxe3 ♕a5 15 ♖xf5 ♗xf5

16 ♕d5+ ♕xd5 17 ♘xd5 ♖c8, as he gets his knight to e5. Surprisingly, 12...♕b6 has rarely been seen since, but since 12 ♗f3 looks good, so this is not so important.

11 f4

The logical way to prevent ...f5-f4. 11 ♕d2 has also been played, but without much success. Motwani-I.Ivanov, British ch 1987, continued 11...♘f7 12 f4 e5 13 ♘xc6 bxc6 14 fxe5 dxe5 15 ♕xd8 ♖xd8 16 ♖ad1 ♗e6 with an equal ending.

11 ... ♗d7

11...♕b6? 12 ♘xf5 ♕xb2 13 ♘xh6+ ♗xh6 14 ♘d5 ♗f5 15 ♗d3 gave White a big plus in Yermolinsky-Chepukaitis, Leningrad 1980.

12 ♔h1!?

This may be White's best, since he can now answer ...♘g4 with ♗g1. 12 h3 was played in Kavalek-Larsen, Sousse izt 1967, when wild complications arose after 12...♕b6 13 ♘xf5 ♕xb2 14 ♘xh6+ ♗xh6 15 ♖c1 ♗g7. Later 12 ♕d2 became the normal move, when in Illescas-Abramovic, Biel 1993, Black was fine after 12...♘g4 13 ♗xg4 fxg4 14 ♖ad1 ♕e8 15 ♘de2 ♕e8 16 b3 ♕g6.

12 ... ♔h8
13 ♖c1 ♖g8

Black plays very directly, but since there are no real targets, he is unlikely to succeed.

14 ♗f3 ♕e8
15 ♖e1 ♖c8

16 b3 ♘g4
17 ♗g1 ♕h5
18 ♘xc6 ♗xc6
19 ♘d5!

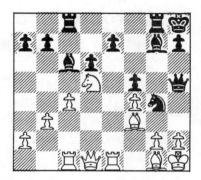

As usual, in open positions, central strategy proves superior to flank action. The black centre is about to collapse.

19...e5 20 ♘e7 e4

Black continues his hunt for White's throat, but White easily rebuffs the attack.

21 ♗xg4 fxg4 22 ♘xc8 ♖xc8 23 ♗d4 ♖g8 24 ♗xg7+ ♖xg7 25 ♕xd6 g3 26 h3 e3 27 ♔g1 e2 28 ♕e5! 1-0

Black's plan was certainly too optimistic, but still this game nicely illustrates White's chances, including positional play in the centre. Black would perhaps do better with a more careful approach, but still it seems that ...f7-f5 simply weakens his position, rather than creating dynamic counter-chances.

7 Maroczy Bind: 6 ♘b3 and 6 ♘c2

Chapter Guide

1 e4 c5 2 ♘f3 ♘c6 3 d4 cxd4 4 ♘xd4 g6 5 c4 ♗g7

6 ♘b3 – *Game 52*
6 ♘c2 d6 7 ♗e2 ♘f6 8 ♘c3 0-0 9 0-0
9...a6 - *Game 53*
9...♘d7
10 ♗d2 ♘c5 11 b4 ♘e6
12 ♔h1 - *Game 54*
12 ♖b1 a5
13 a3 – *Game 55*
13 b5 – *Game 56*
10 f3 – *Game 57*

The lines discussed in this chapter are mainly an attempt by White to avoid the abundance of theory that exists in virtually all of the main lines of the Maroczy Bind. Two moves are considered:

a) 6 ♘b3 has never been very popular and probably never will be. Black simply has easy play against this set-up.

b) However, 6 ♘c2 is much more popular and has been used from time to time by grandmasters such as Ivanchuk, Illescas, Salov and Portisch. Here too Black is fine, but as in most other lines, careful play is required so as not to hand over the initiative to White.

Game 52
Renet-Rantanen
Palma de Mallorca 1989

(1 e4 c5 2 ♘f3 ♘c6 3 d4 cxd4 4 ♘xd4 g6 5 c4 ♗g7)

6 ♘b3

(see following diagram)

This was played twice by Alekhine, but despite his two wins it has never caught on. The rare alternative 6 ♘b5 was twice played by Bronstein, but without much success. The manoeuvre is well known from the Paulsen Sicilian (after 1 e4 c5 2 ♘f3 ♘c6 3 d4 cxd4 4 ♘xd4 e6 5 ♘b5), but there the idea is to force Black to play the weakening ...d7-d6. Here this is not the case, and 6 ♘b5 just looks like it loses time. On the other hand White is still very solid, so it leads to a fairly level game. After 6...♘f6, 7 ♘1c3 is probably the best, e.g. 7...d6 8 ♗e2 0-0 9 ♗e3 a6 10 ♘d4, when White has to play the main line a tempo down! Of course it is possible to play along standard patterns, but Simagin played more creatively with 10...♘xd4 11 ♗xd4 b5!? (sacrificing a pawn) 12 cxb5 axb5 13 ♗xb5 ♗b7 14 0-0 (clever play by Bronstein; he returns the pawn, hoping that his two queenside pawns will counter the black centre) 14... e5 15 ♗e3 ♘xe4 16 ♘xe4 ♗xe4 17 a4, when the wild game Bronstein-Simagin, Moscow 1951, later ended in a draw. Instead of 11...b5!?, 11...♗e6 is a safer way to exploit the extra tempo. Then 12 0-0 ♘xd4 13 ♗xd4 ♖c8 was played in Lutikov-Roizman, USSR 1964, when 13...♕a5, with the standard idea of using the f-rook on the c-file, side-stepping any ♘d5 tricks, gives Black a good position.

In a later game Bronstein tried 7 ♘5c3, but after 7...0-0 8 ♗e2 b6!? (it was of course possible to develop normally with 8...d6, but Black plays more creatively) 9 ♗g5 ♗b7 10 0-0 ♖c8 11 ♘d2 ♘d4, Black had placed his pieces harmoniously, Bronstein-Rantanen, Tallinn 1979.

6   ...   ♘f6
(see following diagram)

6...d6 often transposes, but does sometimes have independent value:

a) Ljubojevic-Short, London 1980, continued 7 ♘c3 a5 8 ♘a4 ♘f6 9 f3 ♗e6 10 ♗e3 0-0 11 ♗e2 ♘d7 with equality. A good plan for Black would be ...b7-b6 followed by ...♘c5, which will force the retreat ♘c3, since capturing on c5 gives Black control over the d4-square. Note that Short did not play 7...♗xc3+. Normally it is good to double the pawns when the knight is on c2, since it is then possible to play ...♕a5 and apply pressure on the weak c-pawns immediately. However, with the knight on b3 this is not possible, and the capture is therefore less attractive.

b) In Schmid-Larsen, Havana 1967, White avoided this possibility with 7 ♗e2 and Larsen responded with one of his typical flank pawn moves: 7...a5!?, and after 8 a4 ♘f6 9 ♘c3 0-0 10 ♗e3 ♘d7 11 ♕d2? (better is 11 0-0; Schmid probably feared 11...♗xc3, but after the inclusion of a2-a4 and ...a7-a5 this is less attractive for Black, since White has targets on the b-file) Larsen now won a pawn with 11...b6 12 ♘d4 ♗b7 13 ♗d1 ♘c5 14 ♘xc6 ♗xc6 15 ♗c2 ♕d7 16 0-0? ♕e6 17 ♘d5 ♘xe4 18 ♕d3 ♘c5 19 ♗xc5 bxc5 20 ♖ae1 ♗e5! 21 f4 ♗xd5 22 cxd5 ♗d4+

and won easily.

6...e6 was played in Alekhine-Gonzalez, Estoril 1940, but this weakens the d6-square, and after 7 ♘c3 a6 8 ♗e2 ♘ge7 9 0-0 0-0 10 ♗f4 the world champion was able to take full advantage.

7 ♘c3 d6
8 ♗e2 0-0

8...♗e6 was played in Alekhine-Sämisch, Vienna 1922, when after 9 0-0 h5?! (bizarre) 10 c5! opened up the game and Alekhine won convincingly.

9 ♗e3

9 0-0 transposes after 9...b6 10 ♗e3.

9 ... b6

This is commonly played, but we think that 9...a5!? deserves serious attention. If 10 a4, Black then continues with ...b7-b6, ...♘d7-c5 and ...♗b7, as in Schmid-Larsen above. And if 10 ♘a4 then 10...♘d7 with the plan of ...b7-b6, ...♘c5 etc. This seems quite promising, and we believe that Black is at least equal.

10 0-0 ♗b7

Again 10...a5!? was interesting.

11 f4

A good move that prevents ...♘e5. The omission of f2-f4 had serious consequences in Hertneck-Hickl, Munich 1988: 11 ♖c1 ♖c8 12 f3? (12 f4!) 12...♘e5 (hitting the c4-pawn) 13 ♘d5 e6 14 ♘xf6+ ♗xf6 15 ♖c2 ♗a6 16 ♕c1, and now after 16...d5! Black won a pawn and later the game.

11 ... ♖c8
12 ♗f3 e5!?

The standard ...♘d7 was safer, but 12...e5!? is an attempt to take over the initiative. Black threatens ...e5xf4 followed by ...♘e5, when

the f3-bishop would be misplaced and the c4-pawn weak. Renet now tries to use the obvious weakness of the backward d-pawn to launch a frontal attack, but Black is already too well developed to have problems with such a simple plan.

13 ♘b5 exf4
14 ♗xf4 ♘e8

Black already has a good game, but now it goes fast downhill for the Frenchman.

15 ♘xd6 ♘xd6
16 ♗xd6 ♗xb2!
17 e5!?

17 ♖ab1 ♗d4+ 18 ♘xd4 ♕xd6 gives Black a nearly winning position due to White's weak pawns.

17 ... ♕g5
18 ♗d5 ♗xa1
19 ♕xa1 ♘d8
20 ♗xf8?

20 ♗xb7 first was better, but it is still not very nice.

20 ... ♗xd5
21 cxd5 ♖c2
22 ♖f2 ♕e3
23 ♕f1

23 ♕d4 ♖c1+ also loses for White.

23 ... ♔xf8
24 e6? ♖xa2

25	exf7	♖xf2
26	♕xf2	♕xb3
	0-1	

Game 53
Spraggett-Andersson
Novi Sad ol 1990

(1 e4 c5 2 ♘f3 ♘c6 3 d4 cxd4 4 ♘xd4 g6 5 c4 ♗g7)

6   ♘c2

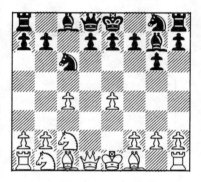

This is a lot more common than ♘b3, but it should not concern Black too much either. White plays the black side of a line in the English opening with an extra tempo (1 c4 c5 2 ♘f3 ♘f6 3 g3 d5 4 cxd5 ♘xd5 5 ♗g2 ♘c7) but it is not enough to guarantee an edge.

6 ... d6

As usual 6...♘f6 normally just transposes after 6 ♘c3 ♗g7 7 ♗e2, but Black also has a couple of other possibilities:

a) 6...b6 7 ♗e2 ♗a6 8 0-0 ♖c8 was tried twice at a high level in the sixties:

a1) Tal-Aronin, Yerevan 1962, continued 9 ♘d2 ♘f6 10 b3 ♕c7 11 f4 0-0 12 ♗b2 b5, when Black won a complicated game, although

White seems to be fine here to us.

a2) In Nei-Larsen, Bewerwijk 1964, White played the stronger 9 ♘ba3, controlling c4 and b5, and after 9...♘f6 10 f3 White was slightly better.

The ...b7-b6, ...♗a6 plan certainly seems playable, and could be an interesting way of taking the game into uncharted territory.

b) 6...♕b6 is another idea to unbalance the position. After 7 ♘c3 ♗xc3+ 8 bxc3 ♕a5 a position from the English Opening arises, where White has in got e2-e4 for free. Unfortunately, this idea has never been tested in practice. It would be interesting to see if White has a convincing answer to Black's simple plan of ...d7-d6, ...♗e6, ...♘e5 and ...♖c8, trying to grab the c4-pawn. Maybe White should simply develop with 9 ♗e2 and sacrifice the c3-pawn, e.g. 9...♕xc3+ 10 ♗d2 ♕e5 11 f3 with good play on the dark squares. Still, it is not clear who is better.

7 ♗e2

7 ♘c3 allows 7...♗xc3+ 8 bxc3 ♕a5 with a transposition to a position from the English Opening with reversed colours, but with no extra tempo for White.

7 ... ♘f6

The aggressive 7...f5 was played in Alexander-Botvinnik, Amsterdam 1954, which continued 8 exf5 ♗xf5 9 0-0 ♘h6 10 ♘d2 0-0 11 ♘f3 ♕d7 12 ♘e3 ♔h8 13 ♘xf5 ♘xf5 and Black was close to equality due to his control over the d4-square. 10 ♘c3 seems more logical, when 10...0-0 11 ♗e3 ♗xc2! 12 ♕xc2 ♘f5, as in Ciric-Hort, Sarajevo 1965, leads to the same kind of position. Both games were drawn, so, although it is slightly weakening, 7...f5 looks like a reliable alternative.

8   ♘c3

Since ...♗xc3 cannot be played now, the knight has to be developed.

8   ...   0-0

An interesting alternative is the immediate 8...♘d7 with the idea of exchanging on c3 and then later playing ...0-0-0. For example:

a) The inexact 9 ♗e3?! runs into 9...♗xc3+ 10 bxc3 ♕a5 11 ♕d2 ♘c5 12 f3 f6!?, intending 13 0-0 ♘a4 14 ♘b4 ♘xc3 and 13 ♘b4 ♘b3!

b) However, this idea completely failed in Stangl-Korchnoi, Nuremberg (rapid) 1994, when after 9 0-0 ♗xc3 10 bxc3 ♘c5 11 f3 ♕a5 12 ♕e1 ♗e6? 13 ♗h6 ♘e4 14 ♗g7 ♖g8 15 ♗d4 0-0-0 16 ♘b4 ♔b8 17 f4 ♘xd4 18 cxd4, it was obvious that Black's strategy had proved inadequate. 12...♘a4, designed to provoke 13 ♗d2 and then continue with ...♗e6, ...0-0-0 etc., is more logical. Still, we think that this is a rather risky strategy, and White should be better.

9   0-0   a6

Not very common, but the Swede always has independent ideas. For 9...♘d7 see Games 54-57.

10   ♖e1

10 ♗g5 is more aggressive and logical. Gufeld-Tal, Dneprotovsk 1970, continued 10...♗d7 11 ♘e3 ♖c8 12 ♕d2 ♖e8 13 ♔h1 ♕a5 14 f4 b5 with a complicated game. 9...a6 certainly seems to be a good way to get out of theory and maintain a solid position with possibilities for outplaying the opponent.

| 10 | ... | ♖b8 |
| 11 | ♗d2 | |

This is too passive.

11	...	♗d7
12	♖b1	♘e8
13	b4	♘c7
14	a4?!	a5!

Fixing the dark squares.

15	b5	♘d4
16	♘xd4	♗xd4
17	♖b3	

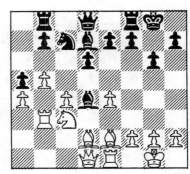

Now it was of course possible to play ...♗g7 followed by ...♘e6-c5 with a nice position, but Black wanted more.

17...e5! 18 ♗f1 ♘e6 19 ♘d5 ♘c5 20 ♖g3 ♗e6 21 ♗e3 ♗xd5 22 ♗xd4

If White were to take back on d5, Black would exchange the bishops, and his knight on c5 would give him a positionally winning game.

22...♘xe4 23 ♖a3 exd4 24 ♕xd4 ♘f6! 25 cxd5 ♘d7! 26 ♖ae3 ♕f6!

Strong play by Black, keeping a big edge.

27 ♕a7 ♘c5 28 ♕xa5 ♖a8 29 ♕c7 ♖xa4 30 ♖f3 ♖f4 31 ♖xf4 ♕xf4 32 g3 ♕f6 33 ♕a5 ♕d8 34 ♕c3 ♖e8

Black uses the fact that every exchange will make the difference between knight on c5 and bishop on f1 even bigger.

35 ♖c1 ♕e7 36 h4 h5 37 ♗g2 ♕e2 38 ♕f6 ♕e5 39 ♕f3 ♔g7 40 ♕d1 ♖a8 41 ♕c2 ♖a3 42 b6 ♖b3 43 ♖b1 ♖xb1 44 ♕xb1 ♕d4 45 ♕c2 ♕b4 0-1

White had had enough. The simple Maroczy Bind strategy of good knight vs. bad bishop was seen here in its purest form.

Game 54
Ivanchuk-Andersson
Tilburg 1990

(1 e4 c5 2 ♘f3 ♘c6 3 d4 cxd4 4 ♘xd4 g6 5 c4 ♗g7 6 ♘c2 d6 7 ♗e2 ♘f6 8 ♘c3 0-0 9 0-0)

9 ... ♘d7!?

The main line. Black puts his knight on c5, where it is often well placed in the Maroczy.

10 ♗d2

The standard move, preventing ...♗xc3. A more testing alternative is the critical 10 ♗e3, since if Black does not take on c3, White's pieces will be the more actively placed:

a) 10...♘c5 11 ♘d4 (11 f3

transposes to note 'b' below after 11...♗xc3 12 bxc3) 11...♗d7 12 ♕d2 ♖c8 13 ♖ad1 ♖e8 14 ♔h1 ♕a5 15 f3 ♘e6 16 ♘b3 ♕b4 17 ♕c2 ♘a5 18 ♘xa5 ♕xa5 19 ♖d5 ♘c5 with approximately equal chances, but perhaps a slight initiative for White, Nimzowitsch-Capablanca, Carlsbad 1929. However, Black can consider 12...♘xd4 13 ♗xd4 ♗c6 with a Classical Maroczy where White has wasted some time with ♘d4-c2-d4.

b) 10...♗xc3 11 bxc3 ♘c5 12 f3 ♕a5 13 ♕d2 ♘a4 does not win a pawn, since after 14 ♘b4 ♘xc3 15 ♘xc6 ♘xe2+ White has 16 ♔f2, which wins a piece because of the possibility of interposing a check on e7. But 13...♘a4 is not Black's best move. After 13...♗e6 14 ♘d4 ♖ad8 15 ♖ab1 b6 16 ♗h6 ♖fe8 17 ♖b5 ♕a3 18 ♘xe6 fxe6 19 h4 ♘d8 20 h5 ♘f7 21 hxg6 hxg6 22 ♗e3 ♔g7 23 ♖f2 ♖h8 24 ♗f1 e5 Black had excellent chances in Stein-Kapengut, Leningrad 1971. Another idea is 12...b6 to develop normally, keeping the queen at home to defend the king. If you do not like these kind of positions for Black, normal play with 11...a5 followed by ...f7-f5, as played with the colours reversed in the English opening, is also possible. Of course, it is to White's advantage that his bishop is on e3 instead of d2, although this is nothing special.

10 ... ♘c5

If the 11 b4 pawn sacrifice scares you, then 10...a5 is playable with a possible transposition. Some independent examples are:

a) 11 ♖c1 ♘c5 12 b3 ♘b4! with a clear edge for Black, Nunn-Petursson, Wijk aan Zee 1990.

b) 11 ♕c1!? ♖e8 12 ♗h6 ♗h8 13 ♕d2 a4 14 ♘a3, Petursson-Donaldson, New York 1991. Now Petursson prefers 14...♕a5 15 ♘ab5 ♘c5 and then ...♗d7 and ...♖ec8 with a good game for Black.

11 b4!?

White hopes to prove dark-squared compensation for the pawn after 11...♗xc3 12 ♗xc3 ♘xe4 13 ♗b2 and now:

a) In Milos-Spangenberg, Buenos Aires 1996, White's strategy worked well: 13...e5 14 ♕e1 ♕g5 15 ♖d1 ♗e6 16 ♔h1 ♕h4 17 ♗f3 f5 18 b5 ♘d8 19 g3 ♕f6 20 ♘e3 ♘f7 21 ♗g2 ♖ac8 22 f3 ♘c5 23 f4, and the bishop on b2 soon became a monster.

b) However, Black's play can be improved. We much prefer Maroczy-expert Tiviakov's 13...♗e6. Black intends quickly to exert pressure on c4 with ...♖c8, ...♘e5 etc. The idea was tried out in Smirin-Tiviakov, Paris 1995: 14 b5 ♘e5 15 ♕d4 ♘f6 16 ♘e3 ♘ed7 17 ♖ad1 a6 18 g4 ♕b6 19 ♕xb6 ♘xb6 20 ♗xf6 exf6 21 ♖xd6 ♘c8 22 ♖d2 axb5 23 axb5 ½-½. Not very informative, but Black's posi-

tion proved sufficiently solid. More testing is 14 a3, as played in Razuvaev-P.H.Nielsen, Viking games 1997, when after 14...a5 15 b5 ♘e5 16 ♘e3 f5 17 ♕d4 ♘f6 18 c5 White opened the position for his bishops and should have won, but I managed to swindle a draw. Afterwards Razuvaev told me you simply cannot take pawns like this. Remembering my unpleasant position, I have to agree with him. Black should retreat his knight...

11 ... ♘e6

White has won some space, but in return Black has play on the dark squares around d4.

12 ♔h1

Since the f2-f4 thrust is difficult to achieve, this is probably a waste of time. It is better to play either 12 ♖b1 (see Games 55 and 56) or 12 ♖c1 a5 13 a3 and now:

a) 13...axb4 14 axb4 ♘ed4 15 ♘xd4 ♘xd4 16 ♗e3 when in Geller-Pigusov, Cappelle la Grande 1992, Black played the thematic 16...e5!, cementing the knight on d4. White played 17 ♘b5, but after 17...♘xb5 18 cxb5 ♗e6 19 b6 f5 20 f3 ♖a3 21 ♕d2 ♖a2 22 ♖c2 ♖xc2 23 ♕xc2 ♕d7 24 ♖c1 f4 25 ♗f2 ♖c8 he was slightly worse due to his doubled pawns.

b) Also possible is 13...♗d7 14 ♘d5 axb4 15 axb4 ♘cd4 16 ♘xd4 ♘xd4 17 ♗g5 ♖e8 18 ♗e3 e5 19 ♗g4 ♗e6 20 h3 ♖a3 with good play for Black, De la Villa Garcia-T.Georgadze, Salamanca 1989.

12	...	♘ed4
13	♘xd4	♘xd4
14	♗d3	a5
15	b5	♘e6
16	♖c1	♘c5
17	♗b1	b6

18   ♗g5   ♗b7

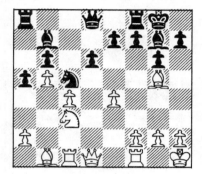

All of Black's minor pieces are excellently placed and he can start preparing breaks with ...f7-f5 or ...d6-d5. The game continued:

19 ♕d2 ♖c8 20 ♘d5 f6 21 ♗e3 e6 22 ♘f4 ♕e7 23 f3 ♖fe8 24 ♖cd1 ♖dc8 25 ♕f2 ♗f8 26 ♖d2

We do not understand this move. It is obvious that Black is playing to break with ...d6-d5 and this could have been prevented by the perfectly natural 26 ♖fe1 with a balanced position. Now Black gets the edge.

26...d5 27 ♘d3 ♕c7 28 cxd5 exd5 29 ♘xc5 ♗xc5 30 ♗xc5 ♕xc5 31 ♕xc5 bxc5 32 ♖fd1 ♔f7 33 exd5 ♖xd5 34 ♖xd5 ♗xd5 35 ♔g1 ♔e6 36 ♖d2 ♖b8 37 a4 ½-½

A strange decision. Black is better centralised and would have had good winning chances after 37...♗b3, threatening ...a5-a4. For example, 38 ♗c2 ♗xc2 39 ♖xc2, then 39...♔d5 followed by ...c5-c4, ...♔c5-b4 etc., which is very difficult for White and totally risk-free for Black. It is notable that in this game White did not even come close to getting active play, since he had to keep the e-pawn de-

fended and could not therefore push the f-pawn to f4 etc.

Game 55
Illescas-Ljubojevic
Linares 1993

(1 e4 c5 2 ♘f3 ♘c6 3 d4 cxd4 4 ♘xd4 g6 5 c4 ♗g7 6 ♘c2 d6 7 ♗e2 ♘f6 8 ♘c3 0-0 9 0-0 ♘d7!? 10 ♗d2 ♘c5 11 b4 ♘e6)

12   ♖b1

12   ...   a5

12...♘cd4 was played in Illescas-Hjartarson, Barcelona 1989, with a level position after 13 ♘xd4 ♘xd4 14 ♗d3 b6 15 ♘e2 ♘xe2 16 ♕xe2 ♗e6. 15 ♘e2 was not very ambitious, but Black is close to equal in any case.

13   a3

13 b5 is seen in the next game.

13   ...   axb4
14   axb4   ♘ed4
15   ♘xd4   ♘xd4
16   ♗d3   ♗d7

After 17 ♖e1 ♖a3 18 ♗f1 ♖e8 19 ♖e3 ♗c6 20 b5 ♗d7 21 ♘d5 ♖a2 22 ♗c3 e5 23 ♘b4 ♖a3?? 24 ♗xd4 White won a piece in Kaidanov-Khasin, Belgrade 1988. The plan with ...e7-e6, which we see in the main game, would also have been strong here. Khasin should have played ...e7-e6 on move 17 or 18 with good prospects.

17 ♕c1

Now Ljubojevic played the key:

17 ... e6!

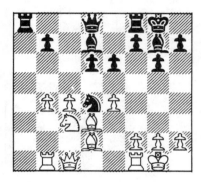

Black wants to follow up with ...♕f6 or ...♕e7 and then double the rooks on the a-file with beautiful co-ordination.

18 ♗h6 ♗xh6 19 ♕xh6 ♕f6 20 ♕c1 ♕g7 21 ♖d1 ♖fc8 22 ♗f1 ♗a4!

Forcing a favourable exchange since 23 ♖e1 ♘c2, 23 ♖d2 ♘b3 or 23 ♖d3 ♗c2 loses the exchange.

23 ♘xa4 ♖xa4 24 ♕b2 e5

Now Black has a dream Maroczy position. Black was winning, but in the end Illescas managed to escape with a draw in 82 moves. Black's play was very instructive and nobody plays 13 a3 anymore.

Game 56
Salov-Adams
Dos Hermanas 1993

(1 e4 c5 2 ♘f3 ♘c6 3 d4 cxd4 4 ♘xd4 g6 5 c4 ♗g7 6 ♘c2 d6 7 ♗e2 ♘f6 8 ♘c3 0-0 9 0-0 ♘d7!? 10 ♗d2 ♘c5 11 b4 ♘e6 12 ♖b1 a5)

| 13 | b5!? | ♘cd4 |
| 14 | b6!? | |

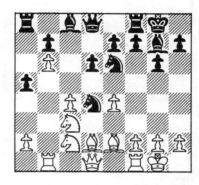

A try for the advantage. If Black gets in ...b7-b6 and ...♗b7 he will have a very solid position.

14	...	♘xc2
15	♕xc2	♗d7
16	♘d5	♗c6
17	♗g4	♘c5
18	♗g5	♗xd5
19	cxd5	

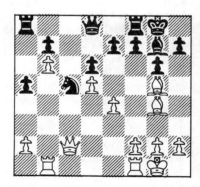

Adams regards this as slightly better for White, but since he wins this game in an instructive manner and only gives alternatives with White gaining equality, it is difficult to place too much faith in this. Black has counterplay against the b6-pawn and his only concern is to keep the knight on c5 defended after a white ♗e3, since the rook cannot go to c8.

19 ... h5!

This strong move forces White to decide where to put his bishop. If he plays it to h3, Black plays 20...♖a6, threatening 21...♗f6! (not 21...♖xb6?? 22 ♗xe7!) which is a typical idea. If White takes on f6, Black gets the e-file and the usual knight vs. light-squared bishop advantage, and also stops all White plans involving an e4-e5-break.

20 ♗e2 ♖c8
21 ♗e3 a4

Not really a pawn sacrifice, since 22 ♗xc5 ♖xc5 23 ♕xa4 ♕a8! wins back the pawn with advantage.

22 ♖b4 a3 23 ♖fb1 ♕d7 24 ♗b5 ♕d8 25 ♗e2 ♕d7

Now Salov should have settled on a draw by repetition. In the game, he was slowly outplayed.

26 ♖c4?! e6! 27 ♖d1 exd5 28 ♖xd5 ♕e6 29 ♗f4 ♖c6

It may look like White is very active, but the opposite is in fact the case. All Black's pieces are placed on good squares, and the a3-pawn is strong.

30 ♗xd6 ♖xd6 31 ♖xd6 ♕xd6 32 ♖xc5 ♕xb6 33 ♖b5 ♕e6

Black followed up with ...♖c8 with the better position and won in 67 moves. As we have seen, Black has just as good chances to win as his opponent in this line, so 11 b4!? does not look like anything to be afraid of.

Game 57
Portisch-Tukmakov
Madrid 1973

(1 e4 c5 2 ♘f3 ♘c6 3 d4 cxd4 4 ♘xd4 g6 5 c4 ♗g7 6 ♘c2 d6 7 ♗e2 ♘f6 8 ♘c3 0-0 9 0-0 ♘d7!? 10 ♗d2 ♘c5)

11 f3

11 ... a5

We wonder why nobody has ever tried 11...♕b6!? Although this looks like a patzer's move, it is not so easy to refute:

a) After 12 ♔h1 ♕xb2 13 ♖b1 ♗xc3 14 ♖xb2 ♗xb2 Black has

rook, knight and pawn for the queen. His position is solid, and he has a strong knight on c5. Only Black can be better.

b) More critical is 12 ♘d5, but 12...♕xb2 13 ♖b1 ♕xa2 14 ♘cb4 ♘xb4 15 ♘xe7+ ♔h8 16 ♗xb4 ♗e6 is better for Black. We have not been able to find a decent way to meet 11...♕b6, which could mean that 11 f3 is actually a mistake!

Instead 11...♗xc3 was played by Spiridonov against Fillip in Sochi 1973. The idea is that after 12 ♗xc3 ♘a4, White cannot preserve the dark-squared bishop without losing a pawn. However, in the game White used his space advantage with 13 ♕d2 a5 14 ♔h1 ♗e6 15 f4 f6 16 ♖ad1 ♔g7 17 ♘e3 ♘xc3 18 ♕xc3 ♕b6 19 ♖f3 ♘b4 20 a3 ♘a6 21 f5 ♗f7 22 fxg6 ♗xg6 23 ♘f5 ♗xf5 24 exf5 ♘b8 25 ♖h3 ♔h8 26 ♖xh7 ♔xh7 27 ♕h3 1-0. Of course, it is possible to improve on Black's play, but 11...♗xc3 looks dubious.

12   ♔h1

Once Black has played ...a7-a5 in this line, White need not fear ...♗xc3 anymore, since Black no longer controls b5 and b6, and the black queen cannot go to a5. The more active 12 ♗e3!? is therefore quite logical. For example, 12...a4 (everybody plays this, but other moves are also possible and in particular the Petursson approach, 12...b6 13 ♕d2 ♖a7 followed by ...♖d7, ...e7-e6, ...♗b7 etc., looks good; Petursson has played the Maroczy for many years, so one should pay extra attention to his ideas. He knows what he is doing!) 13 ♕d2 ♕a5 and now:

a) 14 ♖ac1 was played in Sanz-Zsu.Polgar, Leon 1989, when Black reacted with the ultra-solid 14...♗d7 15 ♔h1 ♖fd8 16 ♖fd1 ♗e8 17 ♘a3 ♔h8. Although Black's last few moves look quite suspicious, she won in 70 moves. Probably Black should prefer either 14...f5 or 14...b6 followed by ...♗b7, ...♖fd8 etc., with a balanced position.

b) 14 ♖ab1 f5 15 exf5 ♗xf5 16 ♖bc1 ♗xc2 17 ♖xc2 ♘b4 18 ♖cc1 a3 19 bxa3 ♗xc3 20 ♖xc3 ♘xa2 21 ♖c2 ♕xd2 22 ♖xd2 ♘c3 23 ♗xc5 dxc5 24 ♖a1 ♖fc8 25 ♖c2 ♘xe2+ 26 ♖xe2 ♔f7 ½-½ Stohl-Malisauskas, Manila ol 1992.

12   ...   f5

A more passive, but solid way of meeting 12 ♔h1 was tried in Conquest-Petursson, Palma de Mallorca 1989: 12...b6 13 ♖c1 ♖a7 14 b3 ♖d7 15 ♕e1 e6 16 ♖d1 ♗b7 and Black had no problems, since he will soon be ready for the ...d6-d5 break.

13   exf5   ♗xf5
14   ♘e3

14 ♗e3!? is an interesting alternative, e.g. 14...♘b4 15 ♘d4 or 14...♗xc2 15 ♕xc2 ♘d4 16 ♕d2

or 14...♔h8 15 ♘d4 with a slight advantage for White in all cases according to Filip, but 14...a4!?, as suggested by David Strauss, seems to provide Black with adequate counterplay.

14   ...   ♘d4!

Black does not care for the bishop pair, since the knights are just as important in the battle for the central squares.

15	♘xf5	♘xf5
16	♖b1	e6
17	b3	♔h8
18	♘b5	d5
19	cxd5	exd5
20	♖c1	b6
21	g4	♘d6
22	♗c3	♘xb5

23	♗xg7	♔xg7
24	♗xb5	d4
25	♖c4	♖f4

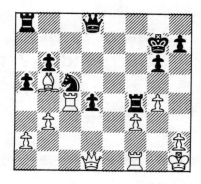

26 a3 ♕d5 27 b4 axb4 28 axb4 ♘e6 29 ♕e2 d3 30 ♕b2 ♔h6 31 ♗c6 ♕xc4 32 ♗xa8 d2 33 ♕b1 ♖d4 0-1

A strategic triumph for Tukmakov. In general the 6 ♘c2 and 6 ♘b3 systems do not give Black much to worry about, and he has the choice between many interesting ideas. Of the two, the 6 ♘c2 system with a quick ♗e3, daring Black to take on c3, seems to be White's best: he gets some attacking chances in return for his spoiled pawn structure, and a complicated game ensues.

8 Maroczy Bind: Gurgenidze Variation

Chapter Guide

1 e4 c5 2 ♘f3 ♘c6 3 d4 cxd4 4 ♘xd4 g6 5 c4 ♘f6 6 ♘c3

Over the past few years the Gurgenidze line has developed from viable sideline to become the most frequently played variation in the entire Accelerated Dragon. In particular, the games of Tiviakov, Antunes, Petursson and a group of Cuban players such as Andres have done much to popularise it.

Black's main idea is to get in the freeing ...b7-b5, but depending on the particular set-up chosen by his opponent, Black has a variety of different plans to choose from, and these are explained in the illustrative games.

Game 58
Polugayevsky-Jansa
Sochi 1974

(1 e4 c5 2 ♘f3 ♘c6 3 d4 cxd4 4 ♘xd4 g6 5 c4 ♘f6 6 ♘c3)

6   ...   ♘xd4?!

This is an inaccurate move order, as it allows White some extra options. Most importantly, White does not need to decide immediately whether he wants to play ♗e2 or f2-f3; here he can wait and place the light-squared bishop on the ideal square d3.

7   ♕xd4   d6
8   ♗g5!

This is the only way to take advantage of Black's move order. Other moves have been tried, but none of them have secured White an advantage:

a) 8 b3 ♗g7 9 ♗b2 0-0 10 ♗e2 ♕a5 11 0-0 ♗e6 12 ♖ac1 ♖fc8 13 ♕d3 a6 14 ♗a1 ♖ab8 with equal chances, Korchnoi-Benko, Buenos Aires 1960.

b) 8 f3 ♗g7 9 ♕f2 (9 ♗e3 0-0

10 ♕d2 transposes to the next game) 9...0-0 10 ♗e2 ♗e6 11 ♗d2 ♘d7 12 0-0 ♕b6 13 ♕xb6 ♘xb6 14 b3 a5 with equality, Klavin-Bannik, USSR 1963.

c) 8 c5 ♗g7 (less advisable is 8...dxc5?! 9 ♕xc5 [Silman and Donaldson give 9 ♕xd8+ ♔xd8 10 ♗f4 ♗e6 11 0-0-0+ ♔e8 12 ♗e3 c4 13 ♖d4 ♘g4 14 ♗xc4 ♘xe3 as equal, but 12 ♘b5 seems to win for White] 9...♗g7 10 ♗e2 0-0 11 ♗f4 with a small advantage for White according to Levy) 9 ♗b5+ ♗d7 10 cxd6 0-0 11 0-0 ♗xb5 12 ♘xb5 a6 13 dxe7 ♕xe7 14 ♘c3 ♖fe8 15 ♖e1 ♖ad8, as in Ciocaltea-Parma, Athens 1968, and now 16 ♕c4 gives equal chances.

8   ...   ♗g7
9   ♕d2   0-0

There is no real point in holding back on castling, as Black will have to do it later anyway. However, other moves have been tried: 9...♗e6 10 ♖c1 ♖c8 11 b3 ♕a5 12 f3 (12 ♗d3?! allows 12...h6 13 ♗e3 ♘g4 14 ♗f4 g5 15 ♗g3 ♘e5 with equality according to Bagirov) 12...h6 13 ♗e3 0-0 14 ♗d3 (14 ♗xh6? ♗xh6 15 ♕xh6 b5! is excellent for Black) 14...♔h7 15 0-0 a6 16 h3 ♘d7 17 f4 f5 18 exf5 ♗xf5 19 ♗e2 with a small but clear advantage for White, Polugayevsky-Beliavsky, USSR ch 1975.

10   ♗d3!

Here 10 ♗e2 transposes to Games 68-72, whereas 10 f3 is analysed in the notes to the next game.

10   ...   ♗e6

Black has not had much luck with the alternatives either:

a) 10...♗d7 11 0-0 a6 12 ♖fe1 ♖b8 13 ♘d5 ♘xd5 14 exd5 f6 15 ♗f4 and White was on top, Khasin-Makarov, USSR 1976.

b) 10...a5 11 0-0 a4?! (11...♗e6!?) 12 ♖ac1 ♗e6 13 ♕c2 with a slight plus for White, Portisch-Reshevsky, Petropolis izt 1973.

11   ♖c1   ♕a5

11...a6 was tried in Morgado-Baumbach, corr 1984/89, but here too White obtained an advantage: 12 0-0 ♖e8 13 ♘d5! ♗xd5?! (White is only slightly better after 13...♘xd5) 14 cxd5 ♘d7 15 b4! ♖c8 16 ♖xc8 ♕xc8 17 ♖c1 ♕b8 18 ♗e2 with a big plus for White. It is surprising to see an Accelerated Dragon specialist like Baumbach end up in such a bad position.

12   0-0

In Nijboer-Van der Weide, Amsterdam 1996, White was successful with 12 ♘d5 ♕xd2+ 13 ♔xd2 ♗xd5 14 cxd5 ♖fc8 15 f3 ♔f8 16 ♗e3 a6 17 b4 e6 18 dxe6 fxe6 19 h4 with a clear edge for White. Since 12...♕xa2 13 ♘xe7+ ♔h8 14 0-0 is also quite uncomfortable for Black, perhaps 12...♕d8 is necessary.

12   ...   a6
13   b3   ♖fc8

14   ♖fe1   ♔f8!

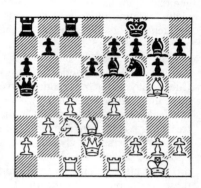

Intending ...b7-b5 without allowing ♘d5. White should now have met this plan with 15 a4! ♖ab8 (15...♕b4!?) 16 ♖c2 ♘g8?! 17 ♖b1 ♕b4 18 ♕c1, intending ♗d2 with a clear advantage for White, as in Spraggett-Zuk, Canada 1983.

15   ♖c2   b5
16   cxb5   axb5
17   ♖ec1   b4
18   ♘b5   ♖xc2
19   ♖xc2   ♗d7
20   ♘c7!

White is slightly better, but in the rest of the game he lets his advantage slip away:

20...♖c8 21 ♕c1 ♕e5! 22 ♖c4

22 ♗f4!? was interesting.

22...♘g4 23 ♗f4 ♕a1 24 h3 ♕xc1+ 25 ♖xc1 ♘e5 26 ♗a6 ♖b8 27 ♗d2 e6 28 ♔f1

Perhaps 28 ♗f1!?

28...♔e7 29 ♗e2 ♘c6 30 ♗b5 ♖b6 31 ♗e2 ♗d4 ½-½

Game 59
Panchenko-T.Georgadze
USSR 1975

(1 e4 c5 2 ♘f3 ♘c6 3 d4 cxd4 4

②xd4 g6 5 c4 ②f6 6 ②c3)

6 ... d6
7 f3

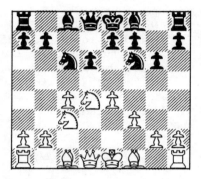

This move was immensely popular in the early seventies, but when it became apparent that White does not have much to show after 12...♛xa2, its popularity slowly died out. These days 7 f3 is rarely seen, and it could therefore serve as a handy surprise weapon, though with accurate play by Black, all White can hope for is equality. The standard 7 ♗e2 is seen in Games 61-72.

7 ... ②xd4

7...♗g7 transposes to the Classical Maroczy with White already committed to f2-f3, but White more or less always plays this move at some point. Note that 7...♛b6? (hoping for either 8 ②c2 or 8 ②b3) is bad because of 8 ♗e3! ♛xb2 9 ②a4 ♛a3 10 ♗c1 ♛b4+ 11 ♗d2 ♛a3 12 ②b5, when the black queen is trapped.

8 ♛xd4 ♗g7
9 ♗e3

Another possibility is 9 ♗g5, but when White has already weakened his dark squares with 7 f3, this

move has less point. Although White has had some good results with this approach, Black should be able to equalise without too much difficulty: 9...0-0 (just as in the line with 7 ♗e2, 9...h6 gives White a small advantage: 10 ♗e3 0-0 11 ♛d2 ♔h7 12 ♖c1 ♗e6 13 b3 ②d7 14 ♗e2, Vaisman-Balogh, Budapest 1975) 10 ♛d2 ♗e6 11 ♖c1 (11 ♗e2 allows 11...♖c8 12 ②d5 b5!?, which may transpose to the note to White's 11th move in Game 70) 11...♛a5 (here Black can try to transpose to Game 70 with 11...♖c8!? 12 b3 a6, when 13 ♗e2 b5 allows the transposition) 12 b3 ♖fc8 13 ②d5 (13 ♗e2 a6 transposes to Game 72) 13...♛xd2+ 14 ♔xd2 ②xd5 15 exd5 (or 15 cxd5 ♗d7, when 16 ♗xe7?? loses to 16...♗h6+, and the pawn-grabbing 16 ♖xc8+ ♖xc8 17 ♗xe7 gives Black a nasty initiative after 17...♗h6+) 15...♗d7 with equality, as 16 ♗xe7? ♗h6+ 17 ♔d1 ♗xc1 18 ♔xc1 ♖e8 19 ♗xd6 ♖e1+ is good for Black.

The above is very similar to the lines in Game 72. For a better understanding of the ideas for both sides, careful study of those lines is recommended.

9 ... 0-0
10 ♛d2 ♗e6

As in the 7 ♗e2 lines, Black must be very careful with the move order. Here, for example, 10...♛a5? allows White to expand on the queenside because his rook is still on a1: 11 a3 ♗e6 12 b4 ♛d8 13 ♖c1 ♖c8 14 ②b5 a6 15 ②d4 ♗d7 16 ♗e2 ♛c7 17 0-0 with a clear advantage for White, Savon-Tal, Sukhumi 1972.

10...♗d7, intending ...a7-a6 and

...b7-b5 has also been tried, but so far this has proved a little too passive to provide equal chances: 11 ♖c1 ♕a5 12 ♗e2 ♖fc8 13 0-0 a6 14 b3 ♗c6 (worse is 14...b5?! 15 c5! ♖c6 16 cxd6 exd6 17 ♖c2 ♖ac8 18 ♘d5 with a clear advantage for White, Polugayevsky-Bednarski, Siegen ol 1970) 15 ♗d4 ♘d7 16 ♗xg7 ♔xg7 17 ♔h1 ♔g8 18 f4 b5 19 ♕b2 bxc4 20 ♗xc4 with a small advantage for White, Suetin-Forintos, Budapest 1970.

An untried idea is 11...a5, intending 12 ♗e2 ♗c6 13 0-0 ♘d7 14 b3 ♘c5 transposing to a Classical Maroczy with White already committed to ♖c1, which is not considered dangerous for Black.

11 ♖c1 ♕a5

In Donaldson-Perelstein, Bermuda 1997, Black was apparently unfamiliar with 7 f3 and chose 11...a6?! here: 12 b3 ♕a5 13 ♘d5 (now ...♕xa2 is no longer possible, and Black will just end up in an inferior endgame) 13...♕xd2+ 14 ♔xd2 ♗xd5 15 cxd5 ♖fc8 16 ♖xc8 ♖xc8 17 g3! with a clear advantage for White.

12 ♘d5

A popular alternative is 12 b3,

but here too Black does not have much to worry about: 12...♖fc8 13 ♗d3 a6 14 ♘a4 (the less accurate 14 ♘e2 was tried in J.Polgar-Antunes, Yerevan ol 1996, which continued 14...♕xd2+ 15 ♔xd2 ♘d7 16 ♘f4 ♘c5 17 ♗e2 a5 18 ♘d5?! [18 h4 is equal] 18...♗xd5 19 cxd5, reaching the position that White was probably hoping for, but she was in for a big surprise: 19...a4! 20 b4? [better is 20 ♗c4, but White hadn't seen Black's next move]

20...♘b3+!! [all of a sudden Black is much better, the passed a-pawn will cost White a rook, leaving Black an exchange up] 21 axb3 ♖xc1 22 ♖xc1 a3 23 ♗b5 a2 24 ♔d3 a1♕ 25 ♖xa1 ♖xa1) 14...♕xd2+ 15 ♔xd2 ♘d7 (this position is almost identical to the main line with 7 ♗e2 and 9 ♗e3, except that the bishop is on d3 instead of e2; however, the position is still equal – see Game 67 for a comparison) 16 f4 f5 17 ♖he1 ♔f8 18 exf5 and Black has no problems: 18...♗xf5 19 ♗e2 h5 20 ♗f3 ♖c7 21 ♘b6 (or 21 ♘c3 e6 ½-½ Polugayevsky-Timman, Hilversum 1973) 21...♘xb6 22 ♗xb6 ♖d7 23 ♗d5 ♖e8 24 ♖e6 ♗f6 25 ♖ce1 a5! 26 a4 ♖a8 27 ♖6e2 ♗g4 28 ♖e4

¹/₂-¹/₂ Boey-Abramov, corr 1975-80.

12 ... ♕xa2!

This is the move that has made it possible for Black to continue playing 7...♘xd4 against 7 f3. Prior to the discovery of 12...♕xa2!, Black had suffered badly in the ending that arises after 12...♕xd2+ 13 ♔xd2 ♗xd5 (unlike most cases when White plays ♘d5, here Black cannot play 13...♘xd5 14 cxd5 ♗d7, because White then has 15 ♖c7) 14 cxd5 ♖fc8 15 ♖xc8 (Kholmov gives 15 ♗e2 e5! 16 dxe6 fxe6 as unclear, but after 16 a4! White has all the chances) 15...♖xc8 16 g3, and White is much better. Two examples are: 16...♖c7 17 ♗h3 ♘d7 18 ♖c1 ♖xc1 19 ♔xc1 ♘c5 20 ♔c2, Kurajica-Huguet, Malaga 1970, and 16...b6 17 ♗h3 ♖c7 18 ♖c1 ♘e8 19 b4 ♖xc1 20 ♔xc1 ♘d7 21 ♗d7, Gheorghiu-Szilagyi, Varna 1971.

13 ♘xe7+ ♔h8

14 ♗d4

For White's alternative, 14 ♗e2, see the next main game. After 14 ♗d4 Black has to decide which rook he will place on e8.

14 ... ♖fe8

14...♖ae8 is generally considered to be stronger in this position because it keeps the f7-square protected. However, we feel that the text move is better, as it offers more possibilities for White to go wrong, whereas the other rook move leads to a more or less forced draw. After 14...♖ae8 15 ♘d5 ♗xd5 (an interesting alternative is 15...♘xd5, although its only outing turned out in White's favour: 16 cxd5 ♗xd5 17 ♗b5 ♗c6 18 ♗c4 ♕a4 19 ♗xg7+ ♔xg7 20 0-0 a5 21 ♕c3+ ♔g8 22 ♖fd1 ♕b4 23 ♕xb4 axb4 24 ♖xd6 with a clear advantage for White, as in Timman-Andersson, Helsinki 1972; but Black can improve with 20...♗b5!, e.g. 21 b3 ♕a6 22 ♕d4+ ♔g8 23 ♖a1 ♕c6 24 ♖xa7 ♗xc4 25 bxc4 ♖c8 with equality) 16 cxd5 and now after 16...♖c8 we have an almost identical position to that which arises after 14...♖fe8, the only difference being that Black here has his rook on f8 instead of e8. One example is Gheorghiu-Hug, Las Palmas 1972: 17 ♗e2 ♖xc1+ 18 ♕xc1 ♘d7 19 ♗xg7 ♔xg7 20 ♕c3+ ♔g8 21 0-0 ♘b6 ¹/₂-¹/₂.

Instead of 16...♖c8, an attempt to take advantage of the protection of the f7-pawn has been suggested by T.Georgadze, who gives the following line: 16...♕xd5 17 ♗c4 ♕h5 18 ♕c3 ♕g5 19 0-0 ♘h5 20 ♗xg7+ ♘xg7 21 ♗d5 ♕e7 22 ♕c7 ♘e6 23 ♕xb7 ♕xb7 24 ♗xb7 ♖b8 25 ♗d5 ♘f4 with a slight advantage for Black. Silman and Donaldson suggest that a draw is probable after 26 ♖c7 ♖xb2 27 ♖xa7 ♖xg2+ 28 ♔h1 ♔g7 29 ♖d7 with a slight, but we still prefer Black after 29...g5, intending

30 ♖xd6 ♖b8 31 ♖g1 ♖xg1+ 32 ♔xg1 ♖b1+ 33 ♔f2 ♖b2+, when Black has the initiative in the endgame. But as Larsen would say: 'Long variation, wrong variation!' White can improve with 18 0-0!, threatening 19 ♕c3, as Black no longer has 19...♕g5 due to 20 f4. The only move is 18...♘d7, which is slightly better for White after 19 ♗xg7+ ♔xg7 20 ♕xd6 followed by ♗d5.

15   ♘d5

In Vaisman-Volchok, corr 1973, White achieved nothing with 15 ♕c3 ♘h5 16 ♗xg7+ (Andersson gives the following line: 16 g4 ♗xg4 17 ♘d5 ♗xf3 18 ♗xg7+ ♘xg7 19 ♕xf3 ♕xb2 20 ♔d1 with an unclear position) 16...♘xg7 17 b4 a5 18 b5 a4 19 ♗e2 a3 20 ♔h2 ♕b2 21 ♘d5 ♗xd5 22 cxd5 f5 and Black even had the better chances. Timman has suggested 17 b3 as better, giving 17...♕a6 18 ♘d5 ♗xd5 19 cxd5 ♕b6 as unclear, but with his control over the dark squares and better development, we believe that Black is better.

15   ...   ♗xd5
16   cxd5   ♖ac8

Both 16...♘xd5? and 16...♕xd5?! are met by 17 ♗c4.

17   ♗e2   ♖xc1+

Also possible is 17...♔g8 18 0-0 ♕a4 19 ♗c3 ♕b3 with equality, Bednarski-Ree, Skopje ol 1972.

18   ♕xc1   ♘d7

18...♕a5+ is inaccurate due to 19 ♕c3 ♕xc3+ 20 bxc3 ♘d7 21 ♔d2 ♖c8 (21...♗xd4?! 22 cxd4 ♘b6 23 ♖a1 was better for White in Donaldson-Silman, Philadelphia 1985) and now both 22 ♖a1 a6 23 ♖b1 ♖c7 24 f4, Polugayevsky-Bednarski, Varna 1972, and 22

♖b1 ♘c5 23 ♔e3, as in Panchenko-Gufeld, Kishnev 1975, are slightly better for White.

19	♗xg7+	♔xg7
20	♕c3+	♔g8
21	♔f2	♘b6
22	♕f6	♖c8
23	h4	♖c2?!

This is not the best, Black has the strong 23...♘a4!, when Pavlov-Adorjan, Bath 1973, continued 24 h5 ♕xb2 25 ♕xb2 ♘xb2 26 ♖a1 a6 27 ♔e3 ♖c2! with a small advantage for Black.

24	h5	♘d7
25	♕d8+	♘f8
26	hxg6	fxg6
27	♕xd6?	

This allows Black to draw immediately, but even after the stronger 27 ♖e1! Black has good drawing chances, e.g. 27...♕a6 28 ♔f1 ♕b6 29 ♕xb6 axb6 30 b4 g5 followed by ...♘g6.

27	...	♖xe2+
28	♖xe2	♕xb2+

The rest of the game was just a series of queen checks:
29 ♔d3 ♕b3+ 30 ♔d4 ♕b2+ 31 ♔c4 ♕c2+ 32 ♔b4 ♕b2+ 33 ♔c4 ♕c2+ 34 ♔b4 ♕b2+ 35 ♔a4 ♕c2+ ½-½

Game 60
Andonovski-Baumbach
Corr 1981-84

(1 e4 c5 2 ♘f3 ♘c6 3 d4 cxd4 4 ♘xd4 g6 5 c4 ♘f6 6 ♘c3 d6 7 f3 ♘xd4 8 ♕xd4 ♗g7 9 ♗e3 0-0 10 ♕d2 ♗e6 11 ♖c1 ♕a5 12 ♘d5 ♕xa2 13 ♘xe7+ ♔h8)

14   ♗e2

14   ...   ♘g8!

This is the only way for Black to continue; gaining time by threatening the b2-pawn and forcing White to decide what to do about his knight on e7.

The alternatives have proven ineffective:

a) 14...♖fe8 15 ♘d5 ♗xd5 16 cxd5 with a clear edge for White, Jansa-Gazik, Sarajevo 1972.

b) 14...♘d7 15 ♗d4 ♖fe8 16 0-0 ♕b3 17 ♗d1 ♕a2 18 ♕c3 ♗xd4 19 ♕xd4+ f6 20 ♘d5 with slightly better chances for White, Andersson-Reshevsky, Palma de Mallorca 1971.

15   ♘xg8

Although 15 ♘d5!? is probably a stronger move, the text is just as popular. After 15 ♘d5!? Black has

to play with care to avoid ending up in a bad position: 15...♕xb2! (for some reason Black often gives preference to 15...♗xd5, which should give White a small advantage with best play: 16 cxd5 ♖fc8 17 0-0 a5 18 ♗d4 ♕a4 19 ♗c3 ♕b3 20 g3 a4 21 ♗xg7+ ♔xg7 22 ♕d4+ f6 23 ♗d1 ♕b5 24 ♖xc8 ♖xc8 25 ♕xa4 ♕xa4 26 ♗xa4 ♖c7 27 ♖f2 with an advantage for White, Cornu-Dusart, corr 1988-90) 16 ♕xb2 ♗xb2 17 ♖b1 ♗g7 18 ♘c7! ♖ac8 19 ♖xb7 ♖b8! 20 ♖xb8 ♖xb8 21 ♘xe6 fxe6 22 ♗xa7 ♖b1+ 23 ♗d1 ♘e7 24 0-0 ♘c6 25 ♗f2 ♗d4 with equal chances, Schmidt-Andersson, Warsaw 1973.

15	...	♔xg8
16	♗xd4	♗xd4
17	♕xd4	♕a5+
18	♔f2	

Also 18 ♕c3 ♕e5 19 0-0 ♖fc8 is fine for Black.

18   ...   ♕e5

Another excellent possibility is 18...♕c5, as in Commons-Browne, USA 1973, which continued 19 ♖cd1 (Browne gives 19 ♖hd1 ♖fd8 20 ♖d2 ♕xd4+ 21 ♖xd4 ♔f8, intending ...♔e7, when Black is fine) 19...♖fc8 20 b3?! (20 ♖d2) 20...a5! 21 ♕xc5 dxc5 22 ♖a1 b5 23 ♖hb1 a4 24 bxa4 bxa4 25 ♖b7 ♖a5 with a small advantage for Black.

19   ♖cd1   ♖fc8

More passive, yet still adequate is 19...♖fd8 20 ♖d2 ♕xd4+ 21 ♖xd4 ♔f8 22 f4 a5 23 g4 f6 24 g4, Ribli-Ghitescu, Kecskemet 1972, and now 24...h6! should provide Black with equality according to Florian.

20   b3

Black does not have any problems after 20 g3, e.g. 20...♖c6 (or

20...a6 21 f4 ♕c5 22 ♕xc5 ♖xc5 23 b3 b5 with equal chances, Tringov-Mista, Varna 1973) 21 f4 ♕xd4+ 22 ♖xd4 ♖b6 23 g4 f6 24 b3 ♖xb3 25 ♖xd6 with equality, Timman-Ree, Amsterdam 1972.

20 ... ♖c6

Or 20...a5 21 ♕xd6 ♕xd6 22 ♖xd6 a4 23 bxa4 ♖xa4 24 ♖b1 ♖a2 25 ♔e3 ♗xc4 26 ♗xc4 ♖xc4 with level chances, Andersson-Hug, Las Palmas 1973.

21 ♕e3

In Pytel-Bednarski, Lublin 1972, White got himself into trouble after 21 ♖d2 ♖b6! 22 ♕e3?! f5! 23 exf5 ♕xe3+ 24 ♔xe3 ♖xb3+ 25 ♔f2 ♗xf5 26 g4?! ♗e6 with a clear advantage for Black.

21 ... a5!?

Black can also try 21...♖b6!? 22 ♖d3 ♕c5 23 ♖a1 a5 with a good game for Black according to Ghizdavu, whose analysis continues 24 ♖a4 ♖b4 25 ♖xb4 axb4 26 f4 ♖a2 27 ♕xc5 dxc5 28 ♔e3 ♔g7 29 g4 b5 with a clear advantage for Black.

22 ♖d4 a4

cause White a lot of grief.

23	...	a3
24	f4	♕f6
25	b5	♖cc8
26	g3	a2
27	♕c3	

Against 27 ♖a1 Baumbach gives the following variation, 27...♗xc4! 28 e5!? dxe5 29 ♖xc4 ♖xc4 30 ♗xc4 exf4 31 ♕e1 fxg3+ with a strong attack. However, Black also has a tactical solution against the text move. The game finished:
27...d5! 28 exd5 ♗xd5 29 ♖c1 ♕b6 30 ♖a1 ♖a3! 31 c5 ♕f6 32 ♕d2 ♖xc5 33 ♕b4 b6 34 ♖dd1 ♖b3 35 ♕a4 ♖b2 36 ♖xd5 ♖xd5 37 ♖xa2 ♖dxb5 38 ♖xb2 ♖xb2 0-1

A powerful game by Baumbach.

Game 61
Franzen-Baumbach
Corr 1994-96

(1 e4 c5 2 ♘f3 ♘c6 3 d4 cxd4 4 ♘xd4 g6 5 c4 ♘f6 6 ♘c3 d6)

7 ♗e2

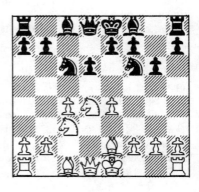

23 b4?
Equal was 23 f4 ♕f6 24 bxa4. Now the black passed a-pawn will

7	...	♘xd4
8	♕xd4	♗g7
9	0-0	

This move is quite harmless and should not cause Black too many problems. Better are 9 ♗e3 (see Games 65-67) and 9 ♗g5 (see Games 68-72). Finally, White can opt for 9 ♗d2 0-0 10 ♕e3, but after 10...♗d7 or 10...♗e6, he will have nothing better than a transposition to the main lines.

9 ... 0-0

Now White invariably chooses to move his queen out the line of the bishop on g7. Here and in the next game we consider 10 ♕d3, while Games 63 and 64 deal with 10 ♕e3.

10 ♕d3

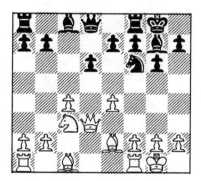

This line has been a favourite of Smejkal for many years and of late also of the young Hungarian Zoltan Almasi. With the white queen on d3, it is harder for Black to achieve ...b7-b5, as the queen gives extra protection to the knight on c3. White's plans for the future lie on the kingside. He intends to exchange the dark-squared bishops and then play f2-f4-f5. Black's counterplay is mainly based on his attempts to get in the freeing ...b7-b5 and exert pressure on the c4- and e4-pawns. Black has a number

of moves to choose from; in this game we shall take a look at 10...♘d7 and 10...a6, while the next game will cover 10...♗e6 and 10...♗d7.

10 ... ♘d7!?

Black targets the queen on d3 and intends to give up his dark-squared bishop under favourable circumstances in order to weaken the white pawn structure. Until quite recently this idea was considered dubious, but at present Black seems to be doing just fine.

Before we continue with the merits of the text move, let us take a look at 10...a6: 11 ♗e3 ♘g4 (for the better alternative 11...♗d7!? – see 10...♗d7 11 ♗e3 a6, which can be found in the next main game) 12 ♗xg4 ♗xg4 13 ♗d4 ♗xd4 14 ♕xd4 ♗e6 (this position can also arise from a different move order: 9 ♗e3 0-0 10 ♕d2 ♘g4 11 ♗xg4 ♗xg4 12 0-0 a6 13 ♗d4 ♗xd4 14 ♕xd4 ♗e6) and now:

a) 15 f4 b5! 16 b3 bxc4 17 f5 ♗d7 18 bxc4 with an unclear position – Silman and Donaldson.

b) 15 ♖fe1 ♖fe8 (both players prepare for ♘d5, but Black could also consider 15...b5!?) 16 b3 ♕a5 17 ♘d5 ♖ac8 18 ♘f4 ♗xc4?! (much better was 18...♕c5, e.g. 19 ♘xe6 fxe6 20 ♕d3 ♖f8! followed by ...b7-b5 with excellent chances for Black) 19 e5! ♗b5 20 ♘d5 ♗c6 21 exd6!, as in Keene-Schmid, Bath 1973. Now, instead of 21...♕xd5? 22 ♕xd5 ♗xd5 23 d7 with a clear edge for White, Black should have tried 21...♖cd8 22 ♘xe7+ ♖xe7 23 ♖xe7 ♕g5 24 f3 ♕xe7 25 dxe7 ♖xd4 26 ♖c1 f5 27 ♖xc6 ♔f7 with a defensible ending according to Keene.

c) 15 b3 (best; White secures his queenside before proceeding on the other flank) 15...♕a5 16 f4 f6 17 ♖ae1! ♖ac8?! (better was 17...♕c5) 18 f5 ♗f7 19 ♘d5, Smejkal-Jansa, Amsterdam 1975, and now Smejkal suggests 19...♖fe8! 20 ♔h1 ♕xa2 21 fxg6 hxg6 22 ♖e3 with an unclear position. However, it seems to us that Black has quite a few problems to solve. Right now his king is under heavy fire; White threatens 23 ♘xf6+ exf6 24 ♕xf6 followed by ♖h3 and mate, so Black's only defence is 22...♗xd5 23 ♕xd5+ ♔g7 and now not 24 ♖g3?!, which is answered with 24...♖c5 25 ♕xb7 ♖e5!, but the simple 24 ♕xb7 when White has somewhat the better chances.

11 ♗g5!?

This is considered best. The alternatives should not worry Black:

a) 11 ♗e3 ♘c5 12 ♕c2 ♗xc3 with a slight plus for Black.

b) 11 ♕g3 ♘c5 12 ♕h4 ♗xc3 13 bxc3 f5 14 ♗g5 (14 exf5 ♗xf5 15 ♗e3!?) 14...♖f7 with an edge for Black, Smit-Parma, Yugoslavia-USSR 1961.

c) 11 ♗d2 ♘c5 12 ♕e3 (Black is a tempo up on the 10 ♕e3 line and is doing fine) 12...♗d7 (equally good is 12...a5) 13 ♖ac1 ♗c6 14 f3 a5 15 b3 e6 16 ♖fd1 ♕e7 17 ♗f1 ♖fd8 18 ♕f2 b6 19 ♗e3 ♗e5 20 ♖c2 ♖ac8 and Black had no worries in Andersson-Tukmakov, Madrid 1973.

11 ... ♘c5
12 ♕e3 ♗d7!?

Two other moves are worth considering:

a) In Z.Almasi-Spangenberg, Buenos Aires 1996, Black tried 12...♘e6?! and stood a bit worse

after 13 ♗h6 ♗xh6 14 ♕xh6. Z.Almasi gives 13 ♗h4! with a clear edge for White as stronger, but Black has a solid position and can defend himself. A possible line 13...♖e8 14 ♖b1 (preparing ♘d5) 14...♗d7 15 ♘d5 ♗c6, intending ...♕d7 followed by ...♗xd5, ...♘d4 and ...e7-e6 or ...e7-e5.

b) A very interesting alternative is 12...♗xc3!?, which was revived by Black in Mohrlok-Kamenets, corr 1992-94. After 13 bxc3

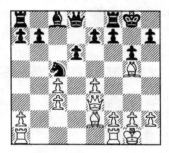

Black played the strong 13...♖e8!, which is an improvement over the previously tried moves: 13...b6? 14 ♗h6 ♖e8 15 f4 ♗b7 16 f5! e6? 17 fxg6 fxg6 18 e5! d5 19 ♖f4 ♘e4 20 cxd5 exd5 21 ♖xe4 dxe4 22 ♗c4+ ♗d5 23 ♕xe4 ♗e6 24 ♕b7 ♖e7 25 ♗xe6+ and White soon won in Smejkal-Jansa, Hradec Kralove 1981, or 13...f6 14 ♗h6 ♖f7 15 f4 f5! 16 exf5 ♗xf5 17 g4 ♗e4 18 f5 ♕b6 19 fxg6 ♖xf1+ 20 ♖xf1 hxg6 21 ♗f3 ♖c8 22 h4 with an initiative for White, Vukcevic-Tennant, corr 1989.

After 13...♖e8! White continued with 14 f4 (also possible is 14 ♖ad1) 14...♕b6 15 ♖ab1 ♕c6 16 e5?! (Mohrlok suggests 16 ♗f3!? and gives 16...♕a6 17 e5 ♗f5 18

♖b2 ♕xc4 19 ♖d1 ♖ac8 with unclear play, but Black is at least equal, so White should perhaps deviate as early as move 14) 16...♕e4 17 ♕f2 ♕c2 18 ♗f3 ♕xf2+ 19 ♖xf2 ♗f5 20 ♖d1 dxe5 21 fxe5 ♖ac8 22 ♗d5, and here Black should have played either 22...b6 23 g4 ♘e6 24 gxf5 ♘xg5 or 22...♘e4 23 ♗xe4 ♗xe4, in both cases with an endgame advantage for Black.

13   ♘d5

A worthless alternative is 13 ♗h6?!, when after 13...♗xh6 14 ♕xh6 ♗c6 15 ♗f3 ♕b6 16 ♕d2 ♕b4 17 ♕e2 e5 White's opening play had been a failure, Pupo-R.Hernandez, Havana 1992.

13   ...   ♖e8
14   ♖ab1   a5
15   ♔h1   ♗c6

The black set-up is very similar to the Classical Maroczy variation, but White's position is unlike any he can achieve in the line mentioned above. Black therefore has to exercise extreme caution in order to stay in the game.

16   f4   ♗xd5
17   exd5   ♘d7!
18   ♕h3!?

White does not fancy allowing ...♕b6, so he tries to prevent this while simultaneously keeping his attack going.

18   ...   ♗f6!
19   ♗g4

19 ♗xf6? exf6 is of course out of the question, as it leaves White with a bad bishop versus a strong knight.

19   ...   ♘c5
20   ♕h4   ♕b6!

A very brave decision. The black queen leaves the defence of the king in order to create some long-term counterplay. However, it was difficult to suggest anything else for Black, e.g. 20...♘e4 21 ♖be1 ♘d2 (21...♘xg5 22 fxg5 ♗g7 23 ♖xf7! ♔xf7 24 ♗e6 ♔f8 25 ♕h7 wins for White) 22 ♖f2 ♘c4 23 ♖f3 followed by ♖h3 with a strong attack for White – analysis by Franzen.

21   f5   ♘e4
22   ♗xf6   ♘xf6

In this situation it would be mistaken to take back with the e-pawn: 22...exf6? 23 fxg6 hxg6 24 ♗e6! fxe6 25 ♕e4 with a clear edge for White according to Franzen.

23   fxg6   hxg6
24   ♗e6!   ♔g7!

The bishop cannot be touched: 24...fxe6? 25 ♕h6 ♔f7 26 ♕h7+ ♔f8 27 dxe6 with mate to follow.

25   ♗xf7!   ♖h8
26   ♕e1   ♖xh2+!

The only move. The bishop was still not to be touched: 26...♔xf7 27 ♕e6+ ♔e8 28 ♖xf6.

27   ♔xh2   ♖h8+
28   ♔g3   ♕d4!
29   ♖d1!

The only way for White to play

for a win. In *Informator* Franzen gives the following analysis of the alternatives:

a) 29 ♕e7?! ♘e4+ 30 ♔f3 (30 ♔f4? ♘g5!; 30 ♔g4? ♘g5! 31 ♖f4 ♖h4 32 ♔xh4 ♕xf4+ 33 g4 ♕h2+ 34 ♔g5 ♕h6 mate) 30...♕d3 31 ♔f4 g5 32 ♔f5 ♘f2 and Black wins.

b) 29 ♖xf6 ♕h4+ 30 ♔f3 ♕xf6+ with an initiative for Black.

c) 29 ♗e6 ♘e4+ 30 ♔f3 (30 ♔f4 ♘g5!; 30 ♕e4 ♕xe4 31 ♖f7+ ♔h6 32 ♖h1+ ♔g5 33 ♖xh8 ♕e5 is better for Black; and 30 ♔g4 ♘f2+ 31 ♔g3 ♘e4+ is a perpetual) 30...♘g5+ 31 ♔e2 ♕xc4+ 32 ♔f2 ♕f4+ with equal chances.

29...♘h5+ 30 ♔f3 ♕f4+ 31 ♔e2 ♘g3+ 32 ♔d3 ♘xf1 33 ♕xf1 ♕xf7 34 ♕xf7+ ♔xf7 35 ♖f1+ ♔e8!

The black king is needed in the defence of the queenside.

36 ♔c3 ♖h2 37 ♖f2 ♖h1 38 ♔b3 ♖h4! 39 ♖c2 b5! 40 a3 bxc4+ 41 ♖xc4 ♖h5 42 ♖d4 ♖e5 43 ♔a4 ♖e2 44 b3 ♖e3 45 ♖d2 ♖c3 46 b4 ½-½

Game 62
Z.Almasi-Tiviakov
Buenos Aires 1996

(1 e4 c5 2 ♘f3 ♘c6 3 d4 cxd4 4 ♘xd4 g6 5 c4 ♘f6 6 ♘c3 d6 7 ♗e2 ♘xd4 8 ♕xd4 ♗g7 9 0-0 0-0 10 ♕d3)

10   ...   ♗e6

10...♗d7 is a fairly new idea. Black will either go for a position very similar to the Classical Maroczy, or attempt to play for ...b7-b5. In both cases the results have been quite good for Black, and

both players should take a serious look at this line. White has tried three ways to develop his bishop in reply:

a) 11 ♗g5 makes little sense. In the game Matthias-Ree, Lippstadt 1992, Black had a clear edge after 11...a6 12 ♖fd1 ♗c6 13 ♖ac1 b5! 14 b4 bxc4 15 ♕xc4 ♗b5! 16 ♘xb5 axb5 17 ♕c2 ♕b6 18 ♗e3?! ♕a6 19 f3 ♖fb8 20 ♖d2 ♕a3, but this was not model play by White.

b) 11 ♗d2 a6 12 ♕e3 ♖b8 13 b4 b5 14 cxb5 axb5 15 f4 ♗c6 16 a4 d5! is also excellent for Black, Fedorowicz-Ree, Cannes 1992, continued 17 exd5 ♘xd5 18 ♘xd5 ♕xd5 19 ♗f3 ♕d6 20 ♗c3 ♗xc3 21 ♕xc3 ♗xf3 22 ♕xf3 bxa4 23 ♖xa4 ♖xb4 24 ♖xb4 ♕xb4 with a useless extra pawn for Black.

c) 11 ♗e3 and now Black has tried four different moves:

c1) 11...♕a5 (this looks strange in combination with ...♗d7-c6, and White can only blame himself for the fact that Black gets a comfortable position in this game) 12 ♗d4 (or 12 a3 immediately) 12...♗c6 13 a3 ♖fc8 14 ♖fe1?! (more logical seems 14 b4 with a space advantage) 14...♕g5!? 15 g3 ♘d7 16 ♗xg7 ♔xg7 17 ♖ad1 a5 18 ♕d4+ ♕f6 19 ♕e3 ♘c5 20 ♗g4 ♖c7 21 f4 e5 22 b4 axb4 23 axb4 exf4 24 gxf4, Smejkal-Sikora Lerch, Czech Team ch 1994, and now 24...♘a4 was best with unclear complications.

c2) 11...a5!? (this move makes a lot of sense, Black would like to enter the Classical Maroczy position after 1 e4 c5 2 ♘f3 ♘c6 3 d4 cxd4 4 ♘xd4 g6 5 c4 ♗g7 6 ♗e3 ♘f6 7 ♘c3 0-0 8 ♗e2 d6 9 0-0 ♗d7 10 ♖c1 ♘xd4 11 ♗xd4 ♗c6

12 ♕d3 a5) 12 b3 (Donaldson gives 12 c5 ♗c6 13 cxd6 exd6 14 ♖ad1 ♖e8 15 f3 d5 as equal) 12...♗c6 13 f3 ♘d7 14 ♖ac1 ♘c5 15 ♕d2 ♗e5 16 ♖fd1 b6 17 ♗f1 ♖a7?! 18 ♖b1 ♖d7 19 ♘e2?! (White should play for b3-b4; hence 19 a3 is correct) 19...e6 20 ♗g5 ♗f6 21 ♗f4 ♗e5 22 ♗g5 ♗f6 23 ♗f4 ♗e5 and a draw was agreed ½-½ Kudrin-Donaldson, Reno 1992.

c3) 11...♗c6 12 b4! (less accurate is 12 ♗d4 or 12 f3) 12...b6 13 ♗d4 a5 14 a3 ♘d7 15 ♗xg7 ♔xg7 16 ♕d4+ ♔g8 17 ♖ad1 axb4 18 axb4 ♖a3 19 f4 ♕c7 20 ♗g4 ♘f6 21 ♗f3 with a small advantage for White, Hellers-Petursson, San Bernardino 1990.

c4) 11...a6 12 a4! (other moves have failed to produce any advantage for White: 12 ♗d4 ♗c6 13 b4 b5 14 cxb5 axb5 15 f3 ♖a3 16 ♕d2 ♕d7 17 ♖fd1 ♖fa8 18 ♖ac1 ♕b7 19 ♖c2 h5 20 ♘b1 ♖3a6 21 ♘c3 ♖a3 22 ♘b1 ♖3a6 23 ♘c3 ½-½ T.Tolnai-Leko, Hungarian ch 1993, or 12 ♖fd1 ♗c6 13 ♕c2 ♕a5 14 ♖ac1 ♖fd8 15 ♕b1 h5!? 16 b4 ♕e5 17 ♗d4 ♕g5 18 ♗f3 b5 with level chances, Schlosser-Leko, Brno 1993) 12...a5 (12...♕a5 is met by 13 b4! ♕xb4 14 a5!, when the queen is in trouble, and 12...♗c6 13 b4 is uncomfortable for Black) 13 c5! dxc5 14 ♗xc5 ♗c6 15 ♕e3! (Black receives some compensation for the pawn after 15 ♕xd8 ♖fxd8 16 ♗xe7 ♖d2) 15...♕d7 16 f3 ♕e6 17 ♘b5 ♗xb5 18 ♗xb5 ♘d7 19 ♗a3 ♘e5 20 ♖ac1 ♖fd8 21 ♔h1, and the pair of bishops secured White a small but clear advantage in Z.Almasi-Khalifman, Wijk aan Zee 1995.

11 ♗d2

Pointless are 11 ♘d5 ♘d7 12 ♖b1 ♘c5 13 ♕c2 f5!? 14 f3 fxe4 15 fxe4 ♖xf1+ 16 ♗xf1 ♗xd5 17 exd5 ♗d4+ 18 ♔h1 ♕f8 19 ♗g5 ♕g7 with level chances, Nagashima-Braga, Sao Paulo 1997, and 11 ♗g5 ♘d7 12 ♕d2 (White aims for a position he could have had with an extra tempo by playing 9 ♗g5 0-0 10 ♕d2) 12...♘c5 13 f3 a5 14 ♔h1 ♖e8 15 ♖ab1 ♕b6 with a good game for Black, Strauss-Donaldson, corr 1981-83.

However, 11 ♗e3 is quite good, when Black has the following options:

a) 11...a6 12 ♗d4 ♘d7 13 ♗xg7 ♔xg7 14 b3 ♕a5 15 f4 ♕c5+ 16 ♔h1 ♘f6 17 ♗f3 ♖ab8 18 ♖ae1 ♖fd8 19 a4 with a small but lasting edge for White in Smejkal-Browne, Milan 1975.

b) 11...♘d7 12 ♗d4 ♗xd4 13 ♕xd4 ♕a5 (Donaldson's suggestion of 13...♕b6!? seems to be much better, e.g. 14 ♕d2 ♖fc8 15 b3 ♘c5 when Black has no problems) 14 b3 a6 15 ♔h1 ♖ac8 16 f4 f6 17 ♖f3 ♔h8 18 ♖e3 g5!? 19 ♘d5 gxf4 20 ♘xf4 ♗f7 21 ♘d5 ♖ce8 22 b4 with a clear edge for

White, Korneev-Permiakov, Omsk 1996.

c) 11...♕a5 12 ♗d4 (this used to be considered quite good for White, but in the light of recent developments, White should probably consider 12 ♖ac1 instead, e.g. 12...♖fc8 13 b3 ♘d7 14 ♕d2 ♘c5 15 f3 a6 16 ♗g5 ♖c7 17 ♖fd1 with a slight edge for White, Ornstein-Popov, Skara 1980; 12 f4 has also been tried, when in Padevsky-Szabo, Kesckemet 1966, Black quickly had the better position: 12...♖fc8 13 b3 ♗g4 14 ♖ac1 b5! 15 ♘d5 bxc4 16 ♘xf6+ ♗xf6 17 ♖xc4 ♖xc4 18 ♕xc4 ♗xe2 19 ♕xe2 ♖c8 20 h3 ♖c3) 12...♖fc8 13 b3 a6 14 f4 b5!? 15 cxb5 axb5 16 ♘xb5.

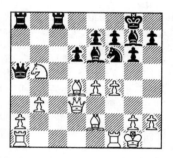

This position was considered clearly better for White on account of Gipslis-Damjanovic, Tallinn 1969, which continued 16...d5? 17 e5 ♗f5 18 ♕e3 ♘g4 19 ♗xg4 ♗xg4 20 a4 ♗d7 21 ♗c3, but Black can easily improve:

c1) 16...♖ab8 17 f5 ♗d7 18 a4 ♕b4 19 fxg6 hxg6 20 e5 ♘h7! 21 ♕e3 dxe5 22 ♗xe5 ♗xe5 23 ♕xe5 ♕xb3 24 ♕xe7 ♖e8 25 ♕xd7 ♖xe2 and White's extra pawn was of no real significance, Hardicsay-Alterman, Hartberg 1991.

c2) 16...♕b4!? 17 ♖fd1 ♖a5 (Black threatens 18...♗d7, intending 19 a4 ♗xb5 20 axb5 ♖xa1 21 ♖xa1 ♘xe4; however, there was no reason for White to go down as he did in this game) 18 ♘c3? ♘xe4! 19 ♕xe4 ♖xc3 20 ♗c4? d5 21 ♕e1 dxc4 22 a3 ♗xd4+ 23 ♖xd4 ♕xb3 and Black won shortly in Messa-Antunes, Reggio Emilia 1986.

11   ...   ♘d7

This is the main line, but Black has other possibilities as well:

a) 11...a6 12 b3 (or 12 ♖ac1 b5! 13 cxb5 axb5 14 ♘xb5 ♖xa2 15 ♗c3 ♖a4 16 b3 ♖a2 17 ♘d4 ♗d7 18 ♘c2 ♕b8 with equal chances, Pablo-Rodriguez Talavera, Menorca 1994) 12...♗d7 (12...♘d7 transposes to the main game and 12...♕b6 to the next line, whereas 12...♖b8!? is an untried suggestion of Fedorowicz's) 13 ♖ac1 b5 14 ♕e3 e6 15 b4 bxc4 16 ♗xc4 ♗b5 17 ♘xb5 axb5, Kestler-Schlick, Germany 1988, and here a draw was agreed after 18 ♗b3, but 18 ♗xb5 seems better, e.g. 18...♖xa2 19 ♖fd1 when White's passed pawn should guarantee him some advantage.

b) 11...♕b6!? 12 b3 ♖fc8 (12...a6) 13 ♖ac1 a6 14 ♔h1 ♕d8?! (14...♘d7!? is to be considered) 15 f4 ♖ab8?! (15...♘d7!?) 16 ♗e3 and White is better, Am.Rodriguez-Hernandez, Holguin 1991.

12   b3   a6

Two other moves have also been tried:

a) 12...f5? is bad for obvious reasons: 13 exf5 ♘c5 14 ♕g3 ♗xf5 15 ♖ad1 is clearly better for White, Savon-Shvedchikov, USSR 1973.

b) 12...♘e5?! gave White an edge in Smyslov-Korchnoi, USSR ch 1961: 13 ♕g3 ♘c6 14 ♔h1 ♘d4 15 ♗d3 ♖c8 16 ♖ad1 a6 17 f4.

c) An interesting new try is 12...♘c5!?, when in Leko-Tiviakov, Groningen 1995, Black quickly obtained equal play: 13 ♕e3 ♗d7! 14 ♖ab1 ♗c6 15 f3 a5.

d) Finally, another Tiviakov idea is 12...a5!? 13 ♖ac1 ♘c5 14 ♕e3 ♗d7!, when Z.Almasi-Tiviakov, Cacak 1996, continued 15 f4?! ♗c6 16 ♗f3 e6 17 ♔h1 ♕e7 18 ♘b5 ½-½. Instead of 15 f4?!, Tiviakov suggests 15 ♖fd1, giving following line: 15...♗c6 16 f3 ♕b6!? 17 ♘d5 ♗xd5 18 exd5 ♘d7 19 ♕xb6 ♘xb6 with equal chances.

13 ♖ac1 ♘e5

Also possible is 13...♕b6, although White is somewhat better after 14 ♔h1 ♕d4 15 ♕c2 ♖fc8 16 f4, Fedorowicz-Zsu.Polgar, Amsterdam 1990, and now best was 16...♘f6 17 f5 ♗d7 18 ♗g5 with a slight pull for White.

Also worth considering is the direct 13...b5. In Luther-Brendel, Groningen 1990, Black equalised easily after 14 cxb5 axb5 15 b4 ♗c4 16 ♕e3 ♗xe2 17 ♕xe2 ♗xc3 18 ♗xc3 ♕b6 19 ♕d2 ♕b7 21 ♕d4 f6 22 ♖c2 ♘c4, but Tiviakov's suggestion 15 ♖c2!? represents a problem for Black.

14 ♕g3

This is probably the way to go, as after 14 ♕e3 Black did not have all that many problems in the game Am.Rodriguez-Antunes, Malaga 1991: 14...♘c6 15 ♘d5 ♘d4 16 ♗d3 ♗d7 17 ♗c3 e5 18 f4 ♗c6 19 f5 ♗xd5 20 exd5 ♕h4! 21 ♖ce1 ♗h6 22 ♕f2 ♕xf2+ 23 ♖xf2 b5.

14 ... ♘c6
15 f4 ♘d4
16 ♗d3 f5!?

Unfortunately for Black, this is the only proper way to continue the game, since for example 16...b5 17 f5 is quite uncomfortable. After 16...f5 Black is left with the usual structural weaknesses: three pawn islands and weak light squares. However, his position is quite active, and White has to play accurately to maintain his advantage.

17 exf5 ♗xf5
18 ♗xf5 ♖xf5
19 ♕d3! ♕d7
20 ♘d5 ♖af8
21 ♗c3

White's advantage is evident. If Black now continues with 21...♘e6, he will have problems on the e-file: 22 ♗xg7 ♔xg7 23 ♕c3+ ♔g8 24 ♖ce1.

21 ... ♘c6
22 ♗xg7 ♔xg7
23 ♕e4 ♖5f7?!

Black wants to centralise and possibly exchange his queen, but it was better to play actively with 23...e5, giving White less time to place his pieces optimally.

24 ♖fe1 ♕f5

25	♕xf5	♖xf5
26	♖cd1	e5

Black must stay active, as 26...♖5f7 27 ♘c7 is rather uncomfortable for him. White is of course still better.

27 ♘c7! ♔g8 28 fxe5 dxe5 29 ♘e6 ♖8f7 30 ♖d2! ♖e7 31 ♘c5 ♔g7 32 ♖d6 ♖f6 33 ♖d5 ♖f8 34 h3 ♖ce8 35 ♖d6 ♖c8

This is inaccurate. It was better to play 35...♘b4 to keep the white knight away from d3.

36 ♘d3 ♖ce8 37 ♖e4 ♖e6 38 ♖d5 ♖6e7 39 ♔h2 ♔f6 40 ♘c5 ♔g7 41 ♖d6 ♖c8 42 ♘d3 ♖ce8 43 b4! a5 44 b5

Instead 44 a3 axb4 45 axb4 would have kept things a little less complicated.

44...♘b4 45 ♘c1 ♖ec7 46 ♖d2 ♖ec7 47 ♖e5+ ♔f6 48 ♖ee2?!

One careless move and the advantage is gone. Correct was 48 ♖e3! a4 49 a3 ♖xc4 50 ♖d6+ ♔g5 51 ♘e2, when White is still clearly better.

48...a4 49 ♖d6+ ♔g5 50 a3 ♖c4 51 ♖e5 ♔h6 52 ♘e2 ♘c2 53 ♘g3 ♖8c5! 54 ♖e7 ♖c7 55 ♘f5+ ♔g5 56 ♖xc7 ♖xc7 57 ♘d4 ♘xd4 58 ♖xd4 ♖c5 ½-½

Game 63
Ivkov-Browne
Wijk aan Zee 1972

(1 e4 c5 2 ♘f3 ♘c6 3 d4 cxd4 4 ♘xd4 g6 5 c4 ♘f6 6 ♘c3 d6 7 ♗e2 ♘xd4 8 ♕xd4 ♗g7 9 0-0 0-0)

10 ♕e3

This move looks quite modest, but do not let your eyes deceive you, it is in fact very ambitious. With the queen on e3 and the bishop on d2, the c3-knight is thoroughly protected, and White will then be ready to start action on the queenside without having to deal with the usual ...b7-b5 tricks. This way of handling the position was quite popular in the late sixties and early seventies. Then it disappeared for a while, but as the ...♘xd4 system has re-emerged as a serious weapon for Black, 10 ♕e3 has once again found a following in top-level chess.

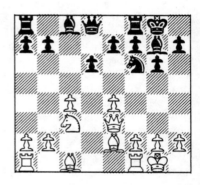

10 ... ♗d7

We feel that this is probably Black's safest option. Of Black's other choices, 10...♗e6 is the most reliable, which often transposes to other lines in the ...♘xd4 system. We shall take a look at this in the next game. 10...a6 has been tried, but always transposes to either 10...♗d7 or 10...♗e6. So let us take a look a 10...♘d7.

(see following diagram)

Although this move is rarely played, it does have some logic to it. Black wants to transpose into a Classical Maroczy, in which the White set-up is somewhat unusual. Black's results in this line have been anything but encouraging to date, but this is mainly due to poor follow-up play. White has tried:

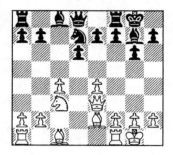

a) 11 b3 ♘c5 (11...♕b6 can be answered with 12 ♘d5, when 12...♕xe3 13 ♘xe7+ ♔h8 14 ♗xe3 ♗xa1 15 ♖xa1 ♖e8 16 ♗d4+ f6 17 ♘xc8 ♖axc8 18 ♗g4 ♖c7 19 ♗xd7 ♖xd7 20 ♗xf6+ ♔g8 21 f3 is better for White, but in Benko-Panno, Palma de Mallorca 1971, Black played more passively: 12...♕d8 13 ♖b1 ♘c5 14 ♗b2 e5 15 f4 ♗h6 16 ♗xe5 dxe5 17 ♕xc5 exf4 18 ♖bd1 and White was clearly better) 12 ♗b2 a5 13 ♖ad1 and here 13...♗d7, intending ...♗c6, would be the obvious way to continue. Nonetheless, two other (quite poor) moves have been played: 13...f5? (nearly always a bad idea) 14 exf5 ♗xf5 15 ♗f3 ♖c8 16 ♖fe1 with a much better game for White, Uhlmann-Matulovic, Skopje 1966, and 13...b6? 14 f4 ♗b7 15 e5 ♕b8 16 exd6 exd6 17 ♗f3 ♖e8 18 ♕d2 ♗xf3 19 ♖xf3 ♕b7 20 f5! and once again White was clearly better in Tatai-Cosulich, Bari 1972.

b) 11 ♗d2 ♘c5 12 ♖ad1 a5 (Geller-Ostojic, Belgrade 1969, saw 12...♗d7 13 ♗e1!? b6 14 f4 ♘a4 15 b3 ♘xc3 16 ♗xc3 ♗xc3 17 ♕xc3 ♕c7 18 ♕g3 with a small edge for White) 13 b3 (13 ♗e1!? is still worth consideration, e.g. 13...a4 14 f4 ♗d7 15 e5) 13...♗d7 14 ♘d5 e6 15 ♘c3 ♗c6 16 ♗e1 ♕e7 17 f3 ♖fe8 (17...♖fd8 is quite possibly stronger, leaving the other rook on the a-file, which will be of use when White eventually breaks with b3-b4) 18 ♗d3 b6 19 ♗c2 ♗e5 20 ♗g3 ♖ad8 21 a3 ♗xg3 22 hxg3 ♕c7 23 b4 ♘d7 24 ♕d4 with an edge for White, Gelfand-Pigusov, Sverdlovsk 1987.

b) 11 ♔h1 (this is probably White's best; he would like to start some kingside action, but does not want the queens to be exchanged) 11...♘c5 12 f4 ♗xc3?! (a dubious idea – White wants to attack and Black gets rid of his dark-squared bishop; the white attack comes to a halt, but the weaknesses in the black position remains, so it was better to play 12...♗d7) 13 bxc3 f5 14 exf5 ♗xf5 15 ♗a3 ♖c8 16 ♗f3 ♕d7 17 ♖ad1 b6 18 ♖fe1 ♖fe8 19 h3 ♕a4 20 ♗xc5 bxc5 21 g4 ♗d7 22 f5 with a strong initiative for White, Smyslov-Furman, USSR 1967.

11 ♗d2

The normal rook moves to b1 and d1 have also been tried:

a) 11 ♖d1 with a further divergence:

a1) 11...a6 12 c5 ♕c7 (Boleslavsky gives 12...♕a5 13 cxd6 exd6 14 ♗d2 ♗c6 with equal chances) 13 cxd6 exd6 14 ♕g3 ♖fe8 with chances for both sides – Salov.

a2) 11...♕a5 12 ♗d2 ♖fc8 13 ♘b5 ♕b6 14 ♕xb6 axb6 15 ♘c3 ♗e6 16 b3 b5! 17 e5 ♘d7 18 ♘xb5 ♘xe5 19 ♗c3 ♗g4 20 ♗xg4 ♘xg4 21 ♗xg7 ♔xg7 22 a4 ♘f6

½-½ Smyslov-Browne, Amsterdam 1971.

a3) 11...♕b6 12 ♕xb6 axb6 13 ♗e3 ♗c6 14 f3 ♘d7 15 ♖dc1 ♘c5 16 ♖c2 ♖fc8 17 ♘d5 ♗xd5 18 cxd5 ♖a3!? 19 ♗f2 ♖ca8 20 ♗c4 b5! 21 ♖ac1 ♖3a4 22 ♗xb5, Illescas-Leko, Leon 1993, and now Black could have maintained equality with 22...♖b4! 23 ♗c4 b5 24 ♗b3 ♘xb3.

b) 11 ♖b1!? and now:

b1) 11...♕b6 was the preferred treatment by Black until quite recently, but Stohl's handling of the game below has cast some clouds over Black's prospects; we therefore suggest that you take a look under 'b2', which seems fine for Black. White has:

b11) Smyslov-Gligoric, Moscow 1971, saw 12 ♕g3 ♖fc8 13 ♗e3 ♕b4 14 ♖fc1 ♗e6 15 ♕h4! (15 b3 ♕xc3! 16 ♖xc3 ♘xe4 is excellent for Black) 15...a6 15 a3 ♕a5 16 b4 ♕d8 17 b4 ♕d8 18 c5 dxc5 19 bxc5 ♕a5! with equal chances.

b12) The actual move order in Stohl-Leko was 12 b3 ♗c6 13 ♕d3, but this allows 12...♕xe3 13 ♗xe3 ♗c6 14 ♘d5 ♗xd5 15 exd5 ♘e4 16 ♖bc1 ♘c3 17 ♖c2 ♘xe2+ 18 ♖xe2 ♗f6 with equality according to Stohl.

b13) 12 ♕d3! ♗c6 13 b3 ♖fc8 14 ♗e3 ♕d8 (14...♕b4 15 ♗d2! ♕b6 16 ♔h1, intending f2-f4, is also good for White) 15 f3 a6, Stohl-Leko, Brno 1993, and here White should have continued 16 a4 a5 17 ♘d5 with a small but clear advantage. Instead he chose 16 ♖fc1?! ♖ab8! 17 ♗a7 ♖a8 18 ♗e3 ♖ab8 19 a4 a5 20 ♘d5 ♘d7 21 ♗g5 ♗xd5 22 exd5 ♗f6 23 ♗e3 ♘c5 with chances for both sides.

b2) 11...a5!? (we feel that this is Black's best shot, though tests are needed before a clear evaluation can be given) 12 a4?! (this is clearly not the critical test of Black's idea; interesting is 12 ♖d1 ♗c6!?, e.g. 13 e5 ♘d7! 14 exd6 exd6 15 ♕g3 [15 ♖xd6 gives Black too much play for the pawn: 15...♖e8 16 ♕d2 ♕e7 17 ♗f1 ♘c5] 15...♘c5! 16 ♕xd6 ♕xd6 17 ♖xd6 ♗xc3 18 bxc3 ♘e4 19 ♖d3 ♖fd8 with equal chances) 16...♗c6 13 f3 ♘d7 14 b3 ♘c5 15 ♗a3?! ♕b6 with a good game for Black, as in Martinez-Bar, Baile Herculaine 1994.

11 ... a6

Several other moves have been tried here:

a) White had an edge after 11...♕b6 in Keres-Lengyel, Tallinn 1975: 12 ♖ab1 ♕xe3 13 ♗xe3 ♖fc8 14 ♖fc1 a6?! (the wrong plan; better was the normal 14...♗c6 15 f3 ♘d7, although White is still slightly better) 15 f3 ♗e6 16 b3 ♔f8 17 a4 a5 18 ♘d5.

b) Once again, Black can consider 11...a5!?, when after 12 ♖fd1 ♗c6, Barcza-Damjanovic, Vrsac 1967, continued 13 ♘d5 ♘d7 14

♗c3 ♗xc3 15 ♘xc3 ♕b6 16 ♕xb6 ♘xb6 17 b3 ♖fc8 with equal chances.

c) 11...♗c6 has also been played on occasion. Kirov-T.Georgadze, Polanica Zdroj 1976, saw 12 ♖ac1 (better is 12 b4, whereas 12 ♖fd1 a5 transposes to the game Barcza-Damjanovic above) 12...e6 (for some reason Georgadze does not bother to play ...a7-a5, which would also be quite good in this position) 13 ♖fd1 ♕e7 14 b4 b6 15 f3 ♖ad8 16 ♗f1 ♖fe8 17 ♗e1 h6 18 a3 ½-½.

12   ♖fd1

The alternatives are:

a) 12 ♘d5?! ♘xd5 13 cxd5 ♖c8 14 ♕b3?! (14 ♗d3 is equal) 14...b5! with a clear plus for Black, Lombardy-Browne, USA 1972.

b) 12 b3 b5?! (12...♗c6!?) 13 cxb5 axb5 14 a4! bxa4 15 bxa4 ♘g4 16 ♕g3 ♘e5 17 ♖fc1 ♕a5 18 ♕g5! With a clear plus for White, Illescas-Alvarez, Oviedo 1991.

c) 12 a4 a5! 13 b3 ♗c6 14 ♖ae1 ♘d7 15 ♗d1 ♘c5 16 ♗c2 b6 17 f4 e6 18 ♘e2 f5 with equality, Ivkov-Adorjan, Amsterdam 1971.

12   ...   ♕b8!

Most common, and probably best, but Black also did fine with 12...♖b8 in Peshina-Rashkovsky, Barnaul 1984: 13 a4?! ♘g4! 14 ♗xg4 ♗xg4 15 ♖e1 ♗e6 16 b3 b5 17 axb5 axb5 18 cxb5 ♖b7 19 ♕d3 ♕b8 with an edge for Black; White will lose both b-pawns.

Another possibility is 12...♗c6, which was tried out in Salov-Dzindzichashvili, New York 1996. After 13 b4 b6 14 ♖ab1 ♘d6 15 h4!? b5 16 a3 bxc4 17 ♗xc4 ♘e5 18 ♗b3 ♗b7, White should have continued with 19 h5 with a small

advantage.

13   a4

If Black achieves ...b7-b5, he equalises easily, e.g. 13 ♖ac1 b5 14 b3 bxc4 15 ♗xc4 ♘g4 16 ♕g3 ♗d4 17 ♖f1 ♕a7 18 ♘e2 ♗e5 19 ♗f4 ♗g7 20 h3 ♘f6 21 ♕d3 ♗b5, Sakharov-Kapengut, USSR 1967.

13   ...   a5
14   ♖ac1

Other moves do not give Black anything to worry about either:

a) 14 b3 ♗c6 15 ♗e1 ♘d7 16 ♖ab1 ♘c5 17 ♘d5 ♖e8 18 f3 b6 with equal chances, Boleslavsky-Averbakh, Moscow 1966.

b) 14 h3 ♗c6 15 ♘d5 ♖e8 16 ♗c3 ♘d7 17 ♗xg7 ♔xg7 18 b3 e5 is also equal, Uhlmann-Kapengut, East Germany-RSFSR 1969.

c) 14 ♖a3 ♗c6 15 ♘d5 ♖e8 16 ♗c3 ♘d7 17 ♗xg7 ♔xg7 18 ♕g5 h6 19 ♕h4 ♘f6 20 ♖h3 ♘g8 21 ♖dd3 ♕d8! 22 e5?! dxe5 23 ♘f6 exf6 24 ♖xd8 ♖exd8 with a good game for Black, Nicevsky-Kapengut, Vilnius 1969.

14	...	♗c6
15	b3	♘d7
16	♘d5	♗xd5
17	exd5	♘c5
18	♖e1	

Not 18 ♕xe7? ♖e8.

18	...	♕c7
19	h4	♖ae8!?
20	♗d1	♕b6
21	♗c2	e5
22	h5	e4!

Black must stay active. The rest of the game went as follows:

23 ♖b1 ♕c7 24 hxg6 hxg6 25 b4

On 25 ♗xa5 Ivkov gives following line: 25...♕xa5 26 b4 ♕a6 27 bxc5 ♕xc4.

25...axb4 26 ♗xb4 ♘a6 27 ♗a3 ♕c4 28 ♕b3 ♕xb3 29 ♖xb3 ♖c8

30 ♗e4 ♘c5 31 ♗xc5 ♖xc5 32 ♖xb7 ♖c4 33 a5 ♖b4 34 ♗c2 ♖xa5 ½-½

Game 64
Sax-Petursson
Valby 1994

(1 e4 c5 2 ♘f3 ♘c6 3 d4 cxd4 4 ♘xd4 g6 5 c4 ♘f6 6 ♘c3 d6 7 ♗e2 ♘xd4 8 ♕xd4 ♗g7 9 0-0 0-0 10 ♕e3)

10   ...   ♗e6

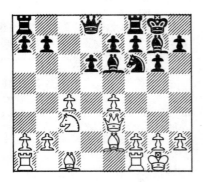

This is Black's most popular response to 10 ♕e3. After 11 ♗d2 ♕b6, play usually transposes to lines which arise after 9 ♗g5 0-0 10 ♕e3 ♗e6 11 0-0 ♕b6. Under this main game, we will take a look at those lines which do not transpose.

11   ♖b1

This is currently White's most common choice. Other possibilities are:

a) 11 ♖d1 ♕c7!? (also possible is 11...♕b6 12 ♕xb6 axb6 13 ♗e3 ♖fc8 14 b3 b5 15 ♘xb5 ♘xe4 with equal chances, Panno-Ree, Las Palmas 1973) 12 ♘b5 ♕c6 13 ♘xa7 ♕xe4 14 ♘b5 ♖fc8 15 b3 d5

16 ♘d4 ♗d7 with equality, Uhlmann-Hecht, Raach 1969.

b) 11 ♗d2 with a new fork:

b1) 11...♘g4?! 12 ♕g3 ♘e5 13 b3 ♘c6 14 h4 ♖c8 15 f4 ♘d4 16 f5! ♘xe2+ 17 ♘xe2 ♗xa1 18 ♖xa1 ♗d7 19 h5 ♕b6+ 20 ♗e3 ♕a5 21 hxg6 fxg6 22 fxg6 g6 23 c5 with a clear plus for White, Khenkin-Neverov, Moscow 1989. Black invested a little too much time in winning the exchange.

b2) 11...♘d7 12 b3 (White also obtained a small edge in Smyslov-Sanguinetti, Mar del Plata 1966, after 12 f4 ♕b6 13 ♕xb6 ♘xb6 14 b3 ♗d7 15 ♖ac1 ♗c6 16 ♘d5) 12...♕b6 (12...a6 transposes to 'b3' below) 13 ♖ac1 ♗d4 14 ♕g3 ♘c5 15 ♕h4 ♗f6 16 ♕f4 a5 17 ♘d5 ♗xd5 18 exd5 ♗e5 19 ♕h6 ♗f6 20 ♕f4 ♗e5 21 ♗e3 e6?! 22 dxe6 fxe6 23 g3! with a clear edge for White, Wojtkiewicz-Gdanski, Warsaw 1993.

b3) 11...a6 12 b3 ♘d7 13 f4 ♕b6 14 ♕xb6 ♘xb6 15 ♖ac1 ♗d4+ 16 ♔h1 ♗d7 17 ♗f3 ♗c6 18 ♖cd1 ♘d7 19 ♗e1 with equal chances, Uhlmann-Browne, Amsterdam 1971.

b4) 11...♕b6!? 12 ♕xb6 (12 b3 ♕xe3 13 ♗xe3 ♖fc8 is fine for Black, while the game Baumbach-Mohring, East Germany 1975, saw 12 ♖ad1 ♕xb2!? 13 ♖b1 ♕a3 14 ♖xb7 ♖fb8 15 ♖fb1 ♖xb7 16 ♖xb7, and now 16...♘d7 was best with chances for both sides) 12...axb6 13 f4 ♖fc8 14 b3 b5! 15 cxb5 ♘xe4!? (possibly better was 15...♘d7) 16 ♘xe4 ♗d4+ 17 ♔h1 ♗xa1 18 ♖xa1, as in Matulovic-Jansa, Vrsac 1979, and here, according to Jansa, Black should have continued 18...♗xb3 19 ♘c3 d5 20 ♗f3 ♗xa2!?

11 ... ♕b6

This is probably the best, but other moves are of interest too:

a) 11...a6 12 a4 (12 ♗d2!? b5? 13 cxb5 axb5 14 ♗xb5 ♗xa2 15 ♘xa2 ♖xa2 16 ♗c4 ♖a8 17 b4 was clearly better for White in Korchnoi-Benko, Curacao ct 1962, but 12...b5? was a mistake, which should be replaced by 12...♘d7) 12...♖c8 13 b3 ♘d7 14 ♘d5 ♖e8 15 ♘f4 ♘f8 16 ♘xe6 ♘xe6 17 ♗g4 ♖c6 18 ♗xe6 fxe6 19 ♕h3 ♕c8 20 ♗e3 e5 21 ♕xc8 ♖exc8 with a drawn ending, Vehi-Antunes, Platja d'Aro 1994.

b) 11...♕a5 (this looks a little odd, as White nearly always develops his bishop to d2, which will force the black queen to move somewhere else, but Black equalises easily enough in this game) 12 ♗d2 ♖fc8 13 ♘d5 ♕d8 14 ♗c3 b5! 15 ♗xf6 ♗xf6 16 ♘xf6+ exf6 17 cxb5 ♗xa2 18 ♖bc1 ♕b6 19 ♕xb6 axb6 20 ♖c6 ♖ab8 21 ♖a1 ♗e6 with equality, Pierrot-Sorokin, Buenos Aires 1994.

c) 11...♘d7 12 ♘d5 (or 12 ♗d2 ♕b6 13 ♘d5 ♗xd5 14 exd5 ♗d4 15 ♕g3 a5 16 b3 ♘c5 17 ♕g4 ♗g7 18 ♔h1 f5 19 ♕f3 ½-½ Wojtkiewicz-Gdanski, Budapest zt 1993) 12...♗xd5 13 exd5 a5 14 b3 (14 ♕xb6 ♘xb6 15 ♗e3 is possibly stronger; endings with a weak pawn on a5 and the queens exchanged usually favour White) 14...♕c7 15 ♗b2 ♗f6 16 ♖fe1 ♖fe8 17 ♗f1 ♕c5 18 ♕h3 ♘e5 19 a4 h5 20 ♕g3 ♘d7 21 h3 ♗xb2 22 ♖xb2 ♕d4 23 ♖be2 ♕f6 24 ♖e3 ♘c5 with equality, Korneev-Sorokin, Russian ch 1996.

12 ♕d3

After this move Black has to be careful not to be pushed off the board. In Eingorn-Malisauskas, Debrecen 1992, White allowed the queen exchange, and soon after most of the remaining pieces departed: 12 b3 ♖fc8 13 a4 (White can still transpose back to our main game with 13 ♕d3) 13...♕xe3 14 ♗xe3 ♘d7 15 ♘d5 ♗xd5 16 cxd5 ♖c2 17 ♗b5 ♘f6 18 ♖fc1 ♖xc1+ 19 ♖xc1 ♘xe4 20 ♖c7 a6 21 ♖xe7 axb5 22 ♖xe4 bxa4 23 ♖xa4 ♖xa4 24 bxa4 f5 and soon drawn.

12 ... ♖fc8
13 b3 a6

13...♕d8?! is both unnecessary and too passive. After 14 ♗g5 a6 15 a4 ♘d7 16 ♘d5 ♗xd5 17 exd5 ♗f6 18 h4 ♕f8 19 ♕e3 a5 20 ♗g4 White has a clear advantage, M.Müller-Herbrechtsmeier, German Bundesliga 1993/94.

14 ♗e3 ♕a5

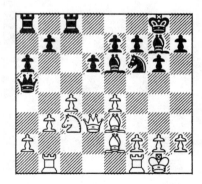

15 ♗d2

Or 15 ♗d4 b5! 16 cxb5 axb5 17 ♕xb5 ♕xb5 18 ♗xb5 ♘xe4 19 ♗xg7 ♘xc3 20 ♗xc3 ♖xc3, when Black cannot be worse.

15 ... ♕b6

Once again ...♕d8 is uncalled for. In Korneev-Antunes, Benasque

1996, White soon dominated due to his massive space advantage: 15...♕d8 16 a4 ♘d7 17 ♘d5 ♘c5 18 ♕e3 a5 19 f4 ♗d7 20 ♗c3 ♗xc3 21 ♘xc3, when Black is without counterplay and can only wait miserably for White to finish him off.

16	♔h1	♗d7
17	f4	♗c6
18	♖be1	♘d7
19	♗g4	e6
20	♗f3	½-½

Game 65
Ivanchuk-Anand
Buenos Aires 1994

(1 e4 c5 2 ♘f3 ♘c6 3 d4 cxd4 4 ♘xd4 g6 5 c4 ♘f6 6 ♘c3 d6 7 ♗e2 ♘xd4 8 ♕xd4 ♗g7)

9   ♗e3

This move used to be considered quite harmless, and was (and, by the way, still is!) a perfect remedy if White wanted to bore his opponent or get a quick draw. But in recent years, players like Ivanchuk have come up with new ideas for White, and Black therefore has to be alert, so as not to end up in a passive, joyless position.

9	...	0-0
10	♕d2	

Also possible is 10 ♕d3, when 10...♗e6 11 0-0 transposes to 9 0-0 0-0 10 ♕d3 ♗e6 11 ♗e3 (see the notes to Game 62).

10	...	♗e6

This is almost exclusively played, but a few other moves have been tried. Most of these merely transpose, but 10...a6!? is interesting. Of course, with 11 ♖c1 or 11 f3 White can aim to transpose into the main lines, but in Yudasin-Antunes, Seville 1993, White explored another path: 11 0-0 ♕a5!? (11...♗e6 is the main line) 12 a3!? (12 ♘d5 ♕xd2 13 ♘xe7+ ♔h8 14 ♗d2 ♘xe4 is okay for Black and 12 f3 is another way to transpose to the main line) 12...♗e6 13 b4 ♕d8! 14 ♖ab1 (on 14 ♖ac1, Yudasin gives 14...♖c8 15 c5 dxc5 16 ♕xd8 ♖fxd8 17 bxc5 ♘g4 18 ♗xg4 ♗xg4 19 ♘d5 ♔f8 with equal chances) 14...b5?! 15 cxb5 axb5 16 ♗xb5 ♖xa3 17 ♗d4 ♕a8 18 ♗d3! ♖c8 19 ♖fc1 with a small but clear advantage for White. But according to Yudasin, Black has better. After 14...♖c8! he gives the following analysis: 15 c5 dxc5 16 ♕xd8 ♖fxd8 17 bxc5 (17 ♗xc5? ♘d7!) 17...b5! 18 cxb6!? (18 ♖fc1 or 18 a4 are both equal) 18...♖xc3 19 b7 ♘d7 20 ♗xa6 ♖xa3 (20...♗e5!) 21 ♗b5 ♘b8 22 ♖fd1 ♖f8 23 ♗c5 with unclear play.

11	0-0

For 11 f3, see Game 67. 11 ♖c1 is also sometimes played, and can be quite tricky for Black if he is not careful. Best is 11...a6 and then 12 f3 (12 0-0 can be found in the next main game) and now:

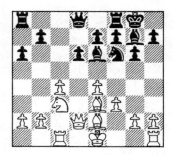

a) This may look like a normal position in the 9 ♗e3 system, but if Black continues with the standard 12...♕a5?!, he soon finds himself in difficulty after 13 ♘d5! Dvoiris-Tiviakov, Podolsk 1993, continued 13...♕xd2+ (unlike in the 7 f3 system, 13...♕xa2 does not work, as White has a bishop on e2 and therefore the pin themes on the e-file do not exist; Ibragimov-Khasin, Gorky 1989, ended quickly after 14 ♘xe7+ ♔h8 15 0-0 ♕b3 16 ♗d1 ♕a2 17 ♗d4 ♖fe8 18 ♘d5 ♗xd5 19 exd5 ♘h5 20 ♗xg7+ ♘xg7 21 ♕c3 and Black resigned, since his queen is lost after 22 ♗b3) 14 ♔xd2 ♗xd5 15 cxd5 ♖fc8 16 b4 (also interesting is 16 g4, when after 16...e6 17 g5 ♘h5!?, White decided to sacrifice a pawn with 18 dxe6 fxe6 19 f4 ♗xb2 20 ♖xc8+ ♖xc8 21 ♖b1 ♗c3+ 22 ♔d3 b5 23 ♖c1 b4 24 f5 d5 25 f6, when Black has plenty of problems, primarily due to his poor minor pieces and White's passed pawn on f6, Adams-Hodgson, Hastings 1991/92) 16...♘d7 17 a4 ♔f8 18 a5 ♗b2 19 ♖c2 ♖xc2+ 20 ♔xc2 ♗f6 21 ♔b3 ♖c8 22 ♖c1 ♖xc1 23 ♗xc1 ♗d4 24 f4 h5 25 h3 ♔e8 26 ♗d2 ♔d8 27 ♔c4 ♗b2 28 ♗e3, and with the bishop pair and a huge space ad-

vantage, White was much better in the endgame, which he went on to win in beautiful style.

b) Instead of 12...♕a5?!, Black has had some success with 12...♖c8 13 b3 b5!? After 14 cxb5 axb5 15 ♘xb5 ♖xc1+ 16 ♕xc1 ♕a5+ 17 ♕d2 ♖a8 an interesting position has arisen.

b1) 18 ♕xa5 does not worry Black: 18...♖xa5 19 ♘c3 ♘d7 20 ♘a4 ♘c5 21 ♗d2 ♖a8! 22 ♗d1 ♘xa4 23 bxa4 ♗xa2 24 a5 ♗d4 25 ♗e2 ♖b8 26 ♗d3 ♖b2 27 ♖f1 ♗b3 ½-½ Shaked-Burtman, Las Vegas 1993.

b2) Of interest is 18 ♘c3, but after 18...♘g4! 19 ♗xd4 ♗xd4 20 ♕xd4 ♖c8 21 ♔d2 (this position is almost identical to the game Frolov-Tangborn, which can be found in the lines with 9 ♗g5 [Game 70] the only difference being the position of the black h-pawn, which in that game was on h6) Black now has 21...♕g5+! (in the above-mentioned game Black played 21...♖xc3? and lost) 22 ♔c2 ♘e3+ 23 ♔b2 ♕xg2 24 ♖e1 (otherwise Black will play 24...♖xc3 and 25...♕xe2) 24...♕f2 25 ♕d2 d5 with a good game for Black.

b3) Somewhat more problematic

seems 18 a3, transposing to Game 70, with the slight difference that the white bishop is on g5 instead of e3.

11 ... ♕a5

12 ♖ab1!?

The alternatives are 12 ♖ac1, which can be found in the next main game, and 12 ♖fc1 and 12 f3, which we shall cover now:

a) 12 ♖fc1!? was first tried in Psakhis-Alterman, Israel 1996. Now 12...♖fc8 13 b3 a6 (13...b5!?) 14 a4 is slightly better for White, and 14 ♖ab1 transposes to this main game, but Alterman wanted to play differently: 12...♘xe4!? (an interesting approach) 13 ♘xe4 ♕xd2 14 ♘xd2 ♗xb2 15 ♗f3. Here Black went wrong with 15...♗xc1?, and after 16 ♖xc1 ♖ac8 17 ♗xb7 ♖c7 18 ♗f3 ♖b8 19 ♗d1! White was clearly better. Instead of 15...♗xc1?, Psakhis suggests 15...♖fb8 16 ♘b3 ♗xa1 17 ♘xa1 ♗d7 18 c5 with chances for both sides.

b) 12 f3 is possible (this position usually arises after 11 f3 ♕a5 12 0-0, but it does not make a whole lot of difference) and here Black has two options, both of which lead to equality:

b1) 12...a6 13 ♖fd1 ♖fc8 14 ♘d5 ♕xd2 15 ♖xd2 ♘xd5 16 exd5 ♗d7 17 a4 e6 18 a5 exd5 19 cxd5 ♗e5 20 f4 ♗f6 with equal chances in the endgame, Blanco-Antunes, Havana 1994.

b2) 12...♖fc8 13 ♖fc1 (or 13 b3 a6 14 ♖fc1 b5 15 cxb5 axb5 16 ♗d4 b4 17 ♘a4 ♘d7 18 ♗xg7 ♔xg7 ½-½ Witke-Detter, Graz 1987) and now:

b21) 13...♗xc4?! 14 ♘d5 ♕xd2 15 ♘xe7+! ♔f8 16 ♗xd2 ♔xe7 17 ♗xc4 ♘d7 18 ♗g5+ with an edge for White in the endgame.

b22) 13...♘d7 14 ♖ab1 ♗xc4 15 ♘d5 ♕xd2 16 ♘xe7+ ♔f8 17 ♗xd2 ♗d4+ (with 13...♘d7 and 14 ♖ab1 inserted, Black plays more actively, as the knight is away from the a1-h8 diagonal; White achieved a very small edge in the game Am.Rodriguez-Minzer, 1997, after the less accurate 17...♔xe7 18 ♗xc4 ♖c6 [18...♗d4+!] 19 ♗b3 ♖ac8 20 ♖xc6 ♖xc6 21 ♖c1 ♖xc1+ 22 ♗xc1) 18 ♔h1 ♔xe7 19 ♗xc4 ♘b6 20 ♗b3 ♖xc1+ 21 ♖xc1 ♖c8 22 ♖xc8 ♘xc8 with an equal ending, Aseev-Vokarev, Russian ch 1996.

b23) 13...a6 14 ♖ab1 ♔f8!? (14...♕d8 transposes to the note after Black's 13th move in the main game) 15 b4 ♕d8 16 c5 ♕d7 17 cxd6 ♕xd6 18 ♕xd6 exd6 ½-½ Am.Rodriguez-Antunes, Mondariz 1994. This looks quite simple for Black, but in Kramnik-Anand, Amsterdam 1996, Black instead tried 14...♖ab8?!, when after 15 b4 ♕d8 16 c5 a5! 17 a3 axb4 18 axb4 ♖a8 19 ♗f1 h5 20 ♕e1 ♘e8 21 ♔h1 ♔f8 White could have maintained a slight edge with 22 ♗g1, but chose instead 22 ♘d5, after which Black equalised with 22...♗xd5 23 exd5 dxc5 24 bxc5 ♕xd5 25 ♖d1 ♕e5 26 ♖d1 ♖xc5! and much later (on move 108!) went on to win the game.

12 ... ♖fc8

On 12...♘g4, Ivanchuk gives the following analysis: 13 ♘d5 (13 ♗d4 ♗xd4 14 ♕xd4 ♕e5 15 ♕xe5 ♘xe5 with equality or 13 b4 ♗xc3! 14 ♕xc3 ♕e5 15 ♕xe5 ♘xe5 with an unclear position) 13...♕xd2 14 ♗xd2 ♗xd5 15 cxd5 ♘f6 16 f3 ♖fc8 17 ♖fc1 with a slight advantage for White.

13 b3

13 b4 looks quite logical, but Black gets a good game after 13...♕d8 14 c5 a5 15 a3 axb4 16 axb4 ♖a3 17 ♘b5 ♖a2 18 ♕d3 d5!, as in Hanel-Stefansson, Vienna 1991.

13 ... ♘d7

Several other moves have also been tried in this position:

a) 13...b5? 14 b4 ♕c7 15 e5! (15 ♘xb5?! ♕b7 is slightly better for Black, but 15 c5 a6 16 ♖fc1 dxc5 17 ♗xc5 ♘d7 18 ♘d5 ♗xd5 19 exd5 ♘xc5 20 bxc5 favours White, Arsovic-Kovacevic, Yugoslavia 1997) 15...dxe5 16 ♘xb5 ♕b7 17 ♖fc1 ♖d8 18 ♕e1 ♘g4 19 ♗c5 e4 20 ♗xg4 ♗xg4 21 ♘c3 ♗f5 22 ♘d5 ♖d7 23 ♗e3 with advantage to White, Ivanchuk-Kovacevic, Belgrade 1997.

b) 13...♘g4 14 ♘d5!? (Ivanchuk's 14 ♗d4 ♗xd4 15 ♕xd4 did not give White anything in the game Korneev-Tiviakov, Linares 1998: 15...♕c5 16 ♕d3 ♘f6 17 ♔h1 ♗d7 18 f4 a5 19 a4?! [19 ♗f3 or 19 ♖be1 were better] 19...♗c6 20 ♘d5 ♖e8 21 ♖bd1 ♖ad8 with approximately level chances) 14...♕xd2 15 ♗xd2 ♔f8 16 ♗g5! (16 ♗xg4 ♗xg4 17 ♗g5 f6 is equal) 16...♘f6! (16...f6?! is too passive: 17 ♗d2 ♘e5 18 f4 ♘c6 19 f5 ♗f7 20 g4 ♘e5 21 ♖bc1 ♗xd5 22 exd5 ♔f7 23 ♗e3 b6 24 h4, and White holds the advantage due to his space advantage and bishop pair, Gelfand-Andersson, Polanica Zdroj 1997) 17 ♘xf6 ♗xf6 18 ♗xf6 exf6 19 ♖bd1 ♔e7 20 f4 ♖c5 21 ♖d4 a5 22 ♖fd1 ♖a6 with a drawn endgame, Tischbierek-Van der Weide, Berlin 1997.

c) 13...a6 (this is probably Black's best choice, as White has yet to show a clear path to an advantage) 14 ♖fc1 and here we have another divergence:

c1) 14...b5?! 15 b4! ♕d8 16 cxb5 axb5 17 ♗xb5 with a clear plus for White – Ivanchuk.

c2) 14...♕b4 15 a3!? (the natural 15 f3 is good for Black: 15...b5! 16 cxb5 axb5 17 a4 ♖xc3! 18 ♖xc3 ♘d5 19 ♖d3 ♘c3 20 ♖c1 ♘xe2+ 21 ♕xe2 bxa4 22 bxa4 ♗c4 23 ♕d2 ♕xa4 24 ♕d1 ♗b2 25 ♕xa4 ♖xa4 26 ♖b1 ♗xd3 27 ♖xb2 with a extra pawn for Black in the ending, Lopez-Nanu, Szeged 1998)

15...♕a5 (not 15...♕xa3?? 16 ♖a1 ♕b4 17 ♖a4 ♕xb3 18 ♗d1! and wins) 16 b4 ♕xa3? (Black is playing to win, but gets too optimistic in the process; correct was 16...♕d8 17 c5 dxc5 18 ♕xd8+ ♖xd8 19 ♗xc5 ♖d7 with a slight edge for White) 17 ♖a1 ♕xb4 18 ♖a4 ♘xe4 19 ♖xb4 ♘xd2 20 ♗xd2 ♖c7 21 ♘a4! ♗d4 22 ♗f3 ♖b8 23 c5 ♗xc5 24 dxc5 dxc5 25 ♖bb1 and White was winning in Al.David-Antunes, Yerevan ol 1996.

c3) 14...♕d8 15 f3 h5!? 16 ♗f1 ♔h7 17 ♘e2 ♕f8 18 ♘d4 ♗d7 19 ♗g5 ♖c5 20 ♖e1 a5 21 a3 ♖ac8 22 b4 axb4 23 axb4 ♖5c7 24 f4?! e5! 25 ♘f3 ♗c6 with an initiative for Black, as played in M.Kaminski-Kveinys, Krynica 1997.

c4) 14...♖ab8!? 15 f3 ♔f8 16 ♗f1 ♕b4! (with the bishop now on f1, it is not quite as easy to take advantage of this move, e.g. 17 a3?! ♕xa3 18 ♖a1 ♕b4 19 ♖a4 ♕xb3 20 ♖b1 ♘xe4 21 ♖xb3 ♘xd2 22 ♗xd2 b5 23 ♖xa6 bxc4 24 ♖xb8 ♗d4+ 25 ♔h1 ♖xb8 and Black is better – Donaldson) 17 ♖c2 b5! 18 a3 ♕xa3 19 ♘xb5 axb5 20 ♖a2 ♕xa2 21 ♕xa2 bxc4 22 bxc4, as in De Firmian-Donaldson, Philadelphia 1997, and now 22...♖xb1 23 ♕xb1 ♗xc4 24 ♗xc4 ♖xc4 is equal.

14   ♖fc1   ♕d8?!

Ivanchuk prefers 14...a6 15 f4 ♖ab8 for Black, but in Oll-Alterman, Krynica 1997, Black tried something else: 14...♕b4 15 ♖c2 a6 16 ♖bc1 ♖ab8 17 f3 ♕a5 18 ♘d5 ♕xd2 19 ♗xd2 ♔f8 20 ♖dc2 f5 21 exf5 ♗xf5 22 ♖d2 with a comfortable edge for White in the endgame.

15   ♘d5   ♘c5
16   ♗f3   a5
17   h4!

With the queenside and the centre under control, Ivanchuk feels it is time for a kingside attack. If now 17...h5, then 18 ♗g5 ♗xd5 19 exd5 ♗f6 20 ♖e1 with a clear advantage for White.

17   ...   ♗xd5
18   exd5   ♕d7
19   ♕e2!?   ♖e8

Also possible is 19...h5, when Ivanchuk intended to break up the kingside with 20 g4 hxg4 21 ♗xg4 f5 22 ♗h3! followed by h4-h5.

20   h5   ♕f5
21   ♖d1   ♗e5?!

Now Black starts to go wrong. Correct was 21...gxh5 22 ♗xh5 ♘e4 23 ♕d3 ♕h5 24 ♕e4 ♗e5 with the better chances for White according to Ivanchuk.

22   g4   ♕c8
23   ♔g2   ♗g7

Now White's attack starts rolling.

24 ♖h1 ♘d7 25 hxg6 hxg6 26 ♖h4 a4 27 ♖bh1 axb3 28 axb3 ♖a1?

The last chance was 28...b5! 29 cxb5 ♕c3.

29 ♖1h3 ♕a8 30 ♖h7 ♕a2?!

The only way to continue the game was 30...♗e5 31 ♗f4 ♗g7!

31 ♖xg7+ ♔xg7 32 ♗d4+ f6 33 ♕e3 ♘f8 34 ♗e4! ♔f7 35 ♖h8! 1-0

Game 66
Shirov-Alterman
Santiago 1990

(1 e4 c5 2 ♘f3 ♘c6 3 d4 cxd4 4 ♘xd4 g6 5 c4 ♘f6 6 ♘c3 d6 7 ♗e2 ♘xd4 8 ♕xd4 ♗g7 9 ♗e3 0-0 10 ♕d2 ♗e6 11 0-0 ♕a5)

12 ♖ac1

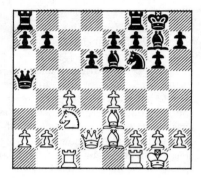

12 ... ♖fc8!?

This used to be considered a mistake, but now it seems that Black actually is doing okay here, particularly considering that Anand used this move to win against Ivanchuk. Conventional wisdom was that Black should not play ...♖fc8 while White can still play f2-f4-f5.

For the more cautious player, we can recommend 12...a6!?, which objectively speaking is probably best, when White has tried:

a) 13 a3!? ♖fc8?! (this leaves Black in a passive position, so we recommend 13...♘d7!, stopping White's b2-b4 ideas, when with ...♖fc8 and ...♘e5 to come, Black can apply pressure on the white queenside, which White was kind enough to weaken with 13 a3) 14 b4 ♕d8 (14...♕xa3 is a little too adventurous after 14 ♖a1 ♕xb4 15 ♖a4 ♕b3 16 ♗d1! with a clear edge for White) 15 c5 dxc5 16 ♕xd8+ ♖xd8 17 ♗xc5 ♔f8 18 f4 ♘d7 19 ♗e3 ♖ac8 20 e5 ♗c4 21 ♗xc4 ♖xc4 22 ♘a4 with a clear advantage for White, Diaz Joaquin-Andres, Camaguey 1987.

b) 13 f4 b5! 14 cxb5 axb5 15 b4? (this allows Black to get on top; equal was 15 f5 b4 16 fxe6 bxc3 17 exf7+ ♔h8 18 ♕xc3 ♕xc3 19 bxc3 ♘xe4 20 ♗d4) 15...♕xb4 16 ♖b1 ♕a3 17 ♖xb5 ♖fc8 18 ♗d4 ♖xc3 19 ♕xc3 ♘xe4 20 ♖b8+ ♖xb8 21 ♕xa3 ♗xd4+ 22 ♔h1 ♘f2+ 23 ♖xf2 ♗xf2 with a clear advantage for Black, Cardoso-Adorjan, Lanzarote 1975.

c) 13 f3 ♖fc8 14 ♘d5?! (better is 14 b3, transposing to a position considered in note 'b' to White's 14th move in the next game) 14...♕xd2 15 ♗xd2 ♘xd5 16 cxd5 (16 exd5 ♗f5 17 b3 ♗d4+ 18 ♔h1 ♗b2 is also comfortable for Black) 16...♗d7 17 b3 ♗d4+ 18 ♔h1 ♗b2 (although it does not seem as if White has done anything drastically wrong, he is already in deep trouble) 19 ♖c4 ♗b5 20 ♖xc8+ ♖xc8 21 ♗xb5 axb5 22 a4 ♖c2 23 ♗h6 b4 24 ♗e3 ♖e2 25 ♗b6 ♗c3 26 ♔g1 ♖b2 27 ♖d1 f5 and Black went on to win, Fishbein-Alterman, Beersheva 1991.

13 b3 a6

14 f4

This used to be considered the refutation of Black's move order. It is certainly quite logical to take advantage of Black's slow, queen-side-oriented play. Other moves do not pose Black any problems. A few examples are:

a) 14 a4 ♘d7 15 ♗d4 ♗xd4 16 ♕xd4 ♕b4 17 ♖b1 ♘c5 18 ♕e3 ♕b6 19 a5 ½-½ Vadasz-Leko, Budapest 1993.

b) 14 ♗f3 ♖c7 15 ♘d5 ♕xd2 16 ♗xd2 ♗xd5 17 cxd5 ♖ac8 18 ♖xc7 ♖xc7 19 ♖c1 ♖xc1 20 ♗xc1 ♘c5 with a level endgame, as in the game K.Müller-Brunner, Altensteig 1992.

c) 14 f3 b5 transposing to note 'b' to White's 14th move in the next main game.

14   ...   b5

Reshevsky once tried 14...♗g4 against a young Fischer, but White had the better position after 15 ♗d3 ♗d7 16 h3 ♗c6 17 ♕f2 ♘d7 18 ♘d5 ♗xd5 19 exd5 b5 20 ♖fe1 ♘c5 21 ♗b1 bxc4 22 ♖xc4, Fischer-Reshevsky, Los Angeles 1961.

15   f5   ♗d7

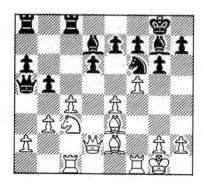

The alternatives are not worth trying for Black:

a) 15...b4? 16 fxe6 bxc3 17 exf7+ ♔f8 18 ♕c2 ♕e5 19 ♗f3 with a clear plus for White,

Shamkovich-Kagan, Netanya 1975

b) 15...gxf5? 16 exf5 ♗d7 17 ♗d4 bxc4 18 ♗xc4, also with a clear edge for White, Lengyel-Matanovic, Budapest 1964.

16   fxg6

The position after Black's 15th move is a key one in this line. White has tried a number of things, but the only move with which he has managed to obtain an advantage is the text continuation. Before we continue let us take a look at some of White's alternatives:

a) 16 ♗d4?! ♘xe4 17 ♕e3 ♘xc3 18 ♖xc3 ♗xd4 19 ♕xd4 e5 20 ♕d2 ♕d8 ½-½ Bobotsov-Hort, Kapfenberg 1970.

b) 16 ♗g5?! ♖c5 17 ♗e3 ♖c7 18 c5 ♖ac8 19 ♖c2 ♖xc5! with better chances for Black, De Firmian-Strauss, Los Angeles 1992.

c) 16 b4?! ♕xb4 17 e5 dxe5 18 fxg6 ♗e6 (White was threatening 19 ♖xf6 followed by ♕xd7) 19 gxf7+ ♗xf7 20 ♗h6 ♗xh6 21 ♕xh6 ♗xc4 22 ♕g5+ ♔h8 23 ♖xf6 ♖g8! and Black was winning, Ivanchuk-Anand, Moscow 1994.

d) 16 g4!? (an untried, yet interesting suggestion of Shamkovich's) 16...b4 (or 16...bxc4 17 g5) 17 ♘d5 ♘xe4? 18 ♕c2 wins for White. We believe that the best way for Black to meet 16 g4 is by playing 16...♗c6!?, maintaining control over the important d5-square even when the black knight is pushed away with g4-g5. Both sides have chances.

16   ...   hxg6
17   c5!?

This is the only way to play for an advantage, although 17 e5?! has been tried quite frequently: 17...b4! 18 exf6 bxc3 19 ♖xc3 ♗xf6 20

♖xf6 (if White moves the c3-rook, Black will exchange the queens and have a slightly better endgame; with 20 ♖xf6 White aims for an attack, but Black's defensive resources are perfectly adequate) 20...exf6 21 ♗f3 ♗c6 22 ♗d4 ♗xf3 23 ♕f4 ♕g5 24 ♕xf3 ♖e8 and although Black has a small advantage, the game soon ended in a draw in Spassky-Panno, Palma de Mallorca 1969.

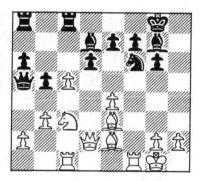

17 ... ♗e6!

In Vitolins-Telman, Kiev 1967, Black soon got into trouble after 17...dxc5? 18 e5 ♘g4 19 ♗f3 ♘xe3 20 ♕xe3 ♖a7 21 ♘d5 ♗e6 22 ♖xc5 ♖d8? (22...♖xc5 23 ♕xc5 ♖d7 24 ♘xe7+ ♔h8 25 ♘c6 ♕d2, although White is still better) 23 ♖c6 ♖ad7 24 ♖xe6! fxe6 25 ♗g4! with a murderous attack.

ECO's suggestion of 17...b4!? was tried out in Mäki-Frois, Thessaloniki ol 1984: 18 ♘d5 ♘xd5 19 exd5 dxc5 20 ♗c4 ♖f8 21 a4 ♕b6 22 ♕f2 ♖ac8 23 d6! e6 24 ♖cd1 ♕c6 25 ♕h4 f5 26 ♖f3 and White had the clearly better chances. Donaldson suggests 20...♗e8 as an improvement, but we believe that White has all the chances after 21

d6 exd6 22 ♕xd6. Black is badly co-ordinated and he has difficulties defending himself against the threat 23 ♕xg6, e.g. 22...♖c6 23 ♗xf7+.

18 ♗f3 dxc5
19 e5 ♘d7!

In the stem game of this line, Parma tried 19...♘g4?, but after 20 ♗xa8 ♗xe5 21 ♗d5 ♘xe3 22 ♗xe6 ♖d8 23 ♕f2 ♘f5 24 ♕e2 ♗d4+ 25 ♔h1 he was lost. The game was soon over: 25...fxe6 26 ♕xe6+ ♔g7 27 ♘e4 ♕c7 28 ♘g5 ♖f8 29 ♕xf5 1-0 Tal-Parma, Bled 1961.

20 ♗xa8 ♖xa8
21 ♕e2 c4

Black already has a pawn for the exchange, and the white e-pawn does not have a very promising future. Therefore White has only one thing left to do if he does not want to die slowly: attack!

22 bxc4 ♗xc4
23 ♕f3 ♖f8
24 ♘d5 ♗xd5
25 ♕xd5 ♘xe5
26 ♗c5 ♖d8

To be considered was 26...♕c7, but it seems as if both parties were happy with the draw that is coming up after the text move. The game concluded:

27 ♕b7 ♕xa2 28 ♗xe7 ♖e8 29 ♖c8 ♖xc8 30 ♕xc8+ ♔h7 31 ♕h3 ♔g8 32 ♕c8+ ♔h7 ½-½

Game 67
Short-Korchnoi
Lucerne 1997

(1 e4 c5 2 ♘f3 ♘c6 3 d4 cxd4 4 ♘xd4 g6 5 c4 ♘f6 6 ♘c3 d6 7 ♗e2 ♘xd4 8 ♕xd4 ♗g7 9 ♗e3 0-0 10 ♕d2 ♗e6)

11   f3   ♕a5

A rare alternative is 11...a6!? After 12 b3 ♕a5 we would be back in the main line, but if White plays 12 ♖c1!?, hoping for 12...♕a5 13 ♘d5!, Black can give 12...b5!? a try, with two possibilities:

a) The critical test may be 13 cxb5 axb5 14 a3, when Donaldson now gives 14...♘d7 15 ♘xb5 ♘c5 16 ♗xc5 dxc5 with some compensation for the pawn. With two strong bishops and pressure against the queenside, Black should be alright, e.g. 17 ♕xd8 ♖fxd8 18 ♘c7 ♗xb2 19 ♖c2 ♖xa3!

b) In Pimenta-Khenkin, Geneva 1994, White played more cautiously: 13 ♘d5 bxc4 14 ♘xf6+ ♗xf6 15 ♗xc4 ♖c8! (Black strives to create some imbalance; the normal 15...♗xc4?! 16 ♖xc4 ♖c8 led to an equal endgame in Braga-Tsuboi, Sao Paulo 1991: 17 ♖xc8 ♕xc8 18 0-0 ♕b7 19 b3 ♖c8 20 ♖c1 ♖c6 21 ♖xc6 ♕xc6) 16 ♗xe6 ♖xc1+ 17 ♕xc1 fxe6 18 ♕d2?! (better was 18 0-0) 18...d5 19 b3 ♕d6 20 0-0 d4 21 ♗h6 ♖c8 22 ♖c1 ♖xc1+ 23 ♕xc1 ♔f7 24 ♗f4 ♗e5 26 ♗xe5 ♕xe5 27 ♕c4 ♕d6 27 ♔f2 d3 28 e5 ♕b6+ 29 ♔f1

♕e3 30 ♕e4 ♕c1+ 31 ♔f2 d2 0-1.

12   ♖c1

Less challenging are 12 ♘d5 ♕xd2+ 13 ♔xd2 ♘xd5 14 cxd5 ♗d7 15 ♖ac1 ♖fc8 16 ♖xc8+ ♖xc8 17 ♖c1 ♖xc1 18 ♔xc1 a6 ½-½ Przewoznik-Malisauskas, Mikolajki 1991, and 12 ♘b5 ♕xd2+ 13 ♔xd2 ♘d7 14 ♖ab1 ♘e5 15 ♖hc1 ♖fc8 16 b3 ♘c6 17 f4 f5 18 ♗f3 fxe4 19 ♗xe4 ♗f5 with a good game, Botvinnik-Matulovic, Belgrade 1970.

12   ...   ♖fc8
13   b3

Nor does 13 ♘d5 promise anything: 13...♕xd2+ 14 ♔xd2 ♘xd5 15 exd5 ♗d7 16 f4 a6 17 b4 a5 18 b5 ♗b2 19 ♖c2 ♗a3 20 ♗d3 ♗c5 with equal chances, A.Sokolov-Velimirovic, Bar 1997.

13   ...   a6

This is pretty much the standard continuation, but other moves are also sufficient for equality:

a) 13...♘d7 14 0-0 a6 15 ♖fd1 b5 16 ♘d5 ♕xd2 17 ♖xd2 ♗xd5 18 ♖xd5 b4 19 g4 ♘c5 20 ♖cd1 a5 21 ♗xc5 ½-½ Larsen-Panno, Buenos Aires 1991.

b) 13...♖ab8 14 ♘a4 ♕xd2+ 15 ♔xd2 ♗d7 16 ♘c3 a6 17 a4 b6 18

g4 ♗e8 19 ♘d5 ½-½ Kavalek-Christiansen, Wijk aan Zee 1982.

14   ♘a4!?

This is White's only real try for an advantage, but with the bishop on e3, Black does not really have too much to worry about, as he can now move his knight to d7 to cover the b6-square.

Apart from 14 ♘a4, White has three other moves at his disposal. None of these are very ambitious and Black equalises without too much difficulty against each of them:

a) 14 ♘d5 (this leads to mass exchanges) 14...♕xd2+ 15 ♔xd2 ♘xd5 16 cxd5 ♗d7 17 ♖xc8+ ♖xc8 18 ♖c1 ♖xc1 19 ♔xc1 ♔f8 20 ♗b6 (or 20 ♔c2 e6 ½-½ Petrosian-Fischer, Buenos Aires 1970) 20...e6 21 ♗d4 ♔e7 22 ♔c2 ♗e5 23 h3 exd5 24 ♗xd5 ♗c6 25 ♗xc6 bxc6 26 ♔g3 ♗c3 with a very drawn ending, Dorfman-Gdanski, Polanica Zdroj 1993.

b) 14 0-0 (this allows Black to play ...b7-b5, and is therefore the only line in which Black can hope for an advantage!) 14...b5 and now we have:

b1) Of course, there is still 15 ♘d5, but with the king away from the centre, White cannot hope for any advantage: 15...♕xd2 16 ♗xd2 ♘xd5 17 cxd5 ♗d4+ 18 ♔h1 ♗d7 19 ♖xc8+ ♖xc8 20 ♖c1 ½-½ Tsarev-Zhachev, Moscow 1988.

b2) Worse is 15 cxb5?! axb5 16 ♖c2? ♖xc3 17 ♕xc3 ♕xc3 18 ♖xc3 ♖xa2 19 ♗xb5 ♘g4 20 fxg4 ♗xc3 with a nightmare ending for White, whose pawns are horribly weak, Sherzer-Honfi, Hungary 1988.

b3) 15 ♘b1 b4! and:

b31) 16 ♖fd1 has been tried, but Black was slightly better after 16...♖ab8 17 h3 ♘d7 18 ♗f1 ♕c7 19 ♕f2 ♘c5 20 ♘d2 a5, Buza-Marasescu, Romania 1988.

b32) Boleslavsky gives 16 a3 ♖ab8 17 ♗f2 ♘d7 18 ♔h1 ♘e5 19 ♗e1 ♘c6 with an edge for Black.

b33) 16 ♔h1 (White has actually managed to pull off a few wins with this move, but only after weak play by Black) 16...♖ab8 17 ♗d4 ♘d7 18 ♗xg7 ♔xg7 19 f4 f6 20 ♕b2 ♕c5 21 ♖cd1 ♖c7 22 ♖d3 a5 and Black had nothing to worry about, Zelcic-Korholz, Cannes 1993.

c) 14 a4!? (by preventing ...b7-b5 and gaining some more space on the queenside, White prepares for the ending that he eventually will force by playing ♘d5; however, the inclusion of a2-a4 does not change the picture a great deal, the likely result is still a draw) 14...♘d7!? 15 ♘d5 ♕xd2+ (an interesting option is 15...♕d8!?, when Herrera and Alzugaray give the following line: 16 a5 ♗xd5 17 exd5 b6 18 axb6 ♘xb6 19 b4 a5 20 bxa5 ♘d7, intending ...♘c5 and ...♕xa5 with a good game for Black) 16 ♔xd2 ♗xd5 17 exd5 (in Vukcevic-Drimer, Leningrad 1960,

White obtained an advantage after 17 cxd5 ♔f8 18 b4 ♗b2 19 ♖c2 ♖xc2+ 20 ♔xc2 ♗g7 21 ♔b3 ♖c8 22 ♖c1, but we think that Black can improve on his play by playing 17...♗b2 instead of 17...♔f8; the idea is to transfer the bishop to b4 via a3, or possibly to exchange off the dark-squared bishops, leaving Black with a good knight versus bad bishop) 17...a5 18 ♔c2 ♖e8 19 ♖he1 e6 ½-½ Dochev-Delchev, Sofia 1994.

14	...	♛xd2+
15	♔xd2	♘d7

16 g4!?

White's most popular and dangerous option. The alternatives have proven quite easy for Black to handle:

a) 16 ♘c3 ♘f6 17 ♘d5 ♘xd5 18 cxd5 ♗d7 19 ♖xc8+ ♖xc8 20 ♖c1 ♖xc1 21 ♔xc1 f5 ½-½ Spassky-Sosonko, Tilburg 1981.

b) 16 ♖c2 ♖c6 (also good is 16...f5 17 ♗d3 ♔f7 18 ♘b6 ♘xb6 19 axb6 ½-½ Chessman-Malisauskas, Norilsk 1987) 17 ♘c3 a5 18 ♖hc1 ♘c5 ½-½ Panno-Reshevsky, Siegen ol 1970.

c) 16 ♖hd1 f5 (or 16...♖cb8 17 c5 dxc5 18 ♘xc5 ♘xc5 19 ♖xc5

♖d8+ 20 ♔e1 ♖xd1+ 21 ♔xd1 ♖c8 with equality, Hort-Vasiukov, Wijk aan Zee 1973) 17 exf5 gxf5 18 ♔e1 ♔f7 19 ♘c3 ♗xc3 20 ♖xc3 b5 21 g4 fxg4 22 fxg4 bxc4 23 bxc4 ♘e5 24 ♖d4 ♖ab8 25 ♖b3 ♖a8 26 ♖c3 ♖ab8 27 ♖b3 ♖a8 ½-½ Kir.Georgiev-Tiviakov, Groningen 1994.

d) 16 h4!? f5 (16...♖ab8!?) 17 exf5 gxf5 18 ♗d3 ♖ab8! 19 ♘c3 ♘c5 20 ♘d5?! (20 ♗b1!?, keeping the bishop and maintaining the pressure on Black's kingside, was a better idea) 20...♔f7 21 g4 ♘xd3 22 ♔xd3 b5 23 ♘f4 bxc4+ 24 bxc4 ♗d7 with a very comfortable endgame for Black, Vaisser-Antunes, Tilburg 1994.

Both players must be aware of the fact that often the positions analysed above, in which Black plays ...f7-f5, also arise from the 9 ♗g5 variation: 9 ♗g5 0-0 10 ♛d2 (or 10 ♛e3 ♗e6 11 ♖c1 ♛b6! 12 ♛d2 ♛b4) 10...♗e6 11 ♖c1 ♛a5.

16 ... ♖c6

A very popular alternative is 16...f5!? and now:

a) 17 gxf5 is harmless for Black after 17...gxf5 18 ♖hg1 ♔h8 19 ♘c3 fxe4 20 ♘xe4 d5 21 ♘g5 ♗g8 22 cxd5 ♗xd5 23 ♖g3 ♖c1 24 ♔xc1 ♘f6 with equal chances, Lau-Zsu.Polgar, New York 1985.

b) But 17 exf5 has caused Black quite a few problems, although objectively speaking, Black is doing alright after 17...gxf5 18 h3 and now:

b1) After the slightly inaccurate 18...♖d8 White's advantage is barely traceable: 19 ♘c3 ♘f6 20 ♖hd1 d5 21 cxd5 ♘xd5 22 ♘xd5 ♖xd5+ 23 ♔e1 ♖xd1+ 24 ♔xd1 ♖d8+ 25 ♔e1 ♔f7 26 ♗c4 ♗e5 27 f4 ♗d6, W.Schmidt-Khasin, Koszalin 1997, but it seems better to leave the knight on a4, as after 19 ♖hd1!? then:

b11) 19...♔f7 20 ♔e1 fxg4 21 hxg4 h5 22 gxh5 ♖h8 23 c5 d5 24 f4 ♘f6 25 c6 bxc6 26 ♖xc6 White had the better ending in Skalik-Gdanski, Polish ch 1994.

b12) If Black instead of 19...♔f7 tries 19...♘f6, then 20 ♘b6 is quite uncomfortable, because then after 20...d5 White no longer has to worry about ...d5-d4, forking the c3-knight and e3-bishop, and can therefore can play 21 c5, threatening 22 ♗f4, when after 21...♖f8 22 ♔e1! fxg4 23 hxg4 ♖bd8 24 c6 White is clearly better. But Black has a couple of other interesting alternatives.

b13) 19...d5!? 20 exf5 (20 cxd5 ♗xd5 21 ♔e1 ♗c6, but not 21 gxf5? ♘e5) 20...♗xf5 21 cxd5 ♘f6 and in this position Black has no problems.

b14) 19...b5!? (with the white knight left on a4, this looks very logical) 20 cxb5 axb5 21 ♘c3 b4 22 ♘b5 fxg4 23 hxg4 ♘e5 with a good game for Black, but 22 ♘a4 is probably better.

b2) Finally, 18...♖f8 19 f4 (less to the point is 19 ♖hf1 fxg4 20 fxg4 ♖ab8 21 ♘c3 ♘e5 ½-½ Liss-Donaldson, Port Erin 1997)

(see following diagram)

and now:

b21) 19...d5 20 cxd5 ♗xd5 21 ♖hd1! ♖ac8 22 gxf5 b5 23 ♖xc8 ♖xc8 24 ♔e1 ♗c6 25 ♘c5 ♘xc5 26 ♗xc5 ♗f6 27 b4! with a clear advantage for White in the endgame, although Black managed to save the draw in Beliavsky-Tiviakov, Groningen 1993.

b22) 19...♘f6!? 20 ♖hg1 ♖ad8 21 ♗b6 ♖c8 22 ♘c3, as in Ivanchuk-Kir.Georgiev, Belgrade 1997, and, according to Ivanchuk, Black could now have chosen between 22...d5!? 23 cxd5 ♖xc3 24 dxe6 ♘e4+ 25 ♔d1 or 22...fxg4 23 hxg4 d5!? 24 f5 (24 cxd5? ♖xc3! or 24 g5 ♘d7!) 24...♗f7 25 ♘d5 ♘xd5 26 cxd5 ♗xd5 with chances for both sides in each case.

b23) 19...♖ad8!? and now:

b231) 20 ♘c3 d5!? (Black must stay active, as after 20...♘f6 21 g5 ♘e4+ 22 ♘xe4 fxe4 23 ♗b6 ♖d7 24 ♔e3 White is much better in the endgame) 21 g5 22 cxd5 ♘f6 23 ♗b6 ♖d7 24 ♔e3 ♖c8! 25 ♗f3 (with his own king in the centre of the action and Black's pieces very active, White has to exercise extreme caution, e.g. 25 ♗c4? ♖d6 26 ♗d4 b5 27 ♗e2 ♖xc3!) 25...e6! 26 ♗d4 (if 26 dxe6 then 26...♖e8 27 ♔f2 ♖xe6 28 ♗e3 ♖d3, when Black's active pieces compensate for the pawn) 26...exd5 27 ♖cg1 ♖e8 28 ♔d2 ♘e4+ 29 ♗xe4 dxe4 30 ♖xg7+ ♖xg7 31 ♗xg7 ♖d8+ 32 ♔e2 ♔xg7 33 ♘d1 ♖d3 with an equal endgame, Am.Rodriguez-Antunes, Matanzas 1994.

b232) 20 ♗f3 fxg4 21 hxg4 d5 22 cxd5 ♘e5 23 ♗e4 ♗xd5 24

♗xh7+ ♔f7 25 ♖h5 ♗xb3+ 26 ♔e2 ♗c4+ 27 ♔e1 ♘xg4 28 ♗b6 ♖d5 with equal chances in the endgame, Riemersma-Van der Weide, Enschede 1996.

b233) 20 ♖hd1 d5 21 cxd5 ♘f6 22 ♘b6 ♘xd5 23 ♘xd5 ♗xd5 24 ♔e1 fxg4 25 ♖xd5 ♖xd5 26 ♗c4 e6 27 ♗xd5 exd5 28 hxg4 ♗b2 29 ♖c2 d4 30 ♗d2 ♗c3 ½-½ Lane-Donaldson, Wrexham 1997.

| 17 | h4 | ♔f8 |

In Soffer-I.Almasi, Budapest 1993, Black mixed his plans: 17...h6 18 ♘c3 f5? 19 ♘d5 ♔f7 20 exf5 gxf5 21 g5 hxg5 22 hxg5 ♘f8 23 f4 ♔e8 24 ♗f3 ♖b8 25 ♘b4 ♖c7 26 ♗b6 ♖d7 27 ♖ce1, when White had a magnificent clamp on the entire black position.

| 18 | h5 | ♖ac8 |
| 19 | hxg6 | hxg6 |

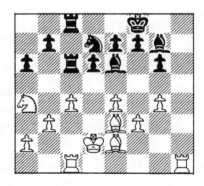

| 20 | g5 |

White does not want to allow the possibility of a freeing ...f7-f5 later on in the game.

| 20 | ... | ♘c5 |
| 21 | ♘c3 | b5! |

The pawn cannot be taken: 22 cxb5 ♗xc3+ 23 ♖xc3 ♘xe4+ 24 fxe4 ♖xc3.

| 22 | ♘d5 | bxc4 |

23	♗xc4	a5
24	♗b5	♗xd5
25	exd5	♖6c7
26	♗c6	♔g8!

Black has to play very carefully, since with a pair of bishops and a weak black pawn on a5, White does not need a whole lot more to win the game. If Black tries to release the tension with 26...e6, White has 27 ♖xc5! exd5 28 ♖xd5 ♖xc6 and now not 29 ♖xa5 ♖c2+ 30 ♔d1 ♖b2 with compensation for the pawn, but 29 ♔e2 with an advantage for White: the weak a- and d-pawns should be all White needs to win. Nor does 27...dxc5 offer Black salvation: 28 ♗xc5+ ♔g8 29 ♗b6 ♖xc6 (not 29...♖e7? 30 d6 ♖xc6 31 dxe7, when the e-pawn decides) 30 dxc6 ♖xc6 31 ♗xa5 (31 ♗e3!?) 31...♖c5 32 ♗b6 ♖xg5 33 ♖h2!, when White's queenside pawns will prove stronger than Black's kingside majority.

| 27 | ♖c4 |

27 ♗xc5 dxc5 28 ♖xc5 e6 is okay for Black.

27	...	e6
28	♖hc1	♖d8
29	♖1c2	exd5
30	♗xd5	♖e7
31	♗d4	♖de8
32	♗xg7	♖e2+
33	♔c3	♖8e3+
34	♔b2	♔xg7
35	♖d4	♘d3+
	½-½	

After 36 ♖xd3 ♖xd3 37 ♖xe2 ♖xd5 the chances are level.

Game 68
Gulko-Petrosian
Biel izt 1976

(1 e4 c5 2 ♘f3 ♘c6 3 d4 cxd4 4

♘xd4 g6 5 c4 ♘f6 6 ♘c3 d6 7
♗e2 ♘xd4 8 ♕xd4 ♗g7)

9   ♗g5

This move has more point than 9
♗e3, as often when Black has developed his queen to a5, White has
the option of 1 ♗xf6 ♗xf6, 2 ♘d5
♕xd2, 3 ♘xf6+, disrupting the
black pawn structure, although
many of these endgames with an
isolated Black d-pawn are in fact
drawn. The drawback of having the
bishop on g5 is that it is sometimes
slightly vulnerable tactically, protected only by the queen. White's
chances of an opening advantage
are certainly better after 9 ♗g5
than 9 ♗e3, but Black should still
be able to keep the balance with
correct play.

9   ...   h6?!

Nowadays this is rarely seen in
top level tournaments, but it is not
really that bad. The main move is
of course 9...0-0, which will be
covered in Games 69-72, but two
other ideas are sometimes seen:

a) It is not particularly good to
postpone castling: 9...♗e6 10 ♖c1
♕a5 (10...0-0!) 11 ♕d2 ♖c8?!
(11...0-0!) 12 f3! and now the po-

sition is already critical for Black:

a1) In the game Geller-Stean,
Teesside 1975, Black suffered a
violent death: 12...♗xc4? 13 ♘d5!
♕xa2 14 0-0 ♘xd5 15 ♖xc4! ♖xc4
16 ♕xd5 ♖a4 17 ♗b5+ ♔f8 18
♖c1 1-0.

a2) Best is 12...0-0 13 ♘d5!
♕xd2+ 14 ♔xd2 ♘xd5 15 cxd5
♗d7 and now 16 b3 with an edge
for White in the endgame, but not
16 ♖xc8 (16 ♗xe7?? ♗h6+)
16...♖xc8 17 ♗xe7?! ♗h6+! 18
♔e1 (18 ♔d3?? ♗b5+ and wins)
18...♖c2 with a good game for
Black.

b) Recently 9...♕a5!? has become quite popular. Usually, it just
transposes to the main lines, but
with 10 ♗d2!?, threatening 11
♘d5, White can avoid these transpositions. In the only examples
given, Black chose to deal with this
threat immediately, moving his
queen to b6 with 10...♕b6. This
bears a resemblance to the line 9
0-0 0-0 10 ♕e3 ♗e6 11 ♗d2 ♕b6,
but White is a tempo up compared
to this line. However, White must
play energetically to retain the initiative. After 11 ♕xb6 axb6:

b1) In Kalesis-Leko, Budapest
1993, White played 12 f3?! ♗e6 13
♔f2 ♘d7 14 ♖hc1 f5 15 exf5 gxf5
16 b3 0-0 17 a4 ♘c5 18 ♖ab1 f4
19 ♘d5 ♗xd5 20 exd5 ♗d4+ and
Black had solved his opening
problems successfully.

b2) A better impression is made
by 12 a4! ♗e6 13 0-0 0-0 14 f4!
♖fc8 15 b3 b5 16 f5, when, already
in a bad position, Black tried to
create some confusion, but White
kept his cool: 16...♗xc4 17 bxc4
b4 18 fxg6 hxg6 19 e5 bxc3 20
exf6 ♗xf6 21 ♖xf6 exf6 22 ♗xc3

with a won endgame for White, Alburt-I.Ivanov, Chicago 1989.

| 10 | ♗e3 | 0-0 |
| 11 | ♕d2 | ♔h7 |

An idea deserving of attention is 11...♕a5!? 12 0-0 ♗e6!? planning to answer 13 ♗xh6 ♗xh6 14 ♕xh6 with 14...♕b4. In its only outing, White did not achieve much: 15 ♖ad1?! ♕xb2 16 ♖d3 ♘xe4 17 ♖b1 ♕c2 18 ♖c1 ♕b2 with equality, Honfi-Makropoulos, Athens 1976. Silman and Donaldson claim that White is clearly better after 15 ♘d5!? ♗xd5 16 exd5 ♕xb2 17 ♖ae1!, intending f2-f4-f5. However, we do not agree with this judgement. In many endgames Black will be better due to the superiority of his knight over White's bishop, and if White insists on an attack with f2-f4, he will weaken his kingside dramatically. A possible line is 17...♖ae8 (or 17...♖fe8!?) 18 f4 (18 ♗d1 b5!) 18...♘e4, threatening ...♕d4+ and ...♕h8. With best play from both sides, the position is probably roughly equal. Instead of 15 ♘d5, White could try 15 ♖ab1, but the chances are about equal after 15...♗xc4 16 ♗xc4 ♕xc4 17 ♕e3.

The correct way for White to take advantage of Black's weak h6-pawn is initially to ignore it, until White has secured his own position, as then Black will have to waste a tempo protecting the h6-pawn. Seen in the light of this recommendation, moves such as 13 ♖ab1, 13 ♖ac1 and 13 ♖fc1 would all be good choices.

| 12 | 0-0 |

White also achieved a slightly better position with 12 f3 ♗e6 13 ♖c1 ♖c8 14 ♘b5!? a6 15 ♘d4

♗d7 16 0-0 ♕c7 17 ♖c2 ♖fd8 18 ♖fc1 e5!? 19 ♘b3 ♗e6 20 ♖c3! ♘d7 21 ♘a1! f5 22 exf5 gxf5 23 ♘c2 in Seirawan-I.Ivanov, USA ch 1992.

| 12 | ... | ♗e6 |

12...♗d7 is too passive here: 13 ♖fd1 ♗c6 14 f3 (or 14 ♕c2 ♕a5 15 ♗d4 with a slight plus, Garcia Martinez-Pinal, Cienfuegos 1983) 14...♕a5 15 ♖ac1 ♖fc8 16 a3 a6 17 ♗f1 ♕d8 18 b4 ♕h8 19 a4 a5 20 b5 ♗d7 21 ♘d5 with the better chances for White, Grünberg-Dumitrache, Romania 1992.

| 13 | ♖ac1 |

This is not White's best move here. Other possibilities are:

a) 13 f3 ♕a5 14 ♖ac1 a6 15 b3 ♖fc8 16 a4 ♘d7 17 ♖c2 (White does not achieve anything after 17 ♘d5 ♕xd2 18 ♗xd2 ♗b2 19 ♖ce1 ♘c5 20 ♗e3 ♗xd5 21 exd5 b6 22 ♗d1 ♗c3 23 ♖e2 ♖c7 with equality, Karasev-Tal, USSR ch 1971) 17...♘c5 18 ♖b1 ♕b4! 19 ♘d5 ♕xd2 20 ♖xd2 ♗xd5 21 ♖xd5 a5 22 ♗d1 ♖c6 23 ♗c2 e6 24 ♖dd1 ♘a6! 25 e5 d5 with equality, as in the game Uhlmann-Andersson, Hastings 1971/72.

b) 13 ♗d4 ♖c8 (an interesting

alternative is 13...♕a5 [threatening 14...♘xe4!] 14 f3 ♖fc8 15 b3 b5!? 15 cxb5 ♘xe4 16 fxe4 ♗xd4+ 17 ♕xd4 ♕xc3 18 ♕xc3 ♖xc3 with a good game for Black, but White is probably slightly better after 14 ♖ad1!?) 14 b3 a6 15 ♕e3 ♘d7 16 ♗xg7 ♔xg7 17 f4 ♕b6 18 ♕xb6 ♘xb6 19 f5 ♗d7 20 ♘d5 with a small edge for White, Timman-Ribli, Amsterdam 1973.

c) 13 f4! (White's most direct and strongest approach) 13...♖c8 14 b3 ♕a5 15 ♖ad1 (in the famous game Larsen-Fischer, Denver 1971, White tried 15 a3 a6 16 f5 ♗d7 17 b4 ♕e5, and now instead of 18 ♖ae1 ♗c6 19 ♗f4 ♘xe4 20 ♘xe4 ♕xe4 21 ♗d3 ♕d4+ 22 ♔h1 ♖ce8 with equal chances, White should have gone for Rabar's 18 ♖ad1 ♗c6 19 ♗d4 ♘xe4 20 ♕e3 ♘xc3 21 ♗xe5 ♘xd1 22 ♖xd1 with a small edge for White, but Black can consider 18...♘xe4 19 ♘xe4 ♕xe4 20 ♗d3 ♕e5, when White still has to prove exactly what he has in return for his pawn) 18...a6 16 ♗d4 ♗d7 (White also gets the better position after 16...b5 17 f5 ♗d7 18 ♗xf6! exf6 19 ♘d5 ♕xd2 20 ♖xd2, Nunn-Van der Sterren, Groningen 1974/75) 17 ♗xf6 exf6 18 ♘d5 ♕c5+ 19 ♔h1 a5 20 f5 with a very comfortable position for White, Nunn-I.Ivanov, London 1987.

| 13 | ... | ♕a5 |
| 14 | f4 | ♖ac8 |

With the weakened structure on the kingside, Black decides it is best to keep a rook on the kingside for protection.

15	b3	a6
16	f5	♗d7
17	h3	

17 c5 ♗b5 is quite messy, as in the game Vera-Marasescu, Timisoara 1982.

18	♗d3	♘d7
19	♘d5	♕xd2
20	♗xd2	♖fe8

Black has equalised, and a draw was soon agreed:

21 ♗b1 ♗d4+ 22 ♔h1 ♔g7 23 fxg6 fxg6 24 ♘f4 ♗f6 25 ♗e3 ½-½

Game 69
Dolmatov-Tiviakov
Rostov na Donu 1993

(1 e4 c5 2 ♘f3 ♘c6 3 d4 cxd4 4 ♘xd4 g6 5 c4 ♘f6 6 ♘c3 d6 7 ♗e2 ♘xd4 8 ♕xd4 ♗g7 9 ♗g5 0-0)

| 10 | ♕e3 |

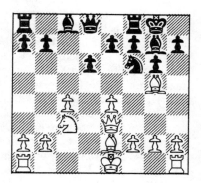

This is a fairly new way of playing the position. Ideally, White wants to place his rooks on c1 and d1 and then push through either c4-c5 or e4-e5. However, if White is not interested in the exchange of queens, this is not the right line for him, since Black often plays ...♕b6. Although 10 ♕e3 is not theoretically any better than 10

♕d2, it certainly gives White more options, as after 10 ♕e3 ♗e6 11 0-0 ♕b6 White can choose 12 ♕d2, when after 12...♕a5 we are back in the 10 ♕d2 lines.

10 ... ♗e6

10...♕a5 is also possible, but after 11 0-0 ♗e6, we will transpose into the note to Black's 11th move. Three rarely played alternatives are:

a) 10...a6 11 0-0 ♗d7 12 ♖fd1 ♖c8 13 h3 ♖e8 14 ♖ac1 with a slight plus for White, Murey-Gelfer, Tel Aviv 1980.

b) 10...♕b6 (in this form ...♕b6 is slightly unusual, but in the game Black soon manages to equalise) 11 ♕xb6 axb6 12 ♔d2 ♗e6 13 a4 ♖fc8 14 b3 ♖a5 15 ♗xf6 (15 ♗e3 ♘d7 is excellent for Black) 15...exf6!? (15...♗xf6 was good enough for equality, but the text move is an interesting attempt to create some action) 16 ♗d3 f5 17 ♖ad1 ♗xc3+ 18 ♔xc3 fxe4 19 ♗xe4 ½-½ Arencibia-Antunes, Cuba 1991, but here 19...d5 is quite interesting. White's only move is 20 b4!, when 20...♖xa4 21 ♗xd5 and 20...♖xc4+ 21 ♔b3 ♖a8 22 ♗xd5 are both about equal, but instead of 21...♖a8, Black can try 21...dxe4!? 22 bxa5 bxa5 with very good chances.

c) 10...♗d7 11 0-0 ♗c6 12 ♖fd1 ♘d7 13 ♗h6 ♕b6 14 ♕xb6 ♘xb6 15 ♗xg7 ♔xg7 16 ♖ac1 a5 17 f3 ♖fc8 18 ♔f2 ♘d7 19 ♔e3 ♘c5 20 ♖c2 ♘a4 and White was just a tiny bit better, Penrose-Damjanovic, Palma de Mallorca 1969.

11 0-0

In Arnason-Petursson, Reykjavik 1989, White was successful with 11 ♖c1 a6!? 12 0-0 b5!? 13 cxb5 axb5 14 a3! ♕b8? 15 ♗xb5, when he was just a pawn up. Arnason suggested 14...♖a5!? as an improvement, but Petursson himself showed the right way for Black the following year against the same player: 11...♕b6! 12 ♕d2 (or 12 b3!?) 12...♕b4!? (12...♕a5 is also playable, but the text is more interesting) 13 f3 and now:

a) Petursson gives 13...♗xc4!? 14 a3 ♕b3 15 ♗xc4 ♕xc4 16 ♘d5 ♕b3 17 ♘xe7+ ♔h8 as unclear. Gallagher disagrees and gives 18 0-0 ♕b6+ 19 ♖f2 ♖fe8 20 ♗xf6 ♗xf6 21 ♘d5 ♕d4 22 ♖c7 with a clear advantage for White, but we think that after 18...♖fe8 Black should have nothing to complain about. In fact, how does White continue? 19 ♕xd6? ♖ad8 20 ♕c5 (20 ♕c7 ♖d7) 20...♘xe4, 19 ♖c7 ♕b6+ and 19 ♘d5 ♘xd5 20 ♕xd5 ♕xd5 21 exd5 ♗xb2 22 ♖c7 ♗d4+ 23 ♔h1 ♔g8 24 ♖xb7 ♖ab8 are all good for Black, but White can keep level chances with 19 ♗xf6! ♗xf6 21 ♘d5 ♕xb2 22 ♕f4! ♗e5! 23 ♕xf7 ♖f8.

b) 13...♖fc8 14 b3 a6 15 ♘a4 ♕xd2+ 16 ♔xd2 ♘d7 17 h4 (or 17 g4 f6 18 ♗e3 f5 – transposing to the note after Black's 16th move in Game 67) 17...f6 18 ♗e3 f5 and we have transposed to the note to White's 16th move in Game 67.

11 ... ♕b6!

An interesting option is 11...♕a5 12 ♖ac1 ♖fc8 13 b3 a6 and now:

a) 14 a4 ♕b4 15 ♗d1 ♕c5! (15...♖ab8 16 ♕e1 gave White a slight edge in Kavalek-Visier, Lanzarote 1973) 16 ♕xc5 ♖xc5 17 ♗e3 ♖cc8 18 ♗f3 ♖ab8 19 a5 ♘d7 20 ♘a4 ♘c5 ½-½ Kavalek-Browne, Las Palmas 1974.

b) 14 ♘a4 ♖ab8 15 c5 with a slight plus for White, Dahlberg-Donaldson, Lone Pine 1981.

c) 14 ♔h1!? (White would like to play f2-f4-f5, but wants to keep the queens on) 14...b5 (14...♕c5!?) 15 f4! bxc4? (now White develops a strong initiative; better was 15...b4, although White is better after 16 ♘d5 ♗xd5 17 exd5 ♕c5 18 ♕xc5 ♖xc5 19 f5) 16 f5! cxb3? 17 fxe6 b2 18 exf7+ ♔f8 19 ♖c2 ♖c5 20 ♗xf6 exf6 21 ♕d3 ♖ac8 22 ♕xd6+ ♔f7 23 ♗g4 ♖8c7 24 ♗e6+ ♔e8 25 ♖d2 1-0 Agnos-Rocha, Linares 1998.

d) 14 f4 ♕c5 15 ♕xc5 ♖xc5 16 ♗f3 and now a further fork:

d1) 16...♖b8?! 17 e5! dxe5 18 fxe5 ♘e8 19 ♗xe7 ♖xe5 20 ♗h4 b5 21 cxb5 ♖c5 22 bxa6! and White was winning in Ciocaltea-Spiridonov, Timisoara 1982.

d2) 16...♔f8!? 17 ♖fd1 ♖b8 18 e5?! (this may give White some initiative on a short-term basis, but Black will eventually be able to free himself; better was 18 a4) 18...dxe5 19 fxe5 ♘d7 20 ♗d5 ♗g4 21 ♖d2 ♘xe5 22 ♗e3 ♖c7 23 h3 ♗f5 24 g4 ♗c8 25 ♗b6 ♖d7 26 ♖f2 (the white position looks pretty impressive, but Black is pretty solid) 26...♔g8! 27 ♖cc2 e6 28 ♗g2 ♘d3, when White had some compensation, but not quite enough in Pajkovic-Govedarica, Centinje 1991.

d3) 16...♖e8!? 17 e5!? dxe5 18 ♗xb7 ♘g4!? (an interesting way of playing; instead of worrying about his queenside, Black immediately starts his counterplay) 19 h3 exf4 20 ♗xf4 ♗d4+ 21 ♔h1 ♘f2+ 22 ♔h2 ♘d3 23 ♖cd1 ♗xc3 24 ♖xd3 ♗e5 25 ♗xe5 ♖xe5 26 ♖fd1 ♔g7

27 ♖1d2 a5 with equal chances in the endgame, Timoshenko-S.Niko-lic, Chelyabinsk 1990.

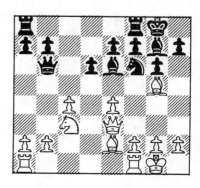

12   b3

At this point White has a number of important alternatives:

a) 12 ♕xb6?! (this is very comfortable for Black; White has to play carefully just to maintain the balance) 12...axb6 13 ♖ac1 (the alternatives are good for Black: 13 b3 ♘d7 14 ♖fc1 ♖fe8 15 ♗d2 ♘c5 16 f3 ♖ec8 17 ♔f1, Christiansen-Donaldson, Los Angeles 1989, and now 17...f5 would have been better for Black, or 13 ♖fc1?! ♖fc8 14 b3 b5! 15 e5 ♘d7 16 ♘xb5 ♗xe5 17 ♗d2 ♘c5 18 ♗f3 ♘xb3! 19 axb3 ♖xa1 20 ♖xa1 ♗xc3 21 ♗xc3 ♖xc3 22 ♖b1 b6 with a big advantage for Black, Runic-Nikcevic, Banja Vrucica 1991) 13...♖fc8 14 b3 b5!

(see following diagram)

and now:

a1) 15 ♘xb5 ♖xa2 16 ♗d3 h6 17 ♗e3 ♘g4 18 ♗d4 ♘e5 19 ♗b1 ♖a6 20 f4 ♘c6 21 ♗xg7 ♔xg7 22 ♖c3 ♗d7 23 ♖g3 ♘b4 with a better game for Black, Larduet-Diaz, Holguin 1991.

a2) 15 ♘d5 ♗xd5 16 cxd5

♘xe4 17 ♗xe7 ♖xc1 18 ♖xc1 ♗d4 19 ♔f1 ♖xa2 20 ♗f3 ♘d2+ 21 ♔e1, Winslow-Gross, New York 1994, and now Black should have continued with 21...♘xf3+ 22 gxf3 ♗e5 with a much better position.

a3) 15 cxb5!? ♖xc3 16 ♖xc3 ♘xe4 17 ♖e3 ♘xg5 18 h4 ♗d4! 19 ♖d3 ♗c5 20 hxg5 ♖xa2 21 ♗f3 b6 with good compensation for the exchange according to Alzugaray and Herrera.

a4) 15 ♗f3 bxc4 16 e5 ♘d7 17 ♗xb7 ♘xe5 18 ♗xa8 ♖xa8 19 ♗xe7 cxb3 (or 19...♘d3 20 bxc4 ♗xc4 21 ♗xd6 ♘xc1 22 ♖xc1 with equal chances) 20 axb3 ♘d3 21 ♖cd1 ♘b2 22 ♖c1 ♘d3 23 ♖cd1 ♘b2 ½-½ Herrera-Andres, Havana 1990.

b) 12 ♖ab1 (Karpov's move, which used to give Black quite a few headaches, though now he seems to be doing fine) 12...♕xe3 13 ♗xe3 ♖fc8 (less to the point is 13...a6?!, as after 14 b3 ♖ac8 15 ♖bc1 ♖fc8 16 ♖fd1 ♘d7 17 ♘d5 ♘c5 18 f3 f5 19 exf5 gxf5 20 ♗f1 ♔f8 22 g3 White had a small advantage, Gavrikov-Andersson, Biel 1993; Karpov mentions 13...♘g4 and gives 14...♗d2 ♖fc8 15 b3 ♗xc3 16 ♗xc3 b5 17 f3 with a slight advantage for White) 14 b3

and now Black has tried a variety of things:

b1) 14...♗d7 15 ♖fd1 ♗c6 16 f3 a5 (the black set-up, which is similar to the Classical Maroczy, is too passive without the queens on the board; Black is left with virtually no counterplay and Karpov, of course, is certainly not the right man to play against in such a position) 17 ♖bc1 ♘d7 18 g3 ♔f8 19 h4 h5 20 ♔f2 ♗e5 21 ♗f1 e6 22 ♖d2 ♘c5 23 ♗g2 ♔e7 24 ♘e2 b6 25 ♖cd1 ♖d8 26 ♗g5+ ♗f6 27 ♗xf6+ ♔xf6 28 e5+ with a clear advantage for White, Karpov-Petursson, Reggio Emilia 1990.

b2) 14...a6!? 15 ♘a4 ♖ab8! (Black had his share of problems after 15...♘d7 in Christiansen-Dzindzichashvili, USA ch 1991: 16 f4! f5 17 exf5 ♗xf5 18 ♖bc1 ♖ab8 19 ♘c3 ♔f8 20 g4 with a clear edge for White) 16 ♘b6 ♖c7 17 ♗f3 ♘d7 18 a4 (Silman and Donaldson mention 18 ♘d5 ♗xd5 19 cxd5 ♘e5 with good chances for Black, e.g. 20 ♗e2 ♖c2 or 20 ♖bc1 ♖bc8 21 ♖xc7 ♖xc7 22 ♖c1 ♖xc1+ 23 ♗xc1 ♘xf3+) ♗c3 19 ♖fd1 ♘xb6 and a draw was agreed in A.Ivanov-Petursson, New York 1991.

b3) 14...♔f8!? 15 f3?! (15 ♗d2!?) 15...♘g4 16 fxg4 ♗xc3 17 ♖bc1 ♗b2 18 ♖c2 ♗a3 19 g5 b5 with a big advantage for Black, Rodin-Pigusov, Podolsk 1992.

b4) 14...♘g4!? 15 ♗xg4 (the only move seen in practice, but instead 15 ♗d2 is possibly stronger: 15...♗xc3 16 ♗xc3 b5 17 f4! [Christiansen] with a powerful initiative for White, e.g. 17...bxc4 18 f5 gxf5 19 exf5 cxb3 20 fxe6 ♖xc3 21 exf7+ ♔f8 22 ♗xg4 bxa2 23

♖b2 and White wins; but Black can improve with 15...♗e5!? 16 ♘d5 ♔f8 17 h3 ♘f6 with chances for both sides – analysis by Silman and Donaldson) 15...♗xc3! (15...♗xg4 16 ♘d5 ♔f8 17 ♗g5 f6 18 ♗e3 is slightly better for White, Stangl-Schindler, German Bundesliga 1989/90) 16 ♗xe6 fxe6 17 f4 a6 18 f5 exf5 19 exf5 b5 20 ♖bc1 ♗f6 21 c5 dxc5 22 ♖xc5 ♖xc5 23 ♗xc5 with a level endgame, A.Ivanov-Donaldson, Reno 1990.

b5) 14...♘d7!? 15 ♘d5 ♗xd5 16 exd5 ♘c5 17 ♖bc1 a5 18 ♖c2 ♘a6! 19 a3 b5 20 ♖fc1 b4 ½-½ Anand-Tiviakov, Groningen 1993. A surprisingly easy draw by Black against Anand. Since this game was played, 12 ♖ab1 has disappeared from high level games.

c) 12 ♕d2 (if handled correctly by Black, this is absolutely harmless) 12...♕a5! (slightly inaccurate is 12...♖fc8 13 b3 and now 13...♕a5 14 ♖ac1 a6 transposes to Game 71, but independent play can arise if Black plays 13...a6 14 ♖ad1 ♕c5, when in Kamsky-Andersson, Reggio Emilia 1991, White did not manage to get any tangible advantage: 15 ♗e3 ♕a5 16 f4 b5 17 f5 ♗d7 18 fxg6 hxg6 19 ♗d4 ♗e6 20 ♗xf6 ♗xf6 21 ♘d5 ♕xd2 22 ♘xf6+ exf6 23 ♖xd2 bxc4 24 bxc4 ♗xc4 25 ♖xf6 ♗e6! 26 ♖xd6 ♖c1+ 27 ♖f1 ♖xf1+ 28 ♗xf1 ♗xa2 29 ♗xa6 with a drawn endgame) 13 ♖ac1 with a transposition to Game 71.

d) Finally, also 12 ♕d3 has been tried, but in Chandler-Pigusov, Sochi 1982, Black equalised easily: 12...♖fc8 13 b3 a6 14 ♗e3 ♕b4 15 ♖ac1 ♖ab8 16 ♗a7 ♖a8 17 ♗d4 b5.

| 12 | ... | ♕xe3 |

12...♖fc8!? is an untried suggestion of Tiviakov's.

| 13 | ♗xe3 | ♘d7 |

13...♘g4 is quite a popular move, e.g. 14 ♗d2 ♗e5 15 ♗xg4 (15 h3 ♘f6 is equal) 15...♗xc3 (Black also equalised in Kalesis-Silman, Budapest 1994: 15...♗xg4 16 ♖ac1 ♗e6 17 a4 ♖fc8 18 ♗e3 a6 19 a5 ♗xc3 20 ♗xc3 f6 21 f4 ♔f7) 16 ♗xc3 ♗xg4 17 ♗d4 ♗d7 18 a4 ♗c6 19 ♖fe1 f6 20 f3 ♔f7 21 ♔f2 h5 with equality, Enders-Kochiev, Balatonbereny 1988. But White should retain a small edge after Tiviakov's 15 g3.

| 14 | ♖ac1 | ♖fc8 |

In Korneev-Polak, Karvina 1992, Black equalised without too much trouble with 14...♘c5: after 15 f3 a5 16 ♖fd1 ♖fc8 17 ♘d5 ♗xd5 18 ♖xd5 b6 19 ♖c2 ♔f8 20 ♗f1 ♖ab8 21 h4 h5 22 g3 ♖d8 23 ♗g2 e6 24 ♖d1 ♔e7 25 ♗f1 ♖d7 the chances were level, but according to Tiviakov, White can play 15 ♘d5! ♗xd5 16 exd5 a5 17 ♖c2! and keep a small advantage.

| 15 | ♘d5 | |

This is the only to play for an advantage. In the game Bernard-

Solozhenkin, Paris 1997, White achieved nothing with 15 f4 ♘c5 16 f5 ♗d7 (16...♗xc3!? Tiviakov) 17 ♘d5 ♔f8 18 ♗g5 ♗d4+ 19 ♔h1 f6 20 ♖cd1 ♗e5 21 fxg6 hxg6 22 ♗f4 ♗xf4 23 ♖xf4 ♔f7 24 b4 ♘e6 when a level endgame was reached.

| 15 | ... | ♔f8 |
| 16 | f4 | a5 |

In his notes in *Informator* Tiviakov mentions 16...♗b2!?, intending 17 ♖b1 ♗xd5 18 cxd5 ♗a3 19 b4 ♖c2!?, but in Dolmatov-Alterman, Haifa 1995, White improved over this analysis with 17 ♖cd1!, when after 17...a5 18 ♖f2 ♗xd5 19 ♖xd5! ♘f6, he could now have obtained a clear advantage with 20 ♖b5! ♘xe4 21 ♗g4 ♘xf2 22 ♗xc8 ♖xc8 23 ♔xf2 ♖c7 24 ♖xa5 – Alterman.

| 17 | f5 | ♗xd5 |
| 18 | exd5 | ♗b2! |

Ideally Black would like to swap the dark-squared bishops, since this would leave him with the traditional good knight versus bad bishop ending, but of course he cannot expect White to co-operate with such a plan.

| 19 | ♖c2 | ♗a3 |

| 20 | ♗h6+ | ♔g8 |
| 21 | h4 | |

White must start some action on the kingside, otherwise Black will take control of the game.

21	...	♘f6
22	h5	gxh5
23	♖c3	♔h8
24	♖h3	b5!?

Drastic measures, but 24...a4 25 ♗xh5 ♘xh5 26 ♖xh5 axb3 27 axb3 ♗b2 was also fine for Black.

25	♗xh5	♘xh5
26	♖xh5	bxc4
27	bxc4	♗b2!

After 27...♖xc4 28 f6 exf6 29 ♖xf6 White would have had compensation for the pawn.

28	♖h4	♗f6
29	♖e4	♖ab8
30	g4	♖b4
31	g5	♗xg5?!
½-½		

Here a draw was agreed, but Black's last move is actually a small mistake. It was better to play 31...♗e5 32 f6 exf6 33 gxf6 ♖bxc4 with a small advantage for Black according to Tiviakov.

Game 70
Mokry-Kallai
Trnava 1985

(1 e4 c5 2 ♘f3 ♘c6 3 d4 cxd4 4 ♘xd4 g6 5 c4 ♘f6 6 ♘c3 d6 7 ♗e2 ♘xd4 8 ♕xd4 ♗g7 9 ♗g5 0-0)

| 10 | ♕d2 | |

This position is by far the most popular in the Gurgenidze variation. The safe 10 ♕d2 keeps the queen safely tucked away from enemy attack, and at the same time it will counter the black queen if it takes up its traditional outpost on a5. White's plan is to expand on the queenside with the support of the rooks, which will usually be put on c1 and d1. In some cases, when Black plays ...♖fc8 before White has played f2-f3, White can take advantage of this by playing for a kingside attack, but we will come to this in the next main game.

10 ... a6!?

This is a fairly new idea. Black abandons the traditional ...♗e6, ...♕a5, ...♖fc8, ...a7-a6 plan and strives for immediate counterplay on the queenside, often sacrificing a pawn with ...b7-b5. So far this concept has proven quite successful, but more games must be played before we can establish a clear idea of the true value of this plan.

11 f3

This is White's most logical response, supporting the e4-pawn. If White does without this move, Black may be able to take advantage of the overloaded white knight to get in ...b7-b5:

a) 11 0-0 ♗e6 and now:

a1) 12 ♖ac1 b5! 13 cxb5 axb5 14 ♗xb5 ♗xa2 15 ♗c6 ♖a6 16 ♘xa2 ♖xa2 17 ♖c2 ♕b8 with

chances for both sides, Ortega-Andres, Holguin 1984.

a2) A better try for advantage is 12 f3 ♕a5, and now instead of 13 ♘d5?! ♕xd2 14 ♘xe7+ ♔h8 15 ♗xd2 ♖fe8 16 ♘d5 ♘xd5 17 cxd5 ♗xd5 18 ♗c3 ½-½ Short-Andersson, Novi Sad ol 1990, White should try 13 ♖fd1!? ♖fc8 14 ♘d5 ♕xd2 15 ♖xd2 ♗xd5 16 cxd5 ♔f8 with a very small plus for White. Black can only sit and wait.

a3) 12 ♖ad1 ♕a5 13 ♗xf6 (or 13 b3 b5!? 14 cxb5 [14 ♗xf6 ♗xf6 15 ♘d5 ♕xd2 16 ♘xf6+ exf6 17 ♖d2 ½-½ Kramnik-Anand, Moscow rapid 1994] 14...axb5 15 ♗xf6 ♗xf6 16 ♘xb5 ♖fb8! 17 b4 ♕b6 18 a3 ♗d7 19 ♘c3 ♗e6 20 ♘b1 ♖a7 21 ♖c1 ♕d4 22 ♕xd4 ♗xd4, when Black's active pieces compensate for his pawn deficit, Sherzer-Karolyi, Hungary 1993) 13...♗xf6 (Nunn and Gallagher suggest 13...exf6!? 14 ♕xd6 f5, when White has some problems with his queenside) 14 ♘d5 ♕xd2 (in Tiviakov-Polak, Oakham 1992, Black found himself in trouble after 14...♕xa2? 15 ♘xf6+ exf6 16 ♕c3! ♕a4 17 ♖xd6 ♖ac8 18 b3 ♕a3 19 ♖fd1 with a big advantage for White) 15 ♘xf6+ exf6 16 ♖xd2 b5! (if it were not for this move, Black would have been clearly worse, but now his counterplay comes just in time) 17 cxb5 axb5 18 a3 ♖fc8 19 f4 f5 20 exf5 gxf5 21 ♖xd6 b4 22 ♖a1 ♖c8 23 ♗f3 bxa3 24 bxa3 (24 ♗xa8 axb2 25 ♖b1 ♖c1+ 26 ♖d1 ♖xd1+ 27 ♖xd1 ♗a2 is a draw) 24...♖a4 25 ♗d1 ♖xf4 with a level endgame, Campora-Morovic, Spain 1994.

b) 11 ♖c1 ♗e6 12 b3 and here

another junction:

b1) 12...♖c8 13 0-0 b5 14 cxb5 axb5 15 ♗xf6 ♗xf6 16 ♘xb5 ♕b6 17 b4!? (Chiburdanidze tried 17 ♘a3!? against Gufeld, at Kuala Lumpur 1994, which then continued 17...♖c5!? 18 ♖xc5 ♕xc5 19 ♘c4 ♗g5 20 ♕c3 f5 21 exf5 ♗xf5 22 b4! ♕c7 23 ♕b3 ♗e6 24 b5 d5 25 ♘e3 ♕e5! 26 ♕d3 and here Black could have maintained equality with 26...d4 27 ♘c4 ♕b5 28 ♕d4 ♖c8 29 ♘d6 ♕d7) 17...♕b7 18 a4 ♕xe4 19 ♘c7 ♖b8 20 ♘xe6 fxe6 21 ♖c4 ♕d5 22 ♕c2 ♗d4 23 ♗f3, Gufeld-Konguvel, Calcutta 1994, and according to Gufeld, Black should now have played 23...♖xf3!? 24 gxf3 ♖f8 with unclear play.

b2) 12...b5 13 cxb5 axb5 14 ♗xb5 ♕a5 15 ♗c6! (prior to this game theory suggested that Black was better; 15 ♗d3 ♖fc8 16 0-0 ♖xc3 17 ♖xc3 ♘xe4 18 ♗xe4 ♗xc3 19 ♕d3 d5 20 ♗f3 ♖a7 21 ♗e3 ♖d7 22 ♗b6 ♕b4 23 ♖d1 d4 24 ♕a6 ♗f5 with better chances for Black, May-Ca.Hansen, corr 1994) 15...♖a6 16 ♘a4! ♖c8 17 ♕xa5 ♖xa5 18 ♗d2 ♖a6 19 ♗b5 ♖xc1+ 20 ♗xc1 ♖a5 21 ♗d3 ♘d7 (Black would like to create some counterplay with ...♘c5, but White continues in accurate fashion) 22 ♗d2 ♖a8 23 ♗b1! ♘c5 24 ♘b6! ♖a7 25 ♔e2 with a clear edge for White, Serper-Donaldson, Las Vegas 1997. White's play was very impressive.

11	...	♗e6
12	♖c1	♖c8

Since 12...♖c8 leads to a drawish position, Black might consider 12...b5!? if he wants to play for a win: 13 cxb5 axb5 14 a3

(possibly better is 14 b4!?, when White developed some initiative in Hellers-Piket, Thessaloniki ol 1988: 14...d5 15 ♗xf6 ♗xf6 16 exd5 ♗xc3 17 ♖xc3 ♕xd5 18 ♕xd5 ♗xd5 19 a3 ♖fc8 20 ♖xc8+ ♖xc8 21 ♔d2 ♖a8 22 ♖a1 ♗c6 with a slight pull for White) 14...♘d7 15 b4 ♖xa3 16 ♘xb5 ♖a2 17 ♕e3 h6 18 ♗h4 g5 19 ♗f2 ♕b8 20 0-0 ♖c8 21 h4 ♗f6 with excellent play for Black, Topalov-Antunes, Candas 1992.

13   b3

A.Ivanov-Pigusov, Biel 1989, saw instead 13 ♘d5 b5! 14 0-0 ♘xd5 15 exd5 ♗d7 16 b3 ♖e8 17 ♗e3 bxc4 18 ♗xc4 ♗b5 19 ♗xb5 axb5 20 ♖c6 ♖a8 21 ♖f2 ♕a5 22 b4 ♕a3 23 ♗d4 ♗xd4 24 ♕xd4 ♕a7 25 ♕c3 ♕a3 ½-½.

13   ...   b5

Also possible is 13...♕a5, leading to the main line after 10...♗e6 but with the difference that here Black has played his queen's rook to c8 instead of the usual king's rook. This rather limits Black's options with regard to the freeing ...b7-b5, so White is slightly better.

14   cxb5

Tukmakov has suggested 14

♘d5, but after 14...♘xd5 15 exd5 ♗d7 we do not feel that Black is worse; for comparison see the A.Ivanov-Pigusov game above.

| 14 | ... | axb5 |
| 15 | ♘xb5 | |

This leads to massive exchanges, but it is probably the only way to play for the advantage. In Szekely-Tangborn, Budapest 1992, 15 0-0 b4 16 ♘b5 ♕a5 17 ♗e3 ♘d7 18 ♘d4 ♘c5 19 ♖fd1 ♖fd8 20 ♗f4 ♗d7 21 ♗c4 ♘e6 was equal. But why not did Black not play 21...e5 here? Unless White does something drastic, he will end up a piece down, but what can he do? 22 a3 is met by 22...♕b6! 23 axb4 ♘e6, so it seems as if White has to go in for 22 ♗g5, when Black is much better after 22...exd4 23 ♗xd8 ♖xd8.

15	...	♖xc1+
16	♕xc1	♕a5+
17	♕d2	♖a8!
18	a3	

This position is almost identical to that which arose in the note to White's 11th move in Game 65, the only difference being that here the white bishop is on g5, but in some examples, such as our main line, transpositions may occur, so one must keep an eye out for these. Possibly better than 18 a3 is 18 ♘c3!?, as in Frolov-Tangborn, Budapest 1992, which went 18...h6 19 ♗e3 ♘g4 20 ♗d4 ♗xd4 21 ♕xd4 ♖c8 22 ♔d2, and now instead of 22...♖xc3? Black should have tried 22...♕g5+! – see Game 65 for analysis.

| 18 | ... | ♗xb3 |
| 19 | ♕xa5 | ♖xa5 |

(see following diagram)

| 20 | 0-0 | |

The best. Other moves have proven even more harmless:

a) 20 ♗d2 ♖a8 21 ♔f2 ♘d7 22 ♖c1 ♘c5 23 ♗e3 ♗a4 24 ♗xc5 dxc5 25 ♖xc5 ♗xb5 26 ♖xb5 ♗d4+, and a draw was agreed, Kuzmin-Zachev, Moscow 1988.

b) 20 ♔f2 ♗a4 21 ♖b1 h6?! (correct was 21...♗xb5! 22 ♖xb5 ♖xa3 23 ♖b8+ ♗f8 24 ♗h6 ♘d7 25 ♖d8 and now 25...♖b3? loses to 26 ♗a6! intending 27 ♗c8, but 25...♖a2! transposes to the main game) 22 ♗d2 ♖a8 23 ♘c7! ♖a7 24 ♘a6! with a small edge for White, as in Tukmakov-Vaganian, USSR 1984.

20	...	♗a4
21	♖b1	♗xb5
22	♖xb5	♖xa3

The game finished:

23 ♖b8+ ♗f8 24 ♗h6 ♘d7 25 ♖d8 ♖a1+ 26 ♔f2 ♖a2 27 g4 f6?? 28 ♔e3?? ♖c2 29 ♗d3 ½-½

Why all the question marks? Well, instead of 28 ♔e3??, White could have won on the spot with IM Strauss' discovery 28 e5!! (28...dxe5 29 ♗e3!, 28...fxe5 29 g5 or 28...g5 29 e6). Hence Black's 27th move was a blunder; correct was 27...g5!, intending ...f7-f6 and ...♔f7, when Black can defend.

Game 71
Kruppa-Tiviakov
St Petersburg 1993

(1 e4 c5 2 ♘f3 ♘c6 3 d4 cxd4 4 ♘xd4 g6 5 c4 ♘f6 6 ♘c3 d6 7 ♗e2 ♘xd4 8 ♕xd4 ♗g7 9 ♗g5 0-0 10 ♕d2)

10	...	♗e6

This natural move is Black's most popular choice. The main line (see the next game) is drawish and quite dull, but the alternatives, as we shall see in this game, are anything but boring.

11 0-0

The main line is 11 ♖c1 followed by 12 f3 (see Game 72) but White also has:

a) Another attempt to enter the main line is 11 f3, but Black does not need to co-operate, since with 11...♖c8 he can benefit from the omission of the move ♖c1. Akesson-Wojtkiewicz, Antwerp 1994, ended in a quick draw after 12 ♘d5 ♘xd5 13 cxd5 ♗d7 14 0-0 f5 15 f3 fxe4 16 fxe4 ♖xf1 17 ♖xf1 ♕c7 ½-½. However, Black has a sharp alternative to 12...♘xd5. In Horak-Dobrovolsky, Luhacovice 1993,

Black tried 12...b5!?,

which is not so easy to meet, e.g. 13 cxb5 ♘xd5 14 exd5 ♗f5 or 13 ♗xf6 exf6! 14 cxb5 ♗xd5 15 ♕xd5 ♕b6! in both cases with a strong initiative for Black. White has massive problems covering all the weak squares in his position. In the game White found the best way to continue: 13 ♖c1 bxc4 14 ♖xc4 ♗xd5 15 exd5 ♕b6 16 b3 a5 17 ♖xc8 ♖xc8 18 ♗c4 ♘d7 19 ♗e3 ♕b4 20 ♕xb4 axb4 21 0-0 ♖a8 22 ♖f2 ♗c3 with some initiative for Black in the endgame.

b) Also possible is 11 ♖d1 a6 12 0-0 ♕c7 (12...♕a5 transposes to the note after White's 11th move in the previous main game) 13 b3 ♖fc8 (worth considering was also 13...♖ac8!?) 14 f4 ♖e8 15 f5 ♗d7 16 ♔h1 ♗c6 17 ♕f4 ♕a5 18 ♖d3 ♕e5 with equality, Renet-Petursson, Reykjavik 1992.

11	...	♕a5

This time Black cannot take advantage of the omission of ♖c1, as White has not weakened his position with 11 f3. Here 11...♖c8?! is met by 12 b3 (or 12 ♖ad1!? ♕a5 13 b3 a6 14 ♘d5! ♕xd2 15 ♘xe7+ ♔h8 16 ♗xd2 ♖ce8, as in the game J.Polgar-Dzindzichashvili, New York 1992, and now White should have continued 17 e5! dxe5 18 ♗b4 with a clear advantage) 12...b5?! (12...a6!?) 13 e5! (not 13 cxb5?! ♖xc3 14 ♕xc3 ♘xe4 15 ♕e3 ♘xg5 16 ♕xg5 ♗xa1 17 ♖xa1 d5 with a small edge for Black, Brodsky-Tiviakov, USSR 1991) 13...dxe5 (also bad is 13...b4? 14 exf6 bxc3 15 ♕xc3 exf6 16 ♗e3 f5 17 ♗d4 ♗xd4 18 ♕xd4 with a horrible position for Black, Uhlmann-Balogh, Budapest 1989) 14 ♕xd8 ♖xd8 15 ♘xb5 a6 16 ♘c3 h6 17 ♗e3 with a large advantage for White, Bologan-Michenka, Ostrava 1993.

12 ♖ac1

White also has:

a) 12 ♖fd1, when after 12...a6 (12...♖fc8 13 ♗xf6 ♗xf6 14 ♘d5 ♕xd2 15 ♖xd2 ♗xd5 ½-½ Uhlmann-Vogt, Nordhausen 1986) 13 ♗xf6 ♗xf6 14 ♘d5 ♕xd2+ 15 ♘xf6+ exf6 (15...♔g7 16 ♘h5+ gxh5 17 ♖xd2 ♖fc8 18 b3 ♖c5 is possibly stronger than the game continuation) 16 ♖xd2 ♖fc8 17 ♖xd6 ♗xc4 18 ♗f3 ♔g7 19 e5 fxe5 20 b3 ♗b5 21 ♗xb7 ♖d8 22 ♖ad1 ♖xd6 23 ♖xd6 ♖a7 24 ♖b6 White had an initiative in the endgame, De Firmian-Finegold, Key West 1994.

b) Just as in the 9 ♗e3 line, 12 ♖ab1 is interesting. Here it has the added bonus that White can exchange on f6 and then play ♘d5, which was not possible after 9 ♗e3. In Geller-Zsu.Polgar, Aruba 1992, Black had some problems after 12...♖fc8 (12...♕b4!?) 13 b4 ♕d8 14 ♗xf6 ♗xf6 15 ♘d5 ♗xd5 16 exd5 a5?! 17 a3 axb4 18 axb4 ♕b6 19 ♖fd1 with a small but clear advantage for White. We think that Black can improve on the 16th move with 16...♗c7, intending

...h7-h5, ...♖ac8 and ...♕f8-g7, or 16...♕d7, intending ...♕f5-e5 or ...e7-e6.

c) White can also try 12 ♖ad1 ♖fc8 13 b3 a6 14 ♗xf6 ♗xf6 15 ♘d5 ♕xd2 16 ♘xf6+ ♔g7 17 ♘h5+ gxh5 18 ♖xd2 ♖c5 19 f4 f6 20 ♖e1!? (20 a4 a5 21 ♖f3 ♖g8 22 f5 ♗f7 23 ♖g3+ ♔h6 24 ♖xg8 ♗xg8 25 ♔f2 ♗f7 26 ♖d3 ♖e5 27 ♔e3 ♗c8 28 ♔f4 ♗c6 with equality, Prie-Trauth, Cannes 1992) 20...♖a7 (20...h4 seems stronger to us, when the chances should be approximately equal) 21 e5 dxe5 22 ♗xh5 b5 23 cxb5 axb5 24 fxe5 ♖xe5 25 ♖xe5 fxe5 26 ♗f3 ♗f5 27 ♔f2 with better chances for White, Reeh-Vatter, Germany 1994.

d) Finally, 12 ♗d3 is also possible, but it seems that Black has no problems after 12...a6 13 ♘d5?! (13 0-0 b5 14 cxb5 axb5 15 ♗xb5 ♗xa2 is equal) 13...♗xa2 14 ♗b1 ♕a4! 15 ♘b6 ♕c6 16 ♘xa8 ♘xe4 17 ♗xe4 ♕xe4 or 15 ♘xe7+ ♔h8 16 0-0 ♖fe8 17 ♕xd6 ♖ad8 18 ♕a3 ♕xa3 19 bxa3 h6 20 ♗xf6 ♗xf6 21 ♘d5 ♗b2 – analysis by Alterman.

12 ... a6
13 b3

13 f3 transposes to the next main game, but White has two other possibilities:

a) So far Black has not had any problems against 13 ♖fd1, after which most of the pieces seem to depart the board after 13...♖fc8 14 ♗xf6 ♗xf6 15 ♘d5 ♕xd2 16 ♘xf6+ ♔g7 (less accurate, but apparently still sufficient, is 16...exf6 17 ♖xd2 b5 18 ♖dc2 f5! 19 f3 fxe4 20 fxe4 ♔f8 21 cxb5 axb5 22 a3 b4! 24 axb4 ♖a4 25 ♔f2 ♖xb4 26 ♔e3 ♔e7, and a draw was soon agreed, Stangl-Sandor, German Bundesliga 1993/94) 17 ♘h5+ (in Agnos-Alterman, Kordítsá 1996, Black almost developed an initiative after the more peaceful 17 ♖xd2 ♔xf6 18 f4 a5 19 a4 ♖c5 20 b3 g5 21 g3 ♖g8) 17...gxh5 18 ♖d2 h4! 19 ♖dc2 a5! 20 f4 f5 21 ♗f3 ♖c7 with a level endgame, Shmuter-Alterman, Rishon-le-Zion 1994.

b) Adams was successful with 13 ♕e3 against Adrian, French Team ch 1991: 13...♖fc8 14 b3 b5?! 15 cxb5 axb5 16 ♘xb5 ♕xa2 17 ♘c7 ♕xb3 18 ♘xa8 ♖xa8 19 ♕xb3 ♗xb3 20 ♗f3, which was all Adams needed to take home the full point. But instead of 14...b5?!, Black should have tried 14...♕c5!? with equal chances.

13   ...   ♖fc8

For a long time 13...b5 was considered to be quite strong, but now the tide has turned, and the general opinion is that White is better:

a) 14 ♗d3 ♖fc8 15 b3 b5 16 ♘d5 ♕xd2 17 ♗xd2 ♘xd5 18 cxd5 ♗d7 with equality, Arnason-Petursson, Reykjavik 1989, and Ye-Yrjölä, Novi Sad ol 1990.

b) 14 b3 b5 and now:

b1) 15 cxb5 axb5 16 ♗xb5 ♖fc8 17 a4 (17 e5!? dxe5 is unclear) 17...♗xb3 18 ♕d3 ♗c4 19 ♗xc4 ♕xg5 20 ♗b5 ♕e5 21 ♘d5 ♘xd5 22 exd5 ♖c3 ½-½ Tseshkovsky-Pigusov, Podolsk 1990.

b2) 15 e5!? dxe5 16 cxb5 axb5 17 ♗xb5 h6! 18 ♗e3 ♘g4 19 ♗c4 ♗xc4 20 bxc4 e4! 21 ♘xe4 ♕e5 with a good game for Black, Casabona-Orseth, corr 1988-93.

b3) 15 ♗f3!? b4 16 ♘a4 ♖ab8 17 ♖fe1 ♖fc8 18 ♕e3 h5? 19 h4 ♗d7 20 ♖xc8+ ♖xc8 21 ♕b6 with a clear advantage for White, Ortega-Andres, Camaguey 1988, but Black can improve: after 18...♗d7! he has no problems.

b4) It is quite possible that 15 ♘d5 is stronger: 15...♕xd2 16 ♘xe7+ ♔h8 17 ♗xd2 ♘xe4 18 ♗a5 ♖ae8 19 ♘d5 ♗xd5 20 exd5 ♘c3 21 ♖xc3 ♖xe2 22 ♗b4 ♖d8 23 a3 ♖b2 24 ♖c6 ♖xb3 25 ♖d1 ♗e5 26 g3 ♖a8 27 f4 a5 28 ♗c5 ♗b2 29 ♗xd6 with a big advantage for White, Wells-Karolyi, Oakham 1993.

14   f4

Aside from 14 f4, White has three alternatives at this point:

a) 14 ♗f3!? ♖ab8 15 ♖fe1 b5?! 16 ♘d5 ♕xd2 17 ♗xd2 ♔f8 18 cxb5 axb5 19 ♘b4! ♘g4 20 ♗e2 ♗d7 21 h3 ♘e5 22 ♖xc8+ ♗xc8 23 ♖c1 with a clear edge for White, Sigurjonsson-Petursson, Reykjavik 1985, but 15...♔f8! improves for Black, leaving the position balanced.

b) 14 ♖fe1 b5?! (just what White was hoping for; correct was 14...♔f8, as ♘d5 has less point when the king is on f8 and, with the white rook on e1, he will achieve nothing by playing f2-f4-

f5) 15 ♘d5 ♕xd2 16 ♗xd2 ♘xd5
17 exd5 ♗d7, Dutreeuw-Donald-
son, Liechtenstein 1994, and here
White could have played 18 ♗g5,
forcing Black to play 18...♗f6 19
♗xf6 exf6 when White is practically a pawn ahead.

c) A third possibility is 14 a4, an
attempt to clamp Black's queenside, but since Black simply plays
14...b5 anyway, it does not make
much sense. The game Gasseholm-
Isajev, corr 1987-92, continued 15
e5 dxe5 16 axb5 axb5 17 ♗f3 e4
18 ♘xe4 ♘xe4 19 ♗xe4 ♕xd2 20
♗xd2 ♖xa2 with a small advantage
for Black.

14   ...   ♖c5

Black must try to stop the white
e- and f-pawns from marching forward. A similar idea is known from
the Yugoslav Attack in the Dragon
variation.

White has a murderously high
percentage score against 14...b5: 15
f5 b4 (even worse is 15...♗d7 16
fxg6 hxg6 17 e5 ♘e8 18 ♘d5
♕xd2 19 ♗xd2 ♖d8 20 ♘xe7+
♔h7 21 ♗f3 ♖a7 22 ♗e3 ♖c7 23
exd6 ♘xd6 24 ♗b6 1-0 Van der
Werf-Ree, Holland 1993) 16 fxe6
bxc3 17 exf7+ ♔f8! (this is the
only way to stir things up;
17...♔xf7?! 18 ♖xc3 [18 ♕d5+
♕xd5 19 exd5 is also good for
White, as in Mainka-Döry, Dortmund 1987] 18...♔g8 19 ♗f3 ♖ab8
20 ♖d3 ♕xd2 21 ♖xd2 with a clear
advantage for White, Uhlmann-
Spiridonov, Decin 1977) 18 ♕f4
♕xa2 (in Barle-Whitehead, Lone
Pine 1979, Black committed sui-
cide with 18...♘xe4? 19 ♗xe7+
♔xe7 20 ♕xe4+ ♔f8 21 ♕f4 h5 22
♗f3 ♖a7 23 ♕g3 with a big advantage for White, but even

stronger is 20 f8♕+! and Black is
busted) 19 e5 dxe5 20 ♕xe5 ♕a3
21 ♗f3 ♖ab8 with a complicated
position, but somewhat better
chances for White in Levy-Silman,
Lone Pine 1975.

15   ♕e3

Other tries are:

a) 15 ♖b1 ♘d5 16 exd5 ♗xc3
17 ♕e3 ♗f5 18 b4 ♗xb4 19 ♖xb4
♕xb4 20 ♕xe7 ♕b6 21 ♕f6
♖cc8+ 22 ♔h1 ♕d8 23 ♕xd8+
♖xd8 24 ♗xd8 ♖xd8 with equality,
Berthelot-Bernard, French Team ch
1996.

b) 15 a3 (White wants to play
f4-f5, and nothing is going to stop
him from doing so!) 15...♕xa3 16
♗xf6 ♗xf6 17 f5 gxf5 18 exf5
♖xf5 19 ♖xf5 ♗xf5 20 ♘d5 ♗g6
21 ♘xf6+ exf6 22 b4 ♖e8 and
Black was slightly better, Adla-
Palacios, Parana 1993.

c) 15 ♗f3 ♖ac8 16 ♕f2!? (not
16 ♕e3 b5! 17 e5 dxe5 18 fxe5
♘d7 19 ♘d5 ♗xd5 20 ♗xd5 e6
with a clear plus for Black, Psak-
his-Pigusov, USSR 1979, or 16
♖cd1 b5 17 ♘d5 ♕d8 18 cxb5
♗xd5 19 exd5 axb5 with a slight
edge for Black, as in the game
Kaiszauri-Spiridonov, Skara 1980)

16...♖c7?! (16...b5 is met by 17 f5! gxf5 18 ♗e3, but Black has 16...♖xg5 17 fxg5 ♕xg5 with control over the dark squares and excellent compensation for the exchange) 17 f5 gxf5 18 ♘d5 ♗xd5 19 exd5 b5 20 ♗e3 ♖b8 21 c5 with a big advantage to White, Krnic-Spiridonov, Athens 1981.

d) 15 ♗d3 (this is considered White's best option; White keeps playing for the f4-f5 advance) 15...b5 (this leads to a small advantage for White, but Black has an interesting alternative: 15...♖xg5! 16 fxg5 ♘g4 with serious compensation on the dark squares) 16 f5 bxc4 17 fxe6 cxd3 18 exf7+ ♔xf7 19 ♗e3 ♖c6 20 ♕xd3 ♖ac8 21 ♗d2 ♕c5+ 22 ♔h1 with a slight edge for White, Orlov-Petrenko, Podolsk 1989.

| 15 | ... | ♖ac8 |
| 16 | ♖b1 | |

In Korchnoi-Wojtkiewicz, Antwerp 1994, White insisted on playing f4-f5. However, after 16 ♘a4 ♖5c6 17 f5 ♗d7 18 ♔h1 ♖e8 (Black aims for a set-up with ...♖e8, ...♖c8, ...♗c6 and ...♘e5 with absolute control; to avoid this White must play very actively) 19 ♘c3 ♖cc8 20 ♗xf6 ♗xf6 21 ♘d5 ♗c6 22 b4 ♕xa2 23 ♘b6 ♖cd8 24 b5 ♗d7 25 ♗g4 g5 26 ♖cd1 ♕b2 27 h4 gxh4 28 ♘xd7 and Black lost on time! After 28...♖xd7 he would have had a good game.

16	...	♕d8
17	a4	a5
18	♔h1	♕f8
19	♖be1	

This is beginning to look uncomfortable for Black. His position is solid but quite passive, and if he waits, White will soon play either e4-e5 or f4-f5. However, Tiviakov has no intentions of being a sitting duck, so he pulls out a weapon which is also quite common in the regular Dragon variation: the positional exchange sacrifice.

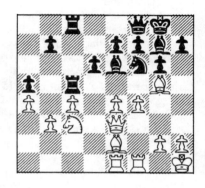

| 19 | ... | ♖xg5! |

In return for the exchange, Black gets excellent control over the dark squares and simultaneously takes the dynamism out of the white position. The chances are level.

20	fxg5	♘d7
21	♘d5	♗e5
22	♗f4	♗xf4
23	♖xf4	

White has exchanged the black dark-squared bishop, but Black still has a strong hold on the central dark squares.

23	...	h6
24	h4	♘e5
25	♖ff1	♖c5
26	gxh6	♔h7
27	h5	♕xh6
28	♕xh6+	♔xh6
29	hxg6	♔xg6

We have now reached an ending, in which only White can play for win, but Black's strong knight will keep the chances equal. White plays on for quite some time before

accepting the draw:
**30 ♖f4 ♘c6 31 ♖h4 ♔g7 32 ♖f1
♘d4 33 ♗d1 ♔g7 34 ♔h2 f6 35
♖e1 ♔f8 36 ♖e3 ♔e8 37 ♖h5
♖xh5 38 ♗xh5+ ♔d7 39 ♖d3 ♘c6
40 ♖c3 ♔c7 41 ♗e8 ♘d4 42 ♖d3
♘c2 43 ♗b5 ♘b4 44 ♖g3 ♗d7 45
♖g7 ♗xb5 46 axb5 ♔d7 47 ♖g3
♔e6 48 ♔g1 ♔e5 49 ♖g7 ♔e6 50
e5 dxe5 51 c5 ♔d7 52 ♖g8 ♘d3
53 c6+ bxc6 54 b6 ♘c5 55 ♖a7
♘b7 56 ♖a7 ♔c8 57 ♖a8+ ♔d7
58 ♖a7 ♖c8 ½-½**

Game 72
Ernst-Tiviakov
Haninge 1992

**(1 e4 c5 2 ♘f3 ♘c6 3 d4 cxd4 4
♘xd4 g6 5 c4 ♘f6 6 ♘c3 d6 7
♗e2 ♘xd4 8 ♕xd4 ♗g7 9 ♗g5
0-0 10 ♕d2 ♗e6)**

| **11** | **♖c1** | **♕a5** |
| **12** | **f3** | |

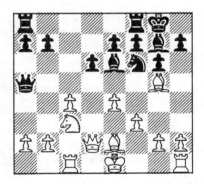

12 0-0 transposes to the previous game.

| **12** | **...** | **♖fc8** |

12...a6 13 b3 ♖fc8 usually transposes, but Kudrin-Ca.Hansen, Satellite Beach 1997, saw Black try 13...b5? Unfortunately he was se-

verely punished for weakening his queenside in such a fashion: 14 ♘d5 ♕xd2+ 15 ♔xd2 ♗xd5 16 cxd5 (compared to the main line, White has everything he could ever dream of: the c-file, the pair of bishops and a black queenside weakened by ...b7-b5) 16...♖fb8 17 ♖c7 ♔f8 18 ♖hc1 ♔e8 19 g3! ♘d7 20 ♗f1 ♗d4 21 ♗h3 ♘f6 22 ♗e3! ♗xe3+ 23 ♔xe3 ♔d8 24 ♔d4 h5 25 a3 b4 26 a4 a5 27 ♖1c2 1-0. White will simply march through in the centre with his pawns, which is precisely what Black must strive to avoid in these endings.

| **13** | **b3** | |

Harmless is 13 ♘d5 ♕xd2+ (13...♕d8 is also for Black, when in Tukmakov-Estevez, Leningrad 1973, Black had equalised after 14 ♘xf6+ exf6 15 ♗e3 f5 16 exf5 ♗xf5 17 0-0 ♕e7 18 ♗f2 ♖e8) 14 ♔xd2 ♘xd5 15 exd5 (or 15 cxd5 ♗d7 16 b3 ♔f8 17 h4 ♗b2 18 ♖b1 ♗c3+ 19 ♔e3 ♗b4 20 ♗d3 f6 21 ♗f4 ♗a3 22 g4 a6 23 b4 ♗b5 with a draw coming up, Loeffler-Vaulin, Koszalin 1997) 15...♗d7 16 b3 e6 17 dxe6 fxe6 18 ♗d3 d5 19 cxd5 ♗xd5 20 ♖xc8+ ♖xc8 21 ♖c1 ♖xc1 22 ♔xc1 with a drawish endgame, Vaganian-Sandor, German Bundesliga 1995/96.

| **13** | **...** | **a6** |

In Jansa-Szabo, Amsterdam 1975, Black tried 13...♗d7 14 0-0 a6 15 f4 ♗c6 16 ♕e3 (16 ♗d3 intending 16...b5 17 f5 is an interesting alternative) 16...b5 17 e5 b4 18 exf6 exf6 19 ♘d5 ♗xd5 20 ♔h4 ♖e8 21 ♕d2 ♗e4 22 f5 ♕c5+ 23 ♔h1 ♗xf5 24 ♗f2 ♕c6 with equality.

| **14** | **♘a4** | |

This move is clearly White's

most ambitious try for an advantage in the main line. Other tries in this position are:

a) 14 0-0 b5 15 ♘d5 ♘xd2 16 ♗xd2 reaching a dead level position that can be found under 9 ♗e3 – note to White's 14th move in Game 67.

b) 14 ♘d5 ♕xd2+ 15 ♔xd2 ♘xd5 (15...♗xd5?! 16 cxd5 ♔f8 17 ♗e3 ♘d7 18 b4 a5 19 ♗b5 ♔e8 20 bxa5 ♔d8 21 ♗xd7 ♔xd7 22 ♖xc8 ♖xc8 23 ♗b6 ♔d7 24 ♖b1 with a clear advantage for White, Herrera-Hergott, Cienfuegos 1996) 16 cxd5 (16 exd5 does not make much difference: 16...♗d7 17 a4 e6 18 dxe6 ♗xe6 19 ♗e3 d5 20 cxd5 ♗xd5 with equal chances, Dolmatov-Lautier, Clermont Ferrand 1989) 16...♗d7 17 h4 (if White takes the pawn on e7, Black gets excellent compensation 17 ♖xc8+ ♖xc8 18 ♗xe7 ♗h6+ 19 ♔e1 ♖c2 20 ♗xd6 ♖xa2, as in Banas-Dobrovolsky, Trnava 1983) 17...f6 18 ♗e3 f5 19 exf5 gxf5 20 g4 fxg4 21 fxg4 ♗b2 22 ♖xc8+ ♖xc8 23 ♖g1 ♗c3+ 24 ♔d1 a5 25 ♗d3 a4 with equality, Mokry-Zsu.Polgar, Trencianske Teplice 1985.

c) 14 a4!? (although it is hardly ever played, this is possibly White's best move) 14...♔f8?! (best is 14...♕b4, e.g. 15 ♘d5 ♕xd2+ 16 ♔xd2 ♘xd5 17 exd5 ♗d7 18 a5 e6 with approximately equal chances, whereas 14...♕d8?! 15 g4 ♘d7 16 h4 ♘c5 17 ♗d1 ♕f8 18 h5 h6 19 ♗e3 g5 20 a5 is clearly better for White, Paneque-Andres, Manzanillo 1989) 15 h4 h5? (15...♕b4!?) 16 ♗d1 ♗d7 17 g4 b5 18 gxh5 gxh5 19 ♗h6 with a strong attack, Kasparov-Merkulov, Tbilisi 1976.

14 ... ♕xd2+

This move used to be played exclusively, but 14...♕d8!? became famous after Krasenkov-Hernandez, Palma de Mallorca 1989. Although it has only been tried a couple of times in high level games since then, we feel that this line deserves more attention. White has tried:

a) 15 0-0 ♗d7 (15...♖ab8?! is too passive, e.g. 16 c5 ♖c6 17 ♖fd1 ♘e8 18 b4 b5 19 ♘c3 ♖b7 20 ♘d5 ♔f8 21 ♗h6 ♗xh6 22 ♕xh6+ ♔g8 23 ♕e3 ♕b8 24 f4 when White was clearly better in Frey-Andres, Camaguey 1987) 16 ♘c3 b5 17 ♖fd1 ♗e8 (17...b4? is just plain bad: 18 ♗xf6 exf6 19 ♘d5 a5 20 ♕e3 ♖c5 21 ♖c2 ♗e6 22 ♖cd2 ♗f8? 23 ♕xb4 and White is winning, Marciano-Spiridonov, French team ch 1996) 18 e5 dxe5 19 ♕xd8 ♖xd8 20 ♖xd8 ♖xd8 21 cxb5 axb5 22 ♘xb5 h6 23 ♗e3 ♘d5 is unclear, Beliavsky-Shabalov, Manila ol 1992.

b) 15 c5 ♘d7! (the Krasenkov-Hernandez game mentioned above took another route: 15...♖c6!? 16 ♔f2! ♕f8 17 ♕b4 ♘d7 18 cxd6, and now instead of 18...♖xd6 19

♕xb7 ♗d4+ 20 ♗e3 ♖b8 21 ♕c7 with a clear edge for White, Hernandez suggests 18...exd6!? 19 ♕xb7 ♗d4+ 20 ♔g3 ♘f6! 21 ♗xf6 ♖xc1 22 ♖xc1 ♗xf6 with an unclear position) 16 cxd6 ♖xc1+ 17 ♕xc1 ♖c8! (everywhere else only 17...♕a5+ 18 ♗d2 with a small advantage is given, but this move is much better) 18 ♕b1 (other queen moves loses at least a piece after 18...b5) 18...b5, and now in Medda-Conti, corr 1982, White lost his head and played 19 dxe7??, which loses to 19...♕c7!, but even after the better move 19 ♘b2 ♕a5+ (or 19...♗c3+ 20 ♔f1 f6 21 dxe7 ♕xe7 with good compensation for the pawn) 20 ♗d2 ♗c3 21 ♕c2 ♗xd2+ 22 ♕xd2 ♕xa2 Black has a clear advantage.

15   ♔xd2   ♘d7

The old main line 15...♖c6 is still playable, when White has tried the following:

a) 16 ♗e3 ♘d7 17 ♘c3 ♖ac8 18 ♘d5 ♗xd5 19 exd5 ♗xc3+ with equality, Reshevsky-Browne, USA ch 1974.

b) 16 h4!? ♔f8 17 ♗e3 ♘h5? (17...♘d7 is much better, when the chances are approximately level) 18 ♘b6 ♖d8 19 g4 ♘g3 20 ♖hg1 ♘xe2 21 ♔xe2 ♗b2 22 ♖cd1 ♗a3 23 f4 with a clearly better game for White, Pigusov-Makarov, USSR 1982.

c) 16 ♘c3 ♖cc8 (Karpov-Kavalek, Nice ol 1974, was better for White after 16...♖ac8 17 ♘d5 ♔f8 18 ♗e3 ♘d7 19 h4; 16...♖e8 is suggested by Karpov in his annotations to the game, when after 17 ♘d5 ♘d7 White cannot take on e7 [18 ♘xe7+?! ♖xe7 19 ♗xe7 f6 20 ♗d8 b6] but 18 g4 ♗d4 19 h4

f6 transposes to our main game) 17 h4 ♔f8 18 ♗e3 ♘h5 19 g4 ♘g3 20 ♖hg1 ♘xe2 21 ♔xe2 b5 22 ♘d5 ♗xd5 23 cxd5 ♗b2 24 ♖xc8+ ♖xc8 25 ♔d3 b4 26 ♖b1 ♖c3+ 27 ♔d2 ♗a3 with an equal endgame, Morris-S.B.Hansen, Copenhagen 1992.

16   g4

After 16 ♗e3, which was tried out in Kramnik-Ivanchuk, London 1994, White achieved a slightly better position after 16...♖ab8 (16...f5!?) 17 ♘c3 ♘e5 (17...f5) 18 ♘d5 ♘c6 19 ♘b6 ♖d8 20 ♖hd1 ♗d4 21 ♗xd4 ♘xd4 22 ♔e3 ♘xe2 23 ♔xe2 f5 24 exf5 ♗xf5 25 ♖d4.

16   ...   ♖c6

After 16 g4 (and the same goes for 16 ♖c2, 16 h4 and 16 ♘c3) Black can transpose to the 9 ♗e3 main line (Game 67) with 16...f6 17 ♗e3 f5. However, 16...♔f8 leads to independent play: 17 h4 (in Zsu.Polgar-Leko, Budapest 1991, Black had no problems after 17 ♗e3 ♖ab8 [not 17...♖c6?! 18 ♘c3 ♘c5 19 ♘d5 ♗d7 20 h4 h6 21 b4 ♘e6 22 f4 ♘d4 23 f5 ♘xe2 24 ♔xe2 with a small edge for White, Dvoiris-Pigusov, Vilnius 1984] 18 g5 f5 19 exf5 gxf5 20 f4 b5 21 cxb5 axb5 22 ♘c3 ♘c5; but Alterman suggests 17 h3!? f6 18 ♗e3 f5 19 exf5 gxf5 20 f4 with a small edge for White) 17...f6 (according to Alterman should Black have played 17...♖c6 18 ♗e3 f5 19 exf5 gxf5 20 g5 d5 21 cxd5 ♗xd5 with equality, but in Averbakh-Popov, Polanica Zdroj 1976, White achieved the better chances after 18 ♖c2 ♘c5 19 ♘c3 a5 20 ♘d5 ♖e8 21 ♗e3) 18 ♗e3 f5 19 exf5 gxf5 20 g5 d5 21 cxd5 ♗xd5 22 ♖hd1 with a small advantage for White, Wang Zili-Alterman, Beijing 1995.

Black wants his bishop out in open air before advancing with ...f7-f6.

19 ♘d5 f6 20 ♗f4 ♗f7 21 g5 ♔g7 22 ♗e3 ♗xe3+ 23 ♔xe3 e6 24 ♘xf6 ♘xf6 25 exf6+ ♔xf6 26 ♖hd1 ♔e7 27 f4 ♖ec8

We have reached an endgame in which White has a tiny edge, but the black position is solid, and the draw is never really in danger.

28 ♖d2 b5 29 ♖cd1 bxc4 30 ♗xc4 ♗e8 31 ♖g1 ♖b6 32 f5 exf5 33 exf5 ♖c5 34 fxg6 ♗xg6 35 ♖g5 ♖xg5 36 hxg5 ♖c6 37 ♔d4 a5 38 ♖e2+ ♔d8 39 ♖e6 ♗f7 40 ♖h6 ♗g6 41 ♗d3 ♗xd3 42 ♔xd3 ♖c5 43 ♖xd6+ ♔c7 44 ♖h6 ♖xg5 45 ♖xh7 ♔b6 46 ♖h6+ ♔c5 47 ♔c3 ♖g3+ 48 ♔b2 ♖g2+ 49 ♔a3 ♔b5 50 ♖h5+ ♔b6 ½-½

17 h4

White still cannot take on e7: 17 ♗xe7 f6 18 g5 (18 c5 ♗h6+) ♔f7 19 ♗xf6 ♘xf6 20 gxf6 ♗h6+.

17	...	♖e8
18	♘c3	♗d4

9   Classical with ♗e2

Chapter Guide

1 e4 c5 2 ♘f3 ♘c6 3 d4 cxd4 4 ♘xd4 g6 5 ♘c3 ♗g7

6 ♘b3 – *Game 73*
6 ♗e3 ♘f6 7 ♗e2 0-0 8 0-0 d5! 9 exd5
         9...♘b4!? – *Game 74*
         9...♘xd5 – *Game 75*

In this chapter we shall deal with the classical lines in which White neither plays 5 c4, entering the Maroczy Bind, nor plays ♗c4 (see Chapters 10 and 11). White hopes that by developing his light-squared bishop to e2, he will be able to transpose to a regular Classical Dragon (normally reached via the move order 1 e4 c5 2 ♘f3 d6 3 d4 cxd4 4 ♘xd4 ♘f6 5 ♘c3 g6 6 ♗e2). However, White's modest set-up often allows Black to play ...d7-d5 in one go, with a good game to follow.

Game 73
Zapata-Garcia Martinez
Sagua la Grande 1984

(**1 e4 c5 2 ♘f3 ♘c6 3 d4 cxd4 4 ♘xd4 g6**)

     5   ♘c3
Since 5 ♘c3 ♗g7 6 ♘b3 allows

Black the option of 6...♗xc3+, White may try 5 ♘b3 if he wants to enter the Karpov variation of the Classical Dragon (1 e4 c5 2 ♘f3 d6 3 d4 cxd4 4 ♘xd4 ♘f6 5 ♘c3 g6 6 ♗e2 ♗g7 7 0-0 0-0 8 ♘b3 ♘c6 9 ♗g5). However, Black can keep the game within the Accelerated Dragon by postponing moving the d-pawn: 5...♗g7 6 ♗e2 ♘f6 7 ♘c3 0-0 8 0-0 a5 9 a4 ♘b4 10 ♗g5 h6 (10...d6 would transpose into the Karpov variation, but on occasion Black has tried the immediate 10...d5: 11 exd5 ♘fxd5 12 ♘xd5 ♘xd5 13 ♗f3 ♘f6 14 ♖e1 ♕c7 15 ♕e2 ♖e8 16 ♕b5 ♔f8 17 c3 with some initiative for White, Kupreichik-Pohl, Schwäbisch Gmünd 1995) 11 ♗h4 g5 12 ♗g3 d5 13 exd5 (13 e5 only helps Black: 13...♘e4 14 ♘xe4 dxe4 15 ♘c5 ♗f5 with excellent chances) and now:

a) Black adopted an interesting

approach in Fishbein-Hodgson, Stavanger 1989: 13...♗f5!? 14 ♘d4 ♗g6 15 ♗c4 ♖c8 16 ♗b3 ♘fxd5 17 ♘xd5 ♘xd5 18 ♖e1 (Black has taken over the initiative, but 18 c3 was to be preferred) 18...♘b4 19 ♗e5 ♘xc2 20 ♗xc2 ♗xc2 21 ♘xd2 ♕xd1 22 ♖axd1 ♖xc2 and Black won the endgame.

b) 13...♘fxd5 14 ♘xd5 ♘xd5 and now:

b1) 15 ♕d2 has been tried: 15...♗e6?! (Donaldson suggests 15...e6! as an improvement, giving 16 c3 ♕b6 17 ♘d4 ♗d7 18 ♘b5 ♖ad8 with equality) 16 ♘c5 ♗xb2 17 ♘xe6 with a slight plus for White, Meijer-Ozolin, Riga 1986.

b2) 15 c3 e5?! (too ambitious: it would have been better to try the solid 15...e6 with about equal chances or Silman's 15...♘f4, e.g. 16 ♗xf4 gxf4 17 ♕xd8 ♖xd8 18 ♖fd1 ♗e6 or 16 ♗b5!? ♕b6 17 ♗xf4 gxf4 18 ♖fe1 e5 in both cases with good play for Black) 16 ♗f3 ♘b6 17 ♕xd8 ♖xd8 18 ♖fd1 ♖xd1 19 ♖xd1 f5 20 ♖d8+ ♔f7 21 ♗h5+ ♔e7 22 ♖e8+ ♔d6 23 ♖g8 and White later won the endgame, Balashov-Winants, Eupen 1994.

5 ... ♗g7

6 ♘b3

6 ♗e3 is seen in Games 74 and 75.

6 ... ♗xc3+

Both theory and practice indicate that Black's chances are inferior after the text, but Suba has suggested a couple of ideas which should prove that Black is okay. However, Black does not need to exchange on c3. After 6...♘f6 7 ♗e2 0-0 8 0-0 he has a few alternatives:

a) 8...a5 9 a4 ♘b4 and now 10 ♗g5 will transpose to the lines given in the note to White's fifth move above and 10 ♗e3 to the 6 ♗e3 lines which are to be found later in the book. However, White can avoid these transpositions with:

a1) 10 f4, when in Unsworth-Theis, corr 1995, Black equalised after 10...♕b6+ 11 ♔h1 d5 12 e5 (12 exd5 ♗f5) 12...♘e4 13 ♘xe4 (or 13 ♘d4 f6 14 exf6 ♗xf6 15 ♗e3 ♘xc3 16 bxc3 ♘c6, Lengyel-Silman, Budapest 1994) 13...dxe4 14 ♗b5 ♗e6 15 c3 ♗xb3 16 ♕xb3 ♘d3.

a2) White can also try 10 ♔h1, but after 10...d5 11 e5 ♘e4 12 f4 f6 (12...♕b6 is the 10 f4 line) 13 exf6 exf6 14 ♘b5 f5 15 c3 ♘c6 16 ♗e3 ♗e6 17 ♖f3 ♗f7 18 ♕g1 g5! Black held the initiative in Zapata-Laflair, New York 1993.

b) 8...b6 9 ♗g5 (9 f4 was successful for White in Franzoni-Nemet, Switzerland 1987: 9...♗b7 10 ♗f3 a5 11 a4 ♘b4 12 ♗e3 ♕b8?! 13 e5 ♘e8 14 ♘b5 ♘c7 15 ♗xb7 ♕xb7 16 ♘xc7 ♕xc7 17 c3 ♘a6 18 ♕d5 with an edge for White; instead of 12...♕b8?! Black could consider 12...d5 or 12...d6, but his set-up looks artificial)

9...♗b7 and now:

b1) After 10 ♔h1?!, Black seized the initiative with 10...♖c8 11 f4 d5 12 exd5 ♘b4 13 ♗f3 ♗a8 14 ♗xf6 ♗xf6 15 a3 ♗xc3 16 axb4 ♗xb2 17 ♖xa7 ♕d6, Hebden-Pavlovic, Vrnjacka Banja 1991.

b2) Nor should Black have any major problems after 10 ♕d2 d6?! (10...♖c8, intending ...♘e5 is stronger, when Skembris gives 11 f4 b5!? as unclear) 11 f4 ♘d7 12 ♖ae1 ♘c5 13 ♗c4! ♘xb3 14 axb3?! (14 ♗xb3!) 14...a6 15 ♘d5 b5 16 ♗d3 f6 17 ♗h4 e6 18 ♘e3 g5 19 ♗g3 gxf4 20 ♗xf4 ♘e7 21 c3 ♖ad8 22 ♘c2 ♘e5 with unclear play, Thorhallsson-Skembris, Kopavogur 1994.

b3) 10 f4 d6 11 ♗f3 ♘d7 12 ♖b1 ♘c5 13 ♘d5 (13 ♘xc5?! bxc5 14 ♘d5 f6 15 ♗h4 e6 16 ♘e3 ♘d4 is good for Black, Timmerman-Van den Bosch, Enschede 1993) 13...f6 14 ♗h4 e6 15 ♘c3 g5!? 16 ♗g3 gxf4 17 ♗xf4 ♘e5 18 ♗g4 ♕e7 19 ♘d4 ♘xg4 20 ♕xg4 ♔h8 and Black was in command in Kotronias-Skembris, Karditsa 1994.

c) 8...e6 9 ♕d6 (best is 9 ♗e3!, e.g. 9...d5 10 exd5 ♘xd5 11 ♘xd5 exd5 12 c3 with a lasting edge for White [Donaldson] while 9 ♗g5 h6 10 ♗h4 g5 11 ♗g3 d5 12 exd5 ♘xd5 13 ♘xd5 exd5 14 ♖b1 a5 15 a4 ♗f5 16 ♗d3 ♗xd3 17 ♕xd3 ♘b4 18 ♕d2 d4 is okay for Black) 9...♘e8 10 ♕g3 ♘b4 11 ♗g5 (11 ♗d1!? d5 12 a3 ♘c6 13 exd5 exd5 14 ♗f3, planning ♖d1 with a small plus – Velicovic) 11...f6 12 ♗f4 ♘xc2 13 ♖ad1 ♘b4 14 ♖fd1 ♘c6 15 ♘b5 ♔h8 16 ♘d6 e5 17 ♗e3 ♘xd6 18 ♖xd6 ♕e8 20 ♗c4 b6!, when White had insufficient compensation for the pawn, Torre-

N.Nikolic, Lugano 1989.

7   bxc3   ♘f6

8   ♗d3

The alternatives should not bother Black too much:

a) 8 ♗c4?! ♘e5 9 ♗e2 d5 ♗h6 dxe4 11 ♕xd8+ ♔xd8 12 ♖d1+ ♔e8 13 ♘c5 ♘ed7 14 ♗b5 a6 15 ♗xd7+ ♘xd7 16 ♘xe4 f6 17 0-0 ♔f7 with a better ending for Black, Raaste-Wedberg, Helsinki 1983.

b) 8 f3!? d5 9 exd5 ♕xd5 10 ♕xd5 ♘xd5 11 ♗d2 0-0?! (11...♗f5!? 12 0-0-0 0-0-0 is a better try) 12 ♗e2 ♖d8 13 h4 ♗f5 14 0-0-0 ♘b6 15 ♘c5 ♘a5 16 g4 ♗e6 17 ♘xe6 fxe6 18 h5 ♘ac4 19 hxg6 hxg6 20 ♗d3 with a clear edge for White, Gomez Baillo-Garbarino, Salta 1987.

c) 8 c4!? ♘xe4 9 ♗h6 d6 10 ♗d3 ♘c5 11 0-0 ♗e6 12 ♕d2 ♕c7 13 ♘xc5 dxc5 14 ♕e3 ♘b4 15 ♗g7 ♘xd3!? 16 ♗xh8 ♘b4 17 ♖ad1 ♖d8 18 ♗e5 ♕c6 19 ♕h6 ♗xc4 20 ♕f8+ ♔xf8 21 ♖d8+ ♕e8 22 ♗g7+ ♔xg7 23 ♖xe8 ♗xf1 24 ♔xf1 ♔f6 with equality, Imanaliev-Yurtaev, Frunze 1987.

d) 8 ♕e2 ♕c7 9 f4 d6 and soon White's pawns will become targets – Suba.

8	...	d5
9	exd5	♕xd5
10	0-0	0-0

Since the main line favours White, Black has to consider trying something different here:

a) 10...♗g4!? 11 ♕e1 0-0 ½-½, J.Fernandez-Zsu.Polgar, Pamplona 1991. This is hardly a test of 10...♗g4. While 11 f3 ♗f5 12 c4 ♕d7 is okay for Black, as 13 ♘c5 fails to 13...♕d4+, the real test is 11 c4!?, but Black should be fine after 11...♕d7 12 ♕e1 0-0 13 ♘c5 ♕c8.

b) 10...♗f5!? (Suba's recommendation) 11 c4 ♕d7 12 ♘c5 ♕c8 (or 12...♕c7 13 ♗b2 ♘g4!? 14 g3 ♘ce5? 15 ♗xf5 gxf5 16 ♘d3 0-0-0 17 ♕e2 with a clear plus for White, Peters-Silman, Los Angeles 1982) 13 ♗h6 (or 13 ♗xf5 ♕xd5 14 ♘xb7 0-0 with good play for Black) ♘g4 14 ♗g7 ♖g8 15 ♗c3 ♕c7 16 g3 0-0-0 17 ♖b1 b6 18 ♘a6 ♕b7 19 c5 ♘ce5, when Black is clearly better – Suba.

11 ♖e1

An important alternative is 11 h3!? In Tolnai-Chernikov, Debrecen 1988, White had a clear edge after 11...♘e5 12 ♘e2 ♕xd1 13 ♖xd1 ♘e4 14 ♗h6 ♘xc3 15 ♗xf8 ♘xd1 16 ♗xe7 ♘c3 17 ♗f1, but for example, both 11...♖d8 and 11...♗f5 seem to provide Black with good chances of equality.

Another possibility is 11 c4, when 11...♕h5 12 ♕xh5 ♘xh5 13 ♖e1 ♖e8 14 ♘c5! f5 (Razuvaev suggests 14...♘g7) 15 ♗e2! is better for White, as in Vogt-Garcia-Martinez, Leipzig 1983, but Black should instead opt for 11...♕d6 12 c5!? (12 ♗b2 ♘g4 13 g3 ♘ge5 14

♕e2 ♘xd3 15 cxd3 ♗h3 16 ♖fe1 e5 is equal, Bokuchava-Rashkovsky, Tbilisi 1972) 12...♕c7 13 h3 a5? (too slow and weakening; better was 13...♗e6 followed by ...♖ad8) 14 ♖e1 ♗e6 15 ♕f3 a4 16 ♗f4 ♕c8 17 ♘d2 ♖d8 18 ♗g5 ♘d4 19 ♕f4 ♘h5 20 ♕h4 ♘h5 20 ♕h4 ♘g7 21 ♘e4 ♘gf5 22 ♕f4 with a clear advantage for White, Kuzmin-Bern, Cappelle la Grande 1994.

11	...	♗g4

12	♕d2!?

Even better is 12 c4! For example, 12...♕d6 13 ♕d2 ♖ad8 14 ♕g5 ♗c8 15 ♗f4 ♕d7 16 h3! ♘h5! 17 ♘c5 ♕d4 18 ♗c7 ♖de8, Ljubojevic-Kir.Georgiev, Thessaloniki ol 1988, and now Georgiev gives 19 ♖ab1 b6! 20 ♘b3 ♕d7 21 ♗h2 followed by c4-c5, when White's two bishops and space advantage guarantee him the better of it.

12	...	♖ad8

Possibly better is 12...♖fd8!?

13 ♕f4!

Meister-Vokac, Ceske 1994, saw instead 13 c4 ♕h5 14 ♕c3 ♗f5 15 ♗b2 e5! 16 ♗e2 ♕h4 17 g3 ♕h6 18 ♗f3 ♘d4 19 ♗xb7 ♘g4 20 h4

♘xc2, when Black was doing very well.

	13	...	♕h5
	14	h3	♗c8
	15	c4	♘e8
	16	♗b2	f6
	17	♗e4	e5
	18	♕e3	♘d6?!

Zapata suggests instead 18...♘c7, intending 19 ♗xc6?! bxc6 20 ♕xa7 ♘e6.

19 ♗d5+ ♔h8 20 f4

Now Black's position is undergoing demolition.

20...♘b4 21 fxe5 ♘xd5 22 cxd5 ♘c4 23 exf6! ♘xb2 24 ♕d4 ♕xd5 25 ♕xb2 ♕d7 26 ♖ad1 ♖xd1 27 ♖xd1 ♔g8 28 ♖d6 d6 29 ♕d4 ♗e6 30 ♘d2 ♗xa2 31 c4 1-0

Game 74
Radulov-Deze
Vrsac 1971

(1 e4 c5 2 ♘f3 ♘c6 3 d4 cxd4 4 ♘xd4 g6 5 ♘c3 ♗g7)

	6	♗e3	♘f6

	7	♗e2

The alternatives mostly transpose into other lines:

a) 7 h3?! 0-0 8 ♕d2 d5 9 exd5 ♘xd5 10 ♘xc6 bxc6 11 ♗d4 ♗xd4 12 ♕xd4 ♕a5 13 ♕a4 ♕b6 14 ♘d1 ♗f5 15 c3 e5 16 ♗a6 ♖ad8 17 0-0 ♘f4 with a plus for Black, Saltaev-Serper, Tashkent 1987.

b) 7 ♘b3 a5 (7...0-0 is likely to transpose into Game 75) 8 ♗b5 0-0 9 0-0 a4 10 ♘xa4 ♘xe4 11 ♘b6 ♖b8 12 c3 f5 13 f4 e6 14 a4 d5 15 a5 g5 16 ♗xc6 bxc6 17 fxg5 e5 with compensation for the pawn, Sisov-Kotkov, USSR 1954.

c) 7 f4 0-0 (7...d6 transposes to the Classical Dragon after 8 ♗e2) 8 e5 ♘e8 9 ♕f3 d6! 10 ♘xc6 bxc6 11 ♕xc6 ♗d7 and Black has excellent compensation for the sacrificed pawn.

d) 7 f3 0-0 8 ♗c4 ♕b6 transposes into lines which can be found under 7 ♗c4 0-0 8 f3 ♕b6 – see Game 87.

	7	...	0-0

It is premature to play ...d7-d5 before castling. The game Filipowicz-Borkowski, Poland 1976, showed why: 7...d5? 8 ♗b5! ♗d7 9 exd5 ♘b4 10 ♗c4 ♖c8 11 ♗b3 ♕a5 12 ♕d2 ♖xc3 13 bxc3 ♘bxd5 14 ♗xd5 ♘xd5 15 c4 and Black had insufficient compensation for the exchange.

	8	0-0

For 8 f4 and 8 ♘b3, see the notes to the next game. The other moves at White's disposal should not bother Black too much:

a) 8 h4? d5 9 ♘xc6 (White should try to limit Black's advantage by 9 exd5 ♘xd5 10 ♘xd5 ♕xd5 11 ♗f3 ♕a5+ 12 c3 ♖d8 or 12...♘xd4) 9...bxc6 10 exd5 ♘xd5 11 ♘xd5 cxd5 12 c3 e5 with an excellent position for Black, Lepeshkhin-Zaitsev, USSR 1958.

b) 8 ♕d2? (a common mistake in this position) 8...d5! and now:

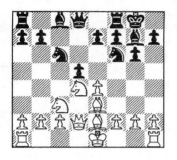

b1) 9 ♘xc6 bxc6 10 e5 (10 0-0-0 ♗e6 11 exd5 cxd5 12 ♗f3 ♕c7 13 ♗d4 ♖d8 is very comfortable for Black, Ciuksyte-Stankovic, Litosmyl 1994) 10...♘d7 11 f4 e6 (11...f6? 12 ♘xd5!) and now 12 ♘a4? can be answered with 12...♘xe5 13 fxe5 ♕h4+.

b2) 9 exd5 ♘xd5 10 ♘xd5 (damage control with 10 ♘xc6 is more advisable; Barczay-Adorjan, Budapest 1978, then continued with 10...bxc6 11 ♖d1 ♗e6! 12 ♗d4 ♗xd4 13 ♕xd4 ♕a5! 14 ♕a4 ♕b6 15 ♕a3 ♖fb8! with a slight plus for Black) 10...♘xd4! (10...♕xd5 is not easy for White to handle either: 11 ♗f3 ♕a5! 12 ♘xc6 bxc6 13 ♗xc6? [better was 13 0-0] 13...♗a6! 14 c3 ♖fd8 15 ♕c1 ♖ac8 16 f4 ♕a5 17 ♕c1 ♖ac8 18 f4 ♕a5 19 ♗f3 ♗xc3+! 20 bxc3 ♖xc3 21 ♔f2 ♖dd3! winning, Ekström-Cvitan, Bern 1988) 11 ♗xd4 (here 11 ♘c3 was to be preferred, though Black of course retains the advantage after 11...♘xe2 12 ♕xe2 ♗f5; to be avoided is the greedy 11 ♘xe7+? ♕xe7 12 ♗xd4 ♗xd4 13 ♕xd4 ♖e8 14 ♕e3 ♕b4+ 15 ♕c3 ♕e4 16 ♕e3 ♕c6 with a nasty attack) 11...♕xd5 12 ♗xg7 ♕xg2!

13 0-0-0 ♔xg7 14 ♕e3 ♕c6 15 ♗d3 ♕e6 (or 15...♗e6 16 h4 h5 17 ♖hg1 ♗g4 with an extra pawn for Black, Crepeaux-Glatmann, Varna 1972) 16 ♕d4+ ♕f6 17 ♕e3 ♗e6 with a big advantage for Black, Ignacio-Donaldson, Anaheim 1985.

8 ... d5!
9 exd5

Or 9 ♘xc6 bxc6 and now:

a) 10 ♗f3 e6 11 exd5 cxd5 12 ♘e2 ♗a6 13 ♖e1 ♘d7 14 c3 ♘e5 with a very good game for Black, Jensen-Ca.Hansen, corr 1996.

b) 10 exd5 cxd5 11 ♗d4 e6 12 a4 a5 13 ♘b5 ♗a6 14 c3 ♘e4! 15 ♗e3 ♖e8 16 ♖fe1 ♕b8 17 ♗d3 ♘d6 18 ♕e2 e5 with clearly better chances for Black, Pilnik-Petrosian, Stockholm izt 1952.

c) 10 e5 is the *ECO* main line, which continues 10...♘e4?! 11 ♘xe4 dxe4 12 ♕xd8 ♖xd8 13 ♖fd1 ♗e6 14 ♗d4 ♖d7 (14...c5!?) 15 a4! with a slight plus for White, Short-Yrjölä, Manila ol 1992. Better is 10...♘d7 11 f4 e6 12 ♘a4 ♕e7 (also good is 12...f6 13 ♘c5 ♕e7 14 ♘xd7 ♗xd7 15 ♕d4 ♖fb8 16 b3 a5 17 c4 a4 with a slight plus for Black, Desch-Donaldson, Portland 1979, or 13 exf6 ♕xf6 14 c3

♕e7 with equality, Fechner-Donaldson, Heidelberg 1979) 13 c4 f6 14 exf6 ♗xf6 15 ♕d2 ♖d8 16 ♖fd1 ♗b7 17 ♖ac1 d4 with a slight edge for Black, Zhukhovitsky-A.Zaitsev, USSR 1962. 10...♘e8 also deserves attention: 11 f4 f6 12 exf6 exf6 13 ♘a4 ♘d6 is unclear.

9   ...   ♘b4!?

For 9...♘xd5, see the next game.

10   d6!?

Clearly best. Other tries are:

a) 10 ♕d2 ♘bxd5 11 ♘xd5 ♘xd5 12 ♗h6 ♗xh6 13 ♕xh6 ♕b6 14 ♘b3 with equality, Calcado-Martinez, Sao Paulo 1992.

b) 10 ♗f3 ♘bxd5 11 ♘xd5 ♘xd5 12 ♗g5, Postler-Baumbach, East Germany 1983, and now 12...♘f6 is equal.

c) 10 ♘b3 ♘bxd5 (alternatively Black could go for 10...♗f5!? 11 ♖c1 ♘bxd5 12 ♘xd5 ♘xd5 13 ♗d4 ♗h6, Anceschi-Makropoulos, Groningen 1972) 11 ♘xd5 ♘xd5 12 ♗d4 e5 (12...♘f6 13 ♗f3 ♕c7 14 ♖e1 ♗f5 15 c3 ♖ac8 16 ♕e2 ♖fe8 17 ♗e5, Hoen-Soos, Lucerne 1979, and 12...♘f4 13 ♗f3 ♗xd4 14 ♕xd4 [Korchnoi] both slightly favour White) 13 ♗c5 ♖e8 14 ♗b5 ♗d7 15 ♗xd7 ♕xd7 16 c4 ♘f6 17 ♕xd7 ♘xd7 18 ♗e3 e4 19 ♘d4 a6 with equality, Jevtic-Twardon, Bydgoszcz 1980.

10   ...   ♕xd6

11   ♘cb5

Inferior is 11 ♘db5?! ♕b8! 12 ♗c5 (12 ♗f3 ♘c6 slightly favours Black) 12...♘c6 13 ♗f3 a6 14 ♘d4? (14 ♗xc6 bxc6) 14...♘xd4 15 ♗xd4 ♖d8 16 ♖e1 ♘g4! 17 ♘d5 ♕xh2+ 18 ♔f1 ♕h4! and Black was winning in E.Bouazis-Balaskas, Caorle 1975.

11   ...   ♕b8

Less dynamic is 11...♕d7 12 c4 a6 13 ♕a4 ♘c6 14 ♖ad1 ♖b8, Bartis-Yudovich, corr 1971, and now Korchnoi gives 15 ♘c3 ♘xd4 16 ♗xd4 with a slight plus for White.

12   c4

12 ♕c1 a6 13 ♘c3 ♘bd5 14 ♘xd5, Minev-Keres, Munich ol 1958, and 12 ♕d2 ♘c6 13 ♗f3 ♗d7 are both equal.

12   ...   a6

Also perfectly playable is 12...♘c6 13 ♘xc6 (or 13 ♕b3 ♘xd4 14 ♗xd4 a6 15 ♘c3 ♘g4 with a slight plus for Black – Andres) 13...bxc6 14 ♘d4 and now Black has:

a) 14...♕xb2? 15 ♘xc6 ♗e6 16 ♘xe7+ ♔h8 17 ♗d4 ♕b7 18 ♘d5! ♘xd5 19 ♗xg7+ ♔xg7 20 ♗f3! ♖ad8 21 ♕d4+ ♔g8 22 ♖fd1 ♖d6 23 cxd5 ♖fd8 24 ♕h4 ♗xd5 25 ♗xd5 ♖xd5 26 ♕xd8+, Estevez-Andres, Cuban ch 1984/85.

b) 14...♗d7 15 ♗f3 ♕c7 16 ♘b3 ♖fd8 17 ♘c5 ♗f5?! (better is 17...♗g4! 18 ♕e2 ♗xf3 19 ♕xf3 ♘d7! with equal chances) 18 ♕e2 e5 19 g4! ♗d7 20 ♖ad1 h6 21 b4 with a clear plus for White, Yanofsky-Benko, Stockholm izt 1962.

c) 14...♕c7!? has been recommended by Andres, who claims equality.

13   ♘c3

13 ♕b3 leaves Black with the initiative after 13...axb5 14 ♕xb4 bxc4 15 ♕xc4 e5 16 ♘b3 ♗e6 17 ♕b5 ♗d7 18 ♕d3 ♗c6 19 ♖fd1 ♘d5 20 ♗c5 ♖e8, Binder-Felegyhazi, Debrecen 1995.

13   ...   e5?!

This thrust is somewhat premature. A wiser course is 13...♕c7 14 ♕b3 (14 ♖c1 ♗d7 is also fine for Black) 14...♘c6 15 ♘xc6 bxc6 16 ♕a3 ♖e8 17 ♗c5 ♖b8 18 ♗f3 ♗e6 with equality, as in Gounder-Balaskas, Caorle 1975. Now White got greedy with 19 ♕xa6?, but found himself losing after 19...♘d7! 20 ♗a3 ♘e5! 21 ♗e4 ♖a8 22 ♘b5 ♕d7 23 ♕b6 ♖ab8 24 ♗xc6 ♖xc6.

14   ♘f3!?

14 ♘c2 also leads to a slight advantage for White after 14...♘c6 15 ♘d5 ♗f5 16 ♘cb4 ♘xb4 17 ♘xb4 ♖d8 18 ♕b3 a5 19 ♘d5, as in B.Martinez-O.Martinez, Cuban ch 1995.

14	...	♗f5
15	♗c5	♖d8
16	♕b3	a5

16...♘d3 17 ♗e7 ♖c8 18 ♗xf6 ♘c5 19 ♗xg7 ♘xb3 20 ♗xe5 ♕a7 21 axb3 ♖d8 22 ♘d5 is very pleasant for White.

17	♖ad1	♗c2
18	♖xd8+	♕xd8
19	♕a3	♘c6
20	♖c1	♗f5
21	♖d1	♘d7
22	♗e3	e4?!

Black is too optimistic and initiates a mistaken plan. The text just weakens the e-pawn and makes the light-squared bishop look foolish. It was better to play 22...♘b4 or 22...♗f8.

23	♘d2	♗xc3?!
24	♕xc3	♕h4
25	h3	♘de5
26	f4!	

Now Black's hopes are crushed. 26...exf3 27 ♘xf3 ♘xf3+ 28 ♗xf3 is very uncomfortable and the game continuation does not present him with much hope either:

26...♘d3 27 ♘xe4 ♗xe4 28 ♗xd3 ♖d8 29 ♔h2 ♘b4 30 ♗e2 ♖xd1 31 ♗xd1 ♕d8 32 ♗e2 ♘c6

32...♘xa2? loses to 33 ♕e5 followed by ♗d4.

33 ♕d2 ♕e7 34 c5 h5 35 ♗c4 ♕f6 36 ♕d7 ♗f5 37 ♕xb7 ♗e4 38 ♕d7 ♔g7 39 ♗d2 ♘d4 40 ♕d6 ♕xd6 41 cxd6 ♘c6 42 d7 1-0

Game 75
Estevez-Andres
Sagua la Grande 1987

(1 e4 c5 2 ♘f3 ♘c6 3 d4 cxd4 4 ♘xd4 g6 5 ♘c3 ♗g7 6 ♗e3 ♘f6 7 ♗e2 0-0)

8   0-0

Here we shall take a look at 8 f4 and 8 ♘b3. For White's other eighth move alternatives, see the previous game.

a) 8 f4 and now of course Black can choose to transpose to a Classical Dragon with 8...d6, but since that is not the subject of this book, we shall to bypass that particular possibility:

a1) After the 'mad' approach 8...e5!?, Grosar-Zsu.Polgar, Portoroz 1991, saw the following continuation 9 ♘db5 exf4 10 ♗xf4 ♘e8 11 0-0 ♘e5 12 ♘d5 a6 13

♘bc3 ♘c7 14 ♘xc7 ♕xc7 15 ♘d5
♕d8 16 ♗e3 b5 (Black has equalised) 17 ♗b6 ♕g5 18 ♗c5 ♖e8 19
♗e3 ♕d8 20 ♗b6 ♕g5 21 ♘c7?
(White should have settled for the draw with 21 ♗e3 ♕d8 22 ♗b6, since after the text Black's well co-ordinated pieces more than compensate for his small material deficit) 21...♗b7 22 ♗f3 f5 23 ♘xe8
♖xe8 24 ♕c1 ♘xf3+ 25 ♖xf3 ♕f6
26 ♗a5 ♖xe4 27 ♖f2 ♕h4 28 ♗c3
♗h6 29 ♗d2 ♗f8 30 ♗e3 ♗d6 31
g3 ♗xg3! 32 ♖g2 ♗xh2+ 33 ♔f1
♕h3 34 ♕d2 ♖xe3 0-1.

a2) 8...d5 9 e5 ♘e4 (also possible is 9...♘e8, intending to break up the centre with ...f7-f6, e.g. 10
♕d2 f6 11 exf6 ♘xf6 12 0-0-0
♘g4 13 ♗xg4 ♗xg4 with equality in Westermeier-Weidemann, German Bundesliga 1981/82) reaching the following position:

10 ♘xe4 dxe4 11 ♘xc6 bxc6 12
♕xd8 ♖xd8 13 ♗c4 ♖b8 14 b3 g5
and now:

a21) 15 ♗xa7 ♖xa8 16 ♗e3
gxf4 17 ♗xf4 ♗a6 18 ♗xa6 ♖xa6
19 ♔e2 f6 and Black held on to the initiative and went on to win in the ending in Tarnowski-Gheorghiu, Bucharest 1961.

a22) Much more difficult to meet is the untried 15 g3!, which

allows White to take back on f4 with the g-pawn if Black decides to exchange. Black is more or less forced to answer with 15...♖b7
(15...a5 16 a4 leaves the a-pawn even more exposed) when 16 ♔f2!
(16 0-0 gxf4 17 gxf4 ♗g4 is fine for Black) 16...♗g4 17 ♗e2 ♗xe2
18 ♔xe2 gxf4 (or 18...f5 19 exf6
♗xf6 20 ♖ad1 and again White is better) 19 gxf4 f5 (or 19...f6 20 e6!
f5 21 ♖ag1 with big problems for Black) 20 ♖ad1 ♖d5 21 c4 ♖a5
with an unclear position, but 20
♖ag1! e6 21 ♖g3 is uncomfortable for Black. It seems better to play
17...♗e6 instead of exchanging on e2, but still White holds the better chances after 18 ♖hd4 ♖dd7
(18...♖bd7 19 ♗xa7) 19 ♗d4 gxf4
20 gxf4 or (best) 19 ♖xd7! ♖xd7
20 ♖d1 ♖xd1 21 ♗xd1 with a won endgame for White, since the black pawns are hopelessly weak. Black can improve with 18...♖c8, but White is still better.

b) After 8 ♘b3 it is also possible to transpose to the Classical Dragon with 8...d6, but Black does best to play for ...d7-d5. However,
8...b6!? 9 f4 ♗b7 is interesting. For example, 10 ♗f3 d6 (not 10...e5?!
11 0-0 ♕e7 12 g3 ♖ad8 13 ♕d2
d5, Milner-Barry-Wade, England
1955, and now 14 ♘d5 ♘xd5 15
exd5 with a clearly better game for White, would have been best) 11
0-0 ♖b8?! (Black could have transposed to the 7 ♗c4 ♕a5 8 0-0 0-0
9 ♘b3 line with 11...♕c7, where he does not have much to worry about) 12 ♖f2! a6 13 ♖d2 with better chances for White, Rhodin-Cladouras, German Bundesliga
1988/89. Instead of 8...b6!? Black should play 8...a5!

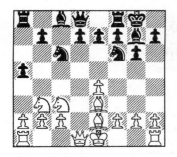

Now if White allows ...a5-a4, Black has easy play:

b11) 9 0-0 a4 10 ♘d4 d5 11 exd5 ♘xd5 12 ♘xd5 ♕xd5 13 ♗f3 ♕c4 (13...♕a5!?) 14 c3 ♘xd4 15 cxd4 ♖d8 with a clear edge for Black, Ravinsky-Vasiukov, Moscow 1958.

b12) 9 a3 a4 10 ♘c1 d6 11 f4 ♗e6 12 ♗f3 ♘a5 13 ♖b1 ♘c4 14 ♗d4 ♕a5 15 0-0 ♖ac8 16 ♘ca2 ♗d7 17 ♔h1 e5 with a clear plus for Black, Zhukovitsky-Suetin, Vilnius 1953.

b13) 9 ♘d5 d6 10 ♘b6 ♖b8 11 f3 ♗e6 12 c4 ♘d7! 13 ♘a4 ♗xc4! 14 ♗xc4 b5 15 ♗xf7+ ♖xf7 16 ♘c3 ♘de5 and Black is on top, Schutt-H.Schmid, corr 1976.

b14) 9 a4 ♘b4, when Black does not have to worry after:

b141) 10 0-0 d5!

b142) 10 f4 d5 11 e5 ♘e4 12 ♗f3 ♗f5 13 ♘d4 ♖c8 14 ♘cb5 f6 15 c3 fxe5!? (15...♘c6 is also fine for Black) 16 ♘xf5 gxf5 17 cxb4 exf4 18 ♗xf4 e5 19 ♗c1 ♔h8 20 ♕e2 axb4 and Black had massive compensation for the sacrificed material in Galkin-Kochiev, St Petersburg 1993.

b143) 10 ♕d2!? d5 11 ♖d1 ♗e6 12 ♘c5 ♘xe4 13 ♘3xe4 dxe4 14 ♘xe6 ♕xd2+ 15 ♖xd2 fxe6 16 c3

♘d5 with the upper hand for Black, G.Garcia-Antunes, Seville 1994.

b144) 10 ♗f3 (this stops ...d7-d5 for now, but apart from that the bishop is not of much use on f3) 10...d6 11 0-0 ♗e6 12 ♖e1 (or 12 ♘d4 ♗c4! 13 ♖e1 ♕c8 14 ♘db5 ♖d8 15 ♖d4 ♖a6 16 b3 e5 17 ♗e3 ♗e6 18 ♕e2 d5 19 exd5 ♗f5! and White had trouble coping with all of Black's threats in Lemrye-Donaldson, Philadelphia 1979) 12...♗xb3 13 cxb3 ♘d7 14 ♗e2 ♖c8 15 ♖c1 ♘c5 16 ♗b5 e6 17 ♗e2 ♕e7 18 ♖d2 ♖fd8 19 ♗c4 f5 and Black was in command in the game Bastrikov-Vasiukov, Yerevan 1955.

8   ...   d5

9   exd5   ♘xd5
10   ♘xd5

White's attempt to exchange everything with 10 ♘xc6 bxc6 backfires after 11 ♗d4 ♘xc3 12 bxc3 ♗e6 13 ♗xg7 ♔xg7 14 ♕d4+ ♕xd4 15 cxd4 ♖ab8, when Black was much better in Stubenrauch-Donaldson, USA 1989.

10   ...   ♕xd5!

Black sacrifices a pawn for the initiative, and in fact White does best to decline the sacrifice. The alternative 10...♘xd4 leads to boring equality. White has tried the following ideas:

a) 11 c4 e5 is equal.

b) 11 ♗c4 ♘c6? (correct is 11...e5 12 c3 ♗e6! with equality) 12 ♗g5 ♗e6 13 ♖e1 ♖e8 14 c3 h6 15 ♗h4 g5 16 ♗g3 with a strong initiative for White, London-T.Taylor, New York 1985.

c) 11 ♗xd4 (White wants to exchange everything down to an ending in which he has a queenside majority, which should offer him the better chances, but practice has shown that Black does not have any problems with best play) 11...♕xd5 12 ♗xg7 ♕xd1 13 ♖fxd1 ♔xg7 and now:

c1) 14 c4 ♗e6 15 c5 a5 (or 15...♖ad8 16 ♗f3 ♖xd1+ 17 ♖xd1 ♖c8) 16 ♗f3 ♖ac8 17 ♖ac1 ♖c7 18 ♖c3 ♖fc8 19 ♖dc1 ♖c8 with equality, Brooks-Donaldson, Columbus 1990.

c2) 14 ♖d2 ♗f5 (or 14...♗e6 15 ♖ad1 ♖fc8 16 ♗f3 ♖ab8 17 c3 b5 18 ♗d5 ♗f5 with equality, Mills-I.Ivanov, Chicago 1985) 15 ♖ad1 ♖ac8 16 c4 ♗e6 17 b3 ♖c7 18 f4 a5 19 ♔f2 ♖a8 with equality, Zso.Polgar-Moldovan, Bucharest 1989.

c3) 14 ♗f3 ♗f5! (somewhat more passive, but still good enough for equality is 14...♗e6 15 b3 ♖ac8 16 c4 ♖ac7 17 h3 ♗d7! 18 ♖d2 ♗c6 19 ♗xc6 bxc6 20 ♖ad1 h5 21 ♔f1 ♔f6 with equal chances, Radulov-Rajkovic, Vrsac 1973) 15 c4 (or 15 ♖d2 ♖ad8 16 ♖ad1 ♖xd2 17 ♖xd2 e5 [17...♖c8! 18 c3 ♖c7 is equal] 18 c3 b6 19 ♖d6 with a slight plus for White, Shakhov-Pakhomov, Simferopol 1989) 15...♖ac8 16 ♖ac1 (or 16 b3 ♖c7 17 ♖d5 ♗e6 18 ♖d4 ♖fc8 19 ♖ad1 a6 20 ♗xd5 ♗xd5 21 ♖xd5 e6 22 ♖d6 b5 with equality, as in Wedberg-Donaldson, Athens 1980) 16...♖c7 17 c5 a5 18 a3 a4 19 ♖d4 ♖a8 20 ♖b4 ♖a7 21 h3 ♗d7 22 ♖cc4 ♗c6 23 ♗xc6 ♖xc6 24 f4 ♔f6 25 ♔f2 ♖a5 26 ♖xa4 ♖xa4 27 ♖xa4 ♖xc5 28 b4 b5 ½-½ Radulov-Forintos, Budapest 1970.

11   ♗f3

Or 11 ♘xc6 ♕xc6 12 c3 ♗e6 13 ♗f3 ♕b5 (13...♕a6 14 ♕c2 ♖ac8 15 ♖fd1 ♖c7 16 ♗d5 ♗f5 is equal, Grann-Wexler, Mar del Plata 1960) 14 ♕c2 ♖fd8 15 a4 ♕c4 16 a5 (White should have tried 16 ♗xb7 ♗f5 17 ♕c1 ♖ab8 18 ♗f3 a5 with some compensation for the pawn) 16...♗d5 17 ♗xd5 ♖xd5 with a slight plus for Black, Leonard-Donaldson, USA 1983.

11   ...   ♕a5!

The alternatives are:

a) 11...♕d7 led to a White advantage in Radulov-Firnhaber, Kiel 1978, after 12 ♘xc6 bxc6 13 c3 ♖b8 14 ♕xd7 ♗xd7 15 ♖fd1 ♗e6 16 ♖d2.

b) Black has also done well with 11...♕c4!? and now:

b1) 12 ♗e2 ♕d5 (12...♕b4!?)

13 ♗f3 repeats the position.

b2) 12 ♗xc6 bxc6 13 c3 e5 14 ♘b3 ♗f5 15 ♕c1 ♖fd8 16 ♘c5 e4 17 ♖d1 ♖d5 with equality, Shabanov-Cherniak, Moscow 1994.

b3) 12 ♘xc6 bxc6 13 c3 (or 13 ♕d3 ♗e6 14 ♕xc4 ♗xc4 15 ♖fd1 ♗xb2 16 ♖ab1 ♗f6 17 ♗xc6 ♗xa2 18 ♗xa8 ♗xb1 19 ♗e4 ½-½ Dely-Aronin, Moscow 1962) 13...♗e6 (also of interest is 13...♖b8, e.g. 14 b3 ♕xc3 15 ♗xa7 ♖b7 16 ♖c1 ♕a5 17 ♗e3 ♕xa2 18 ♗xc6 ♖b8 19 ♗d5 ♗a6 20 ♗xc4 ♗xc4 21 bxc4 ♖fd8, Tverskaya-Kondou, Moscow 1994, or 14 ♗e2 ♕e6 15 ♕c2 a5 16 b3 ♕f5 17 ♗d3 ♕h5 18 ♗e2 ♕h4 19 ♖ac1 ♖d8 20 ♗c4 ♗f5 with some initiative for Black in both cases) 14 ♖e1 (14 ♕c2 a5 15 ♗e2 ♗f5 16 ♗xc4 ♗xc2 17 ♖ac1 ♗f5 is equal, Thomsen-Weemaes, Novi Sad ol 1990) 14...♖fd8 15 ♕e2 ♕xe2 16 ♖xe2 ♗d5 17 ♖c1 a5 with equality, Short-Christiansen, Monaco (rapid) 1993.

12   ♘xc6

A reasonable alternative is 12 c3!? ♘xd4 13 ♗xd4 ♖d8 14 ♕e2 ♗xd4 15 cxd4 e6 16 ♖fd1 ♕b6 17 d5 with equality according to Donaldson, whereas others are not to be recommended:

a) 12 ♘b3 ♕c7 13 c3 ♗f5 14 ♕e2 ♖ad8 15 ♖fd1 ♘e5 16 ♘d4 ♗d7 17 ♗f4 ♘xf3+ 18 ♕xf3 e5 19 ♗g3 ♕c4 with a clear edge for Black, Roll-Donaldson, Philadelphia 1983.

b) 12 ♗xc6 bxc6 and now either:

b1) 13 ♘xc6? ♕c7 14 ♘d4 ♗a6 15 ♖e1 ♖ad8 16 ♕g4 ♗c8 (or 16...e5 17 ♕g3 ♕c8 18 ♘f3 e4 19 ♘g5 ♕xc2 20 ♕h4 h6 21 ♘h3 g5

22 ♕h5 ♖d5 with a clear plus, Dobrito-Vilela, Alcobendas 1994) 17 ♕e4 ♗b7 18 ♕g4 h5 19 ♘b5 ♕c6 20 ♕g5 f6 and Black was winning, Muller-Donaldson, Vancouver 1980.

b2) 13 ♘b3 ♕c7 14 c3 ♗a6 (14...a5!? 15 ♘c5 a4 16 ♘xa4 ♖d8, intending ...♗e6 or ...♗f5 – Donaldson) 15 ♖e1 ♖ad8 16 ♕g4 ♖d5 17 ♕a4 ♗b5 18 ♕xa7 ♕xa7 19 ♗xa7 e5 20 ♖ed1 ♖a8 with strong compensation for the pawn, Casey-Donaldson, Seattle 1979.

12   ...   bxc6
13   ♕c1

Probably White's best chance. The alternatives are:

a) Exchanging the queens with 13 ♕d2? does not ease White's task: 13...♕xd2 14 ♗xd2 ♖b8 15 ♗c3 ♗xc3 16 bxc3 c5 17 ♖fe1 ♗e6 18 c4 ♖fd8 19 ♖e5 ♖b2 20 ♖c1 ♖c8 21 a3 ♔f8 with a slight plus for Black, Nalic-Ca.Hansen, Orlando 1997.

b) Accepting the pawn sacrifice with 13 ♗xc6? gives Black tremendous compensation. After 13...♖b8 Black has a clear edge following:

b1) 14 ♕d5 ♕c7 15 ♗a4 ♖xb2 16 ♕xc5 ♕b7 17 ♗b3 ♗f5 18 ♖ad1 ♖c8 19 ♕xa7 ♕xa7 20 ♗xa7 ♗xc2 21 g4?! ♖c3 22 ♗xc2 ♖bxc2 23 ♖xc2 ♖xc2, as played in Basanta-Donaldson, Bellingham 1987.

b2) 14 ♗f4 ♗a6 15 ♖e1 ♗xb2 16 ♖xe7 ♖fd8 17 ♕b1 ♗f6 18 ♗c7 ♕c3, as in Sherzer-Donaldson, New York 1985.

b3) 14 b4 ♖xb4! 15 ♗d2 ♗xa1 16 ♕xa1 ♕c5 17 ♗xb4 ♕xb4 – analysis by Donaldson.

c) Finally, 13 c3 was played in

Nelson-Turner, British ch 1994, when after 13...♖d8 14 ♕c2 ♗f5 15 ♗e4 ♖ab8 16 ♗xf5 gxf5 18 ♖fd1 ♖d5 19 ♖xd5 cxd5 Black had clearly the better chances.

| 13 | ... | ♖b8 |
| 14 | c3 | c5 |

14...♕c7 15 ♗c5 ♖d8 16 ♖e1 is also okay for Black.

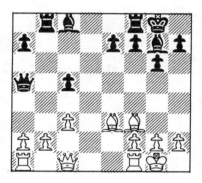

15　♗d5?!

As Black can improve on his next move, White must look here for alternatives:

a) Inferior is 15 a3?, when after 15...c4! 16 ♖d1 ♗e6 17 ♗d4 ♖fd8 18 ♗xg7 ♔xg7 19 ♖xd8 ♕xd8 20 ♗e4 ♖b6 21 ♖b1 ♖d6 Black was clearly better, Glässner-Tangborn, Baden Baden 1987.

b) Interesting is 15 ♖e1!?, Beccera-Diaz, Havana 1992, saw 15...c4 16 ♗g5 f6 17 ♗h6 ♗xh6 18 ♕xh6 e5 19 b4 ♕b6 20 ♗e4 ♗f5 21 ♗xf5 gxf5 when Black's active pieces compensated for the weakened pawn structure.

c) Finally, Andres gives 15 ♖d1 c4! (again!) 16 ♖d5 ♕a6 17 b4 cxb3 18 axb3 ♕e6 as unclear.

15　...　♗f5?!

Stronger is 15...♕b5!, when White has problems protecting his b2-pawn, e.g. 16 ♖b1 ♗f5 17 c4 ♕a5 or 16 b3 ♕d3 or 16 ♗b3 c4.

16	♖d1	♖fd8
17	♗f4	♖bc8
18	♕e3!	

18 ♗c4 is strongly met by 18...♕a4! 19 ♗b3 (19 b3 ♕a5!) 19...♕c6, intending 20...c4 with a slight plus for Black – Andres.

18　...　♖d7

Silman and Donaldson mention 18...c4 19 ♗b7! ♖xd1 20 ♖xd1 ♖d8 21 ♖xd8 ♕xd8 22 h3 a5 23 ♕c5!, when Black's pawns are weak.

19	♗c4	♖cd8
20	♖xd7	♖xd7
21	h3	h5
22	♗e5	♗xe5
23	♕xe5	♕b6
24	b3	♕d6
25	♖e1	

Andres gives the following line 25 ♕xd6 exd6! (25...♖xd6 26 ♖e1 ♔f8 27 ♖e5 slightly favours White) 26 ♖d1 ♗e6! with equality.

| 25 | ... | ♕d2 |
| 26 | a4 | |

26 ♖e2 ♕c1+ 27 ♔h2 h4 is also equal. The game concluded: **26...♗d3! 27 ♗xd3 ♖xd3 28 ♕xe7 ♕xc3 29 ♖e4 ♕xb3 30 ♕xc5 ♕b1+ 31 ♔h2 ♖xh3+! 32 ♔xh3 ♕xe4 33 ♕xa7 ♕f4 34 g3 ♕f3 35 ♔h2 h4 36 ♕b8+ ♔h7 37 ♕f4 hxg3+ 38 fxg3 ♕e2+ 39 ♔g1 ♕e1 40 ♔g2 ♕e2+ 41 ♔g1 ♕e1+ 42 ♔h2 f5 43 ♕c7 ♔h6 44 ♕c2 f4 45 gxf4 ♕h4+ 46 ♔g1 ♕g4+ 47 ♔h1 ♕f3+ ½-½**

10 Main Lines with 7 ♗c4 ♕a5

Chapter Guide

1 e4 c5 2 ♘f3 ♘c6 3 d4 cxd4 4 ♘xd4 g6 5 ♘c3 ♗g7 6 ♗e3 ♘f6 7 ♗c4 ♕a5 8 0-0 0-0

9 ♗b3 d6
>   10 f3   – *Game 76*
>   **10 h3 ♗d7**
>>   **11 ♖e1**
>>>   11...♖ac8 – *Game 77*
>>>   11...♖fe8 – *Game 78*
>>   **11 f4**
>>>   11...♖ac8 12 ♕f3   – *Game 79*
>>>   12 ♘f3   – *Game 80*
>>>   11...♕h5   – *Game 81*
>>>   **11...♘xd4 12 ♗xd4 ♗c6**
>>>>   13 ♘d5 – *Game 82*
>>>>   13 ♕d3 – *Game 83*

9 ♘b3 ♕c7
>   10 ♗g5   – *Game 84*
>   **10 f4 d6 11 ♗e2**
>>   11...a5   – *Game 85*
>>   11...b6!? – *Game 86*

The lines covered in this chapter are more positionally orientated than those to be found in the next chapter (7...0-0 8 ♗b3 a5 and 8...d6). White has a choice of two main ways of countering Black's 7...♕a5. Either:

a) 0-0 and ♗b3, intending ♘d5 to put a central clamp on Black's position, or

b) 0-0 and ♘b3 forcing Black backwards and into the Classical Dragon, when Black has committed himself to the odd looking ...♕c7.

In both lines, Black has to be very careful not to end up in a passive and joyless position with no counterplay, but with best play his chances are no worse than his opponent's.

If as Black you do not like the somewhat passive positions that Black often ends up with after 7...♕a5, we refer you to the next chapter, where more complicated and risky positions occur more frequently.

Game 76
Sax-Andersson
Szirak 1990

(1 e4 c5 2 ♘f3 ♘c6 3 d4 cxd4 4 ♘xd4 g6 5 ♘c3 ♗g7 6 ♗e3 ♘f6 7 ♗c4 ♕a5)

8   0-0

Other moves have proved easy for Black to meet:

a) 8 ♕d2? ♘xe4! 9 ♘xc6 (after 9 ♘xe4 ♕xd2+ 10 ♔xd2 ♘xd4 Black has an extra pawn) 9...♕xc3! 10 bxc3 ♘xd2 11 ♔xd2 bxc6 with a winning endgame for Black, as in D.Hansen-Ca.Hansen, Denmark 1994.

b) 8 f3 ♕b4 9 ♗b3? (better is 9 ♘xc6 bxc6 when Black is at least equal) 9...♘xe4 10 fxe4 (even worse is 10 ♘xc6 ♗xc3+ 11 bxc3 ♕xc3+ 12 ♔e2 dxc6, Gurgenidze-A.Geller, USSR 1959, 13 ♕g1 ♘f6 14 ♗d4 ♕b4 15 ♕e3 0-0, and now Ravinsky gives 16 ♖ad1 b6 winning and Silman and Donaldson give 16 ♗c5 ♕a5 17 ♗xe7 ♖e8 18 ♔f2 ♕f5!, threatening ...♘g4+, and wins) 10...♗xd4 11 ♗xd4 ♕xd4 12 ♕f3 e6! 13 a4 a6 14 h4 h5 15 ♖d1 ♕e5, when Black was just a pawn up in Matulovic-Toran, Palma de Mallorca 1967.

c) 8 ♘b3?! ♕b4! and now:

c1) 9 ♗d3? ♘xe4 10 ♗xe4 ♗xc3+ 11 bxc3 ♕xe4 is plain good for Black, Ramayrat-Silman, Fish-

becks 1992.

c2) Worse is 9 ♕e2? ♘xe4 10 a3 ♘xc3 11 ♗xf7+ ♔f8 12 bxc3 ♕xc3+ 13 ♗d2 ♕e5 and Black was winning in Calvo-Toran, Palma de Mallorca 1968.

c3) 9 ♘d2! (best; the following analysis is by Silman) 9...♕xb2 10 ♘b5! (10 ♘a4 ♕e5! [also good is 10...♕b4 11 c3 ♕a5, Pilnik-Silman, Lone Pine 1975] 11 f4 ♕a5, threatening 12...b5, 12...♕xa4 and 12...♘xe4) 10...♕e5 (10...0-0? 11 c3) 11 f4 ♕b8 12 e5 ♘xe5! (Black also has 12...♘g8!?, intending ...♘h6, or 12...♘g4!? 13 ♕xg4 d5 14 ♕e2 dxc4 15 ♘xc4 0-0 with ...♗e6 and ...f7-f6) 13 fxe5 ♕xe5 14 ♔f2 d5 15 ♗e2 a6 16 ♘d4 ♕c7 followed by ...e7-e5 and White is in difficulties.

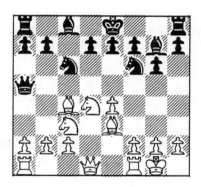

8   ...   0-0

Black has also tried:

a) 8...♕b4? leads to nothing but trouble: 9 ♗b3 (or 9 ♕e2!? ♘g4 10 ♘d5 ♕d6 11 ♕xg4 ♗xd4 12 ♗xd4 ♘xd4 13 ♖ad1 ♕c5 14 ♕h4 f6 15 ♘xf6+, Grankin-Soslov, Riga 1965) 9...♘xe4? (9...0-0 was called for) 10 ♘xc6! bxc6 11 a3! ♘xc3 12 ♕f3 and White was winning in Grabczewski-Filip, Lublin 1967.

b) 8...♘g4?! and now:

b1) 9 ♘xc6 dxc6 10 ♗xd4 ♗xd4 (Black also has 10...e5 11 ♗e3 0-0 with satisfactory play, whereas 11...♘xe3 12 fxe3 favours White since 12...0-0? is met by 13 ♖xf7!) 11 ♕xd4 ♕e5 12 ♕xe5 ♘xe5 13 ♗b3 g5 with equal chances, Usov-A.Geller, USSR 1962.

b2) 9 ♘d5!? ♘xe3 (this gives White a strong initiative, so perhaps 9...d6, but White is still better) 10 fxe3 ♘e5 11 ♘b5 ♘c4 12 ♘bc7+ ♔f8 13 c3 ♖b8 14 b4 ♕a3 15 ♕g4 f6 16 ♕g5 ♔f7 17 e5 when White's attack more than compensated for his material deficit in Litvinov-Litov, corr 1972.

b3) 9 ♕xg4 ♘xd4 10 ♘d5! (Boleslavsky recommends 10 ♕h4!, e.g. 10...♘xc2 11 ♘d5 with a nasty attack or 10...♗f6 11 ♕h6 ♘xc2 12 ♘d5, and this time, too, Black is in deep trouble) 10...♕d8 (10...♘xc2 11 ♕g5 ♕d8 12 ♖ac1 ♘xe3 13 ♘c7+! ♕xc7 14 ♗xf7+ wins for White) 11 c3 ♘c6 12 ♕h4 with a strong attack in Ciric-Ilievsky, Yugoslavian ch 1965.

b4) 9 ♘b3 ♕h5 (9...♘xe3? 10 ♗xf7+) 10 ♗f4 ♗e5 (10...g5!?) 11 ♗xe5! (this is Boleslavsky's move; Ivkov-Lehmann, Beverwijk 1965,

continued less convincingly with 11 ♕f3 g5!? 12 ♗g3 ♘f6 13 ♕e3 ♘g4 14 ♕f3 ♘f6 15 ♕d3 a6, when White's chances are preferable) 11...♘cxe5 12 h3 ♘xc4 13 hxg4 ♕e5 14 f4 ♕d6 15 ♘d5 ♘b6 16 ♕d4 0-0 17 c4 ♘xd5 18 cxd5 b6 19 e5 and Black is lost.

c) 8...d6 again with another choice:

c1) After 9 ♗b3 Black should transpose to the main lines with 9...0-0.

c2) In Kapengut-Romanishin, Gomel 1968, White chose 9 ♘b3, but after 9...♕h5!? (or 9...♕c7) 10 f3 0-0 11 ♕e1 ♗e6 12 ♗e2 d5 Black had equalised.

c3) 9 ♘d5!? (attempting to take advantage of Black's move order) 9...♘xe4?! (9...0-0? 10 ♘xc6 bxc6 11 ♘xe7 loses, and since the text move is very risky Black should try 9...♘e5, though after 10 ♗b3 White is better) 10 ♕f3! ♗xd4 11 ♗xd4 ♘xd4 12 ♕xe4 and White's initiative compensates for the pawn deficit.

c4) 9 ♗b5 ♗d7 10 ♘b3 ♕d8 (10...♕c7!?) 11 ♗e2 0-0 (this is given as slightly better for White by *ECO*, but practice has not verified this judgement) 12 f4 b5! (or 12...a6 13 g4 b5 14 g5 ♘e8 15 ♕d2 b4 16 ♘a4 a5 17 ♖ad1 ♖b8 18 c4 ♘e5 19 ♘ac5 ♘g4 and Black was okay in Suetin-Lehmann, Berlin 1967) 13 a3 (13 ♗xb5 fails to 13...♘g4) 13...a5 14 ♗f3 b4 15 axb4 axb4 (½-½ Short-Miles, Dortmund 1986) 16 ♖xa8 ♕xa8 17 ♘d5 ♘xd5 18 exd5 ♘a5 19 ♘d4 ♘c4 20 ♗f2 ♘xb2 21 ♕e1 ♗f6 22 ♕xb4 ♖b8 ½-½ Carlier-W.Watson, Wijk aan Zee II 1987.

9   ♗b3

For 9 ♘b3, please see Games 84-86. The alternatives in this position are:

a) The positional 9 ♘d5. If Black captures the white knight on d5, White will take back with the e-pawn and start playing against the backward black e-pawn. Black must usually strive to avoid such positions unless he can immediately create counterplay elsewhere. Black has a choice:

a1) 9...♘xe4!? 10 ♘xc6 (10 ♕f3 ♘d2!) 10...dxc6 11 ♘xe7+ ♔h8 12 ♘xc8 (12 ♗d4 ♕d8! is equal) 12...♖axc8 13 c3 ♖cd8 (here T.Georgadze gives 13...f5 as unclear, but in an open position like this White's bishops should guarantee him some advantage) 14 ♕c2 ♘f6 (14...♘d6 15 ♗b3 ♘f5 16 ♗f4 ♗e5 17 ♕e4 is clearly better for White according to Adorjan) 15 ♖fe1 ♕c7?! (Adorjan suggests 15...♘g4!? 16 ♗f4 ♕c5, when White is slightly better) 16 h3 b6 17 ♖ad1 ♔g8 18 a4, Adorjan-Visier, Lanzarote 1975.

a2) Black has also tried 9...♕d8, but without success: 10 ♘xf6+ ♗xf6 11 f4 (also good for White is 11 c3 ♕c7 12 ♕e2 d6 13 f4 ♗d7 14 ♖ae1 ♖ac8 15 ♗d3 ♕a5 16 ♘xc6 ♗xc6 17 f5, Kinzel-Hort, Krems 1967) 11...d6 12 e5! ♗g7 (or 12...dxe5 13 ♘xc6 ♕xd1 14 ♖axd1 bxc6 15 fxe5 ♗xe5 16 ♗h6 ♗g7 17 ♗xf7+! ♔h8 18 ♗xg7+ ♔xg7 19 ♗b3 ♗f5 20 ♖de1 – analysis by Adorjan) 13 e6 f5 14 ♗d5 ♘b4 15 ♗b3 a5 16 c3 ♘c6 17 ♘b5 (intending ♘xd6) 17...a4 18 ♗c4 ♔h8 19 ♕f3 ♖b8 20 ♕f2 b6 21 ♗d5 with a sad position for Black, J.Rodriguez-Kagan, Skopje ol 1972.

a3) 9...♘xd5! 10 exd5 and now play can continue:

a31) 10...♘e5 11 ♗b3 (Levy gives 11 ♗e2!? ♕xd5 12 ♘f5 ♕e6 13 ♘xg7 with compensation for the pawn, but Black should be better) 11...d6 12 h3 (12 c4 ♘g4 13 ♗d2 ♕c5 14 ♗c3 ♘e5 15 ♖c1 ♘xc4 16 ♗xc4 ♕xc4 17 ♘e6?! [17 ♘c6!?] 17...♗xe6 18 ♗xg7 ♕xd5 19 ♗xf8 ♕xd1 20 ♖fxd1 ♔xf8 21 ♖c7 ♖b8! and Black had somewhat better chances in the game Patterson-G.Taylor, Canadian open 1990) 12...♕a6! 13 ♗g5 ♖e8 14 ♖e1 ♗d7 15 c3 ♖ac8 16 ♕d2 ♗f6! 17 ♗h6 (17 ♗xf6 exf6 18 ♕h6 ♘c4 is fine for Black) 17...b5 18 ♖e4 ♕b7 with equal chances, Browne-Silman, Sunnyvale 1974.

a32) Probably better is 10...♘xd4 11 ♗xd4 e5 12 dxe6 (12 ♗c3 ♕c7 13 ♗b3, intending f2-f4, is roughly equal) 12...dxe6 13 ♗xg7 ♔xg7 14 ♕d4+ (14 ♖e1 ♖d8 15 ♕f3 ♕c7 16 ♗b3 ♗d7 17 h4 is clearly better for White according to Adorjan, though Silman and Donaldson suggest 15...♕c5! 16 ♗b3 a5! 17 a4 ♖a6 followed by 18...♖ad6, and 14...♕c5!? 15 ♕d3 b6 16 ♕c3+ ♔g8 17 ♖e5 ♕c6 in both cases with fine play for Black) 14...e5 15 ♕e3 (Gufeld gives 15

♕d6 ♗f5 16 b4 with an initiative for White, but T. Georgadze improves with 15...♖d8 16 ♕e7 ♖d7 17 ♕e8 ♕c7 18 ♖ad1 ♖e7 19 ♕d8 ♗g4 20 ♕xc7 ♖xc7 21 f3 ♗f5 with a clear edge for Black) 15...♗f5 16 ♗b3 ♖ac8 17 ♖ad1 ♗xc2 18 ♖d5 ♕a6 19 ♕xe5 ♕f6 with equality, as in Beliavsky-T.Georgadze, USSR 1973.

b) A similar idea is 9 ♖e1 followed by ♘d5, e.g. 9...d6 10 ♘d5 and now in Pedzich-Baumbach, German Bundesliga 1992, Black kept the balance after 10...♖e8 11 c3 ♗d7 12 b4 ♕d8 13 ♗g5 ♘xd5 14 ♗xd5 ♘xd4 15 cxd4 ♕b6 16 e5 e6.

c) 9 h3 mainly leads to transpositions to the main lines. However, it acquires independent significance if Black tries to exploit it with the dubious 9...♕b4?, when White has 10 ♗b3 ♘xe4 11 ♘d5! ♕a5 (worse is 11...♕d6 12 ♘b5! ♕e5 13 ♗f4 ♕h5 14 ♕xh5 gxh5 15 ♖e1) and here White has so far tried two different paths:

c1) 12 ♕g4 ♘f6 (12...♘d2!? 13 ♕g5! ♘xb3 14 axb3 ♕d8 15 ♘xc6 dxc6 16 ♘xe7+ ♔h8 17 ♖fd1 ♕c7 18 ♗f4 with an edge for White – *ECO*) 13 ♘xc6 bxc6 (13...dxc6!?) 14 ♘xe7+ ♔h8 15 ♕f4 ♗a6 16 ♖fe1 ♘h5 17 ♕d6 favours White Lepeshkin-Demirkhanian, Yerevan 1964.

c2) 12 ♘xc6!? (simpler, but not as convincing as the above) 12...dxc6 13 ♘xe7+ ♔h8 14 ♖e1 ♘c5 15 ♕d6 ♘xb3 16 cxb3 ♕d8 17 ♕xd8!? ♖xd8 18 ♗b6 ♖f8 19 ♘xc8 ♖fxc8 20 ♖xa7 ♖xa7 21 ♗xa7, when White is clearly better, as in the game Hector-Andersson, Haninge 1990.

9 ... d6

Black's attempts to deviate here have not been particularly impressive: 9...♘g4?! (9...b5? 10 ♘d5! ♕d8 11 ♘xf6+ ♗xf6 12 f4 ♗b7 13 e5 ♘xd4 14 ♗xd4 ♗g7 was Minic-Forintos, Pula 1971, when White should have continued with 15 f5!, intending f5-f6) 10 ♕xg4 ♘xd4 and now:

a) White was successful with 11 ♗xd4 in I.Zaitsev-Pavlovichev, Moscow 1965: 11...♗xd4 12 ♘d5 ♘d8? 13 c3 ♗g7 14 f4 d6 15 ♕h4 e6 16 ♘e7+ ♔h8 17 f5! g5 18 ♕xg5 f6 19 ♘g6+ hxg6 20 ♕h4 ♔g8 21 fxg6 ♖e8 22 ♕h7+ ♔f8 23 ♖f3 1-0. But much better is 12...e6! 13 c3 ♗g7 14 ♘e7+ ♔h8 15 ♖ad1 ♕c7 with equality.

b) *ECO* suggests 11 ♕d1 ♘c6 with an edge for White.

c) 11 ♘d5 (aiming for more) 11...♘c6 (11...e6!? 12 ♘e7+ ♔h8 13 ♖fd1 ♘c6! 14 ♘xc8 ♖xc8 15 c3 ♕c7 is better for White) 12 ♕h4 ♖e8 13 c3 d6 14 ♗g5 ♕d8 15 f4 ♗e6 16 f5 ♗xd5 17 ♗xd5 ♘e5 18 fxg6 hxg6 19 ♔h1 ♖f8 20 ♖xf7! ♘xf7 21 ♖f1 ♖f8 22 ♗xe7 ♘d7 23 ♗xf8 ♖xf8 24 ♖f3 ♕a4 25 ♗b3 ♕b5 26 ♕e7 ♕e2 27 ♗xf7+ ♔h7 28 ♖h3+ ♔h6 29 ♗e6 1-0 Hall-Gordon, Canada 1992.

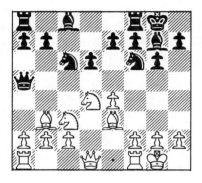

10   f3

Black was threatening to play 10...♘g4, so either 10 f3 or 10 h3 (Games 77-83) is usually played. When he has already castled kingside, 10 f3 does not seem to fit as well into the White set-up as 10 h3 does. On occasion White has also tried the interesting 10 ♘d5!?, which is not easy for Black to meet:

a) 10...♘xe4? 11 ♘xc6 bxc6 12 ♘xe7+ ♚h8 13 ♘xc6 is bad for Black.

b) Not too good either is 10...♕d8?!, in Suetin-T.Georgadze, Lublin 1976, Black soon ended up in a passive position: 11 f3 ♘a5 12 ♕d2 ♘xb3 13 axb3 ♗d7 14 c3 a6 15 b4 ♖e8 16 ♖fd1 ♘xd5 17 exd5 ♖c8 18 ♘b3 e5!? 19 dxe6 ♖xe6 20 ♗d4 ♗f8 21 ♗f2 and due to Black's isolated d-pawn, White had the better prospects.

c) Kapengut's recommendation is 10...♖e8!? and now:

c1) 11 ♗d2 ♕d8 12 ♘b5 ♘xd5? (playing White's game; better was 12...♖b8 13 ♖e1 a6 14 ♘bc3 b5 with counterplay – Baumbach) 13 exd5 ♘a5 14 ♗c3 ♗d7, and now in Estrin-Baumbach, corr 1972,

White should have continued 15 ♗xg7 ♚xg7 16 ♘d4 with much better chances.

c2) 11 ♘xf6+ ♗xf6 12 c3 ♘e5 13 h3 ♕a6 is also comfortable for Black, Kurajica-Bellon, Malaga 1970.

c3) Therefore best is 11 f3 ♗d7 12 c3 ♖ac8 13 ♕d2 ♘xd5 (Black should avoid the endgame and prefer 13...♘e5 with roughly equal chances) 14 exd5 ♘xd4 15 ♗xd4 ♗xd4 16 ♕xd4 ♕c5 17 ♖ad1 ♕xd4+ 18 ♖xd4 with a slight plus for White in the endgame, Sandor-Troyke, played in the German Bundesliga 1994/95.

d) 10...♘xd5! 11 exd5 ♘e5 transposes to line 'a31' in the note to White's ninth move above.

10   ...   ♗d7

Less common is 10...♘xd4 11 ♗xd4 ♗e6 (11...♗d7 is too passive: 12 ♕e2 ♗c6 13 ♖ad1 ♖ad8 14 ♕e3 ♘d7 15 ♘d5 ♗xd5 16 exd5 and White had a typical structural advantage in Ritzmann-Flechsig, corr 1989) and now:

a) 12 ♕d2 ♖fc8 13 ♖fd1 ♘d7 14 ♗xg7 ♚xg7 15 ♕d4+ ♘f6 16 h3 ♕c5 with a level endgame, Damjanovic-Gufeld, Sarajevo 1964.

b) 12 ♘d5?! ♗xd5! (less accurate is 12...♘xd5 13 exd5 ♗xd4+ 14 ♕xd4 ♗d7 15 ♖fe1 ♖fe8 16 ♚h1 ♕c5 17 ♖ad1?! ♕xd4 18 ♖xd4 ♖ac8 with equality, Wallin-Wennström, corr 1978, but White can improve with 17 ♕h4 with a slight plus) 13 exd5 ♘d7 14 ♗xg7 ♚xg7 15 ♕d4+ f6 16 ♚h1 ♕b6 17 ♕e4 ♖f7 18 f4 ♘c5 19 ♕e3 a5 and Black had an edge in Pope-Silman, San Francisco 1974, but this was not exactly model play by White.

c) 12 f4!? (this leads to an almost identical position to the one that arises after 10 h3 ♘xd4 11 ♗xd4 ♗e6 12 f4, which is favourable for White; the question is whether Black can take advantage of White's omission of h2-h3) 12...♘d7 (in Mack-McCue, corr 1989, Black tried 12...♗g4, when after 13 ♕e1 e5 14 fxe5 dxe5 15 ♗e3 ♗e6 16 ♕h4 White was clearly better; however, 13...♘d7 looks like an improvement) 14 ♗xg7 ♔xg7 15 ♗xe6 fxe6 16 ♕g4 ♖f6 with roughly equal chances, but 15 ♘d5 is slightly better for White.

11 ♕d2

11 ♕e1 has been tried on occasion: 11...♖ac8 (11...♖fc8!?) 12 ♖d1 ♖fd8 (12...♕a6, intending ...♘e5-c4, is interesting, while in the game Domnitz-Reshevsky, Netanya 1969, Black tried 12...♖fe8 13 ♕f2 ♘e5 14 ♘de2 b6 15 ♖d4 ♕a6 16 ♖fd1 with slightly better chances for White) 13 ♔h1 (13 ♕f2 does not pose any problems for Black: 13...♘e5 14 ♖d2 b5 15 ♖fd1 ♘c4 16 ♗xc4 bxc4 17 ♘de2 ♖c7 18 ♘f4 ♗c6 when Black was slightly better due to the open b-file in Scarlett-Gibbs, corr 1968) 13...♘e5 (again 13...♕a6, preventing 14 ♕e2, is interesting) 14 ♕e2 a6 15 f4! ♗g4 16 ♘f3 ♘xf3 17 gxf3 ♗e6 18 f5 ♗xb3 19 axb3 ♖c6 20 ♗d4 ♖dc8 21 f4 ♘e8 22 b4 ♕d8 23 fxg6 hxg6 24 f5 ♖c4 25 fxg6 fxg6 26 ♗xg7 ♘xg7 27 ♕g4 ♕e8 28 ♖d5 1-0 Spassky-Gurgenidze, Leningrad 1960.

Untried, but worth a shot is 11 ♘d5, when 11...♘xd5 12 exd5 ♘xd4 13 ♗xd4 ♗xd4 14 ♕xd4 ♕c5 15 ♖ad1 is better for White, but 11...♖fe8 should be okay.

Two rare alternatives are:

a) 11 ♔h1 ♖fc8 12 ♘d5 ♕d8 (12...e6!? 13 ♘xf6+ ♗xf6 14 ♘xc6 ♖xc6) 13 ♕d2 ♘e5 14 c3 ♘c4 (14...b5!?) 15 ♗xc4 ♖xc4 16 b3 ♖cc8 17 c4 ♘xd5, Knoll-Znamenacek, Oberwart 1991, and White should now have played 18 exd5 with an edge.

b) 11 ♘de2!? b5 (perhaps 11...♖ac8!?, intending ...♘e5-c4) 12 a3 ♖ac8 13 ♘f4 ♖fe8 14 ♕e2 ♘e5 15 ♕f2 ♖c7, Nevednichy-Cabrilo, Novi Sad 1993, and according to Nevednichy, White should now have continued with 16 ♘cd5!? ♘xd5 17 ♘xd5 ♖b7 18 ♗d4! with a small edge for White.

11 ... ♖fc8

11...♖fe8 12 ♖ad1 ♖ac8 13 ♘xc6 ♗xc6 14 ♗d4 b6 15 ♖fe1 ♘d7 16 ♗xg7 ♔xg7 17 f4 ♕c5 18 ♔h1 ♘f6 is level, Mikenas-Butnoris, USSR 1974.

12 ♖ad1

12 ... ♖ab8

Black has no problems after 12...♘e5 13 ♕e2 a6 14 f4?! ♗g4 15 ♘f3 ♘xf3+ 16 gxf3 ♗e6 with a slight plus for Black in Borge-Ca.Hansen, Denmark 1995, nor

after 12...♕a6 13 ♕f2 ♘e5 14 ♘d5
♘xd5 15 exd5 ♘c4 16 ♗c1 ♖c5
17 c3 ♖ac8 18 ♘c2 b5 19 ♘e3
♕b7 20 f4 f5 with equal chances,
Kosenkov-Osnos, Moscow 1964.

13	♕f2	a6
14	♘de2	b5
15	♘f4	♕d8
16	♘cd5	♘xd5
17	♘xd5	♗e6

The safest. 17...♗xb2 would
have left Black's kingside very
vulnerable: 18 c3 ♗a3 19 f4 with
plenty of compensation for the
pawn. The game continued:
18 f4 ♗xd5 19 ♗xd5 e6

19...♗xb2 20 f5 is too dangerous
for Black.
**20 ♗b3 ♘a5 21 f5 ♘xb3 22 cxb3
exf5 23 exf5 ♗e5 24 ♗d4**

Interesting is 24 fxg6 hxg6 25
♕f7+ ♔h8 26 ♗d4, but Black can
defend with 26...♗xd4 (26...♕e8
27 ♗xe5 dxe5 28 ♖d7 is very good
for White) 27 ♖xd4 ♕b6.
**24...♕f6 25 fxg6 ♕xf2+ 26 ♖xf2
hxg6 27 ♗e5 dxe5 28 ♖e2 ♖e8 29
♖d5 e4 30 ♖d4 f5 31 ♖d6 ♔f7 32
♖xa6 ½-½**

Game 77
H.Olafsson-Kagan
Randers zt 1982

(1 e4 c5 2 ♘f3 ♘c6 3 d4 cxd4 4
♘xd4 g6 5 ♘c3 ♗g7 6 ♗e3 ♘f6 7
♗c4 ♕a5 8 0-0 0-0 9 ♗b3 d6)

10	h3

(see following diagram)

10	...	♗d7

Black almost always answers
with this natural move, connecting
the rooks and supporting a later
...b7-b5. Other moves fail to im-
press:

a) 10...♘h5?! (hoping for 11
♕d2? ♘xd4 12 ♗xd4 ♗xd4 13
♕xd4 ♘f4 with equality) 11 ♘d5!?
(Parma gives 11 f4!? ♘xd4 12
♗xd4 ♗xd4 13 ♕xd4 ♘xf4 14
♖xf4 e5 15 ♖xf7! with a clear edge
for White, while in Ciocaltea-Bilek,
Bucharest 1968, White tried 11
♘de2 ♗e6 12 g4?! [12 f4 looks
better] 12...♘f6 13 ♘g3?! [13
♘f4! was slightly better for White]
13...♘d7 14 ♗d2 ♘de5 15 f4 ♘c4
16 ♗xc4 ♕c5 17 ♔g2 ♗xd4 and
Black was much better) 11...♕d8
12 ♘f5?! (White cannot resist the
temptation to create complications;
sane and much better was 12 c3 or
12 ♕d2, when Black seems to have
wasted time) 12...gxf5 13 ♕xh5 e6
(13...fxe4!? 14 ♗h6 ♗xh6 15
♕xh6 ♗f5 16 ♘f4 ♔h8 17 ♘h5
♖g8 18. ♗xf7 ♕f8! – Silman and
Donaldson) 14 ♘c3 fxe4 15 ♘xe4
d5 16 ♖ad1 f5 17 ♘g5 h6 18 c4!?
with a mess, but White later won in
Grünfeld-Kagan, Tel Aviv 1986.

b) 10...♘xd4?! 11 ♗xd4 ♗e6
(Parma-Pirc, Beverwijk 1963, continued instead 11...b5 12 ♗xf6
♗xf6 13 ♘d5 ♗xb2 14 ♘xe7+
♔g7 15 ♖b1 ♕c3 16 ♕xd6 and
White had the best of it) 12 f4 (this

may not be the most accurate; Gufeld gives 12 ♖e1!, intending ♘d5, and 12 ♗xe6 fxe6 13 e5!, when in both cases White stands better) 12...♖fc8 (12...♖ac8 13 ♛d3 ♘d7 14 ♗xg7 ♔xg7 15 ♛d4+ ♔g8 16 f5 ♗xb3 17 axb3 ♛b6 18 ♛xb6 axb6 19 ♖a7 is slightly better for White, Gauilanes-D.Rodriguez, Havana 1990, or 12...a6 13 ♛f3 ♛h5? [13...♘d7 was necessary] 14 ♛f2 ♖ac8 15 ♖ae1 ♗c4 16 e5 dxe5 17 ♖xe5+, Tal-Stefanov, Kislovodsk 1966, while 12...♘d7 also gives White an advantage after 13 ♗xg7 ♔xg7 14 ♘d5) 13 ♛d3 ♛c7 14 ♘b5? (14 ♗xe6 fxe6 15 e5 is better) 14...♛c6 15 ♘xa7 ♖xa7 16 ♗xa7 b6 17 ♗xe6 fxe6 18 ♛b3 ♛xe4 19 ♗xb6 ♘xd5 20 ♖ae1 ♛xc2 21 ♛xc2 ♖xc2 22 ♗a7 ♖xb2 23 ♖xe6 ½-½ Ciric-Parma, Ljubljana 1960.

c) 10...♛h5?! was used by Kamsky against Short in their 1994 PCA Candidates match in Linares. Short chose to transpose into the main line, but it would have been interesting to see what Kamsky had in mind against 11 ♛d2! (see line 'c4' below). White has:

c1) 11 f4 ♗d7 (11...♛xd1 12 ♖axd1 ♗d7 13 ♘f3, intending e4-e5, is better for White) transposes into 10 h3 ♗d7 11 f4 ♛h5 – see Game 81.

c2) 11 ♘d5 ♛xd1 12 ♖axd1 ♘xd4 13 ♗xd4 ♘xd5 14 exd5 ♗d7 15 ♖fe1 ♖fe8 is equal – Ubilava.

c3) 11 ♛xh5 ♘xh5 12 ♖ad1 ♘xd4 13 ♗xd4 ♘f4 14 ♖fe1 ♗e6 15 ♘d5 ♗xd5 16 exd5 ♗f6 ½-½ Jonasson-Frey, Reykjavik 1982.

c4) 11 ♛d2! ♗d7 12 ♘de2 ♛a5 13 ♗h6 ♖ac8 14 ♗xg7 ♔xg7 15 f4

with a clear edge for White, Sydor-Filipowicz, Poland 1969.

11 ♖e1

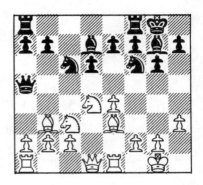

White's intentions with this move are strictly positional, planning to play his c3-knight to d5 to make it more difficult for Black to create counterplay. If Black captures the knight, White will often be clearly better due to his pressure against Black's backward pawn on e7 and general space advantage. The main alternative, 11 f4, is the subject of Games 79-83.

11 ... ♖ac8

11 ... ♖fe8 is seen in the next game. Two rarer alternatives are:

a) 11...♖fc8 12 f4! (this is a strong plan, as Black's rook has left the f-file) 12...♛h5 13 ♘f3 ♖d8? 14 ♛e2 e6 15 ♖ad1 ♗e8 16 ♛f1, intending 17 g4 with a strong attack, Pietzsch-Damjanovic, Sarajevo 1966. Kapengut suggests 13...b5 as an improvement, but even then White has the better chances.

b) 11...♘xd4 12 ♗xd4 ♗c6 (not 12...e5 13 ♗e3 ♗c6 14 ♛xd6 ♘xe4 15 ♘xe4 ♗xe4 16 ♗d2 ♛d8 17 ♛xd8 ♖fxd8 18 ♗g5, winning the exchange) 13 ♘d5 and now:

b1) 13...♗xd5?! 14 exd5 ♖fe8 15 ♕f3 ♘d7 16 ♗xg7 ♔xg7 17 ♖e3 with a strong initiative for White, Sigurjonsson-Bochosian, Tbilisi 1974, or 15 c4 a6 16 ♖c1 ♘d7 17 ♗xg7 ♔xg7 18 ♖c3 ♖ac8 19 ♖ce3 with a clear edge, T.Tolnai-Oney, Komotini 1992.

b2) Eduard Gufeld recommends 13...e5!? but 14 ♗c3 ♕d8 15 ♕d2, intending ♖ad1, gave White the better chances in Todorovic-Kunovac, Zlatibor 1989.

12 ♕e2!

This is White's only real try for an advantage. Less convincing are:

a) 12 ♕d2 ♖fe8 transposing to the next game.

b) 12 ♕d3 (this move was introduced by Ljubojevic, but it does not give Black a hard time) 12...♘e5! (White gains the upper hand after 12...♘xd4 13 ♗xd4 ♖fe8?! [13...♗c6 is not joyful either, as after 14 ♖ad1 ♘d7 15 ♗xg7 ♔xg7 16 ♘d5 White has somewhat the better prospects] 14 f4 ♗c6 15 e5 ♘h5 16 ♕e3 ♗h6 17 e6 f5 18 ♖f1 ♖f8 19 ♖ad1 with a clear plus for White in Ligterink-Kagan, Haifa ol 1976) 13 ♕e2 (White now threatens f2-f4) 13...♕a6! (other tries are worse: 13...♖xc3 14 ♗d2 or 13...b5? 14 a4 b4 15 ♘d5 ♖fe8 16 ♘b5 ♘c6 17 ♖ad1 ♘xe4 18 ♘xa7! and White soon won, Ljubojevic-Sosonko, Wijk aan Zee 1976)

(see following diagram)

13...♕a6! is a brilliant idea of Silman's. Black takes control of the c4-square, and this suffices to generate enough counterplay to compensate for his damaged pawn structure. For example, 14 ♕xa6 bxa6 15 ♖ad1 (15 ♘d5?! ♘xd5 16

♗xd5 ♘c4 17 ♗xc4 ♖xc4 18 c3 ♖b8 19 ♖e2 e5 20 ♘f3 ♖c7 21 ♖d1 ♖f8 22 ♖c1 ♗b5 23 ♖d2 ♗c6 24 ♖e1 f5 with a distinct advantage for Black in Povah-Silman, England 1978) 15...♘c4 16 ♗c1 a5 17 ♘d5?! ♗xd5 18 exd5 ♘b6! and Black was better in Kramer-Ca.Hansen, Denmark 1996. White should have tried 17 a4 to limit Black's queenside activity.

c) 12 ♘d5 ♕d8 (after 12...♖fe8 13 ♗d2 ♕c5 14 ♘f3 ♘xd5 15 exd5 ♘a5 16 ♗e3 ♕c7 17 c3 b5 18 ♗d4 Black ended up in a dead end in L. Bronstein-Kagan, Rio de Janeiro 1979; in Pietzsch-Panno, Lugano 1968, Black tried 15...♘d4 but after 16 ♘xd4 ♗xd4 17 ♗e3 ♗xe3 18 ♖xe3 b5 19 ♕d2 ♖c7 20 ♖ae1 White held the better prospects) 13 ♘b5 ♘xd5 (13...♘xe4? loses to 14 ♘xa7 ♘xa7 15 ♗b6 ♕e8 16 ♗xa7; Black has also tried 13...♕a5, but after 14 a4! ♗e6 15 ♗g5 ♗xd5 16 exd5 ♘e5 17 ♗d2 ♕a6 18 ♕e2 ♖fe8 19 ♗a3 b6 20 a5, he was experiencing great pain in Vasiukov-Roizman, Moscow 1972) 14 exd5 ♘a5 15 ♘d4 b5 16 c3 ♖e8 (this may not be necessary; instead 16...♘c4 is worth consideration, e.g. 17 ♗g5 ♖e8 18 ♕e2 ♕b6 or 17 ♗xc4 ♖xc4 18 ♗g5

♖e8 19 ♕e2 ♕a8 or 17...bxc4!?) 17 ♕d2 (better seems 17 ♘c2 ♕c7 18 ♗d4 ♗h6 with a slight plus, Hennings-Kapengut, Lublin 1973) 17...♘c4 18 ♗xc4 ♖xc4 19 ♘c2 ♕a8 (here T.Georgadze has recommended 19...a5 20 ♗d4 b4 21 ♗xg7 ♔xg7 22 cxb4 ♕c7 23 ♖e2 ♖c8 24 ♘a3 ♖c1, but as Silman and Donaldson correctly point out, Black loses a pawn after 25 ♖xc1 ♕xc1+ 26 ♕xc1 ♖xc1+ 27 ♔h2 axb4 28 ♘c2 ♗b5 29 ♖d2) 20 ♗g5 ♗f8 21 ♖ad1 ♖c5 22 ♗e3 ♖c7 23 ♗h6 ♗f5! 24 ♗xf8 (24 ♘b4 a5 25 ♘c6 e5) ♗xc2 25 ♕xc2 ♖xf8 26 ♕d2 ♖bb8 (intending ...♖bb7, ...♕f8-g7) ½-½ Vogt-T.Georgadze, Lublin 1974.

12   ...   ♘xd4?!

In Sigurjonsson-L.Garcia, Bogota 1978, Black was tempted by 12...♘xe4?, but realised too late that it was actually the losing move: 13 ♘xc6 ♗xc6 14 ♘xe4 ♗xb2 (14...♗xe4 15 ♗d2 is even worse) 15 ♖ab1 ♗g7 16 ♗d2 and Black was lost. However, worth a try is 12...♕h5!?, when White cannot go for the pawn win: 13 ♕xh5 ♘xh5 14 ♘xc6 bxc6 15 ♗xa7 ♗xc3 16 bxc3 c5 or 13 ♘xc6 bxc6 14 ♗xa7 ♕xe2 15 ♖xe2 c5 and White's bishop is lost. Probably best is 13 ♘f3, when White is slightly better.

13   ♗xd4   ♗c6
14   ♖ad1   ♖fe8

14...b5 is possible, but after 15 ♘d5 ♗xd5 16 exd5 White is clearly better.

15   ♕e3!   ♘d7

Worse is 15...b6 16 ♘d5 ♘xd5 17 exd5 ♗b7 18 c3 ♖c7 19 ♗xg7 ♔xg7 20 ♖d4!, and White was having the time of his life in

Lanka-Veremeichik,   Daugavpils 1979.

16	♘d5	♗xd5
17	exd5	♘c5
18	♗xg7	♔xg7
19	♕d4+	♔g8
20	♖e2	b5
21	c3	♖c7
22	♖de1	♘xb3
23	axb3	♕b6
24	♕f4	♕b7

It seems as if Black has solved most of his problems by exchanging all the minor pieces, but he is still left with a very passive position, while the backward a7- and e7-pawns are permanent weaknesses.

25 ♖d2 ♖c5 26 h4 ♕a8 27 ♕f3 h5 28 b4 ♖c4 29 ♖de2 ♔f8 30 g3 a5 31 ♖a1 a4 32 b3 ♖c7 33 bxa4 bxa4 34 ♖da2 ♕c8 35 ♖xa4 ♖xc3 36 ♕f4 ♔g7 37 ♖a8 ♖c1+ 38 ♖xc1 ♕xa8 39 ♕d4+ f6 40 b5

White has used his advantage excellently and created a decisive passed pawn.

40...♕a3 41 ♖c7 ♕a5 42 b6 ♔f7 43 ♔g2 f5 44 ♔h2 ♕e1 45 b7 ♖b8 46 ♔g2 ♕e4+

This leads to a lost endgame, but White was threatening ♖c8 with

penetration on the back rank.
47 ♕xe4 fxe4 48 f3 ♔f6 49 fxe4 e6 50 dxe6 ♔xe6 51 ♔f3 ♗f5 52 ♔e3 d5 53 exd5+ ♔xd5 54 ♔f4 ♔d6 55 ♖g7 1-0

Game 78
Tal-Cu.Hansen
Reykjavik 1986

(1 e4 c5 2 ♘f3 ♘c6 3 d4 cxd4 4 ♘xd4 g6 5 ♘c3 ♗g7 6 ♗e3 ♘f6 7 ♗c4 ♕a5 8 0-0 0-0 9 ♗b3 d6 10 h3 ♗d7 11 ♖e1)

11 ... ♖fe8

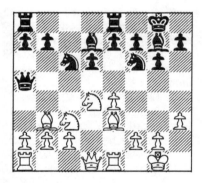

This is probably Black's best answer to 11 ♖e1. For a while Black nullifies White's intention to play ♘d5.

12 ♕d2

This is White's most common try, but not necessarily the best. Other attempts:

a) 12 f4 (this does not seem logical in combination with 11 ♖e1) 12...♘xd4 13 ♗xd4 ♖ad8 (13...e5!? is interesting, although after 14 fxe5 dxe5 15 ♗e3 ♗e6 16 ♕f3 a6 17 ♖f1 ♕c7 18 ♖f2 b5 19 ♗g5 ♘h5 20 ♘d5 White held a strong initiative in Grünfeld-

Nikolic, Belgrade 1989) 14 ♕f3 ♗c6 15 ♖ad1 ♘d7 16 ♗xg7 ♔xg7 17 f5 (it seems wrong to leave the e5-square in Black's hands, but it is hard to come up with anything better, e.g. 17 ♘d5 e6 is also okay for Black) 17...♖f8 18 ♕g3 ♕e5 19 ♕h4 ♘f6 20 ♖d2 e6 21 ♘d5!? ♖fe8 22 fxe6 fxe6 23 ♘c7 ♖e7, Medina-Bellon, Palma de Mallorca 1971, and here 24 ♘xe6 ♖xe6 25 ♗xe6 g5! 26 ♕f2 ♕xe6 27 e5 ♘e4 wins for Black.

b) 12 ♕d3 ♖ac8 (Baumbach mentions 12...♖ad8, intending to meet 13 ♘d5 with ...e7-e6) 13 f4 (more logical is 13 ♖ad1 ♘xd4 14 ♗xd4 ♗c6 15 ♕f3 a6 16 ♘d5 ♘d7 17 ♗xg7 ♔xg7 18 a3!? e6 19 ♘b4 ♕e5 20 c3 ♕e5 21 ♕e3 ♕c5 22 c4 ½-½ Bryson-Baumbach, corr 1989) 13...a6 (better is 13...♘xd4 14 ♗xd4 ♘h5!, as after 15 ♗xg7 ♔xg7 16 ♕f3 ♕c5 17 ♔h2 ♗c6 ½-½, as in Schoneberg-Baumbach, Schwerin 1969, Black has sufficient counterplay on the queenside) 14 ♘f3 (14 ♖ad1 b5 15 a3 ♕c7 16 ♘xc6 ♗xc6 17 ♗c1 ♘d7 18 ♘d5 ♗xd5 19 ♕xd5 ♕c5 was about equal in Walther-Nagorni, corr 1986) 14...♕c7 15 ♖ad1 ♘a5 16 e5 ♘xb3 17 exf6 ♘c5 18 ♕d2 exf6 (also to be considered is 18...♗xf6 19 ♘d5 ♘e4; there could follow 20 ♘xc7 ♘xd2 21 ♘xe8 ♘xf3+ 22 gxf3 ♖xe8 with an interesting endgame) 19 ♕xd6 ♗e6 20 ♕xc7 ♖xc7 21 ♗d4 ♖ec8 22 g4 f5 23 gxf5 gxf5 24 ♖d2 (White tries to improve on Sorokin-Baumbach, corr 1977, which continued 24 ♗xg7 ♔xg7 25 ♘d4 ♔f6 26 ♖e5 ♖d8 27 ♔f2 ♖cd7, when Black had no problems and in fact later won) 24...♗xd4 25 ♘xd4 b5 26 a3 ♖d7

27 ♖e5 f6!? 28 ♖xc5 (this leads to a draw, but the tempting alternative 28 ♖g2+ is no good: 28...♔h8! 29 ♖xc5 ♖xc5 30 ♘xe6 ♖c6 31 ♖e2 ♖dd6 32 ♘f8 ♔g8 33 ♖e8 ♔f7 followed by ...♖c7-e7-e8 and the knight will be lost) 28...♖xc5 29 ♘xe6 ♖xd2 30 ♘xc5 ½-½ Kramer-Ca.Hansen, corr 1995.

c) 12 ♕e2 and now:

c1) Again 12...♘xe4? does not work, since after 13 ♘xc6 ♗xc6 14 ♘xe4 (1-0 Neukirch-Baumbach, Schwerin 1969) 14...♗xe4 15 ♗d2 Black loses a piece.

c2) Also bad is 12...♖ad8? 13 ♖ad1 ♘xd4 14 ♗xd4 ♗c6 15 ♕f3! (Black answers 15 ♘d5 with 15...♘d7 followed by ...e7-e6) 15...b5 16 ♘d5 ♗xd5 17 exd5 ♖c8 18 ♖e3 and Black was suffering, P.Popovic-Renet, Dubai ol 1986.

c3) 12...♘xd4 13 ♗xd4 ♗c6 14 ♖ad1 ♖ac8 15 ♕e3 b6 16 ♘d5! with a nice advantage for White, Vogt-Roizman, East Germany 1969.

c4) 12...♕h5! and now:

c41) 13 ♘f3 ♘e5 14 ♘xe5 ♕xe5 (this has been regarded as equal since Ree-Sosonko, Wijk aan Zee 1976, but things are not that easy) 15 ♕d3 ♗c6 16 ♗d4 ♕a5 17 ♘d5 ♘xd5? (17...♘d7!?) 18 exd5 ♗d7 19 ♗xg7 ♔xg7 20 ♖e3 with a clear edge for White, Gonschior-Lerch, corr 1982.

c42) 13 ♕xh5 has also been tried, when after 13...♘xh5 14 ♖ad1 ♘xd4 15 ♗xd4 ♗c6 16 ♘d5 ♗xd4 17 ♖xd4 ♖ac8 18 e5 ♗xd5 19 ♖xd5 dxe5 20 ♖d7 ♖b8 21 ♖xe5 e6 22 ♖b5 White was winning, De.Markovic-Jelic, Belgrade 1989. Black could try to improve with 14...♘f6 or 15...♘f4.

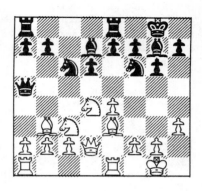

| **12** | **...** | **♖ac8** |

Black has three other valid alternatives:

a) 12...♖ad8 13 ♖ad1 a6 14 ♘f3 ♗c8 15 ♗h6 ♘e5 16 ♘xe5 17 ♕e3 ♗xh6 18 ♕xh6 e6 19 ♕e3 ♔g7 20 ♘b1 ♖d4 21 ♘d2 ♖ed8 with equality, Koch-Ivkov, Dortmund 1989.

b) 12...♘xe4!? 13 ♘xc6 ♕xc3! (or 13...♗xc3?! 14 ♕xc3?! [14 ♘xa5 ♗xd2 15 ♗xd2 ♘xd2 16 ♗d5 is better for White] 14...♕xc3 15 ♘xe7+ ♖xe7 16 bxc3 ♘xc3 17 ♗d4 ♖xe1 ♘b5 19 ♖e7 ♘xd4 20 ♗xf7+ ♔g7 21 ♖xd7 ♔f6 22 c4 b5 with a drawish endgame in Anka-P.Kiss, Dortmund 1988) 14 bxc3 ♘xd2 15 ♘xe7+ ♖xe7 16 ♗xd2 ♖xe1+ 17 ♖xe1 ♗c6 18 ♖e7 d5 19 ♖e3 d5 with equal chances, Kristiansen-Borge, Danish ch 1996.

c) 12...♘xd4 13 ♗xd4 ♗c6, which stops 14 ♘d5 and threatens ...♘xe4.

| **13** | **♘f3** |

In Delacroix-Jenal, corr 1989, White gave 13 ♖ad1 a try, but Black was untroubled after 13...b5 14 a3 ♘e5 15 ♕e2 ♘c4 16 ♗c1 e5.

| **13** | **...** | **a6?!** |

Better was the immediate 13...b5 or 13...♘h5 14 ♖ab1 ♘e5 15 ♗xe5 ♗xe5 16 ♘e2 ♕xd2 17 ♗xd2 ♗b5 18 ♗c3 ♗xe2 19 ♗xe5 dxe5 20 ♕xe2 ♖ed8 with equal play, Koch-Tal, Marseilles 1989.

| 14 | ♖ad1 | b5 |
| 15 | ♗h6 | ♘d8 |

Also possible is 15...♗h8 16 ♘g5 ♕c5 17 f4 (or 17 ♕f4 ♘c4 18 ♘d5 ♗c6 19 c3 ♗xd5 20 ♖xd5 ♗g7 21 ♕h4 e6 22 ♗xg7 ♔xg7 23 ♖xd6 ♘xd6 24 e5 ♕d8 25 exf6+ ♕xf6 26 ♕xh7+ ♔f8 27 ♕h4 ♔g7 28 ♕h7+ ♔f8 29 ♕h4 ½-½, as in the game Chandler-W.Watson, London 1987) 17...♘c4 18 e5!? ♘h5? (18...b4! 19 ♘ce4 ♘xe4 20 ♖xe4 ♗e6 21 ♗xc4 ♗xc4 22 b3 ♗e6 and White has somewhat better chances – Jansa) 19 ♕f2 ♘g7 20 g4 b4 21 ♘d5 ♘e6 22 f5! with a fierce attack, Jansa-W.Watson, Gausdal 1988.

16	♘d4	♖c5
17	a3	♗xh6
18	♕xh6	♖h5
19	♕f4	♗e6
20	♗xe6	♗xe6
21	g4!	♖xh3

T.Georgadze gives 21...♖c5 22 b4 ♕xa3 as interesting.

22 f3

According to T. Georgadze, Black should now have continued with 22...g5 23 ♕xg5+ ♔h8 24 ♕d2 b4 25 ♘d5 ♗xd5 26 axb4 ♕b6 27 ♔g2 ♖xf3 28 ♔xf3 ♗b7 with some compensation for the exchange. Instead, Black unfortunately chose:

22...b4? 23 axb4 ♕xb4 24 ♔g2! ♕xb2 25 ♘d5! ♗xd5 26 exd5 ♘xd5 27 ♕d2 ♖h4 28 ♔g3 ♘c3 29 ♖a1 ♘e2 30 ♘xe2 ♕f6 31 g5 **1-0**

Game 79
Pietzsch-Kapengut
Byelorussia-East Germany 1968

(1 e4 c5 2 ♘f3 ♘c6 3 d4 cxd4 4 ♘xd4 g6 5 ♘c3 ♗g7 6 ♗e3 ♘f6 7 ♗c4 ♕a5 8 0-0 0-0 9 ♗b3 d6 10 h3 ♗d7)

11   f4

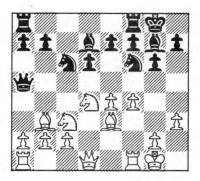

In contrast to 11 ♖e1, with 11 f4 White hopes to get something going on the kingside. Black has a number of different moves and plans at his disposal, most of which, however, are inadequate for equality.

11   ...   ♖ac8?!

Later we will analyse Black's main alternatives 11...♕h5 (Game 81) and 11...♘xd4 (Games 82 and 83). Other tries are:

a) 11...b5 12 ♘d5 (Euwe gives 12 e5! as stronger: 12...dxe5 13 ♘xc6 ♗xc6 14 fxe5 ♘e8 15 ♘d5 ♗xd5 16 ♗xd5 ♖d8 17 ♕f3 ♗xe5 18 ♗xf7 with a clear advantage for White, but there is no reason for Black to allow his opponent to take on f7, so 17...e6 looks like an improvement) 12...♘xd5 13 exd5 ♘xd4 14 ♗xd4 ♕b4 15 ♗xg7

♔xg7 16 c3 ♛c5+ with a fair game for Black, Schoeneberg-Baumbach, East Germany 1966.

b) 11...e5?! 12 ♘xc6 ♗xc6 13 f5! ♖ad8 (things are already a little difficult for Black but in Short-Wagman, Lugano 1986, Black now made things much worse: 13...♗xe4? 14 ♘xe4 ♘xe4 15 fxg6 hxg6 16 ♖xf7! ♖xf7 17 ♗xf7+ ♔xf7 18 ♛f3+ and the game was soon over) 14 fxg6!? hxg6 15 ♗g5 ♘xe4 16 ♘xe4 ♗xe4 17 ♗xd8 ♛xd8 and White has the better chances.

c) 11...♖fc8?! Usually Black has to be very careful when he moves his rook away from f8, as White may take advantage of the lack of protection of the f7-pawn. 12 a3?! (12 ♘f3! clearly favours White) 12...♘xd4 13 ♗xd4 ♗c6 14 ♛d3 ♘d7 15 ♗xg7 ♔xg7 16 ♔h2 ♛c5 17 ♖ae1 b5 ½-½ Ciric-D.Byrne, Vrsac 1969.

d) 11...♖ad8?!

Kan's move from 1936; the idea is to prevent e4-e5, but it is very passive and with correct play White obtains a clear advantage:

d1) 12 f5 ♘e5 (in the stem game Black incorrectly sacrificed a piece with 12...♘xe4?, but was rewarded when White answered 13 ♘d5?,

and Black went on to win in Chekhover-Kan, Leningrad 1936; correct was 13 ♘xe4 ♛e5 14 ♛d3 ♘b4 15 ♛d2 ♛xe4 16 ♖ae1, when Black is much worse) 13 ♛e1 ♗c6 14 ♘xc6 bxc6 15 g4 ♛b4 16 a3 ♛b7 17 ♛h4 d5 with chances for both sides, Damjanovic-Baumbach, Bad Liebenstein 1963.

d2) 12 ♛f3 ♘xd4 13 ♗xd4 ♗c6 14 ♛f2 ♘d7! (of course not 14...♘xe4?? 15 ♘xe4 ♗xe4 16 ♗xg7 ♔xg7 17 ♛d4+) 15 ♗xg7 (15 ♗xa7? only leads to trouble: 15...b6 16 ♗d5 ♗xc3! 17 ♗xc6 ♗b4! winning a piece) 15...♔xg7 16 ♛d4 ♘f6 with equal chances.

d3) 12 ♛d3 (in the game Short-Korchnoi, Garmisch-Partenkirchen 1994, Black now chose to transpose to Game 83 with 12...♗xd4 13 ♗xd4 ♗c6) 12...♘b4! (not 12...♖fe8? 13 ♘f3 ♛c7 14 g4 ♘a5 15 f5 ♗c6 16 fxg6 hxg6 17 ♗xf7+! ♔xf7 18 e5 with a strong attack in Neikirch-Baumbach, East Germany 1967; a nice demonstration of why the rook should stay on f8) 13 ♛e2 (13 ♛d2 ♘a6 followed by ...♘c5 is fine for Black) 13...e5 14 ♘f3 ♘h5 and Black can be satisfied with the position.

d4) 12 ♘f3! (Romanovsky's 1937 recommendation is still considered strongest) 12...b5 (12...♛h5 was tried out in Krogh-Ca.Hansen, Denmark 1995, but Black came up short after 13 ♛d2 b5 14 a3 a5 15 ♛d3 b4 16 axb4 axb4 17 ♛e2 ♗c6 18 e5! dxe5 19 ♖xa5) 13 a3 a6 14 ♛e1 ♛c7 15 ♛h4 ♛b8 16 g4 a5 17 f5 gxf5 18 exf5 a4 19 ♗a2 b4, Kurajica-Hübner, Barcelona 1965, and now instead of 20 ♘d5 b3, better was 20 axb4 ♘xb4 21 g5 with a very strong attack.

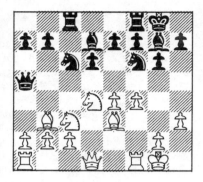

12   ♕f3

For 12 ♘f3! see the next game. The alternatives are less troublesome for Black:

a) 12 f5?! ♘e5 (as the reader will know from the line 11...♖ad8, 12...♘xe4? does not work for Black: 13 ♕xe4 ♕e5 14 ♕d3 ♘b4 15 ♕d2 ♕xe4 16 fxg6 hxg6 17 ♖ae1) 13 ♕e1 ♘c4 14 ♗xc4 ♖xc4 15 ♘b3 ♕c7 16 ♗d4 ♖xd4 17 ♘xd4 ♕b6 with compensation for the exchange, Janosevic-Stein, Sarajevo 1967.

b) 12 ♕d3 ♘b4 (12...♘xd4 13 ♗xd4 ♗c6 transposes to 11...♘xd4 – see Game 83) 13 ♕e2 (13 ♕d2!? ♘a6 14 ♘f3 ♘c5 15 e5 ♘e8 16 ♔h1 was problematic for Black in Gaponenko-M.Calzetta, Buenos Aires 1993; 13...♗c6 may be an improvement) 13...♘a6 14 ♕f3 ♘c5 15 ♖ad1 ♘xb3 16 ♘xb3 ♕c7 17 ♖f2 b6 with equal chances, as in the game Parma-Stein, Yugoslavia-USSR 1965.

12   ...   ♕h5!

Black threatens to equalise by exchanging queens and thereby gains time to start an attack with his queenside pawns. Other possibilities are:

a) 12...♘h5? 13 ♘de2 ♘f6 14 g4, Littleton-Yanofsky, Lugano ol 1968.

b) 12...a6?! 13 ♕f2! ♕h5 14 ♘de2 b5 15 a3 ♔h8 16 ♖ad1 ♘a5, Pietzsch-Szabo, Kecskemet 1966, and now 17 f5! is strong.

c) 12...♘xd4 13 ♗xd4 ♗c6 14 ♖ad1 e6!? (both 14...b5 15 ♕e3 b4 16 ♘d5 ♗xd5 17 exd5, Janosevic-Kagan, Netanya 1971, and 16 e5 ♘e8 17 ♘e4 ♗xe4 18 ♕xe4 e6 19 c3, Hector-Wilder, Cannes 1989 slightly favour White) 15 ♕f2 b6 16 f5 (White goes for the attack, but 16 e5 with equality would have been more advisable) 16...gxf5 17 exf5 e5! 18 ♗e3 d5 19 ♕h4 ♖cd8 20 ♗g5 ♖d6 21 ♗xf6 ♗xf6 22 ♕e1 ½-½ was Janosevic-Schubert, Dortmund 1987. In the final position Black was much better.

13   ♕f2

This is still regarded as the main line, but since Black is at least equal here, White must try something else at some point, perhaps even as early as here. So far, White has also attempted:

a) 13 g4? ♗xg4! 14 hxg4 ♘xg4 15 ♖fd1 ♕h2+ 16 ♔f1 ♘xe3+ 17 ♕xe3 ♘xd4 18 ♖xd4 ♕h1+ and Black was winning in Mesing-Karev, Yugoslavia 1966.

b) 13 ♖ad1 ♘xd4! (13...♘a5 14 g4?! [14 ♕f2! slightly favours White] 14...♘xg4 15 hxg4 ♗xg4 16 ♕h1 ♗xd1 17 ♖xd1 ♕xh1+ 18 ♔xh1 ♘xb3 19 axb3 ♖fe8 with an equal endgame in Mnatsakanian-Stein, Yerevan 1965) 14 ♕xh5 (14 ♗xd4 ♕xf3 15 ♕xf3 ♗c6 16 ♘d5 ♘xd5 17 exd5 ♗d7 18 ♖e3 ♖fe8 19 c3 a5 leads to equality, Rubinetti-Panno, Buenos Aires 1968) 14...♘xh5 15 ♗xd4 ♗xd4+ 16

♖xd4 ♗e6 (inaccurate is 16...♗c6?! 17 ♖d2 ♘f6 18 e5! ♘e4 19 ♘xe4 ♗xe4 20 exd6 exd6 21 c3 with a slight plus for White, Teufel-Toran, Bamberg 1968) 17 ♖f2?! (17 ♖d2 was still equal) 17...a6 (Silman and Donaldson give 17...♘xf4 18 ♖b4 ♗xb3 19 axb3 ♘e6 as good for Black) 18 g4? ♘xf4 19 ♖xf4 ♗xb3 and Black was on top in Teufel-Kestler, Bamberg 1968.

c) 13 ♘xc6!? (White's most recent try, which Kamsky used to win an important game in his candidates match against Anand in Sanghi Nagar 1994, though with correct play Black should be okay) 13...♗xc6 14 g4! ♛a5 15 ♖ad1 (15 g5? loses to 15...♘xe4 16 ♘xe4 d5 17 ♘g3 d4) 15...b5 16 g5 ♘d7 17 f5 and at this point Anand chose 17...♗xc3?! and got into difficulties. In *Informator* Ubilava analyses instead 17...gxf5!:

c1) 18 ♛h5 ♗xc3 19 g6! ♘f6! (19...hxg6 20 ♛xg6+ ♚h8 21 ♛h6+ ♚g8 22 ♚f2 wins for White) 20 ♛h6 ♗xe4 (also interesting is 20...♗xb2, intending ...♛c3) 21 bxc3 (21 ♚f2 hxg6 22 ♛xg6+ ♚h8 23 ♛h6+ ♘h7 24 bxc3 ♖g8 25 ♖g1 ♖xg1 26 ♖xg1 ♛xc3, intending ...♛f6) 21...♛xc3! (21...♖xc3? 22 gxh7+ ♘xh7 23 ♚f2, intending ♖g1 and wins) 22 ♚f2 (22 gxh7+ ♘xh7 23 ♚f3 ♛f6 clearly favours Black) 22...f4! 23 gxf7+ ♚h8 24 ♛f4 (intending ♗d4) 24...♖c4 25 ♗xc4 ♛xc4 26 ♗d4 ♖xf7 with an initiative for Black

c2) 18 ♛f5 e6 19 ♛f4 with chances for both sides.

13 ... b5!

A brilliant idea of Stein's that takes advantage of the tactically weak e4-pawn. The alternatives are too slow to prevent White's kingside build-up:

a) 13...♘a5? (Black intends to sacrifice the exchange on c3, putting more pressure on the e4-pawn, but this plan is easy for White to meet) 14 ♘de2! b6 15 f5! (Black's queen is now caged in, and White just has to catch it!) 15...g5 16 ♛g3 h6 17 ♛h2! ♘c4 18 ♗d4 ♘xb2 19 ♖ae1 ♘c4 20 ♘d5 ♘xd5 21 g4 ♗xd4+ 22 ♘xd4 ♛h4 23 exd5 ♘e5 24 ♖xe5 1-0 Tal-Gazik, Sarajevo 1966.

b) 13...♘b4?! (the same theme: Black wants to play ...♖xc3) 14 ♘de2 a5 15 a3 ♘a6 16 e5 dxe5 17 ♘g3 ♛h4 18 fxe5 ♘h5 19 ♘xh5 ♛xh5 20 ♗xf7+ ♚h8 21 ♛d2 and White is on top, Sakharov-Stein, Tallinn 1965.

14 ♘dxb5

The only move if White wants to battle for the advantage. The alternatives have led to disappointing results for White:

a) 14 ♘xc6 ♗xc6 15 ♗d4 b4 16 e5 (16 ♘d5 ♗xd5 17 exd5 ♘e4 18 ♛e3 ♗xd4 19 ♛xd4 ♘g3 loses an exchange) 16...bxc3 17 exf6 ♗xf6 18 bxc3 ♗xd4 19 cxd4 ♗e4 with a slightly better game for Black, Tsarenkov-Kapengut, USSR 1968.

b) 14 ♘de2 b4 15 ♘g3 ♛h4 16 ♘d5 (16 ♘ce2 ♘a5 17 ♘d4 ♘h5 18 ♘ge2 ♛xf2+ 19 ♖xf2 e5 also favours Black, Sprenger-Scholz, corr 1972) 16...♘xd5 17 exd5 ♘a5 18 ♖ab1 ♗b5 19 ♖fd1 ♘c4 20 ♗xa7 ♘xb2 with an excellent position for Black, Ciocaltea-Panno, Lugano ol 1968.

c) 14 a3 a5 (14...♘a5!? may be better) 15 ♖ad1 (or 15 ♘de2 a4 16 ♘g3 ♛h4 17 ♗a2 b4 with an initiative for Black, Tseshkovsky-Kapengut, Odessa 1968) 15...b4 16 ♘d5 ♘xe4 17 ♛e1 bxa3 18 ♘xc6 ♗xc6 19 ♘xe7+ ♔h8 20 ♘xc8! (20 ♘xc6 ♖xc6 21 ♗d5 ♖xc2 22 ♗xe4 ♖e2 is favourable for Black, Hulak-Romanishin, USSR 1969) 20...♖xc8 21 bxa3 ♗c3 22 ♗d4+ ♗xd4 23 ♖xd4 ♛c5 24 ♛e3 ♘g3 25 ♖fd1 ♘f5 26 ♛f2 ♘xd4 27 ♛xd4+ ♔g8 with a likely draw – Balashov.

14	...	♘xe4
15	♘xe4	♛xb5
16	♖ad1!	

White's best choice, planning c4-c5. The other move tried here, 16 ♘g3, is considered bad: 16...a5!? (or 16...♔h8!? when 17 f5 loses a pawn: 17...♗xf5 18 ♘xf5 ♛xf5 19 ♛xf5 gxf5 20 ♖xf5 e6) 17 a4 ♛b4 18 f5 ♔h8 (18...♛h4 is a suggestion of Silman and Donaldson; one line goes 19 fxg6 hxg6 20 ♗xf7+ ♔h7, when White has a number of threats to meet) 19 ♖ad1 ♛h4 20 ♖d3 ♗e5! (20...♖b8 led to level chances in R.Byrne-Stein, Sarajevo 1967: 21 ♛e1 ♗xf5 22 ♖xf4 ♛xf4!? 23 ♗xf4 ♗xd3 24 ♛d2 ♗a6 25 ♗h6 ♗xh6 26 ♛xh6, when Black should now have

played 26...♘d4 27 ♛e3 ♘xb3 28 ♛xe7 ♘c5 29 ♘f5 gxf5 30 ♛f6+ with a draw) 21 ♗f4 (better is 21 ♗d2, although Black is better after 21...gxf5 22 ♘xf5 ♛xf2+ 23 ♖xf2 ♗xf5) 21...gxf5 22 ♗xe5+ ♘xe5 23 ♖d4 ♛f6 24 ♖d5 (or 24 ♘xf5 ♗xf5 25 ♛xf5 ♘f3+) 24...♖g8 25 ♖xa5 ♛g5 26 ♘e2 ♗c6 27 ♘f4 ♘f3+ 28 ♔h1 ♛xf4 29 gxf3 ♖g3 30 ♗d5 ♖xh3 0-1 Popovych-Sherwin, USA 1968.

16	...	a5
17	c4	♛b4
18	♗d2!	♛b7

Bad is 18...♗d4? 19 ♛xd4 ♘xd4 20 ♗xb4 ♘xb3 21 ♗xd6 exd6 22 axb3.

20 ♗c3 ♘b4 20 ♗xg7 ♔xg7 21 ♛d4+ f6 22 c5 d5!

This practically forces a drawn endgame, whereas 22...♗c6? loses to 23 cxd6 ♗xe4 24 ♖fe1.

23 ♘xd5 ♘xd5 24 ♛xd5 ♛xd5

24...♗c6? 25 ♛e6 ♗xe4 26 ♖d7 wins for White.

25 ♖xd5 ♗c6 26 ♖d4 e5! 27 fxe5 fxe5 28 ♖xf8 ½-½

Game 80
Klundt-Kapengut
Ybbs 1968

(1 e4 c5 2 ♘f3 ♘c6 3 d4 cxd4 4 ♘xd4 g6 5 ♘c3 ♗g7 6 ♗e3 ♘f6 7 ♗c4 ♛a5 8 0-0 0-0 9 ♗b3 d6 10 h3 ♗d7 11 f4 ♖ac8?!)

| 12 | ♘f3! | |

(see following diagram)

| 12 | ... | ♛h5 |

The alternatives suit White fine:

a) 12...b5? (taking away the central control provided by the queen on a5) 13 e5! ♘e8 14 ♘g5 e6 15 ♘ce4 d5 16 ♗c5, Matulovic-

F.Petersen, Kapfenberg 1970.

b) 12...♖cd8?! 13 ♕e1 (also excellent is 13 ♕e2 e5 14 fxe5 ♘xe5 15 ♘xe5 ♕xe5 16 ♗xa7 ♗c6 17 ♖ae1 ♘d7 18 ♕c4 and White had a full pawn extra, G.Garcia-Jimenez, Havana 1969) 13...♗c8 14 ♖d1 (*ECO* suggests 14 g4!?) 14...e6 15 ♕h4 ♘e8? (necessary was 15...♕h5 when after 16 g4 ♕xh4 17 ♘xh4 White has more space) 16 f5! exf5 17 ♖d5 ♕c7 18 ♗g5 ♗e6 19 exf5 ♗xc3 20 fxe6 fxe6 21 bxc3 exd5 22 ♗xd5+ ♔h8 23 ♗xc6 1-0 Kurajica-Kuijpers, Wijk aan Zee 1970.

c) 12...♖fd8?! 13 ♕e1 e6!? (after 13...♗e8, it looked like Black was hit by a steamroller in I.Zaitsev-Dietze, Polanica Zdroj 1970: 14 f5! b5 15 fxg6 hxg6 16 ♕h4 ♘e5 17 ♘g5 ♘c4 18 ♘d5! ♘xe3 19 ♘xe7+ ♔f8 20 ♘xg6+ fxg6 21 ♖xf6+, and Black soon gave up) 14 ♖d1 ♗e8 15 ♘g5 (less aggressive options are 15 ♖f2 b5 16 a3 b4 17 axb4 ♕xb4 18 ♗d2 ♘d7 19 ♘a4 ♕b7 20 ♗c3 ♘b6 with equal chances, Welton-Donnelly, Warwickshire 1993, and 15 ♕f2 d5?! [15...b5 should be okay for Black] 16 exd5 ♘xd5 17

♘xd5 exd5 18 c3 with an edge for White, I.Polgar-Szilagyi, Budapest 1968) 15...h6?! (here 15...d5 was a better try, but White should be better) 16 ♘xe6 fxe6 17 ♗xe6+ ♔f7 18 ♗xc8 ♖xc8 19 ♖xd6 ♗c4, Zuckerman-Toran, Malaga 1968, and now 20 e5! ♗xf1 21 exf6 ♗f8 22 ♖d5 would have won for White.

13 ♕e1

The new move 13 ♕d3 has also served White quite well: 13...b5 14 a3 b4 15 axb4 ♘xb4 16 ♕d2 ♘c6 17 ♗c4 ♘a5 18 ♗e2 ♘c4 19 ♗xc4 ♖xc4 20 ♖xa7 and Black had lost a pawn without compensation in Gild.Garcia-Oblitas, Havana 1992. An improvement for Black is badly needed, but not hard to come by: 14...a5 intending ...a5-a4 or ...b5-b4 looks like a clearly better try.

13 ... b5
14 a3!

Clearly the strongest move, other tries have not been able to offer White any tangible advantage:

a) 14 f5?! b4 15 ♘e2 ♘xe4 16 fxg6 hxg6 17 ♘f4 ♕h7! with a slight edge for Black in Gliksman-Rajkovic, Yugoslavia 1973.

b) 14 e5?! dxe5 15 fxe5 ♘xe5 16 ♘xe5 ♕xe5 17 ♗xa7 ♕xe1 18 ♖axe1 b4 with a completely level endgame – Gufeld.

c) 14 ♖d1!? b4!? (14...a5?! 15 a4 slightly favours White – Korchnoi) 15 ♘d5 ♕xe4 is given by Silman and Donaldson who now continue with 16 f5!? gxf5 17 ♘f4 ♕h6 18 ♘e6 ♕g6 19 ♘xf8 ♖xf8 with plenty of compensation for the exchange. True, but it seems that White can improve by playing 16 ♗xa7!?, when after 16...♘xa7 17 ♘xe7+ ♔h8 18 ♘xc8 Black is obviously lost and 16...e6 fails to 17 ♘b6 ♖c7 18 ♘xd7 ♖xa7 (or 18...♖xd7 19 ♕xe4 d5 20 ♕e3) 19 ♕xe4 d5 20 ♗xd5. Best is probably 16...♗f5 17 g4 ♗xg4 18 ♕xe4 ♗xh3, which leads to a complicated position where White holds the better chances.

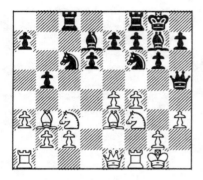

| 14 | ... | a5 |
| 15 | ♖d1 | a4 |

Bad is 15...b4? 16 ♘d5 bxa3 (not 16...♘xe4? 17 ♘b6 ♖cd8 18 ♘xd7 ♖xd5 19 ♗xd5 and wins) 17 ♘xf6 ♗xf6 18 ♖d5+. In *Informator* Maric gives 15...♗e6 16 ♗xe6 fxe6 17 ♘g5 b4 as unclear, but 18 axb4 axb4 (or 18...♘xb4 19 ♖d2 and Black is in deep trouble) 19 ♘e2 ♘d8 20 ♘g3 ♕h6 21 f5 gxf5 22 exf5 ♘d5 23 ♖xd5! exd5 24 ♘e6 wins for White – Gufeld. In Dueball-Klein, West Germany 1968, Black tried 17...♘d8 18 e5 ♘d5 (Boleslavsky gives 18...b4 19 axb4 axb4 20 exf6 exf6 21 ♘de4 fxg5 22 fxg5 ♖xc2 23 ♖xf8+ ♔xf8 24 ♕f1+ ♔e7 25 ♕d3+ ♖c6 26 ♘xd6 and White wins) 19 ♘xd5 exd5 20 ♖xd5, but his position was unenviable.

| 16 | ♗a2 | b4 |
| 17 | ♘d5 | bxa3 |

As we have seen before, 17...♘xe4?? loses to 18 ♘b6 ♖c7 19 ♘xd7 ♖xd7 20 ♗d5.

18 ♘xf6

18 bxa3 ♘xe4! 19 ♘b6 ♘f6 (or even 19...♖c7 20 ♘xd7 ♖xd7 21 ♗d5 ♘c3! 22 ♗xc6 ♖c7 and Black wins the piece back – Gufeld) 20 ♘xc8 ♖xc8 gives Black some compensation for the exchange.

| 18 | ... | ♗xf6 |
| 19 | ♖d5! | |

On 19 e5 dxe5 20 ♖xd7 exf4 21 ♗xf4 axb2 it seems that Black has sufficient compensation for the piece.

| 19 | ... | e5 |
| 20 | ♖xd6 | |

Also possible is 20 bxa3 ♗e6 21 ♖xd6 exf4 22 ♗xf4 ♕c5 23 ♕e3 ♘d8, when Black is doing well according to Levy, but White can improve with 22 ♖xe6 fxe6 23 ♗xe6+ ♔h8 24 ♗xc8 fxe3 25 ♗d7, when Black was a pawn down in Ausinsch-Dauga, corr 1974.

| 20 | ... | exf4 |

21 ♗xf4?

Boleslavsky's recommendation of 21 ♖xf6! is much stronger, e.g. 21...fxe3 22 ♕xe3 (22 bxa3 ♕c5 and Black defends the e3-pawn) 22...axb2 23 ♘g5, when although Black has an extra pawn, he has to prove himself capable of defending against White's threats against his king, Boleslavsky continues:

a) 23...♘b4 24 ♗xf7+ ♖xf7 (or 24...♔g7 25 ♖d6 [*ECO* gives 25 ♕d4 ♔h6 as unclear] 25...♖c7 26 ♖xd7!) 25 ♖xf7 ♘xc2 26 ♕xf4 ♗b5 27 ♘e6.

b) 23...♘e5 24 ♕f4 ♖ce8 25 ♘xf7 ♘xf7 26 ♖xf7.

c) 23...♘d8 24 ♘xf7 ♘xf7 25 ♖xf7 ♖xf7 26 ♗xf7+ ♔g7 27 ♕d4+!

d) 23...♗e8 24 ♕f4 ♘d8 25 e5 h6 26 ♘e4!

e) 23...♗e6 24 ♘xe6 fxe6 25 ♗xe6+ ♔g7 26 ♕f2 ♖b8 27 ♗a2! ♖fc8 28 ♖f7+ ♔h6 29 h4!

This is all very convincing, so it seems that this entire line is almost unplayable for Black, who must deviate at move 11 or 12, unless he can come up with a huge improvement somewhere.

21	...	♕c5+
22	♔h1	♗e6
23	♖xe6	fxe6
24	♗xe6+?	♔g7?

This loses for Black, who should have tried 24...♔h8 when 25 ♗xc8 ♗xb2 26 ♗e3 ♕d6 27 e5 ♕d5 or 25 e5 ♗g7 26 ♗xc8 axb2 27 ♗e3 ♕xc2 would have given him a clear advantage thanks to his passed pawns. However, White had 24 bxa3 with a complicated position and mutual chances.

25	♗xc8	♖xc8

Here 25...♗xb2 did not work due to 26 ♘g5! ♕xg5 (or 26...♘d8 27 ♘e6!) 27 ♗xg5 ♖xf1 28 ♕xf1 a2 29 ♗h6+! ♔xh6 30 ♕xf8+ ♗g7 31 ♕f4+ and mate to follow.

26   bxa3?!

Here White misses another golden opportunity: 26 e5! ♘xe5 (26...♗e7 27 bxa3) 27 ♗xe5 ♗xe5 28 ♘xe5 ♖e8 29 ♖f7+ ♔g8 30 ♕h4 h5 31 ♕f6 and wins – Maric. White is still clearly better though.

26...♖e8 27 ♖f2 ♗c3 28 ♗d2 ♗b2 29 ♘g5 ♗f6

29...♘e5 30 ♗b4 ♕c6 31 c3 ♘d3 32 ♖f7+ ♔g8 33 ♕f1 wins for White – Maric.

30 ♖xf6!

An excellent move that forces the win.

30...♔xf6 31 ♕f1+ ♔e7 32 ♕f7+ ♔d8 33 ♘e6+ ♖xe6 34 ♕xe6 ♔c7 35 ♗f4+ ♔b6 36 ♕d7 ♕xe2 37 ♗e3+ ♔a6 38 ♕c8+ 1-0

Game 81
J.Polgar-Kamsky
Buenos Aires 1994

(1 e4 c5 2 ♘f3 ♘c6 3 d4 cxd4 4 ♘xd4 g6 5 ♘c3 ♗g7 6 ♗e3 ♘f6 7 ♗c4 ♕a5 8 0-0 0-0 9 ♗b3 d6 10 h3 ♗d7 11 f4)

11	...	♕h5!?

This move originates from Kapengut. The reasoning behind it is logical: it is not yet clear where the queen's rook is best placed, while the queen has to move to h5 anyway to start action with the queenside pawns.

12   ♘f3!

Again this knight move is best. The alternatives enable Black to generate sufficient counterplay:

a) 12 ♕xh5 (after this move Black has already equalised) 12...♘xh5 13 ♖ad1 ♖ac8 14 ♔h2 b6 15 g3 ♘a5 16 ♘de2 ♗c6, when Black is already a little better thanks to White's loose pawn structure, Peterson-Troyke, Germany 1991.

b) 12 ♕d2 b5 13 a3 ♘a5 14 ♕f2 ♘xb3 15 cxb3 a5 16 b4 axb4 17 axb4 ♖ac8 with a clear edge for Black, Mnatsakanian-Romanishin, Yerevan 1976.

c) 12 ♖e1 ♖fe8 13 ♗f2 ♘xd4 14 ♗xd4 ♗c6 15 ♘d5 ♗xd5 16 exd5 ♕xd1 17 ♖ad1 a6 18 c3 ♘d7 with equal chances, as in Donchev-Martinovic, Vrnjacka Banja 1984.

d) 12 ♕d3 (White's main alternative to 12 ♘f3) 12...b5! and now:

d1) 13 ♕xb5?? ♘xd4 14 ♕xh5 ♘xh5 and wins.

d2) 13 ♘dxb5 ♘b4 14 ♕c4 a5 15 ♘d4 ♖ac8 16 ♕e2 ♕xe2 17 ♘dxe2 a4! and Black is better.

d3) 13 ♘cxb5 ♘b4 14 ♕c4 a5 15 ♘c3 transposes to 13 ♘dxb5 above.

d4) 13 a4 b4 14 ♘d5 ♘xd5 15 ♗xd5 ♖ac8 16 ♘xc8 (or 16 ♘b5 a5! 17 ♗xc6 ♖xc6 18 ♘a7 ♖c7 19 ♗b6 ♖b7 20 ♕a6 ♖fb8 with very good play for Black – T.Georgadze) 16...♗xc6 17 ♗xa7 ♗xb2 and Black was better in Grabczewski-T.Georgadze, Lublin 1974.

d5) 13 ♖ae1 a5 14 a3 b4 15 axb4 axb4 16 ♘xc6 (16 ♘d5 ♘xd5 17 exd5 ♘xd4 18 ♗xd4 ♗b5! – see note to White's 19th move) 16...♗xc6 17 ♘d5 ♘xd5 18 exd5 ♗d7! (the game Tseshkovsky-Kapengut, Lvov 1973, went 18...♗a4!? 19 ♗xa4 ♖xa4 20 f5 ♕h4 21 ♗f2 ♕f6 22 fxg6 hxg6 23 ♕b3 ♖aa8 24 ♕xb4, and now 24...♖fb8 was better for Black, but according to Ubilava can White improve with 19 ♗c4 ♗xb2 20 ♗d2 with compensation) 19 ♗f2 (best is 19 ♗d4 ♗b5! 20 ♕xb5! ♗xd4+ 21 ♔h1 ♕h4 or 20 ♗c4 ♗xc4 21 ♕xc4 ♖fc8 22 ♕xb4 ♖ab8 23 ♕a4 ♗xd4+ 24 ♕xd4 ♖xc2, when Black is somewhat better in both cases – Ubilava) 19...♖fe8 20 ♖b1 ♕f5! 21 ♕d2 ♗a4 with a clear edge for Black, Short-Kamsky, Linares 1994.

d6) 13 a3!? (the best way to counter ...b7-b5, taking away the b4-square from Black's knight) 13...b4 (also interesting is 13...a6 14 ♘f3 ♖ac8 15 ♖ad1 ♘a5 16 e5 dxe5 17 fxe5 ♗f5 18 ♕d4 ♘d7 with a complete mess, De Firmian-J.Whitehead, San Francisco 1977, e.g. 19 g4 ♕xh3 20 gxf5 ♘xe5) 14 ♘xc6!? (also possible is 14 axb4 ♘xb4 15 ♕d2 a5 with equal chances) 14...bxc3 15 ♘xe7+ ♔h8

16 bxc3 ♖ae8 17 ♕xd6 ♗xh3 18 ♗d4 ♕g4 19 ♖f2 ♖d8 20 ♕xf6 ♖xd4 21 ♕g5 ♖xe4 22 ♘d5 h6 23 ♕xg4 ♗xg4, and now that the madness is over, White has an extra pawn, but the pair of bishops and a better pawn structure provide Black with excellent compensation, as played in De Firmian-Radke, San Francisco 1978.

12	...	b5
13	a3	a5
14	♕d3!	

This has proved quite troublesome for Black. White also has:

a) Less threatening is 14 ♕e1 a4 15 ♗a2 b4 16 axb4 ♘xb4 17 ♗b1 ♕a5 18 g4 ♕c7 19 ♖f2 ♕b7 20 g5 and now of course not 20...♘xe4 21 ♘xe4 ♕xe4 22 c3, but 20...♘h5 when Black was much better in Tsarenkov-Roizman, Minsk 1973.

b) Another strong move for White is 14 ♘d5!, e.g. 14...a4 (14...♗e6 leads to a depressing position for Black: 15 ♕d3 a4 16 ♘xf6+ ♗xf6 17 ♗xe6 fxe6 18 c3 ♖ab8 19 ♔h2 d5 20 e5 ♗h8 21 g4 ♕h6 22 ♘g5, Vujadinovic-G.Todorovic, Kladovo 1992) 15 ♗a2 ♘xd5 16 exd5 ♘a5 17 ♗d4 ♗xd4+ (too passive is 17...♕h6 18

♗xg7 ♕xg7 19 c3 ♖ac8 20 ♕e2 ♖fe8 21 ♘d4, which was not very enjoyable for Black in Wang-Levitan, Manila ol 1992) 18 ♕xd4 ♕f5 19 g4 ♕f6 20 ♖ad1 (20 ♕xf6 exf6, intending ...♘b7-c5, was nice for Black in Wiemer-Finkenzeller, Germany 1990) 20...♕xd4 21 ♘xd4 with a slightly better position for White.

| 14 | ... | a4 |

Here 14...b4 has been suggested as a potential improvement for Black: 15 ♘e2 bxa3 16 ♘g3 axb2 17 ♘xh5 bxa1♕ 18 ♖xa1 ♘xh5 19 c3 with unclear play.

| 15 | ♗d5! | |

Clearly White's strongest move. In Mariasin-Roizman, Minsk 1970, White went for Black's queen with 15 ♘e2?, but Black refuted this easily: 15...♗xh3! 16 gxh3 axb3 17 ♔g2 b4 18 f5 gxf5 19 exf5 ♘e5! and White's position was miserable. Nor can White claim any advantage after 15 ♗a2 b4! 16 ♘e2 ♕a5 (16...bxa3 17 bxa3 ♕a5 is also fine for Black) 17 ♖ae1 ♖ab8 18 ♘ed4 ♘xd4 19 ♗xd4 b3! and Black was better in Dabetic-Novoselski, Cetinje 1993.

| 15 | ... | ♘xd5 |

According to T.Georgadze 15...♖ab8 is met by 16 ♗xc6 ♗xc6 17 ♘d4 ♖fc8 18 f5 with a clear advantage for White. Piket's suggestion of 15...e6!? seems best: 16 ♗xc6 ♗xc6 17 ♗d4 ♖fd8, when Black is okay, but in G.Garcia-Zamura, New York 1994, Black had his share of problems after 17 ♘d4 ♗b7 18 f5! gxf5 19 exf5 e5 20 ♘dxb5 d5 21 ♗c5 ♖fc8 22 ♗e7 d4 23 ♗xf6 ♗xf6 24 ♘e4 ♗h4 25 ♘bd6 ♗a6 1-0. Black can instead try 17...♗d7, intending 18 ♘dxb5

&xb5 19 &xb5 &xe4 20 g4 &xh3
21 &xe4 &g3+ 22 &h1 &g3 with
a draw, but after 18 &f2, intending
19 g4, Black faces new problems.

16   exd5!

An improvement over Gerasi-
mov-T.Georgadze which went 16
&xd5 &ab8 17 c3! &e6
(17...&fe8!? is fine for Black) 18
&ae1 &xd4 19 exd5 &a5 20 &g5
&c4 21 g4! &h6 22 &c1 &f6 and
now White could have settled
things with 23 &e4!

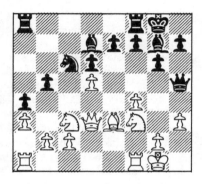

16   ...   &a5
17   &d4!   &h6

Piket analyses 17...&f5 18 &e2
&xd4+ 19 &xd4 &f6 20 &ad1,
intending &e4, or 17...&f5 18 &e3
&c4 19 &f2 &xb2 20 g4. But best
seems 17...&c4!?, e.g. 18 &xg7
&xg7 19 &fe1 &fe8 and Black is
doing fine.

18   &ae1   &fe8

Not 18...&c4? 19 &xe7 &xb2
20 &xg7! &xg7 21 &d4 – Piket.

19   &xb5   &ac8?

According to Piket 19...&ab8
was the only way to keep White's
advantage within limits: 20 &c7
&ec8 21 &c3!, when White is
'only' clearly better. Now on the
contrary, Black's position goes

downhill quickly.

20   b3!   &f5

20...axb3 21 cxb3 &f5 22 &e3
is also very good for White.

21   &d2   &xc2
22   &xa5   &xh3
23   &f2!

Now whatever hopes Black may
have had can be buried. He could
have resigned here, but he strug-
gled on until he eventually lost on
time:

23...axb3 24 &xg7 &xg7 25 &xc2
bxc2 26 &c3+ &g8 27 gxh3 &xf4
28 &f2 &a4 29 &bd4 &a8 30
&xe7 &a5 31 &xa5 &xa5 32 &c2
&d5 33 a4 &a5 34 &e4 f5 35 &b4
&g7 36 &cd4 &f6 37 &b3 &a7 38
a5 g5 1-0

Game 82
Skovgaard-Svensson
Corr 1984

(1 e4 c5 2 &f3 &c6 3 d4 cxd4 4
&xd4 g6 5 &c3 &g7 6 &e3 &f6 7
&c4 &a5 8. 0-0 0-0 9 &b3 d6 10
h3 &d7 11 f4)

11   ...   &xd4!

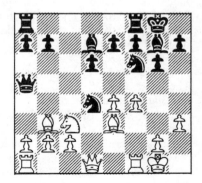

As we saw in the previous
games, Black has his share of

problems after 11...♖ac8 as well as 11...♕h5. The exchange of knights with 11...♘xd4 draws some of the tension from the position, enabling Black to immediately direct his attention towards the weak e4-pawn in combination with a timely ...e7-e5. There is also a certain amount of logic behind this, since in reply to almost any other move, White moves his knight back to f3 to avoid an exchange.

12 ♗xd4 ♗c6

Almost exclusively chosen, but Black has also had some success with 12...e5!? 13 ♗e3 (13 fxe5 dxe5 14 ♗e3 ♗c6 15 ♕f3, intending ♗g5, is an interesting possibility for White) 13...exf4 (13...♗c6? 14 f5 transposes to Short-Wagman, see note 'b' to Black's 11th move in Game 79) 14 ♗xf4 ♗c6 15 ♕f3 ♖ad8 16 ♖ad1 (16 ♘d5 ♗xd5 17 exd5 ♘d7! is nice for Black) 16...♔h8 17 ♖xd6?! (17 ♔h1!? or 17 ♖f2!?, intending ♖fd2, seems better) 17...♕c5+ 18 ♕f2 ♕xf2+ 19 ♖xf2 ♘xe4 20 ♘xe4 ♗xe4 21 ♖fd2 ♖xd6 22 ♗xd6 ♖d8 23 ♗xf7 ♗xc2 24 ♖xc2 ♗d4+ ½-½ Janosevic-Wagman, Bratto 1984. This really went very smoothly for Black, but only time will tell the future of this line.

13 ♘d5

For 13 ♕d3 see the next game. The other alternatives do not present Black with any problems:

a) 13 ♕f3? (neither 13 ♖e1 ♖ad8 14 ♘d5 e5 15 ♗c3 ♕c5+ 16 ♔h1 ♗xd5 nor 13 e5 ♘e8 14 exd6 ♗xd4+ 15 ♕xd4 ♘xd6 give White anything either) 13...♕b4! 14 ♗xf6 ♗xf6 15 ♖fe1 ♕c5+ 16 ♔h1 ♗xc3 17 ♕xc3 ♕xc3 18 bxc3 ♖ac8 with a very enjoyable ending for Black,

Ciocaltea-Furman, Harrachov 1966.

b) 13 ♕e2? ♕b4! 14 ♖fd1 (14 ♖ad1? allows 14...♘xe4! 15 ♗xg7 ♔xg7 16 ♘xe4 [16 ♘d5 fails to 16...♗xd5 and 17...♘g3 winning the exchange, which is why White must play the f-rook to d1] 16...♕xe4 17 ♕d2 ♕f5 18 c3 and now 18...b6 19 ♗d2 ♕f6 20 f5 g5 would have left White without much to hope for, but instead Black chose a disastrous path: 18...♕c5+ 19 ♔h2 f5? 20 ♖fe1 ♖fe8 21 ♗e6 ♗e4 22 b4 ♕b6 23 c4 ♔f6 24 ♖xe4 fxe4 25 f5, and Black was soon dead and buried, Holusija-Gazik, Yugoslavia 1967) 14...♘xe4 15 ♗xg7 ♗xg7 16 ♘xd5 ♕c5? (this only leads to a draw; better was 16...♗xd5 17 ♖xd5 ♕b6+ 18 ♔h2 ♘f6, and White is just a pawn down) 17 ♔h2 ♘f6 18 ♘c7 ♗xg2 19 ♕xe7 ♗xh3 20 ♔xh3 ♕h5+ 21 ♔g2 and a draw was agreed in Hort-Furman, Polanica Zdroj 1967.

c) 13 ♕e1 (this usually leads to a draw) 13...♕b4 14 ♖d1 ♘xe4! 15 ♗xg7 ♔xg7 16 ♘d5 (16 ♘xe4 ♕xe4 17 ♕c3+ [both 17 ♕d2 and 17 ♕f2 lead to positions which can be found under 13 ♕e2] 17...♔g8 18 ♖f2 e6 19 ♖xd6 ♖ad8 was equal in Jacobsen-Kapengut, Ybbs 1968) 16...♕c5+ (16...♕xe1 17 ♖fxe1 ♘c5 18 ♘xe7 ♖fe8 19 ♘xc6 ♖xe1+ 20 ♖xe1 bxc6 21 ♖e7 ♘xb3 22 axb3 and although a draw was agreed here, White was better in the endgame in Kostro-Hort, Polanica Zdroj 1967) 17 ♔h2 ♘f6 18 ♘c7 ♗xg2! 19 ♕xe7 ♗xh3! (certainly not 17...e6?, which gave White a clear edge in Janosevic-Parma, Yugoslavian ch 1964: 18 ♕xe4 exd5 19 ♕d4+ ♕xd4 20

♖xd4 ♖ae8 21 f5) 20 ♔xh3 ♕h5+ with a draw by perpetual check, e.g. in Ostojic-Kaplan, Hastings 1968.

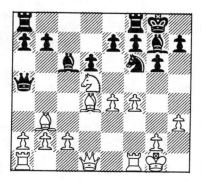

13   ...   ♖ae8!

Three other moves have also been tried:

a) 13...♗xd5?! is too passive: 14 exd5 ♘d7 15 ♗xg7 ♔xg7 16 ♕d4+ ♔g8 17 ♖ae1 ♖ae8 (or 17...♖fe8 18 ♖e3 ♕c5 19 ♕d2 with a slight plus for White, Smit-Razvalayev, USSR 1967) 18 ♔h2, Vasiukov-Ciocaltea, Bucharest 1967, and now Black should have continued with 18...♕c5 19 ♕d3 b5 with a slightly inferior position.

b) Levy mentions 13...♘xd5 14 exd5 ♗d7 15 ♖e1 ♖fe8 16 ♔h2 ♗xd4 17 ♕xd4 ♕c5 18 ♕d2 b5 19 c3 with a slight plus for White, but Black has no prospects of counterplay.

c) Also inaccurate is 13...♖fe8, as Black takes away some of the protection from the f7-pawn. White has tried numerous moves here:

c1) 14 c4?! ♗xd5 15 exd5 ♘d7 16 ♔h1 ♗xd4 17 ♕xd4 ♕c5 and Black's knight is stronger than White's bishop.

c2) 14 ♗c3 ♕c5 15 ♔h2 ♘xd5

16 exd5 ♗b5 17 ♖f3 ♖ac8 with equal chances.

c3) 14 ♘xf6+? exf6 15 f5 ♗e4 16 fxg6 hxg6 17 ♗xf6 ♕c5 18 ♔h1 d5 19 ♕g4 ♕d6 and Black again has a slight pull, Kärker-Yudovic, corr 1966-67.

c4) 14 ♗xf6?! exf6 (14...♕c5+ 15 ♔h2 ♗xd5 [Kapengut suggests 15...♗xf6 16 ♘c7 ♗xe4, when Black has sufficient compensation for the exchange] 16 ♗xg7 ♗xb3 17 ♗c3 ♗c4 18 ♖f3 and White's chances are slightly better due to the weak dark squares on Black's kingside) 15 f5 (interesting is 15 ♕d3!?, intending 15...f5?! 16 exf5 ♗xb2 17 fxg6 hxg6 18 ♘f6+ ♗xf6 19 ♕xg6+ ♗g7 20 ♖xf7+ ♔h7 21 f5 with a decisive attack, yet with 15...♗b5!? 16 c4 ♗c6 Black has a solid position) 15...♖xe4 16 fxg6 (16 ♔h1 ♖ae8 17 ♕d3 g5 18 ♖ad1 ♕c5 19 ♔h2 ♗b5 slightly favours Black, Nonnenmacher-Hecht, German Bundesliga 1987/88) 16...hxg6 17 ♘xf6+ ♗xf6 18 ♖xf6 ♕c5+ 19 ♔h1 d5 20 ♕f3 ♕e7 with equality, as in the game Hector-Donaldson, Malmo 1985/86.

c5) 14 ♖e1!? ♖ac8 15 c3 ♗xd5?! (now Black ends up in a terribly passive position; better was 15...♘xd5 16 exd5 ♗xd4+ 17 ♕xd4 ♗d7) 16 exd5 ♘d7 17 ♗f2! b5 18 a3 ♘b6 19 ♖e4 ♗f8 20 ♕e2, and Black was not enjoying himself in Minic-Bellon, Kapfenberg 1970.

c6) 14 ♕d3 ♖ac8 (or 14...♘xd5 15 exd5 ♗b5 16 c4 ♗xd4 17 ♕xd4 ♗d7 18 ♔h2 ♕c5 with equal chances) 15 ♔h1 ♘xd5 16 exd5 ♕xd4 17 ♕xd4 ♗d7 18 ♖f3 ♕c5 19 ♕d2 a5 20 c3 ♕b5 21 ♖e1 a4 22 ♗d1 e6! is equal, Smit-Murey, USSR 1967.

c7) The best move is 14 f5!, exploiting the fact that Black's previous move took away the protection of the f7-pawn. Play usually continues with 14...♗xd5 (14...♘xe4? loses quickly to 15 fxg6 hxg6 16 ♖xf7!; of interest is 14...♘xd5, though after 15 ♗xg7 ♔xg7 16 exd5 ♗d7 17 fxg6 hxg6 18 ♕d4+, Black's open kingside will soon give him a headache) 15 exd5 ♘d7 (keeping some defenders on the board with 15...b5 seems a lot safer, but Black's lack of counterplay does not promise him a bright future) 16 ♔h1! (both 16 c3 ♗xd4 17 ♕xd4 ♕c5 and 17 cxd4 ♘f6 18 ♕f3 ♕d2 19 ♕f2 ♘e4 20 ♕xd2 ♘xd2 21 ♖f2 ♘xb3 22 axb3 ♖ec8, Browne-Bellon, Malaga 1970, are comfortable for Black) 16...♗xd4 17 ♕xd4 ♕c5 (17...♘e5 is met by 18 f6 and 17...f6 by 18 h4, intending g4-g5) 18 ♕f4 ♘f6 19 ♖ae1 a5 20 c4, with a powerful attacking position for White, as in the game Kelecevic-Rajkovic, Yugoslavian ch 1968.

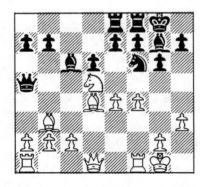

14   ♕e1

White has also tried to seek an advantage with:

a) 14 ♕f3 ♘xd5 15 exd5 ♗b5 16 c4 ♗d7 17 ♗xg7 ♔xg7 18 ♔h1 ♕c5 ½-½ Klovan-T.Georgadze, Tbilisi 1973.

b) 14 ♗xf6 ♕c5+ 15 ♔h1 exf6 (or 15...♗xf6 and now both 16 c3 ♗g7 followed by ...e7-e6 and 16 ♘xf6+ exf6 17 ♗d5 ♗xd5 18 exd5 ♖e8 are good for Black) 16 f5 ♖xe4 17 fxg6 hxg6 18 ♘xf6+ ♗xf6 19 ♖xf6 ♕g5 with equal chances, Acosta-L.Garcia, Bogota 1980.

c) 14 ♘xf6+? exf6 15 f5 is bad because of 15...♗xe4 16 fxg6 hxg6 17 ♗xf6 ♕c5+ 18 ♔h1 ♗xf6 19 ♖xf6 ♗xg2+!

d) 14 ♕d3 ♘xd5 15 exd5 ♗b5 (since White loses material after 16 ♗c4? ♗xc4 17 ♕xc4 ♖c8, he is forced to block off the b3-bishop; Black can then easily break with ...e7-e6) 16 c4 ♗xd4+ 17 ♕xd4 ♗d7 18 ♖ae1 (18 ♔h2 ♕c5 19 ♕d2 e6 is equal, as in the game Van Riemsdijk-Naumann, Wechern 1997) 18...♕c5 19 ♕xc5 dxc5 20 ♖e3 e6 21 ♖fe1 exd5 22 cxd5 ♖xe3 23 ♖xe3 ♖e8 24 ♖xe8+ ♗xe8 25 d6 ♔f8 ½-½ Haupold-Anschutz, corr 1976.

14   ...   ♕xe1
15   ♖axe1   ♘d7

After 15...♘xd5 White got some advantage with 16 ♗xg7 ♔xg7 17 exd5 ♗d7 18 ♖f3 in Ivanovic-Davies, Vrsac 1989, but Black should try 16...♘e3!?, e.g. 17 ♗xf8 ♘xf1 18 ♗xe7 ♖xe7 19 ♔xf1 ♖xe4 20 ♖xe4 ♗xe4 21 ♔f2 ♔f8 22 c3 f6 23 g3 g5, when Black held the draw, F.Olafsson-Pedersen, Athens 1969.

16   ♗xg7   ♔xg7
17   ♖e3   ♘c5
18   ♖d1   ♘xb3
½-½

Game 83
A.Martin-Bellon
Olot 1974

(1 e4 c5 2 ♘f3 ♘c6 3 d4 cxd4 4
♘xd4 g6 5 ♘c3 ♗g7 6 ♗e3 ♘f6 7
♗c4 ♛a5 8 0-0 0-0 9 ♗b3 d6 10
h3 ♗d7 11 f4 ♘xd4 12 ♗xd4
♗c6)

13   ♛d3

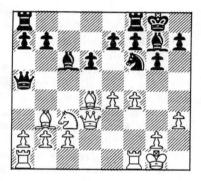

By far White's most popular
move and probably also his strongest. However, it should not worry
Black too much.

13   ...   ♖ad8!

Theory does not think highly of
Black's chances after 13...♘d7, but
Black may be doing okay. After 14
♗xg7 ♔xg7 White now has two
choices:

a) 15 ♖ae1 and now:

a1) 15...♛c5+ 16 ♔h2 b5 17
♗d5 ♖ac8 18 ♗xc6 ♖xc6 19 ♘xb5
♛xc2 20 ♛d4 e5 21 ♛xa7 with a
clear plus for White, Matulovic-
Rajkovic, Vrnjacka Banja.

a2) 15...f6 16 ♛g3!? ♘c5 17
♔h2 ♘xb3 18 axb3 with a slight
advantage for White, Ciric-Parma,
Yugoslavia 1963.

c) 15...♖ac8!? 16 ♛d4+ (16

♛g3!?, intending e4-e5) 16...♔g8
17 ♘d5 ♖fe8 18 ♔h1 ♛c5 19 ♛d2
a5 20 f5 ♗xd5 21 ♗xd5 e6 22 fxe6
fxe6 23 ♛f3 ♘e5 24 ♗b3 ♛c7 25
♖f2 b5 with equal chances, Detko-
Muresan, Brno 1989.

b) 15 ♔h1 ♘c5 (15...♛h5 16
♖ae1 f6 17 ♘d5 ♘c5 18 ♛e3 e5
19 f5 ♖ad8 20 ♘c3 ♘xb3 21 axb3
a6 22 ♖d1 with a slight plus for
White, Soylu-Hifny, Manila ol
1992; 15...♖ac8 has also been suggested, but after the text Black is
doing fine) 16 ♛d4+ f6 and now:

b1) 17 ♗d5 (threatening 18 b4)
17...♛b6 18 ♖ab1 (Zhidkov-Pav-
lenko, USSR ch 1967) and now
18...e6! 19 ♗xc6 with 19...bxc6 or
19...♛xc6 20 b4 ♘a4.

b2) 17 ♖ae1 ♘xb3 18 axb3 ♛c5
19 ♛d2 e6 20 ♖f3 and now instead
of 20...♖fe8 21 ♖d3 with a comfortable edge for White, as in the
old game Matanovic-Simagin, Yugoslavia-USSR 1963, Black should
have played 20...♖ad8! 21 ♖d3 b5!
when the threats are parried.

The direct thrust 13...e5 is mentioned by Gufeld and dismissed
after 14 ♗e3 exf4 15 ♗xf4 'as
Black cannot control the e5-square
in time'. But things are not that
simple: 15...♖ad8!? 16 ♗xd6 (16
♖ad1 ♘h5 is, by transposition,
Lederman-Kagan, Netanya 1975:
17 ♗c1 ♗xc3 18 bxc3 ♛c5+ 19
♗e3 ♛e5 20 ♗h6 ♘g3 21 ♗xf8
and now Black should have continued 21...♖xf8 22 ♖fe1 ♘xe4 23
♛d4 a6 with adequate compensation for the exchange, instead of
21...♛c5+? 22 ♛d4!! ♘e2+ 23
♔h2 ♘xd4 24 cxd4 ♛b6 25 ♗e7
and White was winning) 16...♛b6+
17 ♔h1 ♘xe4 18 ♖xf7!? ♗xf7 19
♗xf7+ ♔h8! 20 ♘xe4 ♗xe4 21

♕xe4 ♕xd6 with some compensation for the pawn due to White's weak kingside. Perhaps White should try 15 ♖xf4.

14 ♖ad1

The main line. The alternatives are not difficult for Black to meet either:

a) 14 f5?! ♘d7 15 ♗xg7 (or 15 ♘d5 ♗xd5 16 ♗xg7 ♔xg7 17 ♗xd5 ♘f6 18 ♖f2 ♕c5 19 c3 e6! 20 b4 ♕b6 21 ♗b3 d5 22 exd5 ♘xd5 23 ♗xd5 ♖xd5 24 f6+ ♔g8 25 ♕f4 ♖f5 with a clear edge for Black, Janosevic-Furman, Harrachov 1966) 15...♔xg7 16 ♕d4+ ♕e5 17 ♖ad1?! (White should have tried 17 ♕xa7, but after 17...♘c5 18 ♖ae1 e6! Black has strong compensation in return for the pawn) 17...♕xd4+ 18 ♖xd4 ♘f6 with a slight pull for Black, Ekblom-Pytel, corr 1992.

b) 14 ♔h1 e5 15 ♗g1 d5! 16 fxe5 dxe4 17 ♕e3 ♕xe5 with a slight edge for Black, Ostojic-Forintos, Belgrade 1967.

c) 14 ♕e3 ♘d7 (14...b6? is too passive: 15 f5! ♘d7 16 ♗d5! ♗xd4 17 ♕xd4 ♘e5 18 b4 ♕a6 19 a4 ♕b7 20 b5 ♗xd5 21 ♘xd5 f6 22 a5, as in Klovsky-Averbakh, USSR 1966) 15 ♗xg7 ♔xg7 16 ♔h2 ♕c5 17 ♕d3 b5 18 a4 (18 ♘d5 is equal) 18...b4 19 ♘b1 e5 20 f5 ♘f6 21 ♘d2 d5! with a slight edge for Black, Matanovic-Bilek, Havana ol 1966.

d) 14 ♖ae1 ♘d7 (14...e5 15 ♗e3 exf4! 16 ♗xf4 d5 17 e5 ♘e4 with equal chances) 15 ♗xg7 ♔xg7 16 ♕d4+ (also good is 16 ♘d5 ♗xd5 17 exd5 ♖fe8 18 ♖e3 with a slight advantage, Juarez-Bellon, Siegen ol 1970, whereas 16 ♔h1 does not lead to any advantage: 16...♘c5 17

♕d4+ ♔g8 [17...e5 18 ♕e3 ♘xb3 19 axb3 exf4 20 ♕xf4 ♕e5 21 ♕xe5 dxe5 22 ♖d1 ½-½ Morgado-Fedorov, corr 1970] 18 ♗c4 ♘d7 19 e5 ♕b6 20 ♕xb6 ♘xb6 21 ♗d3 dxe5 22 ♖xe5 e6 is equal, Matanovic-Cruz, Buenos Aires 1961) 16...♘f6 17 f5 ♕b6 18 ♕xb6 axb6 19 g4 g5 with a slight edge for White, Short-Korchnoi, Garmisch-Partenkirchen 1994.

e) 14 ♘d5 e5!? (clearly the most interesting move, although 14...♘xd5 15 exd5 ♗xd4+ 16 ♕xd4 ♗d7 17 ♖ae1 ♖fe8 18 ♔h1 ♕c5 19 ♕d2 a5 gives equal chances, Klovan-Kapengut, USSR 1965, and 14...♖fe8!? can be given a try) 15 ♘xf6+ ♗xf6 16 ♗c3 ♕c5+ 17 ♔h1 ♗g7 (17...♖b5!? 18 ♕f3 ♗xf1 19 ♖xf1 is not clear, as Black has difficulties releasing himself from the pressure White is exerting on the light squares) 18 f5 ♗h6!? (both 18...d5 and 18...♗b5 are worth considering) 19 fxg6?! (according to Ivkov, White should try 19 ♗d2!? while alternatively, White could go for 19 ♖ad1 or 19 ♖ae1) 19...hxg6 20 ♕g3 ♔g7, and now 21 ♖ad1 is best, Yilmaz-Ivkov, Praia de Rocha 1978.

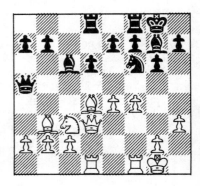

14 ... ♘d7

Best. Other moves leave White with the upper hand:

a) 14...e6?! 15 f5 gxf5 16 exf5 e5 17 ♗e3 d5 18 ♗g5 e4, Bauer-Adrian, French ch 1996, 19 ♕g3 with strong threats.

b) 14...e5?! 15 ♗e3 exf4 16 ♖xf4 with a plus for White (16 ♗xf4 ♘h5 – see 13...e5!?).

c) 14...b5 (Short-Hellers, Wijk aan Zee 1986) 15 ♘d5 with a slight plus for White.

15 ♗xg7 ♔xg7
16 ♔h1

16 f5 ♘e5 17 ♕e3 ♕c5 and 16 ♕e3 ♕c5 are both equal, and 16 ♘d5 is best met by 16...e6 (16...♗xd5 17 exd5 ♘f6 18 ♖de1 ♖d7 19 ♖e3, Tiviakov-Gogoladze, Riga 1987, is the standard good position for White) 17 ♕d4+ e5! 18 fxe5 dxe5 19 ♕d3 ♘c5 20 ♕e3 ♘xb3 21 ♕xb3 ♕c5+ is equal, Matanovic-Tal, Palma de Mallorca 1966. Best is 16 ♕d4+ ♔g8 17 ♔h2 ♕c5 18 ♕d2 b5 (18...♘f6 has been suggested, e.g. 19 ♘d5 ♘xe4 20 ♘xe7+ ♔g7 21 ♕e2 f5) 19 ♘d5 ♗xd5 20 exd5 ♘f6 21 f5 with a clear plus for White, Yilmaz-Tangborn, Budapest 1992.

16 ... ♘c5

Inaccurate is 16...♕c5?! 17 ♘d5 ♗xd5 (17...e6!? may be better, even when met by 18 c4!?) 18 exd5 b5 19 ♖fe1 ♖fe8 20 a4 a6 21 axb5 axb5 22 ♖a1 with a clear edge for White, Mäki-Karkanaque, Malta 1990.

17 ♕d4+ e5
18 fxe5

Black easily obtains a comfortable position after 18 ♕e3 ♘xb3 19 axb3 exf4 20 ♖xf4 ♕e5! 21 ♖df1 a6 and now:

a) 22 ♕f2 f6 23 h4 ♖f7 24 ♔g1 ♖df8! with a slight edge for Black, Jansa-Furman, Harrachov 1966.

b) 22 ♖h4 ♔g8! 23 ♕h6 ½-½, Ciric-Gheorghiu, Beverwijk 1968.

18 ... ♘xb3
19 axb3 dxe5
20 ♕f2 f5!

Inferior is 20...♖xd1 21 ♕f6+ ♔g8 22 ♖xd1 with a slight plus for White.

21 b4!

White wants to remove Black's queen from its protection of the rook on d8. The immediate 21 ♖xd8?!, however, is good for Black: 21...♕xd8 22 ♕xa7 fxe4 23 ♖xf8 ♕xf8 24 ♕e3 (24 ♘d1? only makes things worse: 24...e3 25 ♘xe3 ♕f2! wins for Black) ♕f4 25 ♘d1 ♕f1+ 26 ♕g1 ♕e2 27 ♘e3 h5! with a clear advantage for Black.

21 ... ♕xb4
22 ♖xd8 ♖xd8
23 exf5 g5!

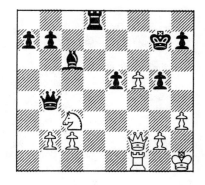

A wonderful idea and a big improvement over 23...♕f4? 24 ♕e1! with a clear plus for White, Shagalovich-Baumbach, Byelorussia-East Germany 1968.

24 f6+ ♔f7

This position is evaluated as unclear by many sources, but Black's strong bishop on c6 gives him the advantage.

25 ♕e3 ♕h4 26 ♔h2

26 ♕xe5?? loses to 26...♕xh3+.

26...g4 27 ♕xe5 g3+! 28 ♕xg3

Unfortunately for White, if 28 ♔g1 then 28...♕d4+ is very good for Black.

28...♕xg3 29 ♔xg3 ♖g8 30 ♔f4 ♖xg2 31 ♔e5 ♖g3

Now the greedy 31...♖xc2? when 32 ♖g1 lets White back into the game.

32 h4 ♖e3+ 33 ♔f4 ♖h3 34 ♖f2 ♖xh4 35 ♔g5 ♖h1 36 ♘e2 h6+ 37 ♔f5 ♖h5 38 ♔g4 ♖g5+ 39 ♔h4 ♖g2 40 ♖xg2 ♗xg2 41 ♘f4 ♗f3 42 ♔g3 ♗d1 43 c3 ♔xf6 44 ♘d5+ ♔e5 45 ♘e3 ♗h5 46 ♔h4 ♗e2 47 ♔g3 ♔e4 48 ♔f2 ♗b5 49 c4 ♗d7 50 ♔e2 a5 51 ♔d2 ♔d4 52 b3 h5 53 ♘g2 ♗f5 54 ♘f4 h4 55 ♘g2 h3 56 ♘e3 ♔e4 57 ♔e2 ♔f4 58 ♘f1 ♗c2 0-1

Game 84
Busquets-Davies
New York 1991

(1 e4 c5 2 ♘f3 ♘c6 3 d4 cxd4 4 ♘xd4 g6 5 ♘c3 ♗g7 6 ♗e3 ♘f6 7 ♗c4 ♕a5 8 0-0 0-0)

9	**♘b3**	**♕c7**
10	**♗g5**	

This is generally considered stronger than the main line 10 f4 (Games 85 and 86). White's intention is to meet ...d7-d6 by an exchange on f6 followed by ♘d5 and ♘xf6+, leaving Black's pawn structure in a shambles. But of course Black need not play ...d7-d6 right away.

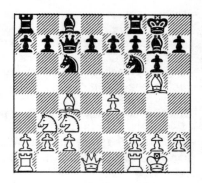

10 ... a6!

ECO's main line is 10...a5 11 a3 (also good is 11 a4 ♘b4 12 ♗e2 ♖d8 [or 12...d6 13 ♘d4 ♗d7 14 ♕d2 ♖fe8 15 ♗h6 with a slight plus for White] 13 ♘d4 ♕e5 14 ♘f3 ♕e6 15 e5 ♘g4 16 ♘b5! ♗xe5 17 h3 ♘f6 18 ♖e1 ♘c6 19 ♗f1 when White's better development and piece co-ordination gave him a strong initiative in Kuzmin-Kapengut, USSR 1972) 11...a4 12 ♘d2 ♕a5 13 ♘d5 d6 14 c3 ♖e8 15 ♘xf6+ with a clear edge for White, Kupreichik-Veremeichik, Minsk 1976. Most sources quote the game Kupreichik-Privara, Stary Smokovec 1975, which went 10...b6 11 f4 ♘a5 12 ♗d5!, when *ECO* amongst others claims a decisive advantage for White, which is only correct if Black continues as in the game: 12...♘xb3? 13 axb3 ♘xd5 14 ♘xd5 ♕c5+ 15 ♔h1 f6 16 b4! ♕d6 17 e5! ♕e6 18 exf6 exf6 19 ♖e1 ♕f7 20 ♖e7 and White soon won. But as Banas has pointed out, things are not that clear after the stronger 12...♗a6! His analysis continues: 13 ♗xa8 ♗xf1 14 e5 (14 ♗xf6 ♗xf6 15 ♘d5 ♕b8) 14...♖xa8 15 ♔xf1 ♕c4+ 16 ♔g1

♘xb3 17 axb3 ♕c5+ followed by
...♘h5 and ...f7-f6 with an unclear
position.

However, the text seems to be
the best move, after which Black
yet has to meet any problems.

11   a4

Black is doing fine after 11
♗xf6 ♗xf6 12 ♘d5 ♕e5 13 ♘b6
♖b8 or 11 f4 b5 12 ♗e2 d6 (or
12...b4 13 ♘d5 ♕a7+ 14 ♔h1
♘xe4 15 ♗xe7 ♘xe7 16 ♘xe7+
♔h8 17 ♗f3 f5 18 ♗xe4 fxe4 19
♕d6 a5 20 ♘c5 ♕b8 21 ♘xd6
♗a6 with a clear edge for Black,
Gudmundsson-Tangborn, Reykjavik 1990) 13 ♗f3 (13 ♗xf6 ♗xf6
14 ♘d5 ♕a7+) 13...♗e6 14 ♘d5
♗xd5 15 exd5 ♘a5 16 ♘xa5 (16
♘d4 ♘c4) ♕xa5 17 ♖e1 ♖fe8 with
roughly equal chances – Silman.

11   ...   ♘b4

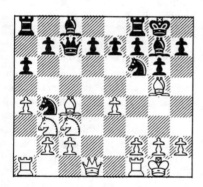

12   ♕e2?!
Better was 12 ♗e2 d6 13 a5
♗d7 (13...♗e6!?) 14 ♕d2 b5 15
axb6 ♕xb6 16 e5 dxe5 17 ♗xf6
♗xf6 18 ♕xd7 ♘xc2 19 ♖ac1
♕xb3 20 ♗d1 ♖ad8 21 ♗xc2
♕xb2 with a slight advantage for
White, Tate-A.Horvath, Budapest
1997. In our main game White is
on a downward slope and it is soon

over.

| 12 | ... | d6 |
| 13 | a5?! | ♘g4! |

Threatening ...d6-d5.

14	f4	b5
15	axb6	♕xb6+
16	♔h1	♘e3
17	♗xe7	♗g4
	0-1	

Game 85
Fischer-F.Olafsson
Bled 1961

(1 e4 c5 2 ♘f3 ♘c6 3 d4 cxd4 4
♘xd4 g6 5 ♘c3 ♗g7 6 ♗e3 ♘f6 7
♗c4 ♕a5 8 0-0 0-0 9 ♘b3 ♕c7)

10   f4
10 ♗e2 usually transposes to the
main line after 10...d6 11 f4, but on
occasion White has tried 11 ♕d2
(11 f3 a6!?) with good results:
11...♘e5 (the somewhat provocative 11...♘g4 seems to be a better
shot at equalising) 12 ♗h6 ♘c4 13
♗xc4 ♕xc4 14 ♗xg7 ♔xg7 15 f4
b6 16 e5! dxe5 17 fxe5 ♘e8 18
♖f4 with a dangerous attack,
Lublinsky-Shabanov, USSR 1961.

| 10 | ... | d6 |
| 11 | ♗e2 | |

Other possibilities are:

a) 11 ♔h1 a6 (11...b6!?) 12 a4 ♘a5 13 ♘xa5 ♛xa5 14 ♕d3 ♗d7 15 f5 ♖ac8 16 fxg6 hxg6 17 ♗d4 ♛h5 18 h3 ♖xc4! 19 ♗xf6 ♗xf6 20 ♛xc4 ♗xh3 21 ♔g1 and White later won, Belov-Utiatsky, USSR 1960, but Black's chances should be no worse after 21...♗e6 followed by ...♔g7 and ...♖h8.

b) 11 h3 ♗d7 (11...b6!?) 12 ♗e2 a5 13 a4 ♘b4 14 ♗f3 ♗c6 15 ♖f2 ♘d7 16 ♘d4 ♖ad8 17 ♖d2 ♖fe8 18 ♛e2 with a slight advantage for White, Timoschenko-Andreev, Voronezh 1973.

The position that has now arisen could also have been reached from the Classical Dragon: 1 e4 c5 2 ♘f3 d6 3 d4 cxd4 4 ♘xd4 ♘f6 5 ♘c3 g6 6 ♗e2 ♗g7 7 ♗e3 0-0 8 ♘b3 ♘c6 9 0-0 ♛c7 10 f4. Although ...♛c7 seems to do less for Black than the usual ...♗e6, ...♘a5 or ...a7-a5, White has yet to demonstrate an advantage in the main lines; Black's position is both solid and dynamic.

11   ...   a5

11...a6?! is too slow: 12 ♗f3 b5 13 ♖f2 ♗b7 14 ♘d5! ♘xd5 15 exd5 ♘a5 16 ♗d4 ♘c4 17 ♗xg7 with a slight plus for White, Ghizdavu-Ribli, Bucharest 1971. However, an interesting alternative is 11...♖d8!?, preparing ...d6-d5, e.g. 12 ♗f3 (possibly stronger is 12 g4, e.g. 12...d5 13 e5 d4 14 ♘b5 ♛b6 15 ♗xd4 ♘xd4 16 ♘5xd4 ♘d5 17 ♛d2 and now according to Boleslavsky can Black should play 17...a5! and after 18 a4 g5 19 fxg5 ♗xe5 with an unclear position) and now:

a) 12...e5!? 13 f5 (not problematic for Black either is 13 ♖f2 ♗e6

14 ♘d5 ♗xd5 15 exd5 exf4 16 ♗xf4 ♘e5 17 ♖c1 ♘fd7 18 c4 ♘c5 19 ♘xc5 ♛xc5 20 ♛b3 ♘xf3+ 21 ♛xf3 ♗d4 22 ♗xe3 ♗xe3 23 ♛xf7+ ♔h8 24 ♛f6 ½-½ Prandstetter-Znamenacek, Prague 1992) 13...d5! 14 ♘b5 ♛b8 15 exd5 (White was successful with 15 fxg6 in Kosenkov-Kubinin, corr 1977: 15...dxe4? 16 gxf7 ♔h8 17 ♛c1 gxf3 18 ♗h6 e4 19 ♛g5 and White was winning, but Black can improve with 15...hxg6 16 exd5 ♗f5! as in the game Dobrovolsky-Karlik below) 15...♗xf5 (15...e4? loses to 16 dxc6! ♖xd1 17 c7!) 16 c4 and now according to Langner Black should continue with 16...a6!? 17 ♘c3 b5 18 cxb5 axb5 19 ♛e2 (19 ♗g5 ♘d4! slightly favours Black) 19...♘b4! with a clear edge for Black, but instead he played 16...♘b4 17 ♗g5 h6 18 ♗xf6 ♗xf6 19 ♗g4 ♗xg4 20 ♛xg4 ♗g7?? 21 ♖xf7! ♔h7 22 ♘c7 ♖f8 23 ♖xf8 1-0 Dobrovolsky-Karlik, Karvina 1989.

b) 12...♗e6 13 ♖f2 (less accurate is 13 ♛d2, when after 13...♗c4 14 ♖fe1 Black could have equalised with 14...e5!; instead he chose 14...d5?! when White held the advantage after 15 e5 ♘e4 16 ♗xe4 dxe4 17 ♛f2 f5 18 exf6 exf6 19 ♘d2 ♘b4 20 ♘dxe4 f5 21 ♘g5, Kupreichik-Kotkov, Sukhumi 1973) 13...♗c4 (Levy claims equality for Black after 13...a5, but after 14 ♘d5 ♗xd5 15 exd5 ♘b4 16 c3 ♘a6 17 a4 White stands better) 14 ♘d5 ♗xd5 15 exd5 ♘a5 16 ♗d4 ♘e8 17 c3 and White is slightly better, Ostojic-Musil, Yugoslavian ch 1968.

c) 12...♗d7 13 ♛e2 ♘a5 14 ♘xa5 ♛xa5 15 ♗f2 ♗c6 16 ♖ab1

♖ac8 17 b4 ♕c7 18 ♖b3 b6 19 ♖d1
e6 is equal, Apicella-Ivkov, Cannes
open 1989.

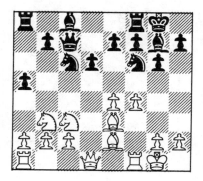

12   a4

Aside from this move, White has
tried a few other things:

a) 12 ♘d2 (12 ♘d5 ♘xd5 13
exd5 a4 is equal) 12...♖b8?!
(according to Baumbach 12...♘b4
would have been a better move, as
13 ♘c4 can be answered with
13...♘g4! and 13 a3 with 13...♘a6
followed by ...♘c5 with good play)
13 h3 ♗d7 14 a3 ♘d8!? 15 ♘c4!
♗c6! 16 ♗b6 ♕c8 17 ♗a7 b5 18
♗xb8 bxc4 19 ♗a7 ♘xe4 20 ♗d4
e5 21 ♘xe4 ♗xe4 22 fxe5 dxe5 23
♗c3 ♕c5+ 24 ♔h2 ♘e6 with
compensation for the exchange,
Khasin-Baumbach, corr 1972.

b) 12 ♘b5?! ♕d7 13 ♘d2 ♘g4
14 ♗xg4 ♕xg4 15 c3 ♕xd1 16
♖axd1 ♗g4 17 ♖de1 ♗d7 18 a4 f5
19 ♖f2 ♖f7 20 exf5 ♗xf5 21 ♘c4
♖af8 with equal chances, Uitumen-
Baumbach, corr 1970.

c) 12 a3 a4 13 ♘d4 ♘xd4 (in a
similar position, but with the a-
pawns on a2 and a7 in the Classical
Dragon ...♕b6 is a good move, but
here it does not deliver: 14 e5!
dxe5 15 fxe5 ♘xe5 16 ♘f5 ♕e6 17

♘xg7 ♔xg7 18 ♕d2 ♔g8 19 ♖ae1
♘c6 20 ♗b5 with a clear edge for
White) 14 ♗xd4 e5 15 fxe5 (15
♗e3 exf4 16 ♗xf4 ♕b6+ 17 ♔h1
♖e8, when Black should be fine
according to Levy) 15...dxe5 16
♗e3 (16 ♘b5? ♕e7 17 ♗c3 ♕c5+
18 ♔h1 ♘xe4 is better for Black)
16...♗e6 17 ♕e1 ♘d7 18 ♖d1 and
now both 18...♖fd8 and Levy's
18...♘b6 gives Black a good game.

12   ...   ♘b4
13   ♖f2!?

This multipurpose move, which
Fischer introduced in this game,
protects the c2-pawn, allows White
to answer ...♗c4 with ♗f3 and
prepares to transfer the rook to d2,
putting an end to Black's hopes of
a ...d6-d5 advance.

However, White's alternatives
are not without importance:

a) 13 ♗f3 ♗g4! 14 ♗xg4?!
(Razuvaev gives 14 ♖f2 ♗xf3 15
♕xf3 ♕c4 as equal) 14...♘xg4 15
♕xg4 ♗xc3 16 bxc3 ♘xc2 17 ♗d4
♘xa1 18 ♖xa1 e5 19 fxe5 dxe5 20
♕g3, Makarichev-Zlotnik, USSR
1978, and now 20...♖fe8 intending
...♕c4 would have been better for
Black.

b) 13 ♖c1 ♗d7 14 ♘d4 ♕c8 15
♕e1 e5! 16 ♘db5 ♗xb5 17 ♗xb5
exf4 18 ♗xf4 ♕c5+ 19 ♔h1 ♘h5
20 ♗e3 and now both 20...♕e5 and
20...♗d4 are quite comfortable for
Black.

c) 13 ♘d4 ♗d7 14 ♘db5 ♗xb5
15 ♗xb5 ♖fd8 (stronger seems
15...♘d7!?) 16 ♖f2 d5?! (once
again 16...♘d7 is interesting; Boleslavsky gives 16...e5 17 ♖d2 exf4
18 ♗xf4 ♘h5 19 ♗xd6 ♖xd6 20
♖xd6 ♘xc2 21 ♖c1 ♘e3 with an
edge for Black, but White can improve with 17 fxe5 dxe5 18 ♕e2,

intending ♖af1 and ♗c4 with pressure on the f-file and the advantage of the pair of bishops in an open position) 17 e5 ♘e4 18 ♘xe4 dxe4 19 ♕e2 e6 20 c3 ♘d3 21 ♖ff1 ♗f8 22 ♗d4 with clearly better chances for White, Dubinin-Rittner, corr 1969.

13   ...   e5

Black has two alternatives, neither of which have given him much success:

a) 13...♗d7 14 ♗f3 ♗c6 15 ♖d2! (stopping Black's dreams of a quick ...d6-d5 advance; Ermenkov-Popov, Sofia 1989, saw a different approach with 15 ♘d5 ♗xd5 16 exd5 ♕c4 17 ♖d2 ♘e4 18 c3 ♘xd2 [better was 18...♘a6] 19 ♘xd2 ♕d3 20 ♗f2 ♘xd5 21 ♗e4 ♘xc3 22 bxc3 ♕xc3 23 ♖c1 ♕f6 24 ♗xb7 with a clear edge for White) 15...♘d7 16 ♘d4 ♘c5 17 ♘cb5! ♕c8 18 c3 ♘ba6 19 ♕c2 ♕e8 20 b3 and White was on top, Heemsoth-Baumbach, corr 1982.

b) 13...♗e6!? 14 ♘d4! ♗c4 15 ♗f3 ♖fd8 16 ♖d2 ♕c8 17 ♘db5 ♘d7 18 ♗g4 (Boleslavsky has recommended 18 ♖b1!, intending 19 b3 or 19 ♘d5) 18...f5! (18...♗xb5? 19 axb5 f5 20 exf5 ♘f6 21 ♗f3 gxf5 22 ♘a4! ♘e4 23 c3 ♘xd2 24 ♕xd2 ♘a6 25 ♘b6 ♕b8 26 ♕xa8 1-0 Westerinen-Jansson, Finland 1969) 19 exf6 ♘xf6 20 ♗b6 (20 ♗f3!?) 20...gxf5 21 ♗xd8 ♕c5+ 22 ♔h1 ♘xg4 with excellent play for the exchange, A.Smith-Petersen, corr 1978.

14   ♗f3   ♗d7
15   ♖d2   ♖fd8
16   ♔h1

16 ♖xd6? is met by 16...♘xc2!

16   ...   ♗c6
17   ♕g1!   ♘d7

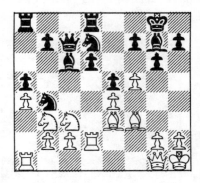

18   ...   b6?!

Here Boleslavsky claims that Black could have kept the chances level with 18...♘c5 19 ♘xc5 dxc5 20 ♖xd8+ ♕xd8 21 ♖d1 ♕e8 22 ♗xc5 ♘xc2. In Hunoldt-Flechsig, corr 1989, White was successful after 19 ♘b5 ♕e7? 20 ♘c5 ♗xb5 21 axb5 dxc5 22 ♗xc5 ♕e8 23 ♖xd8 ♖xd8 24 c3 with a clear edge, but Black can improve with 19...♗xb5! 20 ♘xc5 (20 axb5 ♘xb3 21 cxb3 ♘d7 22 ♗b6 ♗h6! 23 ♖dd1 ♖dc8 with a clear advantage for Black) 20...♗c4! (not 20...dxc5? 21 axb3 and Black has problems with the knight on b4) 21 ♘b3 (21 ♘d3 ♗xd3!? 22 cxd3 ♖a6) 21...♗xb3!? (21...♖a6) 22 ♗b6 ♕c6 23 ♗xd8 ♗h6!

19   ♖ad1   ♘c5

Not 19...♘xc2? 20 ♖xc2 ♗xd4 21 ♘a1 ♗xc2 22 ♘xc2 b5 23 ♕f2 ♖dc8 24 ♘e1 b4 25 ♘d5 with a clear plus for White, Van den Bosch-Druon, corr 1975.

20   ♘b5!   ♕e7

Worse is 20...♗xb5 21 axb5 (threatening 22 ♘xc5 and 23 c3!) 21...♘xb3 22 ♗xb6 and Black loses material.

21	♘xd6	♘xc2
22	♘xc5	♘xe3
23	♕xe3	bxc5
24	♗e2?!	

24 b3! ♕a7 25 ♗e2! would have been even stronger. In the game White's idea is the same, but Black gets the white a-pawn for nothing.

24...♗xa4 25 b3 ♗e8 26 ♗c4 a4 27 ♗d5! ♖xd6!?

27...♖b8 28 ♘xe8 ♕xe8 29 bxa4 is clearly better for White.

28 ♗xa8 ♖d4 29 fxg6 hxg6 30 bxa4 ♗xa4 31 ♖a1 ♕f8?

Better was 31...♗c6 32 ♗xc6 ♕xc6, when Black can play on.

32 ♗d5!

Now Black's poor piece co-ordination becomes evident.

32...♗h6 33 ♖xd4 ♗xe3 34 ♖dxa4 ♕h6 35 ♖f1 ♗f4 36 g3 ♕h3 37 ♖aa1 ♗xg3 38 ♖a8+ 1-0

Game 86
Zagarovsky-Baumbach
Corr 1986

(1 e4 c5 2 ♘f3 ♘c6 3 d4 cxd4 4 ♘xd4 g6 5 ♘c3 ♗g7 6 ♗e3 ♘f6 7 ♗c4 ♕a5 8 0-0 0-0 9 ♘b3 ♕c7 10 f4 d6 11 ♗e2)

11	...	b6!?

Black's best move. The idea behind it is to put pressure on White's e4-pawn and maintain control of the important d5-square if White plays g2-g4-g5 to force the knight away from f6.

Black often follows up with ...♘a5, when if White exchanges on a5 Black, in return for the doubled pawns, gets strong play on the semi-open b- and c- files; while if White does not exchange the knight, it will continue its journey to c4.

12	g4!?

The sharpest, but not necessarily the strongest. Safer alternatives are:

a) 12 ♕d2 ♗b7 13 ♘d5!? (13 ♖ad1 ♘a5 14 ♘xa5 bxa5 15 ♗f3 transposes to note 'b9' below) 13...♘xd5 14 exd5 ♘a5 15 ♘xa5 bxa5 16 c4 and now 16...e6! would have been best, e.g. 17 ♖ac1 ♖fe8 with sufficient counterplay. Instead the game Litvinov-Roizman, Minsk 1973, continued with 16...♗c8?! 17 ♖ab1 a4 18 ♗d3 ♖b8 and now with 19 ♕c2 ♗d7 20 f5 White could have obtained the better chances.

b) 12 ♗f3 ♗b7 and now:

b1) 13 ♖f2?! ♘a5! 14 ♘xa5 bxa5 15 ♗d4 ♘d7 16 ♘d5 ♗xd5 17 exd5 ♗xd4 18 ♕xd4 ♕c5 19 ♖d1 ♖ab8 20 c3 ♖b7 21 ♔f1 ♖ab8 with a clear advantage for Black, Hammie-Silman, USA 1975.

b2) 13 ♘b5?! ♕c8 14 c4 ♘b4 15 ♘d2 ♘d7 16 a3 (16 ♖b1 a6 17 ♘c3 ♗xc3 18 bxc3 ♘d3 19 ♕e2 ♘3c5 is equal, Klovan-Litvinov, Daugavpils 1979) 16...♘c6 17 ♖b1 a6 18 ♘c3 ♘d4 and Black is clearly better, Mukhin-Baumbach, Primorsko 1973.

b3) 13 ♗f2 ♖fe8 (13...♘a5! is

more active and better) 14 ♕d2 ♖ad8 15 ♘d5 ♕c8 16 ♗h4 ♘b8 17 c3 ♘bd7 18 ♖ad1 e6 19 ♘xf6+ ♗xf6 20 ♕f2, Dementiev-Kapengut, USSR 1975, when *ECO* prefers White's chances, but Kapengut gives 20...♗a6 21 ♖fe1 ♗xh4 22 ♕xh4 ♘c5 as equal.

b4) 13 g4 ♘d7 (awfully passive is 13...♖ad8?! 14 g5 ♘e8 15 ♘d5 ♕d7 16 ♗g4 e6 17 ♘d4 ♘xd4 18 ♗xd4 with a slight plus according to Korchnoi; but once again 13...♘a5! seems to be the best way to challenge White, although the text is perfectly playable) 14 ♕d2 ♖ac8 15 ♖ad1 ♘c5 16 ♕f2 ♗xc3 17 bxc3 ♘a4, when Black holds the better prospects, Mysliuvjec-Pähtz, East Germany 1977.

b5) 13 ♘d5 ♘xd5 14 exd5 ♘a5 15 ♘xa5 bxa5 16 c3 ♕c4 with equal chances.

b6) 13 ♕e2 ♘a5 14 ♘xa5 bxa5 15 ♖ad1 ♗c6 16 ♗d4 ♘d7 17 ♗xg7 ♔xg7 18 b3 ♖ac8 19 ♖f2 a4 is equal, Mikhailov-Baumbach, corr 1977.

b7) 13 ♕e1 ♖ac8 (this may seem a bit repetitive, but 13...♘a5! is again the way to go) 14 ♘b5 ♕b8 15 c3 a6 16 ♘5d4, Naschke-Schulz, corr 1981, and now 16...♘xd4 17 ♗xd4 e5 or 16...e6 followed by ...♘d7-c5 would equalise.

b8) 13 ♔h1 ♖ac8 (13...♘a5! 14 ♘xa5 bxa5 15 a4 ♗c6 16 ♕d3 ♘d7 17 ♖ad1 ♘b6 18 b3 ♖ac8 19 ♘e2 ♗b7 20 c4 ♘d7 with good play for Black, Britton-Silman, England 1977) 14 ♖f2 ♖fd8 15 ♖d2 ♕b8 16 a4, Wilken-Melzer, corr 1988, 16...♘a5 17 ♘xa5 bxa5 18 ♕g1 ♗c6! with fine play for Black.

b9) 13 ♕d2!? (probably White's best) 13...♘a5! (slower is 13...♖ac8 14 ♖ad1 ♖fd8 15 ♕f2 ♕b8 16 g4 ♘d7 17 h4 ♘c5 18 h5 ♗a6 19 ♖fe1 e6 20 ♔g2, Kunzelmann-Neubert, corr 1982, 20...♘a5! with excellent chances for Black) 14 ♘xa5 bxa5 15 ♖ad1 ♖fd8! (everything else is good for White: 15...♖fb8 16 ♖f2 ♗c6 17 b3 a4 18 ♗d4 axb3 19 axb3 ♖d8 20 ♘d5, Kupreichik-Kapengut, Minsk 1972, or 15...♗c6 16 e5! dxe5 17 ♗xc6? [much better is 17 fxe5!, e.g. 17...♗xf3 18 exf6 ♗xd1 19 fxg7 ♖fd8 20 ♕f2 with a big edge for White – Silman] 17...♖xc6 18 fxe5 ♘g4 19 ♘d5, Lutzkat-Baumbach, East Germany 1986, and now 19...♖ae8 with unclear complications according to Silman.

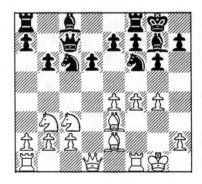

12 ... ♗b7

12...♘e8 looks rather strange, but seems to work for Black, e.g. 13 ♕d2 ♗b7 14 g5 ♘a5 15 ♘d5, Osnos-Sakharov, USSR 1967, 15...♗xd5! 16 ♕xd5 (16 exd5 ♗xb2 is clearly better for Black) 16...♕xc2! with unclear complications – Korchnoi.

13 g5

Once you say 'A' you must say

'B'. Other moves would not be in accordance with the previous one, e.g. 13 ♕d2 ♘a5! 14 ♘xa5 bxa5 15 ♗f3 ♗c6 16 ♖ab1 ♖ab8 17 b3 ♖fc8 with clearly the better chances for Black, K.Nelson-Silman, USA 1975.

13 ... ♘d7
14 ♘d5

Pointless is 14 ♖f2?!, when in the game Tseitlin-T.Georgadze, Barnaul 1969, Black obtained the better position after 14...♖fe8 15 h4 ♘a5 16 ♘d4 a6 17 ♘d5 ♕c8 18 f5 ♗xd5 19 exd5 ♘c4 20 ♗c1 b5 21 h5 ♕c5 22 ♘b3 ♕a7 23 hxg6 fxg6.

14 ... ♕d8

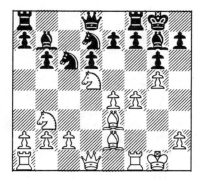

15 ♖b1!?

Korchnoi's recommendation. Other moves do not worry Black:

a) 15 f5 ♗xb2 (bad is 15...♖e8? 16 f6! whereas 15...♘ce5!? seems fine for Black: 16 c4?! [better is 16 ♘d4 or 16 ♕e1] 16...♖e8 17 ♖e1 e6 18 fxe6 fxe6 19 ♘c3 ♘c5 with a clear edge for Black, Kristiansson-Toran, Lugano ol 1968) 16 ♖b1 ♗e5 17 ♕e1 e6 18 ♕h4 exd5 19 f6, Tseitlin-T.Georgadze, and now 19...dxe4! 20 ♗g4 ♔h8 wins for Black.

b) 15 ♘d4 e6! 16 ♘c3 ♘xd4 17 ♗xd4 e5 18 ♗e3 exf4 19 ♗xf4 ♗xc3! 20 bxc3 ♘c5 21 ♕xd6 ♘xe4 22 ♕xd8 ♖axd8 23 ♗f3 ♘c5 with a clear edge for Black in the endgame, Savereide-Silman, USA 1974.

c) 15 c4?! ♖e8 (15...♗xb2 is perfectly playable and bags a pawn) 16 ♕d2 e6 17 ♘c3 ♘c5 18 ♗f3 ♘e7 19 ♘b5 ♘xb3 20 axb3 d5 with unclear complications, Maliszewski-Stachorski, corr 1993.

15 ... ♘c5

Silman's suggestion 15...e6!? 16 ♘c3 ♗xc3 17 bxc3 ♘e7! deserves serious attention, e.g. 18 ♕xd6 ♗xe4 19 ♖ad1 ♘f5 or 18 ♗d3 d5 or 18 f5 exf5 19 ♕xd6 ♗xe4 20 ♖ad1 ♘c5 in all cases with fine chances for Black – analysis by Silman.

Black has also done well with 15...♖e8 16 ♕d2 (16 c4 e6 17 ♘c3 ♘c5 18 ♗f3 ♕e7 19 a3? ♗xc3 20 bxc3 ♘xb3 21 ♖xb3 ♖ac8 wins for Black, Sakrin-Bieluczyk, corr 1983) 16...e6 17 ♘c3 ♘c5 18 ♗f3 ♘e7 19 ♘d4 d5 20 e5 a6 21 h4 ♕c7 22 ♕g2 ♘c6 with about equal chances, Orosz-Keleman, corr 1988.

16 ♗f3

Less logical is 16 ♘xc5, giving Black control over the d4-square: 16...bxc5 17 f5 (17 h4 ♘d4 18 ♗d3 e6 19 ♘c3 a6 20 ♔h2 ♕c7 21 ♗xd4 cxd4 22 ♘e2 ♗g7 23 c3 ♗c6 24 ♘g3 e5 25 ♖f2, Weike-Nagorni, corr 1988, 25...f6! with an initiative for Black) 17...♗d4? 18 ♖f4 ♗e3+ 19 ♘xe3 f6? 20 fxg6 hxg6 21 ♗c4+ ♔g7 22 ♘f5+! 1-0 Martschei-Schlegner, corr 1988, but 17...e6! is difficult for White to handle: 18 ♘c3 ♗d4! 19 ♗xd4

♕xg5+ or 18 f6 exd5 19 fxg7 ♖e8 20 ♕xd5 ♖e7, intending ...♘e5 or ...♘d4, or 18 fxe6 fxe6 19 ♖xf8+! ♕xf8! 20 ♘c7 ♗d4! 21 ♗xd4 ♘xd4 22 ♘xa8 ♕f4! with more than enough compensation.

16	...	e6
17	♘c3	♕e7
18	♕d2	♖fd8
19	♖bd1	

19 ♖be1 ♖ac8 20 h4 ♘a5 21 ♘xa5 bxa5 22 ♕g2 ♗c6 23 ♗xc5 ♗xc3 24 bxc3 dxc5 is equal, Möller-Baumbach, East Germany 1986.

19	...	♘a5!
20	♘xa5	bxa5
21	♕g2?!	

Too optimistic. Baumbach gives 21 ♗d4 ♗xd4 22 ♕xd4 e5 23 ♕d2 exf4 24 ♕xf4 ♘e6 or 24...♖ac8 in both cases with equality.

| 21 | ... | ♖ac8 |
| 22 | ♗d2 | |

Here Baumbach gives 22 ♗d4 as best, but after the obvious moves 22...♗xd4+ 23 ♖xd4 e5 24 fxe5 dxe5 25 ♖xd8 ♖xd8, intending ...♘e6, Black is clearly better.

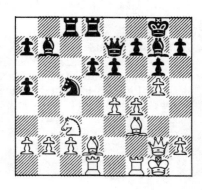

The rest of the game went as follows:

22...♗c6 23 ♖de1?

Now White gets into serious trouble. Correct was 23 ♖fe1.

23...♕b7 24 b3 ♕b6 25 ♕f2

25 ♔h1 loses a pawn to 25...♗xc3 26 ♗xc3 ♘xe4.

25...d5 26 exd5 exd5 27 ♘e2 ♗b5! 28 ♖c1 ♗xe2! 29 ♗xe2 ♘e4 30 ♕xb6 axb6 31 ♗e3

31 ♗e1 ♗b2 32 ♖cd1 ♖xc2 33 ♗d3 ♖c1! wins for Black.

31...d4 32 ♗f2 ♘c3 33 ♗g4 ♖c7 34 ♖a1 ♘d5 35 ♖fd1 ♖xc2! 36 f5 ♘f4 37 ♔f1 gxf5 38 ♗xf5 ♖b2! 39 ♖dc1 d3 40 ♖d1 ♗d4 0-1

A beautiful performance by Baumbach.

11 Main Lines with 7 ♗c4 0-0

This is one of the sharpest systems in the entire Accelerated Dragon. White uses the same set-up as against the standard Dragon variation, hoping to reach that opening by a transposition. Some died-in-the-wool Dragon players, such as Tiviakov, gladly transpose, since with this move order they avoid the critical 9 0-0-0!? in the main line Dragon, because White has already played ♗c4. However, not many Accelerated Dragon players are quite so happy to enter the long theoretical lines of the Dragon, since these differ so much in 'flavour' from their favourite system. Because of this, a number of interesting ideas have been found to get off the beaten track.

Amongst others, the correspondence players Uogele and Ekebjerg have devised some dynamic ways to exploit the fact that the black d-pawn has yet to be moved.

Game 87
Fischer-Panno
Portoroz 1958

(1 e4 c5 2 ♘f3 ♘c6 3 d4 cxd4 4 ♘xd4 g6 5 ♘c3 ♗g7 6 ♗e3 ♘f6 7 ♗c4 0-0)

8   f3?!

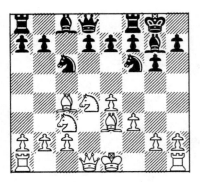

It is interesting to see that even a player of Fischer's class can make serious inaccuracies in the opening. Maybe Fischer believed he was transposing to the main line Dragon (in which he won many miniatures) and just played too quickly. However, White should first play 8 ♗b3 and only then f2-f3 (Games 88-96), when he avoids the following tricks.

8   ...   ♕b6!?

After this move only Black can be better. Still, it is not clear if it is Black's best. 8...e6!? was introduced in Tolush-Lengyel, Warsaw 1961, when White just managed to hold the balance after 9 ♗b3 d5 10 exd5 ♘xd5 11 ♘xd5 exd5 12 0-0 ♕b6 13 c3 ♖e8 14 ♗f2 ♘xd4 15 ♗xd4 ♗xd4+ 16 ♕xd4 ♕xd4+ 17 cxd4 and the ending is drawn. In the later game Szilagyi-Adorjan, Hungary 1972, Adorjan was ready to try 12...♖e8 13 ♗f2 ♕g5!? with an initiative, but did not get the chance, since Szilagyi went for 10 0-0 ♖e8 11 ♘xc6? bxc6 12 ♕e1 ♗a6 13 ♖f2 d4 14 ♖d2 c5, leaving Adorjan with a huge plus. 8...e6!? is certainly not bad, but careful play by White should keep the balance.

We used to believe that Black only had the pleasant choice between 8...♕b6!? and 8...e6!?, but just before finishing the manuscript for this book, *NIC Yearbook 45* drew our attention to 8...d5!? The idea is very similar to Uogele's 9...d5 in the notes to Game 89, and here it seems playable as well. A nice point is 9 ♗xd5 ♘xd5 10 exd5 ♘b4 11 ♘de2 ♗f5 12 ♖c1 ♕a5 13 a3 ♘a2!, which really seems fine for Black. Also in the line 10 ♘xd5 f5!, the fact that the pawn is on a7 rather than a5 favours Black as the b6-square is now well protected. 9 ♘xc6 bxc6 10 exd5 cxd5 11 ♘xd5 e6! 12 ♘c3 ♘d5! 13 ♗xd5 exd5 14 ♘xd5 is given as the critical line, but after 14...♖e8 15 ♔f2 ♗xb2 16 ♖b1 ♗g7 Black clearly has sufficient compensation. However, 8...d5!? has hardly ever been seen in practice so a serious test would be interesting. That it has not been discovered until now, can be explained by the fact that Black has several excellent alternatives and therefore no-one has been searching for new ideas.

9   ♗b3!

Surely White's best way of limiting the damage. 9 a3!?, as in Keres-Larsen, Bewerwijk 1964, also avoids immediate loss of material, but leaves Black with a pleasant edge after 9...d6 10 ♘ce2 ♕a5+ 11 c3 ♘e5 12 ♗a2 ♕a6 13 0-0 ♗d7 14 a4 ♘c4 15 ♗xc4 ♕xc4, when Black was better due to his bishop pair.

Other moves are just bad:

a) 9 0-0? ♕xb2 just leaves Black a pawn up, e.g. the game N.P.Nielsen-Yakovich, Aalborg 1993, went 10 ♘cb5 ♕b4 11 ♕e2 ♕a5 12 ♖fd1 d6 13 ♕f2 ♗d7 14 ♗f1 ♘xd4 15 ♘xd4 ♖fc8 16 c4 with a normal Maroczy position, but the 'slight' difference that White has no b-pawn!

b) Equally depressing is 9 ♕d2? ♘xe4!, since 10 ♘xc6 ♘xd2 11 ♘xe7+ ♔h8 12 ♗xb6 ♘xc4 is just about winning for Black. Nilsson-Geller, Varna 1962, saw instead 10 fxe4 ♗xd4 11 ♗xd4 ♕xd4 12 ♕xd4 ♘xd4 13 0-0-0 ♘c6 14 ♘d5 ♔g7 15 ♗b5 ♖d8, when Black was winning.

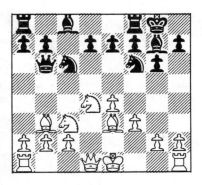

9   ...   ♘xe4?!

This secures an easy draw, but we feel that Black should go for more with the ambitious 9...♘g4!?. In Zagorovsky-Simagin, Moscow 1951, White now tried to avoid damage to his pawn structure with 10 ♘a4?, but was punished after 10...♘xe3 11 ♘xb6 ♗xd4! 12 ♕e2 ♗xb6 13 ♔d2 ♘a5 14 h4 ♘xb3+ 15 axb3 d5! Black's minor pieces became too active and White was blown off the board. So White must enter 10 fxg4 ♗xd4, when he will suffer for a long time due to the black knight, which will eventually find a safe haven on e5:

a) 11 ♗xd4 ♕xd4 (11...♘xd4 12 ♘d5 ♕a5+ 13 c3 ♘c6 followed by ...d7-d6, ...♗e6 etc. is not bad either) 12 ♕xd4 ♘xd4 13 ♘d5 ♘c6 was good for Black in Sakharov-Stein, Kiev 1964. However, not many players would voluntarily defend the position after 14 ♗a4 ♔g7 15 0-0-0 ♖b8 16 h3 b5 17 ♗b3 d6; White's structure is 100% awful.

b) The alternative 11 ♘d5 has given White some success in practice after 11...♕a5+ 12 ♗d2 ♕c5 13 c3. For example, the game Houser-Svarcova, Prague 1989, makes a strong impression: 13...♗g7 14 ♗e3 ♕a5 15 0-0 d6 16 ♕e1!, when White used his weakened structure constructively to attack along the f-file and after 16...♗e6 17 ♕h4 ♗xd5 18 ♗xd5 ♕c7 19 ♖f3 e6 20 ♖h3, he had a winning attack. But simple, and good, seems 12...♕d8 13 c3 ♗g7 followed by ...d7-d6, ...♘e5 etc. when Black will benefit from his superior structure.

9...♘g4 seems like a safe way of

playing for a win.

10   &d5!

Absolutely the only move; everything else loses at least a pawn.

10   ...   ♕a5+
11   c3   &c5

Safe and solid. More ambitious is 11...&xd4!? 12 &xd4 &c5, keeping the extra pawn. After 13 &c4 &e6! (not 13...d6?? when Black had problems with his queen after 14 b4 ♕a4 15 &b3 &xb3 16 axb3 ♕b5 17 c4, Trassaert-Birmingham, Cannes 1990) 14 b4 ♕d8 15 &e3 d6 16 0-0 &c7 17 &h6 &xd5 18 &xd5 ♖e8 19 &g5 &e6, Oszvath-Honfi, Budapest 1963. White has adequate compensation, but no more than that. Pulido-Spangenberg, Seville 1994, saw instead 13 0-0?! &xb3 14 ♕xb3 d6 15 &f2 &e6 16 c4 ♖b8, where White had very little for the pawn. In general, 11...&xd4!? seems fully playable, and if you like to grab pawns and have the patience to defend such positions, this could give you great results.

12   &xc6   bxc6
13   &xe7+   ♔h8
14   &xc8   ♖axc8
15   0-0   ♖cd8
16   ♕c2   ♕b5

Equally good is 16...♖fe8 17 &f2 &xb3 18 axb3 ♕b5 19 ♖fe1 ♖xe1+ 20 ♖xe1 &f6 21 b4 b6 22 ♕e2 ♕xe2 ½-½ W.Watson-Chandler, London 1984.

17   ♖fd1   ♔g8
18   ♖xd8   ♖xd8
19   ♖d1   ♖e8
20   &f2   a5
21   &xc5   ½-½

It is not often that players achieved such an easy draw with the black pieces against Fischer.

Yet, he was probably happy to escape after his opening error. 8 f3?! should certainly not scare Black, and although the choice between 8...♕b6!? 8...e6!? and 8...d5!? certainly is not easy, it is a nice problem to have.

Game 88
Sax-Pigusov
Moscow 1990

(1 e4 c5 2 &f3 &c6 3 d4 cxd4 4 &xd4 g6 5 &c3 &g7 6 &e3 &f6 7 &c4 0-0)

8   &b3!

The critical test. White· avoids ...♕b6 tricks and prepares f2-f3, ♕d2, 0-0-0, h2-h4 etc., following standard Yugoslav Attack patterns. However, in the normal Dragon White only plays &b3 after a knight coming to e5 or a rook to the c-file forces him to do so. This slight difference gives Black some interesting opportunities.

8   ...   a5!?

This tricky move has been popularised by the Lithuanian correspondence player Uogele. His games, together with those of

Petursson and Pigusov have done much to bring this variation to the public eye. Black is waiting for White to play 9 f3, when he will start some serious complications. It is noteworthy that in this game Sax backs off from a theoretical discussion, when normally he is not one to shirk a challenge. 8....d6 is seen in Games 95 and 96.

9 a4!?

Quite a good move, avoiding the tricky lines after 9 f3. White claims 8...a5!? to be positionally suspect; both the b5- and b6-squares look inviting for his minor pieces. The sharper 9 f3 d5 is the subject of Games 89-94.

9 ... ♘g4!
10 ♕xg4

White can force a draw with 10 ♘xc6. Mololkin-Yakovich, Volgograd 1995, saw 10...♘xe3 11 ♘xd8 ♘xd1 12 ♘d5 (both 12 ♘xf7?? ♘xc3 and 12 ♖xd1 ♗xc3+ are better for Black) 12...♖xd8 13 ♖xd1. If the a-pawns had not moved, Black would be better due to his pair of bishops, but here White can exchange a bishop by force: 13...♔f8 14 ♘b6 ♖a6 15 ♘xc8 ♖xc8 16 ♖xd7 ♖b6! (winning back the pawn) 17 ♔e2 ♗xb2 18 ♖hd1 ♖b4 19 ♖d8+ ♖xd8 20 ♖xd8+ ♔g7 21 ♔d3 e6 22 ♖d7 ♔f8 23 f4 ♔e8 24 ♖e7 ♖d4 25 ♔e3 ♖d7 26 ♖xd7 ½-½. Boring, but as in many sharp openings, White often has some way of bailing out with a draw.

10 ... ♘xd4
(see following diagram)
11 ♕h4!

Certainly White's most testing option. 11 ♕d1 is also commonly seen, but if Black plays simple

chess with 11...♘xb3 12 cxb3 d6 followed by 13...♗e6 he is fine, since the b3-pawn is a target. Black's chances were illustrated nicely in Gamarro-Petursson, Buenos Aires ol 1978: 13 ♕d2 ♗e6 14 ♘d5 ♗xd5 15 exd5 ♕d7 16 0-0 b5! and Black was clearly better. He has targets on the b-file, and White has no counterplay.

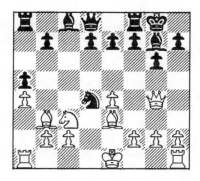

Equally harmless is 11 ♗xd4 ♗xd4 12 ♕g3 due to the simple 12...d6 13 0-0-0 ♗xc3 14 ♕xc3 ♗e6 with equality, Ivanovic-Cebalo, Yugoslavia 1983. Black has exchanged his dark-squared bishop, which normally weakens his king. With counterplay along the c-file, however, Black can maintain the balance. Ambitious attempts to exploit the bishop pair have so far been unsuccessful. For example:

a) Kotronias-Bannikas, Greece 1996, saw 12...e6 13 ♖d1 ♕f6 14 0-0 ♕f6 15 ♖fe1 ♕e5 16 ♖d2 ♗xc3 17 bxc3 ♕xg3 18 hxg3 ♖b8 with an edge for White. Black has difficulties developing without losing pawns, although in the game he 'exchanged' his a- and b-pawns for White's a4-pawn and set up a fortress, drawing after 71 moves.

b) Muhutdinov-Yakovich, St Petersburg 1993, saw 12...d6 13 0-0-0 ♗g7?! 14 h4! ♗e6 15 ♘b5 ♕b6 16 f4 ♖ac8 17 ♗xe6 fxe6 18 ♕b3 ♕c5 19 ♕xe6+ ♔h8 20 c3 ♕c4 21 ♕xc4 ♖xc4 22 g3 ♖xe4 23 ♔d2 and Black was left with positional problems. White is about to put his king on d3 and start playing on the e-file or going for h4-h5. The game ended rather comically with 23...♖xa4 24 ♖he1 e5 25 ♔c2 exf4 26 ♔b3, trapping the rook. It seems strange that Black should not keep his dark-squared bishop, but so far practice indicates that the surprising 13...♗xc3 is Black's best, securing excellent play.

11   ...   ♘xb3

This is the point of inserting the a-pawn moves. Now White will have to take back with the c-pawn, leaving the b3-pawn very weak.

12   cxb3

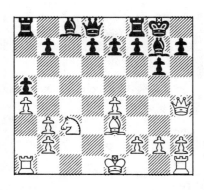

12   ...   ♖a6!?

Seems best. 12...♗f6?! looks strange, but has scored well on its few outings:

a) White has not proven any advantage in the endgame arising from 13 ♗g5 ♗xg5 14 ♕xg5 d6 15 ♘d5 (otherwise 15...♗e6 is just fine) 15...e6 16 ♕xd8 ♖xd8 17 ♘c7 ♖b8, when White even managed to lose in Borocz-Deak, Köbanya 1992, after 18 ♖d1?! ♗d7! 19 ♔e2 ♖bc8 20 ♖c1 ♗c6 21 ♘b5 ♗xe4 22 ♖xc8 ♖xc8 23 ♘xd6 ♖c2+ 24 ♔e3 ♗xg2. Black is just a pawn up.

b) This leaves White with only 13 ♕g3, but 13...d6 14 ♖b1?! ♗e6 15 ♘d5 ♗xd5 16 exd5 ♕d7 17 ♕f4 b5 was good for Black in Reig-Alvarez, Spain 1994. 14 ♖b1?! would never scare anyone. The critical move is 14 ♘d5, as in Hernandez-Alvarez, Cuba 1995, when Black lost horribly after 14...♗xb2 15 ♖b1 ♗g7 16 ♗b6 ♕d7 17 0-0 as he could not develop his pieces. Since we have not found a way to improve upon this line, it seems to more or less refute 12...♗f6?!

13   0-0   ♖e6!?

Nowadays this is standard, but 13...d6 was common until Illijin-Kaidanov, Bled 1989, when after 14 ♘d5 ♖e8 15 ♖ac1 ♖c6 16 ♗g5 f6 17 ♗e3 ♗d7 18 ♖fd1 ♖f8 19 f3 ♗e6 20 ♕f2 White was ready to exploit the weakened queenside. Black tried to mix it, but after 20...f5 21 ♕d2 fxe4 22 fxe4 ♖f7 23 ♖f1 ♕c8 24 ♕xa5 ♗xb2 25 ♖cd1 ♗e5 26 ♖xf7 ♔xf7 27 ♖f1+ ♔e8 28 ♕b5, White was winning.

13...♗f6!?, as played in Hon-Quinn, Hastings 1996, is quite clever. If 14 ♗g5 ♗xg5 15 ♕xg5 d6 16 ♘d5 e6 Black keeps things under control and 16 ♖fd1 ♗e6 is also okay. The game saw 14 ♕g3 d6 15 f4 ♗e6 16 ♖a3 ♔h8 17 f5 gxf5 18 exf5 ♗d7 19 ♕f4 ♗e5 20 ♕h4 ♗c6 21 ♘e4 f6 with a very good position for Black. White's play was unimpressive, but if Black gets in 15...♗e6 he will always be fine. The point of inserting 13...♗f6 14 ♕g3 is that White does not have ♘d5, hitting e7, which won an important tempo in Illijin-Kaidanov. This could be the way to play, and it is our recommendation.

13...♖e6!? is designed to take care of the weak b6-square. Black is planning to play 14...b6 and 15...♗b7, when the b6-square will be safely protected.

14 ♖ad1

14 ♖fe1 led to a victory for White in Topalov-Larsen, Mesa 1992, when White had a huge positional edge after 14...b6 15 ♗h6 ♗b7 16 ♗xg7 ♔xg7 17 ♖e3 f5 18 ♖ae1 fxe4 19 ♘xe4 h6 20 ♘d2 ♖xe3 21 ♕d4+ e5 22 ♕xe3 d6 23 ♘c4.

Black should play as in Emms-Yakovich, Copenhagen 1993, in which Black was fine after 14...b6 15 ♗h6 ♗b7 (15...♗xh6!?) 16 ♖ad1 ♗xh6 17 ♕xh6 ♕c7 18 ♘d5?! ♗xd5 19 exd5 ♖xe3 20 ♕xe3 ♕c5!, though White can improve with 18 ♖d4.

14 ... b6

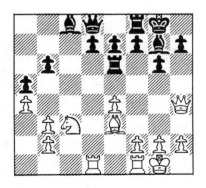

W.Watson-Shabalov, Oslo 1991, saw 14...♗f6 15 ♕g3 ♗xc3!? 16 bxc3 ♖xe4, when White had excellent compensation due to his better development, as well as the presence of the opposite-coloured bishops, which always help the attacker.

If this does not suit White, then 15 ♗g5 is safe, transposing to the main line.

15 ♖d2 ♗b7?!

Pigusov recommends 15...♗f6, giving 16 ♗g5 ♗xg5 17 ♕xg5 ♗b7 as equal. This seems a little too optimistic, since by continuing 18 ♖fd1 ♗c6 19 f3 White should keep some advantage with plans such as like ♘e2-d4 or ♖d4 and b3-b4. Perhaps Black should seek immediate counterplay with 19...f5, but this is somewhat weakening. Although this is playable for Black, we believe that White has a slight plus in these positions. 16 ♕g3 is also possible, but Black will grab the pawn with 16...♗xc3 17 bxc3 ♖xe4, with reasonable chances.

16 ♖fd1 ♗f6
17 ♕g3 ♗c6

Now this is necessary, since the d-pawn needs protection, and Black has no time for pawn grabbing.

18 ♘d5 ♗e5
19 ♕h4 ♗d6
20 ♗xb6 ♕b8

As always in this line, the b6-square is Black's problem. With the pair of bishops there is usually some compensation, but it is not always quite enough.

21 ♗d4 f6 22 ♖d3 ♖f7 23 ♗c3 ♕xb3 24 ♘xf6+ exf6 25 ♖xd6 ♖xe4 26 ♕g3 ♕xa4

Now Black is a pawn up, but the bishop on c3 is a worry for the black king. White has plenty of play on the dark squares.

27 h3 ♛b3 28 ♕d3 ♖e6 29 ♖d4

29 ♖xe6 ♛xe6 30 ♗xa5 ♛e4 31 ♛xe4 ♗xe4 32 ♗c3 is given as slightly better for White, but Black should draw this.

29...♛b5

Now Black is completely equal and the game was drawn in 55 moves. Although 9 a4 is solid and gives White some chances of a small advantage, Black should not worry too much. In particular, 13...♗f6 deserves attention.

Game 89
Shirov-Lautier
Tilburg 1997

(1 e4 c5 2 ♘f3 ♘c6 3 d4 cxd4 4 ♘xd4 g6 5 ♘c3 ♗g7 6 ♗e3 ♘f6 7 ♗c4 0-0 8 ♗b3 a5)

9   f3!?

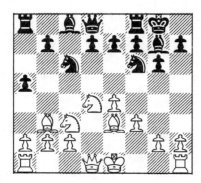

White's most ambitious try. He now threatens 10 a4! with a positional bind since Black no longer has the ...♘g4 trick. However, f2-f3 is slightly weakening, and Black can strike immediately to create complications.

9   ...   d5!

The main idea behind Uogele's 8...a5. Black is a little ahead in development, and gives up a pawn to speed up his mobilisation even further.

10   exd5

This is not considered to be the critical test at the moment, although as we shall see in our next main game, even here new ideas have appeared recently. The main line, 10 ♗xd5, is seen in Games 91-94.

10   ...   ♘b4
11   ♘de2

11 ♘db5?! is generally considered harmless, but it is not all that easy to refute. 11...a4 12 ♘xa4 ♘fxd5 13 ♗d2 ♗d7 14 ♘bc3 ♗xa4 15 ♘xa4 b5 is often given as the easiest way to equalise, but the endgame arising after 16 ♘c3 ♘xc3 17 ♗xc3 ♛xd1+ 18 ♔xd1 ♗xc3 19 bxc3 ♖fd8+ 20 ♔c1 is slightly better for White; he will exchange rooks on the d-file and then use his queenside pawns.

More interesting is 15...♖xa4!? 16 ♗xa4 ♗xb2 17 ♖b1 ♘c3 18 ♗xc3 ♗xc3+ 19 ♔f1 ♛a5 20 ♗b3 ♖d8 with plenty of compensation, after which we feel that Black is definitely not worse.

11   ...   a4!

Certainly Black's best. Short-Kotsur, Lucerne 1997, saw instead 11...e6?! 12 0-0 ♘fxd5 13 ♘xd5 ♘xd5 14 ♗xd5 exd5 15 ♗d4 ♗h6 with transposition to Hector-Hernandez (see below), but with the important difference that White has not wasted time on a2-a3. This really should mean that White is much better, but surprisingly White was not able to prove it, and the game was soon drawn.

| 12 | ♘xa4 | ♘fxd5 |

13   ♗f2?!

Not a serious try for an opening advantage. Later Shirov has admitted that he had simply mixed up two different variations! 13 ♗d2 is seen in the next game, while after 13 ♗d4 Black can choose between:

a) A safe draw with 13...♗xd4 14 ♕xd4 ♗f5 15 ♘ac3 ♘xc2+ 16 ♗xc2 ♘xc3 17 ♕xd8 ♖fxd8 18 ♗xf5 ♘xe2, as in Kostro-Szilagyi, Polanica Zdroj 1969, since 15 ♕d2?! ♗xc2! with the idea of 16 ♗xc2 ♘e3! is far too dangerous for White.

b) If a draw does not suit Black, Uogele's 13...♗f5!? might be worth a shot. Sachs-Uogele, corr 1968, saw 14 ♘ac3? ♗xc2! 15 ♗xc2 ♗xd4 16 ♘xd4 ♘e3 0-1. As pointed out by Silman and Donaldson, the critical test is 14 ♗xg7 ♔xg7 15 ♔f2 e5!?, planning ...♖xa4 and ...♕b6+ with sufficient compensation, which seems to be a reasonable evaluation.

13   ...   ♗f5!

13...♖xa4 14 ♗xa4 ♕a5 15 0-0! and White is winning, Sax-Haik, Smederevska 1982. 15...♕xa4 16

c3 wins back the piece.

| 14 | 0-0 |

14 a3 ♘xc2+! 15 ♗xc2 ♕a5+ 16 b4 ♘xb4 17 axb4 ♕xb4+ 18 ♕d2 ♕xd2+ 19 ♔xd2 ♖fd8+ 20 ♘d4 ♗xd4 21 ♗xd4 ♖xd4+ 22 ♔c3 ♗xc2 23 ♔xd4 ♗xa4 is drawn.

14	...	b5
15	♘ac3	♘xc3
16	♘xc3	♕xd1
17	♖fxd1	♗xc2
18	♗xc2	♘xc2
19	♖ac1	♗xc3
20	♖xc2	♗f6
	½-½	

Not a terribly interesting game, but one that shows that even at the highest level, 8...a5 can be played with success.

Game 90
Sanakoev-Ekebjerg
World corr ch 1994

(**1 e4 c5 2 ♘f3 g6 3 d4 ♗g7 4 ♘c3 cxd4 5 ♘xd4 ♘c6 6 ♗e3 ♘f6 7 ♗c4 0-0 8 ♗b3 a5 9 f3 d5 10 exd5 ♘b4 11 ♘de2 a4 12 ♘xa4 ♘fxd5**)

13   ♗d2!?

This is the critical choice.

13 ... ♗f5!?

Definitely a logical move. In Rogers-Laird, Brisbane 1994, Black thought it was time for immediate sacrifices and played the spectacular 13...♖xa4 14 ♗xa4 ♕a5, hoping for tactics such as 15 ♗b3 ♗xb2 16 ♖b1 ♘e3! with a winning attack. However, Rogers played 15 a3! ♕xa4 16 axb4 ♕c6 17 0-0 ♗xb2 18 ♖a5 when it was apparent that Black had insufficient compensation. In his notes in *Informator*, Ian Rogers suggests 13...♗e6!? as Black's most promising continuation, giving 14 ♘c5 ♗xb2 15 ♖b1 ♗e5 16 ♘xe6 fxe6 17 0-0 with some advantage to White. But by simply playing 14...♗f5!?, we believe that the black position is rather promising, since both 15 a3? ♗xb2 and 15 c3 b6! are good for Black. Therefore 14 ♘c5?! is probably wrong, but Black seems to be fine anyway, and 13...♗e6!? looks like a reliable alternative to the game move.

14 ♘ac3

This is White's safest option, since 14 a3!? has been scoring badly in practice. After 14...b5!? 15 ♘ac3 ♘xc3 16 ♘xc3?! ♘c6 17 ♘xb5 ♘a5 18 ♗c3 ♕b8 19 ♕e2 ♘xb3 20 cxb3 ♖a6 Black certainly had an excellent attack, Enoshi-Greenfeld, Tel Aviv 1988. Better is 16 ♗xc3!?, which led to a quick draw in Lanc-Rantanen, Tbilisi 1987, after 16...♕xd1+ 17 ♖xd1 ♘xc2+ 18 ♔f2 ♗xc3 19 ♘xc3 ♘xa3 20 ♘d5. A critical alternative is 17 ♔xd1!?, when after 17...♖fd8+ 18 ♔c1 ♗h6+ 19 ♔b1 it is not easy to find sufficient play for the pawn.

14 ... ♘xc3

15 ♗xc3 ♗xc3+
16 bxc3!

Necessary, since after 16 ♘xc3 ♕b6, followed by ...♖fd8, Black is fully developed with the white king stuck in the centre.

16 ... ♕xd1+
17 ♔xd1 ♖fd8+
18 ♔c1 ♘a6
19 ♘d4 ♗d7
20 ♖e1 e6

White is a pawn up, but has no hope of making progress, since Black has an excellent blockade on the queenside.

21 ♖e5 ♖dc8 22 ♔d2 ♘c5 23 f4 ♔g7 24 ♖ae1 h5 25 g3 ♖c7 26 ♖5e3 ♗c6 27 ♖e5 ♗d7 28 ♖5e3 ♗c6 29 ♖e5 ½-½

Again a game with absolutely no problems for Black, who even had some interesting alternatives.

Game 91
W.Stern-Ekebjerg
World corr ch 1994

(1 e4 c5 2 ♘f3 g6 3 d4 ♗g7 4 ♘c3 cxd4 5 ♘xd4 ♘c6 6 ♗e3 ♘f6 7 ♗c4 0-0 8 ♗b3 a5 9 f3 d5)

10 ♗xd5!

This seems to be White's best shot at an advantage. White puts an end to Black's tricks with ...a5-a4 at the cost of the bishop-pair.

10 ... ♘xd5
11 ♘xd5?!

This is rather dull. The critical 11 exd5! is examined in Games 92-94.

11 ... f5!?

This rather surprising move tries to open up the position immediately. Less good was 11...e6?! which featured in Berzins-Malisauskas, Yurmala 1995. Black had nothing for the pawn after 12 ♘xc6 bxc6 13 ♘b6 ♖b8 14 ♕xd8 ♖fxd8 15 ♖b1! ♗a6 16 ♘a4.

12 ♘xc6

Necessary. 12 c3 fxe4 13 fxe4 e6 14 ♘xc6 ♕h4+! is already embarrassing.

12 ... bxc6
13 ♘b6 ♖b8
14 ♕xd8 ♖xd8
15 ♖d1!?

This has caused Black some problems in the past, although they now appear to have been solved. White's idea is to return the pawn, and then try to prove that Black's pawns are weak in the endgame. Worse is the move 15 c3, when after 15...♖d3 Black is already better, since White is struggling to co-ordinate his defence.

15 ... ♖xd1+
16 ♔xd1 ♗xb2

Also not bad is 16...fxe4 17 fxe4 ♗xb2 18 ♔e2 ♗e5, Ivanchuk-Zsu.Polgar, Monaco (rapid) 1994. This seems simple and solid.

17 ♘xc8 ♖xc8
18 exf5 gxf5
19 ♔e2

This is the ending that White was heading for, and indeed it seems like he has a slight pull, as the black pawns are weak. Furthermore, White can play on the b-file. However, practice has shown that Black is still okay.

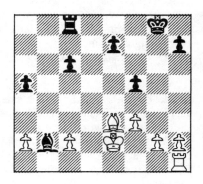

19 ... ♗e5
20 f4!?

The normal move is 20 ♖b1, which gave White the edge in the stem game Kir.Georgiev-Van der Wiel, Wijk aan Zee 1989: 20...♗xh2?! 21 g3! e5 22 ♗f2 f4 23 g4 ♗g3 24 ♗c5.

Yet, in two games shown Hernandez has that 20...♔f7! holds no terrors for Black. Estevez went for 21 ♖b6, Cuba 1989, but had nothing after 21...♗xh2 22 ♖a6 ♗d6 23 ♖xa5 ♔e6 24 a4 ♖g8! 25 ♔f1 ♖b8! as Black is very active. The following year Diaz tried 21 f4!? ♗d6, which transposes to our main game.

20 ... ♗d6
21 ♖b1 ♔f7
22 ♖b6

22 a4 was played in Diaz-Hernandez, Cuba 1990, when Black played 22...♖g8 23 g3 ♖g6 24 ♗d2 ♖h6, creating counterplay.

22 ... ♖b8!

This looks rather dangerous, but it is safe enough.

23	g3	♖xb6
24	♗xb6	a4
25	♔d3	♔g6
26	♔c4	♔h5!

Active counterplay secures the draw. Now White has to weaken his position in order not to let the black king come in:

27 h3 e5! 28 fxe5 ♗xe5 29 ♗f2
½-½

After 29...♗d6 White cannot break through on the queenside. His bishop will constantly have to defend the g3-pawn.

11 ♘xd5?! seems to be nothing to worry about for Black, although it is rather difficult for him to play for a win.

Game 92
Hamarat-Ekebjerg
World corr ch 1994

(1 e4 c5 2 ♘f3 g6 3 d4 ♗g7 4 ♘c3 cxd4 5 ♘xd4 ♘c6 6 ♗e3 ♘f6 7 ♗e3 0-0 8 ♗b3 a5 9 f3 d5 10 ♗xd5 ♘xd5)

11	exd5!

Certainly the critical choice.

11	...	♘b4
12	♘de2	

12 ♘db5?! ♗d7 13 ♘a3? e6 14 d6 ♘d5 15 ♕d3 ♕h4+ 16 g3 ♕b4 17 ♗d2 ♗xc3 18 ♗xc3 ♘xc3 19 ♕xc3 ♖fc8 20 ♕xb4 axb4 21 ♘b1 ♖xc2 left Black with a winning endgame in Semenov-Uogele, corr 1989. Better is 13 a3 ♗xb5 14 axb4 ♗c4 15 bxa5 ♖xa5 16 ♖xa5 ♗xc3+ 17 bxc3 ♕xa5 18 d6 ♖d8 19 ♔f2 ♖xd6 20 ♕a1 after which White survived in Westerinen-Hernandez, Alicante 1989.

12	...	♗f5

12...e6 is seen in Game 94.

13	♖c1	b5

Less exact is 13...♖c8?, which was first seen in Grünfeld-Karlsson, Randers zt 1982, when Black had a bad position after 14 a3! ♘xc2+ 15 ♖xc2 ♗xc2 16 ♕xc2 ♕xd5 17 ♔f2 ♕c4 18 ♖d1 b5. Here 19 ♕d2 is very good, and Rogers has pointed out that 17 a4! is simple and good. Black will not get his usual counterplay, and White's two minor pieces against rook and pawn should be decisive.

13...♖a6?! has been played a little, but without much success. The idea is the piece sacrifice 14 a3 ♖d6!? 15 axb4 axb4. In its first test, Gallagher-Wolff, London (Lloyds Bank) 1994, White was a bit worse after 16 0-0 bxc3 17 ♘xc3 b5! 18 ♕e1 ♖e8 19 ♗c5 ♗xc3 20 ♕xc3 ♕xd5 21 ♖fe1 ♕d7 22 ♖e5? ♖xe5 23 ♕xe2 ♗xc2!

Gallagher, obviously impressed by Black's approach, decided to test it himself against Hector in Geneva 1995. Hector varied with 16 ♗d4!?, keeping an extra pawn after 16...bxc3 17 ♘xc3 ♗h6 18 ♖a1 ♗e6 19 ♕e2 ♗xd5 20 ♘xd5

♖xd5 21 ♗xe7 ♕e8 22 0-0, as Black had no way of profiting from the pin on the e-file.

Just to make things worse, White successfully grabbed the piece in Olivier-Beck, Geneva 1997, after 16 ♘e4!? ♖xd5 17 ♘d2 ♗xb2 18 ♖b1 ♗c3 18 ♕c1. Black tried 18...♖e5!? 19 ♘xc3 ♖xe3+ 20 ♘e2 ♕b6 21 ♘f1 ♖e5 22 g4 ♗e6 23 ♘fg3 ♗c4, but did not get sufficient compensation.

Although 13...♖a6?! has its charming points, it seems to fail for several reasons.

14 a3!?

Generally considered as leading to a drawn ending, but White is more comfortable. 14 0-0 is considered in the next game.

14	...	♘xc2+
15	♖xc2	♗xc2
16	♕xc2	b4
17	♘a4	

The only sensible move, since White tries to slow down Black's initiative by creating threats of his own. Furthermore, he dreams of putting his pawn on b3 and then the knight on c4, when everything will be under control.

17	...	♕xd5
18	♘b6	♕e6
19	♔f2	

The only move seen in practice. Bagirov gives 19 ♘xa8?! ♕xe3 20 ♘c7 ♖c8 21 ♘d5 ♖xc2 22 ♘xe3 ♖xb2 23 axb4 ♖b1+ 24 ♘d1 a4 25 0-0 a3 26 ♘dc3 ♖xb4 27 ♖d1 h5 28 ♖d8+ ♔h7 29 ♖a8 ♖b3 30 ♖c8 ♖b2 31 ♖a8 with a draw by repetition.

This seems correct, but maybe Black can try for more, since White is badly co-ordinated. For example, 20...♗d4!? seems unpleasant for

White as his king is trapped in the middle of the board.

| 19 | ... | ♖ab8 |
| 20 | ♘f4 | ♕a2 |

Compared to the 13...♖c8? line, Black's counterplay is already well under way, as he has created targets on the queenside.

21 axb4 axb4

22 ♖d1!?

The stem game saw 22 ♘fd5 b3 23 ♕e2 ♖b7 24 ♘b4 ♕a5 25 ♘c6 ♕a2 26 ♖d1 ♕xb2 27 ♕xb2 ♗xb2 28 ♖b1 ♗f6 29 ♖xb3 ♖c7 30 ♘b4 e6 ½-½, Klovan-Dorfman, Yerevan 1975.

The critical move is 22 ♕b1!?, inviting Black to play the ending. This is generally dangerous for Black as long as the b-pawns are on the board. It is easier for White's minor pieces to attack Black's pawn than it is for the rooks to get active. Therefore it is Black's strategic goal to exchange the b-pawns, which will nearly 100% guarantee him a draw:

a) He cannot play 22...♕xb2 due to 23 ♕xb2 ♗xb2 24 ♘d7.

b) Black has played 22...♕xb1 23 ♖xb1 a few times, but with little success.

c) 22...b3!?, as seen in Lanka-Priedniek, USSR 1980, is quite clever. The idea is 23 ♘d7?! ♗xb2, which is very dangerous for White. The game continued 23 ♕xa2 bxa2 24 ♖a1 ♗xb2? 25 ♖xa2 ♗c1 26 ♗xc1 ♖xb6 27 ♘d5 ♖b7 28 ♖e2 e6 29 ♘f6+ ♔g7 30 ♘g4 with some chances to White. However, Silman and Donaldson have proved a draw for Black with 24...♖b7 25 ♖xa2 ♖fb8. White's b-pawn is lost and he won't be able to develop an initiative as in the game.

22   ...   b3
23   ♕e2   ♖b7!

Ekebjerg's improvement on Milenkovic-Ujhazi, Kladovo 1992, which came to a beautiful end with 23...♖fd8 24 ♘fd5 e6 25 ♘e7+ ♔h8 26 ♘d7 ♖b7 27 ♘e5 ♖f8 28 ♘xf7+! ♖xf7 29 ♖d8+ ♖f8 30 ♖xf8+ ♗xf8 31 ♗d4+ ♗g7 32 ♕e5! 1-0. Black will be mated. This game was probably the reason why Hamarat gave 22 ♖d1!? a shot, but against one of the world's strongest correspondence players, you should not expect to get your points that easily.

24   ♘c4   e6
25   ♗d4

Around here it looks like White enjoys some initiative, since he is better centralised and Black's queen is rather offside. However, the b2-pawn needs constant protection, and Ekebjerg is sure that Black is okay. This is probably correct in a correspondence game, but in an over-the-board game it may not be so easy.

25   ...   ♖d8
26   ♗xg7   ♕a7+!

An important check, getting the queen back into the game.

27   ♘e3

27 ♔g3 ♖xd1 28 ♗c3 looks attractive, but 28...♗c1 followed by 29...♖xc3 leads to the same type of position as in the game
27...♖xd1 28 ♕xd1 ♔xg7 29 ♘e2 f6 30 ♘f4 ♕b6 31 ♕d3 ♖a7 32 ♔e2 e5 33 ♘fd5 ♕b7 34 ♘c3

34 ♘g4?! may look interesting, but it leads to nowhere after the cool 34...♖b2 35 ♕d2 ♕c8! keeping the balance.
34...♕c6 35 ♕b5 ♕xb5 36 ♘xb5 ♖a1

This ending appears to be critical for Black. It seems that sooner or later the white king will pick up the b3-pawn. However, with active play, Black creates potential counterplay on the kingside, so White has to be careful.
37 ♘c3 f5 38 ♘cd1 ♔f6 39 ♔d2 h5 40 h3 ♔e6 41 ♘f2 ♖g1 42 g4 ♔f6 43 gxf5 gxf5 44 h4 ½-½

44...♖g3 45 ♔e2 ♖g1 46 ♔d2 is a repetition. Probably this line is okay for Black, but it is not easy to play. Over the board it is hard to evaluate which endings are drawn and which are not, though objectively speaking, Black is fine.

Game 93
Prandstetter-Dory
Dortmund 1987

(1 e4 c5 2 ♘f3 ♘c6 3 d4 cxd4 4 ♘xd4 g6 5 ♘c3 ♗g7 6 ♗e3 ♘f6 7 ♗c4 0-0 8 ♗b3 a5 9 f3 d5 10 ♗xd5 ♘xd5 11 exd5 ♘b4 12 ♘de2 ♗f5 13 ♖c1 b5)

14   0-0

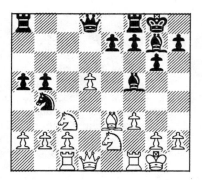

The main line. White does not want an ending with only small winning chances, so he enters a fascinating labyrinth of complications.

14   ...   ♖c8
15   ♘d4!

The only way since 15...♘xc2 was now a threat due to the pin on the c-file. Busquets-Donaldson, New York 1991, saw 15 ♕d2?! ♘xc2 16 ♗f2 ♘b4 17 ♘d4 ♘xd5 18 ♘xf5 ♘xc3 19 ♕xd8 ♘e2+ 20 ♔h1 ♖cxd8 with a slight edge for Black.

15   ...   ♗xd4!?

Uogele's initial idea, winning material at the risk of his own king's safety. The alternatives are:

a) 15...♘xd5?? is a blunder, White picks up a piece with 16 ♘xf5 ♗xc3 17 ♕xd5!

b) Silman and Donaldson suggest 15...♕d7?!, but we think that after 16 g4! ♗xc2 17 ♘xc2 ♗xc3 18 bxc3 ♘xa2 19 ♖a1 ♘xc3 20 ♕d2 White's piece is more important than Black's pawns. He should be able to launch an attack on the black king.

c) More to the point is the exchange sacrifice 15...♖xc3!? 16 bxc3 and now:

c1) Black got a bad position in Oll-Kochiev, Tallinn 1987, after 16...♘xa2 17 ♖a1 ♘xc3 (Kupreichik-Malisauskas, Miedzybrodzie 1991, saw 17...♕xd5 18 ♘xf5 ♕xf5 19 ♖xa2 ♕e6 20 ♖xa5 ♕xe3+ 21 ♔h1 ♕b6 22 ♖a2 ♗xc3 23 ♕e2 e6 24 ♖d1 b4 25 ♖a6 ♕c7 26 ♕e4 ♕c5 27 h4 with good chances of breaking Black's fortress) 18 ♕d2 ♘a4?! 19 ♘xb5 ♘b6 20 ♕xa5 ♘xd5 21 ♗d4 and White was almost winning. However, in his notes in *Informator* Oll indicates that Black could have achieved a drawn ending with 18...♗xd4 19 ♗xd4 ♘xd5 20 ♖xa5 ♗xc2! 21 ♖xb5 ♗d3! 22 ♕xd3 ♘f4 23 ♕e3 ♕xd4 24 ♕xd4 ♘e2+ 25 ♔f2 ♘xd4 which was later proven in Donchev-Fauland, Graz 1987.

Instead of 20 ♖xa5 Oll mentioned 20 g4!? as a possible improvement – and rightly so. It seems that Black is just an exchange down with insufficient compensation. Black has some chances of setting up a fortress, but with the queens still on and pawns on both wings, we think White is close to winning.

An attempt to improve is 18...♕c7!?, which was tried in the

game Ivanovic-Cebalo, Yugoslavian ch 1989. Although Black managed to draw after 19 d6!? exd6 20 ♘xf5 gxf5 21 ♗h6 f4 22 ♗xg7 ♔xg7 23 ♖fe1 d5, we feel this position is dangerous for Black. His king is weak and White should be able to launch an attack. Black's pawns look impressive, but since he needs to concentrate on defending his king, they may end up as weaknesses.

c2) 16...♘xd5 is playable and even led to a Black victory in Gonzales-Pazos, Camaguey 1986. Still, we believe that the position that arises after 17 ♘xf5 gxf5 18 ♗d4 ♘xc3 19 ♗xc3 ♕b6+ 20 ♔h1 ♗xc3 should only hold chances for White.

The exchange sacrifice 15...♖xc3!? is playable, but by combining an attack on Black's king with pressure on his queenside pawns, we feel that White holds realistic winning chances.

| 16 | ♕xd4 | ♘xc2 |
| 17 | ♖xc2 | ♗xc2 |

17...e5? was Uogele's original idea, but this seems to have been more or less refuted. Perman-Uogele, corr 1980, saw 18 ♕xe5

♖e8 19 ♕f4? ♗xc2 20 ♗d4 g5! 21 ♕d2 b4! 22 ♘e4 ♗xe4 23 fxe4 ♖xe4 24 ♗f6 ♕b6+ 25 ♔h1 ♕e3 winning for Black. The later game De Firmian-Forintos introduced the far stronger idea 19 ♕d4! ♖c4 (necessary since 19...♗xc2 20 ♗h6! f6 21 d6 is a transposition to Hector-Pirrot below) 20 ♕d2 ♗xc2 21 ♘xb5 with an eventual win for White, although it is not clear if he is much better. However, this is not so important, since Mors-Bes, corr 1993, saw 18 dxe6!? ♗xc2 19 e7! ♕xe7 20 ♘d5 ♕d8 21 ♘f6+ ♔h8 22 ♘d7+ f6 23 ♘xf8 ♕xd4 24 ♘xg6+ hxg6 25 ♗xd4 with an extra pawn for White, although Black still has reasonable chances to draw. However, we cannot understand why White did not play 21 ♗h6!? f6 22 ♗xf8, which seems to be winning. Maybe Black's best is 18...♕xd4 19 ♗xd4 ♗xc2 20 e7 ♖fe8 21 ♘d5 f5 22 ♘f6+ ♔f7 23 ♘xe8 ♔xe8 24 ♖e1, although White should still be winning.

18	♗h6	e5
19	♕xe5	f6
20	♕d4!?	

20 ♕e6+?! has not been successful so far, and seems to offer Black the better chances in the ending after 20...♖f7 21 ♘e4 ♗xe4 22 fxe4 ♕d7, since both 23 ♖xf6 ♖e8 24 ♕c6 ♕xc6 25 ♖xc6 ♖fe8 26 ♖c5 ♖b7 27 ♗d2 a4 28 d6 ♖xe4 29 ♖d5 ♖d7, as in Smit-Ekebjerg, corr 1991, and 23 ♕xd7 ♖xd7 24 ♖xf6 ♖e7 25 ♖f4 ♖f7 26 ♔f2 ♖c2+ 27 ♔e3 ♖xg2, Gonzalez-Estevez, Havana 1992, leave Black with excellent winning chances. The first game ended in a draw, and Black won the second. Not surprisingly 20 ♕e6+?! is not often seen in

practice anymore.

20 ♕e2?! is just as toothless. After 20...♖f7 21 ♕xc2 b4, Black retains the piece on c3, after which he will start attacking White's rather weak central pawn.

20 ... ♖f7!

20...♖e8 led to an immediate disaster in Hector-Pirrot, Metz 1988, when after 21 d6 ♗f5 22 ♘e4! ♗xe4? 23 ♕a7! Black had lost too much material to avoid being mated. 22...♗xe4 is of course bad, but it is probably not possible to defend Black's position anyhow.

21 ♘xb5

Other moves have not challenged Black's idea. Both 21 d6 b4 22 ♘e4 ♗xe4 23 fxe4 ♖c6 24 e5 fxe5 25 ♕d5 ♕b6+ 26 ♔h1 ♕f7, Kontic-Stanojoski, Kladovo 1990, and 21 ♖f2 ♖c4 22 ♕d2 ♗f5 23 g4 ♗d7 24 ♘e4 ♗xg4 25 b3 ♖b4 26 a3 ♗xf3 27 axb4 ♗xe4 28 bxa5 ♕xd5, as in Pantaleoni-Jaloszyinski, corr 1988, led to trouble for White.

21 ... ♖b7

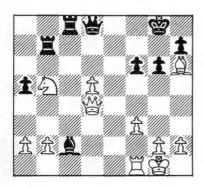

22 ♘c3!?

Two games of Hector's indicate that Black is okay after 22 a4. First Hector-Petursson, Belfort 1988,

continued 22...♕b6 23 ♕xb6 ♖xb6 24 ♗e3 ♖b8 25 ♗f4 ♖b6 26 ♖c1 ♗f5 27 ♗c7 ♖b7 28 d6 ♗d7 28 ♔f2 with some pressure. Hector was happy to repeat the line, but in Clermont Ferrand 1989 Dorfman improved with 25...♖a8! when Hector settled for repetition with 26 ♘c7 ♖b8 27 ♘b5 ♖a8 28 ♘c7. Dorfman probably should have taken the draw now, since after the ambitious 28...♖a7 29 d6 ♗xa4 30 ♖e1 g5 31 ♗e3 ♖b7 32 ♘d5 ♖c2 33 ♘xf6+ ♔f7 34 ♗d4 ♖d2 35 ♗e5 ♖d2 36 ♖c1 a4 37 ♗c3 ♖xd6 38 ♖xc2 ♖xf6 39 ♗xf6 ♔xf6 his reward was an ending a pawn down, which, however, is easily drawn due to the active rook.

22 ... ♕b6
23 ♕xb6

23 ♗e3?! was tried in Borge-P.H.Nielsen, Aarhus 1998, but Black simply played 23...♕xd4 24 ♗xd4 ♖xb2 25 ♘e4?! ♖a2!

23 ... ♖xb6
24 ♖f2!? ♗f5?!

This leads to a difficult ending for Black. We believe Black has a rather safe draw with 24...♖xb2 25 ♗c1 ♖b3! 26 axb3 ♖xc3, when it is almost impossible for White not to end up in a drawn opposite-coloured bishop ending, e.g. 27 ♗b2 ♖c8 28 ♗xf6 ♗xb3 29 d6 ♖c1+ 30 ♖f1 ♖xf1+ 31 ♔xf1 ♗e6 with a drawn endgame. The only way to avoid this type of ending is 27 d6 ♗f5 28 ♗d2 ♖xb3 29 g4!? ♗e6 30 ♗xa5 ♖d3 31 ♗c7 ♔f7, but this, too, is an easy draw, since Black is too active.

If this is correct, then Black has no problems after 15...♗xd4!?

25 ♗e3 ♖b7
26 g4 ♗d7

27 ♘e4 ♔g7
28 ♗d2!

Winning an exchange and the game, since if the bishop gets to c3, Black will have to give up an exchange anyway.

28...♖xb2 29 ♗h6+ ♔xh6 30 ♖xb2 ♗a4 31 ♘xf6 ♔g5 32 ♘e4+ ♔f4 33 ♔f2 ♗c2 34 ♘g3 ♔e5 35 ♖b7 g5 36 ♘f1 a4 37 ♘e3 ♗g6 38 ♖a7 ♗e8 39 ♖xh7 ♖b8 40 ♔g3 ♔d4 41 ♘f5+ ♔xd5 42 ♖h8 ♖a8 43 a3 ♗c6 44 ♖xa8 ♗xa8 45 f4 ♔c4 46 fxg5 ♔b3 47 h4 1-0

White's new queen covers the a1-square just in time.

Game 94
Hector-Hernandez
Thessaloniki ol 1988

(1 e4 c5 2 ♘f3 ♘c6 3 d4 cxd4 4 ♘xd4 g6 5 ♘c3 ♗g7 6 ♗e3 ♘f6 7 ♗c4 0-0 8 ♗b3 a5 9 f3 d5 10 ♗xd5 ♘xd5 11 exd5 ♘b4 12 ♘de2)

12 ... e6!?

A safe way of avoiding the complications arising from 12...♗f5!? Generally, this move leads to quieter positions, since White nor-

mally returns the offered pawn, and then tries to exploit the positional defects of Black's position.

13 a3!?

This seems to be White's best attempt for an advantage. Alternatives are:

a) The latest *ECO* quotes an old recommendation of Korchnoi's, claiming that White is better after 13 ♕d2 exd5 14 ♗d4 ♗xd4?! 15 ♘xd4 ♕h4+ 16 ♔f1 ♘c6 17 ♘db5. This is probably true, but it is really completely irrelevant since Rothaler-Hagberg, corr 1979, saw the much better 14...♗f5!, refuting White's plan since after 15 ♖c1 ♗xd4 16 ♘xd4 ♖e8+ 17 ♔f2?! ♕b6 the game is already close to lost for White, who resigned after 18 ♖hd1? ♘d3+ because 19 cxd3 ♕xd4+ followed by ...♖e3 is terrible. Just as bad is 14 a3 d4! 15 0-0-0 ♘xc2! winning after both 16 ♕xc2 ♗f5 17 ♕d2 dxc3 18 ♘xc3 ♕c7, Hennings-Szilagyi, Varna 1970, when Black has an very easy attack, and 16 ♗f2 ♘a1! 17 ♔b1 ♘b3 18 ♕c2 dxc3! 19 ♖xd8 ♖xd8, as featured in Sammalvuo-Wedberg, Osterkan 1994, where White's unsafe king again gave Black a winning attack.

b) The greedy 13 dxe6?! was tried in Borge-Oblitas, Manila ol 1992. Black had terrific compensation after 13...♗xe6 14 a3 ♘d5 15 ♗d4 ♘xc3 16 bxc3 ♖e8 17 ♔f2 ♕c7 18 ♖b1 ♗xd4+ 19 cxd4 ♖c8 and a winning position after 20 c3 ♗c4 21 ♘g3 ♗d5 22 ♖c1 ♕e7 23 ♕d2 ♕xa3.

c) 13 ♗c5 ♖e8 14 d6 is usually given as unclear, but simply 14...♕g5!, hitting both c5 and g2, is very good for Black.

d) This leaves only 13 0-0, when 13...exd5 14 ♗d4 ♗xd4+ 15 ♘xd4 ♕b6 was okay for Black in Estevez-Hernandez, Holguin 1989. Simpler for Black is 13...♖e8!?, when White has nothing better than 14 a3 transposing to 13 a3.

13	...	♘xd5
14	♘xd5	exd5
15	♗d4	♗h6!?

The positional continuation. 15...♗xd4!? looks awful, since Black risks a white knight ending up on d4, but surprisingly Black has been doing fine in practice. The game Grünfeld-Taylor, New York 1985, illustrated Black's plan rather well. After 16 ♕xd4 ♖e8 17 ♔f2 ♖a6!? 18 ♘c3 ♖c6 19 ♖ad1 ♗f5 20 ♖d2 ♖c4! 21 ♕xd5 ♕b6+ 22 ♔g3 ♕e3 23 h3, Black had a perpetual with 23...♕f4+. However, the prophylactic 18 ♖ae1! gives White an edge. The idea is that 18...♖c6 19 c3! ♖c4 20 ♕d2 followed by ♘d4, as well as 18...♖ae6 19 ♘c3!, seems good for White.

Although 15...♗xd4!? has been scoring well for Black, we find it difficult to believe that his temporary initiative counterbalances White's positional pluses.

16 0-0 ♖a6

This is the usual way of transferring the rook, but the simple 16...♖e8!? seems better to us. The idea is that this rook always belongs on e8, but the other rook may sometimes go to c8 instead of a6. The only example seen in practice is Real-Estevez, corr 1989, when Black was much better after 17 ♘g3?! ♖a6 18 f4 ♕h4 19 ♖e1 ♖ae6 20 ♖xe6 ♗xe6 21 f5 ♗xf5 22 ♘xf5 gxf5 23 ♗f2 ♗e3! In general, we do not think putting the knight on g3 is a good plan. Its ideal square is c3, where it puts pressure on d5. However, if White plays 17 ♘c3!?, Black has 17...♗f5 18 ♖f2 ♖c8 19 ♕f1?! ♖c4! 20 ♖d1 ♗xc2! winning a pawn. White's best might be 17 ♗f2 followed by ♘d4 and c2-c3 etc., hoping to exert pressure on the d-pawn later. Maybe Black should play 17...b6 18 ♘d4 ♗a6 19 ♖e1 ♕d6, when it will not be easy for White to make progress.

17 ♔h1?!

Much better is 17 ♘c3!, immediately putting some pressure on d5, since 18 ♗c5 would already be a threat. 17...♖e8 seems necessary, but then 18 ♕d3, intending 18...♗f5 19 ♕b5!, gives White some advantage. Since it seems that 17 ♘c3! gives White a pleasant position, we recommend 16...♖e8!? as the right move order.

17	...	♖e8
18	♗f2	a4
19	♖e1	♖ae6
20	♘c3	♖xe1+
21	♗xe1	d4
22	♘xa4	♗e3
23	♘c5	♗f5

Black has fine compensation,

since the c2-pawn is easy to attack.
**24 &g3 ♛b6 25 b4 ♛c6 26 a4 ♖c8
27 a5 ♛b5 28 ♖b1 ♛c4 29 ♖b2
♛c3 30 ♛b1 ♖e8 31 ♘e4!**

Avoiding 31 ♘d3? &xd3 32
cxd3 &c1!

**31...&xe4 32 fxe4 ♖xe4 33 ♖b3
♛c4 34 b5 &f4 35 a6 bxa6 36 b6
♛e6 37 b7 &b8 38 ♛a1 ♖e2 39
♛d4 ♛c6 40 ♛d8+ ♔g7 41 ♛d4+
♔g8 42 &f2 ♛c7 43 g3 ♖c2 44
♛f6 ♖d2 45 ♛f3 ♛c2 46 &g1 ♖d1
47 h4 ♛c1 48 ♛e3 ♛c6 49 ♔h2
♛c2+ 50 ♔h1 ♛c6, ½-½**

So far, 12...e6!? have been doing
very well in practice, and White
has no easy way of achieving an
edge. He may get a slight positional
plus, but Black, armed with the
bishop pair, always has some
counter-chances.

Game 95
Lanka-P.H.Nielsen
Moscow ol 1994

**(1 e4 c5 2 ♘f3 ♘c6 3 d4 cxd4 4
♘xd4 g6 5 ♘c3 &g7 6 &e3 ♘f6 7
&c4 0-0 8 &b3)**

8   ...   d6!?

This move is generally used to
transpose to the main line Dragon,
which is outside the scope of this
book. However, the Danish correspondence player Ove Ekebjerg has
popularised an idea which takes
advantage of the fact that White,
compared to the main line Dragon,
has already put his bishop on b3.

**9   f3   &d7
10   h4!?**

Although we consider this to be
more accurate than the common 10
♛d2 (see the next game), for some
reason, 10 h4!? is played only
rarely. To us it seems a good idea
to start the attack immediately.

10   ...   ♘xd4

This may be too dangerous, but
at the time I had not realised just
how strong White's attack is. Unfortunately, no-one has tried 10
h4!? against Ekebjerg, but he
claims that 10...h5!? is fine for
Black. This need practical testing,
and is critical for the entire variation.

11   &xd4   b5!?

This is Black's idea in this line.
Since White's bishop is already on
b3, it is easier for Black to become
active on the queenside.

12   h5!   e6

Limiting the activity of the
bishop on b3, as well as preventing
a white ♘d5, exchanging Black's
important defender on f6. Over the
board I considered the more direct
12...a5!? too. In Vescovi-Afek,
Groningen 1994, White did not
find a way through Black's defences. The game continued 13
hxg6 hxg6 14 ♘d5 ♘xd5 15 &xd5
♖c8 16 &xg7 ♔xg7 17 ♛d4+ f6
18 c3 ♛c7 19 &b3 ♛c5 with
equality. 16 ♛d2!? looks dangerous, but after 16...e6! 17 &xg7

♔xg7 18 ♕h6+ ♔f6, we can only see a perpetual for White. Perhaps the modest 14 a3!?, as in Damjanovic-Begovac, Sombor 1974, is White's best, when he was clearly better after 14...e5?! 15 ♗e3 b4 16 ♘d5 ♘xd5 17 ♗xd5 bxa3 18 ♖xa3, although by analogy to our main game 14...e6!? suggests itself.

13	hxg6	hxg6
14	♕d2	a5
15	a4!?	

White delays his attack for a short while, and makes a positional move instead. The direct 15 ♗e3?! would backfire after 15...a4 16 ♗h6 ♗h8!

15 ... bxa4!

This weakens the queenside, but 15...b4? 16 ♘e2 would allow the white king to live a safe life on the queenside, and give his subordinates plenty of time to organise a mating attack on the other flank. Now, at least, Black has some targets on the queenside.

| 16 | ♘xa4 | ♗c6 |
| 17 | g4!? | |

Motwani-Larsen, London 1989, saw 17 0-0-0 instead. Black won after 17...♖b8 18 ♗c3 d5 19 e5 ♘d7 20 g4? ♕c7 21 ♗xa5? ♕a7, as his attack strikes first. Instead of 20 g4? Larsen gives 20 ♖h3! with a promising attack for White.

| 17 | ... | ♖b8 |
| 18 | ♗e3? | |

This gives Black the opportunity he was hoping for. Instead 18 ♕h2!, threatening ♗xf6, forces 18...♖e8, when 19 ♗e3! followed by ♗h6 probably gives White a winning attack.

18 ... d5!

This classical counterstroke in the centre secures Black excellent chances.

19 e5

19 ♕h2 dxe4! 20 ♗h6 ♖xb3! 21 cxb3 exf3 22 ♗xg7 f2+! arrives just in time.

19 ... ♘d7
20 ♕h2 f6!

Absolutely the only move, since 20...♖e8? loses to 21 ♕h7+ ♔f8 22 ♗h6.

21 ♘c5 ♔f7!!

Actually I am quite proud of this move. It is not often that Black defends like this in the Dragon. Now the e-pawn is defended and ...♖h8 is a threat.

| 22 | ♘xd7 | ♗xd7 |
| 23 | ♕d2! | |

Quite a strong move. It is not easy to admit one's attack is a failure. On d2 the queen maintains some threats.

23 ... fxe5?!

Greedy. Better was 23...♖h8!, keeping the initiative.

24	♖xa5	♖h8
25	♖xh8	♕xh8
26	♖a7	

26 ♖xd5 exd5 27 ♕xd5+ ♔e8 does not promise White more than a perpetual.

26 ... ♔e8

It may seem like Black has lost his co-ordination, but everything is okay; the activity of the black queen secures plenty of counterplay.

27 ♕d3 ♕h1+ 28 ♔e2 e4 29 fxe4 ♗b5 30 ♗a4 ♕g2+ 31 ♔e1 ♕h1+ 32 ♔d2 ♕g2+ 33 ♔e1 ♗c3+!

A nice trick, opening up the b-file, and ensuring that Black gets to the white king first.

34 bxc3 ♗xa4 35 ♕d1??

After 35 ♕e2 ♕h1+ White has serious problems, but now he loses on the spot.

35...♗xc2 0-1

12...e6 has an unbeaten record, but it seems to us that it is just a matter of time before White stops misplaying his rather dangerous attack. However, 10...h5 and 12...a5 seem interesting and deserve testing.

Game 96
Topalov-Tiviakov
Wijk aan Zee 1996

(1 e4 c5 2 ♘f3 ♘c6 3 d4 cxd4 4 ♘xd4 g6 5 ♘c3 ♗g7 6 ♗e3 ♘f6 7 ♗c4 0-0 8 ♗b3 d6 9 f3 ♗d7)

10 ♕d2

White's traditional continuation. He prepares 11 0-0-0 followed by 12 h4, with the standard attack. 10 ♕e2!? is also possible, preventing Black's immediate ...b7-b5. However, the queen is not very well placed on e2, and Black should play 10...♘a5 when he has good chances.

10 ... ♘xd4!?

10...♖c8 is a normal Dragon and is outside the scope of this book. The text move exploits the fact that White already has played the move ♗b3.

11 ♗xd4 b5!

Speeding up Black's counterplay on the queenside.

12 h4!?

This seems to be White's best. 12 a4?! is played just as often, but it tends to steer the game towards a draw after 12...b4 13 ♘d5 ♘xd5 14 exd5 ♗xd4 15 ♕xd4 a5, as proven by Ekebjerg in a number of correspondence games. White has absolutely nothing, e.g. 16 h4 e5 17 dxe6 ♗xe6 18 ♗xe6 fxe6 19 0-0-0 d5 20 ♖de1 ♖a6 21 ♖e5 ♖c6 22 ♔b1 ♕b6 Mallae-Ekebjerg, corr 1977. Even less problematic is 16 0-0 ♕c7! 17 ♖fe1 ♖fe8 18 ♔h1 (18 ♖e2 ♕a7 is drawn as well) 18...e5! 19 dxe6 ♗xe6 20 ♗xe6 ♖xe6 21 ♖xe6 fxe6 with a drawn ending.

14 ♗xd5?! is even worse, and led to an advantage for Black in the game Smith-Ekebjerg, corr 1972: 14...♗xd4 15 ♕xd4 ♖c8 15 ♗b3 ♕a5 16 ♖d1 ♗e6! 17 ♖f1 ♗xb3 18 cxb3 ♖c2 and Black went on to win. 12 a4?! is certainly nothing for Black to worry about, unless he has to win at all costs.

12   ...   a5

12...e6 in the style of the previous game may be possible, and seems to be a viable way of getting off the beaten track.

13   a4!

The sharper 13 h5?! backfires, e.g. 13...e5! 14 ♗e3 a4 15 ♗d5 b4 16 ♘e2 ♘xd5 17 ♕xd5 ♗e6 18 ♕d2 d5!, Tolnai-Leko, Hungary 1992, where Black was much better after 19 hxg6 fxg6 20 ♗c5 ♖f7 21 ♗xb4 ♖d7 22 exd5 ♖xd5 23 ♕e3 ♗f5. Leko gives 19 ♗c5 dxe4! 20 ♗xf8 ♕xf8 21 fxe4 ♕c5 as critical, but it looks as if White is in great difficulties.

14 hxg6!? is given as unclear after 14...exd4 15 ♗xf7+ ♔h8 16 ♕xd4 h6 17 ♕d2 ♘g8 18 ♕xd6 ♗e8 19 ♕xd8 ♖xd8 20 ♗xe8 b4! by Stoica and Nisipeanu, but only Black can win this position. Therefore 13 h5?! must be considered harmless.

13   ...   bxa4

A positional concession, but a necessary one, since 13...b4? 14 ♘d5 ♘xd5 15 ♗xd5 ♗xd4 16 ♕xd4 ♖c8 17 h5! is just bad. Black hopes that the weakened squares on the queenside are not too important, since White's h2-h4 indicates that he will castle queenside. However, White, in turn, can try to exploit these concessions in a positional manner, hoping that h2-h4 will not prove to be a serious weakness later.

14   ♘xa4   e5

This is necessary, as 14...♗e6 15 ♘b6 ♖b8 16 ♘d5 ♗xd5 17 exd5 ♖b5 18 ♖a4 ♕c7 19 h5 ♖a8 20 hxg6 hxg6 21 g4 was good for White in Hort-Forintos, Athens 1969.

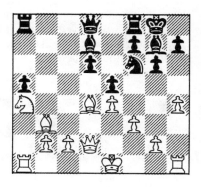

15   ♗b6!

This strong new move seems to pose Black big problems. The older moves are:

a) 15 ♗c3, putting pressure on the a5-pawn, has proven ineffective after the reply 15...♗e6. Both 16 0-0-0 ♗xb3 17 cxb3 ♕b8 18 ♕c2 d5 19 exd5 ♖d8 20 d6 ♖xd6 21 ♖xd6 ♕xd6 22 ♖d1 ♕e6, when Black was better in Lepsenyi-Ekebjerg, corr 1980, and 16 ♗xe6 fxe6 17 0-0-0 d5 18 ♗xe4 ♘xe4, again with a good position for Black, Omelschenko-Ekebjerg, corr 1977, are fine for Black.

b) Not a whole lot better is 15 ♗e3, when Black is doing fine again: 15...♗e6 16 ♘b6?! (16 0-0-0 ♗xb3 17 cxb3 ♖b8 is okay for Black, but probably White's best) 16...♖b8 17 ♘d5 ♗xd5 18 exd5 e4 19 ♗d4 ♖e8 20 ♔d1 ♖b4 21 ♗a4 exf3 22 ♗xe8 ♘e4 and White was blown off the board in Stern-Ekebjerg, corr 1972. Unfortunately these old lines seem academic in the light of 15 ♗b6!

15   ...   ♕b8
16   ♗e3!   ♗e6
17   ♖a3!

These three strong positional

moves give White much the better chances. White simply ignores the fact that he has played h2-h4 and plays along Classical Sicilian lines, trying to exploit the hole on d5.

17   ...   ♕b4?!

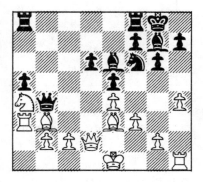

This makes things even worse. The critical test is 17...♕c7!? according to Topalov, when 18 ♗xe6 fxe6 19 ♗b6 ♕c6 20 ♗xa5 ♗h6! seems fine for Black. However, White should forget about winning material and simply play for a better structure with 18 0-0 or 18 ♘c3, which should leave him better.

18   ♘b6   ♖ab8
19   ♕xb4   axb4

20   ♖a5!

Again White is not tempted to win a pawn with a move such as 21 ♖a4, instead he keeps his positional bind by constantly controlling d5.

20...♗xb3 21 cxb3 ♖fd8 22 ♔e2 ♘h5?!

It would have been more practical to play 22...d5!? with drawing chances in the ending resulting from 23 ♘xd5 ♘xd5 24 ♖xd5 ♖xd5 25 exd5 ♖d8 26 ♖d1 ♗f8.

23 ♖c1 f5 24 ♖c7 fxe4 25 fxe4 ♘f4+ 26 ♔d2 ♘e6 27 ♖e7 ♖e8 28 ♘d5 ♖xe7 29 ♘xe7+ ♔f8 30 ♘d5 ♖b7

White has a won position, and now simply with 31 ♖a4, winning a pawn as well as creating two dangerous b-pawns, would have been best. Topalov's 31 ♖a6 was not bad either, but he kept missing wins, and in the end Tiviakov held the draw after 71 moves.

At the moment the Ekebjerg system is in theoretical crisis. Both 10 h4!? and Topalov's 16 ♗e3! seem very promising, so unless some serious repair work is done, this line will probably not be seen much in the future.

12 Lines in which White Captures with ♘xc6

Chapter Guide

1 e4 c5 2 ♘f3 ♘c6 3 d4 cxd4 4 ♘xd4 g6

5 ♘xc6?! – *Game 97*
5 ♘c3 ♗g7 6 ♗e3 ♘f6 7 ♘xc6 bxc6 8 e5
    8...♘g8
        9 f4
            9...f6   – *Game 98*
            9...♘h6   – *Game 99*
        9 ♗d4   – *Game 100*
    8...♘d5 9 ♘xd5 cxd5 10 ♕xd5 ♖b8
            11 ♗c4   – *Game 101*
            11 ♗xa7   – *Game 102*

An early ♘xc6 from White is usually an attempt to punish an inaccuracy on Black's part. However, in the lines given in this chapter, White decides to take on c6 without provocation, attempting to take advantage of Black's modest development. However, this is not particularly easy to do, as Black's position is solid and White is not really very far ahead in development.

Game 97
Vestol-Botvinnik
Moscow ol 1956

(**1 e4 c5 2 ♘f3 ♘c6 3 d4 cxd4 4 ♘xd4 g6**)

5   ♘xc6?!
This early assault should never really succeed. Looking at the position objectively, White is just as undeveloped as his opponent. But even such strong players as grandmaster Alexander Beliavsky have occasionally experimented with this line.

5   ...   bxc6
5...dxc6?! was once played by the great Emanuel Lasker, but that was more than a century ago, and since it only equalises we cannot recommend it: 6 ♕f3?! (6 ♕xd8+ ♔xd8 is equal; 6 ♗d3!?) 6...♘f6 7 h3 ♗e6 8 ♘c3 ♗g7 9 ♗d3 ♘d7 10 ♕g3 ♕b6 11 ♗e2 h5 when Black was better in the game Albin-

Em.Lasker, Hastings 1895.

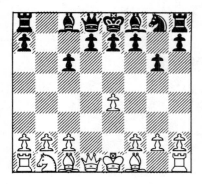

6 ♕d4

The logical follow-up to White's previous move, but White has also tried a number of other moves:

a) 6 ♗e2 ♗g7 7 0-0 ♕b6 8 ♘a3 ♘f6 with a slight plus for Black, Denker-Stoltz, Groningen 1946.

b) 6 ♗d3 ♗g7 7 0-0 ♘f6 8 c4 0-0 9 ♘c3 d5 10 h3 ♖b8 with equal chances, H.Steiner-Stoltz, Groningen 1946.

c) 6 ♗c4 ♗g7 7 0-0 e6!? (Black is playing for ...d7-d5 in one go, but 7...d6 8 ♘c3 ♘f6 is also fine) 8 ♘c3 ♘e7 9 ♖e1 ♕c7 10 ♗g5 d6 11 ♕f3 0-0 is equal, Outerelo-Frois, Cordoba 1991.

d) 6 ♗e3 ♗g7 (6...♘f6!) 7 ♗d4 ♘f6 8 e5 ♘d5 9 c4 ♘f4 followed by ...♘e6 with a good game for Black.

6 ... ♘f6

Also quite common is 6...f6, which White has met with following moves:

a) 7 h4 ♘h6 8 h5 ♗a6 9 ♗xa6 ♕a5+ 10 ♘c3 ♕xa6 with a slight plus for Black.

b) 7 ♗c4 is the most common choice, when Black has several good answers:

b1) 7...e5? (with the white bishop on c4, this is way too weakening) 8 ♕d3 ♘e7 9 ♘c3 ♗b7 10 f4! d5 (or 10...exf4 11 ♗xf4 d5 12 exd5 cxd5 13 ♗b3 ♕a5 14 0-0 0-0-0 15 ♘e4! ♘f5 16 ♘xf6 and wins, Dolginin-Antoshin, USSR 1970) 11 exd5 cxd5 12 ♗b5+ ♔f7 13 fxe5 fxe5 14 0-0+ ♔g7 15 ♗g5 ♕b6+ 16 ♔h1 e4 17 ♕g3 ♕e6 18 ♖f6 and it was soon all over, Buenos-Perez, Cienfuegos 1980.

b2) 7...♕b6 8 ♕d3 ♘h6 9 0-0 ♗g7 10 ♘c3 ♘g4 with equality, Bandal-Schulman, Lugano ol 1968.

b3) 7...♗g7 8 0-0 (or 8 ♘c3 ♘h6 9 0-0 transposing) 8...♘h6 9 ♘c3 ♕b6 (or 9...♘f7 10 ♗e3 0-0 11 ♕d2 e6 12 ♖fd1 ♕a5 13 ♖ab1 ♖c8 14 b4 ♕c7 15 ♗f4 ♘e5 16 ♗b3 ♗f8 17 b5 ♖b8 18 a4 ♗e7 19 ♗g3 ♔g7 20 f4 and White was having a ball in Lasker-Bird, Newcastle 1892) 10 ♕xb6 (10 ♕d3? is met by 10...♘g4! and 10 ♕d1? by 10...♗a6) 10...axb6 11 ♗e3 ♗a6 12 ♗e2 f5 13 ♖fe1 ♗xe2 slightly favours Black, Pilnik-Barcza, Stockholm izt 1952.

b4) 7...♘h6 8 0-0 ♘f7 9 ♗xf7+ ♔xf7 10 e5 ♕b6 11 ♕c4+ d5 12 exd6 ♗e6 13 ♕c3 exd6 with a slight plus for Black, Kapu-Barcza, Hungarian ch 1951.

b5) 7...e6 8 0-0 ♘h6 9 ♘c3 ♘f7 10 ♗e3 ♗g7 11 ♖ad1 0-0 12 ♕d2 f5 13 exf5 gxf5 also slightly favours Black, Schlechter-Lasker, Hastings 1895.

b6) 7...♗a6!? (untried, but deserving a test) 8 ♘c3 (8 ♗b3 does not make any sense as White can no longer castle kingside; nor does 8 ♗xa6 ♕a5+ 9 ♘c3 ♕xa6 make a good impression) 8...♗xc4 9 ♕xc4 e6 and Black follows up with

...♘e7, ...♗g7, ...0-0 and ...d7-d5.

c) 7 c4! (best; it is advisable to restrict Black's options in the centre) 7...e5!? (instead Poljak-Simagin, USSR 1950, saw 7...♘h6 8 ♗e2 ♗g7 9 0-0 0-0 10 c5 f5 11 e5 [Korchnoi suggests 11 ♕a4] 11...♘f7 12 ♗c4 ♕c7 13 ♗xf7+ ♖xf7 14 ♖e1 ♗a6 15 ♘c3 ♖b8 16 ♖b1 d6!? 17 cxd6 exd6 18 exd6 ♕a5 19 ♕h4 ♗xc3 20 bxc3 ♖xb1 21 ♖e8+ with a perpetual) 8 ♕d3 ♗e6 9 ♘c3 ♘h6 10 ♗e2 ♘f7 11 ♗e3 ♕a5 12 0-0 ♗b4 (12...♗e7 is also interesting, although after 13 f4 exf4 14 ♗xf4 d6 Black will have to face h2-h4-h5) 13 ♖fc1 d6, Naselli-Pelikan, played at Buenos Aires 1958, and now instead of the passive 14 ♗f3?!, White should have opted for the more aggressive 14 a3, e.g. 14... ♗xc3 15 b4 ♕d8 16 ♕xc3 d5 17 ♗c5 with an unclear position or 14 ♘d1 (threatening a2-a3 followed by b2-b4) 14...d5 15 a3 ♗e7 16 exd5 cxd5 17 b4 ♕d8 18 b5, when White holds the better chances.

7   e5

7   ...   ♘d5

This seems best, but Black does not have any problems after:

a) 7...♘g8 (the fact that Black is still okay after this move shows that White's entire opening idea is a waste of time) 8 ♗c4 (or 8 e6 ♘f6 9 exf7+ ♔xf7 10 ♘c3, Fluder-Gawlikowski, Poland 1953, and now 10...d5! with a good game for Black) 8...♗g7 9 0-0 f6 10 exf6 (10 ♗xg8 ♖xg8 11 ♕h4 fxe5 12 ♕xh7 ♔f7 13 ♗h6 e6 14 ♗xg7 ♖xg7 15 ♕h6 ♕f6 16 ♕e3 ♕f4 with a slight advantage for Black, Akopian-Faibisovich, Kharkov 1971) 10...♘xf6 11 ♗b3 d5 12 ♗f4 (Korchnoi's recommendation 12 c4 is best met by 12...0-0 13 cxd5 exd5 14 ♘c3 ♗e6 with excellent play for Black) 12...0-0 13 ♗e5 e6 14 ♘c3 c5 15 ♕xc5 ♘d7 16 ♕c6 ♗xe5 17 ♕xa8 ♗xc3 18 bxc3 ♕c7 19 ♗xd5 exd5 20 ♕xd5+ with equal chances.

b) 7...♘h5 and now a further branch:

b1) 8 ♘c3 (untried are 8 ♗c4 ♘g7 9 0-0 and 8 g4 ♘g7 9 ♗c4 a5 and 8 e6 ♗g7 9 exf7+ ♔xf7, but in all cases Black is doing fine) 8...♕b6 9 ♕e4 f5 10 ♕c4 ♗g7 11 f4 d5 12 ♕b3 ♖b8 13 ♗e2 0-0 14 ♕xb6 axb6 15 g3 ♖d8 16 ♗f3 ♗f8 17 b4 e6 18 a3 ♗a6 19 ♗d2 ♘g7 20 ♔f2 ♘e8 21 ♖hb1 ♘c7 with equal chances, Beliavsky-Karlsson, Lucerne ol 1982.

b2) 8 ♗e2 ♘g7 9 ♘c3 (Leonhardt-Reti, Berlin 1920, saw 9 0-0 ♘e6 10 ♕h4 ♗g7 11 f4 ♕b6+ 12 ♔h1 ♘d4 13 ♗d3 ♗a6 with an edge for Black, but Korchnoi mentions 9 ♘d2!? ♘e6 10 ♕h4! as unclear) 9...♘e6 10 ♕e3 ♗g7 11 f4 0-0 followed by ...d7-d6 was better for Black in Adams-Bisguier, USA ch 1954.

8   e6

White attempts to disrupt his opponent's structure, but only helps Black to gain a significant lead in development. Other moves are little better:

a) 8 c4 and now Black can try:

a1) 8...♘c7 9 e6 f6 10 exd7+ ♕xd7 11 ♗e3 ♕xd4 12 ♗xd4 e5 13 ♗c3 with equality, Bendiktsson-Petursson, Iceland 1980.

a2) 8...♘b4 9 ♕c3 c5 10 ♗e2 (Donaldson gives 10 ♗e3 ♗g7 11 ♗xc5 ♘c6 12 f4 d6, which is good for Black, while 10 e6 is also harmless after 10...f6 11 a3 ♘c6 12 exd7+ ♕xd7 13 ♗e3 ♘d4 14 ♘d2 ♗b7 15 ♘b3 a5 Black is clearly better, as in Vartapetyan-Ovsejevich, Nikolaev 1995) 10...♗b7 11 0-0 ♗g7 12 ♗f4 ♘c6 13 ♘d2 d6 14 ♗f3 0-0 with approximate equality, Suchorokov-Isupov, Orel 1992.

a3) 8...♕b6 9 ♕e4 ♘c7 10 ♘c3 ♗g7 11 f4 0-0 12 ♗d2 d5 13 ♕f3 ♗f5 with better chances for Black, Chistiakov-Veresov, USSR 1953.

b) 8 ♗c4 ♕b6 9 c3 ♗g7 10 ♗xd5 cxd5 11 ♕xb6 axb6 12 f4 g5 13 fxg5 ♗xe5 and with a pawn majority in the centre and the pair of bishops, Black clearly holds the better prospects, Yanofsky-Stoltz, Groningen 1946.

8   ...   f6

The alternative 8...♘f6 also offers Black quite good chances:

a) 9 exf7+ ♔xf7 10 ♗e2 ♗g7 11 h4 ♕b6 12 ♕a4 and now 12...e5 gives Black a good game.

b) 9 exd7+ ♗xd7 10 ♗e2 ♗g7 11 0-0 0-0 12 ♘a3 ♗f5! 13 ♕a4 ♕c7, Wolff-Serper, Baguio City 1987, and here 14 ♘c4! would have kept the chances level, but instead White continued 14 ♗f3? and after 14...♘d5 15 ♖e1 ♖ab8 16

c3 ♖fd8 17 ♘c4 ♘b6! 18 ♘xb6 ♖xb6 Black was on top.

9   exd7+

9 c4 may transpose into the 8 c4 line above if Black continues 9...♘b4 10 ♕c3 c5, but in Hart-Silman, USA 1991, Black played 10...a5 and won at great speed: 11 exd7+ ♗xd7 12 ♗e3? (best was 12 ♗e2 to get the white king away from the same diagonal as the queen) 12...♗f5 13 ♘a3 e5 14 ♖d1? ♕b8 15 ♖d2? ♘xa2 0-1.

9   ...   ♗xd7

10   ♗e2

Probably not the best, so White should consider trying something different:

a) Motamedi-Donaldson, Portland 1985, saw 10 ♗c4 e5 11 ♕d1?! (Korchnoi suggests the interesting 11 ♕e4!? intending ♘c3) 11...♗e6 12 ♕e2 (12 h4 can be met with 12...♕a5+ 13 ♗d2 ♕b6 14 ♗b3 a5 15 c4 ♘b4!? 16 ♗xb4 ♗xb4 17 ♘c3 ♖d8 with a clear edge for Black) 12...♗c5 13 0-0 0-0 14 ♘c3 ♕e7 (14...♖f7 15 ♘e4 ♗e7 16 ♗b3 f5 17 ♘c3 ♗f6 slightly favours Black, Abravanel-Haik, Royan 1987) 15 ♗h6 ♖fd8 16 ♘e4 ♗b6 and Black was better.

b) 10 ♗d3 can also be played, although after 10...e5 11 ♕h4 ♗g7 12 0-0 0-0 13 ♖d1 ♕c7 14 ♗c4 ♗e6 15 ♘c3 ♖ad8 Black was already better in Balinas-Donaldson, Reno 1994. At this point White blundered with 16 ♗h6??, which Black met with 16...g5! 17 ♕h5 ♗f7 18 ♗xd5 cxd5 19 ♕h3 ♗xh6 20 ♕xh6 d4 21 ♘b5 ♕b6 22 a4 ♗g6 and while White avoided losing a piece, he could not save his queenside.

| 10 | ... | e5 |
| 11 | ♕d1 | |

In J.Cruz Lima-Garcia Martinez, Cuba 1979, White tried 11 ♕a4 without much success: 11...♖b8 12 c3 ♗g7 13 0-0 0-0 14 ♖d1 ♕c7 15 ♘a3 f5 16 ♘c4 ♔h8 17 ♕c2 ♗e6 18 ♔h1 e4 19 ♗d2 ♖fe8 20 f3 ♗g8 21 ♕c1 e3 22 ♗e1 g5 23 g3 f4 and White was about to be crushed.

11	...	♗g7
12	c3	0-0
13	♘a3	f5!
14	♗c4	♗e6
15	♕a4	♕c7
16	♗e3?!	♔h8
17	♗c5	♖fb8

The game concluded:
18 ♕c2 ♕a5 19 ♗d6 ♖d8 20 ♗e7 ♖e8 21 ♗h4 f4

In his last six moves White has moved his bishop five times, finally putting it on h4 where it does nothing; of course, Black is already much better.

22 0-0 ♗f5 23 ♕e2 h6 24 f3 e4 25 ♗xd5 ♕xd5 26 fxe4 ♖xe4 27 ♕d1 ♖b8 28 ♕c1 ♖e2 29 ♗f2 ♕e4?!

Botvinnik now starts making things more complicated than they ought to be. Simple and good was 29...♖bxb2.

30 b3 f3 31 gxf3 ♕d3?!

Here 31...♕xf3 was best.

32 ♕f4 ♖be8 33 ♗d4?

This just loses. Better was 33 ♖ad1 when although Black is still better, White is still on the board.

33...♗xd4+ 34 ♕xd4 ♕xd4+ 35 cxd4 ♗h3 36 ♖fc1 ♖g2+ 37 ♔h1 ♖ee2 0-1

Game 98
Ulibin-Serper
Tbilisi 1989

(1 e4 c5 2 ♘f3 ♘c6 3 d4 cxd4 4 ♘xd4 g6)

5	♘c3	♗g7
6	♗e3	♘f6
7	♘xc6	

With the black knight on f6, the exchange on c6 makes more sense. Black has to play accurately to avoid falling too far behind in development.

| 7 | ... | bxc6 |

The other possibility is the unambitious 7...dxc6. Play usually continues with 8 ♕xd8+ ♔xd8 and now:

a) 9 ♖d1+ ♔e8 10 f4 ♗e6 11 ♗e2 h5 12 0-0 (better is 12 h3, not allowing Black's knight into g4) 12...♘g4 13 ♗xg4 hxg4 14 ♗d4 ♗xd4+ 15 ♖xd4 f5 16 ♖e1 ♔f7 17 exf5 gxf5 with equality, Lukic-Puc, Yugoslavian ch 1958.

b) 9 ♗c4 ♔e8 10 f3 (better is 10 h3 to take control over e5 with f2-f4, but Black can try 10...♘d7 11 ♗b3 ♗xc3+ when White may find it difficult to make use of his two bishops) 10...♘d7 11 a4 ♘e5 12 ♗b3 ♗e6!? 13 ♗xe6 fxe6 14 0-0-0 ♘c4 15 ♗d4 e5 16 ♗f2 ♗h6+ 17 ♔b1 when Black's doubled e-pawn gives White an insignificant edge, Khasin-Shatskes, Moscow 1961.

c) 9 0-0-0+ and:

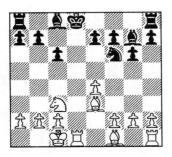

c1) 9...♗d7? 10 ♗e2 e5 11 ♗g5 ♗c7 12 f4! ♗e6 13 f5! gxf5 14 exf5 ♗d7 15 g4 is very unpleasant for Black.

c2) 9...♘d7!? was tried out in Granda Zuniga-Pinal, Havana 1985: 10 ♗c4 f6 11 f4 ♗c7 12 ♖d2 e5 13 g3 ♘b6 14 ♗b3 ♗h3 15 ♘d1 ♖ad8 16 ♘f2 ♖xd2 17 ♗xd2 ♗c8 18 ♖f1 ♘d7 19 ♘d3 exf4 20 ♗xf4+ ♔b6 21 ♗e3+ ♔c7 22 ♘f4 ♘e5 23 ♗e6 ♖e8 ½-½. However, White can improve with 11 ♗e6 ♔c7 12 ♗f4+ ♘e5 13 ♗b3, intending 14 ♗g3 and f2-f4, or 11...♔e8 12 f4 b6 13 a4 in both cases with an edge for White.

c3) 9...♔e8 when White should keep the black knight away from g4:

c31) 10 e5? ♘g4 11 ♘b5 ♗xe5 12 ♗d4 cxb5 13 ♗xb5+ ♔f8 14 ♗xe5 ♘xe5 and White is already lost, Olifer-Bannik, Ukrainian ch 1960.

c32) 10 ♗d4 ♗g4?! (10...♗e6!) 11 f3 ♗e6 12 g4 ♖g8 13 ♗e2 ♗h6+ 14 ♔b1 ♗f4 15 a4 ♘d7 16 ♘a2?! f6 17 ♘c1 ♘e5 18 ♘d3 ♘xd3 19 ♗xd3 ♔f7 is equal, Hamann-Rendboe, Lyngby 1989.

c33) 10 f3 when Black usually answers 10...♗e6 after which White has tried the following options:

c331) 11 ♔b1 ♘d7 12 ♘a4 ♗e5 13 ♘c5 ♘xc5 14 ♗xc5 h5 15 ♗e2 f6 16 h4 ♔f7 17 g4 ♗f4 is equal, Mardle-Fazekas, British ch 1959.

c332) 11 a3 ♘d7 12 ♘d5 ♖c8 13 ♘f4 ♗h6 14 ♗d2 ♘f8 15 ♘xe6 ♗xd2+ 16 ♖xd2 ♘xe6 17 ♗c4 ♖d8 18 ♗xe6 fxe6 with equality, Shianovsky-Gufeld, Ukrainian ch 1960.

c333) 11 ♘e2!? ♗c4?! (this gives a passive position; better is 11...h5 answering 12 ♘d4 with 12...♗d7, intending ...♗h6, ...0-0-0 or ...e7-e5) 12 b3 ♗a6 13 c3 b6 14 g3 ♘d7 15 ♗h3 e6 16 ♖d2 ♔e7 17 ♖hd1 ♖hd8 18 ♗g5+ f6 19 ♘d4! ♘e5 20 ♗f4 ♗b7 21 ♔c2 with a clear edge for White, Varavin-Arzhenkov, Kstovo 1994.

c34) 10 h3! ♗e6 11 f4 h5 12 g3 with a slight plus for White, Rakic-Nedeljkovic, Belgrade 1959.

The recapture on c6 with the d-pawn is a very passive option after which all Black can hope for is a draw. If Black is uncomfortable with the complications that arise after the pawn sacrifice 7...bxc6 8 e5 ♘d5 (Games 101-102), he should opt for 8...♘g8, which will be examined in this and the next two games.

8   e5   ♘g8

Black retreats his knight and accepts the loss of time. Although Black looks terribly undeveloped, he is not in bad shape, as first White has to protect his forward e-pawn, which will allow Black to set up his counterplay.

9   f4

9 ♗d4 is seen in Game 100.

9   ...   f6

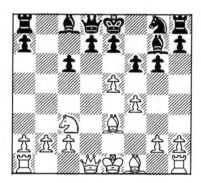

For the more solid alternative 9...♘h6, see the next game.

Three other possibilities deserve attention:

a) 9...d5 10 exd6 (on 10 ♕d2 Strauss gives 10...h5!? 11 0-0-0 ♘h6, intending ...♘f5 and ...0-0, which should be alright for Black) 10...exd6 11 ♗c4 (11 ♗d4 ♘f6 12 ♕d2 0-0 13 0-0-0 ♗e6 14 h3 ♕a5 15 a3 ♖ab8 16 ♘e4 ♕xd2 17 ♘xd2 is equal, Delanoy-Hayoun, Torcy 1991) 11...♘f6 12 0-0 0-0 13 ♕d2 d5 14 ♖ad1 ♕c7 with equality, Kupka-Stefanov, Leningrad 1960.

b) 9...f5 (this move leads to a very rigid structure where White should be somewhat better) 10 ♗c4 e6 11 ♕e2 ♘h6?! (the knight looks silly out here; 12...♘e7 was to be preferred) 12 0-0-0 ♕c7 ½-½ Kr.Georgiev-Ninov, Bulgaria 1988, but White is clearly better in the final position.

c) 9...h5!?, intending ...♘h6-f5, is untried, but definitely worth a shot.

10   ♗d4

In this position White has tried numerous other moves as well:

a) 10 ♗d3? (a sharp but unsound gambit) 10...fxe5 11 f5 d5! 12 fxg6 ♘f6 13 gxh7 e4 and Black is much better, Sapunov-Milev, Bulgaria 1959.

b) 10 f5?! ♕a5! (also good for Black is 10...fxe5 11 fxg6 d5 12 gxh7 ♘f6) 11 exf6 ♘xf6 12 fxg6 ♕e5 (in Vileseco-O. Martinez, Colon 1993, everything was a mess after 12...♘d5 13 ♗d4 e5 14 ♕e2 ♔d8 15 ♗e3 ♖b8 16 ♗d2 ♘f6) 13 ♕d4 ♘g4 14 ♕xe5 ♗xe5 15 ♗g1 hxg6 16 ♗d3 ♔f7 17 0-0-0 ♔g7 with a strong centre and clear advantage for Black in Zaharov-Antoshin, USSR 1964.

c) 10 e6? and now:

c1) 10...dxe6? 11 ♕f3 ♕c7 12 ♗b5! (much stronger than 12 ♘b5 ♕b7 13 ♘d4 ♘h6 14 ♕xc6+ ♔f7 15 0-0-0, Chernikov-Sosonko, Leningrad 1965, and now 15...♘f5! would have left White with only a small advantage) 12...♗d7 13 0-0-0 ♖c8 14 ♗c4 ♘h6 15 ♖he1 ♘f7 16 ♗c5 ♗h6 17 ♖xd7!, Kurkin-Estrin, USSR 1962.

c2) 10...♘h6? 11 exd7+ ♕xd7 12 ♕xd7+ ♔xd7 13 ♗c4 ♔c7 14 0-0 ♘f5 15 ♗c5 ♘d6 16 ♖fe1 with a better game for White, Bole-slavsky-Szilagyi, Debrecen 1961.

c3) 10...d5! By playing around the e6-pawn rather than taking it, Black refutes the pawn sacrifice. 11 f5 ♕d6 12 ♕f3 (or 12 g4? ♕e5 13 ♕f3 transposing to Hennings-Baumbach below) 12...♕e5 13 ♘e2 (also insufficient are: 13 ♗d3 ♗h6 14 ♔f2 ♗xe3+ 15 ♕xe3 gxf5 16 ♕xe5 fxe5 17 ♗xf5 ♘h6 18 ♗h3 ♖f8+ 19 ♔e1 ♘f5, Samole-wicz-Pzorelli, Poland 1959; 13 g4 h5 14 ♘e2 as in the game Hen-nings-Baumbach, East Germany 1961, and now 14...♗h6! 15 ♗d4 hxg4! 16 ♕xg4 ♕xf5 is clearly better for Black or 13 0-0-0 ♕xe3! 14 ♕xe3 ♗h6 15 ♕xh6 ♘xh6 16 fxg6 hxg6 with a huge edge for Black) 13...♗h6 14 ♗f2 gxf5 15 ♕h5+ ♔d8 16 ♗d4 ♕e4 17 c4 ♗xe6 18 ♖d1 ♗e3! when Black is clearly better, Geissert-Baumbach, East Germany 1961.

d) 10 exf6 (this move does not challenge Black) 10...♘xf6 11 ♗e2 0-0 (11...♖b8 12 ♖b1 ♕c7 13 0-0 0-0 14 ♔h1 d6 15 ♗d3 ♔h8 slightly favours Black, Knoppert-Yakovich, Leeuwarden 1994) 12 0-0 d5 (or 12...♕a5 13 ♕d2 ♖b8 14 ♖ab1 d6 15 a3 ♘g4 16 ♗d4 ♗xd4+ 17 ♕xd4 ♕b6 18 ♕xb6 axb6 with equality, Fernandes-Andersson, Novi Sad ol 1990) 13 ♗d4 ♗f5 (13...♖b8 14 ♖b1 a5 15 ♔h1 ♗f5 16 ♗d3 ♕d7 is equal, Edvardsson-Jonasson, Reykjavik 1994) 14 ♗f3 ♖b8 with a slight initiative for Black, Aronin-Geller, Moscow 1951.

e) 10 ♗c4!?

This is White's only good move aside from 10 ♗d4. It is rarely played, so it is worth trying as a surprise weapon:

e1) 10...d5 11 exd6 exd6 11 ♕d2 followed by 0-0-0 is unpleas-ant for Black.

e2) However, Black might con-sider 10...♘h6!?, although it takes a brave man to face 11 0-0 ♘f7 (an attempt to get the king in safety) 12 ♗xf7+ ♔xf7 13 f5!

e3) 10...fxe5 (so far the only move tried in practice) and now:

e31) 11 fxe5 ♕a5 (possible is 11...♗xe5, but White has a strong initiative for the pawn and it will take time before Black's king is safe) 12 0-0! ♕xe5 13 ♗f7+! ♔d8 14 ♕d2 ♘f6 15 ♖ae1 ♕h5? (Gheorghiu gives 15...♕a5 as un-clear, but White has massive com-pensation for the sacrificed pawn, and it is very doubtful that Black will ever free himself) 16 ♖xf6! exf6 17 ♘d5! cxd5 18 ♕a5+ ♔e7 19 ♗g5+! 1-0 Krystall-Burstow, Lone Pine 1976.

e32) Possibly stronger is 11 0-0 exf4 12 ♗xf4 ♘f6 (perhaps 12...d5, intending 13 ♘xd5 cxd5 14 ♗xd5 ♕b6 15 ♔h1 ♗b7, is worth a try, but Black's unsafe king position will provide White with some compensation for the sacri-ficed material) 13 ♗d6! ♗a6 (not 13...exd6? 14 ♖e1+ or 13...♕b6+

14 ♔h1 ♔d8 as in Krystall-Batchelder, USA 1974, and now 15 ♗a3! with excellent compensation for the pawn) 14 ♗xa6 (in the first edition of their book Silman and Donaldson mention the line 14 ♖e1 ♕b6+ 15 ♔h1 ♗xc4 16 ♖xe7+ ♔d8 17 ♖xg7, but what is wrong with 14...♗xc4, when after 15 ♖xe7 ♕xe7 16 ♗xe7 ♔xe7 followed by ...♗e6, Black is much better?) 14...♕b6+ 15 ♔h1 ♕xa6 16 ♖e1, Zajic-Adamski, Trebitz 1959, and now 16...0-0 was best with a small advantage for White.

10 ... ♕a5

The alternatives only lead to discomfort for Black:

a) 10...d5? 11 exd6 ♕xd6 (just as bad is 11...exd6 12 ♕f3 ♘e7 13. 0-0-0 0-0 14 ♗c5 d5 15 ♗c4 ♖b8 16 ♖he1 with clear edge for White, Krogius-Buslaev, Tbilisi 1956) 12 ♕f3 ♕e6+ 13 ♗e2 ♗a6 14 0-0 ♗xe2 15 ♘xe2 with a clear advantage for White, Ivkov-Pirc, Zagreb 1955.

b) 10...fxe5? 11 fxe5 e6?! 12 ♗d3 ♕h4+ 13 g3 ♕e7 14 ♘e4 ♕b4+ 15 ♗c3 ♕b6 16 ♘d6+ ♔e7 17 ♕f3 ♘h6 18 ♕f4 ♔d8 19 ♘c4 ♕c5 20 ♗a5+ and White soon won in Wade-Bilek, Teesside 1972. Black cannot play like this and expect to get away with it, no matter which opening he tries.

c) 10...♘h6 (this move was once recommended by Boleslavsky, but we cannot endorse it; Black is, at best, clearly worse) and now:

c1) 11 exf6!? (11 ♘e4? fxe5 12 fxe5 ♘f5 13 ♗c3 ♕b6! favours Black and 11 ♗d3 0-0 12 0-0 d6 is equal) 11...exf6? (better here is 11...♗xf6 12 ♗xf6 exf6, but after 13 ♕e2+ ♔f7 14 0-0-0 ♖e8 15

♕f3 White is better) 12 ♕e2+! ♕e7 (a little better is 12...♔f7 13 0-0-0 d5 14 ♕f2 ♖e8 15 ♗e2 ♗g4 16 ♗xg4 ♘xg4 17 ♕h4 ♘h6 18 g4, but White is still clearly better, Kaplan-Juhnke, Stockholm 1969) 13 ♘e4 ♔d8 14 ♗c5 ♕e6 15 ♘d6 ♕d5 16 ♕c4 ♕xc4 17 ♗xc4 ♗f8 18 0-0-0 and White is winning, Ostojic-Ree, Wijk aan Zee 1969.

c2) 11 ♗c4! ♘f5 12 exf6 ♗xf6 13 ♗xf6 exf6 14 ♕f3! ♕e7+ 15 ♔d2 ♕d6+ 16 ♔c1 with a clear edge for White, Dückstein-Jansson, Lugano ol 1968.

These examples clearly illustrate how careful Black must be in these lines, particularly since he is so far behind in development.

11 ♕e2

This is no better or worse than other moves. White has also tried:

a) 11 ♗c4?! fxe5 12 fxe5 ♗xe5 13 ♕d3 ♘f6 14 0-0-0 ♗xd4 15 ♕xd4 d5 16 ♕e5 (Baumbach analyses 16 ♖he1 0-0! 17 ♗b3 ♗g4 and 17 ♖xe7 dxc4 18 ♘e4 ♕f5 19 ♕xc4+ ♘d5 as good for Black) 16...0-0 17 ♘xd5 cxd5 18 ♖xd5 ♕b4 19 ♖d4+ ♔h8 20 h4 ♖b8 21 ♗b3 ♖b5! and Black was winning, Masjeev-Baumbach, corr 1972.

b) 11 exf6 ♘xf6 (a safe alternative is 11...♗xf6 12 ♗xf6 ♘xf6, e.g. 13 ♕d4 0-0 14 0-0-0 ♖b8 and Black was doing fine, Ushakov-Kapengut, Minsk 1969) 12 ♗c4 d5 (also possible is 12...♗a6!?) 13 ♗e2 (in Tseitlin-Mikac, Ostrava 1991, White achieved a small advantage after 13 ♗d3 ♖b8 14 ♕d2 0-0 15 ♘e2 ♕xd2+ 16 ♔xd2 ♘d7 17 ♗xg7 ♔xg7 18 ♘d4 ♖f6 19 ♖ae1) 13...0-0 14 0-0 ♖b8 15 ♖b1 ♗f5 16 ♗f3 ♖b4 with equality, Dückstein-Benko, Varna ol 1962. Black can also try Baumbach's suggestion 16...♘e4!? 17 ♗xg7 ♔xg7 18 ♕d4 (18 ♘xe4 dxe4 19 ♕d4+? e5!) 18...♘f6 with equality.

c) 11 b4!?

(an interesting gambit; White sacrifices a couple of pawns in return for a huge lead in development) 11...♕xb4 12 ♖b1 ♕a5 13 ♗c4 fxe5? (Black is asking for trouble; best was 13...♘h6, intending 14 exf6?! ♗xf6! 15 ♗xf6 exf6 16 ♕d4? ♘f5! 17 ♕xf6 ♖f8 and wins or 14 0-0 ♘f5 15 exf6 ♗xf6 16 ♗xf6 ♕c5+! 17 ♔h1 exf6 and Black seems to survive) 14 fxe5 ♗xe5? (better was 14...♘h6) 15 0-0 ♘f6 16 ♘b5! ♗xd4+ 17 ♕xd4 ♖f8 18 ♘d6+ exd6 19 ♕xd6 ♕c3 20 ♖be1+ ♔d8 21 ♕xf8+ and

White was winning here in Diez-F.Petersen, Kapfenberg 1970.

d) 11 ♕d2 (the most important alternative) and now:

d1) Black can try 11...♘h6, although he did not have much luck in its first outing: 12 exf6 exf6 13 ♗c4 (even stronger is 13 0-0-0 0-0 14 ♗c4+ ♔h8 15 ♗b3) 13...d5 14 0-0-0 ♗e6? (Donaldson suggests that Black can take the bishop on c4 and survive after 14...dxc4 15 ♖he1+ ♔f7 16 ♕e2 ♕b4, but after the simple 17 a3, Black will have a hard time defending himself, e.g. 17...♕d6 18 ♗e5 ♕e6 19 ♘e4 with a nasty attack, but this is definitely better than what Black did in the game) 15 ♖fe1 ♔f7 16 ♖xe6 ♔xe6 17 ♕e2+ ♔d7 18 ♘xd5 cxd5 19 ♗c3 ♖ae8 20 ♗b5+ ♔d6 21 ♖xd5+ and Black resigned, Kovalev-Roizman, Minsk 1981.

d2) 11...fxe5 12 fxe5 c5 (in Varavin-Khasin, Elista 1994, Black was successful with the risky 12...♗xe5!?, when after 13 0-0-0 ♘f6 14 ♖e1 ♗xd4 15 ♕xd4 0-0 16 ♖xe7 ♕g5+ 17 ♔b1 d5 18 ♗d3 White appears to hold an advantage, but it proved remarkable little after 18...♗f5 19 ♗xf5 ♕xf5 20 ♖he1 ♖ae8! and Black has few problems) 13 ♗e3 ♗xe5 (after 13...♖b8 14 ♗c4 ♗a6, Black was caught in the middle of a stampede: 15 0-0-0!! ♗xc4 16 ♕xd7+ ♔f7 17 ♖hf1+ ♗xf1 18 ♖xf1+ ♘f6 19 exf6 ♗xf6 20 ♖xf6+ ♔xf6 21 ♘d5+ ♔e5 22 ♗f4+ ♔e4 23 ♕e6+ ♔d4 24 ♗e3+ 1-0, Pavmon-Roizman, USSR 1982) 14 ♗c4 ♘f6 15 0-0 ♗b7 16 ♖ae1 (after 16 ♗f4 ♗d4+ 17 ♔h1 ♗a6 18 ♗xa6 ♕xa6, White did not have enough compensation in Haag-Hennings,

Zinnowitz 1966) 16...0-0-0! 17 ♕e2 d5 with a clear plus for Black, Pieri-P.H.Nielsen, Forli 1992. If White instead of 17 ♕e2 tries 17 ♘d5 he can in fact save himself: 17...♕xd2 18 ♘xe7+ ♔c7 19 ♗xd2 d6! (19...♗xb2? 20 c3! is not what Black has in mind) 20 ♗g5 ♗d4+ 21 ♔h1 ♘e4 22 ♘d5+ ♗xd5 23 ♗xd8+ ♔xd8 24 ♗xd5 ♘f2+ 25 ♖xf2 ♗xf2 with a likely draw.

| | **11** | **...** | **fxe5** |

An interesting idea is 11...c5!? 12 exf6? ♘xf6 13 ♗e5 0-0, Stodola-Chernikov, Pardubice 1994, when compared to the main line, Black has achieved ...c6-c5 and ...0-0 for free and is of course clearly better. White can do better, but how much better? 12 ♗f2 fxe5 13 fxe5 ♘h6, 12 ♗e3 ♘h6 and 12 ♕b5? ♕xb5 13 ♘xb5 cxd4 14 ♘c7+ ♔d8 15 ♘xa8 ♗b7 are all good for Black.

| | **12** | **♗xe5** |

Black stands clearly better after 12 fxe5 ♖b8 (12...♘h6!?) 13 0-0-0 c5.

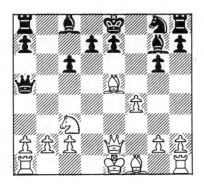

| | **12** | **...** | **♘f6!?** |

Most sources suggest that White is a little better after 12...♗xe5 13

♕xe5 ♕xe5 14 fxe5, but this is not necessarily true: 14...♘h6 (inferior is 14...d5 15 exd6 exd6 16 0-0-0 d5 17 ♗e2 ♘f6 18 ♖d4 0-0 19 ♗f3 ♗f5 20 ♖e1, when White had the better chances in Smrcka-Baumbach, corr 1968) 15 0-0-0 0-0!? (Donaldson gives 15...♘g4 16 ♖e1 0-0 17 ♗c4+ ♔g7 18 h3 ♖f4 19 b3 ♘h6 20 ♖hf1 ♖xf1+ 21 ♖xf1 ♗b7 22 ♖d1 ♖d8 23 ♘e4 which is unpleasant for Black; nor does he equalise after 15...♖f8 16 ♖e1 ♖f5 17 ♗d3 ♖h5 18 ♗e4 with a clear edge for White, Puc-Pirc, Sarajevo 1960) 16 ♗c4+ ♔g7 17 ♖hf1 ♖xf1 18 ♖xf1 d5 19 exd6 exd6 20 ♖e1 ♔f8 and Black had no problems in Delanoy-Van den Bosch, Kecskemet 1991.

| | **13** | **♕c4!** | **♕b6** |
| | **14** | **0-0-0** | **d5** |

In Ulibin-Maliutin, USSR 1988, Black got into deep trouble after 14...d6? 15 ♗d4 c5? 16 ♘d5!, but everyone seems to have forgotten about 14...a5!?, which equalised smoothly for Black in Minic-Parma, Titograd 1965: 15 ♖e1 ♗a6 16 ♕d4 ♕xd4 17 ♗xd4 ♔f7 18 ♗xa6 ♖xa6 19 ♖e2 ♖e8 20 ♖he1 ♖aa8 21 g3 d6.

	15	**♕a4**	**0-0**
	16	**♗d4**	**♕c7**
	17	**♗e5**	**♕b6**
	18	**♗d4**	**♕c7**
	19	**g3**	

White is not in the mood for a draw just yet, which would have been the result after 19 ♗e5, but in this position Black is by no means worse.

| | **19** | **...** | **♗g4!** |

Black wants the bishop in front of the pawns. 19...e6? is horrible: 20 ♗g2! ♗d7 21 ♕a3.

20   ♖d2

Black is also fine after 20 ♖e1 ♗f3 21 ♖g1 c5.

20...♗f3 21 ♗g2 ♗xg2 22 ♖xg2 e6 23 ♕a3?!

Now Black gets the upper hand. Best was 23 ♖e1 c5 24 ♗e5 ♕b6 25 ♖ge2 ♖ac8 with about equal chances.

23...♖ac8 24 ♖e1

24 ♕xa7? ♕xa7 25 ♗xa5 c5 is good for Black according to Serper.

24...c5 25 ♗e5 ♕b6 26 ♖ge2 ♘c6 27 ♘b1! ½-½

Serper gives the following lines: 27...♕b5!? 28 ♘d2 ♖a6 29 ♕b3 ♕xb3 30 ♘xb3 with the idea of 30...♖xa2 31 ♔b1 or 27...♖d8 threatening ...d5-d4 and ...c5-c4.

Game 99
Faulks-Donaldson
Bermuda 1995

(1 e4 c5 2 ♘f3 ♘c6 3 d4 cxd4 4 ♘xd4 g6 5 ♘c3 ♗g7 6 ♗e3 ♘f6 7 ♘xc6 bxc6 8 e5 ♘g8 9 f4)

9   ...   ♘h6!?
(see following diagram)
10   ♕d2

Black does not have much to

fear after 9...♘h6!?, but White also has:

a) 10 ♘e4 0-0 11 ♕d2 d6 with equal chances.

b) 10 ♕f3?! 0-0 11 ♗c4 (or 11 ♗d3 f6 [11...d6 transposes to note 'd' below] 12 exf6 ♗xf6 13 0-0 d5 14 ♗c5 ♕a5 with a slight edge for Black, Witt-Malich, Havana ol 1966) 11...d5! 12 exd6 exd6 13 ♕xc6?! (White takes a little more time than he actually has, but he was already in trouble; Black threatens ...d6-d5-d4) 13...♗d7 14 ♕f3 ♖c8 15 ♗d3 ♗g4 16 ♕d5 ♖e8 17 ♔d2 ♖xe3! 18 ♔xe3 ♕b6+ 19 ♔d2 ♕xb2 and Black soon won, Fichtl-Gereben, Warsaw 1956.

c) 10 ♗e2?! 0-0 11 0-0 ♘f5 (or 11...f6 12 exf6 ♗xf6 13 g4 d5 14 ♗c5 ♕a5 15 b4 ♕d8 16 g5 ♗xc3 17 gxh6 ♗xa1 when White does not have enough for the exchange) 12 ♗f2 h5 13 ♘e4 d6 14 exd6 exd6 15 c3 ♖e8 16 ♗d3 d5 17 ♘g3 ♘e3 18 ♗xe3 ♖xe3 19 f5 ♕b6 20 ♔h1 ♗a6 21 ♗xa6 ♕xa6 22 f6 ♗f8 23 ♘xh5 ♕e2 with an initiative for Black, Rakic-Damjanovic, Portoroz 1961.

d) 10 ♗d3 d6 11 ♕f3 0-0 12 0-0 (12 h3 dxe5 13 fxe5 ♘f5 14 ♗f4

♕a5 15 0-0 ♕b6+ 16 ♔h1 ♘d4 17 ♘f2 ♘e6 18 ♕xb6 axb6 is clearly better for Black, Faulks-Shadade, Bermuda 1995) 12..dxe5 (12...♕c7 is also good) 13 ♕xc6 ♘g4 14 ♗c5 ♗d7 15 ♕a6 exf4 16 ♘d5 ♕b8 17 h3 ♕e5 18 ♘xe7+ ♔h8 19 b4 ♘e3 with a very unpleasant position for White, Rohde-Tarjan, Lone Pine 1975.

e) 10 ♗c4 0-0 11 ♕d2 (11 0-0 d6 12 exd6 exd6 13 ♗d4 ♘f5 [also good is 13...♗xd4+ 14 ♕xd4 ♕b6 15 ♕xb6 axb6 16 ♗d3 ♗f5 17 ♖fd1 d5 when Black is comfortable, Smirin-Davies, Gausdal 1990] 14 ♗xg7 ♔xg7 15 ♕d3 ♕b6+ 16 ♔h1 d5! with a small edge for Black, as in Pilszyk-Brinck-Claussen, Marianske Lazne 1962) 11...d6 12 exd6 exd6 13 0-0-0 ♗g4 14 ♘e2 ♘f5 15 ♗f2 ♖b8 16 ♗b3 a5 17 c3 a4 18 ♗c2 ♕a5 with a strong attack for Black, Rubezov-Sokolsky, corr 1961.

10 ... 0-0
Levy suggests 10...♘f5 11 ♗f2 h5, intending to meet 12 h3 with 12...h4 and if necessary give up the h-pawn to slow down White's kingside attack.

11 0-0-0
White has from time to time prepared g2-g4 with 11 h3 at this point. However, Black has no problems against this slow approach. After 11...d6! (Boleslavsky-Gurgenidze, Riga 1958, saw 11...f6 12 ♗c4+ ♘f7 13 ♗xf7+ ♔xf7!? 14 0-0-0 ♔g8 15 exf6 ♖xf6 16 ♗d4 ♖d6 17 ♕e3 ♖e6 18 ♕f3 ♗xd4 19 ♖xd4 ♕b6 20 ♖e4 ♖xe4 21 ♕xe4 ♖b8 22 ♕xe7 ♕xb2+ 23 ♔d2 ♕b4 with approximately equal chances) 12 0-0-0 ♘f5 13 ♗f2 c5 14 g4 ♘d4 15 ♗g2 ♖b8 16

♗xd4 cxd4 17 ♕xd4 ♕a5 18 ♖he1 ♗a6, threatening ...♖b4 followed by ...♖fb8 with a strong attack, Dückstein-Waller, Austria 1969.

11 ... d6
Recently this has been the most popular of Black's options. However, 11...♕a5!? is possibly stronger: 12 ♗c4 (now Black gets the better of it; critical is 12 h3 ♘f5 13 ♗f2 d6 14 g4 dxe5 15 gxf5 ♗xf5 when Black has two pawns and attacking prospects for the piece; it is hard to say whether this is really enough) 12...♖b8 13 h4 (13 ♕d4?! d6 14 ♕xa7 ♕xa7 15 ♗xa7 ♖a8 16 ♗d4 ♘f5 17 ♖he1 ♗h6! 18 g3 ♘xd4 19 ♖xd4 dxe5 20 ♖de4 exf4 21 gxf4 e5! is very good for Black, Akaba-Boop, USA 1991) 13...d6 14 h5 ♘f5 15 hxg6 hxg6 16 g4 ♘xe3 17 ♕xe3 ♗xg4 18 ♖dg1 ♗f5 is very good for Black, Ravinsky-Zilberstein, Leningrad 1963.

Other moves have proven less successful: 11...f6? 12 ♗c4+ ♔h8 13 h4 fxe5 14 h4 exf4 15 ♗xf4 g5 16 ♗xg5 ♘g4 17 ♕e2 ♘e5 18 h6 ♗f6 19 ♗xf6+ exf6 20 ♖d6 with a killing attack, Shianovsky-Furman, USSR 1960, or 11...d5 12 h4 ♕a5

13 h5 ♖d8 14 hxg6 fxg6 15 ♕d4 ♘f5 16 ♕c5 ♕xc5 17 ♗xc5 ♘g3 18 ♖h2 with a small edge for White, Estrin-A.Zaitsev, corr 1964.

12   h3!?

Boleslavsky's old recommendation. Less good is 12 exd6 exd6 (inferior is 12...♘f5?! 13 ♗f2! [13 d7?! ♘xe3 14 dxc8♕ ♕xd2 15 ♔xd2 ♘xf1+ is just about equal] 13...exd6 14 g4! which slightly favours White) 13 ♗d4 ♗xd4 14 ♕xd4 ♘f5 15 ♕d2 d5 16 ♗d3 (16 g4 is not a worry, as after 16...♘d6 and eventually ...f7-f5 Black has excellent control over the centre) 16...♘d6 17 ♘a4 ♕f6 18 ♘c5 ♖d8 19 c3 ♗f5 20 g3 ♖ab8 21 ♗xf5 ♕xf5 22 ♕d2 ♕f6 23 ♕d4 ♕xd4 24 ♖xd4 with equality, Koch-Birmingham, Val Thorens 1988.

12   ...   ♘f5

Boleslavsky analyses 12...♕a5 13 exd6 exd6 14 g4 ♖b8 15 ♗d4 with a clear advantage for White.

13   ♗f2

Now 13 g4 is met by 13...♗b7 14 ♖g1 ♘d4, intending 15 ♗xd4 cxd4 16 ♕xd4 ♕a5, and very soon White will feel the presence of the black bishops.

13   ...   c5

14	♗c4	♗b7
15	♗d5	♗xd5
16	♕xd5	♖b8
17	g4	♘d4
18	♗xd4	cxd4
19	♖xd4	dxe5
20	fxe5	♕b6
21	♘a4	♕c7
22	♖e1	♖fc8

Black has a pawn less, but the poor co-ordination of the white pieces and the weak pawn provide more than enough compensation. Now Black starts to penetrate the white position.

23 c3 e6 24 ♕d6 ♕a5 25 ♖de4 ♖b5 26 ♕d4 ♖d5 27 ♕e3 ♖cd8 28 ♕f4 ♖d3 29 ♖c4 ♕d5 30 ♖f1 ♖d1+ 31 ♔c2 ♕d3+ 0-1

Game 100
Tringov-Stein
Sarajevo 1967

(1 e4 c5 2 ♘f3 ♘c6 3 d4 cxd4 4 ♘xd4 g6 5 ♘c3 ♗g7 6 ♗e3 ♘f6 7 ♘xc6 bxc6 8 e5 ♘g8)

9   ♗d4

White often plays this move, although Black does not seem to have any problems equalising.

9   ...   ♕a5

The main line. Alternatives are:

a) 9...♕c7 10 e6 ♘f6 11 exf7+ ♔xf7 12 ♗c4+ d5 13 ♗b3 e5 14 ♗c5 ♕a5 15 ♗a3 ♗a6 16 ♕f3 ♖he8 17 0-0-0 ♔g8 18 ♘xd5!? cxd5 19 ♖xd5 ♘xd5 20 ♗xd5+ ♔h8 21 ♗xa8 e4! 22 ♗xe4 ♗b7! 23 ♗xb7 ♖e1+ 24 ♕d1 ♖xd1+ 25 ♖xd1 ♗xe5 with about level chances, E.Kennedy-Biyiasas, USA 1977.

b) 9...♘h6 10 e6 and now:

b1) 10...f6? 11 exd7+ ♗xd7 (even worse is 11...♕xd7 12 ♗c4 ♘f5 13 ♗c5 ♘d6 14 ♗b3 ♗a6 15 ♕d4 ♖d8 16 0-0-0 ♔f8 17 ♕a4 ♕c8 18 ♘e4 ♗h6+ 19 ♔b1 ♗b5 20 ♘xd6 exd6 21 ♖xd6 1-0 Varavin-Myrvold, Gausdal 1993) 12 ♗c4 ♗f5 13 ♕f3 ♕d6 14 h3 ♗e6 15 ♘b5! ♕b4+ 16 c3 ♕xc4 17 ♘c7+ ♔d7 18 b3, Diez del Corral-Velimirovic, The Hague 1966, and now best is 18...♕xd4 19 cxd4 ♔xc7 20 ♖c1 ♗d7 21 d5 with an initiative for White.

b2) Another bad idea is 10...♗xd4? 11 ♕xd4 0-0 12 exd7 ♕xd7 13 ♕xd7 ♗xd7 14 ♗c4! ♖ad8 15 0-0-0 ♘g4 16 ♖d2 ♗c8 17 ♖hd1 with a clear edge for White, Bisguier-Geller, Helsinki ol 1952.

b3) 10...0-0 11 ♗xg7 ♔xg7 12 ♕d4 f6+ 13 exd7 ♗xd7 14 0-0-0 ♗g4 15 f3 ♕xd4 16 ♖xd4 ♗c8 17 ♗d3 ♘f5 18 ♗xf5 gxf5! 19 ♖hd1 ♗e6 20 ♘a4 ♖g8 with an endgame advantage for Black, Troianescu-Ghitescu, Romanian ch 1957.

c) 9...c5?! 10 ♗xc5 (interesting is the less played alternative 10 ♗e3!? ♕c7 11 ♗c4 ♗b7 12 ♕d2 ♕xe5 13 0-0-0 ♘f6 14 ♖he1 0-0 15 ♗g5 ♕xh2 16 f3 ♕c7 17 ♖xe7

♕b6 18 ♕d6! with a powerful initiative for White, Tukmakov-Weichert, Graz 1972; whereas 10 ♕f3 ♖b8 11 ♗xc5 ♕c7 12 ♕e3 ♕xe5 favours Black) 10...♕c7 (inaccurate is 10...♗xe5? 11 ♕d5 ♗xc3+ 12 bxc3 ♕a5 13 ♕xa8 ♕xc3+ 14 ♔d1 ♕xc5 15 ♗a6 ♕d6+ 16 ♗d3 with a clear plus for White) 11 ♗d4 ♗xe5 and now White has tried:

c1) 12 ♗xe5 ♕xe5 13 ♗e2 ♗a6 (13...♘f6!?) 14 ♕d5 ♕xd5 15 ♘xd5 ♗xe2 16 ♔xe2 ♖c8 17 ♘e3! e6 18 c4 ♘f6 19 ♖hd1 ♔e7 20 ♖d3! with a small edge for White in the endgame, Versinin-Voloshin, Litosmyl 1995.

c2) 12 ♗e2 ♘f6 (or 12...♗b7 13 ♗xe5 ♕xe5 14 0-0 ♘f6 15 ♗f3 ♗xf3 16 ♕xf3 0-0 17 ♖fe1 ♕c5 18 ♖ad1 ♖ab8 with equality, Bradvarevic-Pirc, Sombor 1957) 13 ♗xe5 ♕xe5 14 0-0 0-0?! (best was 14...d5! 15 ♗b5+ ♔f8 16 ♗c6 ♖b8 with a good game for Black, whereas 14...♗b7!? transposes to Bradvarevic-Pirc above) 15 ♗f3 ♖b8 16 ♖e1 ♕c5? (16...♕a5!?) 17 ♘a4 ♕a5 18 b3 ♖e8 19 c4 with a clear advantage for White, Ivkov-Pachman, Buenos Aires 1955.

c3) 12 ♘b5 ♕b8 13 f4 ♗xd4 14 ♕xd4 ♘f6 15 0-0-0 0-0 16 ♖e1 ♖e8 17 g4 ♗b7 18 ♖g1 ♗c6 with equality, Estrin-Averbakh, Moscow 1968.

c4) 12 f4 (the only way to maintain the initiative) 12...♗xd4 13 ♕xd4 ♘f6 14 g4 (also promising is 14 0-0-0 0-0 15 ♗c4 ♗b7 16 ♖d2 d5 17 ♗b3 ♖fd8 18 ♖hd1 ♖d7 19 g3 with a slight pull, Tringov-Damjanovic, Ljubljana 1969) 14...♗b7 15 ♖g1 0-0 16 0-0-0 ♖fc8 (Cebalo-Ostojic, Yugoslavian ch

1968, went 16...d5 17 h4? ♘e4 18 ♗g2 ♕xf4+ 19 ♔b1 ♘xc3+ 20 ♕xc3 ♖fc8, but White can do much better: 17 ♕e5! ♕c5 18 ♖g3 ♖fc8 19 ♗g2 with a slight edge) 17 ♖d2 ♖ab8 18 ♖g3 a5 19 ♖e3 d5 20 f5, Dückstein-Stein, Sarajevo 1967.

10 ♗c4

Two other moves have been tried at this point:

a) 10 f4 ♖b8! 11 e6? (best is 11 ♕d2 ♖xb2 12 ♘e4 with some compensation for the pawn) 11...♘f6 12 exf7+ ♔xf7 13 ♗c4+ d5 14 ♗b3 ♖d8 15 ♗e5 ♘g4 16 ♗xg7 ♔xg7 17 ♕d4+ e5! 18 fxe5 c5 19 ♕a4 ♕c7 20 0-0-0 d4 with a clear edge for Black, Kovacs-A.Zaitsev, Debrecen 1970.

b) 10 e6!?

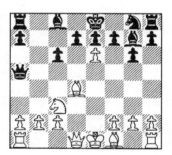

This move, which was once thought plain bad, has in recent years been through a revival, and although it is not considered good for White, it is certainly no longer regarded as bad. Play continues 10...♘f6 11 exf7+ (White can also try 11 exd7+ to split up the black pawn structure, after 11...♗xd7 12 ♕d2 [also possible are 12 ♗d3 0-0 13 0-0 ♖fd8 14 f3 ♖ab8 15 ♕e2 ♖b4 16 ♗c4 ♗e6!? 17 ♗xe6 ♖bxd4, Nadjar-Tugage, Val Thorens 1989, with equality] 12...0-0 13

♘e4 ♕d5 14 ♘xf6+ exf6 15 ♗e3 ♕e6 16 ♖d1 ♖fd8 17 b3 ♕e5 18 f3 ♕e7 19 ♗d3 ♗h6 20 ♔f2 ♗xe3+ 21 ♕xe3 ♕a3 with an initiative for Black, Barcza-G.Horvath, Zalakaros 1994) 11...♔xf7 12 f4!? (12 ♗c4+ is good for Black: 12...d5 13 ♗b3 ♖e8 14 ♗e5 ♘g4 15 ♗xg7 ♔xg7 16 ♕d2 e5 17 0-0-0 ♕c5 18 f3 ♘f6 ♖he1 ♗d7 with a clear edge for Black, Cherkasov-Pekacki, Czestochowa 1992) 12...d5 (12...♖b8 13 ♗c4+ d5 14 ♗b3 ♖b4? [14...♗f5!?] 15 a3 ♖xd4 16 ♕xd4 ♘g4 17 ♕d2 e5 18 h3 ♘h6 19 g4 ♖e8 20 0-0-0 and White was much better, Ulibin-Knezevic, Pula 1990) 13 ♕d2 c5 14 ♗e5 ♖d8 15 ♗e2 d4 16 ♘e4 ♕xd2+ 17 ♘xd2 ♘d5 (17...♗b7!?) 18 ♘c4 ♗e6 19 ♗f3 ♖ac8 and White has a small advantage, Ulibin-M.Garcia, Santa Clara 1991.

10 ... ♗xe5
11 0-0 ♘f6!

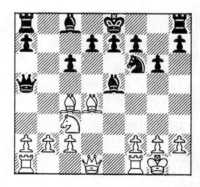

11...f6?! does not make much sense. After 12 ♖e1 ♗xd4 (another weak possibility is 12...♕b4 13 ♗xe5 ♕xc4 14 ♗d6 ♔f7 15 ♘e4 ♕d5 16 ♕f3 ♕f5 17 ♕b3+ ♔g7 18 ♗xe7 ♕e6 19 ♘xf6! ♕xb3 20 ♘e8+ ♔f7 21 ♘d6+ ♔g7 22 axb3

and White won, Haag-Forintos, Hungary 1965) 13 ♕xd4 d5 14 ♗b3 e6? (14...♕b6 was a better try) 15 ♘xd5 cxd5 16 ♗xd5 ♖b8 17 ♗xe6 ♗xe6 18 ♖xe6 and Black was laid to rest in Khudiakov-Alterman, Voronezh 1973.

12   ♖e1   d6!

In Trifunovic-Kort, Noordwijk 1965, Black did not have much luck with 12...♗xd4? After 13 ♕xd4 0-0 14 ♖xe7 ♘h5 15 ♖ae1 d5 16 ♘xd5! cxd5 17 ♗xd5 ♗e6 18 ♖1xe6 it was soon over.

13   ♗xe5

13 ♕e2?? loses on the spot to 13...♘g4 14 ♗b3 ♗xh2 15 ♔h1 e5, as seen in Mestrovic-Stein, Sarajevo 1967.

13	...	dxe5
14	♕e2	♗f5
15	♗b3	e4
16	♕c4	0-0
17	♕xc6	♖ad8
18	♖ad1	♕e5

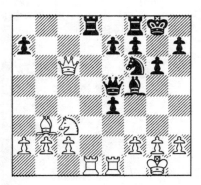

Black has fully equalised and has good centralisation of his pieces.

19 h3 ♖xd1 20 ♘xd1 ♖c8 21 ♕a6 ♖c7 22 ♕e2 a5 23 ♘c3 ♖c5 24 ♕e3 ♕c7 25 ♖d1 ♔g7 26 ♕d2 ♖e5 27 ♘d5 ½-½

(1 e4 c5 2 ♘f3 ♘c6 3 d4 cxd4 4 ♘xd4 g6 5 ♘c3 ♗g7 6 ♗e3 ♘f6 7 ♘xc6 bxc6 8 e5)

8   ...   ♘d5!?

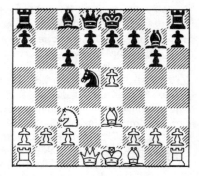

An interesting pawn sacrifice, Black is unwilling to take on the somewhat passive positions that we have seen in the previous three games. At the cost of a pawn, he gets active piece play and a lead in development.

9	♘xd5	cxd5
10	♕xd5	♖b8
11	♗c4	

In this game, we will take a look at the complications that arise after the text move and 11 0-0-0; the next game will deal with 11 ♗xa7.

11 0-0-0 is rather harmless:

a) The commonly played 11...0-0 is not good: 12 ♗xa7! (Levy gives the following analysis after 12 ♗d4: 12...d6 13 exd6 ♗e6 14 ♕c6 ♗xd4 15 ♖xd4 exd6 16 ♕xd6 ♕a5 17 ♕a3 ♕e1+ 18 ♖d1 ♕xf2 19 ♕f3 ♕b6 20 b3 a5 and White's defence is rather difficult)

12...♗b7 13 ♕b5! ♗xg2 14,♕xb8 ♕xb8 15 ♗xb8 ♗xh1 16 ♗c7 ♗c6 17 f4 g5 18 b4 and White had a beautiful set of queenside pawns in Handoko-Bellon, Indonesia 1982.

b) On occasion Black has also tried 11...♕c7, but without much success: 12 f4 0-0 13 ♕c5 ♕b7 14 b3 d6 15 ♕xa7 ♕c6 (or 15...dxe5 16 ♕xb7 ♗xb7 17 ♖g1 exf4 18 ♗xf4 ♖bd8 19 ♖xd8 ♖xd8 20 ♗e3 ♗e4 21 a4 ♗c3 22 ♗e2, when Black has insufficient compensation for the pawn, Zadrima-Anceschi, Forli 1991) 16 ♕xb8 ♗f5 17 ♕xf8+ ♗xf8 18 ♗d3 ♕c3 19 ♔b1 ♗g4 20 ♗d2 ♕d4 21 ♖de1 and White was much better, Colon-Camera, Mar del Plata 1962.

c) 11...♗b7! 12 ♕d4 (in Radulov-Forintos, Hungary 1969, after 12 ♕d2? ♗xe5 13 ♗d4 ♗xd4 14 ♕xd4 0-0 15 ♕xd7 ♕a5 16 ♗c4 ♗xg2 and Black is already much better) 12...0-0 13 f4 (13 ♕xd7 ♕a5! gives Black too much for the pawn) 13...d6 14 ♗c4 ♕c7 15 ♗b3 dxe5 16 fxe5 ♗xg2 17 ♖hg1 ♖bd8 18 ♕xa7 ♕xe5 19 ♗d4 ♕f4+ 20 ♗e3 ♕e5 21 ♗d4 and drawn by repetition, Stein-Nei, USSR 1960.

11   ...   0-0

Black can also hold his own after the less popular, but still playable 11...e6!? 12 ♕c5 ♗b7 and now:

a) 13 0-0?! leaves Black without much to worry about: 13...♖c8 14 ♕b4 ♕c7 (bad is 14...♗xe5? due to 15 ♗xe6! dxe6 16 ♕xb7 0-0 17 c3 with a clear edge for White – analysis by Wedberg; in Dückstein-Karlsson, Lucerne 1979, White played 15 ♖ad1?, but then after 15...♗xh2+ 16 ♔xh2 ♕h4+ 17 ♔g1 ♕e4! 18 f3 ♕xe3 19 ♖f2 ♕b6

Black was much better) 15 f4 (15 ♗g5? is met by 15...♗f8 and 15 ♗b5 is equal after 15...♗xe5 16 ♖fd1 ♗c6, Smit-Gipslis, Amsterdam 1976) 15...a5! 16 ♕b5 ♗xg2 17 ♔xg2 ♕xc4 18 ♕xc4 ♖xc4, Skuja-Gipslis, Riga 1959, and here 19 ♖f3 is best met by 19...d6! (Donaldson), intending to meet 20 exd6 with 20...♔d7 with pressure on White's queenside.

b) More aggressive is 13 0-0-0, but after 13...♖c8 14 ♕b4 ♗xg2 (after 14...♕c7? 15 ♗g5! ♗f8 16 ♕d2 ♗xg2 17 ♖he1 ♗f3 18 ♗b5 White is better, as in the game Muratov-Veresov, Novgorod 1991) 15 ♖hg1 ♗f3 16 ♗g5 f6 17 ♗xe6! (17 exf6 ♗xf6 gives Black nothing to worry about!) 17...♖xd1 18 ♖xd1 ♖c7, Donaldson gives 19 ♕f4 ♖f8 and 19 ♗h4 g5 20 ♕e4 ♕e7 when Black should be fine. We think 19 exf6 ♗xf6 20 ♗f4! is better, although Black can defend after 20...♗g5! 21 ♔b1! ♗xf4 22 ♕xf4 ♖f8 23 ♕e5!? ♖f6! 24 ♗xd7+ ♔f8 with a roughly equal position.

12   0-0-0

White has a number of alternatives, several of which are quite interesting:

a) 12 ♖d1!? (tried once with success, but improvements for Black are not that difficult to come by) 12...♕c7 (12...♖xb2? 13 ♗b3 is embarrassing, but 12...d6!? is interesting) 13 ♗b3 ♗b7? (simple and good is 13...♗xe5) 14 ♕c5! ♕xe5 15 ♕xe5 ♗xe5 16 0-0 ♗a6 17 ♖fe1 ♗xb2 18 ♗h6!, and Black was going down in Holuj-Pogorevici, Bucharest 1959.

b) 12 0-0 and now:

b1) 12...♗b7 was once thought to be mistaken, but matters are not that clear: 13 ♕d3 (best, since other queen moves give Black an easy game: 13 ♕d2? ♕c7 14 ♗b3 ♗xe5 15 f4 ♗xb2 16 ♖ad1 d6, Zvorykic-Volpert, Plovdiv 1959; or 13 ♕d4?! d6 14 ♗f4 dxe5 15 ♕xd8 ♖fxd8 16 ♗e3 a5 17 ♖fd1 e4 18 ♗b6 ♖dc8, Higitian-Kadimova, Debrecen 1992, in both cases with a clear advantage for Black) 13...♗xe5! (13...♕c7? is a mistake due to 14 f4 ♖fd8 15 ♗b3 ♖bc8 16 ♕e2 d6 17 f5 gxf5 18 ♖xf5 and White was much better in Kostro-Kraidman, Budapest 1959) 14 ♗xa7 ♖c8 15 ♗d4 ♗xh2+! (a massive improvement over the old 15...♗xd4, when White is clearly better after 16 ♕xd4 e5 17 ♕g4 d5 18 ♗b3 d4 19 ♖fe1 ♕f6 20 ♖ad1 h5 21 ♕h3 ♖fd8 22 c3 in Langeweg-Geller, Beverwijk 1965) 16 ♔xh2 ♕c7+ 17 ♔g1 ♕xc4 18 ♕xc4 ♗xc4 19 c3 f6 20 ♗e3 ♖a8 with a good game for Black, Lhagvasuren-Bhend, Novi Sad ol 1990.

b2) 12...♕c7 and:

b21) 13 ♗f4 ♗b7 14 ♕d4 d6! 15 ♖fe1 (or 15 exd6 exd6 16 ♕d3 ♗xb2 17 ♖ad1 ♗e5 18 ♗g3 ♖fc8 19 ♗b3 ♕c6 with a slight pull for Black – Donaldson) 15...♖fd8 16 ♕c3 ♖bc8 17 ♗b3 ♕xc3 18 bxc3 dxe5 19 ♗xe5 e6 20 ♗xg7 ♔xg7 21 ♖e3 ♖c7.

b22) 13 f4 d6 14 exd6 exd6 15 ♗b3 ♗e6 16 ♕d2 ♗xb2 17 ♖ad1 ♖fe8 18 h3 ♗c3 19 ♕f2 a5 20 ♗d4 ♗xb3 21 cxb3 a4 22 f5 ♗xd4 23 ♖xd4 axb3 24 axb3 ♖xb3 25 fxg6 hxg6 26 ♖d6 ½-½ Evans-Eliskases, Buenos Aires 1960. Black could consider 15...♗b7!? After 16 ♕g5?! ♗e4 17 c3 a5 18 ♖f2 a4 19 ♗d5? h6 Black was winning in the game Al-Handrani-Antunes, Moscow ol 1994, but 16 ♕d3! ♗xb2 17 f5, threatening 18 fxg6 hxg6 20 ♕xg6+, is very dangerous for Black indeed.

b23) 13 ♕c5 ♕xe5 14 ♕xe5 ♗xe5 15 ♗xa7 ♖a8 16 ♗c5 (or 16 ♗b6 ♗a6 17 ♗xa6 ♖xa6 18 ♗e2 ♗xb2 19 ♖ad1 d6 20 c4 ♖c8 21 ♖d2 ♗a3 22 ♖c2 ♖ac6 with a clear edge for Black, Gdanski-Grigore, Santiago 1990) 16...d6 17 ♗a3 ♗f5 18 ♗d3 ♗xd3 19 cxd3 ♖xa3 20 bxa3 ♗xa1 21 ♖xa1 and 0-1, Abdulghafour-Gonzalez, Moscow ol 1994. Perhaps a little early to resign, but Black was better in the endgame.

c) 12 f4 d6 13 ♗b3 (bad is 13 0-0-0 ♕c7 14 ♗b3 dxe5 15 fxe5 ♗f5 16 ♕c5 ♕xc5 17 ♗xc5 ♖fc8 18 g4 ♗xg4 with a clear edge for Black) and now Black has the following possibilities for his consideration:

c1) 13...♕c7 14 exd6 exd6 15 0-0-0 and Black does not have enough for the pawn.

c2) 13...dxe5 14 ♕xd8 ♖xd8 15 fxe5 ♗xe5 16 ♗c4 ♗e6 when Black is okay – Donaldson.

c3) 13...♗b7!? and now:

c31) 14 ♕d2 dxe5 15 0-0-0 exf4 (also possible is 15...♕c7 16 ♕d7 ♕xd7 17 ♖xd7 ♗xg2 18 ♖g1 ♖b7!) 16 ♗xf4 ♖a8 17 ♕a4 ♕b6 18 ♕xb6 axb6 with about level chances, Hebden-Gerber, London 1987.

c32) Possibly stronger is 14 ♕c4!?, when White won quickly after 14...♗xg2 15 ♖g1 ♗h3 16 0-0-0 a5 17 exd6 exd6 18 ♕a6! ♕f6 19 c3 ♖fc8 20 ♕xa5 ♗f5? 21 ♗d4 ♕h4 22 ♕xf5! gxf5 23 ♗xg7! 1-0, Muir-Stern, corr 1972. However, Black has nothing to fear after 15...♗f3!, keeping White's king in the centre, or 16...♗e6!?, intending 17 ♕a6 ♗xb3 18 axb3 ♕c8!, e.g. 19 ♕xc8 ♖fxc8 20 ♗xa7 ♖xb3 21 ♗d4 ♗h6 22 ♖hf1 dxe5 23 ♗xe5 ♖e3 when White has problems keeping both his bishop and f-pawn on the board: 24 ♗d4 ♖e4, 24 ♖de1 ♖xe1 25 ♖xe1 f6, 24 ♖fe1 ♖xe5!, 24 ♔b1 ♖e2 or 24 ♗c3 e5! 25 ♗d2 exf4 26 ♗xe3 fxe3.

c4) 13...a5 14 0-0 ♗b7 15 ♕c4 ♖c8 16 ♕d3 dxe5 (16...♕c7? allows 17 e6 f5, Gheorghiu-Forintos, Ljubljana 1969, and now Baumbach's suggestion of 18 c3 ♕c6 18 ♕c2 leaves White with an extra pawn) 17 ♕xd8 ♖fxd8 18 f5 e4 19 c3 ♗d5 20 ♗b6 ♖d8 21 ♗c7 ♗xb3

22 ♗xb8 ♗c4 23 ♗c7 ♗xf1 24 ♖axf1 a4 with equal play, as 25 ♖f4 can be met with 25...♖c8 26 ♗a5 gxf5 27 ♖xf5 a3! – Donaldson.

12 ... d6

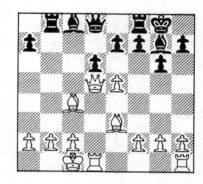

13 ♗xa7 ♖b4

Interesting is 13...♗b7!?, e.g. 14 ♕d3 ♗xg2 15 ♗xb8 ♗xh1 16 ♖xh1 ♕xb8 with roughly equal chances. Best is 15 ♖hg1 ♖b7 16 ♖xg2 ♖xa7 17 exd6 ♕b8! 18 ♗b3 ♖d8 19 ♕d5 e6!, when Black will win back the d6-pawn but White is still better.

14 ♗b3

Frolov recommends 14 ♗c5 ♗e6 (14...e6 15 ♕xd6 ♕xd6 16 ♗xd6! ♖xc4 17 ♗xf8 ♔xf8 18 ♖he1 slightly favours White) 15 ♕xe6 fxe6 16 ♗xe6+ ♔h8 17 ♗xb4 ♗xe5 18 f3, when White has a small advantage. But 14...♗b7!? is worth considering, e.g. 15 ♕d4(d3) ♖xc4! 16 ♕xc4 ♕c7 17 exd6 exd6 18 ♖xd6 ♖c8.

14 ... ♕c7
15 exd6

The normal 15 ♗e3 ♗xe5 leaves Black with plenty of compensation.

15 ... ♕xa7
16 d7 ♖xb3

17   dxc8(♕)

White steers towards the draw. If White takes the rook on b3, matters become uncomfortable for him, e.g. 17 cxb3? ♕xa2 or 17 axb3 ♕a1+ 18 ♔d2 ♗h6+ 19 ♔e2 ♕xb2 and Black has more than enough compensation for the exchange.

17	...	♗xb2+
18	♔b1	♖b8
19	♕h3	♗g7+
20	♔c1	♗b2+
21	♔b1	♗g7+

½-½

Game 102
Kupreichik-Petursson
Reykjavik 1980

(1 e4 c5 2 ♘f3 ♘c6 3 d4 cxd4 4 ♘xd4 g6 5 ♘c3 ♗g7 6 ♗e3 ♘f6 7 ♘xc6 bxc6 8 e5 ♘d5 9 ♘xd5 cxd5 10 ♕xd5 ♖b8)

11   ♗xa7

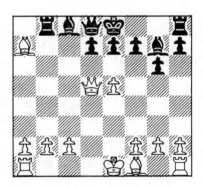

Once recommended by Euwe, this move is now regarded as the main line. Play becomes complex, but more often than not the end result is a draw.

11	...	♖xb2
12	♗d4	

White needs the bishop to protect the important e5-pawn; furthermore, it may end up in trouble if left on a7. Boleslavsky gives the following line after 12 ♗c4? e6 13 ♕c5 ♗f8 14 ♕e3 (14 ♕d4? ♕a5 15 c3 ♖b7 wins) 14...♕a5+ 15 c3 ♗a6 16 ♗xa6 ♕xa6 with a clear advantage for Black.

12   ...   ♖xc2

In an attempt to avoid the drawish main line, Black has recently tried 12...♖b8!? with good results. After 13 ♗c4 0-0 14 0-0 ♗b7 (also adequate is 14...d6, when Delanoy-Pigusov, Mendrisio 1989, went 15 ♖ab1 ♗e6 16 ♖xb8 ♕xb8 17 ♕b5 ♕xb5 18 ♗xb5 dxe5 19 ♗e3 ♗xa2 20 c4 e4 with slightly better chances for Black; his bishop is somewhat offside on a2, which gives White some compensation for the pawn deficit) 15 ♕c5 d6! (best; though 15...♖c8 has also done fine for Black after 16 ♕b4 ♕c7 17 ♗d3 e6 18 ♖fb1 ♗d5 19 ♕b6 ♗xe5 20 ♕xc7 ♗xc7 with about level chances, Kleywegt-Brockmann, Groningen 1994) 16 ♕a3 ♕c8 17 ♗e2 dxe5 18 ♗e3 ♕xc2 19 ♖fe1 ♕c6 with a clear advantage for Black, N.Mitkov-Velimirovic, Kladovo 1991.

An inferior alternative to this is 12...♖b4, Rachels gives 13 c3 ♖b2 14 c4! e6 (14...♗b7 15 ♕c5 d6 16 ♕a3 wins) 15 ♕a8 ♖b7 16 ♗e2 with a clear edge for White.

13   ♗d3   e6

The immediate 13...♖c6 is inaccurate. According to most sources White should be able to get a slight edge, although practice has shown that is not all that easy: 14 0-0 ♗a6 (14...0-0 did not turn out so well for Black in Ulibin-Kozlov, Minsk

1986: 15 a4 ♗b7 16 ♗b5 ♖c7 17 ♕b3 ♕a8 18 ♕g3 ♖fc8 19 a5 ♗a6 20 ♕d3 and White was clearly in control; still another attempt is 14...♕c7!?, when after 15 ♗b5 ♖c2 16 ♕b3 0-0 17 ♗d3 ♖d2 18 ♖fc1 ♕b7 19 ♕c3 ♗h6 20 ♖cb1 ♕a8 21 ♗f1 ♕d5 Black was enjoying himself in Wolter-Ponater, Germany 1991) 15 ♗xa6 ♖xa6 16 a4 (16 ♕b5 ♖c6 17 a4 slightly favours White – Rachels) 16...0-0 17 ♖fd1 ♖a5 18 ♕b7 (or 18 ♕e4 ♕a8 19 ♕c2 ♖c8 20 ♕b3 ♕c6 21 ♕b4 ♖ca8 22 ♕xe7 ♖xa4 with equality, Knoppert-Rubio, as in Velez-Malaga 1991) 18...♕a8 19 ♕b4 ♗xe5 20 ♗xe5 ♖xe5 21 ♖xd7 ½-½ Soltis-Cvitan, Moscow 1989.

14   ♕a8

Or 14 ♕b5 ♖c6 15 0-0 ♗a6 16 ♕b3 ♗xd3 17 ♕xd3 0-0 18 a4 ♕a5 19 ♖fb1 d6 20 ♖b5 ♕a6 21 ♕b3 ♖fc8 with equality, Stein-Nei, USSR 1960.

14   ...   ♖c6

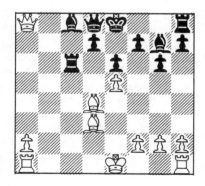

15   0-0

White has two important alternatives:

a) 15 ♗b5!? and now:

a1) Black can try 15...♖c2 with two possible responses:

a11) After 16 0-0 0-0 17 ♕e4 (17 ♖ac1?! ♕c7 18 ♖xc2 ♕xc2 19 f4 d6 20 ♕a7 ♕e4 21 ♔h1 ♗b7 favours Black, Ionescu-Teodorescu, Bucharest 1994) 17...♕c7 18 a4 ♗b7 19 ♕e3 ♖c8 20 ♖fd1 ♗d5 the position was balanced in G.Garcia-L.Garcia, Bogota 1980.

a12) With 16 ♕a3 White tries to prevent Black from castling, though for the moment Black can do without: 16...♕g5 (in Doghri-Bojczuk, Moscow 1991, Black tried 16...♕h4, when after 17 ♕d3 ♕c7 18 0-0 0-0 19 f4 ♗b7 20 ♗b6 ♖c6!? 21 ♗xc6 ♗xc6 22 a4 f6 23 ♗c5 ♖a8 24 ♗d6 ♕g4 25 ♖f2 ♖xa4 26 ♖xa4 ♗xa4 his strong light-squared bishop provided plenty of compensation for the exchange) 17 0-0 ♗xe5 18 ♗xe5 ♕xe5 19 ♖ac1 ♖xc1 20 ♖xc1 ♗b7 21 ♕b4 (White threatens ♗xd7+ and plans to move the a-pawn up along the a-file; had it not been for Black's next move, White would have been winning, but White does have problems finding another way to make progress) 21...♕g5 22 ♗xd7+ ♔d8! 23 ♕b6+ ♔e7! 24 ♕b4+ ♔d8 25 ♕b6+ ½-½, Marin-Ionescu-Popovici, Bucharest 1994.

a2) Black's best is 15...♖a6! 16 ♗xa6 ♕a5+ and now:

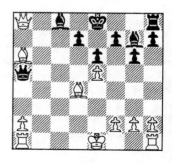

a21) 17 ♔e2 0-0 18 ♗b7! (18 ♕e4? ♗xa6 19 ♔f3 f6! gives Black a winning attack) 18...♕b5+ 19 ♔e3 ♗xb7 20 ♖hb1 ♗h6+ 21 f4 ♗xf4+ 22 ♔xf4 ♕d3 23 ♕xb7 f6! 24 ♖d1?? (this loses on the spot; a draw was around the corner after 24 exf6 ♕xd4+ 25 ♔g3 ♕xe3+ 26 ♕f3 ♕g5+ 27 ♔h3 ♕h6+ 28 ♔g3 ♕g5+ with a perpetual check) 24...g5+ 25 ♔g4 h5+! 26 ♔xh5 ♕h7+ 27 ♔g4 fxe5 28 g3 ♕f5+ 29 ♔h5 ♕h3+ 30 ♔g6 ♕h7+ 0-1 Barczay-Pokojowczyk, Subotica 1981.

a22) 17 ♔f1! 0-0 and now:

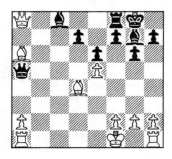

a221) 18 ♕xc8? ♖xc8 19 ♗xc8 ♕b5+ 20 ♔g1 ♕c4 clearly favours Black.

a222) 18 ♕e4 ♕xa6 (18...♗xa6!? 19 ♔g1 d6! 20 ♖e1 ♗b7 21 ♕e3 ♗h6 22 ♕c3 ♕d5 23 f3 ♖c8 24 ♕b2 ♖c4 25 ♗f2 ♗g7 and Black is somewhat better – analysis by Volchok) 19 ♔g1 ♗b7 20 ♕e3 ♕c4! (insufficient is 20...♖a8? 21 h4 ♕c6 22 f3 ♖a4 23 ♔f2 ♕c2+ 24 ♔g3 with a very good game for White, Shianovsky-Volchok, USSR 1960) 21 f3? (21 h4 was better in order to meet 21...♕d5 with 22 ♖h2, but Black has excellent compensation for the exchange; in the game White went down in flames)

21...♗h6! 22 ♕f2 ♕d3 23 ♖e1 ♖c8 24 ♗b6 ♖c2 25 ♕f1 ♕c3 26 ♗f2 (a nice little assembly of white pieces in the corner) 26...♖xa2 27 ♖b1 ♗e3 0-1 Carstens-Blaess, German Bundesliga 1986/87.

a223) 18 ♕a7! ♗xa6+ 19 ♔g1 ♖c8? (Black could have maintained the balance with 19...♗xe5 20 h4 ♕d5! 21 ♗xe5 ♗b7! 22 ♖h2 ♕xe5 23 ♖d1 ♗c6 24 ♕e3 ♕xe3 25 fxe3 ♖a8 26 g3 ♖a3 27 ♖e1 ♗d5 28 ♖b2 ♖xa2 29 ♖xa2 ♗xa2 30 e4 e5 31 g4 ♗e6 ½-½ Wagner-Frendzas, Chania 1997) 20 h4 h5 21 ♖h3 ♗xe5 22 ♖f3 ♖xd4 23 ♕xd4 d5 24 ♕f6 ♕c7 25 ♖e1 ♕d7 26 ♖e5 ♖c1+ 27 ♔h2 ♖c7 28 ♖g3 ♕e7 29 ♖xe6! and White was winning in Rachels-Petursson, Manila izt 1990.

b) Lastly, White has 15 ♕a4, but he runs right into a hurricane. In N.Lücke-Sandor, German Bundesliga 1994/95, White was swept away after 15...♕h4! (also 15...♕c7 16 0-0 ♗xe5 17 ♗b5 ♗xd4 18 ♕xd4 e5 19 ♖fe1 ♖c5 20 a4 0-0 21 ♕b4 d6 22 a5 ♗e6 23 a6 ♖b8 and Black was winning, Loeffler-Claverie, Cannes 1996) 16 g3 ♕g4 17 f4 ♕f3 18 ♔d2 (this clearly illustrates White's problems; Black often breaks with ...d7-d6 in this line, so the d-file is not exactly where the white king belongs) 18...0-0 19 ♖he1 ♕h5 20 ♗e4 ♕xh2+ 21 ♖e2 ♕xg3 22 ♗e3 ♖a6 23 ♕b3 ♕h4 24 ♖h1 ♕d8 and Black soon won.

15   ...   0-0

Here 15...♗a6 leads to a better endgame for White: 16 ♕xd8+ ♔xd8 17 ♗xa6 ♖xa6 18 a4 d6 19 f4! (Boleslavsky gives 19 ♖fd1 ♔d7 20 exd6 ♗xd4+ 21 ♖xd4

♖ha8 22 ♔f1 ♖xd6 with a likely draw) 19...♔d7 20 a5 ♖ha8?! (20...♖c8 was better, but after 21 ♖fd1 ♖c4 22 ♗e3 d5 23 ♖db1 ♗f8 24 ♖b7+ ♔c7 25 ♖xc7+ ♔xc7 26 ♗b6 followed by ♖c1 White has a clear edge according to Klompus) 21 ♗b6 dxe5?! (21...♖c8!?) 22 ♖ac1 ♔e8 23 ♖fd1 ♖xa5 24 ♗xa5 ♖xa5 25 ♖c8 ♔e7 26 ♖c7+ and White was on the road to victory in Klompus-Rettenbacher, corr 1983.

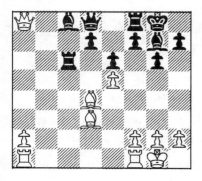

16   ♗b5   ♗a6!
In Sakharov-Veresov, USSR 1960, White got a clear edge after 16...♖c2?! 17 ♕e4 ♕c7 18 a4 ♗b7 19 ♕e3 ♖c8 20 ♖fd1.

| **17** | **♕xd8** | **♖xd8** |
| **18** | **♗xc6** | |

White can also consider 18 a4, when Rajna-Marosi, Budapest 1982, went as follows: 18...♗xb5 19 axb5 ♖c4 20 ♖ad1 ♖b8 21 b6 d6 22 f4 dxe5 23 fxe5 ♖b7 24 ♔f2

♗f8 25 ♔e3 ♗c5 26 ♗xc5 ♖xc5 27 ♖d8+ ♔g7 28 ♖b1 ♖xe5+ 29 ♔d4 ♖e2 30 ♔c5 ♖c2+ 31 ♔b5 ♖xg2 32 ♔c6 ♖xb6+ 33 ♖xb6 ♖xh2 and later a draw.

18	**...**	**♗xf1**
19	**♔xf1**	**dxc6**
20	**♗c3**	**♖d3**

Note how well Black is using his rook to avoid White sending his a-pawn off to the queening square.
21 ♖c1 ♖d5 22 ♖e1
22 f4 g5 is equal.
22...♖c5 23 ♖e3 ♖c4 24 ♗b2 h5 25 ♔e1 ♔h7 26 ♔d1 g5 27 f3 ♖a4 28 a3
This is as far as it gets!
28...c5

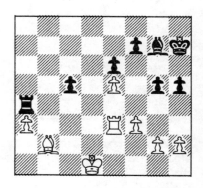

29 ♔c2 c4 30 ♔c3 ♔g6 31 ♖e4 ♔f5 32 ♔d4 g4 33 ♔e3 ♗h6+ 34 ♔f2 ♗f4 35 g3 ♗d2 36 ♖d4 ♗h6 37 fxg4+ hxg4 38 ♔e2 ♗g5 39 ♔f2 ♗h6 ½-½
Neither side can make progress.

13 Semi-Accelerated Dragon

Chapter Guide

1 e4 c5 2 ♘f3 ♘c6 3 d4 cxd4 4 ♘xd4 ♘f6 5 ♘c3 g6?! 6 ♘xc6 bxc6

7 e5 ♘g8 8 ♗c4

    8...♕a5?!   – *Game 103*
    8...♗g7   – *Game 104*

In this line Black plays ...♘f6 before developing his dark-squared bishop. This forces White to put his knight on c3 and thereby excludes White from reaching the Maroczy Bind. However, if it were as easy as that, everyone would play this line, but unfortunately White can play 6 ♘xc6 bxc6 7 e5 with a big lead in development. If Black plays well, he will survive the opening with a passive, yet solid position, but not many leading players are happy to settle for this. The exceptions are Sosonko who played it twice at Wijk aan Zee in 1986 (lost one and won one) and Shamkovich who used it on occasion, not to mention Botvinnik, who once adopted it against Smyslov in their 1958 World Championship match. It is difficult to pinpoint a clear-cut way to an advantage for White, but you always have the feeling that there must be something good for him.

Game 103
Varadi-Sabian
Corr 1985

(1 e4 c5 2 ♘f3 ♘c6 3 d4 cxd4 4 ♘xd4)

4	...	♘f6
5	♘c3	g6?!
6	♘xc6	

At this point there are some other moves which do not transpose into either the standard Dragon variation or the Accelerated Dragon lines. These are as follows:

a) 6 f4 ♕b6 (6...d6 is a Levenfish Dragon, which is absolutely harmless for Black, but also, of course, not the subject matter of this book) 7 ♘f3 (interesting is the untried 7 ♘b3 d6 8 ♘d5) 7...d6 8 ♗c4 ♗g7 9 ♕d3 0-0 10 ♗b3 ♗g4 11 ♗e3 ♕a5 12 0-0 ♗xf3 13 gxf3 ♕h5? (better is Levy's 13...♘d7 followed by ♘c5 with a good game) 14 ♔h1 ♖ad8 15 ♖ad1 ♕h3 16 ♕e2 ♘h5 17 ♖g1 ♔h8 18 ♕f2 ♕c8 and now 19 f5! with clearly better chances for White, as in the game Ljubojevic-Bilek, Teesside 1972.

b) 6 ♗c4 ♗g7 (6...d6? is a well-known mistake which leads to a clear advantage for White after 7 ♘xc6 bxc6 8 e5!, and 6...♕a5?! leads to nothing but problems for Black: 7 0-0 ♗g7 [here Black should go for the lesser evil 7...♕c5 8 ♘xc6 ♕xc4 9 ♘e5 ♕c7 10 ♘d3 with an edge for White, but Black is still in the game] 8 ♘b3 ♕c7 9 ♗g5 0-0 10 f4 b5!? 11 ♗xf6 bxc4 12 ♘d5 ♕b8 13 ♗xg7 ♔xg7 14 ♘d4 e6 15 ♘xc6 dxc6 16 ♕d4+ f6 17 ♘e3 with a clear edge for White, Tal-Benko, Portoroz izt 1958) 7 ♘xc6 bxc6 8 e5 ♘g8 transposing to Game 104.

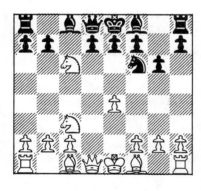

6 ... bxc6

6...dxc6 was once used by Botvinnik, and more recently by GMs Ljubojevic and Karlsson, and although none of the above lost with it, it is not to be recommended. Black hopes for a drawish endgame, but he is in fact very lucky if he gets that. After 7 ♕xd8+ ♔xd8

8 ♗c4 (other moves are possible, but this is clearly the best) 8...♗g7 (best; the old main line is 8...♗e8, when 9 e5 [less energetic is 9 a4 e5 10 f4 ♗e6! 11 ♗xe6 fxe6 12 ♖f1 ♗h6! 13 f5 ♗xc1 14 ♖xc1 ♔e7 with equality, Smyslov-Botvinnik, World ch match 1958] 9...♘d7 10 f4 [or 10 e6 fxe6 11 ♗xe6 ♗g7 12 ♗e3 b6 13 0-0-0 ♗xc3 14 bxc3 ♘c5 15 ♗xc8 ♖xc8 16 ♗xc5 bxc5 17 ♖hf1 with slightly better chances for White, Shirov-Ljubojevic, Buenos Aires 1994] 10...♘c5 11 ♗e3 ♗e6 12 ♗xe6 ♘xe6 13 0-0-0 ♗g7 14 g3 b6 15 ♖d3 ♖d8 16 ♖hd1 ♖xd3 17 ♖xd3 with clearly better chances for White in Hellers-Karlsson, Östersund 1992) 9 f4!? (Karasev has proved that 9 f3 does not promise White anything, e.g. 9...♔e8 10 a4 a5 11 ♗d2 ♘d7 12 0-0-0 e5 13 h4 h5 14 g3 ♘c5 15 ♔b1 ♗e6, Solozhenkin-Karasev, Leningrad 1990, but 9 a4!?, intending 10 h3 and 11 f4, is quite interesting; Silman and Donaldson now give 9...♘g4 10 f4 ♗xc3+ 11 bxc3 ♘f6, which is fine for Black, but 10 f4?! should be replaced by 10 ♗d2 with a slight edge for White) 9...b5 10 ♗d3 e5 11 0-0 ♘d7 12 f5 f6 13 ♗e3 ♗f8 14 fxg6 hxg6 15 a4 b4 16 ♘b1, A.Ivanov-Shabanov, USSR 1986, and now 16...♗e7, intending ...♘c5 and ...♗e6, would have kept White's advantage to a bare minimum.

7 e5 ♘g8

Unlike in the previous chapter, Black does not have 7...♘d5, which is easily refuted: 8 ♘xd5 cxd5 9 ♕xd5 ♖b8 10 e6! f6 (10...fxe6?? allows 11 ♕e5 forking both rooks) 11 ♗f4 with a horrible position for Black, e.g. 11...♖b6 12 ♗b5 ♖xe6+ 13 ♕xe6 ♕a5+ 14 c3 ♕xb5 15 ♕e2 and White was winning, Mikenas-Uogele, Lithuanian ch 1965.

However, an interesting alternative is 7...♘h5!?, e.g. 8 ♗c4 (or 8 ♗e2 ♕a5 9 f4 with a good game for White, whereas 9 ♗xh5 gxh5 10 ♕xh5 ♗g7 11 f4 0-0 12 0-0 f6 13 ♘e4 d5! is playable for Black – Silman and Donaldson) 8...d5! 9 exd6 ♕xd6 10 ♕f3 (or 10 0-0) 10...♗e6 11 ♗b5 ♖c8 12 ♗a6 ♖d8 13 0-0 ♕c7, when Black is only slightly worse, Petrushin-Vizek, Czechoslovakia 1985.

8 ♗c4

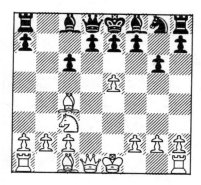

8 ... ♕a5?!

This move is highly dubious; better is 8...♗g7, which can be found in the next main game. Black has two further alternatives:

a) 8...d5?! (Black cannot break in the centre when he is this far behind in development) 9 exd6 ♕xd6 (9...exd6? is even worse: 10 ♕f3 d5 11 ♘xd5! cxd5 12 ♗xd5 ♕e7+ 13 ♗e3 ♖b8 14 0-0 ♗g7 15 ♗f4, John-Janowski, Mannheim 1914) 10 0-0 ♕xd1 11 ♖xd1 ♗h6 12 ♗xh6 ♘xh6 13 ♖d2 ♘f5 14

♘e4 with a clear edge for White in Geller-Stein, USSR ch 1966/67.

b) 8...f5!? (Black is way behind in development and yet he keeps playing pawns moves!) 9 ♗f4 e6 10 ♕d2 ♖b8 11 ♗b3 (White could consider both 11 0-0 and 11 0-0-0 at this point) 11...♖b4!? 12 0-0 ♕c7 13 ♖fe1 ♖xf4! 14 ♕xf4 (it is quite amazing that Black is still in the game: he is an exchange down, and has only developed his queen) 14...♘h6 15 ♖ad1 ♘f7 16 ♕e3 ♗g7 17 f4 g5 18 fxg5 ♗xe5 19 ♕h3, when White is better, but with his pawn majority in the centre and the bishop pair, Black has some counterplay, and actually went on to draw the game in Popovic-Velimirovic, Banja Vrucica 1991.

9 ♗f4

White has two other strong possibilities:

a) 9 ♕e2!? ♗g7 10 f4 ♘h6 11 ♗d2 0-0 12 0-0-0 ♕c7 13 g4 d5 14 exd6 exd6 15 f5 gxf5 16 gxf5 ♗xf5 17 ♖hg1 ♗g6 18 h4 with a dangerous attack for White, Shianovsky-Sherbak, USSR 1960.

b) 9 0-0! ♗g7 (even worse is 9...♕xe5? 10 ♖e1 and now for example 10...♕b8 11 ♕d4 f6 12 ♘e4 ♗g7 13 ♗f4 ♕b6 14 ♘d6+ ♔f8 15 ♕d3 ♗b7 16 ♗xg8 ♖xg8 17 ♕c4 and it was all over, 1-0 Tiviakov-Mugerman, Pinsk 1989) 10 ♕f3! e6 11 ♘e4 ♗xe5 12 ♗f4 ♕c7 13 ♗xe5 ♕xe5 14 ♖fe1 d5 15 ♖ad1 with a strong attack for White, Barvik-Terentiev, USSR 1961.

9 ... ♗g7
10 ♕f3!

In Timman-Korchnoi, Brussels 1991, White was successful with 10 0-0 ♗xe5 11 ♗xe5 ♕xe5 12 ♖e1

♕f4 13 ♖e4 ♕f6 14 ♖e3 d5 15 ♗xd5! with a clear advantage. However, 10 ♕f3 is even better.

| | 10 | ... | e6 |

Nor does 10...f6 help Black to survive: 11 ♗g3 ♗a6 12 b4 ♕b6 13 b5 ♗b7 14 0-0! ♖c8 15 ♘a4 ♕a5 16 ♘c5 ♗a8 17 ♕b3 ♘h6 18 ♘xd7! cxb5 19 ♗xb5 ♗c6 20 ♘xf6+! ♗xf6 21 ♗xc6+ ♖xc6 22 exf6 1-0, was the game Unzicker-Rausis, Daugavpils 1990. White played very accurately; all of Black's moves were responses to white threats.

11	0-0	♗xe5
12	b4	♕c7

12...♕xb4? is answered by 13 ♗xe5 f6 14 ♗xe6!

13	♘b5	♕b8
14	♗xe5	♕xe5
15	♖ad1	d5
16	♖fe1	♕b8
17	♕c3!	

17 ♗xd5! also wins for White: 17...cxd5 18 ♕xd5 ♔f8 19 ♕c5+! ♔g7 (19...♘e7 20 ♖d8+ ♔g7 21 ♖xh8 ♔xh8 22 ♕xe7) 20 ♖d8 ♕b7 21 ♕f8 ♔f6 22 ♘d6 ♕e7 23 ♘e4+ ♔f5 24 ♕xe7 1-0 Geenen-Miranda, Novi Sad ol 1990.

| 17 | ... | f6 |

18	♗xd5!	cxd5
19	♖xd5	♔f7

On 19...♘e7, Bottlik gives: 20 ♘d6+! ♔d7 21 ♖d3 ♘d5 22 ♘e4 ♗a6 23 ♖xd5+ exd5 24 ♘c5+.

20	♖d8!	♕xb5
21	♕c7+	♘e7
22	♖xh8	♕xb4
23	c3	♕h4
24	♕d8	e5
25	♖f8+	♔e6
26	♖e8	1-0

Game 104
De Firmian-Sosonko
Wijk aan Zee 1986

(1 e4 c5 2 ♘f3 ♘c6 3 d4 cxd4 4 ♘xd4 ♘f6 5 ♘c3 g6?! 6 ♘xc6 bxc6 7 e5 ♘g8 8 ♗c4)

| 8 | ... | ♗g7 |

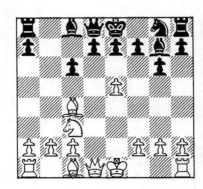

| 9 | ♕f3 |

Also possible is 9 ♕e2 ♘h6 10 ♗f4 0-0 11 0-0-0 ♕b6 12 h4 ♘f5 13 g4 ♘d4 14 ♕e4 ♘e6 15 ♗e3 ♕c7, as in Tarasevich-Karagoiz, USSR 1959, and now 16 ♗xe6 fxe6 17 f4 is clearly better for White. Black has real problems on the kingside; White threatens 18 g5 and 19 h5 with a nasty attack.

In Baker-Shamkovich, New York 1985, White tried 9 0-0, but then Black got away with 9...♗xe5!? (9...♘h6!?) 10 ♖e1 ♗g7 11 ♗f4 d5 12 ♘xd5! cxd5, and now White should have continued with 13 ♕xd5 ♕xd5 14 ♗xd5 g5 15 ♗c7 ♔d7 16 ♗g3 f5 17 ♖ad1 f4 18 ♗xa8+ ♔c7 with an unclear position.

9 ... f5

If Black tries to avoid the main line with 9...e6, White is much better after 10 ♗f4 ♕a5 11 0-0! ♗xe5? (suicidal, but 11...♘e7 12 ♘e4 is also good for White) 12 b4! ♕xc7 13 ♘b5 and White won, Pietzsch-Baumbach, East Germany 1959.

10 ♗f4 e6!

As we should know by now, 10...♕a5? is a bad idea. Pawn snatching when you are far behind in development is suicidal: 11 0-0! ♗xe5 12 b4! ♕c7 13 ♘b5 ♕b8 14 ♗xe5 ♕xe5 15 ♖fe1 ♕b8 16 ♕c3 1-0 Karakas-Polihroniade, Beverwijk 1966.

A better alternative, yet somewhat passive is 10...♖b8!? and now:

a) In Suetin-Bilek, Kecskemet 1972, Black did not have too much trouble after 11 ♗b3 ♕c7 12 0-0 e6 13 ♖fe1 ♘e7 14 ♗g5 ♘d5 15 ♖ad1 0-0 16 ♘xd5 cxd5 17 ♕f4 ♖f7 18 ♗h6 ♗xh6 19 ♕xh6, and now 19...♖b4 would have given equal chances.

b) White tried something different in Daurelle-Koerholz, Cannes 1994: 11 0-0-0 ♖b4 12 ♗xg8?! ♖xg8 13 a3 ♖c4 14 ♘e2 e6 15 ♕b3 ♖e4 16 ♖he1 ♗a6 (White's play leaves an artificial impression, and Black is already taking charge

of the game) 17 ♗e3 ♗c4 18 ♕b7 ♖xe5 19 ♗g5!? ♖b5! 20 ♕xb5 ♕xg5+ 21 f4 ♕xf4+ 22 ♘xf4 ♗xb5 and Black has all the chances to win this endgame.

c) Best is 11 0-0 e6 12 ♖ad1 ♕c7 13 ♖fe1 ♘e7 (13...♘h6 is also possible, but 14 ♕g3 ♘f7 15 h4 is quite uncomfortable for Black) 14 b3 0-0 15 ♕e3 ♕a5 16 h4 ♖f7 17 a3 and White had the better chances in Andersson-Bilek, Teesside 1972.

11 0-0-0

This is the main line, but other moves have also been tried:

a) 11 g4 (tried only once, when White got an excellent position, but Black need not fear this move) 11...fxg4?! (11...♘e7, intending ...0-0, seems to be better, trying to catch up on his development) 12 ♕xg4 ♕a5?! (again this is not advisable, better is 12...♘e7 or 12...♘h6!?, e.g. 13 ♗xh6 ♗xh6 14 ♘e4 0-0 15 ♘f6+ ♖xf6 16 exf6 ♕xf6 with good play for Black) 13 0-0-0 ♗xe5 14 ♗xe5 ♕xe5 15 ♖he1 with more than enough for the pawn, Suetin-Korchnoi, USSR 1954.

b) 11 0-0 (this move is possibly

stronger than 11 0-0-0, but so far it has not been played very often) 11...♘h6 (also possible is 11...♘e7 which may transpose to Andersson-Bilek above) 12 ♖ad1 ♕c7 13 ♖fe1 ♘f7 14 ♕g3 (or 14 ♕e3 ♖b8 15 b3 h6 16 ♗g3 ♕a5 17 ♘a4 ♗f8 18 ♕d3 ♗e7 19 ♗f4 ♕c7, Zivic-Dezelin, Slokobanja 1989, when White was somewhat more active) 14...0-0 (Shamkovich gives 14...g5 as unclear, but one has the feeling that White should be better, although it is pretty difficult to prove, e.g. 15 ♗xg5 ♗xe5 16 f4 ♖g8! or 16 ♕h4 ♖g8!; this is definitely better than the game, where Black ends up bound hand and foot) 15 h4 ♔h8 16 ♘a4 a5?! 17 b3 ♖e8 18 ♕e3 h6 19 g4! ♖g8 20 ♗g3 ♗f8 21 ♕b6! with total control, Short-Sosonko, Wijk aan Zee 1986.

c) 11 h4 ♕c7 (this may already be wrong; perhaps 11...♘h6 was once again the right move) 12 ♕g3 ♖b8 13 h5 g5 14 h6! (the only way to maintain the pressure) 14...♗xh6 15 ♖xh6 ♘xh6 16 ♕xg5 ♘f7 17 ♕g3 ♖b4 18 b3 ♕a5 19 0-0-0 and White develops a strong initiative, Kislov-Groh, Budejovice 1992.

| 11 | ... | ♕c7 |
| 12 | h4 | |

Once again we have some alternatives for White:

a) 12 ♖he1 ♘h6 (in Damjanovic-Gazik, Stary Smokovec 1988, Black ended up in a very sad position after 12...♖b8 13 a3 [preventing Black's ...♖b4xf4 ideas] 13...♘e7 14 h4 ♘d5 15 h5 ♘xf4 16 ♕xf4 ♕a5 17 ♖e3 with a much better position for White) 13 h4 ♘f7 14 ♕e3 ♖b8 15 g4 ♖b4 16 ♗b3? (if possible, White should

never allow Black to sacrifice the exchange on f4 as the e5-pawn will become too weak, and Black will then gain excellent chances due to his pawn majority in the centre and the pair of bishops; in this case 16 b3, despite being weakening, would have been better) 16...♖xf4! 17 ♕xf4 ♘xe5 18 ♕g3 (Black threatened 18...♘d3+) 18...fxg4 19 h5 gxh5 20 ♖h1 ♕a5 21 ♕h4 ♘f3 with a clear advantage for Black, Gaber-Dezelin, Pula 1990.

b) 12 ♖de1!? (this move looks slightly strange, but it is actually quite logical; White wants to break with the h-pawn, so why not keep the rook on h1 and use the other rook to protect the e-pawn, as nothing will be happening on the d-file for some time?) 12...♘h6 (12...♘e7!?) 13 h4 ♘f7 14 ♕g3! ♖b8?! (it is quite possible that 14...♖g8, intending ...♗f8 or ...♗h8 followed by a ...h7-h6, ...g6-g5 plan is better) 15 h5! g5 16 ♗xg5 ♘xg5 17 h6! ♗f6 18 f4! ♖b4 19 b3 ♖g8 20 exf6 ♘f7 21 ♕e3 with a much better position for White, since Black has real problems with his co-ordination, Kiesekamp-Bogdan, Szeged 1998.

c) 12 ♕g3 ♘e7? (12...♘h6!?) 13 h4 h6 14 ♖d6 0-0 15 h5 g5 16 ♗xg5! hxg5 17 h6 and White was winning in Mortishov-Shamkovich, USSR 1951.

d) 12 ♕e3 ♖b8 13 ♗b3 (Kuijf-Sosonko, Hilversum 1987, saw 13 ♖he1 ♕b6 14 ♘a4 ♕xe3+ 15 ♗xe3 ♗xe5 16 ♗xa7 ♗f4+ 17 ♔b1 ♖a8 18 ♗d4 ♖xa4 19 b3 ♖xc4 20 bxc4 e5 21 ♖xe5+ ♔f7 ½-½) 13...♖b4 14 g3 ♘e7 (interesting is Shamkovich's suggestion 14...g5!? 15 ♗xg5 ♕xe5

16 ♕f3 ♘f6 17 ♗f4 ♖xf4!? with an unclear position) 15 a3 ♖b8 16 h4 with the better chances for White, Popovic-Shamkovich, New York 1986.

12 ... ♘h6!

12...♖b8?! is too slow. Black needs to finish his development and put pressure on the e5-pawn, which is White's only weakness. A few examples illustrate the downside to this move: 13 ♖he1 (13 ♗b3?! is less to the point due to 13...♖b4! 14 ♔b1 ♖xf4 15 ♕xf4 ♗xe5 16 ♕d2 ♘f6 17 f3 0-0 18 g4 fxg4 19 fxg4 ♘xg4 20 ♖hg1 ♘f6 with chances for both White and Black, Zontakh-Velimirovic, Belgrade 1993) 13...♖b4 14 b3! ♘h6 15 a3 ♖b8 16 ♗xh6! ♗xh6+ 17 ♔b2 0-0 18 ♕d3 ♖e8 19 ♕d6 when Black is in a bind, Golyan-Mukhin, Alma Ata 1958.

13 ♕g3?!

Shamkovich's 13 ♕e2!? ♘f7 14 ♖de1 followed by ♖h3 and ♖g3 is worthwhile, as is 13 ♖de1!? transposing to the Kiesekamp-Bogdan game, which seems quite attractive.

Silman and Donaldson give 13 h5 g5! 14 ♗xg5 ♘f7 14 ♗f4 ♗xe5 15 ♗xe5 ♘xe5 16 ♕g3 d5 17 ♖he1 f4! without an evaluation, though the exclamation marks indicate that this should be good for Black, but we think that 18 ♘xd5!! should win for White: 18...cxd5 (18...exd5 19 ♕xf4 is obviously murder) 19 ♗b5+ ♗d7! (the only move, as everything else loses on the spot: 19...♘d7 20 ♕g7 ♖f8 21 ♖xe6+; 19...♘c6 20 ♕c3; 19...♔d8 20 ♕g5+; 19...♔f8 20 ♕xf4+; 19...♔e7 20 ♕g5+!) 20 ♕g7 0-0-0! 21 ♗a6+ ♔b8 22 ♕xe5. Furthermore, if Black tries to improve with

15...♕xe5, then 16 ♖he1 ♕a5 17 ♗xe6! decides.

If White does not have any improvements on our main game, this is obviously where he should be looking for an alternative; and there are three good possibilities to choose from.

13 ... ♘f7
14 ♖he1

Better was 14 ♖de1!?, transposing to Kiesekamp-Bogdan above.

14 ... ♖b8
15 ♔b1?!

White cannot play like this, as the game continuation clearly demonstrates. A reasonable alternative is 15 a3 ♕b6 16 b3! (Silman and Donaldson's only playable option for White is 16 ♗b3 c5 17 ♘a4 ♕c6 18 c4 0-0 with an unclear position) 16...♕a5 17 ♔b2 with a good game for White.

15	...	♖b4!
16	♗b3	0-0
17	a3	♖xf4
18	♕xf4	♗xe5
19	♕d2	d5

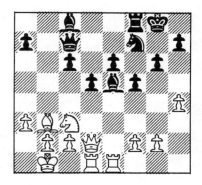

This is exactly what Black is hoping for in this variation. He has tremendous compensation for the exchange and is much better.

20   g3

Another convincing example: 20 ♘e2 ♗d7 21 f4 ♗f6 22 h5 ♖b8 23 hxg6 hxg6 24 ♘d4 ♕d6 25 ♕e3 c5 26 ♘xe6 c4! 27 ♘d4 cxb3 28 cxb3 ♕b6 29 ♕d3 a5 30 ♖e3 ♘d6 31 g4 ♘e4 32 ♘c2 ♖d8 33 g5 ♗b5 0-1 was Ravinsky-Shamkovich, Vilnius 1953.

20	...	♗d7
21	h5	g5!
22	♖e2	♗f6
23	♕e3	♘d6

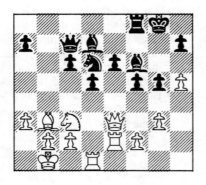

24   ♕c5?

White could have limited his opponent's advantage here with 24 ♘a4 ♘e4 25 ♘c5 f4 26 gxf4 gxf4 27 ♕xe4 dxe4 28 ♘xd7 e3! 29 ♘xf8 ♕e5 30 c3 ♔xf8 31 fxe3 f3 with a clear advantage for Black – Sosonko. The rest of the game is a desperate attempt by White to create some counterplay, which does not succeed at all:

24...♕b8 25 g4 ♘b7 26 ♕e3 f4 27 ♕d2 ♘c5 28 ♔a2 ♕b6 29 ♕e1 ♖b8 30 ♘a4 ♘xa4 31 ♖xe6 ♕d8! 32 ♖xc6 ♗xc6 33 ♕e6+ ♔g7 34 ♕xc6 ♘b6 35 h6+ ♔xh6 36 c3 ♔g7 37 f3 ♖c8 38 ♕b5 ♕e7 39 ♗c2 ♕c5 0-1

Black never let go of his grip. An excellent performance by Sosonko, but before one gets too enthusiastic about this game, one needs to look at White's 13th move alternatives, which are quite troublesome for Black.

14 Hyper-Accelerated Dragon

Chapter Guide

1 e4 c5 2 ♘f3 g6
3 d4 cxd4 4 ♕xd4 ♘f6
3 c3 ♗g7 4 d4 cxd4 5 cxd4 d5 6 e5 ♘c6

The Hyper-Accelerated Dragon (1 e4 c5 2 ♘f3 g6) is often employed by Accelerated Dragon players as a means of avoiding 1 e4 c5 2 ♘f3 ♘c6 3 ♗b5.

Normally White transposes to the main lines of the Accelerated Dragon with 3 d4 cxd4 4 ♘xd4 ♘c6, but 2...g6 gives White some extra options, which constitute the Hyper-Accelerated Dragon, and these are covered in this chapter.

Game 105
Hector-Larsen
London 1991

1	e4	c5
2	♘f3	g6!?
3	d4	

The main alternative, 3 c3, is the subject of Games 108 and 109.

3 h4 is interesting, and quite logical too, if you consider the g6-pawn to be a weakness. It was first played by future World Champion Boris Spassky against Leonid Stein in 1965. Stein did not prevent the threat of h4-h5, and after 3...♗g7 4 h5 ♘c6 5 ♘c3 e6 6 d3 d5 7 ♗g5, White had some initiative, since his h-pawn was highly annoying for Black.

Larsen later tried 3...h5 against Rodriguez in St Martin 1994. This is what one would expect from Larsen, who has always enjoyed pushing his h-pawns. However, Rodriguez, found the g5-square very inviting for his knight, and played a much improved Morra Gambit: 4 d4 cxd4 5 ♗c4 ♘c6 6 c3 dxc3?! (too brave; more sensible was 6...d3 or 6...♘f6 with some edge for White) 7 ♘xc3 ♘f6 8 ♗f4 d6?? (an incredible move from a player of Larsen's class; much better was 8...♗g7, when White will still have to prove his attacking skills, but now it is all over) 9 ♘g5 e6 10 ♘b5 (simply winning the d6-pawn) 10...a6 11 ♘xd6+ ♗xd6 12 ♗xd6 ♕a5+ 13 b4 ♕d8 14 ♖h3 ♘g4 15 ♗b3 a5 16 ♕d2 a4 17 ♗c4 ♕b6 18 ♖d1 f6 19 ♗c5 ♕c7 20 ♘xe6 ♗xe6 21 ♗xe6 ♖d8 22 ♖d3 ♖xd3 23 ♕xd3 ♘ge5 24 ♕b5 ♖h7 25 ♗d6 ♗g7 26 ♕xa4 1-0.

Since this Morra-like gambit looks like a strong reply to 3...h5, perhaps Black should try 3...♘f6, since 4 e5 ♘g4 5 d4 cxd4 6 ♕xd4 h5 7 e6 f6 8 ♗d3 ♖g8 is not very clear, while 5 c3 d6 and 5 h5 ♗g7 also look fine for Black. Still, if White is the creative type, 3 h4 is a good, provocative idea based on sound principles.

3 ♗c4 is quieter, but not without venom. It is very similar to 1 e4 c5 2 ♘f3 d6 3 ♗c4, which Michael Adams has played a few times. However, there is a difference. In that line, after 3...♘f6, White has to defend with the e-pawn with 4 d3, but here White has time for the immediate d2-d4, since Black will not hit the e4-pawn in time. Bronstein-Khasin, Moscow 1961, saw 3 ♗c4 ♗g7 4 0-0 d6 5 c3 ♘f6 6 ♕a4+!? ♗d7 7 ♕b3 0-0 8 e5 ♘g4 9 e6 with a huge plus for White. Later the same year, the game Lutikov-Stein showed how Black should play: 4...♘c6 5 c3 e6! 6 d3 ♘ge7 7 a4 0-0 8 ♘bd2 d5 9 ♗a2 b6 and Black already had the better position. After the immediate 4 c3!?, Bilek has had some success with 4...e6. Against Per Juslin in Boraas 1986, he was worse after 5 d4 cxd4 6 cxd4 d5 7 ♗b5+ ♘c6?!

8 e5 ♗d7 9 ♘c3 f6 10 exf6 ♘xf6 11 ♗xc6 ♗xc6 12 ♗f4 0-0 13 ♗e5, although he later won the game. Three years later, against Chevallier, Val Thorens 1989, he improved with the correct 7...♗d7. After 8 ♗xd7 ♕xd7 9 e5?! ♘c6 10 0-0 f6! 11 exf6 ♘xf6 12 ♘c3 0-0 13 ♖e1 ♘h5, he was already better. The structure is similar to the French Defence, but here in a more active version. In particular the bishop on g7 looks nice. The game finished 14 ♗e3 ♖ad8 15 ♕e2 ♘f4 16 ♕d2? ♘xg2! 17 ♔xg2 e5 18 h3 ♖xf3 19 ♔xf3 ♕xh3+ 20 ♔e2 exd4 21 ♗g5 dxc3 22 bxc3 ♖e8+ 23 ♗e3 d4 0-1.

Not too difficult, but still very attractive. It seems that playing ...e7-e6 and ...d7-d5 immediately secures Black excellent chances.

3 ... cxd4

Also possible is 3...♗g7, intending to use some of the extra options after 4 c4, which can be found in the transpositions chapter. However, White can play 4 d5 with a Schmid Benoni, or the even more scary 4 dxc5!?, when Black should respond 4...♕a5+ 5 ♘c3 ♘f6 6 ♗d3 ♕xc5, but not 5...♕xc5?! 6

♘d5! which has led to some quick disasters for Black. Nunn seems to support the view that 5 c3 ♕xc5 6 ♗e3 ♕c7 7 ♗d4!? is White's most promising line. Although 7...e5?! looks logical, White is much better after 8 ♗e3 ♘f6 9 ♘a3!, e.g. 9...0-0 10 ♘b5 ♕c6 11 ♘xe5 ♕xe4 12 ♘xf7! ♖xf7 13 ♘d6 ♕c6 14 ♗c4 ♗f8 15 ♗xf7+ ♔g7 16 ♘xc8 winning for White, as the knight escapes via a7, Lesiege-Strenzwilk, New York 1992. Best is probably 7...♘f6 8 e5 ♘g4 9 e6 f6, which looks quite playable.

4   ♕xd4!?

As mentioned in the introduction to this chapter, 4 ♘xd4 just transposes to a normal Accelerated Dragon.

4   ...   ♘f6
5   ♗b5

Bronstein's ingenious idea from his game against Zhidkov in 1972. Black played the weak 5...♕a5+, but after 6 ♕c3 he realised that 6...♕xc3 7 ♘xc3 with the threat of e5 followed by ♘d5 can only be parried with 7...a6, and then 8 e5 axb5 9 exf6 with ♘d5 or ♘xb5 next is almost winning for White. Zhidkov swallowed his pride and

played 6...♕d8, but after 7 ♗c4! followed by e5 Black was in big trouble. Still, Legahn tried to improve on this disaster with 6...♘c6 against Fette. However, after 7 ♕xa5 ♘xa5 8 ♘c3 a6 9 e5 ♘g4 10 ♘d5 ♔d8 11 h3 ♘h6 12 ♗e3 he found himself on the wrong side of a miniature.

5 e5 is the subject of the next game and 5 ♘c3 of Game 107.

5   ...   ♘c6

Nowadays nearly the only move played, although we do not find the consequences of 5...a6 to be clear at all. After 6 e5 axb5 7 exf6 e6 (7...♘c6 has been played, but after 8 ♕d5 Black has to play the awkward 8...♘b4 9 ♕b3 e6, after which 10 ♘c3 looks preferable for White) 8 ♘c3 (best; 8 0-0 ♘c6 9 ♕h4 ♖a4! is fine for Black) 8...♘c6 9 ♕h4 Black never got developed in Rührig-Stertenbrink, German Bundesliga 1983/84, after 9...b4?! 10 ♘b5 ♖a5 11 c4! bxc3 12 a4 cxb2 13 ♗xb2 ♗b4 + 14 ♔e2. Instead of 9...b4?!, we find 9...♖a5 more logical. Now ...b5-b4 followed by ...♖h5 cannot be prevented, since 10 a4 bxa4 is okay for Black. Maybe White should try 10 ♗h6 ♗xh6 11 ♕xh6 ♕xf6 12 ♘e4 ♕xb2 13 0-0, which is very unclear.

In summary, after 5...a6, Black is well behind in development. But with the pair of bishops, the rook coming into play via a5 and the f6-pawn being weak, inexact play by White could easily give Black the better game. So, if you find the endgame after 5...♘c6 too difficult to win, 5...a6 is a risky, but not bad winning attempt.

6   ♗xc6   dxc6

6...bxc6 is more ambitious. Black hopes to prove the advantage of the bishop pair and the extra central pawn. The variation is similar to 1 e4 c5 2 ♘f3 ♘c6 3 ♗b5 g6 4 ♗xc6 bxc6 5 0-0 ♗g7 6 ♖e1 ♘f6 7 e5 ♘d5 8 c4 ♘c7 9 d4 cxd4 10 ♕xd4, which has been considered good for White since Kasparov-Salov, Dortmund 1992, when White had easy development due to his space advantage. After 6...bxc6 Black will suffer for the same reasons: 7 e5 ♘d5 8 0-0 (after 8 e6?! Black gets a huge centre after either 8...f6 and 8...♘f6!) 8...♗g7 and now:

a) The attempt to transpose to the above Kasparov game with 9 c4 was less successful in Edelman-Shabalov, New York 1992. After 9...♘b4 Shabalov took advantage of the white queen's early development to d4, and won a messy game after 10 ♘a3 d6 11 c5 ♘d5 12 cxd6 exd6 13 ♗g5 dxe5.

b) 9 ♕h4 (planning ♗h6 to eliminate the bishop pair) 9...f6 (allowing ♗h6; critical was 9...h6 to keep the bishop pair, when after 10 c4 ♘b4 11 ♘c3 ♘d3 12 ♗d2 ♕c7 13 ♘e4 g5 14 ♕g3 ♘xb2 15 ♖ae1 ♔f8 Black survived White's attack and later won in Kengis-Levcenkovc, Riga 1984; still, this looks very dangerous for Black, as after 9...h6 he will hardly ever be able to castle, so 10 a3, preparing c2-c4, or 10 ♘d2 followed by ♘e4 looks like a good idea, but probably this is the kind of position Black has to play if he chooses 6...bxc6) 10 c4 ♘c7 11 ♗h6 0-0 12 ♗xg7 ♔xg7 13 ♘c3 ♘e6 14 ♖ad1 fxe5 15 ♘xe5 ♖f4 16 ♕g3 ♕c7 17 ♖fe1 d6? (losing a pawn, but Black

was much worse anyway) 18 ♘xg6 hxg6 19 ♖xe6 ♗xe6 20 ♕xf4 with an extra pawn in Sax-Tatai, Rome 1986. After 20...♖f8 21 ♕d4+ ♔g8 22 ♖e1 ♗f7 23 ♕h4 e5? 24 ♘e4 1-0.

It seems to us that unless you have very strong nerves and are happy to defend Black's position after 9...h6!?, 6...bxc6 will be unattractive to you, since otherwise White just has a simple position with an edge.

7   ♕xd8+   ♔xd8

This endgame used to be considered as slightly better for White. Yet Larsen does not believe that the right to castle is more important than Black's bishop pair. So he plays very ambitiously, trying to prove Black to be better.

8   ♘c3

In the rapidplay game J.Polgar-Larsen, Melody Amber 1992, White tried 8 e5, but after 8...♘d5 9 ♗d2 ♗g7 10 c4 ♘b6 11 b3 ♗g4 12 ♗c3 ♗xf3 13 gxf3 ♘d7 14 f4 ♘c5 15 ♔e2 ♘c7 16 ♘d2 ♖hd8 17 ♗b4 ♘e6 18 ♗xe7 ♘xf4+ 17 ♔e3 ♗xe5! 18 ♗xd8+ ♖xd8 White found herself completely outplayed. She realised that the planned 19 ♖ad1 would allow mate in three after 19...♖d3 20 ♔e4 ♗d6! with 21...f5 mate! Instead White played 19 ♘f3 and won the endgame a pawn down, but only because Larsen later blundered a rook! 8 e5 is too ambitious, since White is not properly developed.

8   ...   ♗g7

8...♗g4 is also possible, when White did not prove anything in Zarnicki-Larsen, Buenos Aires 1992. The former World Junior Champion played 9 ♘e5, but only had equality after 9...♗e6 10 ♘d3 ♗g7 11 ♘c5 ♗c8 12 ♗f4 b6 13 0-0-0+ ♔e8 14 ♘d3 ♘d7 15 ♖d2 e5. Although 8...♗g4 is playable, it seems more flexible to develop with 8...♗g7 and 9...♔e8 first, and then decide where to put the other pieces.

9 h3

Preventing ...♗g4, but allowing Black to play a plan with ...♘d7, ...e7-e5 and ...♔e7 etc.

9 ♗f4 is more ambitious, since if Black tries the same plan, he gets into trouble after 9...♘d7 10 0-0-0 ♔e8 11 ♗c7!, when White threatens to double rooks on the d-file, after which Black can never free himself. In Arkhipov-P.H.Nielsen, Gistrup 1994, Black managed to draw after 11...b6 12 h4 (not 12 ♖d2 ♗h6 or 12 ♖d3 ♗a6) 12...♗b7 13 h5 ♘c5 14 ♗e5 f6 15 ♗d4 ♘e6 16 ♗e3 ♖g8 17 ♘h4 ♔f7 18 f4, but it was obvious that White enjoyed some initiative.

Instead 9...♔e8 (or 9...♘h5) 10 0-0-0 ♘h5 is more active, and in practice White has not been able to equalise:

a) Schlosser-Lerch, Trnava 1989, saw 11 ♗c7 ♗g4 12 ♖d3 ♗h6+ 13 ♔b1 ♘f4 14 ♗xf4 ♗xf4, when Black was just slightly better.

b) And Kosten-Birmingham, Paris 1988: 11 ♗e5 f6 12 ♗d4 ♗h6+ 13 ♗e3 ♗xe3+ 14 fxe3 e5, when only Black could think of victory. We have not found a way to improve on White's play after 10...♘h5, and if there are no improvements, then the endgame arising after 5 ♗b5 must be considered harmless for Black.

9 ... ♘d7
10 ♗d2

After the more 'aggressive' 10 ♗e3, Rausis simply took on c3. After 10...♗xc3+ 11 bxc3 f6 12 0-0-0 ♔e8 13 ♖he1 e5 14 ♘d2 ♘b6 followed by ...♗e6, Black was much better, Myrvold-Rausis, Gausdal 1995.

10 ... ♔e8
11 0-0-0 ♘e5

Also possible was the standard plan with ...e7-e5 and ...♔e7 etc.

12 ♘d4

White should accept that he has achieved nothing and simplify with 12 ♘xe5 ♗xe5 13 ♘e2 and 14 ♗c3.

12...♘c4 13 ♗g5 f6 14 ♗h4 e5 15 ♘f3 ♔e7 16 ♖d3 ♗e6 17 ♘a4 g5 18 ♗g3 b6 19 b3 ♘d6 20 ♘d2 h5

Now Larsen has a serious initiative. His pieces co-ordinate very well, and he is ready to open the kingside.

21 c4 ♘f7 22 ♖d1 g4 23 hxg4 hxg4 24 f4

Active defence. If White had played passively, Black had plans like ...♗h6-f4 and ...♘g5 or ...♗h6-g5 and ...f6-f5.

24...gxf3 25 ♘xf3 ♗h6+ 26 ♔c2 ♖hg8 27 ♘h4 ♖ad8 28 ♗e1 ♖xd3 29 ♖xd3 ♖g4 30 ♘c3 ♘d6 31 c5

♘xe4 32 cxb6 axb6 33 ♘a4 b5 34 ♘c3 ♗g5

Another strategic triumph for Larsen, but he later allowed his opponent to escape with a draw. It seems to us that the endgame arising after 5 ♗b5 offers as many chances to Black as it does for White.

Game 106
Rozentalis-Tregubov
St Petersburg 1996

(1 e4 c5 2 ♘f3 g6 3 d4 cxd4 4 ♕xd4 ♘f6)

5   e5!?

Generally not considered very strong, but recently Rozentalis has come up with a new idea, which seems promising for White.

5   ...   ♘c6
6   ♕a4

White has to watch out for 6 ♕h4? ♘xe5 and 6 ♕e3 ♘g4 followed by ...♘gxe5. In both cases Black wins a pawn because of ...♕a5+ which wins back the piece.

6   ...   ♘d5
7   ♕e4   ♘db4

This used to be the main move,

but perhaps 7...♘c7 8 ♘c3 ♗g7 is a more solid option and now:

a) In Lutikov-Osnos, Kiev 1964, Black was blown apart after 9 ♗f4 ♘e6?! 10 ♗g3 b6 11 h4 h5 12 ♗c4 ♗b7 13 ♗d5 ♕c8 14 0-0-0 ♘a5 15 ♘g5 ♗h6 16 f4 ♗xg5 17 fxg5 ♘c7 18 ♗xf7+ ♔xf7 19 e6+ ♘xe6 20 ♖hf1 with total destruction. Impressive play by White, but Black could have done better by not giving up control of d5 and playing 9...b6 instead of 9...♘e6?! Silman and Donaldson suggest that 10 ♗c4 ♗b7 11 ♕e2 ♘a5 12 ♗d3 ♘e6 13 ♗g3 ♘c5 14 0-0 0-0 15 ♖ad1 ♕c8 is equal. This is probably right, but 10 ♗c4 seems unnecessary, Black gains a lot of time chasing the bishop. 10 0-0-0 or even stronger 10 h4! seem to be the real tests of 7...♘c7. It looks as if White has good attacking chances, but since Black has no obvious weaknesses, with careful play he should have a fully playable position.

b) The correct answer to 9 ♗c4 was shown as long ago as Trenchard-Blackburne, in 1898! There followed 9...b5!

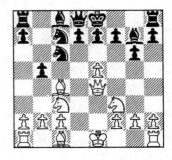

This gains valuable time to develop, as acceptance of the pawn sacrifice with 10 ♗xb5 (10 ♘xb5?? ♘xb5 11 ♗xb5 ♕a5+) is bad. After 10...♘xb5 11 ♘xb5 ♕a5+ 12 ♘c3 ♖b8! (not 12...♗a6 13 ♗d2, when White might keep his pawn) Black wins back the pawn, while keeping all his trumps. Instead of capturing on b5, White played 10 ♗b3 ♗b7 11 ♕e2 ♗a6 12 ♘d5 0-0 13 ♘xc7 ♕xc7 14 ♗f4 ♕a5+ 15 ♕d2 ♕xd2+ 16 ♔xd2 d5! and Black had a level ending.

8   ♘a3!?

A well-known move in the 'c3 Sicilian'. At one time 8 ♗b5 was more popular, but the game Krnic-Sax, 1974, drastically changed the evaluation of the position. After 8...♕a5 9 ♘c3 d5 10 ♕e2 ♗g4 11 0-0 Black has:

a) 11...0-0-0 12 a3 ♗xf3 13 ♕xf3 ♘xe5 14 ♕h3 e6 15 axb4 ♕xa1 16 ♗f4 was winning for White in Romanishin-Kupreichik, USSR 1971, and Adorjan-Sax, Budapest 1973. But still, the move 12...♘d4 as recommended by Donaldson/Silman is far better. After the forced 13 ♘xd4 ♗xe2 14 axb4 ♕xa1 15 ♗xe2 ♗h6! White has to go for the spectacular 16 ♗xh6 ♕xb2 17 ♗d2 with some dubious attacking chances, or the more reasonable 16 ♘b3 ♗xc1 17 ♘xa1 ♗xb2 18 ♘a4 ♗xe5 19 ♘b3, when White definitely has attacking prospects to counter Black's centre. The position should be roughly equal. But Black is just better after...

b) 11...d4! 12 ♘e4 ♗xf3 13 gxf3 d3! 14 ♗xd3 ♘xd3 15 ♗d2 ♕a6 16 ♕xd3 ♕xd3 17 cxd3 ♘xe5 with a far superior ending for Black, since after 18 ♗c3 ♗g7 19 f4 ♘f3+ 20 ♔g2 ♘h4 followed by ...♘f5, White is left with a horrible pawn structure.

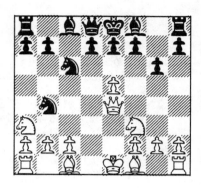

8   ...   d5

8...d6 has also been played. After 9 c3 ♗f5 10 ♕h4 ♘d3+ Black was better in Schmitzer-Brendel, German Bundesliga 1994/95. Far better, however, is 9 ♗b5!, when Black is in trouble.

9   ♕f4   ♗g7

9...♗f5 was tried in Vadasz-I. Polgar, Hungary 1968, when after 10 c3 ♘d3+ 11 ♗xd3 ♗xd3 12 ♘g5 f6 13 exf6 exf6 14 ♕e3+ ♕e7 15 ♘e6 ♘e5 16 ♘xf8 ♖xf8 Black had no problems. 10 ♗b5 seems more testing, but after 10...e6! both 11 ♘d4 ♗xc2! and 11 ♗d2 a6 12 ♗xb4 axb5 13 ♗xf8 ♖a4 seem fine for Black. 9...♗f5 is apparently fine and should be more thoroughly tested.

10   ♗d2   ♘a6?!

Rozentalis recommends instead 10...♕b6, which is certainly better. After 11 c3 ♘a6 12 ♘b5 0-0 Black has more chances of counterplay than in the game. Now White gets a clear edge and Black has no play.

11	♗xa6	bxa6
12	0-0	0-0
13	♗c3	♕c7
14	♖ad1	e6
15	♖fe1	♗b7

16	♕e3	♖fd8
17	♘d4	♖ac8
18	♘xc6	♕xc6
19	♗d4	

Black's position is a disaster, and of course the game is soon over.

19...♗f8 20 ♖d3 a5 21 ♕f4 ♗xa3 22 ♖xa3 ♕xc2 23 ♕h6 ♖d7 24 ♖h3 f5 25 exf6 ♖c4 26 ♖he3! 1-0

Game 107
Van der Wiel-Piket
Wijk aan Zee 1995

(1 e4 c5 2 ♘f3 g6 3 d4 cxd4 4 ♕xd4 ♘f6)

5   ♘c3!?

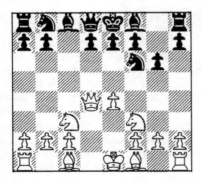

Not played very often, but one of White's best chances to refute 2...g6!?

5   ...   ♘c6
6   ♕a4

At first sight it may look odd to develop the queen this early, but Black will find it very hard to stop the e4-e5 thrust. This will be very annoying, since the queen then takes both e4 and g4 away from the black knight.

6   ...   d6

6...♕c7?! is the only way to stop 7 e5. Not surprisingly, Black runs into even bigger problems, since both 7 ♘d5!? ♘xd5 8 exd5 ♘e5 9 ♗f4 ♘xf3 10 gxf3 and simply 7 ♗g5 are terrible for Black. The white attack is already rolling.

7   e5!

The logical follow-up.

7   ...   ♘g4

Black's most active choice, hitting the f2-pawn in some lines. Other moves have not been as effective:

a) 7...dxe5 8 ♘xe5 ♕d4 9 ♘xc6 ♕xa4 10 ♘xa4 bxc6 was played in the stem game, which was Bonsch Osmolovsky-Khasin, Kiev 1957. White had a huge edge and later won due to the c5-square, which is ideal for a knight. If 8...♗g7, hoping for compensation, it seems as if 9 ♗b5 ♗d7 (9...0-0 10 ♘xc6 bxc6 11 ♗xc6 ♖b8 12 0-0) 10 ♘xc6 bxc6 11 ♗xc6 is nowhere near enough; Black is not that far ahead in development.

b) 7...♘d7 was tried in Walter-Horstmann, Germany 1990, when Black had an acceptable position after 8 exd6 ♗g7!? 9 ♗e2 ♘b6 10 ♕h4 ♕xd6 11 0-0 0-0 12 ♖d1 ♕b4. However, far more critical is 9 dxe7 ♕xe7+ 10 ♗e3 followed by 11 ♗e2 and 12 0-0 to consolidate. Black is well developed, but the white position is difficult to attack. We believe that White has the better chances.

8   exd6

This might be good for White, but Vydeslaver's 8 ♗f4!? is also interesting. The drawback is that the f2-pawn will quite often be hanging. Still, White gets a powerful attack in return: Vydeslaver-

Flash, Beersheva 1993, continued 8...♗g7 9 exd6 ♕b6 10 0-0-0 ♘xf2 11 ♖e1 ♘xh1 12 ♖xe7 ♔f8 13 ♗c4 ♗e6 14 ♗xe6 fxe6 15 ♗g5 ♕b4?! 16 ♕xb4 ♘xb4 17 ♖xb7 with a winning position for White. However, 15...♘xe7 16 ♕d7 h6! 17 dxe7 ♔g8 is not clear at all. Nor is 13 ♘g5 ♗e6 14 ♖xe6 fxe6 15 ♘xe6+ ♔g8 16 ♕c4 ♘e5! 17 ♕d5 ♕c6 18 ♕b3 ♕b6 easy to refute. We have not found anything clear for White, but it still requires a lot of courage to play like this as Black. But on the other hand, after 8 ♗f4 there is no way back, since 8...dxe5 9 ♘xe5 ♘xe5 10 ♗xe5 and 8...♕b6 9 0-0-0 ♘xf2 10 ♘d5 are downright awful for Black.

8 ... ♕xd6
9 ♘b5!?

The direct 9 ♗f4 e5 does not lead anywhere, so White tries this interesting knight twist, hoping to spoil Black's pawn structure.

9 ... ♕b8
10 ♘bd4!?

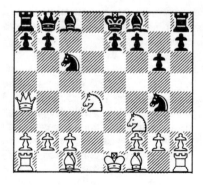

Again 10 ♗f4 is not clear, since after 10...e5 11 ♗g3 ♗g7 12 ♕a3 ♗f8! the bishop returns to g7, when there does not seem to be any way for White to maintain the pres-sure. 10 ♘bd4!? is more subtle. If Black is be forced to take back on c6 with the pawn, the c5-square will be weak. Since 10...♗d7 11 ♘xc6 ♗xc6?? 12 ♕xg4 drops a piece, Black must enter some risky complications in order to avoid the weakening of his pawns.

10 ... ♗g7
11 ♗b5 ♘ge5!?

This move looks risky, but it seems as if Black can afford it. 11...0-0 12 ♘xc6 bxc6 13 ♗xc6 ♗xb2 14 ♗xb2 ♕xb2 15 0-0 ♖b8 16 ♕xa7 is good for White, since although he will lose his extra pawn, the a-pawn is dangerous.

12 ♗f4 0-0

12...♘xf3+ 13 ♘xf3 e5 14 ♗xc6+ bxc6 15 ♕xc6+ ♗d7 16 ♕c3 0-0 is fine for Black, but White has instead 13 gxf3! ♕xf4 14 ♗xc6+ bxc6 15 ♕xc6+ ♔f8 16 ♕xa8 ♗xd4 17 ♕xc8+ ♔g7 18 ♕g4 ♕f6 19 0-0 (19 c3 ♗xc3 20 bxc3 ♕xc3+ 21 ♔e2 ♕b2+ 22 ♔e3 ♕a3+ gives Black a perpetual) 19...♗xb2, when although Black has some compensation for the exchange, White is better. Despite the weakened kingside and c-pawn, White has fair winning chances.

13 ♘xc6

Piket was hoping for the tactical trick 13 ♗xc6 ♘xf3+ 14 ♘xf3 e5!, when all of Black's problems would disappear.

13 ... bxc6
14 ♗xc6 ♕xb2

14...♘xf3+ 15 ♗xf3 e5 16 ♗xa8 exf4 17 ♗f3 ♗xb2 18 ♖d1 ♗c3+ 19 ♔f1 ♗e6, with compensation, has been recommended as an alter-native. White's co-ordination is certainly far from desirable, but by playing h2-h3 and ♔g1-h2 this problem should be solved, leaving White with the better position.

15	♗xe5	♗xe5
16	0-0	♖b8
17	♘xe5	♕xe5
18	♕xa7	♗f5
19	a4!?	

White does not try to defend his small material plus, but starts pushing the a-pawn, which will soon give Black something to worry about.

19	...	♖bc8
20	♗f3	♖xc2
21	a5	♖fc8

With the cute threat of 22...♕xa1! Logically, White now tries to exchange queens, since normally an endgame would make the passed pawn even more valuable. However, he misses a clever defence and should have played the simple 22 h3 with good winning chances.

22	♕e3?	♕xe3
23	fxe3	♗d3
24	♖fd1	

24 ♖fb1 ♖2c3 25 ♖b7 ♖c1+ 26 ♖xc1 ♖xc1+ 27 ♔f2 ♖a1 is drawn.

| 24 | ... | ♗a6 |
| 25 | ♖db1 | ♖8c7! |

This is the point. Now 26 ♖b6 ♖a7 is nothing, since White cannot make progress, and Black will eventually start attacking the a5-pawn.

| 26 | ♖b8 | ½-½ |

After 26...♗d3 27 a6 ♖c1+ 28 ♖xc1 ♖xc1+ 28 ♔f2 ♖a1 29 a7 White threatens ♖d8, picking up the bishop. However, 29...♗f5 solves this problem, leaving White with no way to improve his position.

Although Black managed a draw in this game, it seems to us that 5

♘c3!? is the most testing move in the 4 ♕xd4 variation, and certainly should be played more often. No clear path to equality for Black has been proved as yet.

Game 108
Smyslov-Zsu.Polgar
Vienna 1993

(1 e4 c5 2 ♘f3 g6)

| 3 | c3!? | |

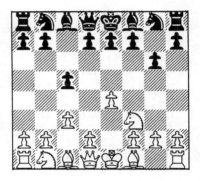

A logical move. White is heading for the Alapin variation (2 c3), hoping to prove that g7-g6 is less effective there.

| 3 | ... | ♗g7 |

3...d5 may be better, hoping after 4 exd5 ♕xd5 5 d4 to transpose to the system 1 e4 c5 2 c3 d5 3 exd5 ♕xd5 4 d4 g6!?, the popularity of which has been increasing in the last few years. Here, however, White is already committed to ♘f3 and therefore loses some of his sharpest options. According to present theory this should be fine for Black. But since this really is a 2 c3 Sicilian position, we will only cover a few independent variations:

a) The stem game is Merenyi-

Capablanca, Budapest 1928, in which Capablanca, won a beautiful ending. White played 4 ♗b5+?!, but after 4...♗d7 5 ♗xd7+ ♕xd7 6 exd5 ♕xd5 7 d4 cxd4 8 ♕xd4 ♕xd4 9 ♘xd4 e5 10 ♘b5 ♔d7! Black was doing fine with his centralised king.

b) Short-Andersson, Tilburg 1990, saw 4 exd5 ♕xd5 5 ♘a3!? (5 d4 is a 'c3 Sicilian') 5...♗g7 6 ♗c4 ♕e4+ 7 ♗e2 ♘f6 8 ♘b5 ♘a6 9 0-0 0-0 10 ♖e1 d5 with reasonable chances for Black. Actually, we are rather sceptical about combining ...g7-g6 with early activity in the centre, but so far no convincing plan has been found for White. So for the time being, 3...d5 is fully playable.

4   d4   cxd4
5   cxd4   d5!

Here, however, we find activity in the centre fully justified, if 6 exd5, Black plays 6...♘f6! Earlier this was evaluated as being better for White, but now theory gives Black the thumbs up: 7 ♗b5+ ♘bd7 8 d6!? (the only critical try, if Black gets time to castle and to play ...♘b6, he will win back the d5-pawn with good play) 8...exd6! (this is the move which gives Black equality; previously, Black went for either 8...♘e4 or 8...0-0, both of which, however, are insufficient for equality), now White has to enter the endgame with 9 ♕e2+ ♕e7 10 ♕xe7+ (10 ♗f4 is possible, leading to quite similar positions after 10...♕xe2+ 11 ♗xe2 ♔e7 followed by ...♘b6+ and ...♗e6 etc.) 10...♔xe7 11 ♘c3 (11 0-0 ♘b6 12 ♘c3 ♗e6 13 ♘g5 ♖ac8 14 ♖e1 a6 15 ♗e2 ♔d7 16 ♘xe6 fxe6 17 ♗g5 ♘fd5 was equal in Timman-

Sax Hilversum 1973) 11...♘b6 12 0-0 ♖d8 13 ♖e1+ ♔f8 14 h3 ♗e6 15 ♘g5 ♗c4 16 ♗f4 h6 17 ♘f3 a6 18 ♗xc4 ♘xc4 19 b3 ♘b6 20 ♖ac1 ♘bd5 21 ♗d2 ♘xc3 22 ♗xc3 ♘d5 with advantage for Black, Christiansen-Larsen, Monaco 1992. This line is similar to 1 e4 c6 2 c4 d5 3 cxd5 cxd5 4 cxd5 ♘f6 5 ♗b5+ ♘bd7 6 ♘c3 g6 7 d4 ♗g7 8 d6 exd6 9 ♕e2+ ♕e7. But there White has 10 ♗f4! ♕xe2+ 11 ♗xe2! followed by ♗f3! with pressure. This is not possible here, so Black is doing fine.

6   e5

6 exd5 ♘f6 leads to a harmless position from the Caro-Kann Defence.

6   ...   ♘c6

Generally, 6...♗g4 is recommended by theory, but for some reason, when this line is played at the top level, Black nearly always prefers 6...♘c6. We have not been able to find any logical explanation for this, since White often answers 6...♘c6 with 7 h3!?, as we shall see in the next game, which is the main motivation to play 6...♗g4!? White's best may be 7 ♗b5+!? with a transposition to the game. Normally, White plays 7 ♘c3, but this is harmless. Black plays 7...♘c6 8 ♗e2 ♘h6! 9 h3 ♗xf3 10 ♗xf3 ♘f5 11 ♗xd5 ♘fxd4 12 f4 0-0 13 0-0 e6 14 ♗xc6 ♘xc6 15 ♗e3 ♕a5 with equal play, as in Ljubojevic-Larsen, Monaco 1992.

Equally harmless was 11 ♗e3 e6 12 0-0 0-0 13 g4?! ♘xe3 14 fxe3 and now instead of 14...♗h6?!, as in Hacker-Kaposzas, Loosdorf 1993, 14...f6! would have left Black somewhat better, since White has merely weakened his position. Even without g2-g4, exchanging on e3 followed by ...f7-f6! is strong, normally leading to equality.

7   &b5!?

White hopes to exploit the c5-square, which will be weak after &xc6. He also removes pressure from the d4-pawn by pinning the knight. 7 h3 is the subject of the next game.

7   ...   &g4

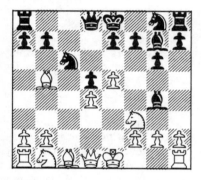

This has been Black's choice in all of the games with 7 &b5!?, but it seems positionally risky to us. However, strong alternatives are difficult to find. 7...&d7 is met with the annoying 8 &c3, hitting the d-pawn, when 8...e6 weakens the dark squares on the kingside.

8   0-0   &h6

8...&b6!? attacks the centre, as well as protecting the queenside, and is an improvement on the game.

9   &bd2   f6!?

The usual way of seeking counterplay in this line. Not 9...0-0 10 &xc6 bxc6 11 h3, and if the bishop retreats, then 12 &b3 is positionally much better for White.

10   h3   &d7

Risky, but 10...&xf3 11 &xf3 is just better for White, who has the bishop pair and better co-ordination of his pieces.

11   exf6   &xf6

Normally Black takes back with the pawn, but since she has not castled yet, White has a check on the e-file.

12	&b3	&f7
13	&c5	&d6
14	&xc6	&xc6
15	&e5	&c8

It is obvious that Black's opening strategy has been a complete failure. Somehow the Hungarian manages to hang on and defend.

16   &e1   &e4!?

Not nice, but a good practical decision, reducing material.

17	&xc6	&xc6
18	&xe4	dxe4
19	&g4	&xd4
20	&xe4	&f6
21	&h6	&f7

Black's position is far from attractive, but at least she is now fully developed and only needs to exchange some pieces on the d-file to be okay.

22	&c1	&d5
23	&c5!?	&xa2

23...♕xc5? 24 ♕e6+ ♔e8 25 ♕xf6 ♖g8 26 ♗g5 is terminal.

24 ♖a5   ♕xb2!

Removing an important queenside pawn. Now Black has good chances of building a fortress after sacrificing her queen.

25 ♕e6+ ♔e8 26 ♖a2

This looks strong, but 26 ♖d5! with the idea of 27 ♖d6 seems to win.

26...♕c3 27 ♗g7!?

This seems to win too, but Black has a trick.

27...♕c1+! 28 ♖e1

28 ♔h2 ♕c7+.

28...♕xe1+! 29 ♕xe1 ♗xg7 30 ♕e4 ♗f6 31 ♕xb7 ♔f7 32 ♖a6 g5 33 g3 ♖hd8 34 ♔g2 ♔g7 35 ♕e4 ♖f8 36 ♖a5 a6 37 h4 h6 38 h5 ♔h8 39 ♕g6 ♗g7 40 ♖xa6 ♖xa6 41 ♕xa6 e5

Although he tried hard, White never found a way through and had to be content with a draw after 51 moves. Even though Black managed to save herself in the end, not many players would like to defend the black position arising after the opening. 8...♕b6, with mutual chances, seems to be critical.

Game 109
Smirin-Ivanchuk
Paris (rapid) 1994

(1 e4 c5 2 ♘f3 g6 3 c3 ♗g7 4 d4 cxd4 5 cxd4 d5 6 e5 ♘c6)

7 h3!?   ♘h6

Since 7 h3!? is rather slow, 7...f6!?, a favourite of the Hungarian GM Bilek deserves attention:

a) Kern played 8 ♗b5 against him, Ludwigsburg 1969, but Black was fine after 8....♗d7 9 ♘c3 fxe5 10 dxe5 e6 11 ♗f4 ♘ge7 12 0-0 0-0 13 ♕d2 ♕a5 14 ♖fe1 ♕b4! 15 ♗h2 ♖xf3! 16 gxf3 ♘d4 and soon won.

b) Much later, in Kecskemet 1992, Fette went for 9 exf6, but Black played the surprising move 9...♘xf6!?, aiming for quick development and not caring much about weak squares. After 10 0-0 0-0 11 ♘c3 a6 12 ♗xc6 ♗xc6, they agreed a draw. Black will play ...♘e4 next, and if 13 ♘e5, then 13...♘d7 equalises.

8 ♘c3   0-0
9 ♗e2

9 ♗b5 was played in Andersson-Dueball, Berlin 1971. Black played 9...♔h8?!, but after 10 0-0 f6 11 ♖e1 fxe5 12 ♗xc6 exd4 13 ♗xh6! White had an extra pawn. Better is the immediate 9...f6!?, when after 10 0-0 fxe5 11 dxe5 e6 12 ♖e1 ♕c7 Black was doing fine in Schweber-Larsen, Buenos Aires 1991.

In general Black should act quickly to take advantage of the fact that he is slightly ahead in development after 7 h3.

9 ...   f6
10 exf6   exf6

It may look as if Black has equalised, since he has eliminated White's space advantage. However, Black's pieces do not co-ordinate very well, and practice has shown that White still has an advantage.

| | **11** | **0-0** | **♘f5** |

11...♘f7?! 12 ♕b3! was good for White in Savon-Bachmann, Dortmund 1975.

| | **12** | **♗f4** | **♗e6** |
| | **13** | **♖e1** | |

13 ♖c1 was successful in Adams-Larsen, Monaco 1992. Larsen now misplayed his position with 13...♖c8 14 ♘a4 ♗f7 15 ♖c3 ♖e8 16 ♗b5 ♖e4 17 ♗xc6 ♖xf4? 18 ♗xb7. Black should of course take back on c6, but White is better.

	13	**...**	**♗f7**
	14	**♗b5**	**♖c8**
	15	**♖c1**	**a6**
	16	**♗f1**	**♖e8**

Again, Black seems to be doing fine, but as we shall see, White's pieces are more actively placed.

| | **17** | **♖xe8+** | **♕xe8** |
| | **18** | **g4!** | |

Since White is very active, he can play this seemingly weakening move as Black is in no position to exploit it.

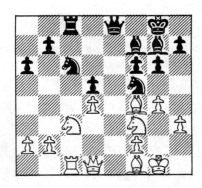

18...♘e7 19 ♕d2 ♕d8 20 ♘a4 g5?!

Black is trying to win space, but he also gives White targets for his attack.

21 ♗g3 ♗g6?! 22 ♘c5 ♕b6 23 ♖e1 ♔f7 24 ♕e3

Now it is nearly over. White is ready for a quick assault and it is striking to notice how easily White manages to develop a huge attack from a seemingly simple and quiet position.

24...♔g8 25 ♗d6 ♖e8

Ivanchuk was probably down to his last few minutes, but even more time would not have saved him.

26 ♕e6+ ♗f7 27 ♕d7 ♗f8 28 ♕xb7 ♕a5 29 ♖e3 ♕xa2 30 ♘d7 ♗g6? 31 ♘xf6+ 1-0

It seems that after 7 h3!? Black should not sit and wait, since White's pressure is long-lasting. Bilek's 7...f6!? with active counterplay seems more promising. However, this is rather academic, since with 6...♗g4! Black avoids 7 h3!? altogether.

15 Guide to Transpositions

Even if your opponent does not play 1 e4, there are several ways to trick him into playing an Accelerated Dragon. This chapter deals with the most common ways to enter the Accelerated Dragon without 1 e4 from White. We shall also look at ways in which White can avoid Black's transpositional attempts.

English and Réti Opening
The most common transposition is probably:
A) 1 c4 c5 2 ♘f3 g6!?
instead of the more normal 2...♘f6 or 2...♘c6. After 2...g6!? White will either have to play the unambitious 3 g3 with a Symmetrical English, which definitely should not scare Black, or go for the official 'refutation' of 2...g6:
3 d4 cxd4 4 ♘xd4 ♘c6
when after 5 e4 we already have the standard Maroczy Bind. Of course, this should not worry the Accelerated Dragon player, but
5 g3
(see following diagram)
may be more annoying. However, after 5...♗g7 6 ♘c2 Black can either choose to play 6...♘f6 with a standard line in which White has committed himself to an early

♘c2 or the more interesting 6...♕b6 or 6...♕a5:

a) Korchnoi answered Spangenberg's 6...♕b6 with 7 ♘d2, but after 7...♘f6 8 ♗g2 0-0 9 0-0 d6 White's knight on d2 was more misplaced than Black's queen, so Black had no problems. Critical is 7 ♘c3, as 7...♗xc3 8 bxc3 ♘e5 will be answered with 9 e4 followed by ♕e2, f2-f4 etc.

b) Better looks 6...♕a5+, as 7 ♘c3 now loses several pawns.

b1) Christiansen played 7 ♘d2 against Leko in New York 1994, when after 7...♘f6 8 ♗g2 0-0 9 0-0 ♕h5 10 e3 ♕xd1 White had almost nothing, although he later managed to win.

b2) More ambitious is 7 ♗d2,

when in the game Rotstein-Klimenko, Simferopol 1991, Black played 7...♕c5, but was crushed after 8 ♘c3 ♕xc4 9 ♘e3 ♕c5 10 ♘ed5 ♗e5 11 f4 ♗b8 12 ♖c1 e6 13 b4 ♕d6 14 ♘e3 a6 15 ♘c4 ♕c7 16 ♗e3 b5 17 ♘b6 ♖a7 18 ♘e4 ♗b7 19 ♗c5 ♕d8 20 ♕d6! Instead of 7...♕c5, 7...♕b6 is the real test, as Black will pick up an important pawn. It is not easy for White to get reasonable compensation, and since 8 ♘c3 ♕xb2 9 ♖b1?? fails to 9...♕xc3!, 8 ♗c3 may be forced, but 8...♗xc3 9 ♘xc3 ♕xb2 looks healthy for Black.

In summary, unless you are afraid of the symmetrical English, both 1 c4 or 1 ♘f3 can be answered with 1...c5 followed by 2...g6 with good chances for an Accelerated Dragon.

Also interesting is:

B) 1 c4 c5 2 ♘f3 g6 3 d4 ♗g7!?

Now White can play 4 d5, which can lead to a Benko Gambit after 4...b5 or a Benoni Defence after 4...d6 or 4...♘f6. However, most players would probably go for

4 e4

trying to get to the Maroczy Bind, which has a reputation of being good for White. Now, of course, it is possible for Black to go back to the well-trodden paths with 4...cxd4, but there are some interesting ways to confuse White:

a) Filipowicz's pet 4...♘a6 is one of them. Normally his games transpose into a Benoni after 5 ♘c3 d6 6 ♗e2 ♘f6 7 0-0 0-0 8 d5. Here Black has avoided a lot of the critical lines, but still it is not everyone's taste to play the Benoni. 8 ♖e1 is also possible, when at first Filipowicz took on d4, leading to a normal Maroczy with the knight misplaced on a6. Later he tried 8...♗g4 and 8...b6, trying to provoke White into playing 9 d5 leading to the normal Benoni structure. Against 8...♗g4 Cvitan did not co-operate and played 9 ♗e3, as after 9...♘d7 10 ♖c1 ♘c7 11 dxc5, 11...dxc5? was bad, since after 12 ♘g5 he realised that 12...♗xe2 would allow 13 ♖xe2, threatening 14 ♖d2. Therefore he had to play 12...♗e6, but suffered after 13 f4. 11...♘xc5 is better, but still with a strange Maroczy. 4...♘a6 may be a possibility for Benoni fans, but we have to admit that it looks optimistic to put a knight on the edge of the board this early.

b) 4...d6 was played in the famous game Smyslov-Botvinnik, World ch match 1957. After 5 ♘c3 ♘c6 6 ♗e3 ♗g4 7 dxc5 dxc5 8 ♕xd8 ♖xd8 9 ♗xc5 ♗xc3 10 bxc3 ♘f6, the usually very well prepared Botvinnik met with the surprising 11 ♘d4 (not 11 ♘d2? ♖xd2!), which allowed Smyslov to keep the extra pawn after 11...♘xe4 12 ♘xc6 bxc6 13 ♗xa7, and with his excellent technique he had no problems converting this into a full point. Since nobody has taken this up since, we have to consider it unplayable for Black.

Much better is 6...♕b6,

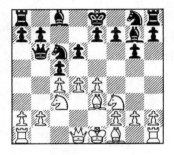

when Nickoloff-Dzindzichash-vili, St John 1988, continued 7 ♘a4 ♕a5 8 ♗d2 ♕c7 9 d5 ♘d4 10 ♘xd4 cxd4 with a transposition to the Modern Defence (1 e4 g6 2 d4 ♗g7 3 c4 d6 4 ♘c3 ♘c6 5 d5 ♘d4 6 ♗e3 c5 7 ♘ge2 ♕b6 8 ♘xd4 cxd4 9 ♘a4 ♕a5 10 ♗d2 ♕c7). This line is considered okay for Black, and White has to look for improvements earlier. 9 dxc5, as played by Letzelter against Forintos, is not one of them, as Black was better after 9...dxc5 10 ♗c3 ♗xc3 11 ♘xc3 ♗g4 12 ♗e2 ♗xf3, since his knight gets the d4-square. 7 ♘d5 looks critical, when the only move is 7...♕a5, hoping for 8 ♗d2 ♕d8 9 ♗c3 ♗g4 with good play. More testing is 8 ♕d2!, when after 8...♕xd2 9 ♗xd2 ♖b8 10 dxc5 dxc5 11 ♗f4 e5 12 ♗e3 White has some initiative, but it is playable for Black. Also possible is 5...♗g4, but after 6 d5 we have a Benoni with Black committed to ...♗g4.

c) 4...♕b6 was played on occasion by Robatsch. His games probably inspired Yudasin to try it

out against Gulko in Beersheva 1993. After 5 dxc5 ♕xc5 6 ♗e2 ♘c6 7 0-0 d6 8 a3 ♗g4 Black had a normal position, but 8 a3 looks strange. Why not 8 ♘c3 instead? White is better after 8...♗xc3 9 bxc3 ♘f6 10 ♕c2, as White will be able to develop normally with ♗e3, ♘d4 etc. with some advantage. 6 ♗d3 was tried twice against Robatsch, but after 6...d6 7 0-0 ♗g4, White could not prove an edge. Cvetkovic tried 8 ♗e3 ♕c7 9 ♘c3, but after the brave 9...♗xc3 10 bxc3 ♘f6, Robatsch won a complicated game. Less ambitious is Vukic's 8 h3, when after 8...♗xf3 9 ♕xf3 ♘c6 10 ♘a3 ♘e5 11 ♕e2 ♘xd3 12 ♕xd3 ♘f6 13 ♖b1 0-0 14 ♗e3 ♕c6 15 f3 ♘d7 16 ♖fc1 f5 17 ♕d5 ♔h8 18 ♕xc6 bxc6 19 exf5 gxf5 he received a lesson in the importance of centre pawns in the endgame.

Since 5 dxc5 does not give White much, he maybe has to gambit his b-pawn with 5 d5, but after 5...♗xb2 6 ♗xb2 ♕xb2 7 ♘bd2 it is difficult to say whether he has enough for a pawn. Overall 4...♕b6 is playable and quite solid.

d) More provocative is 4...♘c6 and now:

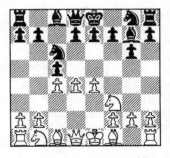

d1) 5 ♗e3 is careless; 5...♕b6 is

an embarrassing reply.

d2) After 5 d5 ♘d4 6 ♘xd4 Black can take back in two ways, but neither has given him much success.

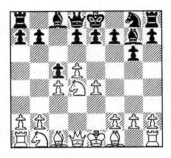

If 6...cxd4 then 7 ♗d3 is the most common followed by 0-0 and b2-b4 with play on the queenside. 7 ♘a3!? may be even stronger as 8 ♘b5 is a threat. 7...a6 is answered by 8 ♗d3 and if 8...e5 then 9 c5!, as played by Akesson against Negulescu in 1980. The point is that 9...♕a5 10 ♗d2 ♕xc5 11 ♖c1 followed by ♘c4 is crushing. Black played 9...♗f8, but after 10 b4 b6 11 ♘c4 bxc5 12 bxc5 ♗xc5 13 ♕a4 f6 14 f4 White had a huge attack and won quickly.

More solid is 6...♗xd4, as Black gets a kind of Benoni, but he will lose time when his bishop is kicked home by a later ♘d2-f3. Ljubojevic tried to keep it on d4 against Smyslov in Wijk aan Zee 1972: 7 ♗d3 d6 8 0-0 e5 9 ♘d2 ♘f6 10 ♘b3 ♗g4 11 ♕e1 ♘h5 12 ♘xd4 cxd4 13 f4 ♕e7 14 fxe5 fxe5 15 ♗d2, but it was now obvious that Black's idea had failed; White is ready for ♗b4, keeping Black's king in the centre. Ljubo tried 15...a5 16 h3 ♗d7 17 ♗xa5 ♘f4, but these kinds of tricks do not

work against Smyslov, who parried it easily with 18 ♖f3 ♖xa5 19 ♕xa5 0-0 20 ♗f1 (1-0, 36). 8...e5 was not exactly a good idea; better was 8...♗g7 followed by ...♘f6, ...0-0 etc., though White still has a small edge.

d3) 5 dxc5 is another possibility if White insists on getting a Maroczy kind of position.

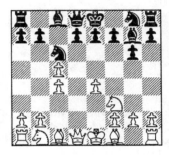

5...♕a5+ is commonly played (although 5...♘f6 has also been tried) when after 6 ♗d2 ♕xc5 7 ♗e2 followed by 0-0, ♗e3 and ♘d4 White gets a Maroczy with Black's queen developed too early. After 5...♕a5+ White sometimes tries 6 ♘c3, hoping for a transposition to the 4...♕b6 variation. If this is not Black's taste, then 6...♗xc3+ 7 bxc3 gives some him interesting options. Black was successful with 7...♕xc3+ in the game Cvetkovic-Lupu, 1990, when he won an unclear game after 8 ♗d2 ♕a3 9 ♗e2 ♘f6 10 0-0 ♘xe4 11 ♗e3 0-0. Probably better is 10 ♕c2, defending the e4-pawn. Then White has the standard compensation on the dark squares, but Black's position is solid and the position is probably about equal. After 7...♘f6, the normally very peaceful Faroe Islands IM Rodgaard played

8 ♘d2 against Gheorghiu at the Novi Sad Olympiad 1990. Black accepted the offered pawns with 8...♕xc3 9 ♖b1 ♘xe4 10 ♖b3 ♕d4 11 ♘xe4 ♕xe4 12 ♖e3 ♕d4 13 ♗d3 ♕xc5 14 0-0 d6, but White had sufficient compensation after 15 ♗e4 ♗e6 16 ♗d5 0-0 17 ♖xe6 fxe6 18 ♗xe6 ♔g7 19 ♗b2 ♖f6, though only enough to draw. 8 ♕c2 is more ambitious, as it keeps more pieces on the board. Then 8...♘xe4 9 ♗e2 ♘xc5 10 0-0 d6 11 ♘d4 ♗d7 12 ♗h6 ♘a4 13 ♗f3 led to a quick finish in Cvitan-Delekta, Katowice 1992: 13...♘e5 14 ♗xb7 ♖b8 15 ♖ab1 ♘b6 16 ♗d5 ♖c8 17 ♕e4 e6 18 ♕f4 exd5 19 ♕f6 1-0. Perhaps Black should have given up the exchange with 9...♕xc3+ 10 ♕xc3 ♘xc3 11 ♗b2 ♘xe2 12 ♗xh8 ♘f4, which seems to offer him excellent chances.

In general, it seems that Black has several reliable ways of heading into unknown territory, but still, just transposing to normal Maroczy positions is the easiest solution to Black's opening problems. Actually, it is our impression that the Maroczy arises just as often after 1 ♘f3 or 1 c4 as after 1 e4. This is probably because the 1 e4 player does not always likes the rather 'positional' games that arise, but prefers sharper lines without a pawn on c4. Another reason why the Maroczy arises so often via the English Opening is that the transposition is really White's only ambitious choice, as he otherwise has to go for some line in the Symmetrical English, which is absolutely fine for Black.

The conclusion is that the Accelerated Dragon player has no prob-

lems with 1 ♘f3 or 1 c4 as he can happily enter Maroczy positions.

King's Indian Main Line

For the player who likes to play the Kings Indian with Black, but feels that the main lines after 1 d4 ♘f6 2 c4 g6 3 ♘c3 ♗g7 4 e4 d6 5 ♘f3 0-0 6 ♗e2 e5 7 0-0 ♘c6 8 d5 ♘e7 are too heavy to study, then

1 d4 ♘f6 2 c4 g6 3 ♘c3 ♗g7 4 e4 d6 5 ♘f3 0-0 6 ♗e2 c5!?

is a way of heading for a Maroczy. If White goes for 7 0-0 cxd4 8 ♘xd4 ♘c6, we have arrived in one of our main lines. Here, however, White is not forced into it, as **7 d5!?**

leads to a Benoni position after **7...e6 8 0-0**

and now 8...exd5 9 cxd5. However, White has already put his bishop on e2, which was popular some twenty years ago, but nowadays is not regarded as particularly dangerous, and the current view is that Black has nothing to complain about. Also interesting is **8...♖e8!?**

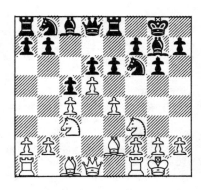

and now 9 ♘d2 ♘a6, not releasing the tension in the centre just yet. The point is that Black can play useful moves such as ...♘c7, ...♖b8, ...a7-a6, ...♗d7 etc. This strategy is more difficult for White to play as he does not have access to the c4-square, which is quite essential for White's play in the Benoni. Therefore White has experimented with 9 dxe6 or 10 dxe6, hoping to prove that the d6-pawn is a weakness, though so far he has not been particularly successful.

a) After 9 dxe6 ♗xe6 10 ♗f4, Black has some interesting options:

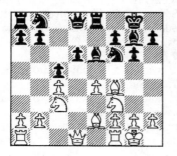

10...♘c6 is often played, but is not our recommendation. Better is 10...♕b6!?, which led to a win for Black in Beliavsky-De Firmian, Reggio Emilia 1989, when Black was better after 11 ♗xd6 ♖d8 12 e5 ♘e8 13 ♘a4 ♕c6 14 b4 cxb4 15 c5 ♕c8 16 ♘d4 ♘xd6 17 ♘xe6 fxe6 18 dxe6 ♗xa1, as White did not have enough compensation. Simplest, however, is Loeffler's excellent discovery namely 10...♗g4! when Black is fine after 11 h3? ♘xe4! 12 ♘xe4 ♖xe4 13 ♗g5 ♕e8 14 ♗d3 ♗xf3 15 ♕xf3 ♖e5 16 ♕xb7 ♘c6 with a huge edge, Prymula-Loeffler, Hradec Kralove 1988. The point is that 12 hxg4 ♗xc3! leaves Black with an extra pawn. Therefore 11 h3? is bad, but if Black gets to play

...♗xf3 followed by ...♘c6-d4, he is just better. 10...♗g4!? has not been played much, but it seems like the best choice to us.

b) 9 ♘d2 ♘a6 10 dxe6 is also possible, since the knight on a6 now takes a long time to get to d4. The white knight, however, also looks oddly placed on d2. After 10...♗xe6 11 ♘b3 ♕b6 12 ♗f4 ♖ad8 13 ♕c1 ♘b4 14 ♖d1 a6 Black was fine in Lukacs-Damljanovic, Lucerne 1988. 9 h3!? exd5 10 exd5 was successful for White in Speelman-Larsen, Hastings 1990, after 10...♕b6?! 11 ♗d3 ♘a6 12 a3 ♗d7 13 ♖b1 ♘h5 14 ♗d2 when White slowly managed to expand (1-0, 36). However, fine for Black is 10...♘e4! 11 ♘xe4 ♖xe4 12 ♗d3 ♖e8 13 ♗g5 ♕b6!? 14 ♖b1 ♘d7 followed by ...♘e5 with equal, but dull play. 13 ♖e1 ♘d7 14 ♗g5 f6!? 15 ♗d2 ♖xe1+ 16 ♕xe1 ♘e5 17 ♘xe5 ½-½ was Volke-P.H.Nielsen, Austria 1997, another good example of the ease of Black's position in this line.

Again White normally goes for the Maroczy with 7 0-0, as this is thought to be good for White. However, many 1 d4 players have never or rarely faced Maroczy positions before, and in our experience they often do very badly in them, since they are more a matter of understanding and experience than just knowing some theory. But it should be noted that the King's Indian move order is just a way to avoid some critical lines, and not a complete repertoire against 1 d4.

Benoni and Benko Gambit
The move order
1 d4 ♘f6 2 c4 c5 3 ♘f3!?

is important if you play the Benko Gambit or the Benoni Defence, or simply if you for some reason forgot to play 2...g6 after 1 c4 c5 2 ♘f3! After
3...cxd4 4 ♘xd4

Black can now go for 4...g6?!, which quite often transposes to the Maroczy after 5 ♘c3 ♗g7 6 e4 etc.

However, 6 g3!? is quite annoying, when White gets a line of the English Opening that is considered quite pleasant for him. Black's problem is that his knight already is on f6 and therefore he does not control the d4-square as in the pure Symmetrical English. So, unless you are willing to play that particular line, this is not a good way of reaching the Maroczy. Instead 3...g6 is possible, hoping for a Benko after 4 d5 b5, but after 4 ♘c3! ♗g7 5 d5!, since White has not yet committed to ♗e2 (as in the King's Indian line above), he can choose whichever set-up he likes against the Benoni.

We hope that the above material gives some ideas of what to do and what not to do in order to reach an Accelerated Dragon from other move orders.

Index of Complete Games

Index of Variations

A detailed summary appears at the start of each chapter.